Market!

Search through the complete book in PDF!

- Access the entire *MCSA/MCSE: Windows Server 2003 Network Infrastructure Implementation, Management, and Maintenance Study Guide*, complete with figures and tables, in electronic format.

- Search the *MCSA/MCSE: Windows Server 2003 Network Infrastructure Implementation, Management, and Maintenance Study Guide*, chapters to find information on any topic in seconds.

- Look up any Key Term, along with other general terms, in the Glossary.

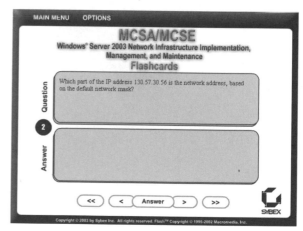

Use the Electronic Flashcards for PCs, Pocket PCs, or Palm devices to jog your memory and prep last-minute for the exam!

- Reinforce your understanding of key concepts with these hardcore flashcard-style questions.

- Download the Flashcards to your Palm device, and go on the road. Now you can study anywhere, any time.

Prepare for Microsoft's tough simulation questions with the WinSim program!

- Use the simulators to guide you through real-world tasks step-by-step, or watch the movies to see the "invisible hand" perform the tasks for you.

MCSA/MCSE: Windows Server 2003 Network Infrastructure Implementation, Management, and Maintenance Study Guide

Exam 70-291

OBJECTIVE	CHAPTER
Implementing, Managing, and Maintaining IP Addressing	
Configure TCP/IP addressing on a server computer.	2
Manage DHCP.	5, 7
Manage DHCP clients and leases.	5
Manage DHCP Relay Agent.	7
Manage DHCP databases.	5
Manage DHCP scope options.	5
Manage reservations and reserved clients.	5
Troubleshoot TCP/IP addressing.	2
Diagnose and resolve issues related to Automatic Private IP Addressing (APIPA).	2
Diagnose and resolve issues related to incorrect TCP/IP configuration.	2
Troubleshoot DHCP.	5, 7
Diagnose and resolve issues related to DHCP authorization.	5
Verify DHCP reservation configuration.	5
Examine the system event log and DHCP server audit log files to find related events.	5
Diagnose and resolve issues related to configuration of DHCP server and scope options.	5
Verify that the DHCP Relay Agent is working correctly.	7
Verify database integrity.	5
Implementing, Managing, and Maintaining Name Resolution	
Install and configure the DNS Server service.	6
Configure DNS server options.	6
Configure DNS zone options.	6
Configure DNS forwarding.	6
Manage DNS.	6
Manage DNS zone settings.	6
Manage DNS record settings.	6
Manage DNS server options.	6
Monitor DNS. Tools might include System Monitor, Event Viewer, Replication Monitor, and DNS debug logs.	6
Implementing, Managing, and Maintaining Network Security	
Implement secure network administration procedures.	3
Implement security baseline settings and audit security settings by using security templates.	3
Implement the principle of least privilege.	3

SYBEX

Exam objectives are subject to change at any time without prior notice and at Microsoft's sole discretion. Please visit Microsoft's Web site (www.microsoft.com/traincert) for the most current listing of exam objectives.

SYBEX

MCSA/MCSE:
Windows Server 2003 Network Infrastructure Implementation, Management, and Maintenance
Study Guide

MCSA/MCSE:
Windows® Server 2003 Network Infrastructure Implementation, Management, and Maintenance
Study Guide

James Chellis

Paul Robichaux

and Matthew Sheltz

San Francisco • London

SYBEX®

Associate Publisher: Neil Edde
Acquisitions/Developmental Editor: Jeff Kellum
Production Editor: Erica Yee
Technical Editor: Dale Liu, Donald Fuller
Copyeditor: Judy Flynn
Compositor: Interactive Composition Corporation
Graphic Illustrator: Interactive Composition Corporation
CD Coordinator: Dan Mummert
CD Technician: Kevin Ly
Proofreaders: Emily Husan, Laurie O'Connell, Nancy Riddiough
Indexer: Ted Laux
Book Designer: Bill Gibson
Cover Designer: Archer Design
Cover Photographer: Colin Peterson, PhotoDisc

SYBEX®

To Our Valued Readers:

Thank you for looking to Sybex for your Microsoft Windows 2003 certification exam prep needs. We at Sybex are proud of the reputation we've established for providing certification candidates with the practical knowledge and skills needed to succeed in the highly competitive IT marketplace. Sybex is proud to have helped thousands of Microsoft certification candidates prepare for their exams over the years, and we are excited about the opportunity to continue to provide computer and networking professionals with the skills they'll need to succeed in the highly competitive IT industry.

With its release of Windows Server 2003, and the revised MCSA and MCSE tracks, Microsoft has raised the bar for IT certifications yet again. The new programs better reflect the skill set demanded of IT administrators in today's marketplace and offers candidates a clearer structure for acquiring the skills necessary to advance their careers.

The authors and editors have worked hard to ensure that the Study Guide you hold in your hand is comprehensive, in-depth, and pedagogically sound. We're confident that this book will exceed the demanding standards of the certification marketplace and help you, the Microsoft certification candidate, succeed in your endeavors.

As always, your feedback is important to us. Please send comments, questions, or suggestions to support@sybex.com. At Sybex we're continually striving to meet the needs of individuals preparing for IT certification exams.

Good luck in pursuit of your Microsoft certification!

Neil Edde
Associate Publisher—Certification
Sybex, Inc.

For my family, as always.
—Matt

Acknowledgments

This book was an exciting and challenging project for a number of reasons. Whereas Windows 2000 Server revolutionized the Windows operating system with the Active Directory and advanced management features, Windows Server 2003 represents an evolution of the previous formula that proved to work so well. In the meantime, Microsoft significantly altered the structure and content of the MCSA and MCSE programs for Windows Server 2003, so authors and trainers have had to change their tactics in order to keep up with the fast-paced certification market. For this book, many great authors, editors, and publishing professionals contributed to the finished product that you now hold in your hands.

First, I must thank Paul Robichaux and James Chellis, my co-authors on this project. This book would not be possible without their technical insight and inspiring leadership.

The editors at Sybex are the next vital component of the production team, and as always they did an excellent job. I must thank Jeff Kellum, Erica Yee, Don Fuller, Dale Liu, and Judy Flynn.

Finally, I would like to thank the excellent layout professionals and illustrators who really give this book a polish uncommon in the industry. Namely Interactive Composition Corporation made this book look and feel great.

Finally, I would like to thank my friends and family who have supported all of my endeavors. I love all of you!

—Matt Sheltz

Contents at a Glance

Contents

Table of Exercises

Introduction

Microsoft's Microsoft Certified Systems Administrator (MCSA) and Microsoft Certified Systems Engineer (MCSE) tracks for Windows Server 2003 are the premier certifications for computer industry professionals. Covering the core technologies around which Microsoft's future will be built, this program provides powerful credentials for career advancement.

This book has been developed to give you the critical skills and knowledge you need to prepare for one of the core requirements of both the MCSA and MCSE certifications in the new Windows Server 2003 track: Managing and Maintaining a Microsoft Windows Server 2003 Environment (Exam 70-291).

The Microsoft Certified Professional Program

Since the inception of its certification program, Microsoft has certified almost 1.5 million people. As the computer network industry increases in both size and complexity, this number is sure to grow—and the need for proven ability will also increase. Companies rely on certifications to verify the skills of prospective employees and contractors.

Microsoft has developed its Microsoft Certified Professional (MCP) program to give you credentials that verify your ability to work with Microsoft products effectively and professionally. Obtaining your MCP certification requires that you pass any one Microsoft certification exam. Several levels of certification are available based on specific suites of exams. Depending on your areas of interest or experience, you can obtain any of the following MCP credentials:

Microsoft Certified Systems Administrator (MCSA) on Windows Server 2003 The MCSA certification is the newest administrator certification track from Microsoft. This certification targets system and network administrators with roughly 6 to 12 months of desktop and network administration experience. The MCSA can be considered the entry-level certification. You must take and pass a total of four exams to obtain your MCSA. Or, if you are an MCSA on Windows 2000, you can take one Upgrade exam to obtain your MCSA on Windows Server 2003.

Microsoft Certified Systems Engineer (MCSE) on Windows Server 2003 This certification track is designed for network and system administrators, network and system analysts, and technical consultants who work with Microsoft Windows XP and Server 2003 software. You must take and pass seven exams to obtain your MCSE. Or, if you are an MCSE on Windows 2000, you can take two Upgrade exams to obtain your MCSE on Windows Server 2003.

MCSE versus MCSA

In an effort to provide those just starting off in the IT world a chance to prove their skills, Microsoft introduced its Microsoft Certified Systems Administrator (MCSA) program.

Targeted at those with less than a year's experience, the MCSA program focuses primarily on the administration portion of an IT professional's duties. Therefore, there are certain Windows exams that satisfy both MCSA and MCSE requirements, namely exams 70-270, 70-290, and 70-291.

Of course, it should be any MCSA's goal to eventually obtain his or her MCSE. However, don't assume that, because the MCSA has to take two exams that also satisfy an MCSE requirement, the two programs are similar. An MCSE must also know how to design a network. Beyond these two exams, the remaining MCSE required exams require the candidate to have much more hands-on experience.

Microsoft Certified Application Developer (MCAD)   This track is designed for application developers and technical consultants who primarily use Microsoft development tools. Currently, you can take exams on Visual Basic .NET or Visual C# .NET. You must take and pass three exams to obtain your MCSD.

Microsoft Certified Solution Developer (MCSD)   This track is designed for software engineers and developers and technical consultants who primarily use Microsoft development tools. As of this printing, you can get your MCSD in either Visual Studio 6 or Visual Studio .NET. In Visual Studio 6, you need to take and pass three exams. In Visual Studio .NET, you need to take and pass five exams to obtain your MCSD.

Microsoft Certified Database Administrator (MCDBA)   This track is designed for database administrators, developers, and analysts who work with Microsoft SQL Server. As of this printing, you can take exams on either SQL Server 7 or SQL Server 2000. You must take and pass four exams to achieve MCDBA status.

Microsoft Certified Trainer (MCT)   The MCT track is designed for any IT professional who develops and teaches Microsoft-approved courses. To become an MCT, you must first obtain your MCSE, MCSD, or MCDBA, then you must take a class at one of the Certified Technical Training Centers. You will also be required to prove your instructional ability. You can do this in various ways: by taking a skills-building or train-the-trainer class, by achieving certification as a trainer from any of several vendors, or by becoming a Certified Technical Trainer through CompTIA. Last of all, you will need to complete an MCT application.

Microsoft recently announced two new certification tracks for Windows 2000: MCSA: Security and MCSE: Security. In addition to the core operating system requirements, candidates must take two security specialization core exams, one of which can be CompTIA's Security+ exam. MCSE: Security candidates must also take a security specialization design exam. As of this printing, no announcement had been made on the track for Windows Server 2003. Check out Microsoft's website at www.microsoft.com/traincert.com for more information.

How Do You Become Certified on Windows Server 2003?

Attaining an MCSA or MCSE certification has always been a challenge. In the past, students have been able to acquire detailed exam information—even most of the exam questions—from online "brain dumps" and third-party "cram" books or software products. For the new exams, this is simply not the case.

Microsoft has taken strong steps to protect the security and integrity of its certification tracks. Now prospective candidates must complete a course of study that develops detailed knowledge about a wide range of topics. It supplies them with the true skills needed, derived from working with Windows XP, Server 2003, and related software products.

The Windows Server 2003 certification programs are heavily weighted toward hands-on skills and experience. Microsoft has stated that "nearly half of the core required exams' content demands that the candidate have troubleshooting skills acquired through hands-on experience and working knowledge."

Fortunately, if you are willing to dedicate the time and effort to learn Windows XP and Server 2003, you can prepare yourself well for the exams by using the proper tools. By working through this book, you can successfully meet the exam requirements to pass the Windows Server 2003 network infrastructure administration exam.

This book is part of a complete series of MCSA and MCSE Study Guides, published by Sybex Inc., that together cover the core MCSA and MCSE operating system requirements, as well as the Design requirements needed to complete your MCSE track. Please visit the Sybex website at www.sybex.com for complete program and product details.

MCSA Exam Requirements

Candidates for MCSA certification on Windows Server 2003 must pass four exams.

> For a more detailed description of the Microsoft certification programs, including a list of all the exams, visit Microsoft's Training and Certification website at www.microsoft.com/traincert.

You must take one of the following client operating system exams:

- Installing, Configuring, and Administering Microsoft Windows 2000 Professional (70-210)
- Installing, Configuring, and Administering Microsoft Windows XP Professional (70-270)

You must also take the following networking operating system exams:

- Managing and Maintaining a Microsoft Windows Server 2003 Environment (70-290)
- Implementing, Managing, and Maintaining a Microsoft Windows Server 2003 Network Infrastructure (70-291)

In addition, you must take one of a number of electives, including:

- Implementing and Supporting Microsoft Systems Management Server 2.0 (70-086)
- Installing, Configuring, and Administering Microsoft Internet Security and Acceleration (ISA) Server 2000, Enterprise Edition (70-227)
- Installing, Configuring, and Administering Microsoft SQL Server 2000 Enterprise Edition (70-228)
- CompTIA's A+ and Network+ exams
- CompTIA's A+ and Server+ exams

Also, if you are an MCSA on Windows 2000, you can take one Upgrade exam: Managing and Maintaining a Microsoft Windows Server 2003 Environment for an MCSA Certified on Windows 2000 (70-292).

MCSE Exam Requirements

Candidates for MCSE certification on Windows Server 2003 must pass seven exams, including one client operating system exam, three networking operating system exams, one design exam, and an elective.

For a more detailed description of the Microsoft certification programs, visit Microsoft's Training and Certification website at www.microsoft.com/traincert.

You must take one of the following client operating system exams:

- Installing, Configuring, and Administering Microsoft Windows 2000 Professional (70-210)
- Installing, Configuring, and Administering Microsoft Windows XP Professional (70-270)

You must also take the following networking operating system exams:

- Managing and Maintaining a Microsoft Windows Server 2003 Environment (70-290)
- Implementing, Managing, and Maintaining a Microsoft Windows Server 2003 Network Infrastructure (70-291)
- Planning and Maintaining a Microsoft Windows Server 2003 Network Infrastructure (70-293)
- Planning, Implementing, and Maintaining a Microsoft Windows Server 2003 Active Directory Infrastructure (70-294)

In addition, you must take one of the following Design exams:

- Designing a Microsoft Windows Server 2003 Active Directory and Network Infrastructure (70-297)
- Designing Security for a Microsoft Windows Server 2003 Network 2000 Server Technologies (70-298)

Finally, you must take one of the following electives:

- Implementing and Supporting Microsoft Systems Management Server 2.0 (70-086)
- Installing, Configuring, and Administering Microsoft Internet Security and Acceleration (ISA) Server 2000, Enterprise Edition (70-227)
- Installing, Configuring, and Administering Microsoft SQL Server 2000 Enterprise Edition (70-228)
- Designing and Implementing Databases with Microsoft SQL Server 2000 Enterprise Edition (70-229)
- The Design exam not taken as a requirement

Also, if you are an MCSE on Windows 2000, you can take two Upgrade exams: Managing and Maintaining a Microsoft Windows Server 2003 Environment for an MCSA Certified on Windows 2000 and Planning, Implementing, and Maintaining a Microsoft Windows Server 2003 Environment for an MCSE Certified on Windows 2000. In addition, if you are an MCSE in Windows NT, you do not have to take the client requirement, but you do have to take the networking operating system, design, and an exam elective.

Windows 2000 and Windows 2003 Certification

Microsoft recently announced that they will distinguish between Windows 2000 and Windows Server 2003 certifications. Those who have their MCSA or MCSE certification in Windows 2000 will be referred to as "certified on Windows 2000." Those who obtained their MCSA or MCSE in the Windows Server 2003 will be referred to as "certified on Windows Server 2003."

If you are certified in Windows 2000, you can take either one Upgrade exam (for MCSA) or two Upgrade exams (for MCSE) to obtain your certification on Windows 2003.

Microsoft also introduced a more clear distinction between the MCSA and MCSE certifications, by more sharply focusing each certification. In the new Windows 2003 track, the objectives covered by the MCSA exams relate primarily to administrative tasks. The exams that relate specifically to the MCSE, however, deal mostly with design-level concepts. So, MCSA job tasks are considered to be more hands-on, while the MCSE job tasks involve more strategic concerns of design and planning.

The Implementing, Managing and Maintaining a Windows Server 2003 Network Infrastructure Exam

The Implementing, Managing and Maintaining a Windows Server 2003 Network Infrastructure exam covers concepts and skills related to installing, managing, and maintaining a Windows Server 2003 network infrastructure. It emphasizes the following elements of network infrastructure support:

- Implementing, Managing, and Maintaining IP Addressing
- Implementing, Managing, and Maintaining Name Resolution
- Implementing, Managing, and Maintaining Network Security
- Implementing, Managing, and Maintaining Routing and Remote Access
- Maintaining a Network Infrastructure

This exam is quite specific regarding Windows Server 2003 network infrastructure requirements and operational settings, and it can be particular about how administrative tasks are performed within the operating system. It also focuses on fundamental concepts of Windows Server 2003's operation. Careful study of this book, along with hands-on experience, will help you prepare for this exam.

Microsoft provides exam objectives to give you a general overview of possible areas of coverage on the Microsoft exams. Keep in mind, however, that exam objectives are subject to change at any time without prior notice and at Microsoft's sole discretion. Please visit Microsoft's Training and Certification website (www.microsoft.com/traincert) for the most current listing of exam objectives.

Types of Exam Questions

In an effort to both refine the testing process and protect the quality of its certifications, Microsoft has focused its Windows XP and Server 2003 exams on real experience and hands-on proficiency. There is a greater emphasis on your past working environments and responsibilities and less emphasis on how well you can memorize. In fact, Microsoft says a certification candidate should have at least six months of hands-on experience.

Microsoft will accomplish its goal of protecting the exams' integrity by regularly adding and removing exam questions, limiting the number of questions that any individual sees in a beta exam, and adding new exam elements.

Exam questions may be in a variety of formats: Depending on which exam you take, you'll see multiple-choice questions as well as select-and-place and prioritize-a-list questions. Simulations and case study–based formats are included as well. Let's take a look at the types of exam questions and examine the adaptive testing technique so you'll be prepared for all of the possibilities.

With the release of Windows 2000, Microsoft stopped providing a detailed score breakdown. This is mostly because of the various and complex question formats. Previously, each question focused on one objective. The Windows Server 2003 exams, however, contain questions that may be tied to one or more objectives from one or more objective sets. Therefore, grading by objective is almost impossible. Also, Microsoft no longer offers a score. Now you will only be told if you pass or fail.

For more information on the various exam question types, go to www.microsoft.com/traincert/mcpexams/policies/innovations.asp.

MULTIPLE-CHOICE QUESTIONS

Multiple-choice questions come in two main forms. One is a straightforward question followed by several possible answers, of which one or more is correct. The other type of multiple-choice question is more complex and based on a specific scenario. The scenario may focus on several areas or objectives.

SELECT-AND-PLACE QUESTIONS

Select-and-place exam questions involve graphical elements that you must manipulate to successfully answer the question. For example, you might see a diagram of a computer network, as shown in the following graphic taken from the select-and-place demo downloaded from Microsoft's website.

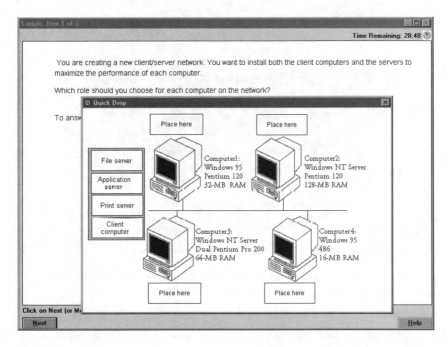

A typical diagram will show computers and other components next to boxes that contain the text "Place here." The labels for the boxes represent various computer roles on a network, such as a print server and a file server. Based on information given for each computer, you are asked to select each label and place it in the correct box. You need to place *all* of the labels correctly. No credit is given for the question if you correctly label only some of the boxes.

In another select-and-place problem you might be asked to put a series of steps in order by dragging items from boxes on the left to boxes on the right and placing them in the correct order. One other type requires that you drag an item from the left and place it under an item in a column on the right.

SIMULATIONS

Simulations are the kinds of questions that most closely represent actual situations and test the skills you use while working with Microsoft software interfaces. These exam questions include a mock interface on which you are asked to perform certain actions according to a given scenario. The simulated interfaces look nearly identical to what you see in the actual product, as shown in this example.

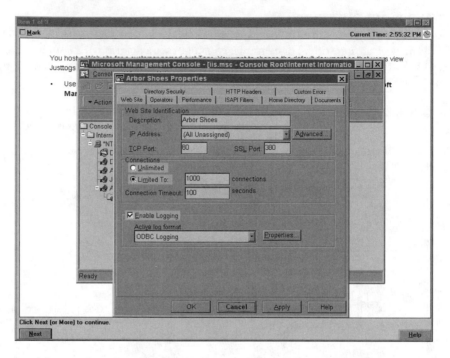

Because of the number of possible errors that can be made on simulations, be sure to consider the following recommendations from Microsoft:

- Do not change any simulation settings that don't pertain to the solution directly.
- When related information has not been provided, assume that the default settings are used.
- Make sure that your entries are spelled correctly.
- Close all the simulation application windows after completing the set of tasks in the simulation.

The best way to prepare for simulation questions is to spend time working with the graphical interface of the product on which you will be tested.

We recommend that you study with the WinSim 2003 product, which is included on the CD that accompanies this Study Guide. By completing the exercises in this Study Guide and working with the WinSim 2003 software, you will greatly improve your level of preparation for simulation questions.

CASE STUDY–BASED QUESTIONS

Case study–based questions first appeared in the MCSD program. These questions present a scenario with a range of requirements. Based on the information provided, you answer a series of multiple-choice and select-and-place questions. The interface for case study–based questions has a number of tabs, each of which contains information about the scenario.

At present, this type of question appears only in most of the Design exams.

Microsoft will regularly add and remove questions from the exams. This is called *item seeding*. It is part of the effort to make it more difficult for individuals to merely memorize exam questions that were passed along by previous test-takers.

Exam Question Development

Microsoft follows an exam-development process consisting of eight mandatory phases. The process takes an average of seven months and involves more than 150 specific steps. The MCP exam development consists of the following phases:

Phase 1: Job Analysis   Phase 1 is an analysis of all the tasks that make up a specific job function, based on tasks performed by people who are currently performing that job function. This phase also identifies the knowledge, skills, and abilities that relate specifically to the performance area being certified.

Phase 2: Objective Domain Definition   The results of the job analysis phase provide the framework used to develop objectives. Development of objectives involves translating the job-function tasks into a comprehensive package of specific and measurable knowledge, skills, and abilities. The resulting list of objectives—the *objective domain*—is the basis for the development of both the certification exams and the training materials.

Phase 3: Blueprint Survey   The final objective domain is transformed into a blueprint survey in which contributors are asked to rate each objective. These contributors may be MCP candidates, appropriately skilled exam-development volunteers, or Microsoft employees. Based on the contributors' input, the objectives are prioritized and weighted. The actual exam items are written according to the prioritized objectives. Contributors are queried about how they spend their time on the job. If a contributor doesn't spend an adequate amount of time actually performing the specified job function, his or her data is eliminated from the analysis. The blueprint survey phase helps determine which objectives to measure, as well as the appropriate number and types of items to include on the exam.

Phase 4: Item Development   A pool of items is developed to measure the blueprinted objective domain. The number and types of items to be written are based on the results of the blueprint survey.

Phase 5: Alpha Review and Item Revision   During this phase, a panel of technical and job-function experts reviews each item for technical accuracy. The panel then answers each item and reaches a consensus on all technical issues. Once the items have been verified as being technically accurate, they are edited to ensure that they are expressed in the clearest language possible.

Phase 6: Beta Exam   The reviewed and edited items are collected into beta exams. Based on the responses of all beta participants, Microsoft performs a statistical analysis to verify the validity of the exam items and to determine which items will be used in the certification exam. Once the analysis has been completed, the items are distributed into multiple parallel forms, or *versions*, of the final certification exam.

Phase 7: Item Selection and Cut-Score Setting   The results of the beta exams are analyzed to determine which items will be included in the certification exam. This determination is based on many factors, including item difficulty and relevance. During this phase, a panel of job-function experts determines the *cut score* (minimum passing score) for the exams. The cut score differs from exam to exam because it is based on an item-by-item determination of the percentage of candidates who answered the item correctly and who would be expected to answer the item correctly.

Phase 8: Live Exam   In the final phase, the exams are given to candidates. MCP exams are administered by Prometric and Virtual University Enterprises (VUE).

Tips for Taking the Windows Server 2003 Network Infrastructure Administration Exam

Here are some general tips for achieving success on your certification exam:

- Arrive early at the exam center so that you can relax and review your study materials. During this final review, you can look over tables and lists of exam-related information.

- Read the questions carefully. Don't be tempted to jump to an early conclusion. Make sure you know *exactly* what the question is asking.

- On simulations, do not change settings that are not directly related to the question. Also, assume default settings if the question does not specify or imply which settings are used.

- For questions you're not sure about, use a process of elimination to get rid of the obviously incorrect answers first. This improves your odds of selecting the correct answer when you need to make an educated guess.

Exam Registration

You may take the Microsoft exams at any of more than 1000 Authorized Prometric Testing Centers (APTCs) and VUE Testing Centers around the world. For the location of a testing center near you, call Prometric at 800-755-EXAM (755-3926), or call VUE at 888-837-8616.

Outside the United States and Canada, contact your local Prometric or VUE registration center.

Find out the number of the exam you want to take, and then register with the Prometric or VUE registration center nearest to you. At this point, you will be asked for advance payment for the exam. The exams are $125 each and you must take them within one year of payment. You can schedule exams up to six weeks in advance or as late as one working day prior to the date of the exam. You can cancel or reschedule your exam if you contact the center at least two working days prior to the exam. Same-day registration is available in some locations, subject to space availability. Where same-day registration is available, you must register a minimum of two hours before test time.

You may also register for your exams online at www.prometric.com or www.vue.com.

When you schedule the exam, you will be provided with instructions regarding appointment and cancellation procedures, ID requirements, and information about the testing center location. In addition, you will receive a registration and payment confirmation letter from Prometric or VUE.

Microsoft requires certification candidates to accept the terms of a Non-Disclosure Agreement before taking certification exams.

Is This Book for You?

If you want to acquire a solid foundation in Windows Server 2003 network infrastructure administration and your goal is to prepare for the exam by learning how to use and manage the new operating system, this book is for you. You'll find clear explanations of the fundamental concepts you need to grasp and plenty of help to achieve the high level of professional competency you need to succeed in your chosen field.

If you want to become certified as an MCSE or MCSA, this book is definitely for you. However, if you just want to attempt to pass the exam without really understanding Windows Server 2003 network infrastructure administration, this Study Guide is *not* for you. It is written for people who want to acquire hands-on skills and in-depth knowledge of Windows Server 2003 network infrastructure administration.

What's in the Book?

What makes a Sybex Study Guide the book of choice for over 100,000 MCPs? We took into account not only what you need to know to pass the exam, but what you need to know to take what you've learned and apply it in the real world. Each book contains the following:

Objective-by-objective coverage of the topics you need to know   Each chapter lists the objectives covered in that chapter.

The topics covered in this Study Guide map directly to Microsoft's official exam objectives. Each exam objective is covered completely.

Assessment Test   Directly following this introduction is an assessment test that you should take. It is designed to help you determine how much you already know about Windows Server 2003 network infrastructure administration. Each question is tied to a topic discussed in the book. Using the results of the assessment test, you can figure out the areas where you need to focus your study. Of course, we do recommend you read the entire book.

Exam Essentials   To highlight what you learn, you'll find a list of exam essentials at the end of each chapter. The Exam Essentials section briefly highlights the topics that need your particular attention as you prepare for the exam.

Key Terms and Glossary   Throughout each chapter, you will be introduced to important terms and concepts that you will need to know for the exam. These terms appear in italic within the chapters, and a list of the key terms appears just after the Exam Essentials. At the end of the book, a detailed glossary gives definitions for these terms, as well as other general terms you should know.

Review questions, complete with detailed explanations   Each chapter is followed by a set of review questions that test what you learned in the chapter. The questions are written with the exam in mind, meaning that they are designed to have the same look and feel as what you'll see on the exam. Question types are the same as questions types in like the exam, including multiple choice, exhibits, and select-and-place.

Hands-on exercises   In each chapter, you'll find exercises designed to give you the important hands-on experience that is critical for your exam preparation. The exercises support the topics of the chapter, and they walk you through the steps necessary to perform a particular function.

Real World Scenarios   Because reading a book isn't enough for you to learn how to apply these topics in your everyday duties, we have provided Real World Scenarios in special sidebars. These explain when and why a particular solution would make sense, in a working environment you'd actually encounter.

Interactive CD   Every Sybex Study Guide comes with a CD complete with additional questions, flashcards for use with an interactive device, a Windows simulation program, and the book in electronic format. Details are in the following section.

What's on the CD?

With this new member of our best-selling MCSE Study Guide series, we are including quite an array of training resources. The CD offers numerous simulations, bonus exams, and flashcards to help you study for the exam. We have also included the complete contents of the Study Guide in electronic form. The CD's resources are described here:

The Sybex E-book for Windows Server 2003 Network Infrastructure Administration   Many people like the convenience of being able to carry their whole Study Guide on a CD. They also like being able to search the text via computer to find specific information quickly and easily. For these reasons, the entire contents of this Study Guide are supplied on the CD, in PDF. We've also included Adobe Acrobat Reader, which provides the interface for the PDF contents as well as the search capabilities.

WinSim 2003   We developed the WinSim 2003 product to allow you to experience the multimedia and interactive operation of working with Windows Server 2003. WinSim 2003 provides both audio/video files and hands-on experience with key features of Windows Server 2003. Built around the Study Guide's exercises, WinSim 2003 will help you attain the knowledge and hands-on skills you must have in order to understand Windows Server 2003 (and pass the exam). Here is a sample screen from WinSim 2003:

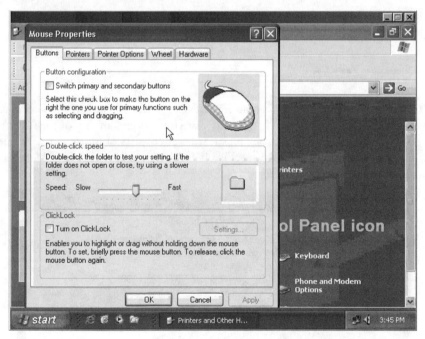

The Sybex Test Engine   This is a collection of multiple-choice questions that will help you prepare for your exam. There are four sets of questions:

- Two bonus exams designed to simulate the actual live exam.
- All the questions from the Study Guide, presented in a test engine for your review. You can review questions by chapter or by objective, or you can take a random test.
- The Assessment Test.

Here is a sample screen from the Sybex Test Engine:

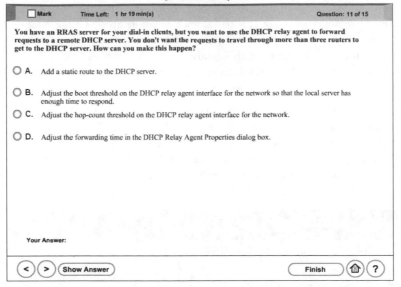

Sybex MCSE Flashcards for PCs and Handheld Devices The "flashcard" style of question offers an effective way to quickly and efficiently test your understanding of the fundamental concepts covered in the exam. The Sybex Flashcards set consists of more than 100 questions presented in a special engine developed specifically for this Study Guide series. Here's what the Sybex Flashcards interface looks like:

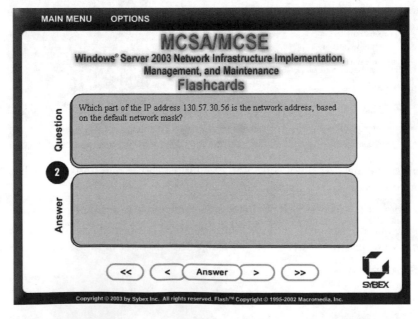

Because of the high demand for a product that will run on handheld devices, we have also developed, in conjunction with Land-J Technologies, a version of the flashcard questions that you can take with you on your Palm OS PDA (including the PalmPilot and Handspring's Visor).

In addition, if you bought this book as part of the MCSA: Windows 2003 Core Requirements or the MCSE: Windows 2003 Certification Kit box sets, you will find two bonus CDs—one including an 180-day evaluation version of Windows Server 2003 and another including two additional practice exams per book. Further information can be found in the readme files on the CDs and instructions on how to install Windows Server 2003 can be found on the bottom of the box set.

How Do You Use This Book?

This book provides a solid foundation for the serious effort of preparing for the exam. To best benefit from this book, you may wish to use the following study method:

1. Take the Assessment Test to identify your weak areas.

2. Study each chapter carefully. Do your best to fully understand the information.

3. Complete all the hands-on exercises in the chapter, referring back to the text as necessary so that you understand each step you take. If you don't have access to a lab environment in which you can complete the exercises, install and work with the exercises available in the WinSim 2003 software included with this Study Guide.

To do the exercises in this book, you must make sure your hardware meets the minimum hardware requirements for Windows Server 2003. See the section "Hardware and Software Requirements" for a list of recommended hardware and software we think you should have in your home lab.

4. Read over the Real World Scenarios to improve your understanding of how to use what you learn in the book.

5. Study the Exam Essentials and Key Terms to make sure you are familiar with the areas you need to focus on.

6. Answer the review questions at the end of each chapter. If you prefer to answer the questions in a timed and graded format, install the Sybex Test Engine from the book's CD and answer the chapter questions there instead of in the book.

7. Take note of the questions you did not understand, and study the corresponding sections of the book again.

8. Go back over the Exam Essentials and Key Terms.

9. Go through the Study Guide's other training resources, which are included on the book's CD. These include WinSim 2003, electronic flashcards, the electronic version of the chapter review questions (try taking them by objective), and the two bonus exams.

To learn all the material covered in this book, you will need to study regularly and with discipline. Try to set aside the same time every day to study, and select a comfortable and quiet place in which to do it. If you work hard, you will be surprised at how quickly you learn this material. Good luck!

Hardware and Software Requirements

You should verify that your computer meets the minimum requirements for installing Windows Server 2003. We suggest that your computer meets or exceeds the recommended requirements for a more enjoyable experience.

The exercises in this book assume that your computer is configured in a specific manner. For the exercises in this book, we assume that your computer should have at least a 3GB drive that is configured with the minimum space requirements and partitions.

Contacts and Resources

To find out more about Microsoft Education and Certification materials and programs, to register with Prometric or VUE, or to obtain other useful certification information and additional study resources, check the following resources:

Microsoft Training and Certification Home Page

www.microsoft.com/traincert

This website provides information about the MCP program and exams. You can also order the latest Microsoft Roadmap to Education and Certification.

Microsoft TechNet Technical Information Network

www.microsoft.com/technet

800-344-2121

Use this website or phone number to contact support professionals and system administrators. Outside the United States and Canada, contact your local Microsoft subsidiary for information.

Prometric

www.prometric.com

800-755-3936

Contact Prometric to register to take an MCP exam at any of more than 800 Prometric Testing Centers around the world.

Virtual University Enterprises (VUE)

www.vue.com

888-837-8616

Contact the VUE registration center to register to take an MCP exam at one of the VUE Testing Centers.

MCP Magazine Online

www.mcpmag.com

Microsoft Certified Professional Magazine is a well-respected publication that focuses on Windows certification. This site hosts chats and discussion forums and tracks news related to the MCSE program. Some of the services cost a fee, but they are well worth it.

Windows & .NET Magazine

www.windows2000mag.com

You can subscribe to this magazine or read free articles at the website. The study resource provides general information on Windows Server 2003, Windows XP, Windows 2000 Server.

Cramsession on Brainbuzz.com

cramsession.brainbuzz.com

Cramsession is an online community focusing on all IT certification programs. In addition to discussion boards and job locators, you can download one of several free cram sessions, which are nice supplements to any study approach you take.

Assessment Test

1. The time to live (TTL) attached to a DNS record _____.

    A. Cannot be used by a resolver, only by servers making recursive queries

    B. Is used only by resolvers

    C. Is used to determine how long to cache retrieved results

    D. Is refreshed each time the record is modified

2. Which of the following settings cannot be adjusted when using RIP?

    A. The RIP version that can be used for incoming and outgoing traffic on each interface

    B. The set of peer routers from which routes will be accepted

    C. The default announcement interval

    D. The location where received RIP routes are stored

3. You want to set up VPN access for 30 users, and the connections must be encrypted. There is a central Windows Server 2003 domain for your users. Which of the following is the most appropriate VPN solution in this case? See Chapter 7 for more information.

    A. L2TP + IPSec

    B. PPTP

    C. Either A or B

    D. None of the above.

4. To enable DHCP-DNS integration, you must do which of the following?

    A. Configure the scope to allow it to use Dynamic DNS only.

    B. Configure the server to allow it to use Dynamic DNS only.

    C. Configure the scope and the server.

    D. Configure the scope or the server.

5. RRAS allows you to create which types of routing-related filters?

    A. Route filters only

    B. Peer filters only

    C. Route and peer filters

    D. Packet filters only

6. What is the IPSec Policy Agent?

    A. It is an optional component that's required when using IPSec with Active Directory.

    B. It is an optional component that's required when using IPSec without Active Directory.

    C. It is an optional component that's required when using IPSec with L2TP.

    D. It is a mandatory component that's required to use IPSec.

7. The seven layers of the OSI model do which of the following?

    A. Map exactly to Windows 2000 networking services and components

    B. Provide a useful conceptual framework for grouping similar services

    C. A and B

    D. None of the above

8. To test whether a DNS server is answering queries properly, you can use which of the following tools?

    A. The ping tool

    B. The nslookup tool

    C. The tracert tool

    D. The ipconfig tool

9. What two modes do RIP routers send updates in?

    A. Link-state database mode

    B. Auto-static update mode

    C. Periodic Update Mode

    D. Border mode

10. You have installed the DHCP Server service on a member server in your domain and have configured a scope, but clients cannot lease an address. What is the most likely cause of this problem?

    A. The scope is not activated.

    B. There are too many DHCP servers.

    C. The DHCP server is not authorized.

    D. The DHCP server is in another subnet.

11. Which of the following statements about Windows Server 2003 Dynamic DNS is true?

    A. DDNS requires a Microsoft DHCP server to work.

    B. The Windows Server 2003 DDNS server can interoperate with recent versions of BIND.

    C. DDNS clients may not register their own addresses.

    D. DDNS only works with Microsoft clients and servers.

12. VPN connections require which of the following? (Choose two.)

    A. The Windows Server 2003 VPN add-on

    B. The name or IP address of the VPN server

    C. The phone number of the VPN server

    D. An existing TCP/IP connection

13. To reject any incoming call from a client that can't use a specified level of encryption, you would do which of the following?

    A. Turn off the No Encryption check box on the Encryption tab of the remote access policy's profile.

    B. Turn off the No Encryption check box on the Security tab of the server's Properties dialog box.

    C. Create a new remote access profile named Require Encryption.

    D. Check the Require Encryption check box in each user's profile.

14. Which of the following is not an OSI layer?

    A. Session

    B. Application

    C. Presentation

    D. Service

15. DHCP address range exclusions are assigned at which level?

    A. Server level

    B. Scope level

    C. Superscope level

    D. Multicast scope level

16. Which of the following is true about IPSec?

    A. Can be used by itself

    B. Can be used only with L2TP

    C. Cannot be used with L2TP

    D. Requires third-party software for Windows 2000 and above

17. Which of the following are true of dynamically maintained routing tables? (Choose all that apply.)

    A. It is automatically maintained by the routing protocols.

    B. It is normally not maintained across reboots.

    C. It may be manually edited from the command line.

    D. It is made up of multiple entries, each containing a network ID, a forwarding address, and a metric.

18. The DHCP relay agent serves which function on the network?

    A. It listens for DHCP messages on a network and forwards them to a DHCP server on another network.

    B. It accepts DHCP messages from multiple networks and consolidates them for a single DHCP server.

    C. It allows DHCP clients to use WINS services.

    D. It relays DHCP requests to a Dynamic DNS server.

19. Which of the following protocols or services is not required for an Active Directory installation?

    A. TCP/IP

    B. DNS

    C. LDAP

    D. NetBEUI

20. You can control VPN access through which of the following mechanisms? (Choose two.)

    A. Individual user account properties

    B. Remote access policies

    C. Remote access profiles

    D. Group policy objects

21. What is a mirrored rule?

    A. It is a single rule that specifies the same source and destination for two different protocols.

    B. It is a single rule that specifies the same source and destination for inbound and outbound traffic.

    C. It is a pair of rules that specify the same source and destination for two different protocols.

    D. It is a pair of rules that specify different source and destination addresses for the same protocol.

22. What is the replication of DNS data from one server to another called?

    A. Replication pass

    B. Zone transfer

    C. Replication transfer

    D. Zone replication

23. If settings on a local machine conflict with settings assigned by a DHCP server, which of the following statements are not true? (Choose all that apply.)

    A. None of the conflicting settings will apply.

    B. The DHCP-assigned settings override the locally assigned settings.

    C. Whichever settings are applied first take effect.

    D. The locally assigned settings override the DHCP-assigned settings.

24. To enable dial-up users to get a pooled IP address, you must do which of the following?

    A. Define an address pool on the IP tab of the server's Properties dialog box.

    B. Define an address pool in the remote access policy.

    C. Add a DHCP address range for the dial-up users.

    D. Disable the DHCP address allocator.

25. Which option is used as a tool to compare your desired security settings with your current security settings?

   A. Security template

   B. Security database

   C. Security profile

   D. Security analyst

26. Which policy types are applied to the computer as opposed to users and groups?

   A. Password policies

   B. Account lockout policies

   C. User rights assignment policies

   D. Security options

27. How do you open the IP Security Monitor in Windows Server 2003?

   A. Start ➤ Run and type **ipsecmon**

   B. Start ➤ Administrative Tools ➤ IP Security Monitor

   C. Start ➤ Accessories ➤ IP Security Monitor

   D. Add the IP Security Monitor snap-in to the MMC

28. What is the name of the file that stores information for a DNS zone?

   A. domain_name.dns

   B. LMHOSTS

   C. ZONES

   D. SERVERS

29. Which of the following statements is true regarding cacheing-only servers?

   A. They are authoritative for a domain

   B. They perform queries

   C. They contain zone files

   D. They participate in zone transfers

30. Which of the following options determines the permissions and restrictions for users dialing in to a remote access server?

   A. Remote access policies

   B. Remote access profiles

   C. Filter lists

   D. Authentication methods

Answers to Assessment Test

1. C. The TTL indicates how long the record may be safely cached; it may or may not be modified when the record is created. See Chapter 6 for more information on TTL.

2. D. The Routing Information Protocol (RIP) implementation in Windows Server 2003 allows you to mix RIP versions, control which peer routers can send you updates, and control how often your router will broadcast updates to others. However, it does now allow you to change where the routing table data is stored. See Chapter 9 for more information.

3. C. L2TP + IPSec and PPTP can both be encrypted, and with the guidelines set forth in the question, either one would do the job.

4. D. You can enable integration either on one scope only or on all scopes on a server. See Chapter 5 for more information.

5. C. Route filters let you accept or ignore individual routes; peer filters give you control over which other routers your router accepts routing information from. See Chapter 9 for more information.

6. D. The IPSec Policy Agent is the component that downloads IPSec policy settings from the local computer or Active Directory. Accordingly, presence is required for IPSec to function. See Chapter 4 for more information.

7. B. The OSI model is a stylized network model that can be used to compare and contrast implementations from different vendors. See Chapter 1 for more information on the OSI model.

8. B. Nslookup allows you to look up name and address information. See Chapter 6 for more information.

9. B, C. In periodic update mode, a RIP router sends out its list of known routes at periodic intervals (which you define). In auto-static update mode, the RRAS router only broadcasts the contents of its routing table when a remote router asks for it. See Chapter 9 for more information.

10. C. If the DHCP server isn't authorized, it will not answer lease requests; therefore, the client will end up with no address. See Chapter 5 for more information.

11. B. DDNS works with BIND 8.2 and later. See Chapter 6 for more information on DDNS.

12. B, D. VPN connections piggyback on top of regular dial-up or dedicated TCP/IP connections, and you must specify the name or address of the server you're calling. See Chapter 7 for more information.

13. A. The profile associated with each remote access policy controls whether that policy will require, allow, or disallow encryption. To force encryption, create a policy that disallows using no encryption. See Chapter 8 for more information.

14. D.   The Session, Application, and Presentation layers are all part of the OSI model, but the Service layer isn't. See Chapter 1 for more information on the OSI layers.

15. B.   Scopes or ranges of addresses can be assigned only at the scope level. The scope range includes the exclusion range. See Chapter 5 for more information.

16. A.   IPSec is a stand-alone protocol included in Windows Server 2003 that can be used by itself or in conjunction with Layer 2 Tunneling Protocol (L2TP). See Chapter 4 for more information.

17. A, C, D.   The routing engines maintain the contents of the routing table, although you may add or remove entries manually. Persistent routes, which are the default, are automatically maintained until you delete them manually. See Chapter 9 for more information.

18. A.   The DHCP relay agent allows you to use a DHCP server that resides on one network to communicate with clients that live on a separate network. See Chapter 7 for more information.

19. D.   NetBEUI is being deprecated, but the other three protocols are required for AD. See Chapter 2 for more information.

20. A, B.   You can allow users to make VPN connections by modifying individual account properties; if you're using a native mode Windows Server 2003 domain, you can also use remote access policies. See Chapter 8 for more information.

21. B.   A mirrored rule that maps a source address of A and a destination of B actually acts as two rules: source A/destination B for outbound traffic and source B/destination A for inbound traffic. See Chapter 4 for more information.

22. B.   *Zone transfer* is the term used for the transfer of resource records from one zone to another. See Chapter 6 for more information.

23. A, B, C.   Local settings always override settings specified by the DHCP server. See Chapter 2 for more information.

24. A.   To assign static IP addresses to dial-up clients, you have to define a pool of addresses on the server; this pool is used instead of allowing DHCP assignments to clients. See Chapter 7 for more information.

25. A.   Using the Security Configuration and Analysis tool, you can compare the security settings defined in a security template with a specific computer's actual security settings. See Chapter 3 for more information.

26. A, B, D.   Security options apply to computers as opposed to users and groups. See Chapter 3 for more information.

27. D.   In Windows Server 2003, IP Security Monitor is implemented as an MMC snap-in. See Chapter 4 for more information.

28. A.   The domain_name.dns file stores name to address mappings for DNS. LMHOSTS is used for WINS, and the other two options are not valid. See Chapter 6 for more information.

29. B.   DNS caching-only servers perform queries and cache the results, but they are not authoritative for any domains, do not contain zone files, or participate in zone transfers. See Chapter 6 for more information.

30. A.   Remote access policies determine who can log on to the remote access server and provide restrictions such as time of day and callback. Profiles determine the settings that apply after a user has successfully logged on. The other two options apply to IPSec and not to RAS. See Chapter 8 for more information.

Chapter

1

Understanding Windows Server 2003 Networking

Microsoft has put an immense amount of time and effort into building Windows Server 2003. It's not fair to say that this operating system is an entirely new product because it still retains a great deal of core code from Windows 2000 and even Windows NT, Internet Information Server, and Exchange Server. Windows Server 2003 is a large, complicated, and very powerful operating system. To use it effectively, you have to understand how it works and how to make it do what you want it to do. This book is a study guide for the Implementing, Managing, and Maintaining a Microsoft Windows Server 2003 Network Infrastructure exam, so it makes sense to lead off with a discussion of the network protocols included in Windows Server 2003—what they're for, how they work, and what you can do with them.

Having a good frame of reference helps when comparing network protocols. To establish such a frame, this chapter will begin with the Open Systems Interconnection (OSI) network model, a sort of idealized way to stack various protocols together.

The OSI Model

The International Organization for Standardization (ISO) began developing the *Open Systems Interconnection (OSI)* reference model in 1977. It has since become the most widely accepted model for understanding network communication; once you understand how the *OSI model* works, you can use it to compare network implementations on different systems.

When you want to communicate with another person, you need to have two things in common: a communication language and a communication medium. Computer networks are no different; for communication to take place on a network composed of a variety of different network devices, both the language and medium must be clearly defined. The OSI model (and networking models developed by other organizations) attempts to define rules that cover both the generalities and specifics of networks:

- How network devices contact each other and, if they have different languages, how they communicate with each other

- Methods by which a device on a network knows when to transmit data and when not to

- Methods to ensure that network transmissions are received correctly and by the right recipient

- How the physical transmission media is arranged and connected

- How to ensure that network devices maintain a proper rate of data flow

- How bits are represented on the network media

The OSI model isn't a product. It's just a conceptual framework you can use to better understand the complex interactions taking place among the various devices on a network. It doesn't do anything in the communication process; appropriate software and hardware do the actual work. The OSI model simply defines which tasks need to be done and which protocols will handle those tasks at each of the seven layers of the model. The seven layers are as follows:

- Application (layer 7)
- Presentation (layer 6)
- Session (layer 5)
- Transport (layer 4)
- Network (layer 3)
- Data-Link (layer 2)
- Physical (layer 1)

You can remember the seven layers using a handy mnemonic, such as "All Pitchers Sometimes Take Naps During Preseason."

Each of the seven layers has a distinct function, which we'll explore a little later in the chapter.

Protocol Stacks

The OSI model splits communication tasks into smaller pieces called subtasks. Protocol implementations are computer processes that handle these subtasks. Specific protocols fulfill subtasks at specific layers of the OSI model. When these protocols are grouped together to complete a whole task, the assemblage of code is called a *protocol stack*. The stack is just a group of protocols, arranged in layers, that implements an entire communication process. Each layer of the OSI model has a different protocol associated with it. When more than one protocol is needed to complete a communication process, the protocols are grouped together in a stack. An example of a protocol stack is TCP/IP, which is widely used by Unix and the Internet—the TCP and IP protocols are implemented at different OSI layers.

Each layer in the protocol stack receives services from the layer below it and provides services to the layer above it. It can be better explained like this: Layer N uses the services of the layer below it (layer N – 1) and provides services to the layer above it (layer N + 1).

For two computers to communicate, the same protocol stacks must be running on each computer. Each layer on both computers' stacks must use compatible protocols in order for the machines to communicate with each other. The computers can have different operating systems and still be able to communicate if they are running the same protocol stacks. For example, a DOS machine running TCP/IP can communicate with a Macintosh machine running TCP/IP (see Figure 1.1).

FIGURE 1.1   Each layer communicates with its counterparts on other network hosts.

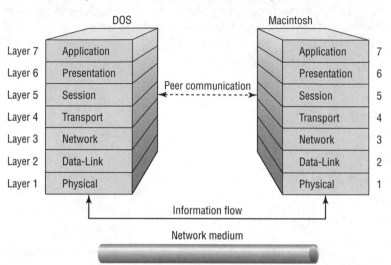

The Physical Layer

The Physical layer is responsible for sending bits from one computer to another. Physical layer components don't care what the bits *mean*; their job is to get the bits from point A to point B, using whatever kind of optical, electrical, or wireless connection that connects the points. This level defines physical and electrical details, such as what will represent a 1 or a 0, how many pins a network connector will have, how data will be synchronized, and when the network adapter may or may not transmit the data (see Figure 1.2).

FIGURE 1.2   The Physical layer makes a physical circuit with electrical, optical, or radio signals.

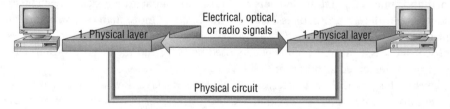

The Physical layer addresses all the minutiae of the actual physical connection between the computer and the network medium, including the following:

- Network connection types, including multipoint and point-to-point connections.

- Physical topologies, or how the network is physically laid out (e.g., bus, star, or ring topologies).

- Which analog and digital signaling methods are used to encode data in the analog and digital signals.

- Bit synchronization, which deals with keeping the sender and receiver in synch as they read and write data.

- Multiplexing, or the process of combining several data channels into one.

- Termination, which prevents signals from reflecting back through the cable and causing signal and packets errors. It also indicates the last node in a network segment.

The Data-Link Layer

The Data-Link layer provides for the flow of data over a single physical link from one device to another. It accepts packets from the Network layer and packages the information into data units called frames; these frames are presented to the Physical layer for transmission. The Data-Link layer adds control information, such as frame type, to the data being sent.

This layer also provides for the error-free transfer of frames from one computer to another. A *cyclic redundancy check (CRC)* added to the data frame can detect damaged frames, and the Data-Link layer in the receiving computer can request that the CRC information be present so that it can check incoming frames for errors. The Data-Link layer can also detect when frames are lost and request that those frames be sent again.

In broadcast networks such as Ethernet, all devices on the LAN receive the data that any device transmits. (Whether a network is broadcast or point-to-point is determined by the network protocols used to transmit data over it.) The Data-Link layer on a particular device is responsible for recognizing frames addressed to that device and throwing the rest away, much as you might sort through your daily mail to separate good stuff from junk. Figure 1.3 shows how the Data-Link layer establishes an error-free connection between two devices.

FIGURE 1.3   The Data-Link layer establishes an error-free link between two devices.

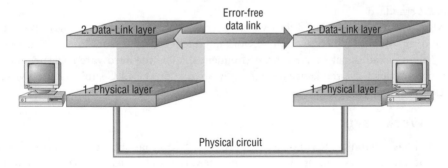

The Institute of Electrical and Electronics Engineers (IEEE) developed a protocol specification known as IEEE 802.X. (802.2 is the standard that divides this layer into two sublayers. The MAC layer varies for different network types and is described further in standards 802.3 through 802.5.) As part of that specification (which today we know as Ethernet), the Data-Link layer is split into two sublayers:

- The *Logical Link Control (LLC)* layer establishes and maintains the logical communication links between the communicating devices.

- The *Media Access Control (MAC)* layer acts like an airport control tower—it controls the way multiple devices share the same media channel in the same way that a control tower regulates the flow of air traffic into and out of an airport.

Figure 1.4 illustrates the division of the Data-Link layer into the LLC and MAC layers.

FIGURE 1.4   The IEEE split the ISO Data-Link layer into the LLC sublayer and the MAC sublayer.

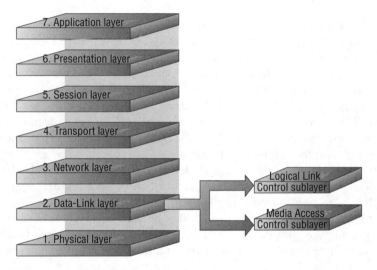

The LLC sublayer provides *Service Access Points (SAPs)* that other computers can refer to and use to transfer information from the LLC sublayer to the upper OSI layers. This is defined in the 802.2 standard.

The MAC sublayer, the lower of the two sublayers, provides for shared access to the network adapter and communicates directly with network interface cards. Network interface cards have a unique 12-digit hexadecimal MAC address (frequently called the hardware Ethernet address) assigned before they leave the factory where they are made. The LLC sublayer uses MAC addresses to establish logical links between devices on the same LAN.

The Network Layer

The Network layer handles moving packets between devices that are more than one link away from each other. It makes routing decisions and forwards packets as necessary to help them travel to their intended destination. In larger networks, there may be intermediate devices and subnetworks between any two end systems. The network layer makes it possible for the Transport layer (and layers above it) to send packets without being concerned with whether the end system is on the same piece of network cable or on the other end of a large wide area network.

To do its job, the Network layer translates logical network addresses into physical machine addresses (MAC addresses, which operate at the Data-Link layer). The Network layer also determines the quality of service (such as the priority of the message) and the route a message will take if there are several ways a message can get to its destination.

The Network layer also may split large packets into smaller chunks if the packet is larger than the largest data frame the Data-Link layer will accept. The network reassembles the chunks into packets at the receiving end.

Intermediate systems that perform only routing and relaying functions and do not provide an environment for executing user programs can implement just the first three OSI network layers. Figure 1.5 shows how the Network layer moves packets across multiple links in a network.

FIGURE 1.5   The Network layer moves packets across links to their destination.

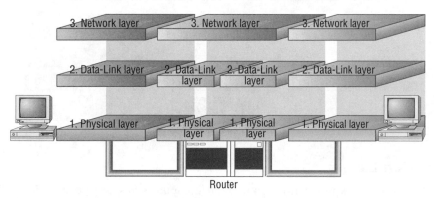

The Network layer performs several important functions that enable data to arrive at its destination. The protocols at this layer may choose a specific route through an internetwork to avoid the excess traffic caused by sending data over networks and segments that don't need access to it. The Network layer serves to support communications between logically separate networks. This layer is concerned with the following:

- Addressing, including logical network addresses and services addresses
- Circuit, message, and packet switching
- Route discovery and route selection
- Connection services, including Network layer flow control, Network layer error control, and packet sequence control
- Gateway services

In Windows Server 2003, the various routing services for TCP/IP, AppleTalk, and Internetwork Packet Exchange/Sequenced Packet Exchange (IPX/SPX) perform Network layer services (see Chapter 9, "Managing IP Routing," for more on these services). In addition, the TCP/IP, AppleTalk, and IPX stacks provide routing capacity for those protocols.

The Transport Layer

The Transport layer ensures that data is delivered error free, in sequence, and with no losses or duplications. This layer also breaks large messages from the Session layer into smaller packets to be sent to the destination computer and reassembles packets into messages to be presented to the Network layer. The Transport layer typically sends an acknowledgment to the originator for messages received (as in Figure 1.6).

FIGURE 1.6   The Transport layer provides end-to-end communication with integrity and performance guarantees.

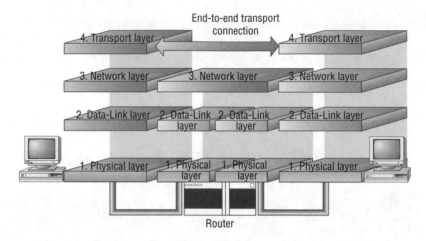

The Session Layer

The Session layer allows applications on separate computers to share a connection called a session. This layer provides services, such as name lookup and security, that allow two programs to find each other and establish the communication link. The Session layer also provides for data synchronization and checkpointing so that in the event of a network failure, only the data sent after the point of failure would need to be resent. This layer also controls the dialog between two processes and determines who can transmit and who can receive at what point during the communication (see Figure 1.7).

FIGURE 1.7   The Session layer allows applications to establish communication sessions with each other.

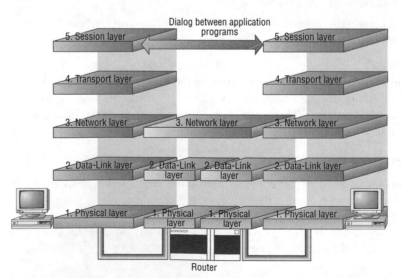

The Presentation Layer

The Presentation layer translates data between the formats the network requires and the formats the computer expects. The Presentation layer performs protocol conversion; data translation, compression, and encryption; character set conversion; and the interpretation of graphics commands.

The network redirector, long a part of Windows networking, operates at this level. The redirector is what makes the files on a file server visible to the client computer. The network redirector also makes remote printers act as though they are attached to the local computer. Figure 1.8 shows the Presentation layer's role in the protocol stack.

FIGURE 1.8   The Presentation layer allows applications to establish communication sessions with each other.

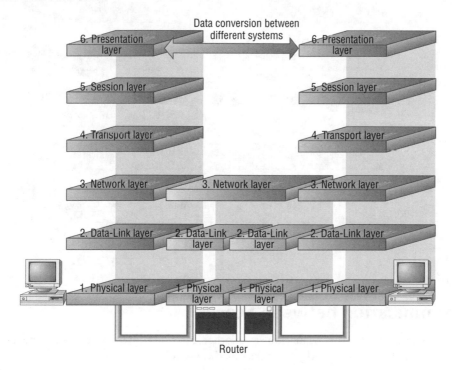

The Application Layer

The Application layer is the topmost layer of the OSI model, and it provides services that directly support user applications, such as database access, e-mail, and file transfers. It also allows applications to communicate with applications on other computers as though they were on the same computer. When a programmer writes an application program that uses network services, this is the layer the application program will access. For example, Internet Explorer uses the Application layer to make its requests for files and web pages; the Application layer then passes those requests down the stack, with each succeeding layer doing its job (as in Figure 1.9).

FIGURE 1.9 The Application layer is where the applications function, using lower levels to get their work done.

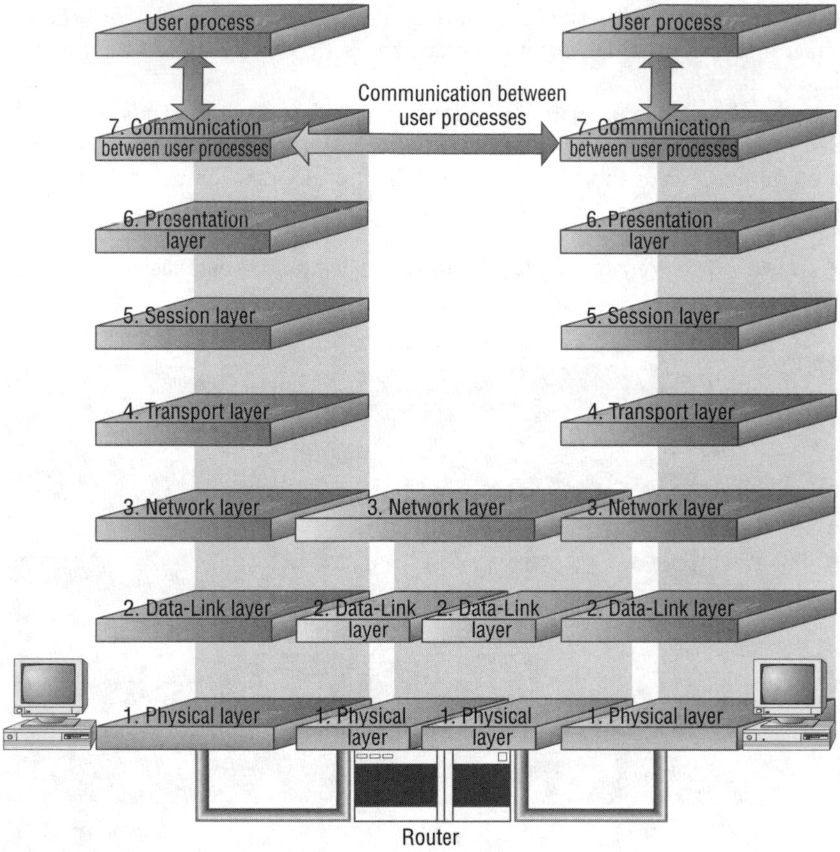

Communication between Stacks

When a message is sent from one machine to another, it travels down the layers on one machine and then up the layers on the other machine, as shown in Figure 1.10.

As the message travels down the first stack, each layer it passes through (except the Physical layer) adds a header. These headers contain pieces of control information that are read and processed by the corresponding layer on the receiving stack. As the message travels up the stack of the other machine, each layer removes the header added by its peer layer and uses the information it finds to figure out what to do with the message contents (see Figure 1.11).

As an example, consider the network we're using while writing this book. It's a TCP/IP network containing several Windows 2000, Windows Server 2003, Macintosh, and Windows NT machines, all connected using the TCP/IP protocol. When we mount a share from our Windows Server 2003 file server on the Mac desktop, at layer 7, the Mac Finder requests something from the Windows Server 2003. This request is sent to the Mac's layer 6, which receives the request as a data packet, adds its own header, and passes the packet down to layer 5. At layer 5, the process is repeated, and it continues until the packet makes it to the Physical layer. The physical layer is responsible for actually moving the bits across the network wiring in the office, so it carries the request packet to a place where the Windows Server 2003 machine can "hear" it. At that point, the request packet begins its journey up the layers on the Windows Server 2003 file server. The header that was put on at the Data-Link layer of the Mac OS is stripped off at the Data-Link layer on the Windows Server 2003 machine. The Windows Data-Link layer driver performs the tasks requested in the header and passes the requests to the next, higher layer. This process is repeated until the Windows Server 2003 file server receives the packet and interprets the request. The Windows Server 2003 would then formulate an appropriate response and send it to the Mac.

FIGURE 1.10 Traffic flows down through the stack on one computer and up the stack on the other.

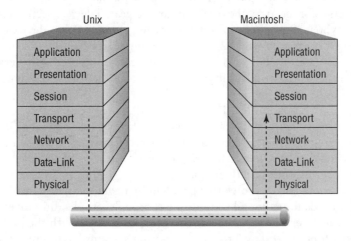

FIGURE 1.11 As packets flow up and down the stacks, each layer adds or removes necessary control information.

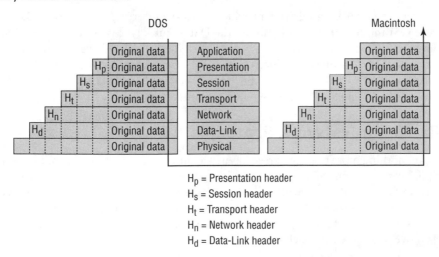

H_p = Presentation header
H_s = Session header
H_t = Transport header
H_n = Network header
H_d = Data-Link header

Microsoft's Network Components and the OSI Model

Because the OSI model is so abstract, it can be hard to tell how its concepts relate to the actual network software and hardware you use in the real world. The following sections will make the link clearer. We will introduce you to the specific protocols that are included with Windows Server 2003 and see how they apply to the various layers of the OSI model.

Device Drivers and the OSI Model

Every hardware device in a computer requires a software-based device driver to make it work. Some drivers—for instance, the driver for an integrated device electronics (IDE) hard disk or for the keyboard—are built into the operating system. Other devices require that drivers be installed separately when the device is attached or installed in the computer. Windows Server 2003 really blurs this distinction because it includes drivers for several hundred different network cards but if your card isn't on the list, you will need to install drivers provided by the manufacturer.

In the past (e.g., when Windows 3.11 was introduced), network drivers were vendor specific, for both the operating system and the card. You might, for instance, have a difficult time if you wanted to put a 3Com Ethernet card and an IBM Token Ring card in the same server. Worse yet, most drivers could only be bound to a single protocol stack and a single card, so you couldn't have two cards using TCP/IP on one server.

A variety of vendors tried to solve this problem by developing driver interfaces that allowed multiple cards to be bound to multiple protocols. Apple and Novell developed the *Open Data-link Interface (ODI)*, and Microsoft countered with the *Network Driver Interface Specification (NDIS)*. Microsoft's operating systems have supported NDIS ever since, making it possible to bind either multiple protocols to one card or the same protocol to multiple cards.

Network adapter cards and drivers provide the services corresponding to the Data-Link layer in the OSI model. In the IEEE model, the Data-Link layer is split into the Logical Link Control (LLC) sublayer—which corresponds to the software drivers—and the Media Access Control (MAC) sublayer—which corresponds to the network adapter. You can think of the drivers as intermediaries between the higher layers and the card hardware that handles the business of forming packets and stuffing them into a wire.

The Basics of Network Protocols

Protocols are nothing more than an agreed-upon way in which two objects (people, computers, home appliances, etc.) can exchange information. There are protocols at various levels in the OSI model. In fact, it is the protocols at a particular level in the OSI model that provide that level's functionality. Protocols that work together to provide a layer or layers of the OSI model are known as a protocol stack or protocol suite. The following sections explain how network protocols move data between machines.

How Protocols Work

A protocol is a set of basic steps that both computers must perform in the right order. For instance, for one computer to send a message to another computer, the first computer must perform the steps given in the following general example:

1. Break the data into small sections called packets.

2. Add addressing information to the packets, identifying the destination computer.

3. Deliver the data to the network card for transmission over the network.

The receiving computer must perform these steps:

1. Accept the data from the network adapter card.

2. Remove the transmitting information that was added by the transmitting computer.

3. Reassemble the packets of data into the original message.

Each computer needs to perform the same steps, in the same way and in the correct order, so that the data will arrive and be reassembled correctly. If one computer uses a protocol with different steps or even the same steps with different parameters (such as different sequencing, timing, or error correction), the two computers won't be able to communicate with each other.

Network Packets

Networks primarily send and receive small chunks of data called *packets*. Network protocols construct, modify, and disassemble packets as they move data down the sending stack, across the network, and back up the OSI stack of the receiving computer. Packets have the following components:

- A source address specifying the sending computer

- A destination address specifying where the packet is being sent

- Instructions that tell the computer how to pass the data along

- Reassembly information (if the packet is part of a longer message)

- The data to be transmitted to the remote computer (often called the *packet payload*)

- Error-checking information to ensure that the data arrives intact

These components are assembled into slightly larger chunks; each packet contains three distinct parts (listed here and seen in Figure 1.12), and each part contains some of the components listed previously:

Header   A typical header includes an alert signal to indicate that the data is being transmitted, source and destination addresses, and clock information to synchronize the transmission.

Data   This is the actual data being sent. It can vary (depending on the network type) from 48 bytes to 4 kilobytes.

Trailer   The contents of the trailer (or even the existence of a trailer) vary among network types, but it typically includes a CRC. The CRC helps the network determine whether or not a packet has been damaged in transmission.

FIGURE 1.12   A packet consists of a header, the data, and a trailer.

| Header | Data | Trailer |

Protocols and Binding

Many different protocol stacks can perform network functions, and many different types of network interface cards can be installed in a computer. A computer may have more than one card, and a computer may use more than one protocol stack at the same time.

The *binding* process is what links the protocol stack to the network device driver for the network interface adapter. Several protocols can be bound to the same card; for instance, both TCP/IP and AppleTalk can be bound to the same Ethernet adapter. In addition, one computer with several interface adapters—for instance, a server that must be able to communicate with both a local area network and a network backbone—can have the same protocol bound to two or more network cards.

The binding process can be used throughout the OSI layers to link one protocol stack to another. The device driver (which implements the Data-Link layer) is bound to the network interface card (which implements the Physical layer). TCP/IP can be bound to the device driver, and the NWLINK Session layer can be bound to the device driver.

Bindings are particularly important to Windows Server 2003 because you'll often want to change the bindings so that protocols you don't need on a particular network aren't bound to some network adapters. For example, it's very common to unbind the NWLINK protocol from the network card connected to a web server's Internet connection.

Determining Connections

There are two ways that communication between computers can be arranged: using connectionless protocols and using connection-oriented protocols. It's important to understand the differences between them because different Windows Server 2003 services use both types.

Connectionless Protocols

It might seem odd to talk about a connectionless protocol for networks, but you use at least two of them just about every day: radio and television. Connectionless systems assume that all data will get through, so the protocol doesn't guarantee delivery or correct packet ordering. Think of shouting a message out of your window to someone walking by outside—there's no guarantee that they'll hear you, but it's quick and easy. These optimistic assumptions mean that there's no protocol overhead spent on these activities, so connectionless protocols tend to be fast. The *User Datagram Protocol (UDP)*, which is part of the TCP/IP protocol standard, is an example of a connectionless Internet transport protocol.

Connectionless systems normally work pretty well on lightly loaded networks like most local area networks. Unfortunately, they break down quickly in large or heavily loaded networks where packets can be dropped due to line noise or router congestion.

All is not lost for connectionless transports, however, because higher-level protocols will know what data has not reached its destination after some time and request a retransmission. However, connectionless systems don't necessarily return data in sequential order, so the higher-level protocol must sort out the data packets.

Connection-Oriented Protocols

Connection-oriented systems work more like your telephone—you have to dial a number and establish a connection to the other end before you can send a message. Connection-oriented protocols pessimistically assume that some data will be lost or disordered in most transmissions. They guarantee that transmitted data will reach its destination in the proper sequence and that all data will get through. To accomplish this, connection-oriented protocols retain the transmitted data and negotiate for a retransmission when needed. Once all the needed data has arrived at the remote end, it can be reassembled into its proper sequence and passed to the higher-level protocols. This means that any application can depend on a connection-oriented transport to reliably deliver data exactly as it was transmitted. Transmission Control Protocol (TCP) is an example of a connection-oriented Internet protocol.

For local area systems where data isn't likely to be dropped, it makes sense to push serialization and guaranteed delivery up to higher-level protocols that are less efficient because they won't be used often anyway. But in wide area networks like the Internet, it would simply take too much time for higher-level protocols to sort out what data had been sent and what was missing, so the transport protocol simply takes measures to guarantee that all the data gets through in order.

Network Protocols and Windows Server 2003

So far, you've been reading a lot of abstract material that might not seem pertinent to Windows Server 2003. Now we'll show you the network protocols included with Windows Server 2003 and how each fits into the models you've read about up to this point.

There are a number of protocol stacks used in the world's networks today. Besides NetWare, AppleTalk, NetBIOS, and TCP/IP, there are a bunch of specialty protocols like IBM's Systems Network Architecture (SNA), Digital's (now HP/Compaq's) DECnet, and others. Even though these protocols actually work at different levels of the OSI model, they fall neatly into three distinct groups, as seen in the following list and in Figure 1.13:

- Application protocols provide for application-to-application interaction and data exchange.

- Transport protocols establish communication sessions between computers.

- Network protocols handle issues such as routing and addressing information, error checking, and retransmission requests.

Microsoft networking products come with three network transports—NWLink IPX/SPX, AppleTalk, and TCP/IP—and each is intended for networks of different sizes with different requirements. Each network transport has different strengths and weaknesses. *NWLink* is intended for medium-sized networks (in a single facility, perhaps) or for networks that require access to Novell NetWare file servers. AppleTalk's primary use is interoperating with Macintosh computers (a topic that's too specialized to discuss further here). *TCP/IP* is a complex transport sufficient for globe-spanning networks such as the Internet, and Microsoft is doing everything possible to position TCP/IP as a one-size-fits-all network protocol. TCP/IP is required to use Active Directory and is the default protocol for Windows Server 2003.

 Windows Server 2003 does not include support for the now defunct NetBEUI protocol. NetBEUI was not routable and Microsoft deemed the protocol unsuitable for enterprise-scale networks.

FIGURE 1.13 The OSI protocol stack can be simplified by grouping its layers into three new categories.

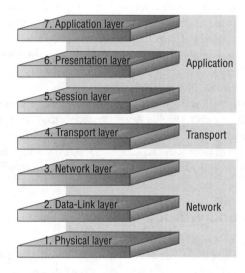

NWLink

NWLink IPX/SPX is Microsoft's implementation of Novell's IPX/SPX protocol stack, which is used in Novell NetWare. In fact, it's fair to say that NWLink IPX/SPX is nothing more than IPX for Windows.

NWLink IPX/SPX is included with Windows Server 2003 primarily to allow Windows Server 2003 to interconnect with legacy Novell NetWare servers and clients. Microsoft clients and servers can then be added to existing network installations, over time easing the migration between platforms and obviating the need for a complete cutover from one networking standard to another.

The advantages of NWLink IPX/SPX include the following:

- It's easy to set up and manage.
- It's routable.
- It's easy to connect to installed NetWare servers and clients.

However, NWLink IPX/SPX has some disadvantages, such as these:

- With NWLink IPX/SPX, it is difficult to exchange traffic with other organizations.

- It has limited support in Windows Server 2003.
- It doesn't support standard network management protocols.

Truly large networks (networks that connect many organizations) may find that NWLink IPX/SPX is difficult to use because there is no effective central IPX addressing scheme—as there is with TCP/IP—to ensure that two networks don't use the same address numbers. IPX doesn't support the wide range of network management tools available for TCP/IP.

TCP/IP

TCP/IP is actually two sets of protocols bundled together: The *Transmission Control Protocol (TCP)* and the *Internet Protocol (IP)*. TCP/IP, and a suite of related protocols, were developed by the Department of Defense's Advanced Research Projects Agency (ARPA, or later DARPA) beginning in 1969. The original goal was to develop network protocols that were robust enough to route communications around damage caused by nuclear war. That design goal was never tested, but some aspects of that design have led to the redundant, distributed whole we call the Internet.

TCP/IP is by far the most widely used protocol for interconnecting computers, and it is the protocol of the Internet. This is because, although ARPA originally created TCP/IP to connect military networks together, it provided the protocol standards to government agencies and universities free of charge. The academic world leapt at the chance to use a robust protocol to interconnect their networks, and the Internet was born. Many organizations and individuals collaborated to create higher-level protocols for everything from newsgroups, mail transfer, and file transfer to printing, remote booting, and even document browsing.

TCP/IP is currently the protocol of choice for most networks because of its rapid and widespread adoption. TCP/IP is used for networks that span more than one metropolitan area or to connect to (or over) the Internet.

TCP/IP has some significant advantages:

- Broad connectivity among all types of computers and servers, including direct access to the Internet
- Strong support for routing, using a number of flexible routing protocols (see Chapter 9 for more on these protocols)
- Support for advanced name and address resolution services (which will be covered in more depth later in this book): the Domain Name Service (DNS), the Dynamic Host Configuration Protocol (DHCP), and the Windows Internet Name Service (WINS)
- Support for a wide variety of Internet-standard protocols, including protocols for mail transport, web browsing, and file and print services
- Centralized network number and name assignment, which facilitates internetworking between organizations

TCP/IP has some disadvantages:

- It's harder to set up than IPX.
- Its routing and connectivity features impose relatively high overhead.
- It's slower than IPX.

Even given these disadvantages, it's the core protocol that Windows Server 2003 depends on for all its network services. In fact, most of this book focuses on TCP/IP and related services.

TCP (and UDP) relies on port numbers assigned by the Internet Assigned Numbers Authority (IANA) to forward packets to the appropriate application process. Port numbers are 16-bit integers that are part of a message header and identify the process that the packet should be associated with.

For example, let's say that a client has a copy of Internet Explorer and a copy of Outlook Express open at the same time. Both applications are sending TCP requests across the Internet to retrieve web pages and e-mail, respectively. How does the computer know which packets to forward to Internet Explorer and which packets to forward to Outlook Express? Every packet destined for Internet Explorer has a port number of 80 in the header, and every packet destined for Outlook Express has a port number of 110 in the header. Table 1.1 contains a list of the major port numbers you might need to know for the exam. You can also visit www.iana.org to get the most current full list of port numbers.

TABLE 1.1   Well-known Port Numbers

Port Number	Description
20	File Transfer Protocol (FTP) data
21	File Transfer Protocol (FTP) control
23	Telnet
25	Simple Mail Transfer Protocol (SMTP)
80	Hypertext Transfer Protocol (HTTP), Web
88	Kerberos
110	Post Office Protocol v3 (POP3)
443	Secure HTTP (HTTPS)

 Real World Scenario

Understanding the OSI Model and Troubleshooting

The company you work for has several regional offices spread around the country. Your job is to make sure the resources on the Windows Server 2003 network, which include manufacturing, inventory, and sales information, are available at all times. If the sales information from the regional offices isn't collected and updated to the manufacturing and inventory programs, the company won't be able to supply its customers effectively. The users of the network aren't particularly interested in the technical nuts and bolts of the system, but they do care when the system is down.

At the same time, you're studying for your MSCE and wondering how the abstract notions of the OSI model are relevant to your job. A support call comes in from a user who can't connect to a printer on a Windows Server 2003 machine in another region where an executive management meeting is taking place. The user is down the hall from you, so you drop everything and run down to take a look.

With the OSI model fresh in mind, you approach the problem in terms of layers of functionality. You ping the address of your router, and it comes back fine. You now know that the Physical, Data-Link, Network, and Transport layers are working fine, which means that you have eliminated cable and basic protocol problems. Your browser also seems to work fine because you can reach random sites. When you ping the name of the Windows Server 2003 machine that hosts the printer, you get the "request timed out" message. But when you ping the IP address directly, the reply shows a healthy connection, implying that you have a name resolution problem. You connect to the printer using a Net Use with the IP address and begin the task of looking at your WINS server.

By breaking down your troubleshooting tactics into the general OSI layers, you can get a better gauge of where the problem lies and which services to look at, depending on where in the OSI model the symptoms appear. Although the OSI model is fairly abstract, when it's applied appropriately, it gives you a structure for thinking about your overall network and provides a framework for following methodical troubleshooting tactics.

Understanding IP Addressing

Understanding IP addressing is critical to understanding how TCP/IP works. An IP address is a numeric identifier assigned to each machine on a TCP/IP network. It designates the location of the device it is assigned to on the network. This type of address is a software address, not a hardware address, which is hard-coded in the machine or network interface card.

In the following sections, you will see how IP addresses are used to uniquely identify every machine on a network.

We're going to assume you're comfortable with binary notation and math for the remainder of this section.

The Hierarchical IP Addressing Scheme

An IP address is made up of 32 bits of information. These bits are divided into four sections (sometimes called octets or quads) containing 1 byte (8 bits) each. There are three methods for specifying an IP address:

▪   Dotted-decimal, as in 130.57.30.56

- Binary, as in 10000010.00111001.00011110.00111000

- Hexadecimal, as in 82 39 1E 38

All of these examples represent the same IP address.

The 32-bit IP address is a structured address, or *hierarchical address*, as opposed to a flat address, or nonhierarchical one. Although IP could have used either flat or hierarchical addressing, its designers chose hierarchical addressing—for a very good reason, as you will see.

What's the difference between these two types of addressing? A good example of a flat addressing scheme is a driver's license number. There's no partitioning to it; the range of legal numbers isn't broken up in any meaningful way (say, by county of residence or date of issuance). If this method had been used for IP addressing, every machine on the Internet would have needed a totally unique address, just as each driver's license number is unique. The good news about flat addressing is that it can handle a large number of addresses, namely 4.3 billion (a 32-bit address space with two possible values for each position—either 0 (zero) or 1 (one)— giving you 2^{32}, which equals approximately 4.3 billion). The bad news—and the reason why flat addressing isn't used in IP—relates to routing. If every address were totally unique, every router on the Internet would need to store the address of each and every *other* machine on the Internet. It would be fair to say that this would make efficient routing impossible, even if only a fraction of the possible addresses were used.

The solution to this dilemma is to use a hierarchical addressing scheme that breaks the address space up into ordered chunks. Telephone numbers are a great example of this type of addressing. The first section of a telephone number, the area code, designates a very large area; the area code is followed by the prefix, which narrows the scope to a local calling area. The final segment, the customer number, zooms in on the specific connection. By looking at a number like 256-233-*xxxx*, you can quickly determine that the number is located in the northern part of Alabama (area code 256) in the Athens/East Limestone area (the 233 exchange).

IP addressing works the same way. Instead of treating the entire 32 bits as a unique identifier, one part of the IP address is designated as the *network address* and the other part as a *node address*, giving it a layered, hierarchical structure.

The network address uniquely identifies each network. Every machine on the same network shares that network address as part of its IP address. In the IP address 130.57.30.56, for example, *130.57* is the network address.

The node address is assigned to, and uniquely identifies, each machine in a network. This part of the address must be unique because it identifies a particular machine—an individual as opposed to a network that is a group. This number can also be referred to as a host address. In the sample IP address 130.57.30.56, *.30.56* is the node address.

The designers of the Internet decided to create classes of networks based on network size. For the small number of networks possessing a very large number of nodes, they created the Class A network. At the other extreme is the Class C network, reserved for the numerous networks with a small number of nodes. The class distinction for networks in between very large and very small is predictably called a Class B network. How you subdivide an IP address into a network and node address is determined by the class designation of your network. Table 1.2 provides a summary of the three classes of networks, which will be described in more detail in the following sections.

TABLE 1.2 Network Address Classes

Class	Format	Leading Bit Pattern	Decimal Range of First Byte of Network Address	Maximum Number of Networks	Maximum Nodes per Network
A	Node	0	1–126	126	16,777,214
B	Node	10	128–191	16,384	65,534
C	Node	110	192–223	2,097,152	254

To ensure efficient routing, Internet designers defined a mandate for the leading bits section of the address for each different network class. For example, because a router knows that a Class A network address always starts with a 0, the router might be able to speed a packet on its way after reading only the first bit of its address. Table 1.2 illustrates how the leading bits of a network address are defined.

Some IP addresses are reserved for special purposes and shouldn't be assigned to nodes by network administrators. Table 1.3 lists the reserved IP addresses.

TABLE 1.3 Special Network Addresses

Address	Function
Network portion of the address set to all 0s (zeros)	This network or subnet (i.e., the network or subnet that you are currently a part of)
Network portion of the address set to all 1s	This network and all related subnets
Network address 127	Reserved for loopback tests. Designates the local node and allows that node to send a test packet to itself without generating network traffic.
Node address of all 0s	Used when referencing a network without referring to any specific nodes on that network. Usually used in routing tables.
Node address of all 1s	Broadcast address for all nodes on the specified network; for example, 128.2.255.255 means all nodes on network 128.2 (Class B address).
Entire IP address set to all 0s	Used by RIP to designate the default route.
Entire IP address set to all 1s (same as 255.255.255.255)	Broadcast to all nodes on the current network; sometimes called an "all 1s broadcast."

In the following sections, we will look at the three different network types.

Class A Networks

In a Class A network, the first byte is the network address, and the three remaining bytes are used for the node addresses. The Class A format is `Network.Node.Node.Node`.

For example, in the IP address 49.22.102.70, *49* is the network address and *22.102.70* is the node address. Every machine on this particular network would have the distinctive network address of *49*; within that network, though, you could have a large number of machines.

The length of a Class A network address is a byte, and the first bit of that byte is reserved, so 7 bits in the first byte remain for manipulation. That means that the maximum number of Class A networks that could be created is 128. Why? Each of the seven bit positions can be either a 0 or a 1; this gives you a total of 2^7 positions: a total of 128. To complicate things further, it was also decided that the network address of all 0s (0000 0000) would be reserved. This means the actual number of usable Class A network addresses is 128 minus 1, or 127. There's actually another reserved Class A address too—127—which consists of a network address of all 1s (111 1111). Because you start with 128 addresses and two are reserved, you're left with 126 possible Class A network addresses.

Each Class A network has 3 bytes (24 bit positions) for the node address of a machine, which means that there are 2^{24}—or 16,777,216—unique combinations. Therefore, there are precisely that many possible unique node addresses for each Class A network. Because addresses with the two patterns of all 0s and all 1s are reserved, the actual maximum usable number of nodes for a Class A network is 2^{24} minus 2, which equals 16,777,214.

Class B Networks

In a Class B network, the first 2 bytes are assigned to the network address, and the remaining 2 bytes are used for node addresses. The format is `Network.Network.Node.Node`.

For example, in the IP address 130.57.30.56, the network address is *130.57* and the node address is *30.56*.

The network address is 2 bytes, so there would be 2^{16} unique combinations. But the Internet designers decided that all Class B networks should start with the binary digits 1 and 0. This leaves 14 bit positions to manipulate; therefore, there are 16,384 (or 2^{14}) unique Class B networks.

This gives you an easy way to recognize Class B addresses. If the first 2 bits of the first byte can only be 10, that gives us a decimal range from 128 up to 191. Remember that you can always easily recognize a Class B network by looking at its first byte—even though there are 16,384 different Class B networks. If the first number in the address falls between 128 and 191, it is a Class B network.

A Class B network has 2 bytes to use for node addresses. This is 2^{16} minus the two patterns in the reserved-exclusive club (all 0s and all 1s), for a total of 65,534 possible node addresses for each Class B network.

Class C Networks

The first 3 bytes of a Class C network are dedicated to the network portion of the address, with only 1 byte remaining for the node address. The format is `Network.Network.Network.Node`.

In the example IP address 198.21.74.102, the network address is *198.21.74* and the node address is *102*.

In a Class C network, the first three bit positions are always binary 110. The calculation is such: 3 bytes, or 24 bits, minus 3 reserved positions leaves 21 positions. There are therefore 2^{21} or 2,097,152 possible Class C networks, each of which has 254 possible node addresses (remember, all 0s and all 1s are special addresses: 256 – 2 = 254).

The lead bit pattern of 110 equates to decimal 192 and runs through 223. Remembering our handy easy-recognition method, this means that (although there are a total of 2,097,152 possible Class C networks) you can always spot a Class C address if the first byte is between 192 and 223.

Each unique Class C network has 1 byte to use for node addresses. This leads to 2^8, or 256, minus the two special club patterns of all 0s and all 1s, for a total of 254 node addresses for each Class C network.

Class D networks, used for multicasting only, use the address range 224.0.0.0 to 239.255.255.255. Class E networks (reserved for future use at this point) cover 240.0.0.0 to 255.255.255.255.

Subnetting a Network

If an organization is large and has lots of computers, or if its computers are geographically dispersed, it makes good sense to divide its colossal network into smaller ones connected by routers. These smaller nets are called *subnets*. The benefits to using subnets include the following:

Reduced network traffic We all appreciate less traffic of any kind, and so do networks. Without routers, packet traffic could choke the entire network. Most traffic will stay on the local network— only packets destined for other networks will pass through the router and over to another subnet. This traffic reduction also improves overall performance.

Simplified management It's easier to identify and isolate network problems in a group of smaller networks connected together than within one gigantic one.

The original designers of the IP protocol envisioned a small Internet with only mere tens of networks and hundreds of hosts. Their addressing scheme used a network address for each physical network. As you can imagine, this scheme and the unforeseen growth of the Internet created a few problems.

To name one, a single network address can be used to refer to multiple physical networks. An organization can request individual network addresses for each one of its physical networks. If these requests were granted, there wouldn't be enough addresses to go around. Another problem relates to routers—if each router on the Internet needed to know about every physical network, routing tables would be impossibly huge. There would be an overwhelming amount of administrative overhead to maintain those tables, and the resulting physical overhead on the routers would be massive (CPU cycles, memory, disk space, and so on). Because routers exchange routing information with each other, an additional, related consequence is that a terrific overabundance of network traffic would result.

Although there's more than one way to approach this problem, the principal solution is the one that will be covered in this book—subnetting. As you might guess, subnetting is the process of carving a single IP network into smaller logical subnetworks. This trick is achieved by subdividing the host portion of an IP address to create something called a *subnet address*. The actual subdivision is accomplished through the use of a *subnet mask*—more on that later.

In the following sections, you will see exactly how to calculate and apply subnetting.

Implementing Subnetting

Before you can implement subnetting, you need to determine your current requirements and plan on how best to implement your subnet scheme. Follow these guidelines:

- Determine the number of required network IDs: one for each subnet and one for each WAN connection.

- Determine the number of required host IDs per subnet: one for each TCP/IP device, including computers, network printers, and router interfaces.

Based on these two data points, create the following:

- One subnet mask for your entire network

- A unique subnet ID for each physical segment

- A range of host IDs for each unique subnet

An organization with a single network address can have a subnet address for each individual physical network. It's important to remember that each subnet is still part of the shared network address but it also has an additional identifier denoting its individual subnetwork number. This identifier is called a subnet address. For example, consider a hotel or office building. Say a hotel has 1000 rooms, with 75 rooms to a floor. You start at the first room on the first floor and number it 1. When you get to the first room on the second floor, you number it 76, and you would keep going until you reach room 1000. Now someone looking for room 521 would have to guess approximately which floor the room was on. If you were to "subnet" the hotel, you would identify the first room on the first floor with the number 101 (1 = Floor 1 and 01 = Room 1), the first room on the second floor with 201, and so on. The guest looking for room 521 would go to the 5th floor and look for room 21.

Subnetting solves several addressing problems. First, if an organization has several physical networks but only one IP network address, it can handle the situation by creating subnets. Next, because subnetting allows many physical networks to be grouped together, fewer entries in a routing table are required, notably reducing network overhead. Finally, these things combine to collectively yield greatly enhanced network efficiency.

Next, you will see how you can benefit from the features of subnetting in your network.

How to Hide Information

One benefit of subnetting is the ability to hide your address scheme from the outside world. Suppose that the Internet refers to Widget, Inc. only by its single network address, 130.57. Suppose as well that Widget, Inc. has several divisions and each is an independent business unit. Because Widget's network administrators have implemented subnetting, the Widget routers use the subnet addresses to route the packets to the correct internal subnet when packets come into its network. Thus, the complexity of Widget, Inc.'s network can be hidden from the rest of the Internet. This is called *information hiding*. Routers on the Internet see only one external address for the Widget network.

Information hiding also benefits the routers inside the Widget network. Without subnets, each Widget router would need to know the address of each machine on the entire Widget network—causing additional overhead and poor routing performance. The subnet scheme eliminates the need for each router to know about every machine on the entire Widget network; their routers need only the following two types of information:

- The addresses of the subnets to which they are attached

- The other subnet addresses

How to Implement Subnetting

Subnetting is implemented by assigning a subnet address to each machine on a given physical network. For example, in Figure 1.14, each machine on Subnet 1 has a subnet address of 1.

FIGURE 1.14 A sample subnet

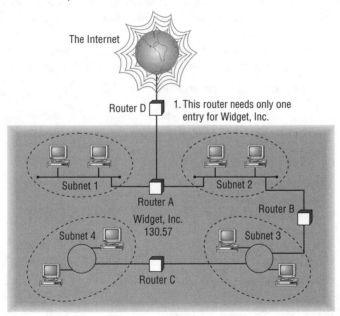

The network portion of an IP address can't be altered. Every machine on a particular network must share the same network address. In Figure 1.14, you can see that all of Widget, Inc.'s machines have a network address of 130.57. That principle is constant. In subnetting, it's the host address that's manipulated; the network address doesn't change. The subnet address scheme takes a part of the host address and recycles it as a subnet address. Bit positions are stolen from the host address to be used for the subnet identifier. Figure 1.15 shows how an IP address can be given a subnet address.

FIGURE 1.15   Network vs. host addresses

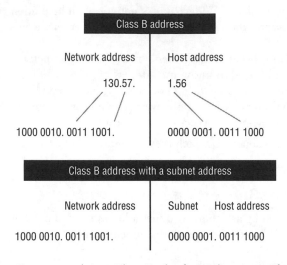

Because the Widget, Inc. network is a Class B, the first 2 bytes specify the network address and are shared by all machines on the network—regardless of their particular subnet. Here, every machine's address on the subnet must have its third byte read 0000 0001. The fourth byte, the host address, is the unique number that identifies the actual host within that subnet. Figure 1.16 illustrates how a network address and a subnet address can be used together.

FIGURE 1.16   The network address and its subnet

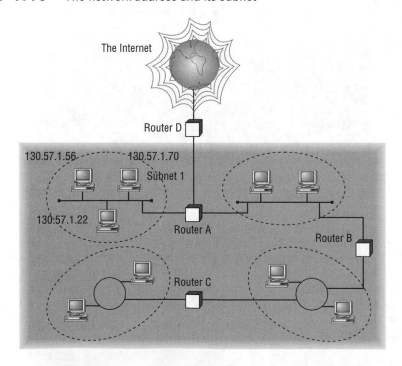

How to Use Subnet Masks

For the subnet address scheme to work, every machine on the network must know which part of the host address will be used as the subnet address. This is accomplished by assigning each machine a subnet mask.

The network administrator creates a 32-bit subnet mask comprising 1s and 0s. The 1s in the subnet mask represent the positions that refer to the network or subnet addresses. The 0s represent the positions that refer to the host part of the address. This combination is illustrated in Figure 1.17.

FIGURE 1.17 The subnet mask revealed

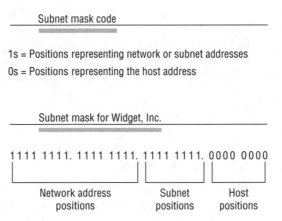

In our Widget, Inc. example, the first two bytes of the subnet mask are 1s because Widget's network address is a Class B address, formatted as `Network.Network.Node.Node`. The third byte, normally assigned as part of the host address, is now used to represent the subnet address. Hence, those bit positions are represented with 1s in the subnet mask. The fourth byte is the only part in our example that represents the unique host address.

The subnet mask can also be expressed using the decimal equivalents of the binary patterns. The binary pattern of 1111 1111 is the same as decimal 255. Consequently, the subnet mask in our example can be denoted in two ways, as shown in Figure 1.18.

FIGURE 1.18 Different ways to represent the same mask

Subnet mask in binary: 1111 1111. 1111 1111. 1111 1111. 0000 0000

Subnet mask in decimal: 255   .   255   .   255   .   0

(The spaces in the above example are only for illustrative purposes.
The subnet mask in decimal would actually appear as 255.255.255.0.)

Not all networks need to have subnets and therefore don't need to use subnet masks. In this case, they are said to have a *default subnet mask*. This is basically the same as saying they don't have a subnet address. The default subnet masks for the different classes of networks are shown in Table 1.4.

TABLE 1.4   Special Network Addresses

Class	Format	Default Subnet Mask
A	Network.Node.Node.Node	255.0.0.0
B	Network.Network.Node.Node	255.255.0.0
C	Network.Network.Network.Node	255.255.255.0

Once the network administrator has created the subnet mask and assigned it to each machine, the IP software applies the subnet mask to the IP address to determine its subnet address. The word *mask* carries the implied meaning of "lens" in this case—the IP software looks at its IP address through the lens of its subnet mask to see its subnet address. An illustration of an IP address being viewed through a subnet mask is shown in Figure 1.19.

FIGURE 1.19   Applying the subnet mask

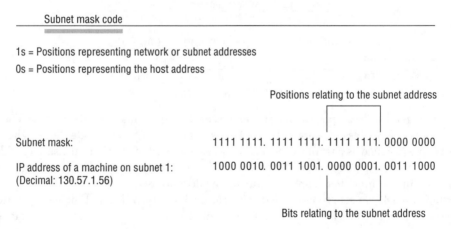

Subnet mask code

1s = Positions representing network or subnet addresses
0s = Positions representing the host address

Positions relating to the subnet address

Subnet mask: 1111 1111. 1111 1111. 1111 1111. 0000 0000

IP address of a machine on subnet 1:   1000 0010. 0011 1001. 0000 0001. 0011 1000
(Decimal: 130.57.1.56)

Bits relating to the subnet address

In this example, the IP software learns through the subnet mask that, instead of being part of the host address, the third byte of its IP address is now going to be used as a subnet address. The IP software then looks in its IP address at the bit positions that correspond to the mask, which are 0000 0001.

The final step is for the subnet bit values to be matched up with the binary numbering convention and converted to decimal. In the Widget, Inc. example, the binary-to-decimal conversion is simple, as illustrated in Figure 1.20.

By using the entire third byte of a Class B address as the subnet address, it is easy to set and determine the subnet address. For example, if Widget, Inc. wants to have a Subnet 6, the third byte of all machines on that subnet will be 0000 0110 (decimal 6 in binary).

Using the entire third byte of a Class B network address for the subnet allows for a fair number of available subnet addresses. One byte dedicated to the subnet provides eight bit positions.

Each position can be either a 1 or a 0, so the calculation is 2^8, or 256. Because you cannot use the two patterns of all 0s and all 1s, you must subtract 2 for a total of 254. Thus, Widget, Inc. can have up to 254 total subnetworks, each with up to 254 hosts.

FIGURE 1.20   Converting the subnet mask to decimal

Binary numbering convention

Position/value: ← (continued)	128 64 32 16 8 4 2 1	
Widget third byte:	0 0 0 0 0 0 0 1	
Decimal equivalent:	0 + 1 = 1	
Subnet address:	1	

Although the official IP specification limits the use of 0 as a subnet address, some products actually permit this usage. Microsoft's TCP/IP stack allows it, as does the software in most routers (provided you enable this feature). This gives you one additional subnet. However, you should not use a subnet of 0 (all 0s) unless all of the software on your network recognizes this convention.

How to Calculate the Number of Subnets

The formulas for calculating the maximum number of subnets and the maximum number of hosts per subnet are as follows:

- 2^x *number of masked bits in subnet mask* – 2 = maximum number of subnets
- 2^x *number of unmasked bits in subnet mask* – 2 = maximum number of hosts per subnet

In the formulas, *masked* refers to bit positions of 1, and *unmasked* refers to positions of 0. The downside to using an entire byte of a node address as your subnet address is that you reduce the possible number of node addresses on each subnet. As explained earlier, without a subnet, a Class B address has 65,534 unique combinations of 1s and 0s that can be used for node addresses.

If you use an entire byte of the node address for a subnet, you then have only 1 byte for the host addresses, leaving only 254 possible host addresses. If any of your subnets will be populated with more than 254 machines, you have a problem. To solve it, you would then need to shorten the subnet mask, thereby lengthening the host address; this gives you more available host addresses on each subnet. A side effect of this solution is that it shrinks the number of possible subnets.

Figure 1.21 shows an example of using a smaller subnet address. A company called Acme, Inc. expects to need a maximum of 14 subnets. In this case, Acme does not need to take an entire byte from the host address for the subnet address. To get its 14 different subnet addresses, it needs to snatch only 4 bits from the host address ($2^4 - 2 = 14$). The host portion of the address has 12 usable bits remaining ($2^{12} - 2 = 4094$). Each of Acme's 14 subnets could then potentially have a total of 4094 host addresses; 4094 machines on each subnet should be plenty.

FIGURE 1.21   An example of a smaller subnet address

Acme, Inc.

Network address:	132.8 (Class B; net.net.host.host)
Example IP address:	1000 0100. 0000 1000. 0001 0010. 0011 1100
Decimal:	132 . 8 . 18 . 60

Subnet Mask Code

1s = Positions representing network or subnet addresses
0s = Positions representing the host address

Subnet mask:

Binary:	1111 1111. 1111 1111. 1111 0000. 0000 0000
Decimal:	255 . 255 . 240 . 0

(The decimal 240 is equal to the binary 1111 0000.)

Positions relating to the subnet address

Subnet mask: 1111 1111. 1111 1111. 1111 0000. 0000 0000

IP address of a Acme machine: 1000 0100. 0000 1000. 0001 0010. 0011 1100
(Decimal: 132.8.18.60)

Bits relating to the subnet address

Binary-to-Decimal Conversions for Subnet Address

Subnet mask positions:	1	1	1	1	0	0	0	0
	↓	↓	↓	↓				
Position/value: ← (continue)	128	64	32	16	8	4	2	1
Third byte of IP address:	0	0	0	1	0	0	1	0
Decimal equivalent:						0 + 16 = 16		
Subnet address for this IP address:						16		

Applying Subnetting

Sometimes subnetting can be confusing. It can be quite difficult to remember all those numbers. You can step back a minute and take a look at the primary classes of networks and how to subnet each one. You'd start with Class C because it uses only 8 bits for the node address, so it's the easiest to calculate. In the following sections, we will look at how to subnet the various types of networks.

Class C

If you recall, a Class C network uses the first 3 bytes (24 bits) to define the network address. This leaves you 1 byte (8 bits) with which to address hosts. So, if you want to create subnets, your options are limited because of the small number of bits left available.

If you break down your subnets into chunks smaller than the default Class C, then figuring out the subnet mask, network number, broadcast address, and router address can be kind of confusing. Table 1.5 summarizes how you can break a Class C network down into one, two, four, or eight smaller subnets, with the subnet masks, network numbers, broadcast addresses, and router addresses. The first 0 bytes have simply been designated x.y.z. (Note that the table assumes you can use the all-0 subnet, too.)

TABLE 1.5   Class C Subnets

Number of Desired Subnets	Subnet Mask	Network Number	Router Address	Broadcast Address	Remaining Number of IP Addresses
1	255.255.255.0	x.y.z.0	x.y.z.1	x.y.z.255	253
2	255.255.255.128	x.y.z.0	x.y.z.1	x.y.z.127	125
	255.255.255.128	x.y.z.128	x.y.z.129	x.y.z.255	125
4	255.255.255.192	x.y.z.0	x.y.z.1	x.y.z.63	61
	255.255.255.192	x.y.z.64	x.y.z.65	x.y.z.127	61
	255.255.255.192	x.y.z.128	x.y.z.129	x.y.z.191	61
	255.255.255.192	x.y.z.192	x.y.z.193	x.y.z.255	61
8	255.255.255.224	x.y.z.0	x.y.z.1	x.y.z.31	29
	255.255.255.224	x.y.z.32	x.y.z.33	x.y.z.63	29
	255.255.255.224	x.y.z.64	x.y.z.65	x.y.z.95	29
	255.255.255.224	x.y.z.96	x.y.z.97	x.y.z.127	29
	255.255.255.224	x.y.z.128	x.y.z.129	x.y.z.159	29
	255.255.255.224	x.y.z.160	x.y.z.161	x.y.z.191	29
	255.255.255.224	x.y.z.192	x.y.z.193	x.y.z.223	29
	255.255.255.224	x.y.z.224	x.y.z.225	x.y.z.255	29

For example, suppose you want to chop up a Class C network, 200.211.192.x, into two subnets. As you can see in the table, you'd use a subnet mask of 255.255.255.128 for each subnet. The first subnet would have network number 200.211.192.0, router address 200.211.192.1, and broadcast address 200.211.192.127. You could assign IP addresses 200.211.192.2 through 200.211.192.126—that's 125 different IP addresses. (Notice that heavily subnetting a network results in the loss of a progressively greater percentage of addresses to the network number, broadcast address, and router address.) The second subnet would have network number 200.211.192.128, router address 200.211.192.129, and broadcast address 200.211.192.255.

Now, you may be wondering how you can subnet a Class C network as in Table 1.5. If you use the $2^x - 2$ calculation, the subnet 128 in the table doesn't make sense. It turns out that there's a legitimate reason to do it this way:

1. Remember that using subnet zero is not allowed according to the RFCs, but by using it you can subnet your Class C network with a subnet mask of 128. This uses only 1 bit, and according to your calculator, $2^1 - 2 = 0$, giving you zero subnets.

2. By using a router that supports subnet zero, you can assign 1–127 for hosts and 129–254, for hosts, as stated in the table. This saves a bunch of addresses! If you were to stick to the method defined by RFC standards, the best you could gain is a subnet mask of 192 (2 bits), which allows you only two subnets ($2^2 - 2 = 2$).

To determine the first subnet number, subtract the subnet mask from 256. Our example yields the following equation: $256 - 192 = 64$. So 64 is your first subnet.

To determine a second subnet number, add the first subnet number to itself. To determine a third subnet number, add the first subnet number to the second subnet number. To determine a fourth subnet number, add the first subnet number to the third subnet number. Keep adding the first subnet number in this fashion until you reach the actual subnet number. For example, 64 plus 64 equals 128, so your second subnet is 128. And 128 plus 64 is 192. Because 192 is the subnet mask, you cannot use it as an actual subnet. This means your valid subnets are 64 and 128.

The numbers between the subnets are your valid hosts. For example, the following are valid hosts in a Class C network with a subnet mask of 192:

- The valid hosts for subnet 64 are in the range 65–126, which gives you 62 hosts per subnet (using 127 as a host would mean your host bits would be all 1s). That's not allowed because the all-1s format is reserved as the broadcast address for that subnet.

- The valid hosts for subnet 128 are in the range 129–190. you might be asking yourself what happened to 191–254? The subnet mask is 192, which you cannot use, and 191 would be all 1s and used as the broadcast address for this subnet. Anything above 192 is also invalid for this subnet because these are automatically lost through the subnetting process.

As you can see, this solution wastes a lot of addresses: 130 to be exact. In a Class C network, this would certainly be hard to justify—the 128 subnet is a much better solution if you only need two subnets.

But what happens if you need four subnets in your Class C network?

By using the calculation of 2^x *number of masked bits* $- 2$, you would need 3 bits to get six subnets ($2^3 - 2 = 6$). What are the valid subnets and what are the valid hosts of each subnet? Let's figure it out.

11100000 is 224 in binary and would be the subnet mask. This must be the same on all workstations.

You're likely to see test questions that ask you to identify the problem with a given configuration. If a workstation has the wrong subnet mask, the router could "think" the workstation is on a different subnet than it actually is. When that happens, the misguided router won't forward packets to the workstation in question. Similarly, if the mask is incorrectly specified in the workstation's configuration, that workstation will observe the mask and send packets to the default gateway when it shouldn't.

To figure out the valid subnets, subtract the subnet mask from 256; 256 − 224 = 32, so 32 is your first subnet. The other subnets would be 64, 96, 128, 160, and 192. The valid hosts are the numbers between the subnet numbers, except the numbers that equal all 1s. These numbers would be 63, 95, 127, 159, 191, and 223. Remember that using all 1s is reserved for the broadcast address of each subnet.

The valid subnets and hosts are as follows:

Subnet	Hosts
32	33–62
64	65–94
96	97–126
128	129–158
160	161–190
192	193–222

You can add one more bit to the subnet mask just for fun. You were using 3 bits, which gave you 224. By adding the next bit, the mask now becomes 240 (11110000).

By using 4 bits for the subnet mask, you get 14 subnets because $2^4 - 2 = 14$. This subnet mask also gives you only 4 bits for the host addresses, or 14 hosts per subnet. As you can see, the amount of hosts per subnet gets reduced rather quickly when subnetting a Class C network.

The first valid subnet for subnet 240 is 16 (256 − 240 = 16). Your subnets are then 16, 32, 48, 64, 80, 96, 112, 128, 144, 160, 176, 192, 208, and 224. Remember that you cannot use the actual subnet number as a valid subnet, so 240 is invalid as a subnet number. The valid hosts are the numbers between the subnets, except for the numbers that are all 1s—the broadcast address for the subnet.

The following are valid subnets and hosts:

Subnet	Hosts
16	17–30
32	33–46

Subnet	Hosts
48	49–62
64	65–78
80	81–94
96	97–110
112	113–126
128	129–142
144	145–158
160	161–174
176	177–190
192	193–206
208	209–222
224	225–238

Class B

Because a Class B network has 16 bits for host addresses, you have plenty of available bits to play with when figuring out a subnet mask. Remember that you have to start with the leftmost bit and work toward the right. For example, a Class B network would look like X.Y.0.0, with the default mask of 255.255.0.0. Using the default mask would give you one network with 65,564 hosts.

The default mask in binary is 11111111.11111111.00000000.00000000. The 1s represent the network, and the 0s represent the hosts. So when creating a subnet mask, the leftmost bit(s) will be borrowed from the host bits (0s, not 1s) to become the subnet mask. You use the remaining available bits for hosts.

If you use only 1 bit, you have a mask of 255.255.128.0. This mask will be somewhat harder to subnet than the Class C 128 subnet mask. With 16 bits, you typically don't need to worry about a shortage of host IDs, so using 128 just isn't worth the trouble. The first mask you should use is 255.255.192.0, or 11111111.11111111.11000000.00000000.

You now have three parts of the IP address: the network address, the subnet address, and the host address. A 192 mask is figured out the same way as a Class C network address, but this time you'll end up with a lot more hosts.

There are two subnets because $2^2 - 2 = 2$. The valid subnets are 64 and 128 ($256 - 192 = 64$ and $64 + 64 = 128$). However, there are 14 bits (0s) left over for host addressing. This gives you 16,382 hosts per subnet ($2^{14} - 2 = 16,382$).

The valid subnets and hosts are as follows:

Subnet	Hosts
64	X.Y.64.1 through X.Y.127.254
128	X.Y.128.1 through X.Y.191.254

You can add another bit to the subnet mask, making it 11111111.11111111.11100000 .00000000 or 255.255.224.0. There are six subnets ($2^3 - 2 = 6$). The valid subnets are 32, 64, 96, 128, 160, and 192 ($256 - 224 = 32$). The valid hosts are listed here:

Subnet	Hosts
32	X.Y.32.1 through 63.254
64	X.Y.64.1 through 95.254
96	X.Y.96.1 through 127.254
128	X.Y.128.1 through 159.254
160	X.Y.160.1 through 191.254
192	X.Y.192.1 through 223.254

Therefore, if you use a 255.255.224.0 subnet mask, you can create six subnets, each with 8190 hosts.

You can add a few more bits to the subnet mask and see what happens. If you use 9 bits for the mask, it gives you 510 subnets ($2^9 - 2 = 510$). With only 7 bits for hosts, you still have 126 hosts per subnet ($2^7 - 2 = 126$). The mask looks like this:

11111111.11111111.11111111.10000000 or 255.255.255.128

You could add even more bits and see what you get. If you use 14 bits for the subnet mask, you get 16,382 subnets ($2^{14} - 2 = 16382$), but this gives you only two hosts per subnet ($2^2 - 2 = 2$). The subnet mask would look like this:

11111111.11111111.11111111.11111100 or 255.255.255.252

You may be wondering why you would ever use a 14-bit subnet mask with a Class B address. This approach is actually very common. Think about having a Class B network and using a subnet mask of 255.255.255.0. You'd have 254 subnets and 254 hosts per subnet. Imagine also that you have a network with many WAN links. Typically, you'd have a direct connection between each site. Each of these links must be on its own subnet or network. There will be two hosts on these subnets—one address for each router port. If you used the mask described earlier (255.255.255.0), you would waste 252 host addresses per subnet. Using the 255.255.255.252 subnet mask, you have many, many subnets available—each with only two hosts.

You can use this approach only if you are running a routing algorithm like Enhanced Interior Gateway Routing Protocol (EIGRP) or Open Shortest Path First (OSPF), which we will talk about later in this book. These routing protocols allow what is called Variable Length Subnet Masks (VLSMs). VLSM allows you to run the 255.255.255.252 subnet mask on your interfaces to the WANs and run 255.255.255.0 on your router interfaces in your LAN. It works because routing protocols like EIGRP and OSPF transmit the subnet mask information in the update packets that it sends to the other routers. RIP doesn't transmit the subnet mask and therefore cannot use VLSM.

Class A

Class A networks have a ton of bits available. A default Class A network subnet mask is only 8 bits, or 255.0.0.0, giving you a whopping 24 bits for hosts to play with.

If you use a mask of 11111111.1111111.00000000.00000000, or 255.255.0.0, you'll have 8 bits for subnets, or 254 subnets ($2^8 - 2 = 254$). This leaves 16 bits for hosts, or 65,534 hosts per subnet ($2^{16} - 2 = 65534$). Instead, you could split the 24 bits evenly between subnets and hosts, giving each one 12 bits. The mask would look like this: 11111111.11111111.11110000.00000000, or 255.255.240.0. How many valid subnets and hosts would you have?

The answer is 4094 subnets each with 4094 hosts ($2^{12} - 2 = 4094$). Knowing which hosts and subnets are valid is a lot more complicated than it was for either Class B or C networks.

The second octet will be somewhere between 1 and 254. However, the third octet you will need to figure out. Because the third octet has a 240 mask, you'll get 16 (256 – 240 = 16) as your base subnet number. The third octet must start with 16 and will be the first subnet, the second subnet will be 32, and so on. This means that your valid subnets are

X.1-254.16.1 through X.1-254.31.254

X.1-254.32.1 through X.1-254.47.254

X.1-254.48.1 through X.1-254.63.254

and so on for the remaining bits.

New to Microsoft is the way that address ranges are written. For example, an address of 131.107.2.0 with a subnet mask of 255.255.255.0 is listed as 131.107.2.0/24 because the subnet mask contains 24 1s. An address listed as 141.10.32.0/19 would have a subnet mask of 255.255.224.0, or 19 1s (default subnet mask for a Class B plus 3 bits). This is the new nomenclature used in all Microsoft exams and is referred to as Classless Inter-Domain Routing (CIDR) notation.

Summary

The following list includes some of the important topics covered in this chapter:

- How the OSI networking model is organized into seven layers: Physical, Data-Link, Network, Transport, Session, Presentation, and Application.

- What each level of the OSI stack does. The Physical layer is responsible for sending bits from one computer to another. The Data-Link layer provides for the flow of data over a single physical link from one device to another. The Network layer moves packets between devices that are more than one link away from each other. The Transport layer ensures that data is delivered error free, in sequence, and with no losses or duplications. The Session layer allows applications on separate computers to share a connection called a session. The Presentation layer translates data between the formats the network requires and the formats the computer expects. Finally, the Application layer is the topmost layer of the OSI model, and it provides services that directly support user applications, such as database access, e-mail, and file transfers.

- Windows Server 2003 includes support for AppleTalk, NWLink, and TCP/IP. TCP/IP is the primary protocol in use today, and Microsoft encourages you to use TCP/IP exclusively, if possible.

- The 32-bit IP address is a structured or hierarchical address that is used to uniquely identify every machine on a network. You learned how to determine available IP addresses and implement subnetting.

Exam Essentials

Understand what subnetting is and when to use it.   If an organization is large and has many computers, or if its computers are geographically dispersed, it's sensible to divide its large network into smaller ones connected by routers. These smaller networks are called subnets. Subnetting is the process of carving a single IP network into smaller, logical subnetworks.

Understand subnet masks.   For the subnet address scheme to work, every machine on the network must know which part of the host address will be used as the subnet address. The network administrator creates a 32-bit subnet mask consisting of 1s and 0s. The 1s in the subnet mask represent the positions that refer to the network or subnet addresses. The 0s represent the positions that refer to the host portion of the address.

Key Terms

Before you take the exam, be certain you are familiar with the following terms:

binding	Open Systems Interconnection (OSI)
cyclic redundancy check (CRC)	OSI model
default subnet mask	packet payload
hierarchical address	packets
information hiding	protocol stack
Internet Protocol (IP)	Service Access Points (SAPs)
Logical Link Control (LLC)	subnet address
Media Access Control (MAC)	subnet mask
network address	subnets
Network Driver Interface Specification (NDIS)	TCP/IP
node address	Transmission Control Protocol (TCP)
NWLink	User Datagram Protocol (UDP)
Open Data-link Interface (ODI)	

Review Questions

1. You have a large IP routed network using the address 137.25.0.0; it is composed of 20 subnets, with a maximum of 300 hosts on each subnet. Your company continues on a merger and acquisitions spree, and your manager has told you to prepare for an increase to 50 subnets, with some of them containing more than 600 hosts. Using the existing network address, which of the following subnet masks would work for that requirement from your manager?

    A. 255.255.252.0

    B. 255.255.254.0

    C. 255.255.248.0

    D. 255.255.240.0

2. You are brought into a small company that occupies two floors of a building that has had two separate networks for some time. The company now wants these two networks to share some information files such as documents, spreadsheets, and databases. You determine that one of the networks is a NetWare 3.x LAN and the other is a Windows NT peer-to-peer network running NetBEUI. The NetWare LAN has a printer that you want users on the NT network to be able to use. Other than any client software, what protocol will you have to install for the Windows NT workstations to be able to access the NetWare printer?

    A. NetBEUI

    B. TCP/IP

    C. AppleTalk

    D. NWLink

    E. DLC

3. The company you work for is growing dramatically via acquisitions of other companies. As the network administrator, you need to keep up with the changes because they affect the workstations and you need to support them. When you started, there were 15 locations connected via routers, and now there are 25. As new companies are acquired, they are migrated to Windows Server 2003 and brought into the same domain as another site. Management says that they are going to acquire at least 10 more companies in the next 2 years. The engineers have also told you that they are redesigning the company's Class B address into an IP addressing scheme that will support these requirements and that there will never be over 1000 network devices on any subnet. What will be the appropriate subnet mask to support this network when the changes are completed?

    A. 255.255.252.0

    B. 255.255.248.0

    C. 255.255.255.0

    D. 255.255.255.128

4. You work for a small printing company that has 75 workstations. Most of them run standard office applications like word processing, spreadsheet, and accounting programs. Fifteen of the workstations are constantly processing huge graphics files and then sending print jobs to industrial-size laser printers. The performance of the network has always been an issue, but you have never addressed it. You have now migrated your network to Windows XP and Windows Server 2003 and have decided to take advantage of the routing capability built into the Windows Server 2003. You choose the appropriate server and place two NICs in the machine, but you realize that you have only one network address, 201.102.34.0, which you obtained years ago. How should you subnet this address to segment the bandwidth hogs from the rest of the network while giving everyone access to the entire network?

    A. 255.255.255.192

    B. 255.255.255.224

    C. 255.255.255.252

    D. 255.255.255.240

5. A packet is sent from one computer to another across a network. Various protocols move the packet down the OSI stack from the sending computer and up the OSI stack to the receiving computer. How do the protocols know where to send the packet?

    A. Each packet has a trailer that contains source and destination addresses.

    B. Each packet has a header that contains an alert signal and source and destination addresses.

    C. The data portion of every packet stores all the source and destination information.

    D. Special packets, called header packets, that contain only source and destination addresses are sent first. Every packet that follows the header packet is sent to the destination address contained in the header packet.

6. You have been engaged at a large automobile manufacturing organization to help company officials understand and alleviate their network traffic overutilization rates. After discussions with the network administrator, you discover that the organization was initially running only TCP/IP but they recently installed NetBEUI as well. After some investigation, you are told the reason for the dual protocols: The administrator was told that they were going to have to support several NetBIOS applications on the network. To permit this NetBIOS support, the administrator then directed several staff members to add the NetBEUI stack to the workstations and, in the bindings, to place NetBEUI first. Now the network is having performance problems. What mistake did this administrator make?

    A. Because NetBEUI was placed at the top of the binding list, the workstations are trying to communicate through NetBEUI first, even though the resource to which they are trying to connect uses only TCP/IP.

    B. Because NetBEUI was placed at the top of the binding list, NetBEUI is being used to communicate with the TCP/IP-based servers and is less efficient in communicating with a different protocol.

    C. NetBEUI is unnecessary for a client's communication with a NetBIOS program.

    D. Although TCP/IP needs NetBEUI in order to communicate with a NetBIOS program, NetBEUI needs to be bound directly to the TCP/IP stack so that they will work together properly.

7. The Integrated Network Computing company is a software development house that writes small utility programs for a wide range of networks. In addition to supporting their Windows Server 2003 network, you are responsible for verifying that some of the applications that are developed function properly. During these tests, you have to install transport protocols from other development houses that are used by various systems. You have worked out the issues surrounding the different protocols working on Windows Server 2003 by requiring the protocol developers to make sure their protocols are compliant with what standard?

    A. ODI

    B. DLC

    C. NDIS

    D. NetBIOS

8. You work for Carpathian Worldwide Enterprises, which has more than 50 administrative and manufacturing locations around the world. The size of these organizations varies greatly, with the number of computers per location ranging from 15 to slightly fewer than 1000. The sales operations use more than 1000 facilities, each of which contains 2 to 5 computers. Carpathian is also in merger talks with another large organization; if the merger materializes as planned, you will have to accommodate another 100 manufacturing and administrative locations, each with a maximum of 600 computers, as well as 2,000 additional sales facilities. You don't have any numbers for the future growth of the company, but you are told to keep growth in mind. You decide to implement a private addressing plan for the entire organization. More than half of your routers don't support Variable Length Subnet Masking. What subnet masks would work for this situation? (Choose all that apply.)

    A. 255.255.224.0

    B. 255.255.240.0

    C. 255.255.248.0

    D. 255.255.252.0

    E. 255.255.254.0

9. You administer a very large network that consists of Windows 2000 and XP Professional and Windows Server 2003 computers. You want to implement DNS, DHCP, and WINS, and every computer must have access to the Internet and services on non-Windows machines. You want to be able to configure the network from a central location. Which network protocol provides the ability to do all these things?

    A. NetBEUI

    B. NWLink

    C. TCP

    D. TCP/IP

10. You are the administrator for a Windows NT network that has been internally focused on basic file and print services. You have been charged with upgrading your network to Windows Server 2003 and also allowing the users of the network to find information on the Internet. Currently, the network is running NWLink because of routing needs between two locations and a lack of IP experience. You need to change the network protocol to TCP/IP to support Internet connectivity. What primary layers in the OSI model do you need to consider to allow the workstations to access the Internet for simple browsing? (Choose all that apply.)

    A. Physical layer

    B. Network layer

    C. Application layer

    D. Presentation layer

    E. Transport layer

11. You have just been asked to troubleshoot intermittent communication problems on a fairly old network for a company that builds and repairs elevator motors. You have determined that the network is a straightforward thin-coax Ethernet Windows NT LAN running TCP/IP. The company wants to upgrade to Windows Server 2003, hoping that the now-stable platform will resolve the intermittent problems. You perform the upgrade; all goes smoothly, and initially everything seems to function properly. However, the intermittent problems show up again. What layer in the OSI model is the most likely place for the problems to be occurring?

    A. Physical layer

    B. Data-Link layer

    C. Network layer

    D. Transport layer

    E. Session layer

12. You are working at a manufacturing company that occupies an entire city block. Management informs you that they have acquired another business on the other side of town that previously had been a supplier to your company. The Windows Server 2003 network that you have been supporting now needs to be connected to the new location through a router. You also have several NetBIOS applications that need to continue functioning properly. What protocols are available for you to use to ensure that these criteria are met? (Choose all that apply.)

    A. NWLink

    B. TCP/IP

    C. XNS

    D. NetBEUI

13. The company you work for manufactures handballs and has an Intel PC–based Windows Server 2003 network. To cut packaging costs, the management of the company has acquired a graphics arts company. Its network is entirely Macintosh based and is currently using Apple-Talk as the protocol to communicate among workstations. You have to integrate the two networks so that they can easily share information. What protocols must you have on your network for communication among all the workstations on this network?

   A. AppleTalk

   B. TCP/IP

   C. NWLink

   D. NetBEUI

14. You administer a network that contains 175 machines. Your manager has assigned the network the IP address 192.168.11.0 with the default subnet mask of 255.255.255.0. A router that has one WAN interface and eight LAN interfaces connects this network to the corporate WAN.

You want to subnet the network into three subnets, and you want to reserve a few addresses for a fourth subnet, just in case you need it later. You decide that Subnet A will contain 25 computers, Subnet B will contain 50 computers, and Subnet C will contain 100 computers.

In the following exhibit, select the network addresses and subnet masks in the Choices column and place them in the appropriate boxes in the other three columns. Each item may be used only once.

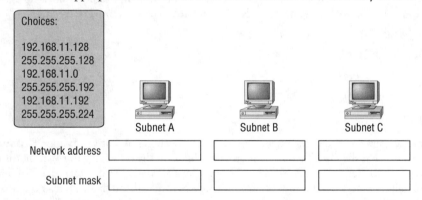

15. Your multinational company has a Windows NT and Novell NetWare network that is built on several subnetworks. To provide interoperability, you have been using NWLink on the NT network and IPX for the NetWare network. You have been told that the Windows NT network must be migrated to Windows Server 2003 because it's less expensive to administer. You know that the administrative cost benefits are a result of utilizing Active Directory, so you include this service in your migration plan. What are you going to have to do immediately in order to install and begin using Active Directory on this network?

   A. Change the protocol to TCP/IP.

   B. Make sure that you install a copy of Active Directory on the NetWare servers as well as on the Windows 2003 Server computers.

   C. As you upgrade the Windows NT servers, make sure that you choose to upgrade some of them as domain controllers so that you can install Active Directory on them.

   D. Install NetBEUI in order to provide connectivity for the NetBIOS components of Windows Server 2003.

Answers to Review Questions

1. **A.** A Class B address with a default subnet mask of 255.255.0.0 will support up to 65,534 hosts. To increase the number of networks that this network will support, you need to subnet the network by borrowing bits from the host portion of the address. The subnet mask 255.255.252.0 uses 6 bits from the hosts area and will support 62 subnetworks while leaving enough bits to support 1022 hosts per subnet.

    The subnet mask 255.255.248.0 uses 5 bits from the hosts and will support 30 subnetworks while leaving enough bits to support 2046 hosts per subnet. 255.255.252.0 is probably the better answer because it leaves quite a bit of room for further growth in the number of networks while still leaving room for more than 1000 hosts per subnet, which is a fairly large number of devices on one subnet. The subnet mask 255.255.254.0 uses 7 bits from the hosts area and will support more than 120 networks, but it will leave only enough bits to support 500 hosts per subnet. The subnet mask 255.255.240.0 uses 4 bits from the hosts and will support only 14 subnetworks, even though it will leave enough bits to support more than 4000 hosts per subnet.

2. **D.** Older NetWare networks are based on the IPX protocol. There must be a common protocol in order for two network devices to communicate. Because there is no server to run the gateway for NetWare services, each NT workstation must have NWLink loaded. Also, the NetWare client must be installed on the workstations so that they will be able to connect to the printer.

3. **A.** The network mask applied to an address determines which portion of that address reflects the number of hosts available to that network. The balance with subnetting is always between the number of hosts and individual subnetworks that can be uniquely represented within one encompassing address. The number of hosts and networks that are made available depends upon the number of bits that can be used to represent them. This scenario requires more than 35 networks and fewer than 1000 workstations on each network. If you convert the subnet masks as described in the chapter, you will see that the mask in choice A allows for more than 60 networks and more than 1000 hosts. All of the other choices are deficient in either the number of networks or hosts that they represent.

4. **A.** The subnet mask 255.255.255.192 borrows 2 bits from the hosts, which allows you to build two separate networks that you can route through the Windows server. This will allow you to have 62 hosts on each segment. You'll be cutting it close, but this will work.

    The subnet mask 255.255.255.224 borrows 3 bits from the hosts; this allows you to create 6 networks, which you don't need, and leaves only enough bits for 30 hosts. The subnet mask 255.255.255.252 borrows 6 bits from the hosts; this allows you to create more than 60 networks, which you don't need, and leaves only enough bits for 2 hosts. The subnet mask 255.255.255.240 borrows 4 bits from the hosts; this allows you to create 15 networks, which you don't need, and leaves only enough bits for 15 hosts.

5. **B.** Each packet typically consists of three parts: a header, data, and a trailer. The header includes the source and destination addresses.

6.   C. NetBEUI and NetBIOS are separate entities. NetBEUI is a transport protocol that has a Net-BIOS interface. However, each protocol that comes with Windows Server 2003 has a NetBIOS component and can be used to communicate with NetBIOS programs. Although the binding order of protocols can have a performance effect on communication across the network, it has nothing to do with the problem described here. The extra protocol is simply consuming unnecessary network bandwidth.

7.   C. Network Driver Interface Specification (NDIS) provides a standard way for protocols to bind to the data link drivers in Windows Server 2003. This is what allows Windows Server 2003 to support so many protocols. As long as a developer supports NDIS, the protocol will load in Windows Server 2003. However, this will not make it interoperate with the Windows Server 2003 services. The applications will have to be written to the specific protocols.

8.   B, C, D. When you add up the locations that currently need to be given a network address, the total is 3150, and the maximum number of hosts at any one of these locations is less that 1000. The subnet masks need to support those requirements. The subnet masks given in options B, C, and D will provide the address space to support the outlined requirements. The subnet mask 255.255.240.0 supports more than 4000 subnets and 4000 hosts. The subnet mask 255.255.248.0 supports more than 8000 subnets and more than 2000 hosts. The subnet mask 255.255.252.0 supports more than 16,000 subnets and more than 1000 hosts.

Although each of these subnet masks will work, at the rate that this company is growing, 255.255.252.0 is probably the best mask to prepare for the future. It's unlikely that there will ever be more than 1000 hosts on any given network. In fact, that number would probably cause performance problems on that subnet. Therefore, it's better to have more subnets available to deploy as the company grows.

The subnet mask 255.255.224.0 supports more than 2000 subnets—an insufficient number to cover the locations. The subnet mask 255.255.254.0 supports more than 32,000 subnets but only 500 hosts per subnet, which are not enough hosts to cover all the locations.

9.   D. TCP/IP is the most widely used protocol for interconnecting computers, and it is the only protocol used on the Internet. It works well with very large networks.

10.   A, B, C, D, E. TCP sits at the Transport layer, and IP at the Network layer, and both are necessary to route requests through the Internet. However, you also need a browser such as Netscape or Internet Explorer to provide the HTTP calls to actually connect to the various websites; the browser sits at the Application layer. But any end-to-end communication uses all the levels of the OSI model at some point because each layer communicates with the layer below and the layer above to form the complete chain.

11.   A. The Physical layer is concerned with signaling, specifically through electrical, optical, or radio signals. The high voltage associated with large motors can easily cause an interruption in the signaling of coax cable. There have been many cases of people running network cable through elevator shafts in a building because of their ease of access, only to have the network malfunction every time someone summons the car. The other layers are associated with software and are beyond the reach of most electrical interference unless it affects the entire workstation.

12. A, B. Both NWLink and TCP/IP are routable and both can function properly with NetBIOS applications because they are both Microsoft's versions and have the interface for proper communication. XNS is a routable protocol but is not provided with Windows Server 2003, and with the overwhelming popularity of TCP/IP, XNS is generally no longer used in networks. NetBEUI, although it supports the NetBIOS programs, is not routable.

13. B. Although Macintosh computers can use AppleTalk to communicate with each other, these computers can also run TCP/IP, so AppleTalk won't be necessary when these two networks are merged. You could add AppleTalk to the servers in the network, and the two machine types could share files back and forth, but if you can reduce the number of protocols on any network, it's a best practice to do so.

14.

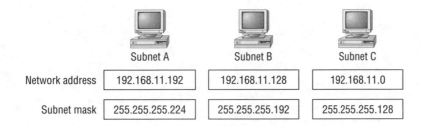

	Subnet A	Subnet B	Subnet C
Network address	192.168.11.192	192.168.11.128	192.168.11.0
Subnet mask	255.255.255.224	255.255.255.192	255.255.255.128

The network address 192.168.11.192 with a subnet mask of 255.255.255.224 is perfect for Subnet A because it supports up to 30 hosts. The network address 192.168.11.128 with a subnet mask of 255.255.255.192 is perfect for Subnet B because it supports up to 62 hosts. The network address 192.168.11.0 with a subnet mask of 255.255.255.128 is perfect for Subnet C because it supports up to 126 hosts. That still leaves the network address 192.168.11.224 with a subnet mask of 255.255.255.224 available for a fourth subnet later.

15. A. Active Directory requires TCP/IP in order to function. Even though you can have TCP/IP and IPX coexisting on the same network, it's not beneficial to have multiple protocols because they increase the level of support necessary for the network. Active Directory does not run on NetWare, and NetBEUI is not required for NetBIOS communication. Finally, Active Directory can be installed and uninstalled on any Windows Server 2003 computer. It's a service that is added rather than a particular type of server that is installed.

Chapter 2

Installing and Configuring TCP/IP

MICROSOFT EXAM OBJECTIVES COVERED IN THIS CHAPTER:

✓ **Configure TCP/IP addressing on a server computer.**

✓ **Troubleshoot TCP/IP addressing.**

- Diagnose and resolve issues related to APIPA.
- Diagnose and resolve issues related to incorrect TCP/IP configuration.

✓ **Troubleshoot connectivity to the Internet.**

✓ **Monitor network traffic. Tools might include Network Monitor and System Monitor.**

Windows Server 2003 includes support for the same network protocols as Windows 2000 and NT 4. Some of these protocols, like TCP/IP, have assumed new importance. Others, like NetBEUI, are being quietly phased out. This chapter will focus on how to configure and troubleshoot TCP/IP. By the time you finish this chapter, you'll know how to set configuration parameters for TCP/IP and configure the bindings that attach protocols to particular network interface cards (NICs). You'll also learn how to monitor and troubleshoot TCP/IP and Internet connectivity using built-in tools such as Network Monitor, ping, ipconfig, and tracert.

Configuring Basic TCP/IP Settings

TCP/IP is installed automatically as part of the Windows Server 2003 setup process and cannot be removed. Likewise, it cannot be installed manually. You have the opportunity to configure TCP/IP settings in the Configure Your Server Wizard, which appears automatically after bootup. When you install TCP/IP, it defaults to using Dynamic Host Configuration Protocol (DHCP) for automatic configuration, which will be explained in the next section and later in this book. If you want to use DHCP for automatic configuration you certainly can—servers typically use static addressing—however, as a network administrator (and because you will be tested on it), you should know how to manually configure a TCP/IP connection.

If you were under the impression that TCP/IP is difficult to configure, configuring it using Windows Server 2003's Internet Protocol (TCP/IP) Properties dialog box may surprise you. TCP/IP actually requires only two pieces of information to function:

- The IP address you want to use for this system
- The subnet mask that corresponds to the network subnet the client is on

Figure 2.1 shows the Internet Protocol (TCP/IP) Properties dialog box. You get this dialog box by selecting Start ➤ Control Panel ➤ Network Connections ➤ Local Area Connection icon, selecting the Internet Protocol (TCP/IP) protocol, and clicking the Properties button. Of course, if you have multiple network adapters in a single computer, you can set independent TCP/IP properties for each adapter. Depending on what you want to do, you'll use either the automatic configuration buttons or the text fields.

FIGURE 2.1   The basic TCP/IP Properties dialog box

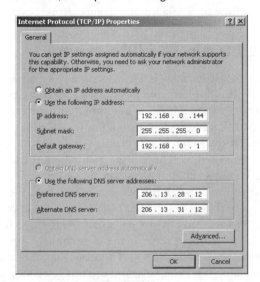

The Default Gateway and DNS Settings

In Figure 2.1, you may notice settings for the default gateway and DNS. Before we go on, you should know what these terms mean and what the default gateway and DNS are used for.

The *default gateway* is used to route traffic between your computer and computers on different subnets. Each gateway has an IP address (to which the client sends outbound packets). When deciding where to send packets bound for other networks, Windows Server 2003 will examine its internal TCP/IP routing table to see whether it already knows how to get packets to the destination network. If so, it uses that route. If not, it uses the default gateway.

The Domain Name System (DNS) is a set of protocols and services that allows users of the network to utilize hierarchical, user-friendly names instead of IP addresses when looking for network resources. This system is used extensively on the Internet and in many private enterprises today. If you've used a web browser, Telnet application, FTP utility, or other similar TCP/IP utilities on the Internet, then you have probably used a DNS server.

The DNS protocol's best-known function is mapping user-friendly names to IP addresses. For example, suppose the FTP site at Microsoft had an IP address of 157.55.100.1. Most people would reach this computer by specifying `ftp.microsoft.com` instead of its alienating IP address. Besides being easier to remember, the name is more reliable. The numeric address could change for any number of reasons, but that name can remain in spite of the change. If you want your clients to use DNS, you must specify one or more DNS servers in the TCP/IP Properties dialog box. The DNS servers keep records of name-to-address mappings and provide clients with the address information they need to communicate effectively using the DNS service. You will learn more about DNS and how to configure DNS servers in Chapter 6.

Now that you understand the basic elements of the Internet Protocol (TCP/IP) Properties dialog box, we'll show you how to configure the various settings.

Configuring Automatic TCP/IP Settings

The Dynamic Host Configuration Protocol is a server-based service that is designed to automate configuration of TCP/IP clients. You can put one or more DHCP servers on your network, program them with a range of network addresses and other configuration parameters, and let clients automatically obtain IP addressing information without manual intervention. With appropriate DHCP configurations, your TCP/IP clients—running any operating system that has DHCP support—can be configured with little or no manual intervention from you.

If you're configuring a Windows 2000 Professional or XP Professional machine, chances are probably pretty good that you're using DHCP with it. In that case, the default TCP/IP settings will work fine for you because they configure the TCP/IP stack to get configuration parameters from any available DHCP server. You can mix and match DHCP and non-DHCP machines on the same network as long as they use addresses in the same subnet range. On a single client, you can use DHCP to get everything except DNS server addresses if you want to. In the Internet Protocol (TCP/IP) Properties dialog box, you have two options for configuring the computer for automatic addressing:

- To configure a computer to get its TCP/IP configuration information from a DHCP server, leave the Obtain An IP Address Automatically radio button selected.

- If you're using DHCP for basic IP addressing and you want to accept DNS server addresses from the DHCP server as well, leave the Obtain DNS Server Address Automatically radio button selected.

The biggest thing to be aware of before enabling any DHCP clients is that you need a DHCP server for them to talk to. Windows 98, 2000, XP, and Server 2003 computers have a feature built into them called Automatic Private IP Addressing (APIPA) that can cause unintended consequences when you enable DHCP on the client without a DHCP server present. For instance, if you switch a client into DHCP mode, it will pick an address in the 169.254.$x.y$ Class B address space—and unless that address space is already in use on your network, your client will have difficulty talking to other computers on the network. More precisely, all the clients that can't reach the DHCP server will have addresses in the same range, and they'll be able to see only each other. Each time a client fails to contact a DHCP server, it picks an address from the 169.254 range and broadcasts it; if no other client answers the broadcast, the client uses the address as if it were manually assigned. However, the client "knows" that this isn't a real DHCP address, so it keeps attempting to renew its lease every 5 minutes (leases are discussed in more depth in Chapter 5, "Managing the Dynamic Host Configuration Protocol"). Once it succeeds, it transparently switches to the DHCP address.

There is a new feature in Windows Server 2003 called Alternate Configuration. Using Alternate Configuration, if a DHCP server is unavailable, you can have the computer switch to an alternate static configuration instead of the 169.254.$x.y$ range. Take a look at it. Open the Internet Protocol (TCP/IP) Properties dialog box. Make sure that the computer is configured to obtain its IP address automatically. If it is, then at the top of the dialog box, click the Alternate

Configuration tab. Notice that the Automatic Private IP Address radio button is selected by default. Click the User Configured radio button. You can now enter a complete alternate static configuration including a default gateway and two DNS and WINS servers. Figure 2.2 shows you what the Alternate Configuration tab looks like.

FIGURE 2.2   The Alternate Configuration tab

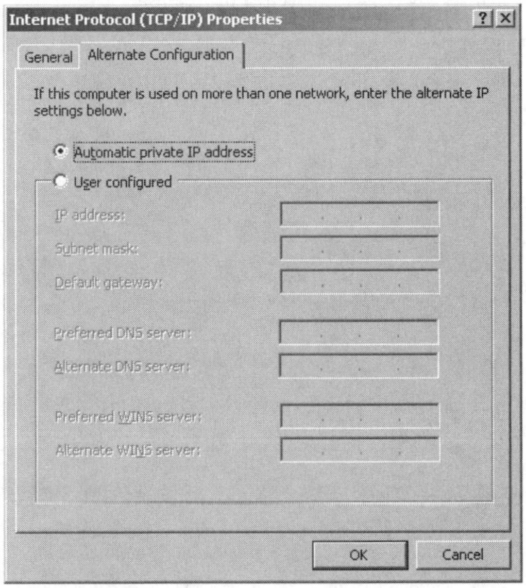

You might wonder when you would use an alternate configuration. There are two possibilities. The first possibility would be if, for instance, you had Windows Server 2003 installed on a portable computer and you need to dial up an ISP that doesn't support DHCP. Another possibility is for system backup. Although very expensive, it's possible to have secondary servers online configured in the alternate address scheme ready to accept requests when the DHCP server goes down. The problem here is keeping the primary servers and the secondary servers in sync. In any of these cases, Alternate Configuration is a new and very viable feature.

If you *do* have DHCP servers, you should verify that at least one of them is authorized. Here's one caveat that's mentioned in Microsoft's documentation: A Windows 2000 Server or a Windows Server 2003 machine running the DHCP server service *must* have a static IP address. Don't expect to be able to use the DHCP client on your servers if you're running DHCP or DNS services on them.

In Exercise 2.1, you will learn how to configure a Windows Server 2003 computer to use DHCP as a client.

EXERCISE 2.1

Configuring a Windows Client to Use DHCP

1.   Select Start ➢ Control Panel ➢ Network Connections.

2. Right-click the Local Area Connection icon and choose Properties. If you have more than one LAN adapter, choose the one you want to configure.

3. The Local Area Connection Properties dialog box appears. Select Internet Protocol (TCP/IP) from the This Connection Uses The Following Items list.

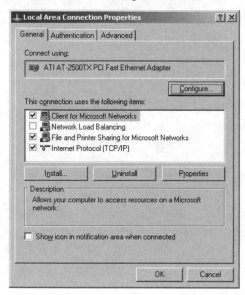

4. Click the Properties button. The Internet Protocol (TCP/IP) Properties dialog box appears.

5. To turn on DHCP, click the Obtain An IP Address Automatically radio button.

6. To enable your client to get DNS server information from the DHCP server, select the Obtain DNS Server Address Automatically radio button.

7. Click OK to close the Internet Protocol (TCP/IP) Properties dialog box.

8. Click OK to close the Local Area Connection Properties dialog box.

Configuring Manual TCP/IP Settings

We recommend not using DHCP on servers because they're not nearly as dynamic as clients. Ideally, you won't reboot servers unless they *need* it, and you won't be moving them around. Therefore, the "dynamic" in DHCP isn't really useful, and its other benefits are outweighed by the comfort that comes from knowing that your server has a correct and unchanging IP configuration. If you want to configure the TCP/IP settings yourself, start by selecting the

Use The Following IP Address radio button in the Internet Protocol (TCP/IP) Properties dialog box and then fill in the other fields as follows:

- In the IP Address field, enter the IP address you want to use for this machine. Remember that Windows Server 2003 won't verify that the address is unique or that it matches the local subnet. The most common mistake people make with this field is to enter an address that doesn't match the address range they're using on their network or adding an address that is already in use on another machine.

- In the Subnet Mask field, enter the appropriate subnet mask for your network.

- Enter the gateway or router address you want the computer to use in the Default Gateway field if you want this machine to be able to route packets to other networks. Again, make sure it's right.

- If you're using DNS on your network, check the Use The Following DNS Server Addresses radio button and enter the first DNS server you want this client to talk to in the Preferred DNS Server field. It's critical to get this right on a Windows Server 2003 network because DNS is required for Active Directory services (see Chapter 3, "Administering Security Policy," for more information on Active Directory). If you want to specify another server (which we recommend) to use when the preferred server is unavailable or can't resolve a DNS query, enter it in the Alternate DNS Server field. (You can also specify additional servers, as you'll see in the following section on the Advanced TCP/IP Settings dialog box.) The preferred DNS server should be the DNS server that is physically closest to the client computer. It's important to note that manual DNS settings override DNS settings obtained from a DHCP server.

Exercise 2.2 shows you how to manually configure an IP address on any Windows Server 2003 computer.

> Before attempting Exercise 2.2 on your network, be sure to choose an IP address *not* in use by any other host or device on your network!

EXERCISE 2.2

Manually Configuring TCP/IP

1. Select Start ➢ Control Panel ➢ Network Connections.

2. Right-click the Local Area Connection icon and choose Properties. If you have more than one LAN adapter, choose the one you want to configure.

3. The Local Area Connection Properties dialog box appears. Select Internet Protocol (TCP/IP) from the This Connection Uses The Following Items list.

4. Click the Properties button. The Internet Protocol (TCP/IP) Properties dialog box appears.

5. To manually enter an IP address, click the Use The Following IP Address radio button. Enter your IP address, subnet mask, and default gateway in the relevant fields.

EXERCISE 2.2 *(continued)*

6. To manually configure your computer's DNS server settings, select the Use The Following DNS Server Addresses radio button. Enter the names of your DNS servers in the relevant fields.

7. Click OK to close the Internet Protocol (TCP/IP) Properties dialog box.

8. Click OK to close the Local Area Connection Properties dialog box.

Configuring Advanced TCP/IP Settings

The Advanced button in the Internet Protocol (TCP/IP) Properties dialog displays several settings that are not available elsewhere. The Advanced TCP/IP Settings dialog box contains four tabs you can use to extend and override the settings from the simpler dialog box shown in Figure 2.1.

In the following sections, you will see how to configure advanced TCP/IP settings not available in the standard TCP/IP dialog box.

Expanding the Basic Settings

In the basic configuration dialog box you saw earlier, you can enter one IP address, one subnet mask, and one default gateway. For the majority of systems, that's enough. But what if you want to configure a machine that can communicate on multiple IP addresses? For example, if you're setting up an IIS server, you may want it to answer to multiple IP addresses on a single physical network connection (such as the connection that links your server to the Internet). Adding multiple IP addresses in this manner is called *multihoming*. You may also want to specify multiple default gateways so that an outbound packet sent by your systems can be sent to whichever gateway is most efficient. You can do both of these things on the IP Settings tab of the Advanced TCP/IP Settings dialog box. Figure 2.3 shows what it looks like.

Your options on the IP Settings tab include the following:

IP Addresses   The IP Addresses control group lists the IP addresses currently defined for this network adapter. You can add new address bindings, edit existing bindings, or remove an additional address with the buttons at the bottom of the control group. Once you add an address here and close all open network properties dialog boxes (including the Local Area Connection dialog box), any changes you make here will become effective.

Default Gateways   The Default Gateways control group shows the routing gateways that are currently defined for the computer you are working on. If you specify more than one default gateway, the system chooses a gateway by selecting the one that has the lowest cost, which you can enter arbitrarily. If that gateway is down, or if it can't get packets to the destination system, Windows Server 2003 will try the next-most-expensive gateway. This process repeats until the packets arrive at their destination or until the system runs out of gateways to try. If the costs (metrics) are equal on two different gateways, the server will load-balance the connection.

FIGURE 2.3   The IP Settings tab of the Advanced TCP/IP Settings dialog box

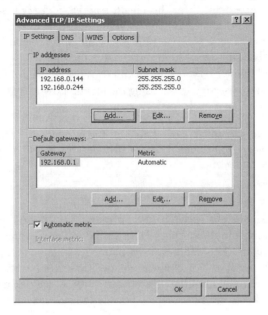

Configuring Advanced DNS Settings

The DNS tab, shown in Figure 2.4, may look kind of confusing, but the controls on it are all reasonably easy to understand.

FIGURE 2.4   The DNS tab of the Advanced TCP/IP Settings dialog

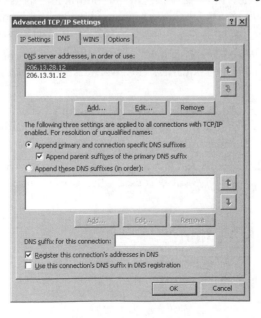

First, you should understand the DNS Server Addresses, In Order Of Use list. This list shows all the DNS servers currently defined for this client. Any DNS query is sent to the first server. If that server doesn't produce an answer, the query goes to the next one in the list after a 1-second delay. This process continues until a server returns a valid answer or until all the servers have been tried. This list can contain up to 20 different DNS servers.

You can add, edit, and remove servers with the buttons below the list, and you can change the order of a server in the list by selecting it and using the up and down arrows to the right of the list.

The DNS server list is used only for the network interface you're configuring. This allows you to use different DNS servers for NICs that are connected to different networks.

The remaining settings pertain only to this connection (or network adapter, to be more precise):

Append Primary And Connection Specific DNS Suffixes   This radio button controls whether DNS will automatically append the primary DNS suffix and any connection-specific suffixes when it makes DNS requests. This can best be explained with an example. Say your primary DNS suffix is hsv.chellis.net and your connection-specific suffix is eng.hsv.chellis.net. When this radio button is active, and you initiate a DNS query for a machine named hawk, DNS will first look for hawk.hsv.chellis.net and then for hawk.eng.hsv.chellis.net.

Append Parent Suffixes Of The Primary DNS Suffix   This checkbox (which is only active when Append Primary And Connection Specific DNS Suffixes is selected) forces the resolver to tack on parent suffixes of the primary suffix. Using the preceding example, if you couldn't find *hawk* in either eng.hsv.chellis.net or hsv.robichaux.net, this would force DNS to look in robichaux.net and then old.net.

Append These DNS Suffixes (In Order)   This radio button and its associated controls allow you to provide a list of suffixes for DNS. These are used in place of the primary and connection-specific suffixes, and they override any suffixes passed by the DHCP servers.

DNS Suffix For This Connection   This field allows you to specify the default connection suffix you want to append to DNS queries. This overrides any suffix that may be specified by the DHCP server.

Register This Connection's Addresses In DNS   This checkbox, which is on by default, tells the DHCP client to register its name and IP address with the nearest dynamic DNS (DDNS) server. (See Chapter 6 for more information on dynamic DNS.)

Use This Connection's DNS Suffix In DNS Registration   This checkbox controls whether the primary or connection-specific DNS suffix is used when your client registers itself with the DDNS service.

Configuring WINS Clients

In the previous chapter, you learned that NetBIOS works by broadcasting network resource information—such as which shares a server offers and where the domain master browser is—so that any client can hear what its peers have to offer. Broadcasts work OK for smaller networks, but they generate a lot of unnecessary and undesirable clutter in larger networks. Because NetBIOS packets aren't routable, the problem is even worse: Not only do all those broadcasts clutter the network, they don't even do any good because only machines on the local subnet can hear them.

Microsoft solved the routability problem by offering NetBIOS over TCP/IP (also known as NBT). However, NBT still sends out broadcasts. Although NBT broadcasts do allow NetBIOS-style name resolution on TCP/IP networks, Microsoft's designers realized that it was possible to come up with an even better solution, and the Windows Internet Name Service (WINS) was created.

WINS listens to NBT broadcasts and collates them in a central source. In this role, it effectively serves as a clearinghouse for NetBIOS naming information. If your clients are configured to use a WINS server, they can resolve NBT addresses without using broadcasts. This significantly decreases the load on the network and actually makes NBT a viable (although dying) solution on larger networks.

In the following sections, you will see how to configure WINS client information.

Node Types

Before we get into the specifics of how to configure a WINS client, you should understand some terminology that you need to know. You know that NBT typically uses broadcasts unless your clients are configured to use a WINS server. More specifically, the method that the client uses depends upon the client's node type, as listed in Table 2.1. The node type is determined by the NBT settings that you configure (or don't configure) in the WINS tab. A client's node type can be altered in the Registry, but you should use the DHCP or default settings whenever possible.

TABLE 2.1   NetBIOS Node Types

Node type	Description
b-node (broadcast)	Broadcasts NBT queries for name registration and resolution. The default for Windows 2000, XP, and Windows Server 2003 client machines not configured with WINS.
p-node (peer-peer node)	Uses a NetBIOS name server (or a WINS server) to resolve NetBIOS names and does not use broadcasts.
m-node (mixed)	Similar to b-node by default. If it cannot resolve a name, reverts to p-node.
h-node (hybrid)	Similar to p-node by default, and if it cannot resolve a name reverts to b-node. The default for Windows 2000, XP, and Windows Server 2003 client machines that are configured with WINS.

Configuring WINS Client Information

The WINS tab (see Figure 2.5) offers you a small group of controls for configuring how (if at all) your client uses WINS for name resolution.

FIGURE 2.5 The WINS tab of the Advanced TCP/IP Settings dialog box

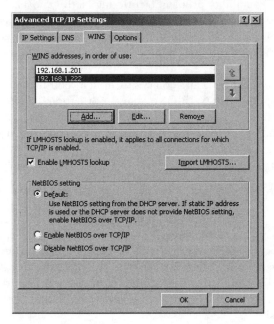

The controls are as follows:

WINS Addresses This list and its related controls show you which WINS servers you have defined for this client. By default, this list will be empty, so you have to manually add WINS servers to it if you want to use WINS.

As with DNS, the WINS code will send WINS resolution requests to the servers on this list in the order of their appearance. You add, remove, and change server addresses with the buttons below the list, and you change the ordering of the servers by selecting a server and using the up and down arrow buttons along the list's right side. You can have up to 12 WINS servers on the list.

LMHOSTS The next group, which falls immediately below the WINS address list group, controls whether or not the old-style *LMHOSTS file* is used as a source for address resolution information. The LMHOSTS file is a text file that contains NetBIOS name-to-address mappings. Computers can reference this file to resolve names to IP addresses, or they can use the traditional broadcasts or WINS methods. The Enable LMHOSTS Lookup checkbox controls whether or not Windows Server 2003 will use the computer name to IP mappings in the LMHOSTS file before querying a WINS server. When you check this box, LMHOSTS lookups are enabled for all connections that are using TCP/IP, not just the one whose properties you're editing. The Import LMHOSTS button allows you to read the contents of a file into the WINS name cache, which is handy if you want to load a set of name mappings without keeping a file around on disk.

NetBIOS Setting   The final controls are the three radio buttons at the bottom of the dialog box. They control whether NetBIOS over TCP/IP is active at all. In the past, NetBEUI was the only transport that could carry NetBIOS traffic, but it wasn't routable and had poor performance on large networks. As you saw earlier, Windows Server 2003 includes support for NBT, even though we expect its use to diminish as networks move toward pure TCP/IP. Here's what each button does:

- Default: Use NetBIOS Setting From The DHCP Server button forces this particular client to use the DHCP server's setting instead of manual WINS settings or the LMHOSTS file. If this button is *not* selected, whatever setting is in force will override the DHCP server's setting.

- The Enable NetBIOS Over TCP/IP button is selected to override a DHCP setting. It allows this client to exchange NetBIOS traffic with servers using TCP/IP as a transport.

- The Disable NetBIOS Over TCP/IP button turns off NBT, which is handy when you want to totally rid your network of all NetBIOS traffic, even when it's encapsulated.

   You initially enter the client's NBT name during Windows Setup.

Configuring a Windows Server 2003 machine as a WINS client is detailed in Exercise 2.3.

EXERCISE 2.3

Configuring a Windows Server 2003 Machine as a WINS client

1. Select Start ➤ Control Panel ➤ Network Connections.

2. Right-click the Local Area Connection icon and choose Properties. If you have more than one LAN adapter, choose the one you want to configure.

3. The Local Area Connection Properties dialog box appears. Select Internet Protocol (TCP/IP) from the This Connection Uses The Following Items list.

4. Click the Properties button. The Internet Protocol (TCP/IP) Properties dialog box appears.

5. Click the Advanced button. The Advanced TCP/IP Settings dialog box appears.

6. Click the WINS tab.

7. Click the Add button. When the TCP/IP WINS Server dialog box appears, enter the IP address for your WINS server and click the Add button. The first WINS server on the list should be the server physically closest to the client machine. You can enter additional WINS server addresses and reorder the servers as necessary if you like.

8. Click OK to close the Advanced TCP/IP Settings dialog box.

9. Click OK to close the Internet Protocol (TCP/IP) Properties dialog box.

10. Click OK to close the Local Area Connection Properties dialog box.

Real World Scenario

Multiple Protocols Are Nice but Inefficient

Your company has been running Windows NT, Novell NetWare, and even some Banyan that has been floating around for years. There are also connections to old mainframe controllers that still use Data Link Control (DLC). Over the years, the connections to these various operating systems have been created piecemeal by adding the clients and protocols at each workstation. This is a common approach, particularly on networks that have grown over time as each special-interest group kept control of its piece of the network. The interoperability features of Windows Server 2003 (as well as Windows NT before it), specifically the ability to run multiple protocols, are phenomenal. With the Network Driver Interface Specification (NDIS) and the similar Transport Driver Interface (TDI) (applied at the transport layer rather than the Network layer), you can run just about as many protocols as you would like. But the ease of this functionality can also cause problems at the other end because running multiple protocols creates an increase in bandwidth consumption and multiple points of management.

Although you can't just throw out the other systems, there are ways to approach the problems caused by this interoperability. Because it is now accepted globally, every major operating system today supports TCP/IP. This provides an opportunity to remove the other protocols on the network, such as IPX and NetBEUI, which are fading out of use. Each protocol stack brings its own overhead to the network. If you have Windows NT or Windows 9.*x* machines on your network with multiple protocols, you also have multiple instances of services that ride on top of those protocols. For example, if you're running NWLink and TCP/IP, there is a complete browser service (not the Internet kind of browser) that handles NetBIOS requests. This type of redundancy isn't efficient—it just provides another level of complexity where something can go wrong, thus adding to support efforts.

In the future you'll see the maturity of protocol interoperability applied at the other end of the OSI stack. Using technologies such as XML and HTTP, the network client is becoming simply the browser that can be used to access information across different underlying platforms. Until then, the best practice is to work toward the goal of a unified client and to minimize the number of protocols on your network, as well as the number of clients, if possible. Although the functionality is there to support more protocols and more clients, this is another case where more is not necessarily better.

Configuring Network Bindings

A *network binding* links a protocol to an adapter so that the adapter can carry traffic using that protocol. For example, if we say, "TCP/IP is bound to the onboard Ethernet port on our laptop," we're telling you a few things: TCP/IP is installed, our onboard Ethernet port has a driver that supports TCP/IP, and the adapter is configured to send and receive TCP/IP traffic. In Chapter 1,

"Understanding Windows Server 2003 Networking," you read about the NDIS driver specification and its benefits. One of those benefits is the ability to bind more than one protocol to a NIC. That's how your Windows Server 2003 machine can run TCP/IP, NetBEUI, and AppleTalk at the same time, even if it has only one network card.

Windows Server 2003 automatically creates bindings when you install a protocol or when you check or uncheck the checkboxes in the Properties dialog box of a particular NIC. You can change these bindings manually; for example, it's commonly considered good practice to unbind NetBEUI and NWLink from adapters that are connected to, or visible from, the Internet. You access the Windows Server 2003 binding list from within the `Network Connections` folder, which can be opened by selecting Start ≻ Control Panel, right-clicking Network Connections, and selecting Open from the pop-up menu. Click on a local NIC (like the standard Local Area Connection item), choose the Advanced menu, and select Advanced Settings. You'll see the Advanced Settings dialog box, shown in Figure 2.6. This dialog box is divided into two distinct areas.

FIGURE 2.6   Adjusting bindings with the Advanced Settings dialog box

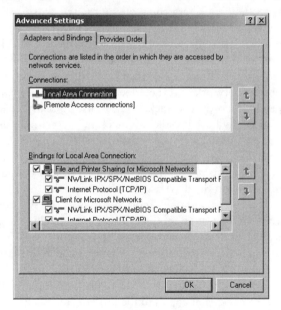

The Connections list shows all the connections available on your computer. They're listed in the order that they'll be used for services. For example, in Figure 2.6, you can see that TCP/IP services (as well as everything else) will first use the LAN connection; if the requested action can't be taken there, the services will use a remote access connection instead. You can change the order in which connections are used by selecting a connection and using the up and down arrow buttons to the right of the list.

The Bindings list shows you which protocols and services are bound to the selected connection. For example, Figure 2.6 shows that the File and Printer Sharing for Microsoft Networks and Client for Microsoft Networks services are bound to the LAN adapter and that the NWLink and TCP/IP protocols are bound to the File and Printer Sharing for Microsoft Networks and Client for Microsoft Networks services. What this dialog box tells you is which services are available on a connection. Beneath each service, you'll see a list of which protocols that service can use. Checking and unchecking services has the same effect as checking or unchecking items in the Adapter Properties dialog box.

The one benefit is that you can turn individual protocols on or off on a per-service basis. You can also control the order in which the protocols are used. This is a valuable optimization because many protocols have some sort of built-in retry behavior. Changing the bindings so that the most frequently used protocols are at the top of the list for each service means that the services never waste time trying the wrong protocol; instead, they'll try the most likely choice first, falling back to other protocols only if the first protocol fails.

Monitoring Network Traffic

Sometimes the best way to see what's happening on your network is to watch the traffic as it passes. A tool called Network Monitor is included with Windows Server 2003. This tool is a direct descendant of the Windows NT Network Monitor, which in turn is based on the same-named tool provided with the Systems Management Server (SMS) product. Network Monitor is a network analyzer (or "sniffer" after the Network General Sniffer toolset). Network analyzers capture raw traffic from the network and then decode it just as the protocol stack would. Because they don't depend on a protocol stack, you can use an analyzer to monitor traffic for protocol types you don't actually have installed; for example, you might use Network Monitor to capture and decode AppleTalk packets while troubleshooting a Mac connectivity problem, even without having AppleTalk on your workstation.

Network Monitor comes in two pieces: the application—which you install on Windows Server 2003 (see Figure 2.7)—and the driver, which you typically install on Windows 2000 or XP Professional client machines, although most versions of the Windows operating system can use the Network Monitor driver. To monitor traffic on a machine, it must have the driver installed (it's automatically installed when you install the application). The driver is required because it puts the network card into *promiscuous mode*, in which the card will accept packets not addressed to it—obviously a requirement to monitor overall network traffic.

Network Monitor allocates a big chunk of RAM to use as a *capture buffer*. When you tell it to start capturing network packets, it copies to the buffer every packet it sees on a particular NIC, gathering statistical data as it goes. When you stop the capture process, you can analyze the buffered data in a variety of ways, including by applying *capture filters* that screen out packets you're not interested in.

Before you install and use Network Monitor, there are a couple of caveats you need to know about. First, the Windows Server 2003 Network Monitor only works with Windows 2000 or XP clients—if you want to use it to monitor Windows NT, 95, or 98 clients, you need the Network Monitor drivers from the SMS CD. More importantly, the Windows Server 2003 version of Network Monitor allows you to watch traffic to and from only the server that it's installed on; the SMS version of Network Monitor supports watching traffic anywhere on your network.

FIGURE 2.7   The main Network Monitor window

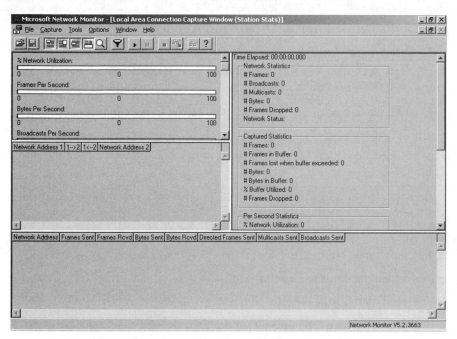

Windows Server 2003 also includes a tool called System Monitor, which is used to monitor just about everything that goes on in the computer. The processor, memory, disk, and most importantly, the network can all be monitored in the System Monitor utility. The System Monitor does not provide as much information about network traffic as Network Monitor, but it's great for obtaining a quick graphical representation of the status of your network. In many cases, this is quicker and easier than deciphering the complex information that Network Monitor presents.

In the following sections, you will see how to install and use Network Monitor and System Monitor to monitor network traffic.

Installing the Network Monitor Driver and Application

If you want to use Network Monitor to capture packets from a machine that doesn't already have Network Monitor on it, you need to install the Network Monitor driver on the target machine. Once you've installed the Network Monitor driver on at least one other machine, you can install the Network Monitor application itself and start monitoring. Exercise 2.4 explains this process. In this exercise, you'll install the Network Monitor driver and the Network Monitor application.

Be forewarned that many organizations watch their network very closely for signs of network analyzer use, so completing this exercise may raise an alarm in your IT department. You may be prompted for the Windows Server 2003 CD, too, so have it handy.

EXERCISE 2.4

Installing the Network Monitor Driver and Application

Installing the Network Monitor Driver

1. Open the Network Connections folder by clicking Start ➢ Control Panel ➢ Network Connections ➢ Local Area Connection.

2. When the Local Area Connection Status window appears, click the Properties button.

3. When the Properties dialog box appears, click the Install button. The Select Network Component Type dialog box appears. Click Protocol in the Component list and click the Add button.

4. The Select Network Protocol dialog box appears. Select Network Monitor Driver and click the OK button.

5. Once the driver's installed, the Properties dialog box reappears. Click the Close button. Click the Close button on the Local Area Connection Status dialog box as well.

Installing the Network Monitor Application

6. Select Start ➢ Control Panel ➢ Add Or Remove Programs.

7. When the Add Or Remove Programs dialog box appears, click the Add/Remove Windows Components button, which opens the Windows Components Wizard.

8. Select the Management And Monitoring Tools item and then click the Details button.

9. Check the box next to the Network Monitor Tools item and then click OK, which returns you to the Windows Components Wizard.

10. Click Next in the Windows Components Wizard.

11. After the necessary files are copied, click Finish to close the wizard.

12. Click the Close button to close the Add Or Remove Programs dialog box.

How to Use Network Monitor

Network Monitor is a complicated tool; it's made for complicated tasks and its interface reflects that. This section isn't going to teach you how to troubleshoot subtle network problems with Network Monitor, but it will explain how to use Network Monitor to do some simple tasks that will give you a good head start on learning to use it well enough to pass the exam (and, it is hoped, to solve the occasional problem, too).

When you first start Network Monitor, it will ask you to choose a network to monitor. The list of networks you see will depend on the number of NICs you have installed; if you have only one NIC, Network Monitor will automatically select the correct network for you and you'll see the Network Monitor window.

The following list explains what you'll see in the main Network Monitor window (you can turn specific panes on and off with the Window menu):

- The Graph pane, in the upper-left corner, displays bar graphs of current network utilization, including the number of frames, bytes, broadcasts, and multicasts captured per second. This pane updates only when a capture is in progress.

- The Session Stats pane, located in the middle of the left side, shows information about connections captured during the current session. This information includes the source and destination network addresses and how many packets have gone in each direction between the two endpoints.

- The Total Stats pane, which occupies the right side of the window, lists a variety of interesting statistics, including the total number of unicast, broadcast, and multicast frames that Network Monitor captures, plus the amount of data currently in the capture buffer. Like the Session Stats pane, this pane's contents are continuously updated during a capture.

- The Station Stats frame, located at the bottom of the window, tells you what's been happening on the machine running Network Monitor.

Now that you have an idea of what the different sections of the Network Monitor window represent, you can begin to capture data, as you will see in the following section.

Capturing Data

When you capture data (the process is detailed in Exercise 2.5), you're just filling up a big buffer with the packets as they arrive. Network Monitor doesn't attempt to analyze them at that point. To control capture activity, you can use either the toolbar buttons (the ones that use the standard start, stop, and pause symbols) or the commands in the Capture menu: Start, Stop, Stop And View, Pause, and Continue.

Starting and stopping a capture is pretty straightforward, although you may need to adjust the buffer size upward from its default of 1Mb. You do this using the Capture ➢ Buffer Settings command. Once you start the capture, Network Monitor will continue working until you've filled the buffer or stopped the capture. At that point, you can view the data or save it to a disk file for later analysis with the File ➢ Save As command.

In Exercise 2.5, you'll use Network Monitor to gather a full capture buffer so you can experiment with display filters in the next exercise.

Computers with video cards manufactured by Nvidia may experience problems running Network Monitor. Certain Nvidia GeForce driver implementations install a file named nview.dll, which is the same file name used by Network Monitor. To solve this problem, use the /basevideo switch in your boot.ini file, as described in the *Windows Server 2003 Study Guide*, by Lisa Donald and James Chellis.

EXERCISE 2.5

Capturing Data with Network Monitor

1. Install Network Monitor as described in Exercise 2.4. Open the Network Monitor application by selecting Start ➢ Administrative Tools ➢ Network Monitor. The first time you use the Network Monitor application, you will be prompted to select an interface to monitor. Select the Local Area Connection to continue with this exercise.

2. Use the Capture ➢ Buffer Settings command to increase the capture buffer size to 2Mb. This gives you room for 4096 frames of data.

3. Start a capture with the Capture ➢ Start command. While the capture is going, use a web browser to request a web page from the machine you're running Network Monitor on. (This step is necessary for the next exercise.)

4. Let it run until the buffer is full; you can tell by watching the "# Frames in Buffer" line in the Captured Statistics section of the Total Stats pane. Then click the Stop button to stop the capture.

5. Save the capture buffer to disk with the File ➢ Save As command. You'll need it for the next exercise.

Viewing Data

After you stop a capture, you can view the accumulated data with the Capture ➢ Display Captured Data command. This opens a new window: the Frame Viewer (see Figure 2.8). This window lists every captured frame, summarizing its source and destination address, the time at which it was captured (relative to the start of the capture operation), the network type, and the protocol in use. Although the display of all this data is interesting, it's more likely that you'll need to use Network Monitor's filtering functions to pick out just the data you want.

FIGURE 2.8   The Frame Viewer window

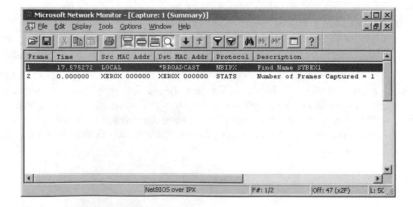

If you want to see the full contents of an individual frame, just double-click it. This causes two new panes to appear in the Frame Viewer window: The Detail pane is in the middle, and the Hex pane is at the bottom (see Figure 2.9). This gives you an easy way to inspect, bit by bit, the contents of any captured frame in the buffer.

FIGURE 2.9   The Frame Viewer window with the Detail and Hex panes visible

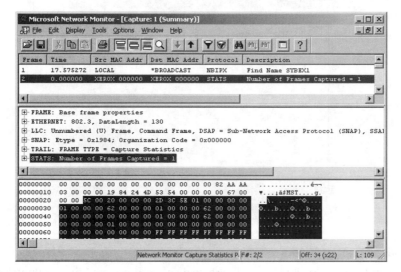

Using Filters

You can create two types of filters in Network Monitor:

- Capture filters screen out unwanted packets before they're recorded to the capture buffer.
- Display filters display some packets but not others.

We will look at each of these filters in the following sections.

Working with Capture Filters

You create and manage capture filters using the Capture ➤ Filters command, available from the standard Network Monitor window. This displays the Capture Filter dialog box (see Figure 2.10).

The rule to remember when using the Capture Filter dialog box is that filters are grouped in a tree. The default filter says that any SAP/ETYPE (Service Access Point or Ethernet Type—both of these tags mark packets with the protocol they're using) will be captured. This is because the three conditions under the root of the tree all use the AND modifier. While you can use AND, OR, and NOT for your own filters, you can't remove the original tree branches.

Say, for example, that you want to create a filter that captures traffic going to port 80 on a particular machine. Capture filters don't care about ports, but you can create a filter based on the address by selecting the SAP/ETYPE branch and using the Edit button to capture only IP packets. Next, edit the (Address Pairs) item to specify the proper destination address. To find packets with a particular payload, specify a pattern to capture that traffic with the (Pattern

Matches) branch. (Unfortunately, that's about all you can do with capture filters in the Windows Server 2003 version of Network Monitor; there are a bunch of additional features that only work in the SMS version.)

FIGURE 2.10 The Capture Filter dialog box

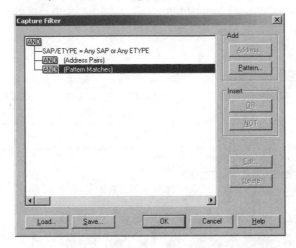

Working with Display Filters

Once you've captured some data, you can create display filters that give you much finer control over what you see. This is handy because it's difficult to pick out the few frames you're looking for from a full capture buffer. You create display filters while you're looking at the Frame Viewer window. Use the Display ➤ Filter command to bring up the Display Filter dialog box (see Figure 2.11).

FIGURE 2.11 The Display Filter dialog box

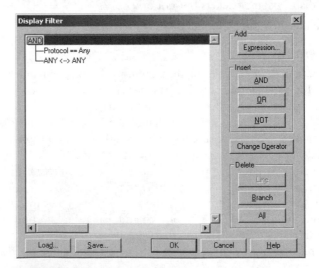

The mechanics of this dialog box work just like they do in the Capture Filter dialog box, but you can do some additional things, as you will see in the next exercise.

Using the capture buffer from Exercise 2.5, you can create a display filter to limit what appears in the Frame Viewer. In Exercise 2.6, you will see how to create a display filter.

Creating a Display Filter

1. If you have quit Network Monitor since the previous exercise, reopen it and then use the File ➤ Open command to reopen the capture buffer you saved. Otherwise, select Capture ➤ Display Captured Data to open the Frame Viewer window. The capture information should be intact from the previous exercise.

2. When the Frame Viewer window appears, use the Display ➤ Filter command to open the Display Filter dialog box.

3. Select the Protocol == Any line and click the Edit Expression button. You'll see the Protocol tab of the Expression dialog box.

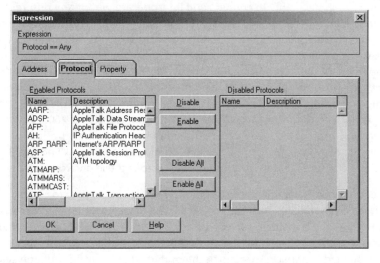

4. Click the Disable All button to remove all the protocols. The filter screens out any protocol that's disabled.

5. Select HTTP in the Disabled Protocols list and click the Enable button. Now HTTP should be the only enabled protocol. Click the OK button. Optionally, select the ANY <--> ANY filter and use the Edit Expression button to add an address rule to the filter. Normally you don't need to do this because the Windows Server 2003 version of Network Monitor monitors traffic between only your computer and one other at a time.

6. Click the OK button in the Display Filter dialog when you're done. The Frame Viewer window reappears, but notice that the frame numbers (in the leftmost column) are no longer consecutive—the filter is screening out any traffic that doesn't match its criteria.

7. Double-click a frame to see its contents. Because you're looking at unencrypted HTTP packets, you can clearly see the requests and responses.

 Real World Scenario

Network Interoperability

Your company has been deploying LAN technology for years. The problem is that each department has been free to choose its own favorite technology products. The result of this unbridled freedom has been chaos in terms of methodical and cost-effective support. You, the network administrator, have the task of building bridges to all of these independent islands of technology until a plan can be put into place to consolidate the various technologies.

One of the most flexible aspects of Windows Server 2003—and, for that matter, of Windows 2000 and NT—is the ability to connect and interoperate with many different types of backend systems. Macintoshes, mainframes, minicomputers, Unix workstations, NetWare, and even Banyan have all been connected to Windows Server 2003 rather easily. There were several issues with connectivity to dissimilar systems; these are slowly vanishing one by one, although some remnants still exist in individual networks. For example, in the past, there was a large issue with the transport protocols of the different systems. TCP/IP won that battle, and all the remaining operating systems support TCP/IP. Now there remains the issue of the actual clients. If you need to communicate with NetWare, Unix, and Windows 2000, you might have a common transport protocol, but you still may need to have specific proprietary clients to access each system. However, even this issue is beginning to go away. Windows Server 2003 comes with all the clients necessary to communicate across these diverse systems.

Although the acceptance of common protocols and clients would appear to create a domain of simplicity, instead we see complexity created by the overall growth of the internetworking system itself. But the real issue that is now rearing its head is the question of how to manage all these clients. Windows 2000 and XP desktops, cellular phones, PDAs, and other household devices that are being developed all need to be integrated into the full information system. This is why services such as DHCP, DNS, IPSec, and Active Directory and virtual private networks (VPNs) are so critical to understand. A solid and well-designed core of Windows Server 2003 services that support the Windows 2000 and XP clients creates a supportable foundation for the onslaught of clients that are coming down the developmental chute.

Monitoring Network Activity with System Monitor

The *System Monitor* utility is used to collect and measure the real-time performance data for a local or remote computer on the network. Through System Monitor, you can view current data or data from a log file. When you view current data, you are monitoring real-time activity. When you view data from a log file, you are importing a log file from a previous session.

System Monitor enables you to do the following tasks:

- Collect data from your local computer or remote computers on the network. You can collect data from a single computer or multiple computers concurrently.

- View data as it is being collected in real time or view it historically (that is, collected data).

- Have full control over the selection of what data will be collected by choosing which specific objects and counters will be collected.

- Choose the sampling parameters that will be used, meaning the time interval that you want to use for collecting data points and the time period that will be used for data collection.

- Determine the format in which data will be viewed—in graph, histogram, or report view.

- Create HTML pages for viewing data.

- Create specific configurations for monitoring data that can then be exported to other computers for performance monitoring.

When you first start System Monitor, as shown in Figure 2.12, you will see that three counters are tracked by default (as opposed to previous versions of System Monitor, which did not track any counters by default). The default counters that are tracked contain some of the most useful performance data:

- Memory > Pages/Sec

- PhysicalDisk > Avg. Disk Queue Length

- Processor > % Processor Time

FIGURE 2.12   System Monitor

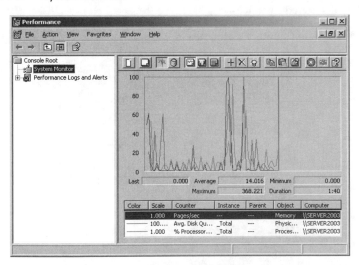

You will learn about counters in the section "Organization of System Monitor" later in this chapter.

In this book, we use the format *performance object > counter*. For example, Memory > Pages/Sec denotes the Memory performance object and the Pages/Sec counter.

Each counter is listed at the bottom of the System Monitor utility. The fields just above the counter list will contain data based on the counter that is highlighted in the list, as follows:

- The Last field displays the most current data.

- The Average field shows the average value of the counter.

- The Minimum field shows the lowest value that has been recorded for the counter.

- The Maximum field shows the highest value that has been recorded for the counter.

- The Duration field shows how long the counter has been tracking data.

The following sections describe how System Monitor is organized, how to add counters to track data, and how to use and configure network-specific counters.

Organization of System Monitor

System Monitor allows you to track performance-related data about your computer using a hierarchical structure for specifying what should be tracked. When you click the Add button on the System Monitor toolbar, the Add Counters dialog box appears. As you can see in Figure 2.13, counters are added based on the following:

- The local computer or counters from another computer

- Performance objects

- All counters or specific counters

- All instances of selected instances

FIGURE 2.13   Add Counters dialog box

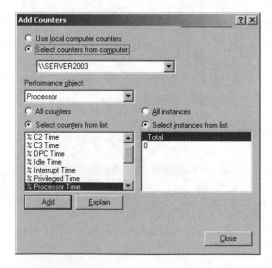

By default, any counters that are added to System Monitor track the local computer. However, you can specify that you want to track counters on a remote computer. This option allows you to track performance data for several computers within a single System Monitor session.

Windows Server 2003 organizes system resources that affect system performance into categories called performance objects. The sum of all of the performance objects represents your system. Depending on the configuration of your server, you will see different performance objects listed. Examples of performance objects include Paging File, Memory, Process, and Processor.

Each performance object has an associated set of counters. Counters are used to track specific information regarding the performance object. For example, the performance object Memory allows you to track counters for Page Reads/sec and Page Writes/sec.

Instance

Each performance object can consist of one or more instances. Performance objects like Memory and Cache will always have one instance. Performance objects like Print Queue or Processor can have multiple instances if you have more than one print queue or processor installed on your computer. By using the instance option, you can track data for all instances—for example, all print queues or specific instances such as the Laser print queue.

Adding Counters

To add additional counters to System Monitor, use the following steps:

1. In System Monitor, click the Add button on the toolbar. This brings up the Add Counters dialog box.

To see information about a specific counter, select it and click the Explain button in the lower-left corner of the Add Counters dialog box. System Monitor will display text regarding the highlighted counter.

2. In the Add Counters dialog box, select the Use Local Computer Counters radio button to monitor the local computer. Alternatively, select the Select Counters From Computer radio button and choose a computer from the drop-down list to select counters from a specific computer. You can monitor remote computers if you have administrative permissions on that computer. This option is useful when you do not want the overhead of System Monitor running on the computer you are trying to monitor.

3. Select the performance object from the drop-down list.

4. Select the All Counters radio button to track all the associated counters, or select the Select Counters From List radio button and choose specific counters from the list box below.

You can select multiple counters of the same performance object by Shift+clicking contiguous counters or Ctrl+clicking noncontiguous counters.

5. Select the All Instances radio button to track all the associated instances, or select the Select Instances From List radio button and choose specific instances from the list box below.

6. Click the Add button to add the counters for the performance object.

7. Repeat steps 2 through 6 to specify any additional counters you want to track. When you are finished, click the Close button.

Using System Monitor, you can monitor and optimize the traffic that is generated on the specific Windows Server 2003 computer. You can monitor the network interface (your network card), and you can monitor the network protocols that have been installed on your computer.

Key Counters to Track for the Network Subsystem

The following are two of the counters that are useful for monitoring the network subsystem:

Network Interface > Bytes Total/Sec   Measures the total number of bytes that are sent or received from the network interface and includes all network protocols.

TCPv4 > Segments/Sec   Measures the number of bytes that are sent or received from the network interface and includes only the TCP protocol.

Normally, you monitor and optimize the network subsystem from a network perspective rather than from a single computer. For example, you can use a network protocol analyzer to monitor all of the traffic on the network to determine if the network bandwidth is acceptable for your requirements or if the network bandwidth is saturated.

Tuning and Upgrading the Network Subsystem

The following suggestions can help to optimize and minimize network traffic:

- Use only the network protocols you need. For example, use TCP/IP and don't use NWLink and NetBEUI.

- If you need to use multiple network protocols, place the most commonly used protocols higher in the binding order.

- Use network cards that take full advantage of your bus width. For example, use 32-bit cards instead of 16-bit cards.

- Use faster network cards. For example, use intelligent (CPU based) and/or larger buffer network cards.

In Exercise 2.7, you will monitor your network subsystem.

EXERCISE 2.7

Monitoring the Network Subsystem

1. If System Monitor is not already open, select Start ➢ Administrative Tools ➢ Performance.

2. In the System Monitor window, click the Add button on the toolbar.

EXERCISE 2.7 *(continued)*

3. In the Add Counters dialog box, select the following performance objects and counters:

   - Select Network Interface from the Performance Object drop-down list, select Bytes Total/Sec in the counter list box, and click the Add button.

   - Select TCPv4 from the Performance Object drop-down list, select Segments/Sec from the counter list box, and click the Add button.

4. Click the Close button. You should see these counters added to your chart.

5. To generate some activity, copy some files between your domain controller and the member server.

6. Note the Network Interface > Bytes Total/Sec and TCPv4 > Segments/Sec counters. These numbers are cumulative. Use them in your baselines to determine network activity.

Troubleshooting Network Protocols

Knowing how to effectively troubleshoot network problems is an essential part of managing even small networks, and Microsoft expects you to understand basic troubleshooting principles and how to apply them in Windows Server 2003 networking. Fortunately, you probably already know what to check; now you'll read about a set of tools that you can use to verify the proper functioning of your network. More importantly, you'll learn how to use those tools the right way at the right time.

Analyzing Recent Changes

When someone complains that their network is broken, your first impulse should be to ask what changed. This might seem weird, but it's actually very practical. If a system is working and then it stops working, obviously something has changed somewhere—either as the result of an explicit change or by accident. Once you can identify what has, or has not, changed, you're ready to start looking for effects of the change and ways to fix whatever's gone wrong.

For example, one of the servers in our home office is a reliable old Intergraph TD-30. It's been running Windows Server 2003 since very early in the beta cycle, and it just keeps trucking along, never giving us any trouble. It happens to have a front-mounted power switch. When we can't contact it, our first suspicion is that it's been powered off.

The first sign of network trouble is usually pretty obvious, too: one machine can't talk to another. If you think back to the OSI networking model from Chapter 1, you'll remember that computers can communicate at several different layers. Using the preceding example, if we look at the back panel of hawk, our primary Windows Server 2003 machine, we can see that its NIC has some LED lights that indicate network activity. Those lights blinking don't tell us anything about what kind of network data is being carried by the Transport, Application, Session, or

Presentation layers—all it tells us is that the Physical layer components are sending and receiving something. To really understand what the problem is, we would have to use various trouble-shooting tools, as you will see in the following sections.

Pinpointing the Cause of the Problem

You can often save yourself a lot of unnecessary time and effort when troubleshooting a problem by doing something simple: stopping to think about the problem. It's hard to keep your wits about you when something's wrong with your network and end users are asking why. But if you can clearly identify the problem source, you're well on your way to being able to effectively resolve it without any time-wasting detours.

In the following sections, you will learn how to identify network problems and begin to formulate a plan based on the data that you gather.

What Kind of Problem Is It?

Sometimes figuring out what kind of problem you're dealing with can be the most frustrating part of troubleshooting. Getting a phone call or a pager message that says, "The network is down" doesn't tell you much. Is it your connection to the Internet? Your e-mail server? A file server somewhere on your LAN? Without knowing what specific service or connection is unavailable, you won't know what to start fixing.

Some types of problems immediately suggest a solution. For example, if a client calls and says they get DNS errors when trying to connect to websites, our first two thoughts are that someone's changed their DNS settings or that their DNS servers are down. Likewise, if a user reports a problem reaching a particular share on a server, the problem may be on the client, the server, or the intervening network. If you can, gather as many details about how the problem is manifesting itself (including exact error messages), when it started, and whether or not it's consistent before you try to figure out what the problem is. Knowing these things beforehand can guide you to an easy, quick solution if it's a problem you've seen and fixed before—but only if you *know* you've seen it before!

Who's Having the Problem?

Knowing which users or computers are affected by a problem is very important, because that gives you insight into possible causes (including user mistakes) and helps you select a course of action. In this section, you'll learn how to identify problems based on the users that report errors.

If One User Reports a Problem

If one user on your network has a problem, more often than not the problem stems from some change the user made. Windows contains a lot of interrelated components, and it's not evident to most people that a simple change they made in component A may have unexpected side effects on component B. When troubleshooting an end user problem, your first question should always involve whether or not they've changed anything on the machine. This includes changing Control Panel settings, installing or removing software, rebooting, or any other action that might have directly or indirectly changed the state of the machine. If you can find out what's changed, that will give you a list of potential places to start looking.

For example, a junior administrator at a company complained that he could no longer see the network after performing some work on his designated server. As it turned out, he had turned his machine into a DHCP server while experimenting, which meant that his previously assigned DHCP address could no longer be used. He'd picked another IP address at random, which turned out not to work with the company's network configuration. Knowing what changed helped to pinpoint and fix the problem quickly.

If Several Users Report the Same Problem

Multiuser troubleshooting is, paradoxically, both easier and harder than single-user trouble-shooting. Most of the time one user can't change anything that will affect other users on the network, so you generally don't have to worry about that variable. On the other hand, the kinds of changes that can accidentally affect connectivity for many users at once are more likely to be things you as a network administrator changed. The first step in fixing this kind of problem is identifying its scope. Is everyone on the network affected? Are only people in one workgroup or on one floor of a building affected? Is the problem limited to the lack of one key service (like DNS), or is all network traffic affected? Answering this type of question helps you isolate where the problem's occurring so you can concentrate your efforts on that area.

Here's an example: While on a consulting assignment in Texas, users at the site we were visiting began reporting that inbound Internet mail wasn't arriving as expected. We checked the Exchange server and found that it was okay. What else could have changed? It turned out that the DNS entry for the mail server had been improperly altered by someone at the company's ISP, so mail couldn't be delivered until things were fixed. Knowing that the problem affected *everyone* helped us find the right solution instead of assuming another cause.

Checking Physical Connections

Physical layer connectivity is absolutely critical. If you don't have a physical connection to the network you want to talk to, you can't send packets to it. So, when you first notice a network problem, be sure to verify that all of your network cables are correctly connected; that your hub, router, or switch has power; and so on. Take a look at the activity or "heartbeat" lights on your NIC, hub, or switch to see whether the Physical layer is reporting any type of activity.

Knowing something about the scope of the outage helps, too—if all your users begin complaining at once that the network is down, it's unlikely to be the fault of one user's network cable. On the other hand, if a single user is having trouble with the network, it's unlikely that a router or switch is to blame. If you've properly identified exactly who's having trouble, that may suggest a cause based on your knowledge of the physical topology.

If you verify that all of the physical connections are okay, with power and cabling all in good order, and you still have no connectivity, that indicates that the problem probably resides within a higher layer.

Using Ipconfig

Windows Server 2003 includes a useful tool called *ipconfig*. As its name implies, it's used to con-figure, and to see the configuration of, TCP/IP interfaces on your local machine. Typing `ipconfig` into a Windows Server 2003 command prompt window will present you with a summary of your current IP configuration, including the local DNS name, the IP addresses, and the subnet masks configured for all adapters on the computer. Figure 2.14 shows an example of this output.

FIGURE 2.14   The output from the `ipconfig` command

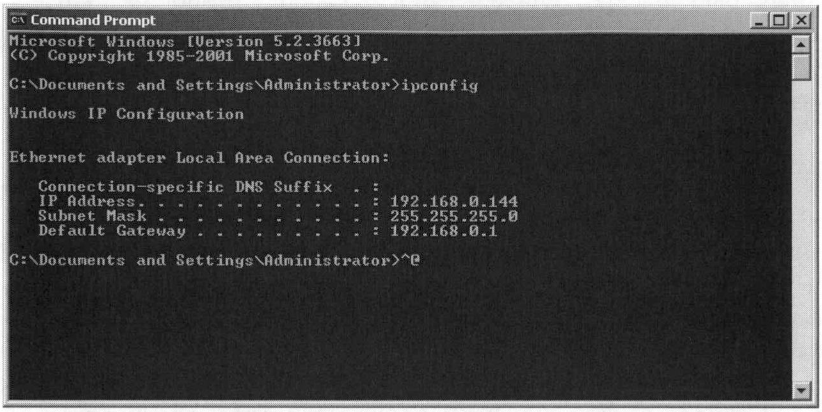

You can use the `ipconfig` command in this mode to get a quick snapshot of the machine's IP configuration, even if it's using DHCP. For example, if you see that the problem machine has no IP address assigned, even though there's a DHCP server, it suggests the possibility that the DHCP server isn't authorized in Active Directory.

There's a switch of particular interest to troubleshooters: `/all`. The `/all` switch causes ipconfig to display everything it knows about the current IP configuration on all installed adapters. In addition to the DNS information and IP address that it ordinarily displays, you'll also get the MAC address of each NIC, the present WINS configuration (if any), and the IP addresses being used for the preferred and alternate DNS servers. Figure 2.15 shows an example of the `ipconfig /all` output.

FIGURE 2.15   The output from `ipconfig /all`

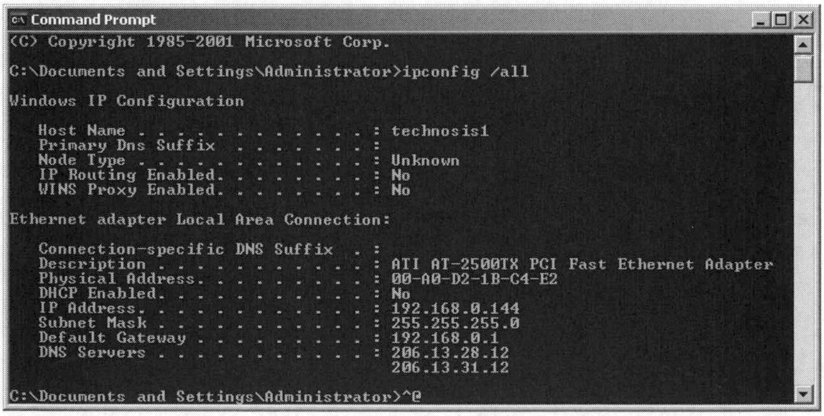

If you're familiar enough with your network to know what IP address configurations should look like, often a quick check with ipconfig will tell you where the problem lies. For example, you might notice that an adapter that should be DHCP enabled isn't, or vice versa. Even if you're not familiar with the details of your network, though, knowing how to find the IP addresses and subnet masks in use on your computers can be very valuable.

In Exercise 2.8 you will use ipconfig to view your current IP configuration.

EXERCISE 2.8

Checking Configurations with Ipconfig

1. Open a command prompt window by selecting Start ➤ Run, entering **cmd** in the Run dialog box, and clicking OK.

2. At the command prompt, type `ipconfig`. Notice that you see an abbreviated display containing the machine's connection-specific DNS suffix, its IP address, subnet mask, and default gateway.

3. Type `ipconfig /all`. Note that a great deal more information is displayed, including information on multiple adapters (if you have more than one).

Using Ping, Tracert, and Pathping

The next step up from Physical layer troubleshooting is tracing the route that packets take, or are attempting to take, between the source and destination. Once you've verified that all of the physical connections are in good shape, the next step is to see whether you can send *any* type of packet between points A and B.

TCP/IP includes a protocol called the *Internet Control Message Protocol (ICMP)*. ICMP is designed to pass control and status information between TCP/IP devices. One type of ICMP packet, popularly known as a ping packet, tells the receiving system to send back an ICMP response. This gives you confirmation of whether or not the ICMP ping packet reached the target, which in turn tells you whether or not you can get packets from place to place. Because name resolution and application services depend on lower-level protocols, this sort of "Is this thing on?" test is the next logical step after testing the underlying physical connection. The ping and tracert tools both use ICMP to help sniff out network problems. Unfortunately, this test is not foolproof because many routers purposely block ICMP traffic, which is used in denial of service attacks.

The Ping Tool

When you ping a remote computer using the *ping* utility in its default mode, your computer will send out four ICMP ping packets and measure the time required before each packet's corresponding response arrives. When it finishes, ping gives you a helpful summary showing the number of packets sent and received; the minimum, maximum, and average round-trip times; and a percentage indicating how many ping packets got no response. Figure 2.16 represents a sample session that pings the machine at IP address 206.13.28.12.

What does this tell you? First of all, you can see that all of the packets you sent arrived and that there are approximately five hops in between this machine and your target. You know the latter because the time to live, or TTL, value is 250. By default, the TTL on the packets that ping sends out is set to 255, and each routing device that routes the packets subtracts 1 from the TTL value. When a packet's TTL hits 0 (zero), it is dropped.

FIGURE 2.16   Results of the ping command

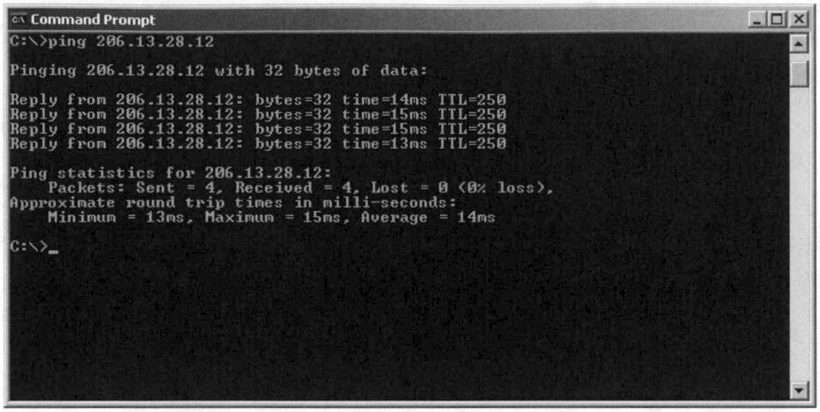

```
Command Prompt                                                    _ □ ×
C:\>ping 206.13.28.12

Pinging 206.13.28.12 with 32 bytes of data:

Reply from 206.13.28.12: bytes=32 time=14ms TTL=250
Reply from 206.13.28.12: bytes=32 time=15ms TTL=250
Reply from 206.13.28.12: bytes=32 time=15ms TTL=250
Reply from 206.13.28.12: bytes=32 time=13ms TTL=250

Ping statistics for 206.13.28.12:
    Packets: Sent = 4, Received = 4, Lost = 0 (0% loss),
Approximate round trip times in milli-seconds:
    Minimum = 13ms, Maximum = 15ms, Average = 14ms

C:\>_
```

More importantly, this ping session shows that data is flowing normally between your machine and the target. Because all of the ping packets got there (notice the "0% loss" line near the bottom), you can comfortably say that any network problems on this link aren't because of a routing problem. Packets are flowing normally between here and there.

How would you identify a problem using this data? The most obvious way to tell is when ping times out without getting *any* packets back from the remote end. That's a big red flag indicating that either you typed the IP address wrong or that something is blocking traffic between the two ends of the connection. Likewise, high rates of packet loss signal that something is wrong somewhere along the path between the machines.

The Tracert Tool

When your plumbing is stopped up, you can tell because your sink or shower won't drain—but knowing that it won't drain doesn't tell you where the blockage is. Likewise, the ping utility can tell you whether or not packets are flowing, but it won't necessarily tell you where the problem is. Windows Server 2003 includes a tool called *tracert* (pronounced "traceroute" after the original Unix version) that takes advantage of the TTL in each IP packet to map out the path that the packets are taking as they flow to a remote system. Recall that each device that routes a packet decrements its TTL. Tracert begins by sending one ICMP ping packet with a TTL of 1. That means that the first router or gateway to encounter it will send an ICMP response, decrement the ping packet's TTL, notice that the TTL is now 0, and drop the packet. At that point, tracert sends a second packet with a TTL of 2. The first device responds and decrements the TTL and then routes the packet to the next hop. The next device in the chain responds to the ping, decrements the TTL, and drops the original packet. This process continues with tracert gradually incrementing the TTL until the packet finally reaches the desired destination host.

As it sends these packets, tracert keeps a running log of which hosts along the route have responded and which ones haven't. You can use this information to figure out where the stoppage is. For example, take a look at the tracert session in Figure 2.17. As you can see, the tracert completed successfully. If a failure occurs, you will notice a time-out at the relevant hop in the route.

FIGURE 2.17   Output of the tracert command

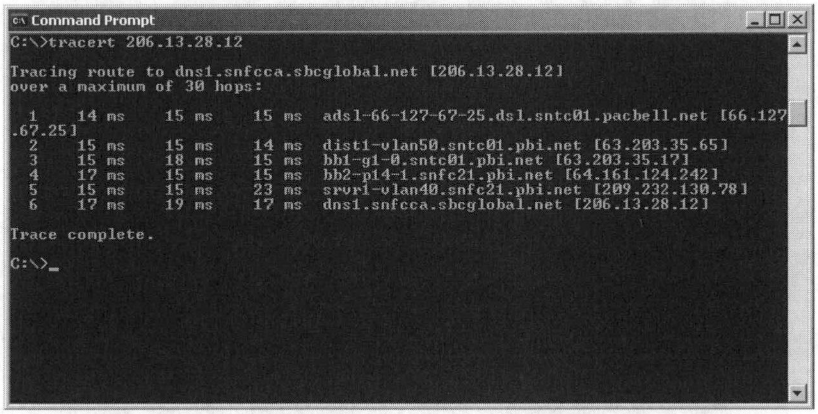

The Pathping Tool

The pathping tool provides the functionality of both ping and tracert and adds some of its own features into the mix as well. A sample pathping output is shown in Figure 2.18. The first list in the output is the route that the packet takes to reach the destination. This is similar to the output of the tracert command. You will have to wait for several seconds (25 per hop, to be exact) until the next list appears. The two rightmost columns provide the most useful information. The Address column indicates the address of the node or link that the hop went to. The This Node/Link Last/Sent % column indicates the packet loss that occurred at that point in the route. Typically, the packet loss should be 0, but if you are having routing problems, you might spot a malfunctioning router by seeing where along the line you are losing packets.

The most useful switch to know is the -n switch, which only displays the IP address of each hop rather than resolving each name.

Using Nslookup

Another thing that the tracert session shows you is that DNS resolution is working properly—after all, you typed in the DNS name for Microsoft's server and your DNS server was able to turn that into an IP address. Most of the time, you'll use troubleshooting tools like ping and tracert with IP addresses because you frequently need to verify that packets can be moved at the IP level before trying to use higher-level services like DNS. Name resolution is very important to Windows Server 2003 because of the way it uses DNS service records to locate network resources. In addition, users will want to type UNC paths by using easy-to-remember names like minuteman, not IP addresses.

FIGURE 2.18   Pathping output

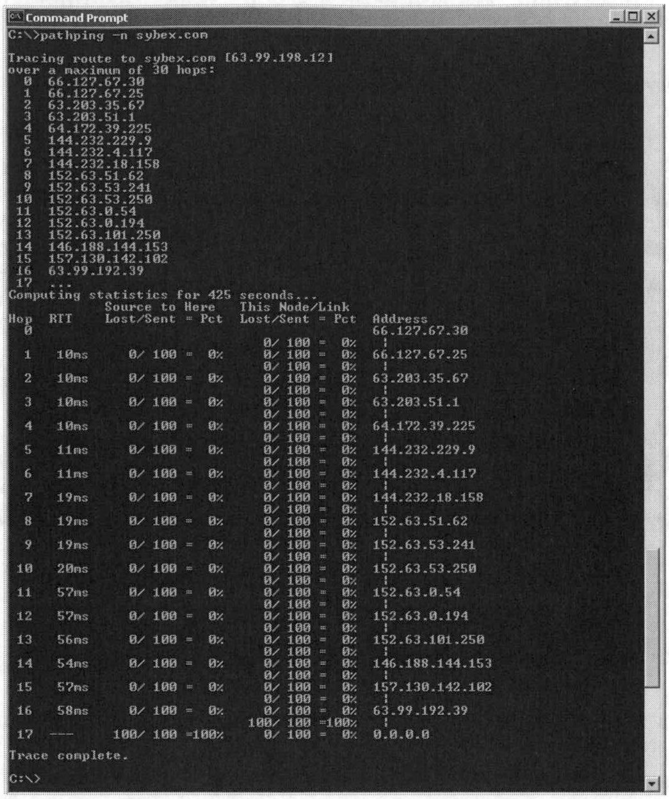

```
Command Prompt                                                    _|□|x|
C:\>pathping -n sybex.com

Tracing route to sybex.com [63.99.198.12]
over a maximum of 30 hops:
  0  66.127.67.30
  1  66.127.67.25
  2  63.203.35.67
  3  63.203.51.1
  4  64.172.39.225
  5  144.232.229.9
  6  144.232.4.117
  7  144.232.18.158
  8  152.63.51.62
  9  152.63.53.241
 10  152.63.53.250
 11  152.63.0.54
 12  152.63.0.194
 13  152.63.101.250
 14  146.188.144.153
 15  157.130.142.102
 16  63.99.192.39
 17  ...
Computing statistics for 425 seconds...
                Source to Here   This Node/Link
Hop  RTT     Lost/Sent = Pct   Lost/Sent = Pct  Address
  0                                               66.127.67.30
                                 0/ 100 =  0%
  1  10ms     0/ 100 =  0%       0/ 100 =  0%     66.127.67.25
                                 0/ 100 =  0%
  2  10ms     0/ 100 =  0%       0/ 100 =  0%     63.203.35.67
                                 0/ 100 =  0%
  3  10ms     0/ 100 =  0%       0/ 100 =  0%     63.203.51.1
                                 0/ 100 =  0%
  4  10ms     0/ 100 =  0%       0/ 100 =  0%     64.172.39.225
                                 0/ 100 =  0%
  5  11ms     0/ 100 =  0%       0/ 100 =  0%     144.232.229.9
                                 0/ 100 =  0%
  6  11ms     0/ 100 =  0%       0/ 100 =  0%     144.232.4.117
                                 0/ 100 =  0%
  7  19ms     0/ 100 =  0%       0/ 100 =  0%     144.232.18.158
                                 0/ 100 =  0%
  8  19ms     0/ 100 =  0%       0/ 100 =  0%     152.63.51.62
                                 0/ 100 =  0%
  9  19ms     0/ 100 =  0%       0/ 100 =  0%     152.63.53.241
                                 0/ 100 =  0%
 10  20ms     0/ 100 =  0%       0/ 100 =  0%     152.63.53.250
                                 0/ 100 =  0%
 11  57ms     0/ 100 =  0%       0/ 100 =  0%     152.63.0.54
                                 0/ 100 =  0%
 12  57ms     0/ 100 =  0%       0/ 100 =  0%     152.63.0.194
                                 0/ 100 =  0%
 13  56ms     0/ 100 =  0%       0/ 100 =  0%     152.63.101.250
                                 0/ 100 =  0%
 14  54ms     0/ 100 =  0%       0/ 100 =  0%     146.188.144.153
                                 0/ 100 =  0%
 15  57ms     0/ 100 =  0%       0/ 100 =  0%     157.130.142.102
                                 0/ 100 =  0%
 16  58ms     0/ 100 =  0%       0/ 100 =  0%     63.99.192.39
                                100/ 100 =100%
 17  ---     100/ 100 =100%      0/ 100 =  0%     0.0.0.0

Trace complete.
C:\>
```

Part of troubleshooting network problems involves understanding how and when network name resolution is used as well as how to test whether or not it's working properly. By now you understand the importance of making sure the DNS server addresses are set properly. Naturally, that should be the first thing you check when you notice that a client's getting DNS-related error messages. It's usually a good idea to check whether or not other clients are having related problems, too, because the problems caused by losing your DNS servers won't necessarily manifest themselves at once. Windows Server 2003 DNS can maintain a cache of addresses, so if the DNS server dies after the address is stored in the cache, the client won't have a problem until the cached record reaches its TTL, expires, and is deleted.

The *nslookup* tool allows you to query a DNS server to see what information it holds for a host record. You can query for a single piece of information from the command line, as in this example:

```
F:\>nslookup mail.chellis.net
Server:  hawk.chellis.net
Address:  192.168.0.144
Name:  mail.chellis.net
Address:  209.68.1.225
```

Note that this session tells you what DNS server the query was made against, as well as what the answer is. If you run nslookup with no command-line arguments, it goes into interactive mode, in which you can make several queries in a row:

```
F:\>nslookup

Default Server:  hawk.chellis.net

Address:  192.168.0.144

> www.naismith-engineering.com

Server:  hawk.chellis.net

Address:  192.168.0.144

Non-authoritative answer:
Name:  www.hosting.swbell.net
Addresses:  216.100.99.6, 216.100.98.4, 216.100.98.6
Aliases:  www.naismith-engineering.com

> fly.hiwaay.net
Server:  hawk.chellis.net
Address:  192.168.0.144

Non-authoritative answer:
Name:  fly.hiwaay.net
Address:  208.147.154.56

> www.apple.com
Server:  hawk.chellis.net
Address:  192.168.0.144

Non-authoritative answer:
Name:  www.apple.com
Address:  17.254.0.91
```

You can use the `server ipAddress` command to switch resolution to the server at the specified IP address. That's very useful when your regular DNS server is down or can't seem to resolve a particular address. For example, look at this nslookup session, which begins when you switch to an (improperly configured) DNS server named minuteman:

```
> server minuteman

Default Server:  minuteman.chellis.net
```

```
Address:  192.168.0.201

> www.chellis.net

Server:  minuteman.chellis.net

Address:  192.168.0.201

DNS request timed out.

timeout was 2 seconds.

DNS request timed out.

timeout was 2 seconds.
*** Request to minuteman.chellis.net timed-out
```

So, minuteman can't find the answer. No problem; switch to an alternate server named hawk:

```
> server hawk

DNS request timed out.

timeout was 2 seconds.
*** Can't find address for server hawk: Timed out
```

Because minuteman is misconfigured, it can't find hawk's address. Try again with the IP address:

```
> server 192.168.0.144

DNS request timed out.

timeout was 2 seconds.

Default Server:  [192.168.0.144]
Address:  192.168.0.144

> www.chellis.net
Server:  [192.168.0.144]
Address:  192.168.0.144

Name:  www.chellis.net
Address:  209.68.1.225
```

As you can see, you can now resolve www.chellis.net's IP address using the hawk server.

Summary

In this chapter, we showed you how to configure and troubleshoot network protocols. Specifically, you learned the following:

- How to configure client and server machines with dynamic and static IP addresses
- How to configure client and server machines to use the DNS, WINS, and DHCP services offered by Windows Server 2003, including advanced configuration options available in the Advanced TCP/IP Settings dialog box
- How to configure network bindings to bind and unbind protocols to services and to rearrange the order of protocol bindings
- How to install and use the Network Monitor driver on target machines and the Network Monitor application on the server
- How to view network activity in System Monitor
- How to troubleshoot network problems using the following tools: ipconfig, ping, tracert, pathping, and nslookup

Exam Essentials

Know how to configure TCP/IP settings.   TCP/IP requires only two pieces of information to function: the IP address you want to use for the system and the subnet mask that corresponds to the network subnet the client is on. If you're configuring a Windows XP Professional machine, you're probably using DHCP with it. In that case, the default TCP/IP settings will work fine because they configure the TCP/IP stack to get configuration parameters from any available DHCP server.

Know how to configure DNS on network clients.   In the Internet Protocol (TCP/IP) Properties dialog box, you can select either the Obtain DNS Server Address Automatically radio button (which you can do only when DHCP is enabled) or the Use The Following DNS Server Addresses button, in which case you must enter the address of the DNS server manually. You can configure advanced DNS settings by clicking the Advanced button of the properties dialog box.

Know how to configure WINS clients.   The WINS client configuration options in Windows Server 2003 are buried in the Advanced TCP/IP Settings dialog box. On the WINS tab, the WINS Addresses, In Order Of Use list and its related controls show you which WINS servers you have defined for the client you're configuring. The Enable LMHOSTS Lookup checkbox controls whether or not Windows Server 2003 will use the computer name-to-IP mappings in the LMHOSTS file before querying a WINS server. The three radio buttons at the bottom of the dialog box control how NetBIOS over TCP/IP is configured.

Understand network bindings.   A network binding links a protocol to an adapter so that the adapter can carry traffic using that protocol. Windows Server 2003 automatically creates bindings when you install a protocol or when you check or uncheck the checkboxes in the Properties dialog box of a particular NIC.

Know how to use Network Monitor to monitor network traffic.   Network Monitor allocates a big chunk of RAM to use as a capture buffer. When you tell it to start capturing network packets, it copies to the buffer every packet it sees on a particular NIC, gathering statistical data as it goes. When you stop the capture process, you can analyze the buffered data in a variety of ways.

Know how to use System Monitor to monitor network traffic.   The System Monitor utility is used to collect and measure the real-time performance data for a local or remote computer on the network. System Monitor graphically displays network activity according to the counters that you add. For instance, the Network Interface > Bytes Total/Sec counter measures the total number of bytes that are sent or received from the network interface and includes all network protocols.

Know the steps for troubleshooting network protocols.   First, figure out what the problem is. Gather as much information as possible about how the problem is manifesting itself (including exact error messages), when it started, and whether or not it's consistent. Knowing which users or computers are affected by a problem is very important because it gives you insight into possible causes (including user mistakes) and helps you select a course of action. When you first notice a network problem, be sure to verify that all of your network cables are correctly connected; that your hub, router, or switch has power; and so on.

Know how to use the ipconfig tool.   Ipconfig is used to view configuration of TCP/IP interfaces on your local machine. Typing **ipconfig** into a Windows Server 2003 command prompt window will produce a neat summary of your current IP configuration, including the local DNS name, the IP addresses, and the subnet masks configured for all adapters on the computer.

Know how to use the ping tool.   When you ping a remote computer using the ping utility in its default mode, your computer will send out four ICMP ping packets and measure the time required before each packet's corresponding response arrives. When it finishes, ping gives you a helpful summary showing the number of packets sent and received; the minimum, maximum, and average round-trip times; and a percentage indicating how many ping packets got no response.

Know how to use the tracert tool.   The tracert tool takes advantage of the TTL in each IP packet to map out the path that the packets are taking as they flow to a remote system. Tracert begins by sending one ICMP ping packet with a TTL of 1. That means that the first router or gateway to encounter it will send an ICMP response, decrement the ping packet's TTL, notice that the TTL is now 0, and drop the packet. At that point, tracert sends a second packet with a TTL of 2. The first device responds and decrements the TTL, then routes the packet to the next hop. The next device in the chain responds to the ping, decrements the TTL, and drops the original packet. This process continues with tracert gradually incrementing the TTL until the packet finally reaches the desired destination host.

Know how to use the pathping tool.   The pathping tool provides the functionality of both ping and tracert and adds packet loss information as well. The most useful switch to know is the -n switch, which only displays the IP address of each hop rather than resolving each name.

Know how to use the nslookup tool.   The nslookup tool allows you to query a DNS server to see what information it holds for a host record. You can query for a single piece of information from the command line, or if you run nslookup with no command-line arguments, it goes into interactive mode, in which you can make several queries in a row.

Key Terms

Before you take the exam, be certain you are familiar with the following terms:

capture buffer

capture filters

default gateway

Internet Control Message Protocol (ICMP)

ipconfig

LMHOSTS file

multihoming

network binding

nslookup

ping

promiscuous mode

System Monitor

tracert

Review Questions

1. You administer a network that consists of several Windows XP workstations and two Windows Server 2003 machines. You are having a hard time diagnosing network problems for a particular XP user, so you decide to use Network Monitor to sniff the packets that the computer is sending and receiving. From your Windows Server 2003 machine, you open Network Monitor, but you discover that you cannot see any packets transmitted to or from the target machine. What is most likely the problem?

   A. The packets from the XP machine in question are not reaching the intended destination.

   B. The Network Monitor application must be used on the local machine.

   C. A copy of Network Monitor on the other Windows Server 2003 machine on the network is overriding the output from the Windows XP machines.

   D. The target computer does not have the Network Monitor driver installed.

2. For several years you have been administering a small network that is fully contained in one building. You recently finished the migration from Windows 2000 to Windows Server 2003 and changed the protocol from NetBEUI to TCP/IP. You have just learned that a very large company that houses a network that contains several subnets connected by routers has acquired your company. Because you are not fully up to speed on all the details of TCP/IP, the acquiring company's IS department is going to send you a preconfigured router with the network address that you provided to them. After the line is installed, you receive the router and power it up. The network administrator of your new IS department checks out the router connections, and everything looks good. However, when you try to connect to resources on the other networks, the attempts fail. All the local workstations continue to function properly, but none of them can access anything across the router. When you ping the router interface, however, you get the proper response. What is most likely the problem?

   A. You have provided an incorrect subnet mask.

   B. You are running the wrong version of TCP/IP.

   C. You have not provided a default gateway address.

   D. You have not provided any DNS information.

   E. You have provided an incorrect IP address.

3. For several years you have been administering a small network that is fully contained in one building. You recently finished the migration from Windows 2000 to Windows Server 2003 and changed the protocol from NetBEUI to TCP/IP. You have just learned that a very large company that houses a network that contains several subnets connected by routers has acquired your company. Because you are not fully up to speed on all the details of TCP/IP, the corporate administrators are going to send you a preconfigured router with the network address that you provided to them. After the line is installed, you receive the router and power it up. The network administrator of your new IS department checks out the router connections, and everything looks good. However, when you try to connect to resources on the other networks, the attempts fail. All the local workstations continue to function properly, but none of them can access anything across the router. What would you do to troubleshoot this problem?

   A. Ping the new router from one of the workstations.

   B. Run nslookup to the new router.

   C. Run ipconfig on the workstations.

   D. Run winipcfg on the workstations.

   E. Run nbtstat on a server.

4. Your company has two locations, with most of its resources contained in the corporate location, which is in Chicago. You have been administrating a Windows NT network that uses LMHOST files to provide the addressing information for the NetBIOS requests for services across the routers. You've heard a great deal about WINS, but you've never implemented it because the LMHOSTS files have worked fine and WINS hasn't been a high priority. Now you are finally in the process of upgrading your Windows NT network to Windows Server 2003, and you decide to install WINS. You take your test machine and rename the LMHOSTS file. Now the machine can't reach any of the servers that it could reach previously. What is most likely causing the problem?

   A. You need to enable the client by entering it in the WINS server.

   B. You need to run DHCP and enable the client by entering it in the DHCP server.

   C. You need to enable the client by entering the WINS server at the client.

   D. You need to enter the WINS server in the LMHOSTS file and rename it properly to place the initial client entry in the WINS server.

   E. You need to reboot the client to flush out the old name/address mappings.

5. You want to install two network cards on one computer. You definitely want to configure the IP address of one of the cards manually. How must you configure the other card?

   A. Both cards must be configured manually.

   B. Both cards must be configured dynamically.

   C. One card must be configured manually, and the other must be configured dynamically.

   D. Both cards can be configured either manually or dynamically.

6. The company that you work for has two separate divisions: one that handles sporting event ticketing and one that handles leasing event venues. They are completely separate from a financial operations perspective, but they are located in the same building, connected by a single router. You are the administrator for both divisions. Even though the companies are managed separately, they share some of their IS resources, such as their Internet connection and an IIS server that is physically on the ticketing side of the company. One of the workstations in the venue side of the house cannot connect to any of the resources on the other side, including the Internet. The machines are configured as follows:

IIS server:

Node address	192.23.64.23/24
Gateway	192.23.64.1/24

Router:

Ticketing interface	192.23.64.1/24
ISP interface	10.2.223.23/28
Venue interface	204.45.36.1/24

Problem workstation:

Node address	204.45.36.2/24
Gateway	10.2.223.23/28

What do you need to do to allow the workstation to access the Internet?

A. Change the IIS server gateway to 10.2.223.23/28.

B. Change the ISP interface to 192.23.64.1/24.

C. Change the workstation gateway to 204.45.36.1/24.

D. Change the workstation gateway to 192.23.64.1/24.

7. Your company has decided to upgrade your Windows 2000 network to Windows Server 2003. You start with the servers and complete the migration of the Windows 2000 servers and services to Windows Server 2003 with no trouble. The DHCP and WINS servers provide their services properly with few issues. You leave the WINS configurations and DHCP scopes as they were before. Your Windows 2000 DHCP server was configured to deliver the default gateway, but the DNS servers were manually configured. You have your support technicians begin the process of upgrading the Windows 2000 workstations to Windows XP Professional. During the process, they notice that there is an option to obtain DNS automatically, and they select that option in order to match the Obtain An IP Address Automatically option. When they attempt to browse the Internet, they can't locate any resources. What is the most likely cause of the problem?

A. The technicians need to restart the machine for the changes to take effect.

B. The DHCP server does not have the DNS information.

C. The DHCP configuration from the Windows 2000 server that was migrated will not properly serve the Windows XP Professional workstations.

D. You need to manually remove the old DNS entries from the Advanced menu tab.

8. You have been hired as a consultant to research a network-related problem at a small organization. The environment supports many custom-developed applications that are not well documented. A manager suspects that one or more computers on the network are generating excessive traffic and bogging down the network. You want to do the following:

   - Determine which computer(s) is/are causing the problems.

   - Record and examine network packets that are originating to/from specific machines.

   - View data related to only specific types of network packets.

   What tool should you use?

   A. Tracert

   B. Pathping

   C. Nslookup

   D. Network Monitor

9. You work as a network administrator for a small company. The company network consists of 100 workstations and 2 Windows Server 2003 computers. All of the workstations use TCP/IP exclusively, but the servers use TCP/IP and NWLink because they need to connect to some older NetWare servers. You provide support for the workstation users, but you maintain almost no communication with the NetWare administrators. One day the workstation users complain that they cannot connect to any resources on one of the Windows Server 2003 computers. You cannot reach the NetWare administrators to see if they are having trouble connecting as well. What should you do to begin diagnosis? Choose the best answer.

   A. In System Monitor, add the Network Interface > Bytes Total/Sec counter to the display.

   B. In System Monitor, add the TCPv4 > Segments/Sec counter to the display.

   C. Install the Network Monitor driver on one of the workstations and the Network Monitor application on the working Windows Server 2003 computer. Monitor network activity on the workstation.

   D. Install System Monitor on one of the workstations and add the Network Interface > Bytes Total/Sec counter to the display.

10. You have spent a great deal of time upgrading your 500-node network from Windows 2000 to Windows XP and Windows Server 2003. During the migration, you finally took advantage of the centralized management that DHCP brings to TCP/IP by redesigning your IP subnets and creating the scope necessary to cover all the workstations. You have activated the scope. You haven't implemented Active Directory yet, but you plan to do that after you confirm that everything works fine. During the weekend of the final rollover, at each workstation you run a script that edits the Registry to convert the IP configuration from static IP addressing to support DHCP; then you reboot all the machines. You test a few random machines and connect them to resources across your routers, and they all connect to the servers appropriately. On Monday morning, you receive a flurry of phone calls from users who complain that the Internet connection is down. You check the Internet connection from your Windows Server 2003 server, and the connection is fine. What is the probable cause of this problem?

    A. The subnet mask is incorrect on some of the workstations.

    B. The default gateway is incorrect.

    C. The DNS configuration on the workstations is overriding the configuration in the DHCP server.

    D. The IP address scheme that you created is not valid.

    E. The WINS server is not configured properly.

11. A machine suddenly loses Ethernet network connectivity shortly after you hear a loud crash coming from the room where the computers are stored. Everything else on the machine appears to be working normally. You check the TCP/IP properties and find that they are in order. What is most likely the cause of the problem?

    A. The network card is damaged.

    B. The DNS properties need to be reset.

    C. One of the other machines on the network has been damaged.

    D. The machine's network cable is either broken or dislodged.

12. Your users are complaining of intermittent problems with various websites. You have run tracert to various sites repeatedly, encountering no problems whatsoever. What would be the best command to use to determine intermittent router operation?

    A. `nbtstat -n`

    B. `netstat`

    C. `ping -a`

    D. `pathping`

13. A Windows Server 2003 computer on your network that receives its address dynamically was working fine until the DHCP server went down. After the DHCP server failed, the computer in question could not communicate with any other computer on the network, all of which reverted to APIPA. Using the `ipconfig` command, you found that the computer has an address of 208.41.13.2. Your internal network normally uses the 10.*x.y.z* range. What do you suspect the problem to be?

A. The APIPA address failed due to a duplicate address.

B. The computer was manually configured incorrectly.

C. This particular computer has an alternate configuration of 208.41.13.2.

D. The computer is disconnected from the network.

14. In the following exhibit, where would you click to manually configure more than two DNS servers?

A. Use The Following IP Address

B. Obtain DNS Server Address Automatically

C. OK

D. Advanced

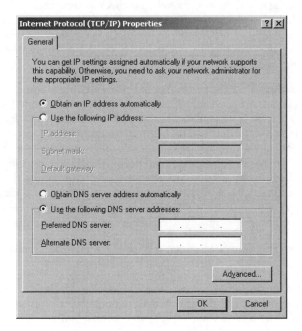

Answers to Review Questions

1. **D.** To use Network Monitor, you must install the Network Monitor driver on the target machine and the Network Monitor application on the server. The first option is the reason that you would be running Network Monitor in the first place. Option B is not true because Network Monitor is typically used by one machine to monitor the activity of another. Option C is simply not correct; a single server typically would not ruin the network output of other machines on the network.

2. **C.** You need to provide a default gateway address so that the computer can route packets to other subnets and networks. When a packet is formed and is addressed to a different subnet, the local IP stack looks to a special address in its configuration to forward the packet to. This is called the default gateway. If the default gateway isn't configured, all local IP traffic will function properly, but the machines missing this gateway configuration won't be able to reach any other networks. If the subnet mask or IP addresses were incorrect, local communication would not work properly. The DNS configuration is used for name resolution and would not result in this type of failure.

3. **A.** Because you just added a new router and none of the machines can access information beyond the router, the first thing you should do is check to see if the workstations can even talk to the router at all. If they can, then the problem is either with the link between the new router and the next point of contact or with the router itself. If the workstations cannot successfully ping the new router, then you might want to double-check the workstation configurations with the `ipconfig` command.

4. **C.** By default, the list of WINS servers that the client will use is empty. Because WINS is a central database that needs to be reached, each client needs to know the IP address ahead of time. In addition to the address, the client needs to be WINS enabled, which means that it must have a NetBIOS p-node or h-node so that it knows to try to find a WINS server. The machine's entry is made in the WINS server through the communication from the client. You can enter a static entry into the WINS server, but the client still needs to be WINS enabled to work properly. You can use DHCP to load the WINS server addresses and/or modify the NetBIOS node type, but you don't have to run DHCP in order to run WINS. WINS replaces the need for LMHOSTS files, and they aren't used to locate WINS servers. You don't need to reboot the client to flush out old name mappings.

5. **D.** Any adapter can use either DHCP or manual addressing without reference to what the other adapters are using.

6. **C.** The workstation gateway address is the address that IP uses to send packets that are off the network. Regardless of whether the ultimate destination is to the IIS server on the other LAN or an address somewhere on the Internet, the only way packets can reach this destination is if they first reach the gateway that can contact other routers to forward the packets. You do not make the gateway address the address of a particular machine that you want to reach.

7. B.   The previous DHCP configuration didn't have the DNS information in it because the DNS addresses were manually entered in the DNS client. Once you choose the Obtain DNS Server Address Automatically option, the previous manual information is lost—just as it is with the standard IP address information when you choose Obtain An IP address Automatically. You don't need to reboot the machine when you change the DNS address in Windows 2000 or Windows Server 2003. The DHCP configuration information in the Windows 2000 version is maintained when it's upgraded to Windows Server 2003.

8. D.   Through the use of the Network Monitor application, you can view all of the network packets that are being sent to or from the local server. Based on this information, you can determine the source of certain types of traffic, such as pings. The other tools can provide useful information, but they do not allow you to drill down into the specific details of a network packet, nor do they allow you to filter the data that has been collected based on details about the packet.

9. B.   In this case, you would want to add the TCPv4 > Segments/Sec counter to the display in System Monitor. This will provide you with an idea of whether or not TCP/IP is generating any traffic on the server. Adding the Network Interface > Bytes Total/Sec counter to the display will include the NWLink traffic in the display (and as far as you know, it's still working fine) and could hide the fact TCP/IP is malfunctioning. The Network Monitor solution won't help to diagnose problems on the bad server, and the final option wouldn't help solve the problem either.

10. C.   A static DNS configuration will override the DHCP configuration that was negotiated with the DHCP client. Because the Registry was edited from static IP to DHCP, the DNS information wasn't changed and is still entered as static information, overriding the DHCP configuration. With the incorrect DNS configuration, the workstations cannot resolve a URL into the IP addresses necessary to connect to resources on the Web. If the subnet mask and IP addresses were incorrect, they would not be able to communicate on the local network. The default gateway is accurate because you were able to make connections across the routers. WINS is not involved with web services browsing.

11. D.   A quick check of physical connectivity can keep you from wasting time looking for other, nonexistent problems. The majority of networking problems occur at the Physical layer.

12. D.   `Pathping` can be useful for diagnosing intermittent problems because it performs operations over a period of time. For example, if a router outside your network is having intermittent problems, `pathping` will display packet loss at those times. At the same turn, `pathping` will display no packet loss when that router is working properly, so you can see why users are experiencing such intermittent problems.

13. C.   Windows Server 2003 provides a way to specify an alternate APIPA configuration in cases where it cannot reach a DHCP server. In this case, all of the computers on the network reverted to the default APIPA address range, but the computer in question was probably configured with one of these alternate addresses.

14. D.   Click the Advanced button to display the Advanced TCP/IP Settings dialog box. You can then configure additional DNS servers in the DNS tab of that dialog box.

Chapter

3

Administering Security Policy

MICROSOFT EXAM OBJECTIVES COVERED IN THIS CHAPTER:

✓ **Implement secure network administration procedures.**

- Implement security baseline settings and audit security settings by using security templates.
- Implement the principle of least privilege.

✓ **Install and configure software update infrastructure.**

- Install and configure software update services.
- Install and configure automatic client update settings.
- Configure software updates on earlier operating systems.

✓ **Troubleshoot server services.**

- Diagnose and resolve issues related to service dependency.
- Use service recovery options to diagnose and resolve service-related issues

Like its predecessor, Windows 2000 Server, Windows Server 2003 enables you to administer security at a granular level to control a variety of options for user rights as well as the behavior of applications and the operating system itself. This is accomplished through the use of security policies at the local or domain level.

Security settings can be applied at the site, domain, OU, or local level and are configured through Group Policy. Account policies are used to control the logon process, such as password and account lockout configurations. Local policies are used to define security policies for the computer, such as auditing, user rights, and security options.

The Security Configuration and Analysis tool is a Windows Server 2003 utility that you can use to analyze your security configuration. Using any of a set of standardized security templates, this utility compares your actual security configuration to your desired configuration.

In this chapter, you will learn about these different security types and tools, as well as how to manage security in a Windows Server 2003 environment using Group Policy and local security policies and how to use the Security Analysis and Configuration utility.

In addition you will learn about the software update tools included with Windows Server 2003. Windows is an ever-changing operating system that requires occasional updates to run properly. The most important updates are the security updates that Microsoft releases whenever vulnerabilities are found in any of its products. Microsoft always makes sure to fix these leaks as soon as possible, usually within 24 hours of their discovery. In order to protect your system, you need to make sure that you apply updates as soon as they become available. The update tools included with Windows Server 2003 provide you with a way to do this.

Finally, we will look at Windows Server 2003 services. Services range from the print spooler service to the DNS service, and provide a great variety of functionality to the operating system. You will learn how to use the Services utility to start, stop, and examine the services that are enabled on your server.

An Overview of User and Group Accounts

If you haven't already passed the 70-290 exam (Managing and Maintaining a Microsoft Windows Server 2003 Environment), then you might benefit from a quick overview of how user and group accounts operate in the Windows Server 2003 environment. In this section, we'll cover both local and domain accounts, but note that the 70-291 exam focuses primarily on domain accounts.

User Accounts

A computer that is running Windows XP Professional or Windows Server 2003 (configured as a member server) has the capability to store its own user accounts database. The users that are stored at the local computer are known as *local users*.

Active Directory is a directory service that is available with the Windows 2000 Server and Server 2003 platforms. It stores information in a central database that allows users to have a single user account for access to resources across the enterprise network. The users and groups that are stored in Active Directory's central database are called *Active Directory users* or *domain users*.

You will learn more about Active Directory in the next section.

If you use local user accounts, they are required on each computer that the user needs access to within the network. For this reason, domain user accounts are commonly used to manage users on medium to large networks.

On Windows XP Professional computers and Windows 2003 member servers, you create and manage local users through the *Local Users and Groups* utility. On Windows Server 2003 domain controllers, you manage users with the Microsoft *Active Directory Users and Computers (ADUC)* utility.

The Active Directory is covered in detail in *MCSE: Windows 2003 Active Directory Planning, Implementation, and Maintenance Study Guide* by Anil Desai with James Chellis (Sybex, 2003).

When you install Windows Server 2003, there are several built-in user accounts that are created by default. The following accounts are the two most important accounts that are created:

- The *Administrator* account, which is a special account that has full control over the computer. You provide a password for this account during Windows Server 2003 installation. The Administrator account can perform all tasks, such as creating users and groups, managing the file system, and setting up printing.

- The *Guest* account, which allows users to access the computer even if they do not have a unique username and password. Because of the inherent security risks associated with this type of user, this account is disabled by default. When this account is enabled, it is given very limited privileges.

By default, the name Administrator is given to the account with full control over the computer. You can increase the computer's security by renaming the Administrator account, and then creating an account named Administrator without any permissions. This way, even if a hacker is able to log on as Administrator, the intruder won't be able to access any system resources.

Microsoft recommends that all passwords contain an uppercase character, a lowercase character, a symbol, and a number; for example, instead of using oscar, you might use 0sc@R.

Microsoft recommends that you never log on as a user with administrator privileges because of the security risks that can arise. Many viruses hide themselves on the computer in the form of a Trojan horse. They typically cannot cause damage unless a user logs on as an administrator because of the way permissions work in Windows Server 2003. The best way to avoid this problem and still perform your duties as systems engineer is to use an account with limited permissions for day-to-day operations and use the runas command whenever you need to perform tasks as an administrator.

The runas command allows you to run executable files, Control Panel items, and the Microsoft Management Console (MMC) with administrator permissions that apply to only a particular process. You typically should use the runas command by right-clicking an item and selecting Run As from the pop-up menu. Then you can enter any valid username and password, and that user's access settings will apply to the file or process that you run.

Group Accounts

On a Windows Server 2003 member server, you can use only local groups. A *local group* resides on the Windows Server 2003 member server's local database.

On a Windows Server 2003 domain controller in Active Directory, you can have security groups and distribution groups. A *security group* is a logical group of users who need to access specific resources. You use security groups to assign permissions to resources. A *distribution group* is a logical group of users who have common characteristics. Distribution groups can be used by applications and e-mail programs (for example, Microsoft Exchange). Distribution groups contain no Access Control Lists (ACLs) and therefore have no permissions. This allows these groups to execute at very high speed.

Windows Server 2003 domain controllers also allow you to select group scope, which can be domain local, global, or universal. The scope types are used as follows:

- *Domain local groups* are used to assign permissions to resources. Local groups can contain user accounts, universal groups, and global groups from any domain in the tree or forest. A domain local group can also contain other domain local groups from its own local domain.

- *Global groups* are used to organize users who have similar network access requirements. Global groups can contain user and global groups from the local domain.

- *Universal groups* are used to logically organize global groups, and they appear in the global catalog (a special listing that contains limited information about every object in Active Directory). Universal groups can contain users (not recommended) from anywhere in the domain tree or forest, other universal groups, and global groups.

On Windows XP Professional computers and Windows Server 2003 member servers, you create and manage local groups through the Local Users and Groups utility. On Windows

Server 2003 domain controllers, you manage groups with the Microsoft Active Directory Users and Computers (ADUC) utility.

Security Policy Types and Tools

Windows Server 2003 enables you to manage security settings at either the local computer level or the site, domain, and OU level. Domain security policies override local policies.

You manage policies with Group Policy and the appropriate object:

- To manage *local policies*, you use Group Policy with the Local Computer Group Policy Objects (GPOs).
- To manage *domain policies*, you use Group Policy with the Active Directory Domain Controller GPOs.

We will begin by discussing Active Directory Group Policies, and see how GPOs apply at different levels within the directory. Then we will look at Group Policies at the local computer level.

Group Policies within Active Directory

If Windows Server 2003 is installed with Active Directory, group policies can be applied as Group Policy Objects (GPOs). Group policies contain configuration settings for the following options:

Software   Software policies are used to configure system services, the appearance of the desktop, and application settings.

Scripts   Scripts are special instructions that can be configured to run when the user logs on or off the computer or when the computer is started or shut down.

Security   Security policies define how security is configured and applied at the local computer or through Active Directory.

Application and file deployment   Application and file deployment policies are used to assign and publish applications or to place files in the user's desktop, within a specific folder (for example, the Start Menu folder), or within Favorites.

 You create GPOs at the domain and OU level through the Active Directory Users and Computers MMC snap-in. You create GPOs at the site level through the Active Directory Sites and Services MMC snap-in.

Before we get into the specifics of how GPOs apply to sites, domains, and OUs, you will need to understand the basic principles behind Active Directory, as we will see in the next section.

Quick Overview of Active Directory

Within Active Directory, you have several levels of hierarchical structure. A typical structure will consist of domains, organizational units (OUs), and sites. Other levels exist within Active Directory, but this section focuses on domains, organizational units, and sites in the context of using GPOs.

Domains

The *domain* is the main unit of organization within Active Directory. Within a domain, there are many domain objects (including users, groups, and GPOs). Security can be applied to each domain object to specify who can access the object and the level of access they have. The Active Directory data for each domain is stored on one or more Windows 2000 Server or Windows Server 2003 computers specifically configured as domain controllers. If you use multiple domain controllers (for redundancy or for multiple physical locations) then you must replicate the Active Directory data between them on a regular basis in order to maintain a consistent database.

Determining the Domain Functional Level

Windows Server 2003 Active Directory introduces a new concept called domain and forest functionality. This is similar to the idea of mixed mode and native mode in Windows 2000 Active Directory, so much so that those two modes are actually included as a part of domain and forest functionality. However, Microsoft refers to these modes as *functional levels*, and adds a third functional level appropriately called *Windows Server 2003 functional level*. When you are installing a Windows Server 2003 domain controller, you must determine which functional level you will support: Windows 2000 Mixed, Windows 2000 Native, or Windows Server 2003.

Windows 2000 Mixed domain functional level is the default option when you are installing a domain controller. It is designed to allow backward compatibility with Windows NT 4 and earlier domain models. If you need to support Windows NT domain controllers for one or more domains within your environment, you should choose Windows 2000 Mixed domain functional level for those domains. However, as long as you are using Windows 2000 Mixed domain functional level, certain Active Directory features (such as universal groups and group nesting) are unavailable.

If your environment does not require support for Windows NT domain controllers within any of your domains but does require support for Windows 2000 domain controllers, then you can choose to implement your domains in Windows 2000 native domain functional level. Windows 2000 native domain functional level allows for most of the functionality of the Active Directory for all domain controllers, but it does not allow for backward compatibility with Windows NT 4. Since this means that Windows NT domain controllers cannot be used in Windows 2000 native domain functional level Active Directory domains, it's an important decision. Note also that domains cannot be converted from Windows 2000 native domain functional level back to Windows 2000 mixed domain functional level. Windows 2000 native domain functional level does not offer the full functionality of Active Directory supported by Windows Server 2003, so you should consider upgrading all of your domain controllers if you want to use some of the new features of Active Directory.

If you know that you will only be running Windows Server 2003 domain controllers, you can install Active Directory in the Windows Server 2003 domain functional level. This level adds all of the functionality of Active Directory, as shown in Table 3.1.

TABLE 3.1   Comparing Domain Functional Levels

Domain Functional Feature	Windows 2000 Mixed	Windows 2000 Native	Windows Server 2003
Ability to rename domain controllers	Disabled	Disabled	Enabled
Logon Timestamp updates	Disabled	Disabled	Enabled
Kerberos KDC key version numbers	Disabled	Disabled	Enabled
InetOrgPerson objects can have passwords	Disabled	Disabled	Enabled
Converts NT groups to domain local and global groups	Disabled	Enabled	Enabled
SID history	Disabled	Enabled	Enabled
Group nesting	Enabled for Distribution Groups, disabled for Security Groups (note that Domain Local Security Groups can still have Global Groups as Members)	Enabled	Enabled
Universal Groups	Enabled for Distribution Groups, Disabled for Security Groups	Enabled	Enabled

In addition to domain functional levels, Windows Server 2003 includes added forest functionality over Windows 2000. Forest functionality applies to all of the domains in a forest. There are two levels of forest functionality: Windows 2000 and Windows Server 2003. Windows 2000 forest functionality is the default and supports Windows NT 4, Windows 2000, and Windows Server 2003 domain controllers. All of the new forest functionality features of Windows Server 2003 are supported exclusively by Windows Server 2003. The new features include:

Global Catalog replication enhancements   When an administrator adds a new attribute to the global catalog, only the changes are replicated to other global catalogs in the forest. This can significantly reduce the amount of network traffic generated by replication.

Defunct schema classes and attributes   You can never permanently remove classes and attributes from the Active Directory schema, but you can mark them as defunct so that they cannot be used. When forest functionality is raised to Windows Server 2003, you can redefine the defunct schema attribute so that it occupies a new role in the schema.

Forest trusts   Previously, system administrators had no easy way of granting permission on resources in different forests. Windows Server 2003 resolves some of these difficulties by allowing trust relationships between separate Active Directory forests. Forest trusts act much like domain trusts, except that they extend to every domain in two forests. Note that all forest trusts are intransitive.

Linked value replication   Windows Server 2003 introduces a new concept called linked value replication. In Windows 2000, if changes were made to a member of a group, the entire group would be replicated during the replication process. With linked value replication, only the user record that has been changed is replicated. This can significantly reduce network traffic associated with replication.

Renaming domains   Although the Active Directory domain structure was originally designed to be flexible, there were several limitations. Due to mergers, acquisitions, corporate reorganizations, and other business changes, you may need to rename domains. You can now change the DNS and NetBIOS names for any domain, as well as reposition a domain within a forest. Note that this operation is not nearly as simple as just issuing a `rename` command. Instead, there's a specific process you must follow to make sure that the operation is successful. Fortunately, when you properly follow the procedure, Microsoft supports domain renaming.

Other features   In addition to the Windows Server 2003 forest functional features just listed, Windows Server 2003 also supports improved replication algorithms and dynamic auxiliary classes. These improvements are designed to increase performance, scalability, and reliability.

Organizational Units

Within a domain, you can further subdivide and organize domain objects through the use of *organizational units (OUs)*. This is one of the key differences between Windows NT domains and Windows 2000 and 2003 domains: the NT domains were not able to store information hierarchically. Windows 2003 domains, through the use of OUs, allow you to store objects hierarchically—typically based on function or geography.

For example, assume that your company is called ABCCORP. You have locations in New York, San Jose, and Belfast. You might create a domain called ABCCORP.COM with OUs called NY, SJ, and Belfast. In a very large corporation, you might also organize the OUs based on function. For example, the domain could be ABCCORP.COM and the OUs might be SALES, ACCT, and TECHSUPP. Based on the size and security needs of your organization, you might also have OUs nested within OUs. OUs that contain other OUs are called parents, and OUs that are contained within parent OUs are called children. The relationships between nested OUs are called parent-child relationships. As a general rule, you will want to keep your Active Directory structure as simple as possible.

Sites

Domains and OUs can be thought of as logical groupings of network resources. In the preceding example, you saw that it might make sense to organize OUs by location or by department, according to your preference or the needs of the network. In contrast, *sites* organize the Active Directory into distinct physical locations. Sites are primarily used for directory replication purposes. Consider what happens when you have two physically separate locations that share a common directory. Without frequent replication, the two directories would become horribly disjointed and practically useless. However, if you set up sites in the directory for each location, you can schedule replication to occur at regular intervals and maintain a consistent database.

Delegation of Administrative Control

OUs are the smallest component within a domain to which permissions and Group Policy can be assigned. Let's look specifically at how administrative control is set on OUs.

The idea of *delegation* involves a higher security authority that can give permissions to another. As a real-world example, assume that you are the director of IT for a large organization. Instead of doing all of the work yourself, you would probably assign roles and responsibilities to other individuals. For example, you might make one system administrator responsible for all operations within the Sales domain and another responsible for the Engineering domain. Similarly, you could assign the permissions for managing all printers and print queues within the organization to one individual while allowing another to manage all security permissions for users and groups.

In this way, the various roles and responsibilities of the IT staff can be distributed throughout the organization. Businesses generally have a division of labor to handle all of the tasks involved in keeping the company's networks humming along. Network operating systems, however, often make it difficult to assign just the right permissions. Sometimes, the complexity is necessary to ensure that only the right permissions are assigned. A good general rule of thumb is to provide users and administrators with the minimum permissions they require to do their jobs. This ensures that accidental, malicious, and otherwise unwanted changes do not occur.

In the world of the Active Directory, the process of delegation is used to define the permissions for administrators of OUs. When considering implementing delegation, there are two main concerns to keep in mind: parent-child relationships and inheritance settings.

Parent-Child Relationships

The OU hierarchy you create will be very important when considering the maintainability of security permissions. As we've already mentioned, OUs can exist in a parent-child relationship. When it comes to the delegation of permissions, this is extremely important. You can choose to allow child containers to automatically inherit the permissions set on parent containers. For example, if the North America division of your organization contains 12 child OUs, you could delegate permissions to all of them by placing security permissions on the North America division. This feature can greatly ease administration, especially in larger organizations, but it is also a reminder of the importance of properly planning the OU structure within a domain.

 You can delegate control only at the OU level and not at the object level within the OU.

Inheritance Settings

Now that you've seen how parent-child relationships can be useful for administration, you should consider the actual process of inheriting permissions. Logically, the process is known as *inheritance*. When permissions are set on a parent container, all of the child objects are configured to inherit the same permissions. This behavior can be overridden, however, if business rules do not lend themselves well to inheritance.

Application of Group Policy

One of the strengths of Windows operating systems is that they offer users a great deal of power and flexibility. From installing new software to adding device drivers, users can be given the ability to make many changes to their workstation configurations. This level of flexibility is also a potential problem. Inexperienced users might inadvertently change settings, causing problems that can require many hours to fix.

In many cases (and especially in business environments), users will require only a subset of the complete functionality provided by the operating system. In the past, however, the difficulty associated with implementing and managing security and policy settings has led to lax security policies. Some of the reasons for this are technical—it can be very tedious and difficult to implement and manage security restrictions. Other problems have been political—users and management might feel that they should have full permissions on their local machines, despite the potential problems this might cause.

One of the major design goals for the Windows Server 2003 platform (and specifically, Active Directory) was manageability. Although the broad range of features and functionality provided by the operating system can be helpful, being able to lock down types of functionality is very important.

That's where the idea of group policies comes in. Simply defined, group policies are collections of permissions that can be applied to objects within Active Directory. Specifically, Group Policy settings are assigned at the site, domain, and OU level and can apply to user accounts, computer accounts, and groups. Examples of settings that a system administrator can make using group policies include the following:

- Restricting access to the Start menu
- Disallowing the use of Control Panel
- Limiting choices for display and Desktop settings

Group Policy Objects and Active Directory

GPOs are stored within Active Directory on all domain controllers in the *systemroot* \Sysvol folder by default. Within each root folder, there is a policy file called Gpt.ini that contains information about the group policy.

When GPOs are created within Active Directory there is a specific order of inheritance (meaning how the polices are applied within the hierarchical structure of Active Directory). When a user logs on to an Active Directory domain, depending on where GPOs have been applied within the hierarchical structure of Active Directory, the order of application is as follows:

1. Local computer policy
2. Site (group of domains)
3. Domain
4. OU

If there are any conflicts between settings, the site policy overrides the local policy. Next, the domain policies are applied. If the domain policy has any additional settings, they will be applied to the configuration. If there are any conflicts in settings, the domain policy overrides the site policy. Next, the OU policies are applied. Again, any additions to the settings will be applied. If there are any conflicts in settings, the OU policy overrides the domain policy. Finally, if there are conflicts between computer and user policy settings, the user policy settings are applied.

The following options are available for overriding the default behavior of application of GPOs:

No Override   The No Override option is used to specify that child containers can't override the policy settings of higher-level GPOs. In this case, the order of precedence would be that site settings override domain settings and domain settings override OU settings, assuming that No Override is set at both levels. You would use the No Override option if you wanted to set corporate-wide policies without allowing administrators of lower-level containers to override your settings. This option can be set on a per-container basis, as needed.

Block Inheritance The Block Inheritance option is used to allow the child container to block GPO inheritance from parent containers. You would use this option if you did not want child containers to inherit GPO settings from parent containers and only wanted the GPO you had set for your container to be applied.

If there is a conflict between the No Override and the Block Inheritance settings, the No Override option would be applied.

 It is essential that you understand the order in which policies are applied for GPOs, both for the exam and for troubleshooting in the real world.

How Policies Are Applied to Different Network Clients

If your network consists of only Windows Server 2003 and 2000 Server computers, you can use GPOs to manage your computers' configuration settings. Backward compatibility for NT 4 is maintained in Windows Server 2003. If you want to manage configuration settings for NT 4 users within the domain, you would use NT System Policy files; these can be configured from the `poledit` command, which calls the System Policy Editor utility.

By default the following administrative templates, which are used to apply Group Policy settings to the Registry, are used by Windows Server 2003:

- `System.adm`
- `Intres.adm`
- `Winnt.adm`
- `Windows.adm`
- `Common.adm`

The function of each template is defined in Table 3.2.

TABLE 3.2 Administrative Templates Defined

Administrative Template	Description
System.adm	Template used by Windows 2000 and higher clients.
Inetres.adm	Template used to set Internet Explorer (IE) settings for Windows 2000 and higher clients.
Winnt.adm	User interface options used by Windows NT clients. To configure options for Windows NT clients, use the System Policy Editor (`Poledit.exe`).

TABLE 3.2 Administrative Templates Defined *(continued)*

Administrative Template	Description
Windows.adm	User interface options used by Windows 95/98 clients. To configure options for Windows 95/98 clients, use the System Policy Editor (Poledit.exe).
Common.adm	User interface options that are common to both Windows NT 4 and Windows 95/98 clients.

Administering Local Computer Policy

You can manage local computer policies by adding the Group Policy snap-in to the MMC. Once you have added the snap-in, you will see an option called Local Computer Policy. When you expand the Local Computer Policy snap-in, you'll see Computer Configuration, as shown in Figure 3.1. There are many options here that can be configured for local computer policies.

FIGURE 3.1 Local computer policies

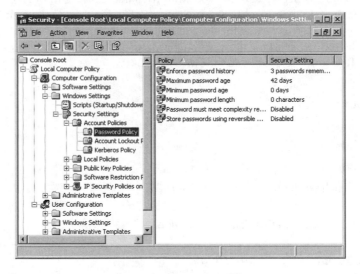

The options that can be set are shown in Figure 3.1. The most common options that you would configure for Local Computer Policy are defined in the following sections. You may want to refer back to this image to better understand where in the hierarchy particular policy settings can be found.

To conduct your policy management tasks, you can add the Local Computer Policy snap-in to the Microsoft Management Console (MMC). On a domain controller you can access the domain policies by selecting Start ➢ Administrative Tools ➢ Domain Security Policy.

In Exercise 3.1, you will add the Local Computer Policy and Event Viewer snap-ins to your member server.

 All of the exercises in this chapter, except Exercise 3.7, should be completed from a member server.

EXERCISE 3.1

Creating a Management Console for Security Settings

1. Select Start ➢ Run, type **MMC** in the Run dialog box, and click the OK button to open the MMC.

2. From the main menu, select File ➢ Add/Remove Snap-In.

3. In the Add/Remove Snap-In dialog box, click the Add button.

4. Select the Group Policy Object Editor option and click the Add button.

5. The Group Policy Object specifies Local Computer by default. Click the Finish button.

6. Select the Event Viewer option and click the Add button.

7. The Select Computer dialog box appears with Local Computer selected by default. Click the Finish button. Then click the Close button.

8. In the Add/Remove Snap-In dialog box, click the OK button.

9. Select File ➢ Save As. Save the console as Security in the drive:\Documents and Settings\ All Users\Start Menu\Programs\Administrative Tools folder and click the Save button.

You can now access this console by selecting Start ➢ Administrative Tools ➢ Security.

 You can also edit Local Computer Policy Settings by using the command-line utility Gpedit.msc. To use this utility, select Start ➢ Run and at the Run dialog box, type **Gpedit.msc** and click the OK button.

Configuring Security Settings

You configure security settings through Computer Configuration ➢ Windows Settings ➢ Security Settings. There are three main options that can be configured for Windows Settings:

▪   Account policies

▪   Local policies

▪   Public key policies

Using Account Policies

Account policies are used to specify the user account properties that relate to the logon process. They allow you to configure computer security settings for passwords, account lockout specifications, and Kerberos authentication within a domain.

After you have loaded the MMC snap-in for Group Policy, you will see an option for Local Computer Policy. To access the Account Policies subfolders, expand Local Computer Policy, Computer Configuration, Windows Settings, Security Settings, and Account Policies.

If you are on a Windows Server 2003 member server, you will see two folders: Password Policy and Account Lockout Policy. If you are on a Windows Server 2003 computer that is configured as a domain controller, you will see three folders: Password Policy, Account Lockout Policy, and Kerberos Policy. The account policies available for member servers and domain controllers are described in the following sections.

Setting Password Policies

Password policies ensure that security requirements are enforced on the computer. It is important to note that the password policy is set on a per-computer basis; it cannot be configured for specific users.

The password policies that are defined on Windows Server 2003 member servers are described in Table 3.3. On Windows Server 2003 domain controllers, all of these policies are configured as "not defined."

TABLE 3.3   Password Policy Options

Policy	Description	Default	Minimum	Maximum
Enforce Password History	Keeps track of user's password history	Remember 3 passwords	Same as default	Remember 24 passwords
Maximum Password Age	Determines maximum number of days user can keep valid password	Keep password for 42 days	Keep password for 1 day	Keep password for 999 days
Minimum Password Age	Specifies how long password must be kept before it can be changed	0 days (password can be changed immediately)	Same as default	999 days
Minimum Password Length	Specifies minimum number of characters password must contain	0 characters (no password required)	Same as default	14 characters
Passwords Must Meet Complexity Requirements	Allows you to install password filter	Disabled	Same as default	Enabled

TABLE 3.3   Password Policy Options *(continued)*

Policy	Description	Default	Minimum	Maximum
Store Password Using Reversible Encryption For All Users In The Domain	Specifies higher level of encryption for stored user passwords	Disabled	Same as default	Enabled

The password policies are used as follows:

- The Enforce Password History option is used so that users cannot reuse the same password. Users must create a new password when their password expires or is changed.

- The Maximum Password Age option is used so that after the maximum number of days has passed, users are forced to change their password.

- The Minimum Password Age option is used to prevent users from changing their password several times in rapid succession in order to defeat the purpose of the Enforce Password History policy.

- The Minimum Password Length option is used to ensure that users create a password, as well as to specify that it meets the length requirement. If this option isn't set, users are not required to create a password at all.

- The Passwords Must Meet Complexity option is used to prevent users from using items found in a dictionary of common names as passwords.

- The Store Password Using Reversible Encryption For All Users In The Domain option is used to provide a higher level of security for user passwords.

In Exercise 3.2, you will configure password policies for your computer. It is assumed that for this and the remaining exercises in this chapter, you have completed Exercise 3.1 to create the security management console.

EXERCISE 3.2

Setting Password Policies

1. Select Start ➢ Administrative Tools ➢ Security and expand the Local Computer Policy snap-in.

2. Expand the folders as follows: Computer Configuration, Windows Settings, Security Settings, Account Policies, Password Policy.

3. Open the Enforce Password History policy. In the Effective Policy Setting field, specify five passwords remembered. Click the OK button.

4. Open the Maximum Password Age policy. In the Local Policy Setting field, specify that the password expires in 60 days. Click the OK button.

5. Select Start ➢ Command Prompt. At the command prompt, type **gpupdate** and press Enter.

6. At the command prompt, type **exit** and press Enter.

Real World Scenario

Updating Your Group Policies

You are the administrator of a large network. You have been making changes to your member server's local computer policies and notice that none of the options are being applied. You wait over 30 minutes and the changes are still not there. At this point, you are beginning to think you edited something improperly.

If you edit your group policies and your changes are not taking effect, it is because the group policies are only applied every 90 minutes to computers by default. You can force your policies to be updated by typing gpupdate at a command prompt.

Setting Account Lockout Policies

The *account lockout policies* are used to specify how many invalid logon attempts should be permitted. You configure the account lockout policies so that after x number of unsuccessful logon attempts within y number of minutes, the account will be locked for a specified amount of time or until the administrator unlocks it. The account lockout policies are described in Table 3.4.

TABLE 3.4 Account Lockout Policy Options

Policy	Description	Default	Minimum	Maximum	Suggested
Account Lockout Threshold	Specifies number of invalid attempts allowed before account is locked out	0 (disabled, account will not be locked out)	Same as default	999 attempts	5 attempts
Account Lockout Duration	Specifies how long account will remain locked if Account Lockout Threshold is exceeded	0 (but if Account Lockout Threshold is enabled, 30 minutes)	Same as default	99,999 minutes	5 minutes
Reset Account Lockout Counter After	Specifies how long counter will remember unsuccessful logon attempts	0 (but if Account Lockout Threshold is enabled, 5 minutes)	Same as default	99,999 minutes	5 minutes

 The account lockout policies are similar to the policies banks use to handle ATM access code security. You have a certain amount of chances to enter the correct access code. That way, if someone stole your card, they would not be able to continue attempting to guess your access code until they got it right. Typically, after three unsuccessful attempts at your access code, the ATM machine takes the card. Then you need to request a new card from the bank. Account lockout policies work in the same fashion.

In Exercise 3.3, you will configure account lockout policies and test their effects. It is assumed that for this and the remaining exercises for configuring policies, you have access to at least two user accounts other than Administrator that can be deleted if they become corrupted.

 Creating and managing user accounts is a topic that goes beyond the scope of this book. For more information, see the MCSE: Windows Server 2003 Study Guide, by Lisa Donald and James Chellis.

EXERCISE 3.3

Setting Account Lockout Policies

1. Select Start ➢ Administrative Tools ➢ Security and expand the Local Computer Policy snap-in.

2. Expand the folders as follows: Computer Configuration, Windows Settings, Security Settings, Account Policies, Account Lockout Policy.

3. Open the Account Lockout Threshold policy. In the Local Policy Setting field, specify that the account will lock after three invalid logon attempts. Click the OK button.

4. The Suggested Value Changes dialog box appears. Accept the default values for Account Lockout Duration and Reset Account Lockout Counter by clicking the OK button.

5. Log off as Administrator. Try to log on as any user other than Administrator with an incorrect password three times.

6. After you see the error message stating that account lockout has been enabled, log on as Administrator.

7. To unlock the user's account, open the Local Users and Groups snap-in in the MMC, expand the Users folder, and double-click the locked-out user. In the Account tab of the Properties dialog box, click to remove the check from the Account Is Locked Out checkbox. Then click OK.

Setting Kerberos Policies

The *Kerberos policies* are used to define Kerberos authentication settings. Kerberos version 5 is a security protocol that is used in Windows Server 2003 to authenticate users and network services. This is called dual verification, or *mutual authentication*.

When a Windows Server 2003 is installed as a domain controller, it automatically becomes a *key distribution center (KDC)*. The KDC is responsible for holding all of the client passwords and account information. Kerberos services are also installed on each Windows Server 2003 client and server.

The Kerberos authentication involves the following steps:

1. The client requests authentication from the KDC using a password or smart card.

2. The KDC issues the client a ticket-granting ticket (TGT). The client can use the TGT to access the ticket-granting service (TGS), which allows the user to authenticate to services within the domain. The TGS issues service tickets to the clients.

3. The client presents the service ticket to the requested network service. This service ticket authenticates the user to the service and the service to the user, for mutual authentication.

The Kerberos policies are described in Table 3.5.

TABLE 3.5 Kerberos Policy Options

Policy	Description	Default Local Setting	Effective Setting
Enforce User Logon Restrictions	Specifies that any logon restrictions will be enforced	Not defined	Enabled
Maximum Lifetime For Service Ticket	Specifies the maximum age of a service ticket before it must be renewed	Not defined	600 minutes
Maximum Lifetime For User Ticket	Specifies the maximum age for a user ticket before it must be renewed	Not defined	10 hours
Maximum Lifetime For User Ticket Renewal	Specifies how long a ticket may be renewed before it must be regenerated	Not defined	7 days
Maximum Tolerance For Computer Clock Synchronization	Specifies the maximum clock synchronization between the client and the KDC	Not defined	5 minutes

Using Local Policies

As you learned in the previous section, account policies are used to control logon procedures. When you want to control what a user can do after logging on, you use local policies. With local policies, you can implement auditing, specify user rights, and set security options.

To use local policies, first add the Local Computer Policy snap-in to the MMC (see Exercise 3.1). Then, from the MMC, follow this path of folders to access the Local Policies folders: Local Computer Policy, Computer Configuration, Windows Settings, Security Settings, Local Policies.

There are three folders in Local Policies: Audit Policy, User Rights Assignment, and Security Options. These policies are covered in the following sections.

Setting Audit Policies

The *audit policies* are used to audit events that pertain to user management. By tracking certain events, you can create a history of specific tasks, such as user creation and successful or unsuccessful logon attempts. You can also identify security violations that arise when users attempt to access system management tasks that they do not have permission to access.

When you define an audit policy, you can choose to audit success or failure of specific events. The success of an event means that the task was successfully accomplished. The failure of an event means that the task was not successfully accomplished.

By default, auditing is not enabled, and it must be manually configured. Once auditing has been configured, you can see the results of the audit through the Event Viewer utility. The audit policies are described in Table 3.6.

TABLE 3.6   Audit Policy Options

Policy	Description
Audit Account Logon Events	Tracks when a user logs on, logs off, or makes a network connection
Audit Account Management	Tracks user and group account creation, deletion, and management actions
Audit Directory Service Access	Tracks directory service accesses
Audit Logon Events	Audits events related to logon, such as running a logon script or accessing a roaming profile
Audit Object Access	Audits access to files, folders, and printers
Audit Policy Change	Tracks any changes to the audit policy
Audit Privilege Use	Tracks each instance of a user exercising a user right.
Audit Process Tracking	Tracks events such as activating a program, accessing an object, and exiting a process
Audit System Events	Tracks system events such as shutting down or restarting the computer, as well as events that relate to the security log within Event Viewer

Auditing too many events can degrade system performance due to the high processing requirements. Auditing can also use excessive disk space to store the audit log. You should use this utility judiciously.

In Exercise 3.4, you will configure audit policies and view their results.

EXERCISE 3.4

Setting Audit Policies

1. Select Start ➤ Administrative Tools ➤ Security and expand the Local Computer Policy snap-in.

2. Expand the folders as follows: Computer Configuration, Windows Settings, Security Settings, Local Policies, Audit Policy.

3. Open the Audit Account Logon Events policy. In the Local Policy Setting field, under Audit These Attempts, check the boxes for Success and Failure. Click the OK button.

4. Open the Audit Account Management policy. In the Local Policy Setting field, under Audit These Attempts, check the boxes for Success and Failure. Click the OK button.

5. Log off as Administrator. Attempt to log on with an account name that does not exist. The logon should fail (because there is no user account with that username).

6. Log on as Administrator. Open the MMC and expand the Event Viewer snap-in (added in Exercise 3.1).

7. From Event Viewer, open the security log. You should see the audited events listed in this log.

Assigning User Rights

The *user rights* determine what rights a user or group has on the computer. User rights apply to the system. They are not the same as permissions, which apply to a specific object.

An example of a user right is the Back Up Files And Directories right. This right allows a user to back up files and folders even if the user does not have permissions through the file system. The other user rights are similar in that they deal with system access as opposed to resource access. The user rights assignment policies are described in Table 3.7.

TABLE 3.7 User Rights Assignment Policy Options

Right	Description
Access This Computer From The Network	Allows a user to access the computer from the network.
Act As Part Of The Operating System	Allows low-level authentication services to authenticate as any user.
Add Workstations To Domain	Allows a user to create a computer account on the domain.
Adjust Memory Quotas For A Process	Allows a user to change the maximum memory that can be consumed by a process.

TABLE 3.7   User Rights Assignment Policy Options *(continued)*

Right	Description
Allow Log On Locally	Allows a user to interactively log on to this computer. This is required by logons initiated by pressing the Ctrl+Alt+Del sequence and may be required by some service or administrative applications that can log on users. If you define this policy for a user or group, you *must* ensure that the Administrators group also has this right!
Allow Log On Through Terminal Services	Allows a user to log on as a Terminal Services client.
Back Up Files And Directories	Allows a user to back up all files and directories regardless of how the file and directory permissions have been set.
Bypass Traverse Checking	Allows a user to pass through and traverse the directory structure even if that user does not have permissions to list the contents of the directory.
Change The System Time	Allows a user to change the internal time of the computer.
Create A Pagefile	Allows a user to create or change the size of a page file.
Create A Token Object	Allows a process to create a token if the process uses the NtCreateToken API.
Create Permanent Shared Objects	Allows a process to create directory objects through the Windows Server 2003 Object Manager.
Debug Programs	Allows a user to attach a debugging program to any process.
Deny Access To This Computer From The Network	Allows you to deny specific users or groups access to this computer from the network.
Deny Logon As A Batch Job	Prevents specific users or groups from logging on as a batch job.
Deny Logon As A Service	Prevents specific users or groups from logging on as a service.
Deny Logon Locally	Denies specific users or groups access to the computer locally.
Deny Log On Through Terminal Services	Prevents specific users or groups from logging on to the computer as a Terminal Services client.

TABLE 3.7   User Rights Assignment Policy Options *(continued)*

Right	Description
Enable Computer And User Accounts To Be Trusted For Delegation	Allows a user or group to set the Trusted For Delegation setting for a user or computer object.
Force Shutdown From A Remote System	Allows the system to be shut down by a user at a remote location on the network.
Generate Security Audits	Allows a user, group, or process to make entries in the security log.
Increase Scheduling Priority	Specifies that a process can increase or decrease the priority that is assigned to another process.
Load And Unload Device Drivers	Allows a user to dynamically unload and load Plug and Play device drivers.
Lock Pages In Memory	This user right is no longer used in Windows Server 2003 (it was originally intended to force data to be kept in physical memory and not allow the data to be paged to the page file).
Log On As A Batch Job	Allows a process to log on to the system and run a file that contains one or more operating system commands.
Log On As A Service	Allows a service to log on in order to run the specific service.
Manage Auditing And Security Log	Allows a user to manage the security log.
Modify Firmware Environment Variables.	Allows a user or process to modify the system environment variables.
Perform Volume Maintenance Tasks	Allows a user or group to run maintenance tasks (for instance, remote defragmentation) on a volume. Beware that this provides file system access and is thus a security risk.
Profile Single Process	Allows a user to monitor nonsystem processes through tools such as the Performance Logs and Alerts utility.
Profile System Performance	Allows a user to monitor system processes through tools such as the Performance Logs and Alerts utility.
Remove Computer From Docking Station	Allows a user to undock a laptop through the Windows Server 2003 user interface.

TABLE 3.7 User Rights Assignment Policy Options *(continued)*

Right	Description
Replace A Process Level Token	Allows a process to replace the default token that is created by the subprocess with the token that the process specifies.
Restore Files And Directories	Allows a user to restore files and directories regardless of file and directory permissions.
Shut Down The System	Allows a user to shut down the local Windows Server 2003 computer.
Synchronize Directory Service Data	Allows a user to synchronize data associated with a directory service.
Take Ownership Of Files Or Other Objects	Allows a user to take ownership of system objects.

In Exercise 3.5, you will apply a local user rights assignment policy.

EXERCISE 3.5

Setting Local User Rights

1. Select Start ➢ Administrative Tools ➢ Security and expand the Local Computer Policy snap-in.

2. Expand folders as follows: Computer Configuration, Windows Settings, Security Settings, Local Policies, User Rights Assignment.

3. Open the Log On As A Service user right. The Local Security Policy Setting dialog box appears.

4. Click the Add User Or Group button. The Select Users Or Groups dialog box appears.

5. Enter a valid user. Click the Add button. Then click the OK button.

Defining Security Options

Security options are used to configure security for the computer. Unlike user rights, which are applied to a user or group, security options apply to the computer.

Windows Server 2003 features over 70 potential security options, depending on how your server is configured. Unlike its predecessor, Windows 2000 Server, which lumped all of the nearly 40 options together, Windows Server 2003 organizes the security options under subcategories. Table 3.8 describes the new categories of security options.

TABLE 3.8 Security Options Categories

Category	Description
Accounts	Options that control the status of (Enabled|Disabled) and allow you to rename the Administrator and Guest accounts, as well as an option to limit local account use of the blank password to local logon only
Audit	Options that control security related to auditing, including the option to shut down the system immediately if unable to log security audits
Devices	Options that control access to removable media, printers, docking stations, and that control unsigned driver installation behavior
Domain Controller	Options that apply specifically to security on domain controllers
Domain Member	Options for digital encryption, machine account passwords, and session keys
Interactive Logon	Options for logging on interactively, including whether to display the last username, whether or not to require Ctrl+Alt+Del, whether to display a custom message for users attempting to log on, and the number of previous logons to cache in the event a domain controller is not available
Microsoft Network Client	Options to configure digitally signed communications and unencrypted passwords
Microsoft Network Server	Options to configure digitally signed communications, session idle time, and whether to disconnect clients when logon hours expire
Network Access	Options to configure 10 anonymous network access settings
Network Security	Options to configure network security at a granular level
Recovery Console	Options to configure behavior of the Recovery Console, including floppy access and automatic administrative logon
Shutdown	Options to allow system shutdown without requiring logon and/or to clean the virtual memory page file on shutdown
System Cryptography	Options related to encryption, hashing, and signing
System Objects	Options to configure the behavior of system objects, including whether to require case insensitivity for non-Windows systems
System Settings	Options to configure additional settings (it is unlikely that you will need to change them)

In Exercise 3.6, you will define some security options and see how they work. For this exercise, it is assumed that you have completed all of the previous exercises in this chapter.

EXERCISE 3.6

Defining Security Options

1. Select Start ➢ Administrative Tools ➢ Security and expand the Local Computer Policy snap-in.

2. Expand folders as follows: Computer Configuration, Windows Settings, Security Settings, Local Policies, Security Options.

3. Open the policy Interactive Logon: Message Text For Users Attempting To Log On. In the Local Policy Setting field, type **Welcome to all authorized users**. Click the OK button.

4. Open the policy Interactive Logon: Prompt User To Change Password Before Expiration. In the Local Policy Setting field, specify three days. Click the OK button.

5. Select Start ➢ Command Prompt. At the command prompt, type **gpupdate** and press Enter.

6. At the command prompt, type **exit** and press Enter.

7. Log off as Administrator and log on as another user.

8. Log off and log on as Administrator.

Using Public Key Policies

Using public key policies allows you to set options so that computers can automatically submit requests to Certificate Authorities in order to install and access public keys, which are associated with cryptography.

You can also specify the Data Recovery Agents that are used in conjunction with Encrypting File System (EFS).

EFS is covered in greater detail in *MCSA/MCSE: Windows Server 2003 Environment Management and Maintenance Study Guide* by Lisa Donald and James Chellis (Sybex, 2003).

Administering the Local Computer's System Policies

System policies are accessed from the Local Computer Policy MMC snap-in under Computer Configuration, Administrative Templates, System.

You are likely to configure the following policy settings through System Policies:

- User profiles policies
- Logon policies
- Disk quota policies
- Group Policy policies
- Windows file protection policies

To edit a policy, double-click the policy name. For the most part, you only have two options: enabled or disabled. In a few cases, you must specify a single numeric value, such as in the Timeout For Dialog Boxes policy, but configuring policies is never more complicated than that. Each of these are discussed in more detail in the following sections.

User Profiles Policies

In Windows 2000 Server, *user profile* policy settings were grouped with the logon policy settings. Windows Server 2003 separates them under a new category, User Profiles, for a cleaner administrative interface. Table 3.9 describes the most commonly configured options available.

TABLE 3.9   User Profiles Policy Options

User Profiles Policy	Description
Delete Cached Copies Of Roaming Profiles	Specifies that a local copy of the roaming profile should not be saved to the local computer. Normally, you want to save a local copy of a roaming profile because loading a copy locally is faster than loading from a network drive.
Do Not Detect Slow Network Connections	By default, the system will try to detect slow links and respond to slow links differently than it does to faster links. Setting this policy disables the detection of slow links.
Slow Network Connection Timeout For User Profiles	Allows you to specify what a slow network connection is.
Wait For Remote User Profile	Specifies that if a roaming profile is used, the roaming (network) copy of the profile should be used rather than a locally cached copy of the profile.
Prompt User When Slow Link Is Detected	Notifies users of a slow link and prompts them to select whether they will use a locally cached copy of a user profile or the roaming (network) copy.
Timeout For Dialog Boxes	Allows you to configure the default time-out value that will be used to display dialog boxes.

TABLE 3.9   User Profiles Policy Options *(continued)*

User Profiles Policy	Description
Log Users Off When Roaming Profile Fails	Specifies that if a roaming profile is not available, the user should be logged off. If you do not enable this option and a roaming profile fails to load, the user will use a locally cached copy or the default user profile.
Maximum Retries To Unload And Update User Profile	Determines the number of retries the system will take if it tries to update the portions of the Registry that store user profile information and the update is not successful.

Logon Policies

Logon policies are used to specify how logon events, such as logon scripts and access of user profiles, are configured. The logon policy options are described in Table 3.10.

TABLE 3.10   Logon Policy Options

Logon Policy	Description
Run Logon Scripts Synchronously	Specifies that the logon scripts should finish running before the Windows Explorer interface is run. Configuring this option can cause a delay in the appearance of the Desktop.
Run Startup Scripts Asynchronously	Allows the system to run startup scripts asynchronously, that is, simultaneously. Otherwise, if you have multiple startup scripts, a startup script can't run until the previous script has finished running.
Run Startup Scripts Visible	Displays the startup script instructions as they are run.
Run Shutdown Scripts Visible	Displays the shutdown script instructions as they are run.
Maximum Wait Time For Group Policy Scripts	Specifies the maximum amount of time that the system will wait for scripts (logon, startup, and shutdown) to be applied before scripts stop processing and an error is recorded. This value is 600 seconds (10 minutes) by default.

Disk Quota Policies

Disk quota policies are used to specify how the computer will be used for disk quota configuration. The disk quota policy options are described in Table 3.11.

Disk quotas are covered in greater detail *MCSA/MCSE: Windows Server 2003 Environment Management and Maintenance Study Guide* by Lisa Donald and James Chellis (Sybex, 2003).

TABLE 3.11   Disk Quota Policy Options

Disk Quota Policy	Description
Enable Disk Quotas	Forces the system to enable disk quota management on all NTFS volumes for the computer.
Enforce Disk Quota Limit	Specifies that if disk quotas are configured, they should be enforced.
Default Quota Limit And Warning Level	Allows you to configure the default quota limit for quota management and the disk use threshold at which users see a warning message.
Log Event When Quota Limit Exceeded	Specifies that if users reach their quota limit, an entry will be added to the Event Viewer application log.
Log Event When Quota Warning Level Exceeded	Specifies that if users reach their warning limit, an entry will be added to the Event Viewer application log.
Apply Policy To Removable Media	Extends the disk quota policies that are applied to fixed disks to removable media that are formatted as NTFS.

Group Policy Policies

Group Policy policies are used to specify how group policies will be applied to the computer. The Group Policy policy options that are commonly configured are described in Table 3.12.

TABLE 3.12   Group Policy Options

Group Policy	Description
Turn Off Background Refresh Of Group Policy	Prevents group policies from being updated if the computer is currently in use.
Apply Group Policy For Users Asynchronously During Startup	Specifies that the computer can display the Windows Desktop before it finishes updating the computer's Group Policy.

TABLE 3.12   Group Policy Options *(continued)*

Group Policy	Description
Group Policy Refresh Intervals For Computers	Specifies the interval rate that will be used to update the computer's Group Policy. By default, this background operation occurs every 90 minutes, with a random offset of 0–30 minutes.
Group Policy Refresh Intervals For Domain Controllers	Specifies the interval rate that will be used to update the domain controller's Group Policy. By default, this background operation occurs every 5 minutes.
User Group Policy Loopback Processing Mode	Specifies how group policies are applied when a user logs on to a computer with this option configured. You can specify that the group policy is replaced or merged with other policy settings.
Group Policy Slow Link Detection	Defines what a slow link is for the purpose of applying and updating group policies.
Registry Policy Processing	Specifies how Registry policies are processed, such as whether Registry policies can be applied during periodic background processing.
Internet Explorer Maintenance Policy Processing	Determines when Internet Explorer Maintenance polices can be applied.
Software Installation Policy Processing	Determines how often software installation policies are updated. This option does not apply to local policies.
Folder Redirection Policy Processing	Specifies how folder redirection policies are updated.
Scripts Policy Processing	Specifies how shared script policies are updated.
Security Policy Processing	Specifies how security policies are updated.
IP Security Policy Processing	Specifies how IP security policies are updated.
EFS Recovery Policy Processing	Specifies how encryption policies are updated.
Disk Quota Policy Processing	Specifies how disk quota policies are updated.

Windows File Protection Policies

The *Windows file protection policies* are used to specify how Windows file protection will be configured. The Windows file protection policy options are described in Table 3.13.

TABLE 3.13   Windows File Protection Policy Options

Windows File Protection Policy	Description
Set Windows File Protection Scanning	Determines the frequency of Windows File Protection scans.
Hide the File Scan Progress Window	Suppresses the display of the File Scan Progress window.
Limit Windows File Protection Cache Size	Specifies the maximum amount of disk space that can be used by Windows File Protection.
Specify Windows File Protection Cache Location	Specifies an alternate location to be used by the Windows File Protection cache.

Analyzing Security Configurations with The Security Configuration and Analysis Tool

Windows Server 2003 includes a utility called *Security Configuration and Analysis*, which you can use to analyze and help configure the computer's local security settings. This utility works by comparing your actual security configuration to a security template configured with your desired settings.

The following steps are involved in the security analysis process:

1. Using the Security Configuration and Analysis utility, specify a working security database that will be used during the security analysis.

2. Import a security template that can be used as a basis for how you would like your security to be configured.

3. Perform the security analysis. This will compare your configuration against the template that you specified in step 2.

4. Review the results of the security analysis.

5. Resolve any discrepancies indicated through the security analysis results.

The Security Configuration and Analysis utility is an MMC snap-in. After you add this utility to the MMC, you can use it to run the security analysis process, as described in the following sections.

Specifying a Security Database

The security database is used to store the results of your security analysis. To specify a security database, take the following steps:

1. In the MMC, right-click the Security Configuration and Analysis snap-in and select the Open Database option from the pop-up menu. If you select the Security Configuration and Analysis snap-in in the MMC, the contents of the right pane explain how to open an existing database and how to create a new one, as shown in Figure 3.2.

FIGURE 3.2   Opening a security database

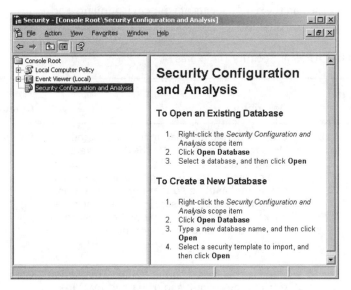

2. The Open Database dialog box appears. In the File Name text box, type the name of the database you will create. By default, this file will have a .sdb (for security database) extension. Then click the Open button.

3. The Import Template dialog box appears. Select the template that you want to import. You can select a predefined template through this dialog box. In the next section, you will learn how to create and use a customized template file. Make your selection and click the Open button.

Importing a Security Template

The next step in the security analysis process is to import a security template. The security template is used as a comparative tool. The Security and Configuration Analysis utility compares the security settings in the security template to your current security settings. You do not set security through the security template. Rather, the security template is where you organize all of your security attributes in a single location.

> As an administrator, you can define a base security template on a single computer and then export the security template to all the servers in your network.

In the following sections you will see how to import a security template, which actually consists of two steps: creating a template and then opening it for further analysis.

Creating a Security Template

By default, Windows Server 2003 ships with a variety of predefined security templates, which are stored in *systemroot*\Security\Templates. Each of the templates defines a standard set of security values based on the requirements of your environment. The template groups that are included by default are defined in Table 3.14.

TABLE 3.14   Default Security Templates

Standard Security Template	Description	Default Templates
Default security (Setup security.inf)	Created during installation for each computer. Used to set security back to the default values as configured during installation, with the exception of user rights. User rights are modified by some applications so that the applications will run properly. If user rights were also set back to default values, some of the applications that were installed on the computer might not function.	Setup security
Compatible (Compatws.inf)	Used for backward compatibility. This option relaxes the default security used by Windows 2000 and higher so that applications that ran under Windows NT and are not certified for Windows 2000 and higher will still run. This template is typically used on computers that have been upgraded and are then having problems running applications.	Compatws
Secure (Secure*.inf)	Implements recommended security settings for Windows 2000 and higher in all security areas except for files, folders, and Registry keys.	Securedc, Securews
Highly secure (Hisec*.inf)	Defines highly secure network communications for Windows Server 2003 computers. If you apply this security template, Windows Server 2003 computers can communicate only with other Windows Server 2003 computers. In this case, the computers would not communicate with clients such as Windows 95/98 or even Windows NT 4 computers.	Hisecdc, Hisecws

TABLE 3.14   Default Security Templates *(continued)*

Standard Security Template	Description	Default Templates
Dedicated domain controller (DC Security.inf)	Provides a higher level of security for dedicated domain controllers. This option assumes that the domain controller will not run server-based applications, which would require a more lax security posture on the server.	DC security
System root security (rootsec.inf)	Defines the root permissions. By default, these permissions are defined for the root of the system drive. Can be used to reapply root directory permissions if they are inadvertently changed, or the template can be modified to apply the same root permissions to other volumes. This template propagates only the permissions that are inherited by child objects and does not overwrite permissions explicitly defined on child objects.	Rootsec

You create security templates through the Security Templates snap-in in the MMC. You can configure security templates with the items listed in Table 3.15.

TABLE 3.15   Security Template Configuration Options

Security Template Item	Description
Account Policies	Specifies configurations that should be used for password policies, account lockout policies, and Kerberos policies
Local Policies	Specifies configurations that should be used for audit policies, user rights assignments, and security options
Event Log	Allows you to set configuration settings that apply to Event Viewer log files
Restricted Groups	Allows you to administer local group memberships
Registry	Specifies security for local Registry keys
File System	Specifies security for the local file system
System Services	Sets security for system services and the startup mode that local system services will use

After you add the Security Templates snap-in to the MMC, you can open a sample security template and modify it, as follows:

1. In the MMC, expand the Security Templates snap-in and then expand the folder for *systemroot*\Security\Templates.

2. Double-click the sample template that you want to edit. There are several sample templates, including securews (for secure Windows server) and securedc (for secure domain controller).

3. Make any changes you want to the sample security template. Changes to the template are not applied to the local system by default. They are simply a specification for how you would like the system to be configured.

4. Once you have made all of the changes to the sample template, save the template by highlighting the sample template filename, right-clicking, and selecting the Save As option from the pop-up menu. Specify a location and a filename for the new template. By default, the security template will be saved with an .inf extension in the *systemroot*\Security\Templates folder.

Opening a Security Template

Once you have configured a security template, you can import it for use with the Security Configuration and Analysis utility, assuming that a security database has already been configured. To import a security template, in the MMC, right-click the Security Configuration and Analysis utility and select the Import Template option from the pop-up menu. Then highlight the name of the template file you wish to import and click the Open button.

Performing a Security Analysis

The next step is to perform a security analysis. To run the analysis, simply right-click the Security Configuration and Analysis utility and select the Analyze Computer Now option from the pop-up menu. You will see a Perform Analysis dialog box that allows you to specify the location and filename for the error log file that will be created during the analysis. After this information is configured, click the OK button.

When the analysis is complete, you will be returned to the main MMC window. From there, you can review the results of the security analysis.

Reviewing the Security Analysis and Resolving Discrepancies

The results of the security analysis are stored in the Security Configuration and Analysis snap-in, under the security item you've configured (see Table 3.15). For example, to see the results for password policies, double-click the Security Configuration and Analysis snap-in, double-click Account Policies, and then double-click Password Policy. Figure 3.3 shows an example of security analysis results for password policies.

The policies that have been analyzed will have an *x* or a check mark next to them, as shown in Figure 3.3. An *x* indicates that the template specification and the actual policy do not match. A check mark indicates that the template specification and the policy do match. If any security discrepancies are indicated, you should use the Group Policy snap-in to resolve the security violation.

FIGURE 3.3   Viewing the results of a security analysis

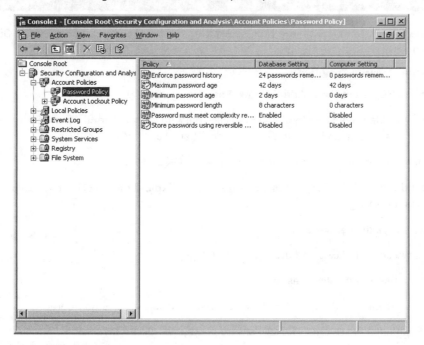

In Exercise 3.7, you will use the Security Configuration and Analysis utility to analyze your security configuration. In this exercise, you will add the Security and Configuration Analysis snap-in to the MMC, specify a security database, create a security template, import the template, perform an analysis, and review the results. For this exercise, it is assumed that you have completed all of the previous exercises in this chapter.

EXERCISE 3.7

Using the Security Configuration and Analysis Tool

Adding the Security and Configuration Analysis Snap-In

1.   Select Start ➢ Administrative Tools ➢ Security.

2.   Select File ➢ Add/Remove Snap-In.

3.   In the Add/Remove Snap-In dialog box, click the Add button. Highlight the Security Configuration and Analysis snap-in and click the Add button. Then click the Close button.

4.   In the Add/Remove Snap-In dialog box, click the OK button.

Specifying the Security Database

5.   In the MMC, right-click Security Configuration and Analysis and select Open Database.

6.   In the Open Database dialog box, type **sampledb** in the File Name text box. Then click the Open button.

7. In the Import Template dialog box, select the template securews and click the Open button.

Creating the Security Template

8. In the MMC, select File ➢ Add/Remove Snap-In.

9. In the Add/Remove Snap-In dialog box, click the Add button. Highlight the Security Templates snap-in and click the Add button. Then click the Close button.

10. In the Add/Remove Snap-In dialog box, click the OK button.

11. Expand the Security Templates snap-in and then expand the *systemroot*\Security\ Templates folder.

12. Double-click the securews file.

13. Select Account Policies and then Password Policy.

14. Edit the password policies as follows:

   ▪ Set the Enforce Password History option to 10 passwords remembered.

   ▪ Enable the Passwords Must Meet Complexity Requirements option.

   ▪ Set the Maximum Password Age option to 30 days.

15. Highlight the securews filename, right-click, and select the Save As option.

16. In the Save As dialog box, place the file in the default folder and name the file servertest. Click the Save button.

Importing the Security Template

17. Highlight the Security Configuration and Analysis snap-in, right-click, and select the Import Template option.

18. In the Import Template dialog box, highlight the servertest filename and click the Open button.

Performing and Reviewing the Security Analysis

19. Highlight the Security Configuration and Analysis snap-in, right-click, and select the Analyze Computer Now option.

20. In the Perform Analysis dialog box, accept the default error log file path and click the OK button.

21. When you return to the main MMC window, double-click the Security Configuration and Analysis snap-in.

22. Double-click Account Policies and then double-click Password Policy. You will see the results of the analysis for each policy, indicated by an *x* or a check mark next to the policy.

Managing Software Installation and Maintenance

To keep your Windows operating systems up-to date and secure, you use Windows Update, Automatic Updates, Microsoft Software Update Services, and the Microsoft Baseline Security Analyzer:

- *Windows Update* attaches to the Microsoft website through a user-initiated process and allows Windows users to update their operating systems by downloading updated files (critical and noncritical software updates).

- *Automatic Updates* extend the functionality of Windows Update by automating the process of updating critical files. With Automatic Updates, you can specify whether you want updates to be automatically downloaded and installed or whether you just want to be notified when updates are available.

- *Microsoft Software Update Services (SUS)* is used to deploy a limited version of Windows Update to a corporate server, which in turn provides the Windows updates to client computers within the corporate network. This allows clients that are limited to what they can access through a firewall to still keep their Windows operating systems up-to-date.

- *Microsoft Baseline Security Analyzer (MBSA)* is a utility you can download from the Microsoft website to ensure that you have the most current security updates.

In the following sections, you will learn how to use these tools.

Windows Update

Windows Update is available through the Microsoft website and is used to provide the most current files for the Windows operating systems. Examples of updates include security fixes, critical updates, updated help files, and updated drivers.

Windows Update is available through the Help And Support page on the Microsoft website (Figure 3.4). To search for new updates, click the Scan For Updates link on the Welcome To Windows Update screen (Figure 3.5).

The results of the Windows Update search will be displayed on the left-hand side of the Windows Update screen. You will see options for the following:

- Pick Updates To Install, which lists what updates are available for your computer and includes the following categories:

  - Critical Updates And Service Packs

  - Windows Server 2003 Family

  - Driver Updates

- Review And Install Updates, which allows you to view all updates you have selected to install and installs the updates

- View Installation History, which allows you to track all of the updates you have applied to your server

- Personalize Windows Update, which customizes what you see when you use Windows Update
- Get Help And Support displays help and support information about Windows Update.

FIGURE 3.4   Help And Support

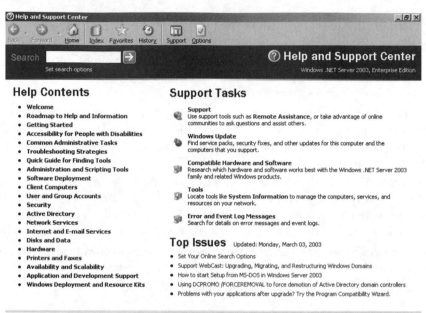

FIGURE 3.5   Windows Update

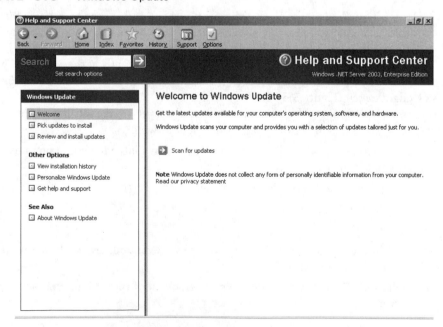

Sometimes the updates that are installed require that the computer be restarted before they can take effect. In this event, Windows Update uses a technology called chained installation. With chained installation, all updates that require a computer restart are applied before the computer is restarted. This eliminates the need to restart the computer more than once.

> The information that is collected by Windows Update includes operating system and version number, Internet Explorer version, the software version information for any software that can be updated through Windows Update, Plug and Play ID numbers for installed hardware, and region and language settings. Windows Update will also collect the product ID and product key to confirm that you are running a licensed copy of Windows, but this information is retained only during the Windows Update session and is not stored. No information that can be used to personally identify users of the Windows Update service is collected.

You will use Windows Update in Exercise 3.8.

EXERCISE 3.8

Using Windows Update

1. Select Start ➤ Help And Support.

2. The Help And Support Center dialog box appears.

3. Under Support Tasks, click the Windows Update option.

4. The Welcome To Windows Update screen appears. Click Scan For Updates.

5. Windows Update will look for all available updates based on your computer's configuration.

6. All updates for your computer will be listed. Click on each option for Critical Updates And Service Packs, Windows Server 2003 Family, and Driver Updates and check the updates you want to install.

7. Click Review And Install Updates. In the Total Selected Updates section, click the Install Now button.

Windows Automatic Updates

Automatic Updates extend the functionality of Windows Update by automating the update process. With Automatic Updates, Windows Server 2003 recognizes when you have an Internet connection and will automatically search for any updates for your computer from the Windows Update website.

If any updates are identified, they will be downloaded using Background Intelligent Transfer Services (BITS). BITS is a bandwidth-throttling technology that only allows downloads to occur using idle bandwidth. This means that downloading automatic updates will not interfere with any other Internet traffic.

If Automatic Updates detects any updates for your computer, you will see an update icon in the notification area of the Taskbar.

> In order to configure Automatic Updates, you must have local administrative rights to the computer on which Automatic Updates are being configured. Requiring administrative rights prevents users from specifying that critical security updates not be installed. In addition, Microsoft must digitally sign any updates that are downloaded.

You configure Automatic Updates by selecting Start ➢ Control Panel ➢ System and clicking the Automatic Updates tab. You will see the dialog box shown in Figure 3.6.

FIGURE 3.6   The Automatic Updates tab in the System Properties dialog box

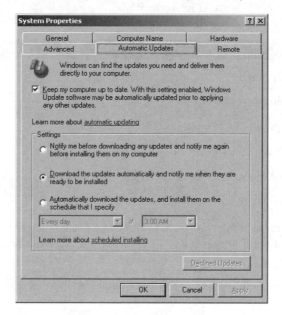

You enable Automatic Updates by checking the option, Keep My Computer Up To Date. With this setting enabled, Windows Update software may be automatically updated prior to applying any other updates.

The following settings can be applied to Automatic Updates:

- "Notify me before downloading any updates and notify me again before installing them on my computer." This option will prompt you to accept the downloading of any updates and you will be required to verify that you want the updates installed.

- "Download the updates automatically and notify me when they are ready to be installed." This is the default setting. Updates will automatically downloaded as a background process, but you must verify that you want to install the updates.

- "Automatically download the updates, and install them on the schedule that I specify." This option allows you to specify the days and times you want Windows to search for updates, such as, for example, during nonbusiness hours. You still have to verify that you want the updates installed prior to the updates being applied to your server.

The bottom of the Automatic Updates tab has a Declined Updates button. If Windows Update notifies you of an update and you decline it, you can click this button at a later time and still access the update.

You will configure Automatic Updates in Exercise 3.9.

EXERCISE 3.9

Configuring Automatic Updates

1. Select Start ➤ Control Panel ➤ System and click the Automatic Updates tab.

2. Verify that the Keep My Computer Up To Date option is checked.

3. Under Settings, select the "Automatically download the updates, and install them on the schedule that I specify" option. Select Every Sunday at 2:00 A.M. and click the OK button.

Using Software Update Services

Software Update Services (SUS) is used to leverage the features of Windows Update within a corporate environment by downloading Windows updates to a corporate server, which in turn provides the updates to the internal corporate clients. This allows administrators to test and have full control over what updates are deployed within the corporate environment.

SUS is designed to work in medium-sized corporate networks that are not using Systems Management Server (SMS).

We'll cover these topics in the following sections:

- Advantages of using SUS
- SUS server requirements
- Configuring the SUS servers
- SUS client requirements
- Configuring the SUS clients

 As this book is being written, the current version of SUS is SUS 1.0 with Service Pack 1.

Advantages of Using SUS

There are many advantages to using SUS:

- SUS allows an internal server within a private intranet to act as a virtual Windows Update server.

- Administrators have selective control over what updates are posted and deployed from the public Windows Update site. No updates are deployed to client computers unless they are first approved by an administrator.

- Administrators can control the synchronization of updates from the public Windows Update site to the SUS server either manually or automatically.

- Automatic Updates can be configured on client computers to access the local SUS server as opposed to the public Windows Update site.

- SUS checks each update to verify that it is digitally signed by Microsoft. Any updates that are not digitally signed are discarded.

- Administrators can selectively specify whether clients can access updated files from the intranet or from Microsoft's public Windows Update site, which is used to support remote clients.

- Updates can be deployed to clients in multiple languages.

- Administrators can configure an SUS statistics server to log update access, which allows them to track which clients have installed updates. The SUS server and the SUS statistics server can coexist on the same computer.

- Administrators can manage SUS servers remotely using HTTP or HTTPS if their web browser is Internet Explorer 5.5 or higher.

SUS Server Requirements

To act as an SUS server, the server must meet the following requirements:

- Must be running Windows 2000 Server with Service Pack 2 or higher or Windows Server 2003

- Must be using Internet Explorer 5.5 or higher

- Must have all of the most current security patches applied

- Must be running Internet Information Services (IIS)

- Must be connected to the network

- Must have an NTFS partition with 100MB free disk space to install the SUS server software and 6GB of free space to store all of the update files

If your SUS server meets the following system requirements, it can support up to 15,000 SUS clients:

- Pentium III 700MHz processor

- 512MB of RAM

Installing and Configuring the SUS Server

SUS should run on a dedicated server, meaning the server will not run any other applications except IIS, which is required. Microsoft recommends that you install a clean or new version of Windows 2000 Server or Windows Server 2003 and apply any service packs or security-related patches.

You should not have any virus-scanning software installed on the server. Virus scanners can mistake SUS activity as a virus.

Installing an SUS Server

The following steps are used to install the SUS server:

1. Download the SUS software from the Microsoft website. The URL for accessing the SUS homepage is `http://go.Microsoft.com/fwlink/?linkid=6930`. Scroll down to "Download SUS Server with Server Pack 1 (SP1)" and click it once. The download file is called `Sus10Sp1.exe`. The SUS software is available in English and Japanese.

2. Double-click on `Sus10Sp.exe` to install the SUS server.

3. The Welcome To The Microsoft Software Update Services Setup Wizard screen appears. Click the Next button.

4. The End-User License Agreement screen appears. Carefully read the agreement and select the I Accept The Terms In The License Agreement button. Click the Next button.

5. The Choose Setup Type screen appears. You can select Typical (which installs Microsoft Software Update Services with default settings) or Custom (which customizes the installation and settings) Click Typical to install the SUS with default settings.

6. The Ready To Install screen appears and a download URL is specified, as shown in Figure 3.7. The download URL is `http://yourservername` by default. Click the Install button.

FIGURE 3.7 Ready To Install screen

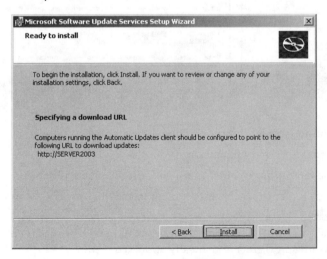

7. The Completing The Microsoft Software Update Services Setup Wizard screen appears. Click the Finish button.

8. The SUS administration website will automatically open in Internet Explorer.

Configuring an SUS Server

In the following sections you will learn how to set the SUS server options, set synchronization, approve updates, view the synchronization log, view the approval log, and monitor the SUS server.

SETTING SUS SERVER OPTIONS

You can configure the SUS server using the following steps:

1.   If the SUS administration website is not open, you can open it from Internet Explorer through the URL `http://yourservername/SUSadmin`.

2.   The Software Update Services screen appears (Figure 3.8). Click Set Options.

FIGURE 3.8   Microsoft Software Update Services

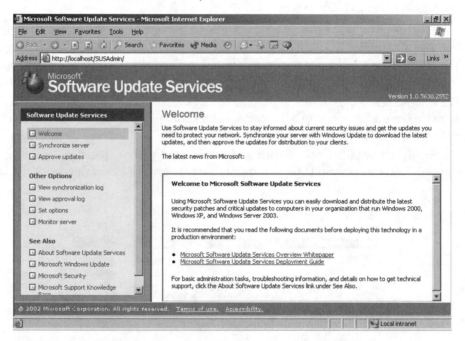

3.   In the Set Options screen, shown in Figure 3.9, there are options to do the following:

- Select a proxy server configuration
- Specify the name your clients will use to locate this update server
- Select which server to synchronize content from (Microsoft Windows Update servers or a local Software Update server)
- Select how you want to handle new versions of previously approved updates; that is, whether you want them automatically approved or not
- Select where you want to store updates (maintain the updates on a Microsoft Windows Update server or save the updates to a local update folder)

- Synchronize installation packages for certain locales (specify locales/languages that you are storing update packages for)

Click the Apply button when you are done with your configuration settings.

FIGURE 3.9   The Set Options screen

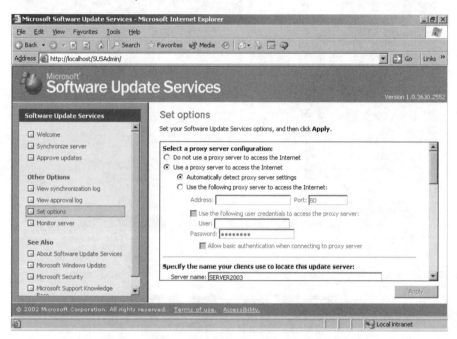

SETTING SUS SERVER SYNCHRONIZATION

By default, SUS server synchronization is not defined. You can manually synchronize your server with the Windows Update server or you can set a synchronization schedule to automate the process. The following steps are used to configure SUS Server synchronization:

1. From the Software Update Services screen, click Synchronize Server.

2. The Synchronize Server screen appears (Figure 3.10).

3. You can select Synchronize Now (which forces a manual synchronization) or Synchronization Schedule. To set a synchronization schedule, click the Synchronization Schedule button.

4. The Schedule Synchronization—Web Page Dialog screen appears (Figure 3.11). You can specify that you will not use a synchronization schedule (which means you will need to manually synchronize your server) or you can synchronize your server using the specified schedule. You would typically schedule updates during nonpeak network hours. When you are done, click the OK button.

FIGURE 3.10   The Synchronize Server screen

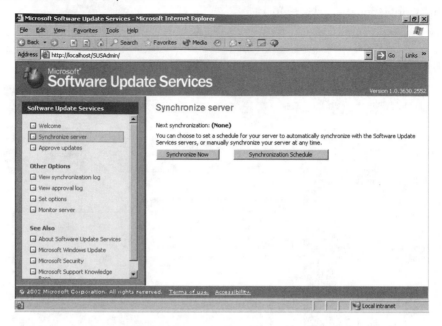

FIGURE 3.11   The Schedule Synchronization—Web Page Dialog screen

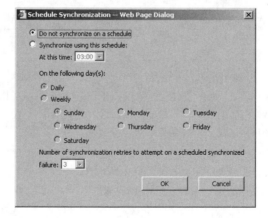

APPROVING UPDATES

Before updates can be deployed to SUS clients, the administrator must approve the updates. To approve updates, from the Software Update Services screen, click Approve Updates. The Approve Updates screen appears (Figure 3.12).

VIEWING THE SYNCHRONIZATION LOG

To view the synchronization log, from the Software Update Services screen, click View Synchronization Log. The Synchronization log will appear (Figure 3.13).

FIGURE 3.12   The Approve Updates screen

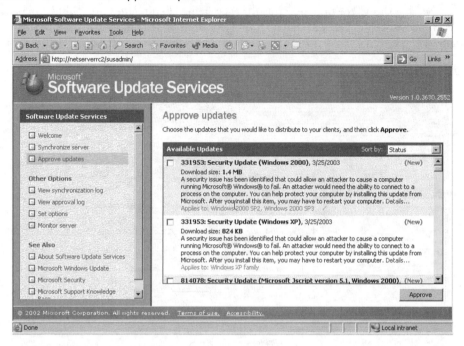

FIGURE 3.13   The Synchronization Log screen

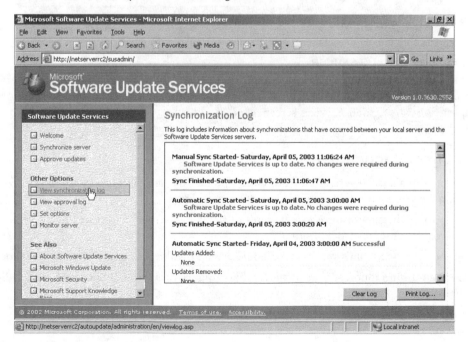

VIEWING THE APPROVAL LOG

The approval log shows the update status for each item. The update status will be marked as New, Approved, Unapproved, Updated, or Temporarily Unavailable. From the Software Update Services screen, click View Approval Log. The approval log appears (Figure 3.14).

FIGURE 3.14 The Approval Log screen

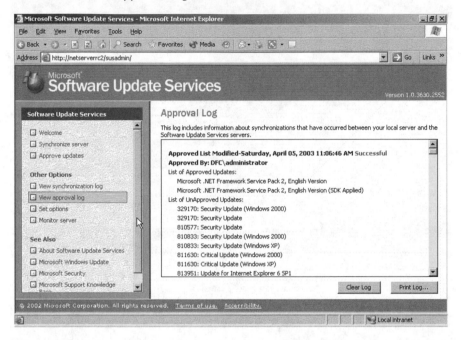

MONITORING THE SUS SERVER

The Monitor Server option allows you to see what updates have been cached into the server memory. If the memory cache does not load automatically, you can click the Refresh button. From the Software Update Services screen, click Monitor Server. The Monitor Server screen appears (Figure 3.15).

SUS Client Requirements

SUS clients run a special version of Automatic Updates that are designed to support SUS. The following enhancements to Automatic Updates are included:

- Support so the client can receive updates from an SUS server as opposed to the public Microsoft Windows Update site

- Support so the administrator can schedule when downloading of updated files will occur

- Configuration support so that clients can be configured via Group Policy or through editing the Registry

- Support for allowing updates when an administrative account or non-administrative account is logged on

FIGURE 3.15   The Monitor Server screen

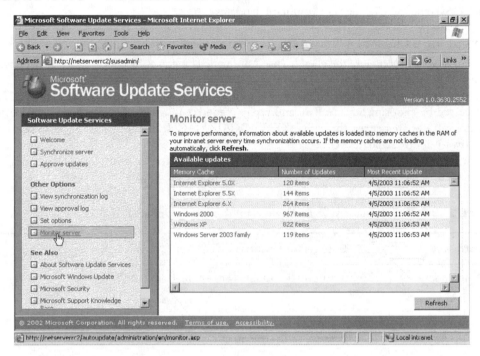

The following client platforms are the only ones that SUS currently supports:

- Windows 2000 Professional (with Service Pack 2 or higher)
- Windows 2000 Server (with Service Pack 2 or higher)
- Windows 2000 Advanced Server (with Service Pack 2 or higher)
- Windows XP Home Edition (with Service Pack 1 or higher)
- Windows XP Professional (with Service Pack 1 or higher)
- Windows Server 2003 (all platforms)

Configuring the SUS Clients

There are two methods for configuring SUS clients. The method you use depends on whether you use Active Directory in your network.

In a nonenterprise network (not running Active Directory), you would configure Automatic Updates through Control Panel using the same process that was defined in the section "Windows Automatic Updates" earlier in this chapter. Each client's Registry would then be edited to reflect the location of the server that will provide the automatic updates.

Within an enterprise network, using Active Directory, you would typically see automatic updates configured through Group Policy. Group policies are used to manage configuration and security setting via Active Directory. Group Policy is also used to specify what server a client will use for Automatic Updates. If Automatic Updates are configured through Group

Policy, the user will not be able to change Automatic Updates settings by choosing Control Panel ➢ System and clicking the Automatic Updates tab.

Configuring a Client in a Non–Active Directory Network

The easiest way to configure the client to use Automatic Updates is by choosing Control Panel ➢ System and clicking the Automatic Updates tab. However, you can also configure Automatic Updates through the Registry. The Registry is a database of all of your server settings and can be accessed by choosing Start ➢ Run and typing **regedit** in the Run dialog box. Automatic Updates settings are defined through HKEY_LOCAL_MACHINE\Software\Policies\Microsoft\ Windows\WindowsUpdate\AU.

The Registry options that can be configured for Automatic Updates are specified in Table 3.16.

TABLE 3.16   Registry Keys and Values for Automatic Updates

Registry Key	Options for Values
NoAutoUpdate	0 Automatic Updates are enabled (default).
	1 Automatic Updates are disabled.
AUOptions	2 Notify of download and installation.
	3 Auto download and notify of installation.
	4 Auto download and schedule installation.
ScheduledInstallDay	1 Sunday.
	2 Monday.
	3 Tuesday.
	4 Wednesday.
	5 Thursday.
	6 Friday.
	7 Saturday.
UseWUServer	0 Use public Microsoft Windows Update site.
	1 Use server specified in WEServer entry.

To specify what server will be used as the Windows Update server, you edit two Registry keys, which are found at HKEY_LOCAL_MACHINE\Software\Policies\Microsoft\Windows\ WindowsUpdate:

- The WUServer key sets the Windows Update server using the server's HTTP name; for example, http://intranetSUS.

- The WUStatusServer key sets the Windows Update intranet SUS statistics sever by using the server's HTTP name; for example, http://intranetSUS.

Configuring a Client in an Active Directory Network

If the SUS client is a part of an enterprise network using Active Directory, you would configure the client via Group Policy. To configure Group Policy on a Windows Server 2003 domain controller, you would take the following steps:

1. Select Start ➤ Run. In the Run dialog box, type **MMC**.

2. From the MMC console, select File ➤ Add/Remove Snap-In.

3. In the Add/Remove Snap-In dialog box, click the Add button.

4. In the Add Standalone Snap-In dialog box, select Group Policy Object Editor and click the Add button.

5. For Group Policy Object, click the Browse button, select Default Domain Policy, and click the OK button.

6. In the Select Group Policy Object dialog box, click the Finish button. In the Add Standalone Snap-In dialog box, click the Close button. In the Add/Remove Snap-In dialog box, click the OK button.

7. Expand Default Domain Policy, Computer Configuration, Administrative Templates, Windows Components, Windows Update to access the Windows Update settings shown in Figure 3.16.

FIGURE 3.16   Group Policy settings for Windows Update

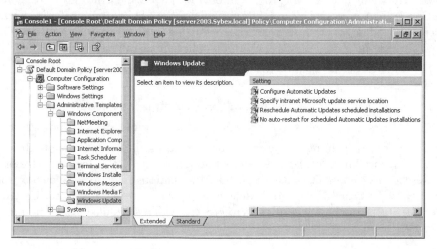

8. Double-click the Configure Automatic Updates option. The Configure Automatic Updates Properties dialog box appears (Figure 3.17). The Automatic Updates options that can be configured through Group Policy are as follows:

- Whether Automatic Updates are not configured, enabled, or disabled.

- How automatic updating is configured. The options are Notify For Download And Notify For Install, Auto Download And Notify For Install, and Auto Download And Schedule The Install.

- The schedule that will be applied for the install day and the install time.

FIGURE 3.17   Configure Automatic Updates Properties dialog box

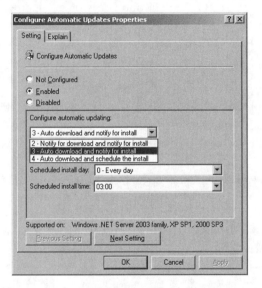

9. To configure which server will provide automatic updates, click the Next Setting button in the Configure Automatic Updates Properties dialog box. This brings up the Specify Intranet Microsoft Update Service Location Properties dialog box, shown in Figure 3.18. The properties that can be configured through group policy are as follows:

- The status of the intranet Microsoft update service location as not configured, enabled, or disabled

- The HTTP name of the server that will provide intranet service updates

- The HTTP name of the server that will act as the intranet SUS statistics server

10. To configure rescheduling of automatic updates, click the Next Setting button in the Specify Intranet Microsoft Update Service Location Properties dialog box. This brings up the Reschedule Automatic Updates Scheduled Installations Properties dialog box, shown in Figure 3.19. You can enable and schedule the amount of time that Automatic Updates waits after system startup before it attempts to proceed with a scheduled installation that was previously missed.

FIGURE 3.18   The Specify Intranet Microsoft Update Service Location Properties dialog box

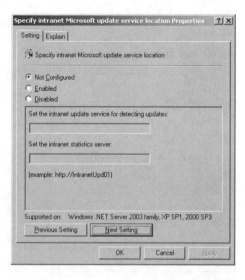

FIGURE 3.19   The Reschedule Automatic Updates Scheduled Installations Properties dialog box

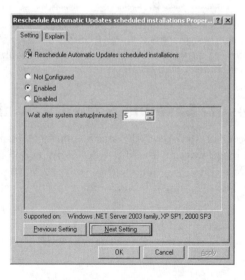

11. To configure auto-restart for scheduled Automatic Updates installations, click the Next Setting button in the Reschedule Automatic Updates Scheduled Installations Properties dialog box. This brings up the No Auto-Restart For Scheduled Automatic Updates Installations dialog box, shown in Figure 3.20. This option is used if the computer is required to restart after an update. You can choose to wait until the next time the computer is restarted or to restart the computer automatically as a part of the update.

FIGURE 3.20 The No Auto-Restart For Scheduled Automatic Updates Installations dialog box

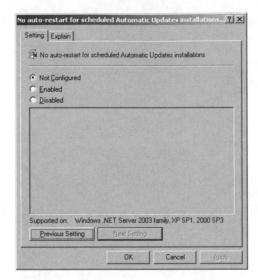

12. When you are done making setting changes, click the OK button.

There are security templates called Wuau.adm (for Windows 2000 Server), which is available through the Software Update Services installation, and System.adm (for Windows Server 2003), which automatically applies the group policy settings that are used by SUS.

Using the Microsoft Baseline Security Analyzer

The Microsoft Baseline Security Analyzer (MBSA) is a security assessment utility that can be downloaded from the Microsoft website. It verifies whether your computer has the latest security updates and whether there are any common security violation configurations that have been applied to your computer. The following programs and operating systems are scanned by MBSA:

- Windows NT 4
- Windows 2000
- Windows XP
- Windows Server 2003
- IIS 4 and 5
- Internet Explorer, versions 5.01 and higher
- SQL Server 7 and SQL Server 2000
- Microsoft Office 2000 and Microsoft Office XP
- Windows Media Player, versions 6.4 and higher

To use MBSA, the computer must meet the following requirements:

- Must be running Windows NT 4, 2000, Windows XP, or Windows Server 2003 (MBSA is not supported by Windows 95, Windows 98, or Windows Me)

- Must be running Windows Explorer 5.01 or higher

- Must have an XML parser installed for full functionality

- Must have the Workstation and the Server service enabled

- Must have Client for Microsoft Networks installed

 MBSA replaces the Microsoft Personal Security Advisor (MPSA) that was an application previously used to scan for possible security threats to your computer.

MBSA can be run through a GUI version from Start All Programs ➢ Microsoft Baseline Security Analyzer, or you can open a command prompt, change the path to *Drive*:\Program Files\Microsoft Baseline Security Analyzer, and type **mbsa** (after Mbsasetup.msi has been downloaded and installed from the Microsoft site) or use **Mbsacli.exe** from the command-line.

Using the GUI Version of MBSA

Once you have installed MBSA, you can access it from Start ➢ All Programs ➢ Microsoft Baseline Security Analyzer or by opening the command prompt and executing Mbsa.exe. This brings up the Baseline Security Analyzer utility, shown in Figure 3.21. You can select from Scan A Computer, Scan More Than One Computer, or View Existing Security Reports.

FIGURE 3.21   Baseline Security Analyzer

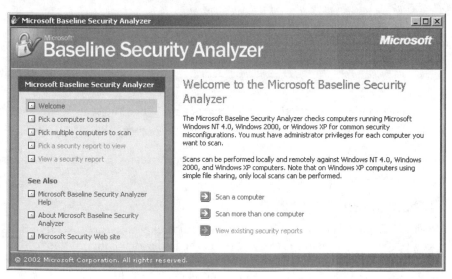

When you click Scan A Computer, the Pick A Computer To Scan dialog box appears (Figure 3.22). You can specify that you want to scan a computer based on computer name or IP address. You can also specify the name of the security report that will be generated. The following are options for the security scan:

- Check For Windows Vulnerabilities
- Check For Weak Passwords
- Check For IIS Vulnerabilities
- Check For SQL Vulnerabilities
- Check For Security Updates (If you use this option and are using SUS, you can specify the name of the SUS server that should be checked for the security updates.)

FIGURE 3.22   The Pick A Computer To Scan dialog box

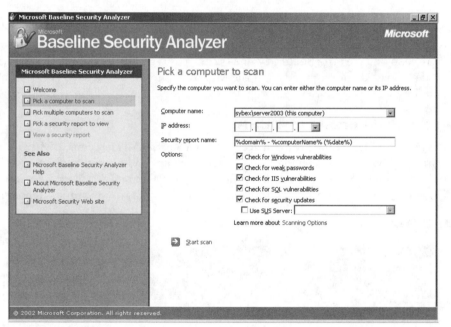

Once you have made your selections, click Start Scan. When the scan is complete, the security report will be automatically displayed. Figure 3.23 shows the View Security Report dialog box.

If you have scanned multiple computers, you can sort the security reports based on issue name, score (worst first), or score (best first).

Using *Mbsacli.exe*

If you use MBSA from the command-line utility `Mbsacli.exe`, there are several options that can be specified. You type **`Mbsacli.exe /hf`** (from the folder that contains `Mbsacli.exe`, which is `Drive:\Program Files\Microsoft Baseline Security Analyzer`) and can then customize the command execution with the options defined in Table 3.17.

FIGURE 3.23 The View Security Report dialog box

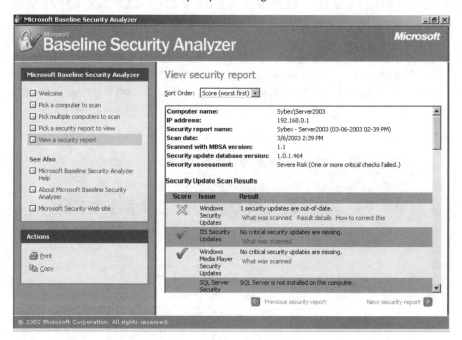

TABLE 3.17 Mbsacli.exe /hf Command-Line Options

Option	Description
-h *hostname*	Scans the specified host. You can specify that you want to scan multiple host computers by separating the hostnames with a comma.
-fh *filename*	Scans the NetBIOS names of each computer that is to be scanned and saves the information as text within the filename you specify.
-i *xxxx.xxxx.xxxx.xxxx*	Scans a computer based on the specified IP address. You can scan multiple computers by IP address by separating the IP addresses with a comma.
-fip *filename*	Scans the computer's IP addresses within the text file that was specified, up to a maximum of 256 IP addresses.
-d *domainname*	Scans the specified domain.
-n	Specifies that all of the computers on the local network should be scanned.

Managing Windows Server 2003 Services

A service is a program, routine, or process that performs a specific function within the Windows Server 2003 operating system. You manage services through the Services window, shown in Figure 3.24. You can access this window in a variety of ways, including through the Computer Management utility (right-click My Computer in the Start menu, select Manage, expand Services and Applications, and then expand Services), through Administrative Tools, or as an MMC snap-in.

FIGURE 3.24   The Services window

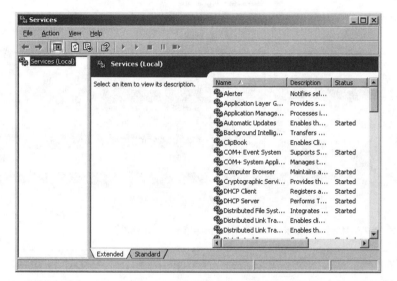

For each service, the Services window listing shows the name, a short description, the startup type, and the logon account that is used to start the service. To configure the properties of a service, double-click it to open its Properties dialog box. This dialog box contains four tabs of options for services, which are described in the following sections.

Configuring General Service Properties

The General tab of the service Properties dialog box (see Figure 3.25) allows you to view and configure the following options:

- The service display name
- A description of the service
- The path to the service executable
- The startup type, which can be automatic, manual, or disabled
- The current service status
- Startup parameters that can be applied when the service is started

You can use the buttons in the Service Status section of the dialog box to start, stop, pause, or resume the service.

FIGURE 3.25   The General tab of the service Properties dialog box

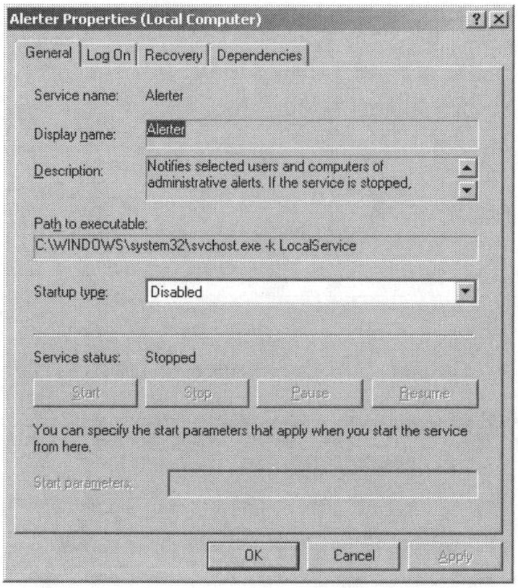

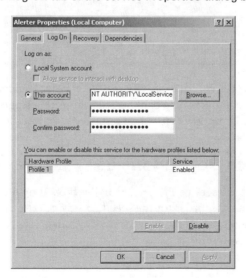

Configuring Service Log On Properties

The Log On tab of the service Properties dialog box, shown in Figure 3.26, allows you to configure the logon account that will be used to start the service. You can choose to use the local system account or specify another logon account.

FIGURE 3.26   The Log On tab of the service Properties dialog box

At the bottom of the Log On tab, you can select hardware profiles to associate the service with. For each hardware profile, you can set the service as enabled or disabled.

Configuring Service Recovery Properties

Use the Recovery tab of the service Properties dialog box, shown in Figure 3.27, to configure what action will be taken if the service fails to load. For the first, second, and subsequent failures, you can select from the following actions:

- Take No Action
- Restart The Service
- Run A File
- Reboot The Computer

FIGURE 3.27   The Recovery tab of the service Properties dialog box

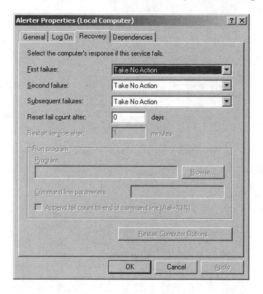

If you choose to run a file, you then specify the file and any command-line parameters. If you choose to reboot the computer, you can then configure a message that will be sent to users who are connected to the computer before it is restarted.

Checking Service Dependencies

The Dependencies tab of the service Properties dialog box, shown in Figure 3.28, lists any services that must be running in order for the specified service to start. If a service fails to start, you can use this information to determine what the dependencies are and then make sure that each dependency service is running.

FIGURE 3.28   The Dependencies tab of the service Properties dialog box

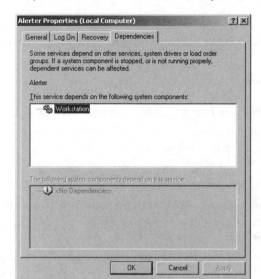

At the bottom of the Dependencies tab, you can see if any other services depend on this service. You should verify that there are no services that depend on a service that you are about to stop.

 **Real World Scenario**

Using Windows Server 2003 Services

Your company uses several applications that require a user to be logged on as a service. Some of the applications have specific instructions for setup, whereas other applications leave the specific configuration up to the administrator.

The problem with many of the applications is that they require the service to log on as a user with administrative rights. This could easily be a potential security violation, but there are steps you can take to manage your service accounts.

Consider using a naming convention so that you can easily identify the service accounts. For example, you could place a # sign in front of all service accounts. If you have a virus scanner that uses a service account, you would create #VirScan as the user account that will be used to log on. Under user rights, you will typically assign this user account the Logon As A Service right. You should also make sure that the user account has a difficult password composed of alphanumeric and nonalphanumeric characters. If your domain uses password restrictions, you should configure the service accounts so that their passwords never expire.

Summary

In this chapter, you learned about the security features of Windows Server 2003. We covered the following topics:

- Security settings can be applied at the local or domain level. To manage local security policies, use Group Policy with the local computer Group Policy Object. To manage domain security policies, use Group Policy with the domain policy Group Policy Object.

- Account policies control the logon process. The three types of account policies are password, account lockout, and Kerberos policies.

- Local policies control what a user can do at the computer. The three types of local policies are audit, user rights assignment, and security options policies.

- The Security Configuration and Analysis utility is used to analyze your security configuration. You run this utility to compare your existing security settings to a security template configured with your desired settings.

- You can manage software installation and maintenance with Windows Update, Automatic Updates, Microsoft Software Update Services, and Microsoft Baseline Security Analyzer.

- The Services utility is used to manage startup options for services, stop services, configure log on and service recovery properties, and check service dependencies.

Exam Essentials

Understand how to configure security settings using Group Policy Objects.   Know which options can be configured through GPOs. Understand how GPOs are applied through Active Directory. Understand the order of application of GPOs. Know how to override the default behavior of GPO execution.

Know how to define and configure account policies.   Understand how to configure the options for password policies, account lockout policies, and Kerberos policies.

Know how to define and configure local policies.   Understand how to configure the options that can be configured in the Audit Policy, User Rights Assignment, and Security Options folders.

Know how to define and configure system policies.   Understand how to configure User Profiles, Logon, Disk Quota, Group Policy, and Windows File Protection options.

Be able to use the Security Configuration and Analysis Tool.   Know how to use the Security Configuration and Analysis utility along with security templates to analyze the security of your Windows Server 2003 computers.

Understand the different ways to keep Windows up-to-date.   Windows includes four tools for performing updates: Windows Update, Automatic Update, Microsoft Software Update Services, and Microsoft Baseline Security Analyzer. Windows Update attaches to the Microsoft website through a user-initiated process and allows Windows users to update their operating systems by downloading updated files (critical and noncritical software updates). Automatic Update extends the functionality of Windows Update by automating the process of updating critical files.

Microsoft Software Update Services (SUS) is used to deploy a limited version of Windows Update to a corporate server, which in turn provides the Windows updates to client computers within the corporate network. Microsoft Baseline Security Analyzer (MBSA) is a utility you can download from the Microsoft website to ensure that you have the most current security updates.

Know how to manage services   You manage services through the Services window. For each service, the Services window listing shows the name, a short description, the startup type, and the logon account that is used to start the service. To configure the properties of a service, double-click it to open its Properties dialog box.

Key Terms

Before you take the exam, be certain you are familiar with the following terms:

account lockout policies	key distribution center (KDC)
Account policies	local group
Active Directory	local policies
Active Directory users	local users
Active Directory Users and Computers (ADUC)	Local Users and Groups
Administrator	logon policies
audit policies	Microsoft Baseline Security Analyzer (MBSA)
Automatic Updates	Microsoft Software Update Services (SUS)
delegation	mutual authentication
disk quota policies	organizational units (OUs)
distribution group	Password policies
domain	Security Configuration and Analysis
domain local groups	security group
domain policies	Security options
domain users	sites
Global groups	universal groups
Group Policy policies	user profile
Guest	user rights
inheritance	Windows file protection policies
Kerberos policies	Windows Update

Review Questions

1. You recently made changes to the GPOs on your Windows Server 2003 domain controller. You notice that the changes are not being applied automatically when new users log on. Using the following exhibit, which option can you set so that new changes to the GPO are applied within 10 minutes for any computers that are logged onto the network?

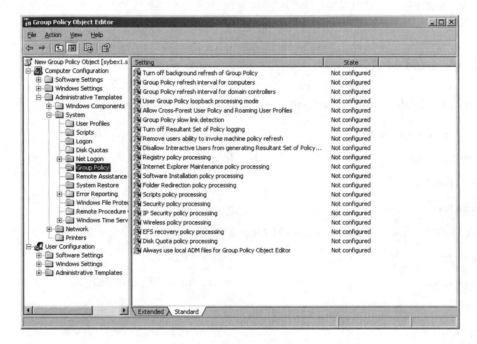

A. Enable and configure the group policy for Apply Group Policy For Computers Asynchronously During Startup.

B. Enable and configure the group policy for Apply Group Policy For Users Asynchronously During Startup.

C. Enable and configure the group policy for Group Policy Refresh Interval For Computers To 10 minutes.

D. Enable and configure the group policy for Group Policy Refresh Interval For Domain Controllers To 10 minutes.

2. You are the administrator of the TESTCORP.COM domain. You have configured Local Security Options for the Default Domain Policy object. You have delegated administrative control to the DENVER.TESTCORP.COM domain and the BELFAST.TESTCORP.COM domain to the respective local administrators. You want to make sure the local administrators do not define any group policies that might conflict with the settings you have specified. What should you configure?

A. Configure the No Override option on the TESTCORP.COM domain GPO.

B. Configure the Block Inheritance option on the TESTCORP.COM domain GPO.

C. Configure the Always Apply Root Level GPO option on the TESTCORP.COM domain GPO.

D. Nothing. Your options will override any local options by default.

3. You suspect that someone is attempting to log on to your domain using the Administrator account. You want to track when users log on successfully or unsuccessfully in the domain. Based on the following exhibit, which auditing event should you enable?

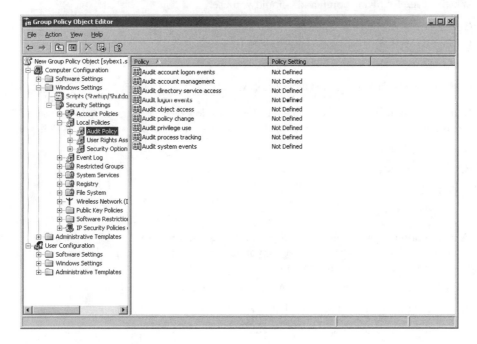

A. Audit Account Logon Events

B. Audit Account Management

C. Audit Logon Events

D. Audit Process Tracking

4. You are the administrator of a Windows Server 2003 network that uses Active Directory. Your network includes Windows Server 2003 domain controllers, Windows Server 2003 member servers, and XP Professional computers. You are concerned that the security on your network is susceptible to network attacks. You want to use the Security Configuration and Analysis snap-in to tighten the network's security. Which of the following options can be applied using this tool? (Choose all that apply.)

    A. Track changes to security options

    B. Create and apply group policies

    C. Set a working database of security options

    D. Import an existing security template

5. You are the network administrator for a Fortune 500 company. You are responsible for all client computers at the central campus. You want to make sure that all of the client computers are secure. You decide to use MBSA to scan your client computers for possible security violations. You want to use the command-line version of MBSA to scan your computers based on IP address. Which of the following commands should you use?

    A. `Mdsacli.exe /hf -i` *xxxx.xxxx.xxxx.xxxx*

    B. `Mdsacli.exe /ip` *xxxx.xxxx.xxxx.xxxx*

    C. `Mbsa.exe /hf -ip` *xxxx.xxxx.xxxx.xxxx*

    D. `Mbsa.exe /ip` *xxxx.xxxx.xxxx.xxxx*

6. You need to quickly edit the Group Policy for a Windows Server 2003 member server. Which of the following command-line utilities could you use to access the Local Computer Policy utility?

    A. `EditGPO.exe`

    B. `GPOEdit.exe`

    C. `EditGPO.msc`

    D. `Gpedit.msc`

7. One common use of the Services utility is to disable the Print Spooler service in order to stop a queue of print jobs. What steps would you take to stop the Print Spooler service, and then restart it? Choose all options that apply.

    A. Select Start ➤ All Programs ➤ Accessories ➤ Services

    B. Select Start ➤ Administrative Tools ➤ Services

    C. Double-click the Print Spooler service

    D. Right-click the Print Spooler service and select Edit from the pop-up menu.

    E. Click the Pause button, then click the Start button.

    F. Click the Stop button, then click the Start button.

    G. Choose Manual from the Startup Type list.

8. Your network requires an extraordinary level of security. You want to configure the Windows Server 2003 domain controllers so that only Windows 2000 clients can communicate with them. Based on your requirements, which of the following security templates should you apply to your servers?

A. `Securedc.inf`

B. `Hisecdc.inf`

C. `Dedicadc.inf`

D. `W2kdc.inf`

9. You are concerned about network security. You want to know as much as you can about the security protocols that are used in conjunction with Windows Server 2003. Which of the following security protocols is used with Windows Server 2003 to authenticate users and network services?

A. Kerberos version 5

B. C2\E2 Security

C. KDS Security

D. MS-CHAP

10. You are the administrator of the TESTCORP.COM domain. You have configured a GPO for your domain so that users have to change their passwords every 45 days. You want to ensure that users do not immediately reuse their old password. Which password policy specifies that users cannot reuse passwords until they have cycled through a specified number of unique passwords?

A. Enforce Password History

B. Use Unique Passwords

C. Require C2/E2 Encryption Standards

D. All Passwords Must Use High Level Standards

11. You suspect that one of your administrators is creating new users so that they can look at the Payroll folder, which has folder auditing enabled. Which audit policy should you enable so that you can track when a user or group is created, deleted, or has management actions generated?

A. Audit Object Access

B. Audit Logon Events

C. Audit Account Management

D. Audit Process Tracking

12. You are the network administrator for a Fortune 500 company. You are responsible for all client computers at the central campus. You want to make sure all of the client computers have the most current software installed for their operating systems, including software in the categories Critical Updates and Service Packs, Windows Server 2003 Family, and Driver Updates. You want to automate the process as much as possible, and you want the client computers to download the updates from a central server that you are managing. You decide to use Software Update Services. The SUS server software has been installed on a server called SUSServer. You want to test the SUS server before you set up group policy within the domain. You install Windows XP Professional with the latest service pack on a test client. Which of the following Registry entries needs to be made for the client to specify that the client should use SUSServer for Windows Update? (Choose all that apply.)

A. HKEY_LOCAL_MACHINE\Software\Policies\Microsoft\Windows\WindowsUpdate\ AU\UseWUServer and specify 0 data

B. HKEY_LOCAL_MACHINE\Software\Policies\Microsoft\Windows\WindowsUpdate\ AU\UseWUServer and specify 1 for data

C. HKEY_LOCAL_MACHINE\Software\Policies\Microsoft\Windows\WindowsUpdate\ AU\WUServer and specify http://SUSServer

D. HKEY_LOCAL_MACHINE\Software\Policies\Microsoft\Windows\WindowsUpdate\ AU\WUServer and specify SUSServer

E. HKEY_LOCAL_MACHINE\Software\Policies\Microsoft\Windows\WindowsUpdate\ WUServer and specify http://SUSServer

F. HKEY_LOCAL_MACHINE\Software\Policies\Microsoft\Windows\WindowsUpdate\ WUServer and specify SUSServer

13. Your Windows Server 2003 computer also acts as an IIS server that allows anonymous access. You want to minimize security risks as much as possible. Which of the following security options will enable you to specify additional restrictions for anonymous connections?

A. Additional Restrictions For Anonymous Users

B. Impose Additional Security For Anonymous Users

C. Tight Security For Anonymous Users

D. Audit Access Of Anonymous Users

14. You have recently applied security options for your Windows Server 2003 computer. When you attempt to verify the security settings, they appear as if they have not been applied. What command-line utility can you use to force an update of the new security policies?

A. secupdate

B. gpupdate

C. secrefresh

D. secpol

15. You have configured group policies on your Windows Server 2003 domain controllers. Your Windows 2000 clients use the group policies, but the Windows NT 4 clients do not have the group policies applied. Which command-line utility is used to create and manage system policies for Windows NT 4 clients on Windows Server 2003?

    A. `poleditor`

    B. `syspoled`

    C. `poledit`

    D. `editpol`

Answers to Review Questions

1. C. Group Policy Refresh Intervals For Computers specifies the interval rate that will be used to update the computer's Group Policy. By default, this background operation occurs every 90 minutes.

2. A. The No Override option is used to specify that child containers can't override the policy settings of higher-level GPOs. In this case, the order of precedence would be that site settings override domain settings and domain settings override OU settings. The No Override option would be used if you wanted to set corporate-wide policies without allowing administrators of lower-level containers to override your settings. This option can be set on a per-container basis as needed.

3. A. The Audit Account Logon Events policy is used to track events such as when a user logs on, logs off, or makes a network connection. The Audit Logon Events policy is used to track events such as running a logon script or accessing a roaming profile.

4. C, D. Through the Security Configuration and Analysis snap-in, you can analyze an existing template against your current configuration to identify any weakness in your security settings. This utility, Analyze Computer Now, does not configure any security options. The Configure Computer Now utility does change the security settings and should only be used with extreme caution.

5. A. If you use MBSA from the command-line utility Mdsacli.exe, there are several options that can be specified. You type **Mdsacli.exe /hf** (from the folder that contains Mdsacli.exe) and then customize the command execution with an option such as /i *xxxx.xxxx.xxxx.xxxx*, which specifies that computer with the specified IP address should be scanned.

6. D. You can edit group policies through the Group Policy MMC snap-on or by using the command-line utility Gpedit.msc. To use this utility, select Start ➢ Run and, at the Run dialog box, type **Gpedit.msc** and click the OK button.

7. B, C, F. First, select Start ➢ Administrative Tools ➢ Services. Then, double-click the Print Spooler service. Finally, click the Stop button, then click the Start button.

8. B. The Hisecdc.inf security template defines highly secure network communications for Windows Server 2003 computers. If you apply this security template, Windows Server 2003 computers can communicate only with other Windows Server 2003 computers. In this case, the computers would not communicate with older clients such as Windows 95/98 or even Windows NT 4 computers.

9. A. Windows Server 2003 uses the Kerberos version 5 security protocol to authenticate users and services through a mutual authentication process.

10. A. When the Enforce Password History option is set, users cannot reuse the same password. Users must create a new password when their password expires or is changed.

11. C. The Audit Account Management policy is used to track user and group creation, deletion, and management actions.

12. B, E.   The Registry key HKEY_LOCAL_MACHINE\Software\Policies\Microsoft\Windows\ WindowsUpdate\AU\UseWUServer can be set to 0 to use the public Windows Update server or 1, which means that you will specify the server for Windows Update in the HKEY_LOCAL_ MACHINE\Software\Policies\Microsoft\Windows\WindowsUpdate key. The WUServer key sets the Windows Update server using the server's HTTP name; for example, http://intranetSUS.

13. A.   The Additional Restrictions For Anonymous Users security option allows you to impose additional restrictions, such as not allowing access without explicit anonymous permissions.

14. B.   If you edit your security policy and notice that your changes are not taking effect, it may be because the group policies are only applied periodically. You can force your policies to be updated by issuing the command `secedit /refreshpolicy machine_policy` for computers and `secedit /refreshpolicy user_policy` for user settings.

15. C.   In Windows Server 2003, you access the System Policy Editor with the command-line utility `poledit`. This utility is used to create and manage system policies for Windows NT 4 clients.

Chapter

4

Managing IP Security

MICROSOFT EXAM OBJECTIVES COVERED IN THIS CHAPTER

✓ Monitor network protocol security. Tools might include the IP Security Monitor Microsoft Management Console (MMC) snap-in and Kerberos support tools.

✓ Troubleshoot network protocol security. Tools might include the IP Security Monitor MMC snap-in, Event Viewer, and Network Monitor.

The ability to control network traffic is a key part of system administration. Many organizations want to protect their network traffic from eavesdropping and tampering, but it's been very difficult to do so because of the obstacles involved. Interoperability is the most obvious hurdle, but there are a lot of subtle pitfalls associated with trying to secure network traffic in a robust yet easily managed way.

The Internet Engineering Task Force (IETF) addressed this problem some time ago, and the result was the *Internet Protocol Security Extensions (IPSec)*. IPSec is a set of extensions to the basic Internet Protocol (IP). The IPSec Extensions allow secure communication over the unsecure Internet Protocol (IP) and is not a replacement for IP.

In this chapter, you'll learn how to install and configure IPSec and how to use the default security policies. You'll also learn how to define your own security policies and filters to customize the level of protection available to computers on your network.

Understanding How IPSec Works

The original specifications for IP made no provisions for any kind of security. That wasn't accidental; it stemmed from two completely different causes. One was the expectation that users and administrators would continue to behave fairly well and not make serious attempts to compromise other people's traffic. The other was that the cryptographic technology needed to provide adequate security wasn't widely available, or even widely known about.

As the Internet expanded, it became clear that robust authentication and privacy protection were desirable, but they aren't included in version 4 of the IP specification (which is the currently adopted standard). As the installed base of IP-capable devices grew, so too did the complexity of devising a security protocol that wouldn't interfere with the operation of all those devices. Finally, in the late 1990s, vendors began releasing products that incorporated the IP Security Extensions (better known as just IPSec) into IP version 4.

A number of major vendors, including Microsoft, Cisco, Nortel, and RSA Security, are shipping IPSec products. However, the standard itself is still somewhat in flux; if you're thinking of implementing IPSec in a mixed-vendor network, make sure your devices can all talk to each other. Refer to RFC 1825 for additional information on IPSec.

The whole idea behind IPSec is that it operates at the Network layer and that users and applications never need to be aware of whether their traffic is being carried over a secure connection or not. In IPSec terminology, there are clients and servers, but that's a little misleading. Any

Windows 2000 Server, Windows XP, or Windows Server 2003 machine may be an IPSec client or server—an *IPSec client* is the computer that attempts to establish a connection to another machine, and an *IPSec server* is the target of that connection. By choosing appropriate client and server settings, you can fine-tune which computers will use IPSec to talk to each other.

IPSec provides two services: a way for computers to decide if they trust each other (*authentication*) and a way to keep network data private (*encryption*). The IPSec process calls for two computers to authenticate each other before beginning an encrypted connection. At that point, the two machines can use the Internet Key Exchange (IKE) protocol to agree on a secret key to use for encrypting the traffic between them. This process takes place in the context of IPSec security associations (SAs), which you will learn about later in this chapter.

As if that weren't enough, the Windows Server 2003 implementation of IPSec explicitly supports the idea of policy-based security. Instead of running around changing security settings on every machine in a domain, you can set policies that configure individual machines, groups of machines within an organizational unit or domain, or every Windows 2000, XP, or Server 2003 machine on your network.

When you use IPSec to encrypt or authenticate connections between two machines—called *end-to-end mode* (or *transport mode*) because network traffic is protected before it leaves the originating machine—it remains secured until the receiving machine gets it and decrypts it. There's a second application: using IPSec to secure traffic that's being passed over someone else's wires. This use of IPSec is called *tunnel mode* because it's used to encrypt traffic to pass over (or through) a tunnel, usually established by the Layer 2 Tunneling Protocol (L2TP).

In this chapter, and on the exam, when you see "IPSec tunnel mode," assume that it means IPSec for tunneling, not for VPN traffic. When you see L2TP mentioned, you can safely assume that it means "L2TP + IPSec." See Chapter 7, "Managing Remote Access Services," for more details on the differences.

In the following sections you will see how IPSec is used to secure IP communications, and you will begin to learn how IPSec is integrated into Windows Server 2003.

IPSec Fundamentals

IPSec has two separate features: authentication and encryption. You can use them together or separately, and each feature has a number of options and parameters you can adjust to fine-tune security on your network.

Authentication protects your network, and the data it carries, from tampering. This tampering might take the form of a malicious attacker sitting between a client and a server, altering the contents of packets (referred to as a man-in-the-middle attack), or it might take the form of an attacker joining your network and impersonating either a client or a server. IPSec uses an *authentication header (AH)* to digitally sign the entire contents of each packet. This signature provides three separate benefits:

Protection against replay attacks   If an attacker can capture packets, save them until a later time, and send them again, then they can impersonate a machine after that machine is no longer on the network. This is called a replay attack. IPSec's authentication mechanism prevents replay attacks by including the sender's signature on all packets.

Protection against tampering   IPSec's signatures provide data integrity, meaning that an interloper can't selectively change parts of packets to alter their meaning.

Protection against spoofing   Normally when you hear about authentication, it refers to the process of a client or server verifying another machine's identity. IPSec authentication headers provide authentication because each end of a connection can verify the other's identity.

Authentication protects your data against tampering, but it doesn't do anything to keep people from seeing it. For that, you need encryption, which actually obscures the payload contents so that it can't be read as it goes by. To accomplish this, IPSec provides the *Encapsulating Security Payload (ESP)*. ESP is used to encrypt the entire payload of an IPSec packet, rendering it undecipherable by anyone other than the intended recipient. ESP only provides confidentiality, but it can be combined with AH to gain maximum security.

In the following sections you will see how IPSec is integrated into Windows Server 2003, and the specific details of the IPSec negotiation process.

IPSec and Windows Server 2003

Microsoft's IPSec implementation is actually licensed from, and was written by, Cisco, which guarantees good compatibility with other standards-based IPSec clients. There are some other Windows Server 2003 features that make IPSec more useful, especially Group Policy. Imagine a large network of computers, some running IPSec. When two computers want to communicate, it would be ideal if they could automatically take advantage of IPSec if both ends supported it. You'd also want to ensure that the security settings you wanted were applied to all IPSec-capable machines. With Windows NT, and with most other operating systems, that would mean hand-configuring each IPSec machine to use the settings you wanted.

The solution lies in the Windows Server 2003 Group Policy mechanism. First, you specify the IPSec settings you want to use on your network. Then each Windows 2000, XP, or Server 2003 machine runs a service called the IPSec Policy Agent. When the system starts, the Policy Agent connects to an Active Directory server, downloads the IPSec policy, and then passes it to the IPSec service. (You will learn more about the Policy Agent in the "Security Policies" section later in this chapter.)

Windows Server 2003 adds several new IPSec features that were either not present in or significantly enhanced since Windows 2000. Some of the features simply add extra layers of security to IPSec, but others actually enhance or replace the management and monitoring tools that you would use in the workplace:

IP Security Monitor   The IP Security Monitor is new for Windows Server 2003. This tool is now implemented as an MMC snap-in and adds several enhancements to the old version. You can now monitor IPSec information on the local computer as well as on remote machines, view details of all IPSec policies, view generic and specific filters, view statistics, view security associations, customize the display, and search for specific filters by IP address.

Stronger cryptographic master key (Diffie-Hellman)   IPSec now includes support for the much stronger Group 3 2048-bit Diffie-Hellman key exchange. The complexity of this key exchange significantly increases the difficulty of computing the secret key. However, if you require backward compatibility with Windows 2000 and Windows XP, you must use Group 2 (medium), which provides a 1024-bit key exchange. You should never use Group 1 (low).

Command-line management with *netsh* You can now configure IPSec using the updated netsh command, which replaces the Ipsecpol.exe tool in Windows 2000. With netsh, you can script and automate IPSec configuration.

Persistent policies You can now create a persistent policy for a computer if a local or Active Directory–based policy cannot be applied. The persistent policy is always active and cannot be over-ridden by any other policy. Persistent policies can be applied only by using the netsh command.

Removal of default traffic exemptions Previously, all broadcast, multicast, Internet Key Exchange (IKE), Kerberos, and Resource Reservation Protocol (RSVP) traffic was exempt from IPSec by default. Now, only IKE traffic is exempt because IKE is required for estab-lishing IPSec-secured communication.

IPSec functionality over NAT IPSec ESP packets can now pass through Network Address Translation (NAT) that allow UDP traffic with a feature called User Datagram Protocol-Encapsulating Security Payload (UDP-ESP) encapsulation.

IPSec support for Resultant Set of Policy (RSoP) Resultant Set of Policy (RSoP) is a new feature of Windows Server 2003 that provides the ability to see exactly how the various policies within the domain will apply to a specific user or computer. IPSec provides an extension to the RSoP console that you can use to view detailed settings for the IPSec policy that is being applied.

The IPSec Negotiation Process

Internet Security Association and Key Management Protocol (ISAKMP) and the IKE protocol provide a way for two computers to agree on security settings and exchange a security key that they can use to communicate securely. In IPSec, a *security association (SA)* provides all the information needed for two computers to communicate securely. The SA contains a policy agreement that controls which algorithms and key lengths the two machines will use, plus the actual security keys used to securely exchange information. Think of this agreement as a contract: It specifies what each party is, and is not, willing to do as part of the agreement.

There are two steps to this process: main mode and quick mode.

First, in main mode, the two computers use the ISAKMP to establish a security agreement. This is called the ISAKMP SA. To establish the ISAKMP SA, the two computers must agree on the following three things:

- Which encryption algorithm they'll use: (DES, triple DES, 40-bit DES, or none)
- Which algorithm they'll use for verifying message integrity (MD5 or SHA-1)
- How connections will be authenticated (using a public-key certificate, a shared secret key, or Kerberos)

Once the ISAKMP SA is in place, the two machines can use the Oakley protocol to securely agree on a shared master key. This key, called the ISAKMP master key, is used along with the algorithms negotiated in the ISAKMP SA to establish a secure connection.

After the secure connection is brought up, the two machines start another round of negotiations called quick mode. These negotiations cover the following:

- Whether the Authentication Header (AH) protocol will be used for this connection
- Whether the Encapsulating Security Payload (ESP) protocol will be used for this connection
- Which encryption algorithm will be used for the ESP protocol
- Which authentication protocol will be used for the AH protocol

After these negotiations are finished, the two machines end up with two new SAs: one for inbound traffic and another for outbound traffic. These SAs are called IPSec SAs to distinguish them from the ISAKMP SA. At this point, Oakley is used again to generate a new set of session keys. The master ISAKMP key is used whenever new SAs are negotiated; once the SA negotiation finishes, though, the communications using that SA are protected using the SA-specific keys.

The AH protocol provides data integrity and authentication. There are two features that give AH its security. The first security feature is that the packet signature (which is contained in the AH itself) is computed on the entire packet—payload and headers. That means that an attacker can't modify any part of the packet, including the IP or TCP/UDP header. The second security feature is that the AH is placed between the IP header and the TCP or UDP header; this adds further tamper proofing.

The ESP protocol is designed to deliver message confidentiality. Take a look at a sample ESP packet (Figure 4.1) to see how it accomplishes this. This packet is more complex in construction than the AH packet because ESP alone provides authentication, replay proofing, and integrity checking. It does so by adding three separate components: an ESP header, an ESP trailer, and an ESP authentication block. Each of these components contains some of the data needed to provide the necessary authentication and integrity checking. To prevent tampering, an ESP client has to sign the ESP header, application data, and ESP trailer into one unit, and ESP is used to encrypt the application data and the ESP trailer to provide confidentiality. The combination of this overlapping signature and encryption operation provides good security.

FIGURE 4.1 An ESP packet

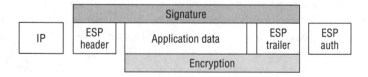

Security Filters

A security filter ties security protocols to a particular network address. The filter contains the source and destination addresses involved (using a netmask for either specific hosts or networks), the protocol used, and the source and destination ports allowed for TCP and UDP traffic. For example, you can define a filter (as you will see later in this chapter) that specifies exactly what kind of IPSec negotiations you're willing to allow when a machine in your domain contacts a machine in the microsoft.com domain. Recall that IPSec connections have two sides: inbound and outbound. That means that for each connection, you need to have two filters: one inbound and one outbound. The inbound filter is applied when a remote machine requests security on a connection, and the outbound filter is applied before sending traffic to a remote machine.

Let's say that you want to create a rule to allow any machine in the `chellis.net` domain to use IPSec when talking to any computer in the `microsoft.com` domain. For this to work, you need the following four filters:

- A filter for the `chellis.net` domain for outbound packets with a source of `*.chellis.net` and a destination of `*.microsoft.com`. (You can use DNS names and wildcards in filters.)

- A filter for the `chellis.net` domain for inbound packets, this time with a source of `*.microsoft.com` and a destination of `*.chellis.net`.

- An inbound filter in the `microsoft.com` domain that specifies a source of `*.chellis.net` and a destination of `*.microsoft.com`.

- An outbound filter in the `microsoft.com` domain that specifies a source of `*.microsoft.com` and a destination of `*.chellis.net`.

If any of these filters are missing or misconfigured, the IPSec negotiation process will fail and IPSec won't be used. If they're all there, when you try to establish an FTP connection from `hawk.chellis.net` to `exchange.microsoft.com`, the outbound filter on your domain will fire and it will trigger IPSec to request a security negotiation with Microsoft's machine. If everything goes well and the filters are okay, you'll end up with two IPSec SAs on your machine and the connection will be secured.

You normally group filters into *filter lists* for ease of management. Because you can store any number of individual filters into a filter list, you can easily build rules that enforce complicated behavior and then distribute those rules throughout your network as necessary.

Security Methods

Each IPSec connection uses a security method. A *security method* is a connection that uses a prespecified encryption algorithm with a negotiated key length and key lifetime. You can use one of the two predefined security methods (High or Medium, as you will see later in this chapter), or you can create your own by specifying which security protocols (AH or ESP), encryption algorithms, and key lifetimes you want to use for a particular connection.

When your computer is negotiating with a remote IPSec peer, the ISAKMP service works its way down the list of methods you've specified, trying to use the most secure method first. As soon as your ISAKMP and the one on the other end agree on a method, it then establishes communications using that method.

 Windows Server 2003 supports the Data Encryption Standard (DES) and Triple DES (3DES) encryption algorithms. 3DES is more secure than DES because it processes each block of data three times.

Security Filter Actions

Filters specify a source and destination, but they also have to specify what action should take place when the criteria specified in the filter matches. Using the IP Security Policy Management snap-in (as you will see later in this chapter) you can use the following five separate security *filter actions* in each filter (though you can't combine them in the same filter):

- The Permit action tells the IPSec filter to take no action. It neither accepts nor rejects the connection based on security rules, meaning that it adds zero security. This action is also called the *passthrough action* because it allows traffic to pass through without modification. In general, you'll use it for applications like Windows Internet Name Service (WINS) servers, where there's no security-sensitive data involved.

- The Block action causes the filter to reject communications from the remote system. This prevents the remote system from making any type of connection, with or without IPSec.

- The two actions Accept Unsecured Communication, But Always Respond Using IPSec and Allow Unsecured Communication With Non-IPSec Aware Computers allow you to interoperate with computers that aren't configured with IPSec. The Accept Unsecured Communication, But Always Respond Using IPSec policy says that it's okay to accept unsecured connections but that your machines will always ask for an IPSec connection before accepting the unsecured request. This action allows you to handle both unsecured and secured traffic, with a preference for IPSec when it's available. The Allow Unsecured Communication With Non-IPSec Aware Computers action allows your machines to accept insecure connections without attempting to use IPSec; as such, we recommend that you not use it, but instead use the Accept Unsecured Communication, But Always Respond Using IPSec action.

- Enabling session key perfect forward secrecy (PFS) ensures that master key keying material cannot be used to derive more than one session key.

- The Use These Security Settings action lets you specify which security methods you want used on connections that trigger this filter. This option allows you to specify custom settings for either individual computers or remote networks.

The upcoming section "Managing Rules with the Rules Tab" discusses an additional filter action as well as a little more about when to use, or not use, each of these actions.

Security Policies

A security policy is a set of rules and filters that provide some level of security. Microsoft includes a number of prebuilt policies, and you can create your own. (In fact, you'll have to create your own policies for things like Dynamic Host Configuration Protocol DHCP and remote access servers.)

You assign policies to computers in a number of ways. The easiest way is to store the policy in Active Directory and let the *IPSec Policy Agent* apply it to the applicable machines. Once an IPSec policy is assigned to a machine through Active Directory, it remains assigned—even after the machine leaves the site, domain, or organizational unit (OU) in which it was given the original policy—until another policy is provided. You can also assign policies directly to individual machines. In either case, you can manually unassign policies when you no longer want a policy in place on a specific machine.

There are three policies you need to be familiar with in the IP Security Policy Management snap-in:

- The Client (Respond Only) policy specifies that a Windows 2000, XP, or Server 2003 IPSec client will negotiate IPSec security with any peer that supports it but that it won't attempt to initiate security. Let's say you apply this policy to a Server 2003 computer. When it initiates outbound network connections, it won't attempt to use IPSec. When someone opens a connection to it, though, it will accept IPSec if the remote end asks for it.

- The Secure Server (Require Security) policy specifies that all IP communication to or from the policy target must use IPSec. In this case, all DNS, WINS, and web requests and everything else that uses an IP connection either has to be secured with IPSec or will be blocked. This may not be what you want unless you plan to implement IPSec on your entire network.

- The Server (Request Security) policy is a mix of the two other policies. In this case, the machine will always attempt to use IPSec by requesting it when it connects to a remote machine and by allowing it when an incoming connection requests it. This policy provides the best general balance between security and interoperability.

 Be sure you understand the difference between the three default policies! You will probably see more than one question on the exam that requires knowledge of the default policies.

IPSec Authentication

IPSec supports three separate authentication methods. Which ones you'll use will depend on what kind of network you have (for example, with or without Active Directory) and to whom you're talking. Because the first thing an IPSec client and server want to do is authenticate each other, they need some way to agree on a set of credentials to use. The Windows Server 2003 version of IPSec supports three different authentication methods; they're used only during the initial authentication phase of building the SAs, not to generate encryption keys:

Kerberos   *Kerberos* is the default authentication protocol for any Windows 2000/2003/XP computer. If Kerberos fails, the computer will automatically switch to NTLM authentication. Kerberos is a widely supported open standard that offers good security and a great deal of flexibility. Because it's natively supported in Windows Server 2003, it's the default authentication method. Many third-party IPSec products include Kerberos support. Note that only Windows 2000 and Server 2003 domain controllers running in Windows Server 2003 or Windows 2000 native domain functional level support Kerberos authentication; Windows 2000 and Server 2003 member servers and NT 4 servers do not.

Certificates   *Certificates* are public-key certificates used for authentication. When you use certificate-based authentication, each end of the connection can use the other's public certificate to verify a digitally signed message. This provides great security, with some added overhead and infrastructure requirements. As you add machines to a domain in Windows

Server 2003, they're automatically issued *machine certificates*, which only apply to specific computers rather than users, that can be used for authentication; if you want to allow users and computers from other domains or organizations to connect to your IPSec machines, you'll need to explore certificate solutions that allow cross-organization certification.

Preshared Keys   *Preshared keys* are reusable passwords. The preshared key itself is a word, code, or phrase that both computers know. The two machines use this password to establish a trust, but they don't send the plain-text phrase over the network. However, the unencrypted key is stored in Active Directory, so Microsoft recommends against using it in production (because anyone who can see the key can impersonate you or the remote computer). However, most of the time you use this mode only when you need to talk to a third-party IPSec product that doesn't yet support certificate or Kerberos authentication.

 Real World Scenario

IPSec in Practice

You want to establish a connection to a file server run by Sally. You and Sally are both members of the same Windows Server 2003 domain, so you can use the Windows Server 2003 default Kerberos authentication. Recall that this entire process is utterly transparent to users on both machines as well as to most intervening routers and network devices. The negotiation and agreement process is transparent to both the users and the applications they're using.

When your computer boots, the IPSec Policy Agent service starts. It connects to Active Directory and downloads the current IPSec policy for the domain. If this connection attempt fails, your machine will keep trying until it successfully gets an IPSec policy because, without one, the IPSec stack doesn't know what to do.

When the policy is retrieved, policy settings are passed to the ISAKMP/Oakley subsystem and to the actual IPSec drivers in the kernel.

When you initially attempt to make a connection to any foreign machine, your computer's IPSec driver will check the active IPSec policy to see whether any IP filters are defined. These filters specify destination networks, traffic types, or both; for the destination or traffic type, the filter also specifies whether IPSec is mandatory, optional, or forbidden.

After your IPSec driver determines that it's allowed to use IPSec when talking to machines on Sally's subnet, it will use ISAKMP to establish an ISAKMP SA with Sally's server.

When Sally's machine sees the incoming ISAKMP request from your workstation, her ISAKMP service replies to the request and the two machines negotiate an ISAKMP SA as described earlier. This SA includes a shared secret key that can be used to establish connection-specific SAs.

Now that an ISAKMP SA has been established, the two machines have everything they need to establish a pair of IPSec SAs, so they do so. Once those negotiations are complete, each computer has two IPSec SAs in place: one for outbound traffic and one for inbound.

Your request (whatever it is) is processed by the IPSec stack on your computer. Your IPSec code uses AH and/or ESP to protect the outbound packets and then transfers them to the lower-level parts of the IP stack for delivery to Sally's server. When her server gets the packets, it uses Sally's IPSec stack to decrypt them (if necessary), verify their authenticity, and pass them up the TCP/IP stack for further processing.

Installing IPSec

The components necessary for a Windows Server 2003 machine to act as an IPSec client are already installed by default when you install Windows Server 2003. However—also by default—there's no policy that requires the use of IPSec, so the default behavior for Windows Server 2003 machines is to not use it. The good news is that you don't really have to "install" IPSec; you just have to install the tool you use to manage it and then start assigning policies and filters to get the desired effect.

In the following sections, you will learn how to enable IP security policies on a Windows Server 2003 computer.

The IP Security Policy Management Snap-In

IPSec is managed through the IP Security Policy Management snap-in (referred to as the IPSec snap-in throughout this chapter). There's no prebuilt MMC console that includes this snap-in, so you have to create one by opening a console and adding the snap-in to it. When you install the IPSec snap-in, you must choose whether you want to use it to manage a local IPSec policy, the default policy for the domain your computer is in, the default policy for another domain, or the local policy on another computer. This gives you an effective way to delegate control over IPSec policies should you choose to do so.

Exercise 4.1 leads you through the process of installing the snap-in for managing a local policy and then activating IPSec on the local computer.

EXERCISE 4.1

Enabling IPSec on the Local Computer

1. Click Start ➢ Run, type **MMC**, and click OK. An empty MMC console window appears.

2. Select File ➢ Add/Remove Snap-In. When the Add/Remove Snap-In dialog box appears, click the Add button.

3. In the Add Standalone Snap-In dialog box, select IP Security Policy Management and click the Add button.

EXERCISE 4.1 *(continued)*

4. The Select Computer Or Domain dialog box appears. Select the Local Computer (default setting) radio button and then click the Finish button.

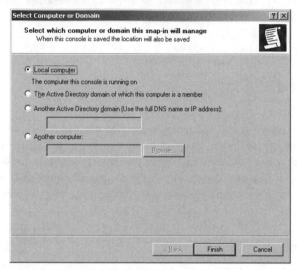

5. Click the Close button in the Add Standalone Snap-In dialog box.

6. Click the OK button in the Add/Remove Snap-In dialog box.

7. Select the IP Security Policies On Local Computer node in the MMC. Note that the right pane of the MMC lists the three predefined policies discussed earlier in this chapter.

8. Right-click the Server (Request Security) policy and choose the Assign command.

9. Verify that the entry in the Policy Assigned column for the selected policy has changed to Yes.

This process in and of itself doesn't do much to improve your security posture because all it does is enable your local computer to accept IPSec connections from other computers. The real payoff comes when you start applying IPSec policies in Active Directory, which we'll show you how to do next.

Configuring IPSec

You can configure IPSec by modifying the default policies, creating your own policies that embody the rules and filters you want to use, and controlling how policies get applied to computers in your management scope.

You manage policies at a variety of levels, depending on where you want them applied. However, you always use the IPSec snap-in to manage them, and the tools you use to create new policies or edit existing ones are the same whether you're using local or Active Directory policy storage. Because Group Policy management is outside the range of this book, the following sections will focus instead on how you customize and control the IPSec settings themselves.

Creating a New Policy

To create a new policy, right-click the IP Security Policies folder in the snap-in and choose the Create IP Security Policy command. This activates the IP Security Policy Wizard, which allows you to create a new policy. You still have to manually edit the policy settings after it's created. The first two screens of the wizard are pretty straightforward; the first page tells you what the wizard does, and the second page allows you to enter a name and description for the policy.

Once you have entered the name and a description of your policy, the Requests For Secure Communications page (see Figure 4.2) asks you whether you want to use the *default response rule* or not.

FIGURE 4.2   The Requests For Secure Communications page

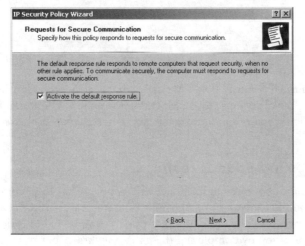

The default response rule is what governs security when no other filter rule applies. For example, let's say you've set up security filters to accept secure connections from *.microsoft.com, *.cisco.com, and *.apple.com. When your server gets an incoming IPSec request from hawk .chellis.net, you'd probably expect IPSec to reject the connection—and it will, unless you leave the default response rule turned on. That rule basically accepts anyone who requests a secure connection. Paradoxically, for maximum security, you might want to turn it off so that you only accept IPSec connections from known hosts. However, you can customize the settings associated with the default rule.

If you choose not to use the default response rule, the wizard will skip the rest of the steps and take you directly to the completion page.

If you choose to use the default response rule, you still have to configure an authentication method for it. To do this, you will use the Default Response Rule Authentication Method page (see Figure 4.3). You can choose one of the three authentication methods mentioned earlier. By default, Kerberos is selected, but you can choose a certificate authority or a preshared key instead. (If you choose to use a preshared key, make sure that you enter the same key on both ends of the connection.)

FIGURE 4.3   The Default Response Rule Authentication Method page

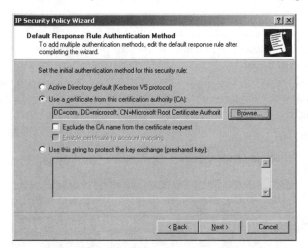

The final page of the IP Security Policy Wizard contains a checkbox labeled Edit Properties. Click it to access the actual settings embedded within the policy after you finish the wizard. You will learn about policy properties in more detail later in the chapter in the section "Configuring IPSec Policies."

Storing Policies in Active Directory

So far, you've read only about managing policies that apply to the local computer. You can also use the IPSec snap-in to create and manage policies that are stored in Active Directory, from which they can be applied to any computer or group of computers in the domain. You actually accomplish this application by completing these three separate, but related, steps:

1. Target the IPSec snap-in at Active Directory and then open it while you're logged in with a privileged account.

2. Edit or create the policy you want to apply using the tools in the snap-in.

3. Use the Group Policy snap-in to attach the policy to a site, domain, or organizational unit.

The first two steps are discussed throughout this chapter, but you should first take a minute to read about the third step. Because you can assign group policies to any site, domain, or organizational unit, you have the ability to fine-tune IPSec policies throughout your entire organization by using an appropriately targeted policy.

For example, in Active Directory Users and Computers, you can create an organizational unit (OU) and then create a new Group Policy Object (GPO) that applies only to that OU.

Finally, you can change the settings in the GPO so they enforce the IPSec policy you want applied to computers in the OU.

You don't actually use the IPSec snap-in to assign policies; you use it to configure them and to create policies that live in Active Directory. When you want to actually apply a policy to some group in the directory, you use the Group Policy snap-in itself.

In Exercise 4.2, you will configure a default IPSec policy for all domain computers. You must have administrative access to the domain for this to work.

EXERCISE 4.2

Enabling IPSec for an Entire Domain

1. Click Start ➢ Run, type **MMC**, and click OK. An empty MMC console window appears.

2. Select File ➢ Add/Remove Snap-In. When the Add/Remove Snap-In dialog box appears, click the Add button.

3. In the Add Standalone Snap-In dialog box, select Group Policy Object Editor and click the Add button.

4. The Select Group Policy Object dialog box appears. Click the Browse button to bring up the Browse For A Group Policy Object dialog box.

5. Select Default Domain Policy and click the OK button.

6. Click the Finish button in the Select Group Policy Object dialog box.

7. Click the Close button in the Add Standalone Snap-In dialog box and then click the OK button in the Add/Remove Snap-In dialog box.

8. Select Domain Policy ➢ Computer Configuration ➢ Windows Settings ➢ Security Settings ➢ IP Security Policies on Active Directory *DomainName*.

9. Select the IP Security Policies On Active Directory *DomainName* item. The right side of the MMC window lists the available policies, including the three predefined policies and any new ones you've added using the IPSec Policy Wizard.

10. Right-click the Server (Request Security) policy and select the Assign command. Notice that the Policy Assigned column for that policy now reads Yes.

11. Save the console for later use.

IPSec policies are subject to the same rules that other objects assigned by group policy are subject to. Even though this book isn't about Group Policy Objects, it's useful to understand those rules so you'll know how IPSec policy assignment really works.

The first rule is simple: A policy applied at the domain level will always override a policy assigned to the local computer (when you're logged on to the domain, of course).

The second rule is equally simple: A policy applied to an organizational unit always takes precedence over domain-level policies. That means that if you have conflicting policies at the domain and OU levels, the settings in the OU policy will be used unless overrides are in place.

The third rule is a little more complex: If you have a hierarchy of OUs set up in Active Directory, the policy for the lowest-level OU overrides the others. For example, let's say you have an OU named Sales, with subordinate OUs for North America and South America. If you assign two different IPSec policies to the Sales and North America OUs, the North America settings will take precedence.

The fourth rule is subtle but important: If you assign an IPSec policy through Group Policy and then remove the Group Policy Object used to assign the policy, *the policy remains in effect*. When the IPSec Policy Agent looks for the policy while the GPO is missing, the agent assumes that the GPO server is temporarily unavailable. It then uses a cached copy of the policy, which means that you have to unassign the policy before removing the GPO you used to assign it and then either refresh the policy on each client computer or wait for the automatic refresh to take place.

Assigning and Unassigning Policies

Whether you're defining policies that affect one computer or a multinational enterprise network, you assign and unassign IPSec policies the same way—by right-clicking the policy in question and using the Assign and Unassign commands.

When a policy is assigned, it takes effect the next time IPSec policies are refreshed—you may remember that the IPSec Policy Agent downloads the policy information for a computer when the computer is restarted. If you're using Group Policy to distribute your IPSec settings, you can force a policy update using the Group Policy snap-in.

Other Policy Management Features

If you know how to create new policies, assign them, and set their properties, you already know almost everything you'll need to know to manage IPSec (though we haven't covered the mechanics of changing policy settings just yet). There are a few additional features that you may find useful in your IPSec implementation.

Forcing a Policy Update

If you want to force one machine to update its IPSec policy, just stop and restart the IPSec Policy Agent service on that machine. When the service starts, it attempts to retrieve the newest available policy from Active Directory or the local policy. Once the policy has been loaded, it's immediately applied. Restarting the Policy Agent forces it to update and reapply the correct policy. This can be useful when you're trying to troubleshoot a policy problem or when you want to be sure that the desired policy has been applied.

By default, the IPSec Policy Agent will update policies every 180 minutes, although you can change that setting. Alternately, you can use the `gpupdate /target:computer /force` command to refresh the local computer's policy settings.

Policy Management with the Pop-Up Menus

Using the context menu (which comes up when you right-click a policy), you can rename, delete, or import and export policies. The commands to import and export policies might seem unnecessary, but they occasionally come in handy if you're not using Active Directory.

For example, let's say you have a small network of computers using Windows 2000 Professional and XP Professional. You can create local IPSec policies on one machine and then export them from the source computer and import them to the remaining machines. Doing so ensures a consistent set of IPSec policies without requiring that you have an Active Directory domain controller present.

 Real World Scenario

Using IPSec in a Security Architecture

Security has always been important at your organization, but recently it has moved to front and center. You have been told to secure every aspect of the information system. You already have many pieces of your company's security shield in place. However, you still have TCP/IP packets going over the wire, and you realize that these packets can be collected and viewed, breaching your security.

You know that IPSec is a strong candidate for completing your company's security architecture and that Windows Server 2003 supports IPSec very well. In fact, it's so simple to implement that you are considering jumping immediately into the fray. This is a common mistake.

The setup for many Windows Server 2003 services—even Windows Server 2003 itself, for that matter—is so easy that many people launch the IP Security Policy Wizard and go to town. One service that's going to strongly resist this method of installation is IPSec. The installation may go smoothly, but it probably won't work. Just a small technicality! One thing to keep in mind about IPSec is that it's a tool for implementing a security policy. You must create a security policy that reflects both what you are trying to accomplish with IPSec and what features or configuration methods are appropriate to make that happen.

Although you know the immediate benefit that IPSec can bring to your organization, you need to take the time to fully understand the IPSec components that will fulfill your implementation. These include authentication, negotiation of encryption, and negotiation of integrity. If there are problems in these components or in others, IPSec won't work. Also keep in mind that these configuration components need to match on both sides of the communication path between the machines.

Configuring IPSec Policies

Once you create a new policy using the IP Security Policy Wizard, you still have to customize it. You do this with the policy Properties dialog box, from which you can add, remove, and manage rules, filter lists, and security actions. There are two separate tabs in the Properties dialog box: The General tab covers general policy-related settings like the policy name, and the Rules tab gives you a way to edit the rules associated with the policy. You will see how to configure settings on both of these tabs in the following sections.

Setting General Properties with the General Tab

In the General tab of the policy Properties dialog box (see Figure 4.4), you can change the policy name and description, which appear in the IPSec snap-in. It's a good idea to use meaningful names for your policies so that you'll remember what each one is supposed to be doing. Use the Check For Policy Changes Every field to change the interval at which clients who use this policy will check for updates. The default value of 180 minutes is OK for most applications because you're unlikely to be changing the policies that frequently.

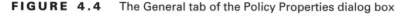

FIGURE 4.4 The General tab of the Policy Properties dialog box

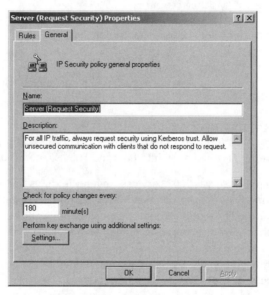

The Settings button allows you to, via the Key Exchange Settings dialog box, change the key exchange settings used by this particular policy (see Figure 4.5). You can use the controls in this dialog box to control how often the policy requires generation of new keys, after either a certain amount of time (8 hours by default) or a certain number of sessions. The Master Key Perfect Forward Secrecy (PFS) option specifies whether or not you want to reauthenticate the SA for every session. Enabling this option provides a higher level of security than leaving it disabled, but performance could be adversely affected. The Methods button displays a list of security methods that will be used to protect the key exchange; the policy always tries the highest-level security from the method list first, such as 3DES, then drops down to less secure methods if the remote end can't handle them.

Managing Rules with the Rules Tab

The Rules tab of the policy Properties dialog box allows you to change the rules included with the IPSec policy. Take a look at Figure 4.6 and you'll see what the rule set for the Server (Request Security) policy looks like.

FIGURE 4.5   The Key Exchange Settings dialog box

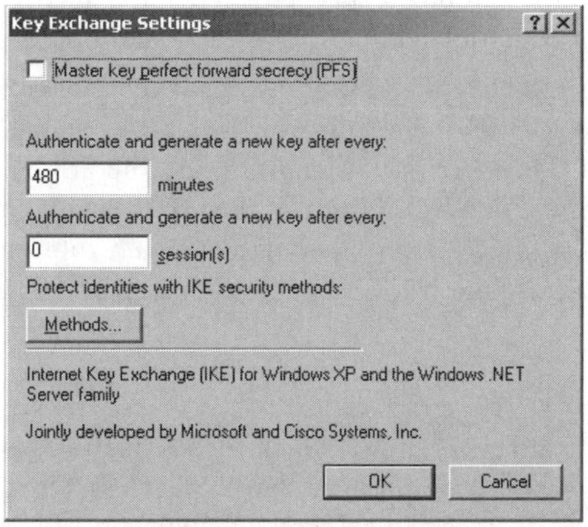

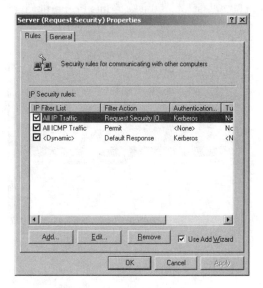

FIGURE 4.6   The Rules tab of the Policy Properties dialog box

Here are the most important things to recognize on this tab:

- There are three rules, each of which ties a filter list to a filter action and authentication method. A single policy can contain an unlimited number of rules. It's common to have a number of rules that are applied in different situations. It's also common to have many different policies defined in a single Active Directory domain or local policy store.

- Each rule has a checkbox next to it that controls whether or not the rule is actually active. You can use these checkboxes to turn on or off individual rules within a policy.

- The Add, Edit, and Remove buttons let you manipulate the list of rules. Note that rules aren't evaluated in any particular order, so there's no need to reorder them.

- The Use Add Wizard checkbox controls whether or not the Security Rule Wizard is used to add a new rule (by default, this box is checked). When it's unchecked and you click the Add button, the Edit Rule Properties dialog box appears, enabling you to set up things by hand.

When you select a rule and click the Edit button or when you create a new rule and the Use Add Wizard checkbox is cleared, the Edit Rule Properties dialog box appears (there is one associated with each rule). There are five different tabs in the Edit Rule Properties dialog box. The Create New IP Security Rule Wizard fills out the tabs for you based on the selections you make, but you should know which settings belong with each rule so you can fill out the tabs by hand. Therefore, instead of taking you through each step of the wizard, we'll go over each tab's settings.

The IP Filter List Tab

The IP Filter List tab (see Figure 4.7) shows which filter lists are associated with this rule. The filter lists defined on your server will appear in the IP Filter Lists list. You can choose any one of them to be applied as a result of this rule. If you like, you can add or remove filter lists here or in the Manage IP Filter Lists And Filter Actions dialog box, covered in the next section.

FIGURE 4.7   The IP Filter List tab of the Edit Rule Properties dialog box

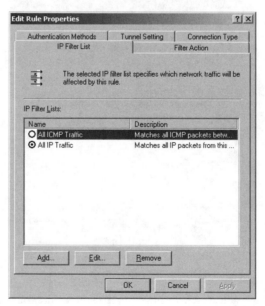

The Filter Action Tab

The Filter Action tab (see Figure 4.8) shows all of the filter actions defined in the policy. You can apply any filter action to the rule. Remember that you combine one filter list with one filter action to make a single rule, but you can group any number of rules into one policy. You can use the Add, Edit, and Remove buttons to add, edit, and remove the filter action. The Use Add Wizard checkbox controls whether adding a new filter action starts up the IP Security Filter Action Wizard (which you'll get to in the next section) or opens the Properties dialog box.

FIGURE 4.8   The Filter Action tab of the Edit Rule Properties dialog box

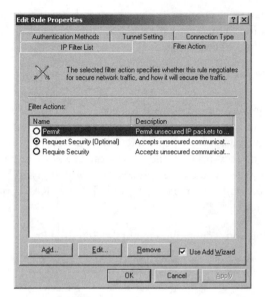

The Authentication Methods Tab

The Authentication Methods tab (see Figure 4.9) allows you to define one or more authentication methods that you want a particular rule to use. You can have multiple methods listed; if so, IPSec will attempt to use them in the order of their appearance in the list. You have the same three choices mentioned earlier: Kerberos, certificates, or preshared keys.

FIGURE 4.9   The Authentication Methods tab of the Edit Rule Properties dialog box

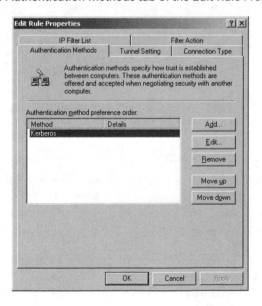

The Tunnel Setting Tab

On the Tunnel Setting tab, you can specify that this rule forms an IPSec tunnel with another system (or *tunnel endpoint*). You'll read more about it in the section "Configuring IPSec for Tunnel Mode" later in this chapter.

The Connection Type Tab

Use the Connection Type tab (see Figure 4.10) to specify which kind of connections this IPSec rule applies to. For example, you might want to specify different rules for dial-up and LAN connections depending on who your users are, where they're connecting from, and what they do while connected. Your basic choice is simple: There are three radio buttons that you use to select which type of connections this rule applies to. The All Network Connections button is selected by default, so when you create a new rule, it will apply to both LAN and remote access connections. If you want the rule to cover only LAN or RAS connections, just select the corresponding radio button.

FIGURE 4.10   The Connection Type tab of the Edit Rule Properties dialog box

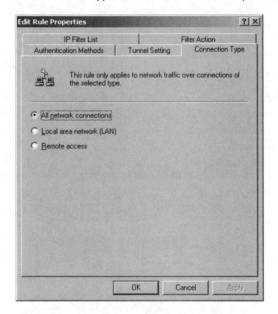

Managing Filter Lists and Actions

Although you can manage IP filter lists and filter actions from the Edit Rule Properties dialog box, it makes more sense to use the management tools provided in the snap-in. This is because the filter lists and actions are stored with the policy, not inside individual rules. The filter lists and actions you create in one policy scope (say, the default domain policy) are available to all policies within that scope.

You can manage filter lists and filter actions using the corresponding tabs in the Edit Rule Properties dialog box, but that obscures the fact that these items are available to any policy. Instead, you can use the Manage IP Filter Lists And Filter Actions command from the pop-up menu (right-click the IP Security Policies item or anywhere in the right-hand pane of the IPSec snap-in). This command displays the Manage IP Filter Lists And Filter Actions dialog box, which has two tabs. Most of the items on these tabs are self-explanatory because they closely resemble the controls you've already seen. In particular, the function of the Add, Edit, and Remove buttons (as well as the Use Add Wizard checkbox) should be evident by this point. Instead of rehashing the controls, let's take a look at the process of defining a new filter list and an action to go with it.

Adding IP Filter Lists and Individual Filters

There are two default IP filters set when you install Windows Server 2003: one for all IP traffic and one for all Internet Control Message Protocol (ICMP) traffic. Let's say that you're a little more selective, though. Perhaps you want to create an IPSec policy to secure web traffic between your company and its law firm. You'd first have to open the Manage IP Filter Lists And Filter Actions dialog box, at which point you'd see the Manage IP Filter Lists tab shown in Figure 4.11.

FIGURE 4.11   The Manage IP Filter Lists tab

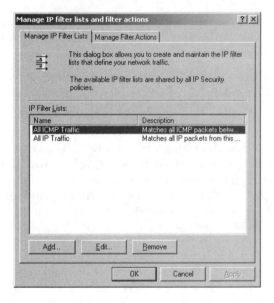

Because filter lists aren't used in order, there's no need to reorder items in the list, though you can add, edit, and remove them. When you edit or add a filter list, you'll see the IP Filter List dialog box (see Figure 4.12). This dialog box allows you to name and describe the filter list and then add, remove, or edit the individual filters that make up the list.

When you edit or add an individual filter, there are three categories of information you need to know:

The source and destination addresses you want the filter to use.   These can be single IP addresses, single DNS names (at any level, so that `hawk.chellis.net`, `chellis.net`, and `.net` are all valid), or IP subnet. There are also special "my" and "any" addresses (e.g., My IP Address, Any IP Address) that you can use to indicate the source and destination.

FIGURE 4.12   The IP Filter List dialog box

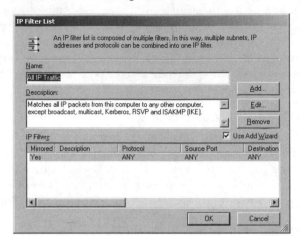

Whether you want the filter to be mirrored.   A *mirrored filter* automatically filters its opposite—if you set up a filter from your IP address to a remote address and configure it to allow only port 80, with mirroring you'll also get a filter that allows traffic from the remote end back to you on port 80.

The protocols and ports to which you want the filter to apply.   You can choose any protocol type (including TCP, UDP, ICMP, EGP, RDP, and RAW), and you can either select individual source and destination ports or use the From Any Port and To Any Port radio buttons we will discuss later.

You use the IP Filter Properties dialog box to get this information into the filter. When you use the Add or Edit buttons in the IP Filter List dialog box, you'll see the Properties dialog box for the appropriate filter (the new one or whichever one you'd selected before clicking the Edit button). This dialog box has three tabs: Description, Addresses, and Protocol. The Description tab is used to name and describe the filter. We will look at the other two tabs in the following sections.

THE ADDRESSES TAB

The Addresses tab (see Figure 4.13) is where you specify the source and destination addresses you want this filter to match. For the source address, you can choose to use the IP address assigned to the IPSec server (My IP Address), any IP address, a specific DNS domain name or IP address, or a specific IP subnet. Likewise for the destination address, you can choose the IPSec computer's address, any IP address, or a specified DNS name, subnet, or IP address. You use these in combination to specify how you want the filter to trigger. For example, you could create a rule that says, "Match any traffic from my address to IP address *a.b.c.d.*" You could also create a rule that does what the All IP Traffic filter does: matches any traffic from your IP address (on any port) to any destination.

You can also use the Mirrored checkbox to specify a reciprocal rule. For example, the mirrored rule of the "All IP Traffic" rule matches traffic coming from any IP address on any port back to your IP address. Mirroring makes it easy to set up filters that cover both inbound and outbound traffic.

FIGURE 4.13   The Addressing tab of the IP Filter Properties dialog box

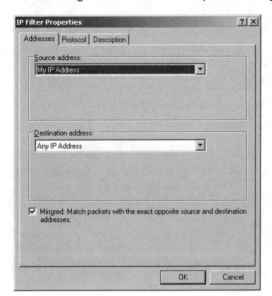

THE PROTOCOL TAB

The Protocol tab (see Figure 4.14) lets you match traffic coming from or sent to a particular port using a specified protocol. This is useful because UDP source port 80 and TCP destination port 80 are entirely different. You use the Select A Protocol Type pull-down menu and the Set The IP Protocol Port control group to specify the protocols and ports you want this filter to match.

FIGURE 4.14   The Protocol tab of the IP Filter Properties dialog box

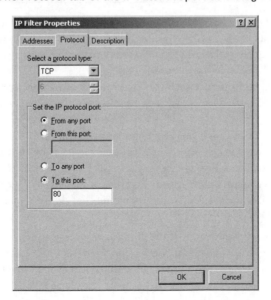

Adding a New Filter Action

The Manage Filter Actions tab (see Figure 4.15) shows you which filter actions are defined in the current group of IPSec policies. You can add, edit, or remove filter actions to meet your needs. As part of Windows Server 2003, you get three filter actions—Permit, Request Security (Optional), and Require Security—that will more than likely meet most of your needs, but it's still a good idea to know how to create policies yourself instead of depending on Microsoft to do it for you.

FIGURE 4.15   The Manage Filter Actions tab

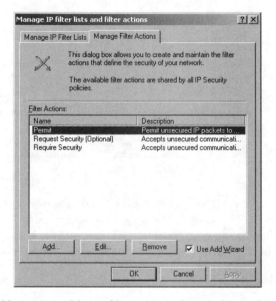

You can use the Add button to add new filter actions that can be used in any policy you define. The Use Add Wizard checkbox is normally checked, so by default you'll get the IP Security Filter Action Wizard. However, let's go through the property pages associated with a filter action so you can see what's in one.

When you click the Add button with the Use Add Wizard checkbox off, the first thing you see is the Security Methods tab of the New Filter Action Properties dialog box (see Figure 4.16).

You use this tab to select which methods you want this filter action to use. In lieu of the permit and block methods, you can select the Negotiate Security radio button to build your own custom security methods, choosing whatever AH and ESP algorithms meet your needs. The three checkboxes under the security methods list control what this IPSec computer will do when confronted with a connection request from a machine that doesn't speak IPSec. The options include the following:

- The Accept Unsecured Communication, But Always Respond Using IPSec checkbox configures this action so that incoming connection requests will always be answered with an IPSec negotiation message. If the other end cannot use IPSec, the computer is allowed to accept the incoming request without any security in place.

FIGURE 4.16   The Security Methods tab of the New Filter Action Properties dialog box

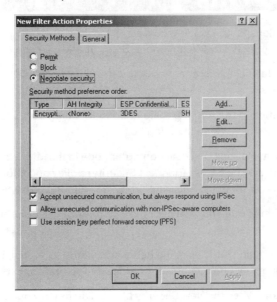

- The Allow Unsecured Communication With Non-IPSec-Aware Computers checkbox configures the action to allow any computer—IPSec capable or not—to communicate. Any machine that can't handle IPSec will get a normal, insecure connection. By default, this box isn't checked; if you check it, you must be certain that your IPSec policies are set up properly. If they're not, some computers that you *think* are using IPSec may connect without security.

- The Use Session Key Perfect Forward Secrecy (PFS) determines whether existing master key keying material can be used to derive a new session key. When session key PFS is enabled, a new Diffie-Hellman key exchange is performed to generate new master key keying material before the new session key is created. Session key PFS does not require main mode reauthentication and uses less resources than master key PFS.

In Exercise 4.2, you assigned the Server (Request Security) policy so that it would always be used. In Exercise 4.3, you'll tweak it some. By default, all IPSec policies you create will be transport mode (as opposed to tunnel mode) policies. This is also true of the default local computer and domain IPSec policies. In this exercise, you'll modify the local computer's Server (Request Security) policy settings to improve its interoperability.

EXERCISE 4.3

Customizing and Configuring the Local Computer IPSec Policy and Rules for Transport Mode

1. Click Start ➢ Run, type **MMC**, and click OK. An empty MMC console window appears.

2. Select the File ➢ Add/Remove Snap-In command. When the Add/Remove Snap-In dialog box appears, click the Add button.

3. In the Add Standalone Snap-In dialog box, scroll through the snap-in list until you see the one marked IP Security Policy Management. Select it and click the Add button.

4. The Select Computer dialog box appears. Select the Local Computer radio button and then click the Finish button.

5. Click the Close button in the Add Standalone Snap-In dialog box, and then click the OK button in the Add/Remove Snap-In dialog box.

6. Select the IP Security Policies On Local Computer node in the MMC. In the right-hand pane of the MMC, right-click the Server (Request Security) policy and choose the Properties command. The Server (Request Security) Properties dialog box appears.

7. Select the All IP Traffic rule and then click the Edit button. The Edit Rule Properties dialog box appears.

8. Switch to the Filter Action tab. Select the Request Security (Optional) filter action and then click the Edit button. The filter action's Properties dialog box appears.

9. Click the Add button. When the New Security Method dialog box appears, click the Custom radio button and then click the Settings button.

10. In the Custom Security Method Settings dialog box, check the Data And Address Integrity Without Encryption (AH) checkbox, and in the drop-down list, select SHA1. Using the drop-down lists under (ESP), set Integrity to SHA1 and Encryption to 3DES.

11. First check the Generate A New Key Every checkbox and set the key generation interval to 24,000 Kbytes. (Kbytes must be in the range 20,480–2,147,483,647Kb.) Then click the next Generate A New Key Every checkbox and specify a key generation interval of 1800 seconds.

12. Click the OK button in the Custom Security Method Settings dialog box and then click OK in the New Security Method dialog box.

13. When the IP Filter Properties dialog box appears, use the Move Up button to move the custom filter you just defined to the top of the list.

14. Click the OK button in the IP Filter Properties dialog box.

15. Click the Close button in the Edit Rule Properties dialog box and then click the OK button in the Server (Request Security) Properties dialog box.

Configuring IPSec for Tunnel Mode

Until now, we've primarily been discussing IPSec in transport mode. As you read earlier, you can also use IPSec in tunnel mode. You can use IPSec tunnels to do a number of useful and interesting things. For example, you can establish a tunnel between two subnets—effectively linking them into an internetwork—without needing to have a private connection between them.

IPSec tunneling isn't intended as a way for clients to establish remote access VPN connections; instead, it's what you'd use to connect your Windows Server 2003 network to a remote device (for instance, a Cisco PIX) that doesn't support L2TP + IPSec or the Point to Point Tunneling Protocol (PPTP). You can also build a tunnel that directly connects two IP addresses.

Either way, you establish the tunnel by building a filter that matches the source and destination IP addresses, just as you would for an ordinary transport mode. You can use ESP and AH on the tunnel to give you an authenticated tunnel (AH only), an encrypted tunnel (ESP only), or a combination of the two. You control this behavior by specifying a filter action and security method. However, when you build a tunnel, you can't filter by port or protocol; the Windows Server 2003 IPSec stack doesn't support it.

To construct a tunnel properly, you actually need two rules on each end: one for inbound traffic and one for outbound traffic. Microsoft warns against using mirroring on tunnel rules. Instead, if you want to link two networks, you'd need to specify settings as the ones shown in Figure 4.17. Each side's rule has two filter lists. The Atlanta filter lists specify a filter for outgoing traffic that has the Seattle router as a tunnel endpoint and then another filter for incoming traffic from any IP subnet that points back to the Atlanta tunnel endpoint. In conjunction with these filter lists, you'd specify a filter action that provided whatever type of security was appropriate for the connection.

FIGURE 4.17   Filter lists for a simple tunnel

Filter list 1:
    Filter from any IP address to specific IP subnet 10.3.*
    Tunnel endpoint of 10.3.1.254
    Authentication and security methods to taste
Filter list 2:
    Filter from specific IP subnet 10.3.* to any IP address
    Tunnel endpoint of 10.1.1.254
    Authentication and security methods to taste

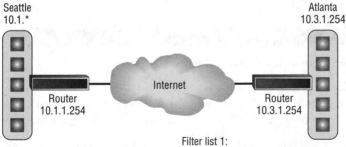

Seattle
10.1.*

Atlanta
10.3.1.254

Internet

Router
10.1.1.254

Router
10.3.1.254

Filter list 1:
    Filter from any IP address to specific IP subnet 10.1.*
    Tunnel endpoint of 10.1.1.254
    Authentication and security methods to taste
Filter list 2:
    Filter from specific IP subnet 10.1.* to any IP address
    Tunnel endpoint of 10.3.1.254
    Authentication and security methods to taste

You specify whether a connection is tunneled or not on a per-rule basis using the Tunnel Setting tab of the Edit Rule Properties dialog box. Select Server (Request Security), right-click, and select Properties. In the Properties dialog box, select the All IP Traffic rule and click Edit Rule Properties dialog box, select the Tunnel Setting tab (see Figure 4.18). The two radio buttons specify whether this rule establishes a tunnel or not. The default button, This Rule Does Not Specify An IPSec Tunnel, is self-explanatory. To enable tunneling with this rule, select The Tunnel Endpoint Is Specified By This IP Address and then fill in the IP address of the remote endpoint.

FIGURE 4.18   The Tunnel Setting tab of the Edit Rule Properties dialog box

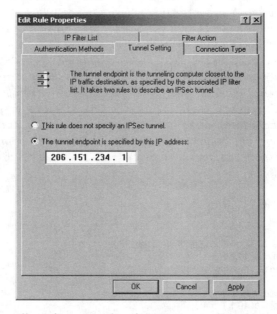

In Exercise 4.4 you will configure a policy for IPSec tunnel mode.

EXERCISE 4.4

Configuring a Policy for IPSec Tunnel Mode

This lab requires you to use two separate machines to which you have administrator access. Let's call them machine A and machine B. Before you start, you'll need their IP addresses, and you'll need to have their local IPSec policies open in an MMC console. First, configure machine A:

1. Right-click the IP Security Policies On Local Computer node, then choose the Create IP Security Policy command. The IP Security Policy Wizard appears. Click Next.

2. Name your policy Tunnel To B and then click the Next button.

3. On the Requests For Secure Communication page, turn off the Activate Default Response Rule checkbox and click the Next button.

EXERCISE 4.4 *(continued)*

4. When the summary page for the wizard appears, make sure the Edit Properties checkbox is on and then click Finish. The Tunnel To B Properties dialog box appears. Click the Add button on the Rules tab. The Welcome To The Create IP Security Rule Wizard begins. Click Next.

5. In the Tunnel Endpoint page of the wizard, select The Tunnel Endpoint Is Specified By The Following IP Address and enter the IP address of machine B. Click Next.

6. In the Network Type page, select Local Area Network (LAN). Click Next.

7. Select the All IP Traffic radio button. Click Next.

8. Select the Request Security (Optional) radio button on the Filter Action page. Click Next.

9. In the Authentication Method page, select Active Directory Default (Kerberos V5 protocol). Click Next.

10. Clear the Edit Properties checkbox, click Finish, then OK.

Now repeat steps 1–10 on machine B, creating rules using the appropriate IP addresses and names (e.g., Tunnel To A, the IP address to machine A) in steps 2–5.

Managing and Monitoring IPSec

Now that you know how to configure IPSec, it's time to learn how to manage and monitor it. The management aspects of IPSec are pretty simple because about 90 percent of your workload will be building filter lists, rules, and filter actions that correctly specify the traffic and hosts you want protected. The remaining 10 percent will be monitoring and troubleshooting the rules we have established.

There are a number of ways you can monitor IPSec on your computers, but the two most useful methods are viewing the security associations and traffic flowing between specific computers in IP Security Monitor and checking the event log for IPSec-related events, as you will see in the following sections.

Using IP Security Monitor

In Windows Server 2003, the IP Security Monitor is implemented as an MMC snap-in. The snap-in allows you to view details about IPSec policy at either the domain or local level and provides you with a way to view main mode and quick mode statistics. In addition, you can view active SAs and execute complex filters.

 You can only use IP Security Monitor to monitor Windows XP or Server 2003.

To begin, you must install the IP Security Monitor in the MMC. Exercise 4.5 shows you how to add the snap-in.

EXERCISE 4.5

Adding the IP Security Monitor to the MMC

1.   Click Start ➢ Run, type **MMC**, and click OK.

2.   Select Add/Remove Snap-In on the File menu and click the Add button.

3.   Select IP Security Monitor in the list of snap-ins and click the Add button. Click Close and then click OK. You should return to the MMC, and the snap-in appears in the left pane.

4.   To save the MMC, select File ➢ Save and specify a name and a location in which to save the console.

The IP Security Monitor snap-in is shown in Figure 4.19. The local computer appears in the IP Security Monitor snap-in by default. If you want to monitor other machines on the network, you can easily add them by right-clicking IP Security Monitor in the left pane and selecting Add Computer. If you are in a domain, you must have administrative privileges for the domain in order to add remote machines to the console window.

FIGURE 4.19   The IP Security Monitor snap-in

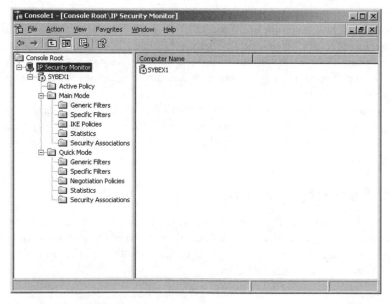

To view the details of the policy assigned to the machine you are monitoring, expand IP Security Monitor, *ServerName*, Active Policy. The policy details as described earlier in this chapter are listed in the right pane, as seen in Figure 4.20.

FIGURE 4.20   Active Policy details

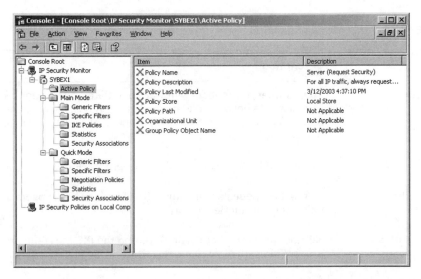

You can also use IP Security Monitor to view IP Security statistics for main mode and quick mode negotiations. To do this, click the Statistics node under either Main Mode or Quick Mode. The various statistics appear in the right pane and display information such as the number of bytes sent and received, send/receive and negotiation or authentication failures, and much more. The main mode statistics are shown in Figure 4.21.

FIGURE 4.21   Main mode statistics

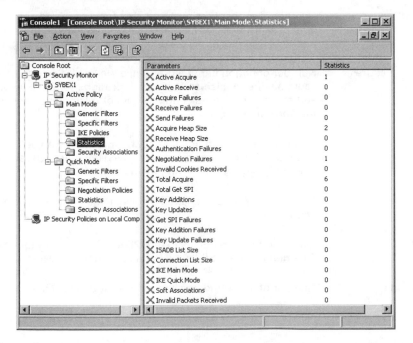

Table 4.1 lists the main mode statistics and what they track.

TABLE 4.1 Main Mode Statistics

Statistic	Description
Active Acquire	The number of requests required to initiate an IKE negotiation to establish SAs between IPSec-enabled machines. Includes the current request and any requests waiting in line (typically 0 unless the load is particularly high).
Active Receive	Number of IKE messages waiting for processing.
Acquire Failures	Number of requests to establish SAs between IPSec peers that have failed since last IPSec restart.
Receive Failures	Number of errors that occurred during the IKE message receive process since the last IPSec restart.
Send Failures	Number of outbound IKE messages that failed since the last IPSec restart.
Acquire Heap Size	Number of successful outbound requests for SAs between IPSec peers.
Receive Heap Size	Number of successful incoming IKE messages.
Authentication Failures	Number of authentication errors that have occurred since the last IPSec restart. Errors could be due to mismatched authentication methods or misconfigured authentication method configuration.
Negotiation Failures	Number of negotiation failures since the last IPSec restart. Failures could be due to mismatched authentication methods, incorrect authentication method configuration, or mismatched security methods or settings.
Invalid Cookies Received	Number of cookies that could not be matched to an active main mode SA. Cookies are stored in received IKE messages and are used to identify the corresponding main mode SA.
Total Acquire	Total number of requests to establish a main mode SA since IPSec was restarted.
Total Get SPI	Total number of requests to the IPSec driver for a unique Security Parameters Index (SPI), which matches inbound packets with SAs.
Key Additions	Number of outbound quick mode SAs added to the IPSec driver.
Key Updates	Number of inbound quick mode SAs added to the IPSec driver.

TABLE 4.1   Main Mode Statistics *(continued)*

Statistic	Description
Get SPI Failures	Number of failed requests to the IPSec driver for a unique SPI.
Key Addition Failures	Number of failed outbound quick mode SAs added to the IPSec driver.
Key Update Failures	Number of failed inbound quick mode SAs added to the IPSec driver.
ISADB List Size	Total number of successful main mode entries, pending main mode negotiations, and failed or expired main mode negotiations.
Connection List Size	Number of pending quick mode negotiations.
IKE Main Mode	Total number of successful SAs that have been created in main mode since last IPSec restart.
IKE Quick Mode	Total number of successful SAs that have been created in quick mode since last IPSec restart.
Soft Associations	Number of SAs created with non-IPSec-enabled machines but allowed by the computer's policy to communicate. Soft associations are not IPSec secure.
Invalid Packets Received	Number of IKE messages with invalid header fields, incorrect payload lengths, or incorrect cookie values. Usually the result of retransmitted IKE messages or mismatched preshared keys.

Table 4.2 lists the quick mode statistics and what they track.

TABLE 4.2   Quick Mode Statistics

Statistic	Description
Active Security Associations	Total number of active quick mode SAs.
Offloaded Security Associations	Total number of active quick mode SAs accelerated by special hardware, such as a NIC that supports SA acceleration.
Pending Key Operations	Number of IPSec key exchanges that have been queued but not completed.
Key Additions	Number of successful quick mode SAs added since last restart.
Key Deletions	Number of successful quick mode SAs deleted since last restart.

TABLE 4.2 Quick Mode Statistics *(continued)*

Statistic	Description
Rekeys	Total number of rekeyed quick mode SAs since last restart.
Active Tunnels	Number of active IPSec tunnels.
Bad SPI Packets	Total number of packets affected by a bad SPI since the last restart. Usually this means that a packet is attempting to use an expired SA. This statistic could be high if rekey intervals are short and the number of SAs is great or during a packet spoofing attack.
Packets Not Decrypted	Number of packets that failed to decrypt since the last restart. This could happen if a packet fails a validation check.
Packets Not Authenticated	Number of packets whose source could not be verified by the computer. High values could indicate packet spoofing, modification attack, or corruption by network devices.
Packets With Replay Detection	Number of packets with an invalid sequence number since the last restart.
Confidential Bytes Sent	Total number of bytes sent that were encrypted under ESP.
Confidential Bytes Received	Total number of bytes received that were encrypted under ESP.
Authenticated Bytes Sent	Total number of bytes sent that were authenticated under AH or ESP.
Authenticated Bytes Received	Total number of bytes received that were authenticated under AH or ESP.
Transport Bytes Sent	Total number of bytes sent in transport mode since last restart.
Transport Bytes Received	Total number of bytes received in transport mode since last restart.
Bytes Sent In Tunnels	Total number of bytes sent in tunnel mode since last restart.
Bytes Received In Tunnels	Total number of bytes received in tunnel mode since last restart.
Offloaded Bytes Sent	Total number of bytes sent with hardware offload since last restart.
Offloaded Bytes Received	Total number of bytes received with hardware offload since last restart.

IP Security Monitor is also useful for viewing the filters that apply to the machine that you are monitoring. Without the IP Security Monitor, it can be difficult to remember which filters apply to which machines. You can easily determine the nature of the filters on your network by clicking the Generic Filters and Specific Filters nodes under the Main Mode and Quick Mode categories. The filters appear in the right window pane along with several details such as the filter name, source, destination, and so forth. The Details displayed relate to the topics discussed in setting up the IPSec parameters in this chapter.

Finally, IP Security Monitor displays the policies and SAs of the computer that you are monitoring. You can double-click a policy to see the AH and ESP types that are in use, as well as the key lifetimes and PFS settings for each method. The Security Associations node is useful for troubleshooting communications between two computers. You should ensure that the server's IP address is listed in the Me column and that the client's IP address is listed in the Peer column. If not, the SA is invalid.

Using Event Logging

If you turn on auditing for logon events and object access, you'll get a wealth of logged information in the Event Viewer that can be very useful when you're trying to troubleshoot a problem. In particular, IPSec logs events when it establishes a security association. Those event messages tell you what policy, filter, and filter actions were used, plus which security methods were active on the connection. Table 4.3 lists the most common event log messages you'll see and describes what they mean.

TABLE 4.3   Interesting IPSec Event Log Messages

Event ID	Appears In	Description
279	System log	Generated by the IPSec Policy Agent; shows which policy was installed and from where it came.
284	System log	Generated by the IPSec Policy Agent; appears when the agent can't fetch a policy.
541	Security log	Indicates that an IPSec SA was established.
542	Security log	Indicates that an IPSec SA was closed. This happens when you terminate a connection to a remote machine. (May also appear as event 543, depending on the type of SA.)
547	Security log	Indicates that IPSec SA negotiation failed, so no SA could be established.

In Exercise 4.6, you'll turn on auditing for logon events and object access. In order to see anything in the log, you'll need at least two IPSec-capable machines that can talk to each other.

It doesn't matter which of these two machines you use to do this exercise provided that you have administrative access to it.

EXERCISE 4.6

Monitoring IPSec Logon Activity

If you are using a domain controller, you should load the console you saved in Exercise 4.2 and skip steps 2 through 5 of this exercise. If you are running a stand-alone or workgroup server, then proceed normally.

1. Click Start ➢ Run, type **MMC**, and click OK. An empty MMC console window appears.

2. Select File ➢ Add/Remove Snap-In. When the Add/Remove Snap-In dialog box appears, click the Add button.

3. In the Add Standalone Snap-In dialog box, scroll through the snap-in list until you see the one marked Group Policy Object Editor. Select it and click the Add button.

4. The Select Group Policy Object dialog box appears. Leave Local Computer set as the focus and click the Finish button.

5. Click the Close button in the Add Standalone Snap-In dialog box and then click the OK button in the Add/Remove Snap-In dialog box.

6. Find and select the Audit Policy folder (Local Computer [or domain] Policy, Computer Configuration, Windows Settings, Security Settings, Local Policies, Audit Policy).

7. Double-click the Audit Logon Events entry. When the Local Security Policy Setting dialog box appears, check the Success and Failure checkboxes and then click the OK button.

8. Double-click the Audit Object Access entry. When the Local Security Policy Setting dialog box appears, check the Success and Failure checkboxes and then click the OK button.

9. Establish an IPSec connection from the *other* machine to the one whose local security policy you just modified.

10. Examine the event log and ascertain whether the IPSec negotiation succeeded or failed.

Monitoring IPSec Activity in Network Monitor

You saw how to use Network Monitor back in Chapter 2. In that chapter, you learned how to examine IP activity on your computer. Network Monitor also includes parsers for the ISAKMP (IKE), AH, and ESP protocols. When you examine captured data in Network Monitor, look for "ISAKMP", "AH", or "ESP" in the protocol column. If they aren't present, then you can be sure that no IPSec policy is enabled on your computer. If the protocols are listed, you can double-click them to display the IPSec activity that you captured in more detail.

The Network Monitor parsers for ESP can parse inside the ESP packet only if null-encryption is being used and the full ESP packet is captured. Network Monitor cannot parse the encrypted portions of IPSec-secured ESP traffic when encryption is performed in software. However, if encryption is being performed by an IPSec hardware offload network adapter, the ESP packets are decrypted when Network Monitor captures them and as a result, can be parsed and interpreted into the upper-layer protocols. If you need to diagnose ESP software-encrypted communication, you must disable ESP encryption and use ESP-null encryption by changing the IPSec policy on both computers.

Troubleshooting IPSec

Troubleshooting IPSec can be tricky. Microsoft's online help does a good job of explaining the various ins and outs, but the basic principles aren't that hard to understand. First, of course, you need to verify that you have basic, unsecured TCP/IP connectivity to the remote system. Because IPSec operates atop IP and UDP, if you can't get regular IP datagrams to the destination, you won't be able to get IPSec packets there either. That means you need to perform all the standard connectivity and name resolution tests (including making sure the network cable's plugged in!) before you dive into IPSec troubleshooting. The following sections provide an overview of the additional steps you can take to diagnose IPSec problems.

Identifying Common IPSec Issues

The most common issue associated with IPSec is that the two computers cannot communicate over the secured connection. You can perform some basic steps to help alleviate any problems that might arise:

- Stop IPSec on both computers and attempt a ping from both ends. If the ping is not successful, then there is something wrong with the underlying connection. Otherwise, the source of the problem is most likely the IPSec configuration.

- Restart the IPSec Policy Agent and use the IP Security Monitor to confirm that the two machines have matching SAs.

- Use the IPSec Policy Management tool to ensure that the IPSec policies are assigned to both computers and that they are compatible with each other.

Verifying That the Right Policy Is Assigned

If you don't have an IPSec policy assigned, or if you have the wrong one in place, your communication efforts may fail. There are several ways to check the policy to see whether it's the right one or not:

- Check the event log for event ID 279; that's the IPSec Policy Agent's way of telling you what policy it has applied.

- Check main mode in IP Security Monitor to determine if a security association was established and then check the Statistics folder, paying close attention to any failures (negotiation failures, authentication failures, acquire failures, send failures, etc.).

- Look in the appropriate Group Policy Object (including the local computer policy) to see whether an IPSec policy is assigned. The IPSec snap-in will warn you that a group policy–based IPSec policy is assigned when you try to edit local policies on a computer.

Checking for Policy Mismatches

If you have policies applied on each end but you still can't establish a connection, it's possible that the policies don't match. To verify whether or not this is the case, review the event log and look for event ID 547. If you find any, read the descriptive text carefully because it can give you great clues. Make sure that the authentication and security methods used in the two policies have at least one setting in common.

Summary

The following topics were covered in this chapter:

- How IPSec provides increased network security by providing or requiring authentication and/or encryption over the normal IP protocol.

- How to install the IPSec management snap-in and configure IPSec policies.

- How to use the built-in security policies: Server (Request Security), Client (Respond Only) and Server (Require Security).

- How to build your own custom security policies and filters.

- How to monitor IPSec using IP Security Monitor, the Event Viewer, and Network Monitor.

- How to troubleshoot IPSec by verifying that the right policy is assigned and checking for policy mismatches.

Exam Essentials

Understand how IPSec works.   IPSec operates at the Network layer, and users and applications never need to be aware of whether or not their traffic is being carried over a secure connection. IPSec primarily provides two services: a way for computers to decide whether they trust each other (authentication) and a way to keep network data private (encryption). The Windows Server 2003 implementation of IPSec explicitly supports the idea of policy-based security.

Know how to install IPSec.   The components necessary for a Windows 2000, XP, or Server 2003 machine to act as an IPSec client are installed by default when you install Windows Server 2003. However—also by default—there's no policy that requires the use of IPSec, so the default behavior for these Windows machines is to not use it. You don't really have to install IPSec; you just need to install the tool you use to manage it and then start assigning policies and filters to get the desired effect. IPSec is managed through the IP Security Policy Management snap-in.

Know how to create and configure IPSec policies. You can configure IPSec by modifying the default policies, creating your own policies that embody the rules and filters you want to use, and controlling how policies get applied to computers in your management scope. You can create new policies by right-clicking the IP Security Policies folder in the snap-in and choosing the New IP Security Policy command. You can customize a policy with the policy's Properties dialog box, where you can add, remove, and manage rules, filter lists, and security actions.

Know how to manage filter lists. You can manage filter lists and filter actions by using the corresponding tabs in the Edit Rule Properties dialog box, but that obscures the fact that these items are available to any policy. You can instead use the Manage IP Filter Lists And Filter Actions command from the pop-up menu. This command displays the Manage IP Filter Lists And Filter Actions dialog box.

Know how to configure IPSec for tunnel mode. You establish the tunnel by building a filter that matches the source and destination IP addresses, just as you would for an ordinary transport mode. You can use ESP and AH on the tunnel to give you an authenticated tunnel (AH only), an encrypted tunnel (ESP only), or a combination of the two. You control this behavior by specifying a filter action and security method. To properly construct a tunnel, you need two rules on each end: one for inbound traffic and one for outbound traffic.

Know how to monitor IPSec. IP Security Monitor is now the preferred troubleshooting tool in IPSec. Know how to determine if a security association was established and if the association is receiving errors in transmission or reception. Know how to enable IPSec logging. IPSec logs events when it establishes a security association, and you can examine the event log to view IPSec statistics and auditing. Know the IPSec command-line tool that is now included as a switch in `netsh`.

Know how to troubleshoot IPSec. First, you need to verify that you have basic, unsecured TCP/IP connectivity to the remote system. Also, if you don't have an IPSec policy assigned, or if you have the wrong one in place, your communication efforts may fail. Finally, if you have policies applied on each end but you still can't establish a connection, it's possible that the policies don't match.

Key Terms

Before you take the exam, be certain you are familiar with the following terms:

authentication	default response rule
authentication header (AH)	Encapsulating Security Payload (ESP)
certificates	encryption

end-to-end mode

filter actions

filter lists

Internet Protocol Security
Extensions (IPSec)

IPSec client

IPSec Policy Agent

IPSec server

Kerberos

machine certificates

mirrored filter

passthrough action

preshared keys

security association (SA)

security method

transport mode

tunnel endpoint

tunnel mode

Review Questions

1. Your employer, Miracle Wonder Software and Development Company, has a Windows Server 2003 network that supports 30 development engineers and 25 administrative people, including accounting, human resources, and management staff. There are also 10 salespeople, who have been trying to sell Miracle Wonder's products to first-time customers. The startup atmosphere has attracted many competent people, but the company's recent attempts to cut costs has made the climate less attractive for a significant number of employees. Because you are concerned that your software code is less than secure, you implement IPSec for all the developers and their storage server. Everything works fine in terms of accessing the files, but you want to ensure that the IPSec is working properly on your network. How should you do that?

   A. Check IP Security Monitor Main Mode, Security Associations to ensure that an SA was established and then check Main Mode, Statistics to ensure that the association is free of errors.

   B. Run System Monitor to analyze the IPSec traffic, and make sure that it is encrypted.

   C. Run `ipsecview` to start the IP Security Viewer and view IPSec statistics.

   D. Run the L2TP monitor to check for the tunneled IPSec encryption.

2. You administer a network that contains 200 Windows 2000 and XP Professional machines and 10 Windows Server 2003 machines. One of the Windows Server 2003 computers, named CLASS1, contains highly classified information, so you decide to implement IPSec on that machine. Management wants you to monitor CLASS1 frequently to ensure that data never enters the wrong hands. Which of the following actions would allow you to monitor IPSec on CLASS1?

   A. Use System Monitor to monitor key exchange traffic.

   B. Use Network Monitor to analyze network traffic.

   C. Load IP Security Monitor in an MMC window and point it to the computer named CLASS1.

   D. Use Computer Management to verify IPSec policy assignment.

3. You have gone to great lengths to secure your network by using firewalls, secured routers, and strong remote access authentication. You also have built a thorough physical security system in which all the users need badges to enter the facilities and each door that a badge opens is tracked and reported. Although you feel comfortable that the perimeter of the network is secure, you still have extremely sensitive information on your network that is passed among various employees. You want to make certain that no one on the inside of the network can capture any packets on the wire and read any of the data. What IPSec component do you need to employ in order to achieve this objective?

   A. AH authentication

   B. IPSec packet filtering

   C. ESP encryption

   D. AH encryption

4. Joanne wants to change the interval at which her default domain IPSec policy is refreshed from the standard 3 hours to 24 hours. To implement this change, which of the following should she do?

    A. Right-click the policy and use the Change Refresh Time command.

    B. Open the General tab of the policy's Properties dialog box and adjust the Check For Policy Changes Every field.

    C. Open the Schedule tab of the policy's Properties dialog box and adjust the Check For Policy Changes field.

    D. Use a scheduled job to stop and restart the IPSec Policy Agent service.

5. Your company has government contracts for collecting economic information that's used to create reports, which in turn are used in congressional reports. Your company obtains this information from various contracted organizations in many countries and then collates it. It's extremely important that the information received by your company is verified as coming from each of the contracted organizations. You have implemented IPSec to secure the information. When you configure IPSec, how can you ensure that the information is coming from the appropriate sources?

    A. Configure AH to provide authentication of the source of each IP packet.

    B. Configure AH to provide encryption of the IP packets.

    C. Configure ESP to provide encryption of the IP payload.

    D. Configure ESP to provide authentication of the IP payload.

6. Malik has been assigned the task of building an IPSec rule that will secure all HTTP traffic sent to a particular external site. Which of the following is the best way to accomplish this?

    A. Create a new policy that specifies the external site as a destination and uses the All IP Traffic IP filter list and the Require Security action.

    B. Enable the Request Security (Optional) policy.

    C. Enable the Require Security policy.

    D. Create a new policy that specifies the external site as a destination and uses a custom filter list for source and destination port 80 on the TCP protocol.

7. The security and integrity of the data on your native mode Windows Server 2003 network is of paramount importance to the management of your company. You have seven locations that communicate with each other frequently, and all of them use their access to the Internet on a regular basis. You have been charged with securing the traffic in all communications among the managers and executive staff of the company. To accomplish this, you plan to implement IPSec to provide the authentication and encryption of the specified communications. What will you need to change in order for IPSec to function properly across your network?

   A. Modify the applications on the network that the managers and executives use to support IPSec.

   B. Upgrade the managers' and executives' NIC cards to support IPSec.

   C. Upgrade the router software to pass the IPSec traffic to the other locations.

   D. Enable IPSec on your computers to accept IPSec connections from other computers.

8. Marie is trying to isolate an IPSec failure on an otherwise working network. She checks the event log and finds event ID 547,which is a record of the failure. From this log, which probable cause can Marie establish?

   A. Negotiation failed because there is a policy mismatch between the two computers.

   B. The IPSec Policy Agent cannot fetch a policy.

   C. An IPSec SA was closed.

   D. An IPSec SA was not established.

9. You have just been informed that your company has signed a contract with another company to complete a joint Windows Server 2003 application software development project. This project is going to involve a great deal of source-code sharing between the two organizations, and there is considerable concern about protecting the communications between the companies. Both companies are running Windows Server 2003 in native mode, and both have enabled IPSec to ensure the security of data transfers. Both companies want to control the IPSec security protocols and limit IPSec communication between the two company networks. Your company's domain is panacea.com, and the other company's domain is hearth.com. You create a security filter with the source of panacea.com and a destination of hearth.com. The administrator of hearth .com creates a security filter with a source of hearth.com and a destination of panacea.com. When you test the connection, the IPSec negotiation process fails, and the traffic is not secured. What is the most likely cause of this problem?

   A. The companies are running different service packs that relate to IPSec.

   B. Nothing. The users need to choose when to transfer data using IPSec.

   C. Both inbound and outbound filters have not been created.

   D. The configuration of your security filters is the opposite of what it should be.

10. You administer a small domain consisting of a single domain controller running Windows Server 2003, a Windows Server 2003 member server that doubles as a remote access server and a file store, 500 clients running Windows XP Professional, and several remote users running a wide variety of operating systems. You must ensure that all communication with the DC is secure, and you would prefer that all internal communication with the member server be secure. Communication among the local clients and between the remote users and the member server does not necessarily need to be secure. Drag the default IPSec policies to the correct location within the network. Note that some options may be used more than once and some options might not be used at all.

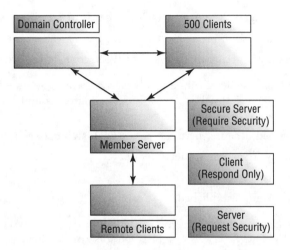

11. Staff members in your human resources department are becoming increasingly concerned about liability surrounding the privacy of employee information. They have sound policies in place to control access to information such as health, salary, and other personal data, but they have learned that if information gets out and it wasn't secured properly, the company could be liable for damages. It's your job to make sure the HR and accounting systems are secure when HR employees are moving information around. However, those systems must remain open to staff in other departments. You immediately implement IPSec on the HR and accounting servers and on the machines of the employees in those two departments. To allow regular connections to the servers from the other departments and at the same time require IPSec connections from the machines that deal with the confidential information, what security filter actions should you specify? (Choose all that apply.)

    A. Permit

    B. Block

    C. Accept Unsecured Communication, But Always Respond Using IPSec

    D. Allow Unsecured Communication With Non-IPSec Aware Computers

    E. Use These Security Settings

12. You want to set up an IPSec tunnel between two sites in different cities. How should you use filter lists at each site?

A. Each site should have two filter lists. One list should specify for outbound traffic a filter that points back to itself as the endpoint, and the other list should specify for inbound traffic a filter that has the other site as an endpoint.

B. Each site should have one filter list that specifies for outbound traffic a filter that has the other site as an endpoint and for inbound traffic a filter that points back to itself as the endpoint.

C. Each site should have two filter lists. One list should specify for outbound traffic a filter that has the other site as an endpoint, and the other list should specify inbound traffic a filter for that points back to itself as the endpoint.

D. Each site should have one filter list that specifies for outbound traffic a filter that points back to itself as the endpoint and for inbound traffic a filter that has the other site as an endpoint.

13. You have been told to implement a strong security infrastructure for your hospital in preparation for the government-required HIPPA regulations. You have a secure perimeter with a firewall and access control lists on your routers. However, the only security in place on your internal LAN is the access control lists on your Windows 2003 Servers that are providing applications and data. In addition, you have basic password-protected applications that are running on mainframes and Unix machines in the hospital. Where you do not have security is on the wire throughout your network. You put a plan in place to implement IPSec so that it will provide authentication and encryption for packets going over the wire. However, you don't want to break any applications or prevent access to any applications anywhere in the hospital until you have demonstrated that IPSec can work across all the platforms within the hospital. With this in mind, you enable IPSec on all your Windows 2003 Servers and workstations and then begin to implement IPSec on the other platforms within the hospital to test interoperability. Which Microsoft prebuilt policies should you assign to the Windows Server 2003 machines until you have fully tested IPSec interoperability?

A. Client (Respond Only)

B. Secure Server (Require Security)

C. Server (Request Security)

D. Client (Request Only)

14. You are the administrator of a Windows Server 2003 network in a top-secret security organization that communicates sensitive information (as opposed to secret information) with another top-secret security organization on a need-to-know basis through a semipublic network. The information that you send to the other organization needs to be authenticated and encrypted. The same is true for the information that you receive from it. In addition, neither organization wants any information about the identity of the other side to be transmitted across the network connection. The technical staffs of the organizations put together a plan based on IPSec in order to provide the necessary security for the communications. What IPSec authentication method should they use to meet the requirements?

    A. Kerberos version 5

    B. Public/private key from a certificate authority

    C. Preshared key

    D. Kerberos version 4

15. You work as a system administrator for a small business incorporating two Windows Server 2003 computers, one of which is configured as a domain controller, and 100 Windows XP Professional workstations. You must ensure that all communication between all computers is secure. You configure Group Policy in Active Directory so that all of the clients use customized security policies. After you do this, all communication between the clients and the servers fails. You open Network Monitor on the domain controller and capture network activity for the local computer. What protocols should you examine in the log to begin to diagnose IPSec activity? Choose all that apply.

    A. ISAKMP

    B. AH

    C. NBT

    D. ESP

Answers to Review Questions

1. A.   IP Security Monitor is the main troubleshooting tool in IPSec. It will determine if a security association was established and whether the association was error free.

2. C.   Because IP Security Monitor is a snap-in, it can be pointed to a local machine or any remote machine in the system. You require administrative privileges to accomplish any of these tasks.

3. C.   Encapsulating Security Payload (ESP) provides confidentiality by encrypting the payload (data) in each packet that transverses the network. ESP also provides other benefits, such as authentication and integrity, by signing the payload and providing dedicated sequence numbers. The main benefit in this scenario is that the payload cannot be viewed. AH authentication is used to ensure that the packet received is from the person or machine from whom you expected the packet; it protects against spoofing. AH by itself doesn't provide encryption. Packet filtering is used to control basic communication and prevent denial of service attacks or undesirable paths.

4. B.   The Check For Policy Changes Every field on the General tab specifies how often the IPSec Policy Agent should look for and redownload policy settings.

5. A.   Using AH with ESP provides authentication and encryption to ensure that the data you are receiving has not been seen by any unauthorized eyes, has not been tampered with by anyone, and is from the person you expected. AH provides authentication and a signature to grant integrity for the entire packet, but it doesn't provide encryption. ESP encrypts the data in the packet. It also offers signature and authentication for the actual data. AH and ESP together virtually ensure that the packet received is from the appropriate person, that the data in the packet is from that person, and that no one has altered the packet or seen the information inside. However, the question specifically asks how you can ensure that "information is coming from the appropriate sources," so the only truly correct answer is A.

6. D.   The method described in option A will secure other types of traffic. The method in option B may fail to establish a secure connection to the target site. The method in option C will shut down all non-IPSec communication to all destinations. Option D will specify the external site and secure all of the HTTP traffic between both sites.

7. D.   The components necessary for a Windows Server 2003 machine to act as an IPSec client are installed by default. However, also by default, the policy required for using IPSec is not turned on, and so it lies dormant. You enable IPSec through the IP Security Policy Management snap-in and choose to use it to manage local IPSec policy, your domain, or the policy of another domain. IPSec works at the Network layer, and applications are no more aware of using IPSec than they would be aware of using any lower-level OSI component. If the NICs or routers support IP—and virtually all of them do—then they will support IPSec.

8. A.   The presence of event ID 547 indicates that negotiation failed. Marie should make sure that the authentication and security methods used in the two policies have at least one setting in common.

9. **C.** You need inbound and outbound filters for both domains, and only outbound filters have been created. You also need to create an inbound security filter for `panacea.com` with a source of `hearth.com` and a destination of `panacea.com`. In addition, the administrator of `hearth.com` needs to create an inbound security filter with a source of `panacea.com` and a destination of `hearth.com`. Service packs could be an issue in the future, and they should always be watched. But service packs are not an issue in this specific situation and are certainly not the most likely source of the problem. Users and applications are entirely unaware of IPSec and don't need to take any action to utilize it. The outbound filters are configured appropriately.

10.

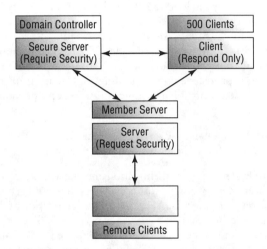

The DC requires secure communication at all times, so you should use the Secure Server (Require Security) default policy on the DC. The member server should use a secure connection whenever possible, so you should apply the Server (Request Security) default policy. The clients should use secure connections with the DC and the member server, but when communicating amongst themselves they don't require security at all, so you should select the Client (Respond Only) default policy. You have very little control over the remote clients, so you shouldn't count on assigning them any particular default policy.

11. **C, E.** An Accept Unsecured Communication, But Always Respond Using IPSec action will always request an IPSec connection before it allows an unsecured request. If all the machines that process confidential information are configured to use IPSec, these connections will be secure. The Use These Security Settings action lets you customize the behavior of the server, and you could, of course, configure it to work in the Accept Unsecured manner. An Allow Unsecured Communication With Non-IPSec Aware Computers action means that the computer does not prefer IPSec and will not request an IPSec connection unless it's requested by the client. A Permit action tells the IPSec filter to take no action. The Block action prevents remote systems from making any type of connection.

12. **C.** Each side needs two filter lists: one for inbound traffic and one for outbound traffic.

13. C.   Server (Request Security) is a combination of Client (Respond Only) and Secure Server (Require Security). This policy will always attempt to use IPSec by requesting it when it connects to a remote machine and by allowing IPSec when an incoming connection requests it. This will give you flexibility as you enable IPSec on the other machines because it will allow communication even if IPSec is not utilized. Client (Respond Only) will attempt an IPSec negotiation if the other machine requests it, but it will never attempt it on its own outward-bound connections. Keep in mind that *client* in this context is not necessarily a computer workstation; it only refers to the machine that is initiating the connection. Secure Server (Require Security) specifies that all IP communication must use IPSec. Obviously, this will have an impact on a network that is not completely IPSec enabled and interoperable. Client (Request Only) is not a valid option.

14. B.   A certificate from a valid CA provides the necessary authentication and also maintains the identity of the computer that is initiating the connection. Coordination is required between the technical staffs to agree on the certificate configuration. If Kerberos authentication is used, the computer identity is unencrypted until encryption of the entire identity payload takes place during the authentication process, thus leaving the identity exposed. A preshared key should be used for interoperability testing and must be entered manually into the IPSec policy and stored there unencrypted.

15. A, B, D.   In Network Monitor IPSec activity appears as ISAKMP, AH, or ESP under the protocol column of the capture display. If none of these protocols are present, then the server probably doesn't have an IPSec policy assigned to it. If ISAKMP appears but AH and ESP do not, then the client and server policies probably do not match.

Managing the Dynamic Host Configuration Protocol (DHCP)

MICROSOFT EXAM OBJECTIVES COVERED IN THIS CHAPTER:

✓ **Manage DHCP**

- ▪ Manage DHCP clients and leases.
- ▪ Manage DHCP databases.
- ▪ Manage DHCP scope options.
- ▪ Manage reservations and reserved clients.

✓ **Troubleshoot DHCP**

- ▪ Diagnose and resolve issues related to DHCP authorization.
- ▪ Verify DHCP reservation configuration.
- ▪ Examine the system event log and DHCP server audit log files to find related events.
- ▪ Diagnose and resolve issues related to configuration of DHCP server and scope options.
- ▪ Verify database integrity.

In Chapter 2, we briefly discussed the Dynamic Host Configuration Protocol (DHCP) and how to configure DHCP clients. Planning for and using DHCP in Windows Server 2003 is pretty straightforward, but there's a lot you need to know to make sure your installation proceeds without trouble.

In this chapter, you'll learn how to install and manage DHCP, including how to set up plain DHCP scopes, superscopes, and multicast scopes. You'll also learn how to set up integration between Dynamic DNS and DHCP as well as how to authorize a DHCP server to integrate with Active Directory.

Overview of DHCP

DHCP's job is to centralize the process of IP address and option assignment. Simply put, you can configure a DHCP server with a range of addresses and other configuration information and let it assign IP parameters like addresses, default gateways, DNS server addresses, and so on. DHCP is defined by a series of Request for Comments (RFCs), notably 1533, 1534, 1541, and 1542. In brief, here is the DHCP process:

1. When TCP/IP starts up on a DHCP-enabled client, a special message is sent out requesting an IP address and a subnet mask from a DHCP server.

2. Any DHCP server that hears the request checks its internal database and replies with a message containing the information the client requested. The contents of this message vary depending on how the DHCP server is configured—there are numerous pieces of information that you can specify to pass to the client on a Windows Server 2003 DHCP server.

3. When the client accepts the IP offer, the address is then extended to the client for a specified period of time, called a *lease*. If the DHCP server has given out all the IP addresses in its range, it won't make an offer; if no other servers make an offer, the client's TCP/IP initialization will fail.

In the following sections, we will examine the advantages and disadvantages of DHCP and take a closer look at the DHCP process.

Advantages and Disadvantages of DHCP

DHCP was designed from the start to simplify network management. It has some significant advantages, such as the following:

- DHCP capability is bundled with Windows Server 2003, so adding it to your network doesn't cost anything extra.

- Once you enter the IP configuration information in one place—the server—it's automatically propagated to clients, eliminating the chance that a user will misconfigure some parameters and require you to fix them.

- Configuration problems are minimized, clearing up a labyrinth of possible situations that lead to big messes and obscure, hard-to-find problems.

- IP addresses are conserved because DHCP assigns them only when a client requests one.

- IP configuration becomes almost completely Plug and Play. In most cases, you can plug in a new system (or move one) and then watch as it receives a configuration from the server.

Unfortunately, there are a few actual and potential drawbacks of DHCP:

- Not all DHCP client implementations work properly with Windows Server 2003's DHCP server.

- If you put incorrect information into your DHCP server, it will automatically be delivered to all of your DHCP clients, meaning you may have to visit each machine and reconfigure it.

- It can become a single point of failure for your network. If you only have one DHCP server and it's not available, clients won't be able to request or renew leases.

- If you want to use DHCP on a multisegment network, you must either put a DHCP server or relay agent on each segment or ensure that your router can forward Bootstrap Protocol (BootP) broadcasts.

The DHCP Lease Process

The DHCP lease process is a pretty simple. There are four stages involved:

1. DHCP discovery
2. DHCP lease offer
3. DHCP Lease request
4. DHCP lease acknowledgment

At the end of the process (and if all goes well), the client will have an IP address and whatever other parameters the DHCP server owner wanted to supply. Because an IP address is required to communicate with other devices on a TCP/IP network, the DHCP negotiation happens very early in the Windows boot cycle.

Each network adapter in a system has its own IP address; if you have multiple NICs that are configured to use DHCP, in the following sections you'll see the lease process occurring for each DHCP-aware NIC.

In the following sections, we will discuss each of the stages of the DHCP lease process, as well as the details of the lease renewal and lease release processes. In addition, you will see how to renew and release a lease, and we'll take a closer look at some `ipconfig` switches that are particularly useful in the context of DHCP.

Step 1: DHCP Discovery

The first step in the DHCP lease process is the *discovery* stage. It's triggered the first time a client's DHCP-configured TCP/IP stack starts or when you switch from using an assigned IP address to using DHCP. It can also occur when a specific IP address is requested but unavailable or immediately after a formerly used IP address is released.

At the time of the lease request, the client doesn't know what its IP address is, nor does it know the IP address of the server. To work around this, the client uses 0.0.0.0 as its address and 255.255.255.255 for the server's address. It then sends out a broadcast *DHCP discover message* on UDP port 68 and destination port 67. The discover message contains the hardware MAC address and NetBIOS name of the client.

Once the first discover message is sent, the client waits 1 second for an offer. If no DHCP server responds within that time, the client repeats its request four more times at 2-, 4-, 8-, and 16-second (plus a random amount of time from 0 to 1000 milliseconds) intervals. If the client still doesn't get a response, it will revert to Automatic Private IP Addressing (APIPA) and continue to broadcast discover messages every 5 minutes until it gets an answer. With APIPA, the Windows client will automatically pick what it thinks is an unused address (from the 169.254.*x.y* address block) instead of waiting indefinitely for an answer. Even though an address has been assigned, the DHCP client will continuously poll every 5 minutes for a DHCP server and then switch back to using a DHCP-assigned address when the server becomes available.

 You'll recall from Chapter 2 that the discover message broadcasts won't be heard outside the client's local subnet unless your routers support BootP forwarding or the DHCP relay agent, which is discussed in more detail in Chapter 7.

Step 2: DHCP Lease Offer

In the second phase of the DHCP lease process, any DHCP server that received the discover message broadcast and that has valid address information to offer responds with an offer message. (This feature allows you to configure multiple DHCP servers so that you're protected against a single-point failure.)

You must register the Windows Server 2003 DHCP server in Active Directory, and it won't begin offering leases until it successfully registers in the directory (more on this later in the chapter, in the section "Authorizing DHCP for Active Directory"). The offer message is a proposal from the server to the client, and it contains an IP address, a subnet mask, a lease period (in days), and the IP address of the DHCP server offering the proposal. The IP address being offered is temporarily reserved so that the server doesn't offer the same address to multiple clients. All offers are sent directly to the requesting client's hardware MAC address.

Step 3: DHCP Lease Selection

Once the client has received at least one offer, the third phase of the DHCP lease process begins. In this phase, the client machine will select an offer from those it received. Windows 2000, XP, and Server 2003 typically accept the first offer that arrives. To signal acceptance, the client broadcasts an acceptance message containing the IP address of the server it selected. It has to be broadcast so that the servers whose offers weren't selected can un-reserve (pull back) the addresses they offered.

Step 4: DHCP Lease Acknowledgment

Once the chosen DHCP server receives the acceptance message from the client, it marks the selected IP address as leased and sends an acknowledgment message, called a *DHCPACK*, back to the client. It's also possible that the server might send a negative acknowledgment, or *DHCPNACK*, to the client. DHCPNACKs are most often generated when the client is attempting to renew a lease for its old IP address after that address has been reassigned elsewhere. Negative acceptance messages can also mean that the requesting client has an inaccurate IP address resulting from physically changing locations to an alternate subnet.

The DHCPACK message includes any DHCP options specified by the server along with the IP address and subnet mask. When the client receives this message, it integrates the parameters into the TCP/IP stack, which can then proceed just as though the user had manually given it new configuration parameters.

 Manually configured entries on the client override any DHCP-supplied entries.

This four-step process may seem overly complicated, but each step is necessary. The aggregate result of these steps is that one server assigns one address to one client. For example, if each server offering a lease immediately assigned an IP address to a requesting workstation, there would soon be no numbers left to assign. Likewise, if the DHCP client controlled whether it accepted or rejected the lease (instead of waiting for a DHCPACK or DHCPNACK message), a slow client could cause the server to mark an assigned address as free and assign it somewhere else—leaving two clients with the same offer.

DHCP Lease Renewal

What happens when the lease expires or needs to be renewed? No matter how long the lease period is, the client will send a new lease request message to the DHCP server when the lease period is half over. If the server hears the request message and there's no reason to reject it, it sends a DHCPACK to the client. This will reset the lease period, just as signing a renewal rider on a car lease does.

If the DHCP server isn't available, the client realizes that the lease can't be renewed. The client can then use the address for the rest of the lease period; once 87.5 percent of the lease period has elapsed, the client will send out another renewal request. At that point, any DHCP server that hears the renewal could respond to this *DHCP request message*, which is a request for a lease renewal, with a DHCPACK and renew the lease.

Any time the client gets a DHCPNACK message, it must stop using its IP address immediately and start the leasing process over from the beginning by requesting a brand-new lease.

When a client initializes TCP/IP, it will always attempt to renew its old address. Just as with any other renewal, if the client has time left on the lease, it will continue to use the lease until its end. If the client is unable to get a new lease by that time, all TCP/IP functions will stop until a new, valid address can be obtained.

DHCP Lease Release

Although leases can be renewed repeatedly, at some point they're likely to run out. Furthermore, the lease process is an "at will" process—the client or server can cancel the lease before it ends. In addition, if the client doesn't succeed in renewing the lease before it expires, the client loses its lease and reverts to APIPA. This release process is an important function that's useful for reclaiming extinct IP addresses formerly used by systems that have moved or switched to a non-DHCP address.

Ipconfig Lease Options

Ipconfig has some options that make it particularly handy for DHCP clients: the /renew and /release switches. These switches allow you to request renewal of or give up your machine's existing address lease. This might not seem that useful because you can essentially do the same thing by toggling the Obtain An IP Address Automatically button in the Internet Protocol (TCP/IP) Properties dialog box, but it is useful especially when you're setting up a new network.

For example, we spend about a third of our time teaching MCSE classes, usually in temporary classrooms set up at conferences, hotels, and so on. Laptops are used in these classes, with one brawny laptop set up as a DNS/DHCP/DC server. Occasionally, a client will lose its DHCP lease (or not get one, perhaps because a cable has come loose), and the quickest way to fix it is to pop open a command-line window and quickly type **ipconfig /renew**.

In addition, you can configure DHCP to assign options only to certain classes. Classes are defined by you or another administrator as groups of computers that require identical DHCP options. The /setclassid *classID* switch is the only way to assign a machine to a class.

More specifically, the switches do the following:

ipconfig /renew   Instructs the DHCP client to request a lease renewal. If the client already has a lease, it requests a renewal from the server that issued the current lease. This is equivalent to what happens when the client reaches the half-life of its lease. If the client *doesn't* currently have a lease, the process is identical to what happens when you boot a DHCP client for the first time: It initiates the DHCP mating dance, listens for lease offers, and chooses one it likes.

ipconfig /release   Forces the client to immediately give up its lease by sending the server a DHCP release notification. The server updates its status information and marks the client's old IP address as "available," leaving the client with no address bound to its network interface. When you use this command, most of the time it will be immediately followed by ipconfig /renew. The combination releases the existing lease and gets a new one, probably with a different address. (It's also a handy way to force your client to get a new set of settings from the server before lease expiration time.)

ipconfig /setclassid *classID*   Sets a new class ID for the client. You will see how to configure class options later in this chapter, in the section "Setting Scope Options." For now, you should know that the only way to add a client machine to a class is to use the ipconfig /setclassid *classid* command. Note that you need to renew the client lease for the class assignment to take effect.

If you have multiple network adapters in a single machine, you can provide the name of the adapter (or adapters) you want the command to work on, including an asterisk (*) as a wildcard.

For example, one of our servers has two network cards: one's an Intel EtherExpress (ELNK1), and one's a generic 100Mbps card. If we want to renew DHCP settings for both adapters, we can type **ipconfig /renew** *. If we just want to renew the Intel EtherExpress card, we can type **ipconfig /renew ELNK1.**

Understanding Scope Details

By now you should have a good grasp of what a lease is and how it works. To properly learn how to configure your servers to hand out those leases, though, you need to have a complete understanding of some additional topics. You can start with the concept of a *scope*, which is a contiguous range of addresses. There's usually one scope per physical subnet, and a scope can cover a Class A, Class B, or Class C network address. DHCP uses scopes as the basis for managing and assigning IP addressing information.

A *superscope* is an administrative convenience. It allows you to group two or more scopes together even though they're actually separate. In reality, a superscope is just a list of its child scopes. Microsoft's DHCP snap-in allows you to manage IP address assignment in the superscope, though you must still configure other scope options individually for each child scope.

Each scope has a set of parameters you can configure. These parameters, or scope options, control what data is delivered to DHCP clients to complete the DHCP negotiation process with a particular server. For example, the DNS server name, default gateway, and default network time server are all separate options that can be assigned. More properly, these settings are called option types; you can use any of the types provided with Windows Server 2003, or you can specify your own.

The scope defines what IP addresses could potentially be assigned, but you can influence the assignment process in two additional ways by specifying the following:

- Any IP addresses within the range that you *never* want automatically assigned. These addresses are called excluded addresses, or *exclusions*, and they're off-limits to DHCP. You'll typically use exclusions to tag any addresses that you never want the DHCP server to assign at all.

- Any IP addresses within the range for which you want a permanent DHCP lease. These addresses are known as *reservations* because they essentially reserve a particular IP address for a particular device.

How do you know whether to use a reservation or an exclusion? The key is what you want to do with the addresses. Obviously you don't want them assigned to "ordinary" clients, but why not? You should exclude a range of addresses if you don't want them to participate in DHCP at all. If you're using devices like laptops and you want them to get DHCP settings without getting a new address each time they restart, you can use reservations.

The range of IP addresses that the DHCP server can actually assign is called its *address pool*. For example, say you set up a new DHCP scope covering the 192.168.1 subnet; that gives you 255 IP addresses in the pool. After adding an exclusion from 192.168.1.240 to 192.168.1.254, you're left with $255 - 14 = 241$ IP addresses in the pool. That means (in theory, at least) that you can service 241 unique clients at one time before you run out of IP addresses.

By design, the DHCP protocol is intended to allow clients and servers on the same IP network to communicate. RFC 1542 sets out how BootP (on which DHCP is based) should work in circumstances in which the client and server are on different IP networks. If there's no DHCP server available on the network where the client's located, you can use a *DHCP relay agent* to forward DHCP messages from the client to the DHCP server's network. The relay agent acts like a radio repeater, listening for DHCP client requests and retransmitting them on the server's network. You will see how to configure a DHCP relay agent in Chapter 7.

Installing DHCP

Installing DHCP is easy because the Windows Server 2003 installation mechanism is used. Unlike some of the other services you'll see in this book, the actual installation installs just the service and its associated snap-in, starting it when the installation is complete. At that point, it's not delivering any DHCP service, but you don't have to reboot.

There are several ways to install the Windows Server 2003 networking services components. Exercise 5.1 presents just one method. In the next chapter, you will see how to install the DNS server component using an alternate method. Both methods would work for either component.

EXERCISE 5.1

Installing the DHCP Service

1. Select Start ➢ Control Panel ➢ Add or Remove Programs.

2. Click the Add/Remove Windows Components icon. The Windows Components Wizard opens and lists all of the available components.

3. Select the Networking Services item from the component list and click the Details button.

4. When the Subcomponents Of Network Services list appears, make sure Dynamic Host Configuration Protocol (DHCP) is selected and click the OK button.

5. Click the Next button to continue the Windows Components Wizard.

6. If prompted, enter the path to the Windows Server 2003 distribution files.

7. Click Finish to close the Windows Components Wizard.

When you install the DHCP server, the DHCP snap-in is installed, too. You can open it by using the Start ➢ Administrative Tools ➢ DHCP command. The snap-in is shown in Figure 5.1.

FIGURE 5.1 The DHCP snap-in

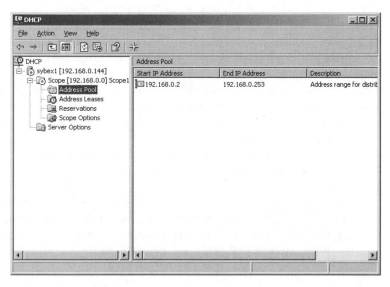

As you can see, it follows the standard MMC model. The left-hand pane shows you which servers are available; you can connect to servers other than the one you're already connected to. Each server contains subordinate items grouped into folders. Each scope has a folder, which is named after the scope's IP address range. There's also a separate folder, Server Options, that holds options that are specific to a particular DHCP server. Within each scope, there are four subordinate views that show you interesting things about the scope, such as the following:

- The Address Pool view shows you what the address pool looks like.

- The Address Leases view shows one entry for each current lease. Each lease shows the computer name to which the lease was issued, the corresponding IP address, and the current lease expiration time.

- The Reservations view shows you which IP addresses are reserved and which devices hold them.

- The Scope Options view lists the set of options you've defined for this scope.

Once you've installed a server, your next step is to authorize the DHCP server in Active Directory. We will look how to do this in the next section.

Authorizing DHCP for Active Directory

Authorization, which actually creates an Active Directory object representing the new server, helps keep unauthorized servers off your network. Unauthorized servers can cause two separate kinds of problems: They may hand out bogus leases, or they may fraudulently deny renewal requests from legitimate clients.

When you install a DHCP server using Windows Server 2003 and Active Directory is present on your network, the server won't be allowed to provide DHCP services to clients until it's been authorized. If you install DHCP on a member server in an Active Directory domain or on a stand-alone server, you'll have to manually authorize the server. When you authorize a server, you're really adding its IP address to the Active Directory object that contains a list of the IP addresses of all authorized DHCP servers.

At start time, each DHCP server queries the directory, looking for its IP address on the "authorized" list. If it can't find the list, or if it can't find its IP address on the list, the DHCP service fails to start. Instead, it logs an event log message indicating that it couldn't service client requests because the server wasn't authorized.

Exercise 5.2 shows you how the process to authorize a DHCP server works. Note that this will work only for DHCP servers in Active Directory domains.

 DHCP authorization works only with Windows 2000 Server and Server 2003 DHCP servers. To authorize a DHCP server, you must be logged on as a member of the Administrators or Enterprise Admins groups.

EXERCISE 5.2

Authorizing a DHCP Server

1. Select Start ➤ Administrative Tools ➤ DHCP to open the DHCP snap-in.

2. Right-click the server you want to authorize and choose the Authorize command.

3. Wait a short time (30–45 seconds) to allow the authorization to take place.

4. Right-click the server again. Verify that the Unauthorize command appears in the pop-up menu; this indicates that the server is now authorized.

 You can unauthorize a previously authorized server by right-clicking it and using the Unauthorize command.

Creating and Managing DHCP Scopes

You can use any number of DHCP servers on a single physical network if you divide the range of addresses you want assigned into multiple scopes. Each scope contains a number of useful pieces of data, but before you can find out what they are, you need to understand some additional terminology.

You can perform any of the following steps to manage DHCP scopes:

- Create a scope
- Configure scope properties
- Configure reservations and exclusions
- Set scope options
- Activate and deactivate scopes
- Create a superscope
- Create a multicast scope
- Integrate Dynamic DNS and DHCP

We will look at each step in the following sections.

Creating a New Scope

Like many other things in Windows Server 2003, the process of creating a new scope is driven by a wizard. The overall process is simple, as long as you know beforehand what the wizard is going to ask. If you think about what defines a scope, you'll be well prepared. You need to know the following:

- The IP address range for the scope you want to create
- Which IP addresses, if any, you want to exclude from the address pool
- Which IP addresses, if any, you want to reserve
- Values for the DHCP options you want to set, if any

This last item isn't strictly necessary for creating a scope because the wizard doesn't ask for any options. However, to create a useful scope, you'll need to have *some* options to specify for the clients.

To create a scope, select a DHCP server in the DHCP snap-in and use the Action ➤ New Scope command. That starts the New Scope Wizard. We will look at each page of the wizard in the following sections.

Setting the Screen Name

The Welcome page of the wizard tells you that you've launched the New Scope Wizard. The Scope Name page allows you to enter a name and description for your scope. These will be displayed by the DHCP snap-in, so it's a good idea to pick a sensible name for your scopes so that other administrators will be able to figure out what the scope is *for*.

Defining the IP Address Range

The next page, the IP Address Range page (Figure 5.2), is where you enter the start and end IP addresses for your range. The wizard does minimal checking on the addresses you enter, but it does automatically calculate the appropriate subnet mask for the address range you enter. You can modify the subnet mask if you know what you're doing.

FIGURE 5.2   The IP Address Range page of the New Scope Wizard

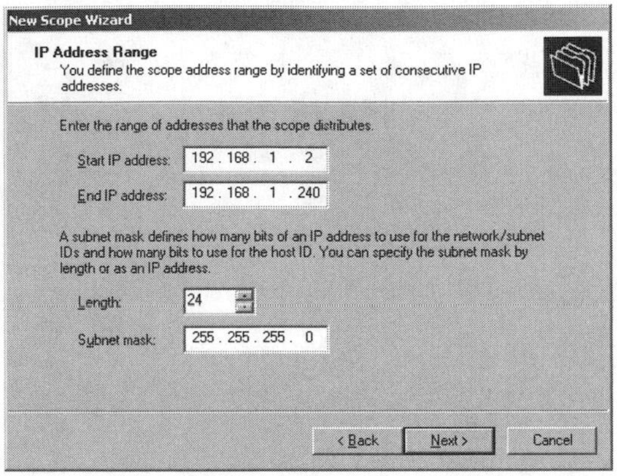

Adding Exclusions

The Add Exclusions page (Figure 5.3) allows you to create exclusion ranges as part of the scope creation process. To exclude one address, put it in the Start IP Address field. To exclude a range, fill in a start and end address. Remember that you can always add exclusions later, but it's best to include them when you create the scope so that no excluded addresses are ever passed out to clients.

FIGURE 5.3   The Add Exclusions page of the New Scope Wizard

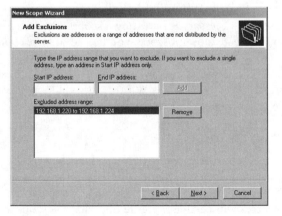

Setting a Lease Duration

The Lease Duration page (Figure 5.4) allows you to set the lease duration. By default, new leases start with a duration of 8 days and 0 hours. You may find that a shorter or longer duration makes sense for your network. If your network is highly dynamic, with lots of arrivals, departures, and moving computers, set a short lease duration; if it's less active, make it longer. Remember that renewal attempts begin when half of the lease period is over, so don't set them *too* short.

FIGURE 5.4   The Lease Duration page of the New Scope Wizard

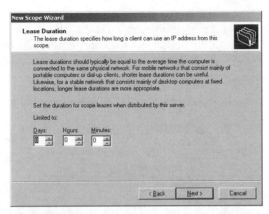

Configuring Basic DHCP Options

The Configure DHCP Options page allows you to choose whether you want to configure basic DHCP options (including the default gateway and DNS settings). If you choose to configure these options, you'll have to go through some additional pages, which are discussed in the following sections. If you choose not to configure options, you can go back and do so later; if you choose to take that route, make sure you don't activate the scope until you've configured the options you want assigned.

Configuring a Router

The first Option Configuration page is the Router (Default Gateway) page (Figure 5.5), in which you to enter the IP addresses of one or more routers that you want to use as gateways for outbound traffic. Type in the IP addresses of the routers you want to use and then use the Up and Down buttons to put the addresses in the order in which you want clients to use them when attempting to send outgoing packets.

FIGURE 5.5   The Router (Default Gateway) page of the New Scope Wizard

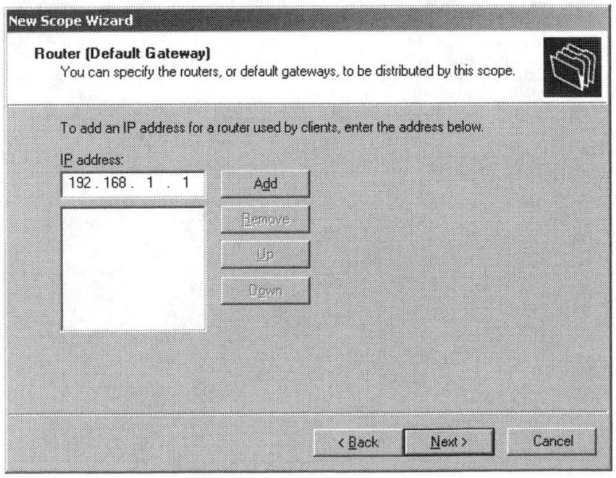

Providing DNS Settings

On the Domain Name And DNS Servers page (Figure 5.6), you specify the set of DNS servers and the parent domain you want passed down to DHCP clients. Normally, you'll need to specify at least one DNS server by filling in its DNS name or IP address; you can also specify the domain you want Windows Server 2003 to use as its base domain for all connections that don't have their own connection-specific suffixes defined.

FIGURE 5.6   The Domain Name And DNS Servers page of the New Scope Wizard

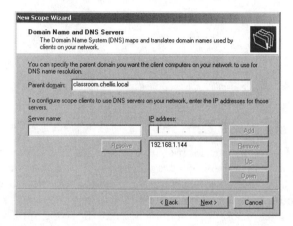

Providing WINS Settings

If you're still using Windows Internet Name Service (WINS) on your network, you can configure DHCP so that it passes WINS server addresses to your Windows clients (though if you want the Windows clients to honor it, you'll also need to define the WINS/NBT Node Type option for the scope). As on the DNS server page, on the WINS Servers page (Figure 5.7) you can enter the addresses of several servers, moving them into the order in which you want clients to try them. You may enter the DNS or NetBIOS name of each server, or you can enter an IP address.

FIGURE 5.7   The WINS Servers page of the New Scope Wizard

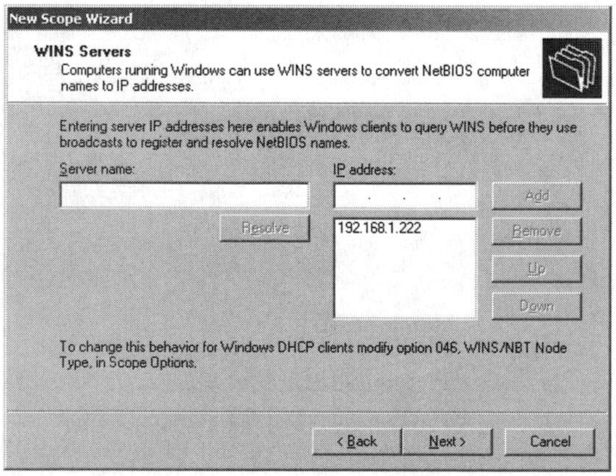

Activating the Scope

The Activate Scope page allows you the option to activate the scope immediately after creating it. By default, the wizard will assume you want the scope activated unless you select the No, I Will Activate This Scope Later radio button, in which case the scope will remain dormant until you manually activate it.

Be sure to verify that there are no other DHCP servers assigned to the address range you choose!

In Exercise 5.3, you will create a new scope for the 192.168.0 private Class C network.

EXERCISE 5.3

Creating a New Scope

1. Open the DHCP snap-in by selecting Start ≻ Administrative Tools ≻ DHCP.

2. Right-click the server on which you want to create the new scope and choose New Scope. The New Scope Wizard appears.

3. Click the Next button on the Welcome page.

4. Enter a name and a description for your new scope and click the Next button.

5. In the IP Address Range page, enter **190.168.0.2** as the start IP address for the scope and **192.068.0.250** as the end IP address. Leave the subnet mask controls alone (though when creating a scope on a production network you might need to change them). Click the Next button.

6. In the Add Exclusions page, click Next without adding any excluded addresses.

7. In the Lease Duration page, set the lease duration to 3 days and click the Next button.

8. In the Configure DHCP Options page, click the Next button to indicate that you want to configure default options for this scope.

9. Enter a router IP address (in this case, **192.168.0.1**) in the IP Address field and then click the Add button. Once the address is added, click the Next button.

10. In the Domain Name And DNS Servers page, enter the IP address of a DNS server on your network in the IP address field, such as 192.168.0.251, and click the Add button. Click the Next button.

11. On the WINS Servers page, click the Next button to leave the WINS options unset and display the Activate Scope page.

12. If your network is currently using the 192.168.0.*x* range, select the No, I Will Activate This Scope Later radio button. Click the Next button. When the Wizard Summary page appears, click the Finish button to create the scope.

Changing Scope Properties

Each scope has a set of properties associated with it. Except for the set of options assigned by the scope (more about this in the next section), these properties can be seen on the General tab of the Scope Properties dialog box (Figure 5.8). Some of these properties, like the scope name and description, are self-explanatory. Others require a little more exposition:

- The Start IP Address and End IP Address fields allow you to set the size of the scope. The subnet mask is automatically calculated for you based on the IP addresses you enter.

- The settings in the Lease Duration For DHCP Clients group control how long leases in this scope will be valid. You can choose either the Limited To or Unlimited radio button. If you choose to set lease duration limits, you use the Days, Hours, and Minutes controls to govern how long the leases will remain in use.

FIGURE 5.8   The General tab of the Scope Properties dialog box

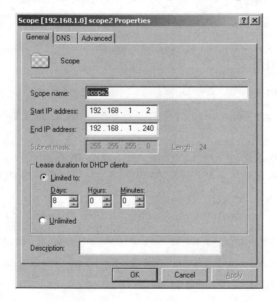

 Don't confuse the process of setting properties of the scope with setting the options associated with the scope—they're two entirely different operations.

When you make changes to these properties, bear in mind that they have no effect on existing leases. For example, say you create a scope from 172.30.1.1 to 172.30.1.199. You use that scope for a while and then edit its properties to reduce the range from 172.30.1.1 to 172.30.1.150. If a client has 172.30.1.180—an address legal under the scope before you changed it—the client will retain that address but will not be able to renew it.

Managing Reservations and Exclusions

After defining the address pool, the next step is to create whatever reservations and exclusions you want used to reduce the size of the pool. In the following sections, you will see how to add and remove exclusions and reservations.

Adding and Removing Exclusions

When you want to exclude an entire range of IP addresses, you need to add that range as an exclusion. Normally, you'll want to do this before you enable a scope because that prevents you from accidentally issuing any of the excluded IP addresses. In fact, you can't create an exclusion that includes a leased address—you have to get rid of the lease first.

Here's how to add an exclusion range:

1. Open the DHCP snap-in and find the scope to which you want to add an exclusion.

2. Expand the scope so you can see its Address Pool item.

3. Right-click Address Pool and then use the New Exclusion Range command. (You can select Actions ➢ New Exclusion Range as well.)

4. When the Add Exclusion dialog box appears (see Figure 5.9), enter the IP addresses you want to exclude. To exclude a single address, type it into the Start IP Address field. To exclude a range, put the ending address of the range into the End IP Address field.

FIGURE 5.9   The Add Exclusion dialog box

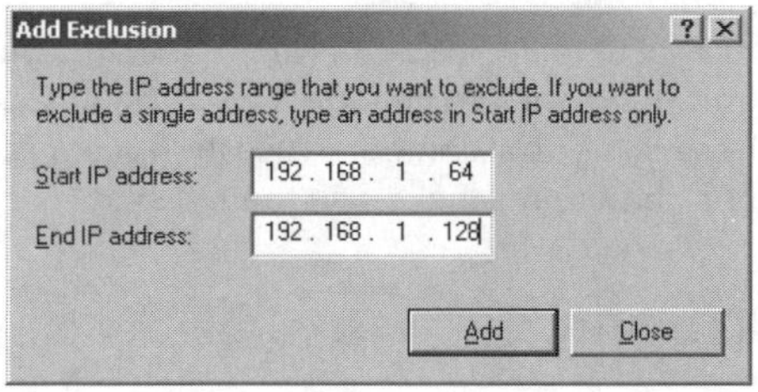

5. Click the Add button to add the exclusion.

When you add exclusions, they appear in the Address Pool node under the scope where you add them. To remove an exclusion, just right-click it and use the Delete command. After confirming your command, the snap-in removes the excluded range and it becomes immediately available for issuance.

Adding and Removing Reservations

Adding reservations is simple as long as you have the MAC address of the device for which you want to create a reservation. Because reservations belong to a single scope, you create and remove them within the Reservations node beneath each scope. You add reservations by right-clicking the scope and selecting New Reservation. This displays the New Reservation dialog box, shown in Figure 5.10.

FIGURE 5.10   The New Reservation dialog box

New Reservation	? X

Provide information for a reserved client.

Reservation name: Instructor machine

IP address: 192 . 168 . 1 . 205

MAC address: 00-C0-4F-4C-04-25

Description: Fixed location instructor machine

Supported types
- ○ Both
- ● DHCP only
- ○ BOOTP only

Add   Close

At a minimum, when you create a new reservation you must enter the IP address and MAC address for the reservation. If you like, you can also enter a name and description. You can also choose whether the reservation will be made by DHCP only, BootP only (useful for remote-access devices that use BootP), or both.

To remove a reservation, right-click it and select Delete. This removes the reservation but does nothing to the client device.

There's no way to change a reservation once it's been created—you'll have to delete it and re-create it to change any of the associated settings. To find the MAC address of the local computer, use the `ipconfig` command. To find the MAC address of a remote machine, use the `nbtstat -a` *computername* command.

Setting Scope Options

Once you've installed a server, authorized it in Active Directory, and fixed up the addresses pool, the next step is to set scope options, such as router (i.e., default gateway) and DNS server addresses, that you want sent out to clients. You must configure the options you want sent out before you activate a scope. If you don't, clients may register in the scope without getting any options, rendering them virtually useless. Scope options, along with the IP address and subnet mask that you configured earlier in this chapter, complete the standard TCP/IP settings that you saw in Chapter 2.

In the following sections, you will learn how to configure and assign scope options on the DHCP server.

Understanding Option Assignment

There are five different (and slightly overlapping) ways to control which DHCP options are doled out to clients:

Predefined options   Predefined options are like option templates that are available in the Server, Scope, or Client Options dialog boxes.

Server options   Server options are assigned to all scopes and clients of a particular server. That means if there's some setting you want *all* clients of a DHCP server to have, no matter what scope they're in, this is where you'd assign them. However, note that more specific options (like those that are set at the class, scope, or client level) will override server-level options. That gives you an escape valve; it's a better idea, though, to be careful about which options you assign if your server manages multiple scopes.

Scope options   If you want a particular option value assigned only to those clients in a certain subnet, select that scope as the base for the option. For example, it's common to specify different routers for different physical subnets; if you have two scopes corresponding to different subnets, each scope would probably have a separate value for the router option.

Class options   The idea behind class options is that you should be able to assign different options to clients in different classes. For example, Windows 2000, XP, and Server 2003 machines recognize a number of DHCP options that Windows 98 and Mac OS machines ignore. By defining a new Windows 2000 Or Newer class on the clients (using `ipconfig/setclassid` command you saw earlier), you could assign those options only to machines that report themselves as being in that class. The problem is that you need to have clients that are smart enough to do so, and most of them aren't.

Client options   If you want to force certain options onto a specific client, you can do so— provided the client is using a DHCP reservation. You actually attach client options to a particular reservation. They'll override any scope, server, or class option. In fact, the only way to override a client option is to manually configure the client. The DHCP server manages client options.

Client options override Class options, Class options override Scope options and Scope options override Server options.

Assigning Options

You can use the DHCP snap-in to assign options at the scope, server, reserved address, or class level. The mechanism you use to assign these options is identical; the only difference is where you set the options. When you create an option assignment, remember that it applies to all the clients in the server or the scope *from that point forward*. Option assignments aren't retroactive, and they don't migrate from one scope to another.

To actually *create* a new option and have it assigned, select the scope or server where you want the option assigned, select the corresponding Options node, and select Action ➢ Configure Options. (To set options for a reserved client, right-click its entry in the Reservations node and select Configure Options.) You'll then see the Configure Options dialog box (Figure 5.11), which lists all of the options you might potentially want to configure.

To select an individual option, check the box next to it and then use the controls in the Data Entry control group to enter the value you want associated with the option. Continue to add options until you've specified all the ones you want attached to the server or scope and then click the OK button.

You saw how to assign classes to individual machines earlier in the chapter. Now you will learn how to configure the DHCP server to recognize your customized classes and configure options for them. In Exercise 5.4, you will create a new user class and configure options for the new class.

FIGURE 5.11 The Scope Options dialog box

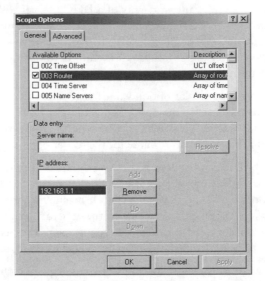

Configuring User Class Options

1. Open the DHCP snap-in by selecting Start ➢ Administrative Tools ➢ DHCP.

2. Right-click the DHCP server and select Define User Classes.

3. Click the Add button in the DHCP User Classes dialog box.

4. In the New Class dialog box, enter a descriptive name for the class in the Display Name field. Enter a class ID in the ID field. Typically, you will enter the class ID in the ASCII portion of the ID field. You should make sure that the computers you want to use in the class have been configured with the `ipconfig /setclassid` command as described earlier in this chapter. When you are done, click the OK button.

5. The new class appears in the DHCP User Classes dialog box. Click the Close button to return to the DHCP administrative tool.

6. Right-click either the Server Options or a Scope Options node (depending on if you want to set the class options at the server or scope level) and select Configure Options.

7. Click the Advanced tab. Select the class you defined in step 4 from the User Class pull-down menu.

8. Configure the options that you want to set for the class. Click OK when you are done. Notice that the options you configured (and the class that they are associated with) appear in the right pane of the DHCP window.

Activating and Deactivating Scopes

When you've completed the steps in Exercise 5.4 and you're ready to unleash your new scope so that it can be used to make client assignments, the final required step is activating the scope. When you activate a scope, you're just telling the server that it's okay to start handing out addresses from that scope's address pool. As soon as you activate a scope, addresses from its pool may be assigned to clients. Of course, this is a necessary precondition to getting any use out of your scope.

If you later want to stop using a scope, you can, but beware: It's a permanent change. You turn off a scope by deactivating it, but when you do, DHCP tells all clients registered with the scope that they need to release their leases and renew them someplace else—the equivalent of a landlord who evicts his tenants when the building is condemned! Don't deactivate a scope unless you want clients to stop using it immediately.

Creating a Superscope

A superscope allows the DHCP server to provide multiple logical subnet addresses to DHCP clients on a single physical network. You create superscopes with the New Superscope command, which triggers the New Superscope Wizard.

     You can only have one superscope per server.

To create a superscope, follow these steps:

1. Open the DHCP snap-in by selecting Start ≻ Administrative Tools ≻ DHCP.

2. Follow the instructions in Exercise 5.3 to create two scopes: one for 192.168.0.2-192.168.0.127 and one for 192.168.1.12-192.168.1.127.

3. Right-click your DHCP server and choose the New Superscope command. The New Superscope Wizard appears. Click the Next button.

4. In the Superscope Name page, name your superscope and click the Next button.

5. The Select Scopes page appears showing a list of all scopes on the current server. Select the two scopes you created in step 2 and then click the Next button.

6. The Wizard Summary page appears; click the Finish button to create your scope.

7. Verify that your new superscope appears in the DHCP snap-in.

You may notice that you can delete a superscope by right-clicking it and choosing the Delete command. A superscope is just an administrative convenience, so you can safely delete one at any time—it doesn't affect the "real" scopes that make up the superscope.

In the following section, you will see how to add and remove scopes from a superscope and how to activate and deactivate a superscope.

Adding and Removing Scopes from a Superscope

Adding a scope to an existing superscope is a matter of finding the scope you want to add, right-clicking it, and using the Action ≻ Add To Superscope command. This causes the snap-in to show you a dialog box listing all of the superscopes known to this server; pick the one you want the current scope appended to and click the OK button.

If you later want to remove a scope from a superscope, open the superscope and right-click the target scope. The pop-up menu provides a Remove From Superscope command that will do the deed.

Activating and Deactivating Superscopes

Just as with regular scopes, you can activate and deactivate superscopes. The same restrictions and guidelines apply: You must activate a superscope before it can be used, and you must not deactivate it until you want all your clients to lose their existing leases and be forced to request new ones. To activate or deactivate a superscope, right-click the superscope name and select Activate or Deactivate, respectively, from the pop-up menu.

Creating Multicast Scopes

Multicasting occurs when one machine sends data to an entire network rather than specifically addressing each machine on the destination network. IP multicasting is becoming increasingly common as the amount of network bandwidth available on the average network increases. It's much more efficient to *multicast* a video or audio stream to multiple destinations than it is to broadcast it to the same number of clients, and the increased demand for multicast-friendly network hardware has resulted in some head scratching about how to automate the multicast configuration.

In the following sections, you will learn about the protocol that controls multicasting, MADCAP, and how to build and configure a multicast scope.

Understanding the Multicast Address Dynamic Client Allocation Protocol (MADCAP)

DHCP is normally used to assign IP configuration information for *unicast* (or one-to-one) network communications. It turns out that there's a separate type of address space assigned just for multicasting: 224.0.0.0–239.255.255.255. However, multicast clients also need to have an ordinary IP address: Clients can participate in a multicast just by knowing (and using) the multicast address for the content they want to receive.

How do clients know what address to use? Ordinary DHCP won't help because it's designed to assign IP addresses and option information to one client at a time. Realizing this, the Internet Engineering Task Force (IETF) defined a new protocol: *Multicast Address Dynamic Client Allocation Protocol (MADCAP)*. MADCAP provides an analog to DHCP, but for multicast use. A MADCAP server issues leases for multicast addresses only. MADCAP clients can request a multicast lease when they want to participate in a multicast.

There are some important differences between DHCP and MADCAP. First, you have to realize that the two are totally separate. A single server can be a DHCP server, a MADCAP server, or *both;* there's no implied or actual relation between the two. Likewise, clients can use DHCP and/or MADCAP at the same time—the only requirement is that every MADCAP client has to get a unicast IP address from *somewhere.*

Next, remember that DHCP can assign options as part of the lease process but MADCAP cannot. The only thing MADCAP does is dynamically assign multicast addresses.

The Windows Server 2003 online help has a comprehensive checklist that covers how to set up IP multicasting.

Building Multicast Scopes

When you want to create a new multicast scope, right-click the server where you want the scope created and choose the New Multicast Scope option. Most of the steps you go through when creating a multicast scope are identical to those required for an ordinary unicast scope, so you'll see the differences highlighted in Exercise 5.5.

EXERCISE 5.5

Creating a New Multicast Scope

1. Open the DHCP snap-in by selecting Start ➢ Administrative Tools ➢ DHCP.

2. Right-click your DHCP server and choose New Multicast Scope. The New Multicast Scope Wizard appears. Click the Next button on the Welcome page.

3. In the Multicast Scope Name page, name your multicast scope (and add a description if you'd like). Click the Next button.

4. The IP Address Range page appears. Enter a start IP address of **224.0.0.0** and an end IP address of **224.255.0.0**. Adjust the TTL to 1 to make sure that no multicast packets escape your local network segment. Click the Next button when you're done.

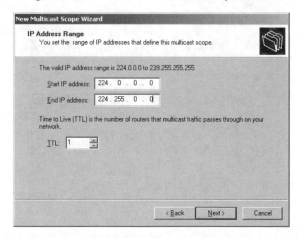

5. The Add Exclusions page appears; click its Next button.

6. The Lease Duration page appears. Normally you leave multicast scope assignments in place somewhat longer than you would with a regular unicast scope, hence the default lease length of 30 days. Click the Next button.

7. The wizard asks you if you want to activate the scope now. Click the No radio button and then the Next button.

8. The Wizard Summary page appears; click the Finish button to create your scope.

9. Verify that your new multicast scope appears in the DHCP snap-in.

Setting Multicast Scope Properties

Once you create a multicast scope, you can adjust its properties by right-clicking the scope name and selecting Properties.

The Multicast Scope Properties dialog box has two tabs. The General tab (Figure 5.12) allows you to change the scope's name, its start and end address, its Time to Live (TTL) value, its lease duration, and its description—in essence, all of the settings you provided when you created it in the first place.

FIGURE 5.12 The General tab of the Multicast Scope Properties dialog box

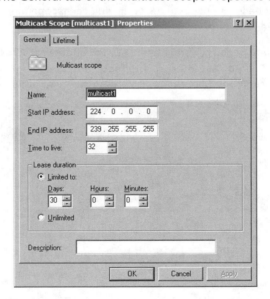

The Lifetime tab (see Figure 5.13) allows you to limit how long your multicast scope will be active. By default, a newly created multicast scope will live forever, but if you're creating a scope to provide MADCAP assignments for a single event (or a set of events that cover a limited duration), you can specify an expiration time for the scope. When that time is reached, the scope disappears from the server, but not before making all its clients give up their multicast address leases. This is a nice way to make sure the lease cleans up after itself when you're done with it.

FIGURE 5.13   The Lifetime tab of the Multicast Scope Properties dialog box

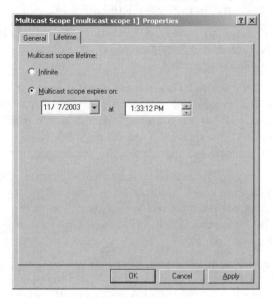

Integrating Dynamic DNS and DHCP

DHCP integration with Dynamic DNS is a simple concept but powerful in action. By setting up this integration, you can pass addresses to DHCP clients while still maintaining the integrity of your DNS services. There are actually two separate ways that the DNS server could potentially be updated. One way is for the DHCP client to tell the DNS server what its address is. This method is easy to understand, but it's insecure because there's no way to trust the client. The default Windows Server 2003 method is better: The DHCP server tells the DNS server when it registers a new client. This method relies on the likelihood that the DHCP server is more trustworthy than some random client.

However, neither of these updates will take place unless you configure the DHCP server to use Dynamic DNS. There are actually two separate ways to make this change: If you change it at the scope level, it will apply only to the scope, but if you change it at the server level, it will apply to all scopes and superscopes served by the server. Whichever of these options you choose depends on how widely you want to support Dynamic DNS; most of the sites we visit have enabled DNS updates at the server level.

You also have to instruct the DNS server to accept Dynamic DNS updates. For more on how to do so, see Chapter 6, "Installing and Managing Domain Name Service (DNS)."

To actually update the settings at either the server or scope levels, you need to open the scope or server properties, which you do by right-clicking the appropriate object and choosing

Properties. When you do, you'll see the General tab, which lets you adjust some general settings for the object you've just opened. In the DNS tab (Figure 5.14), you'll see the following:

Enable DNS Dynamic Updates According To The Settings Below   This checkbox controls whether or not this DHCP server will attempt to register lease information with a DNS server. It must be checked to enable Dynamic DNS.

Dynamically Update DNS A And PTR Records Only If Requested By The DHCP Clients
This radio button (which is on by default) tells the DHCP server to register the update only if the DHCP client asks for DNS registration. When this button is active, DHCP clients that aren't hip to DDNS won't have their DNS records updated. However, Windows 2000, XP, and Server 2003 DHCP clients are smart enough to ask for the updates.

Always Dynamically Update DNS A And PTR Records   This radio button forces the DHCP server to register *any* client to which it issues a lease. This setting may add DNS registrations for DHCP-enabled devices that don't really need them, like printer servers; however, it allows other clients (like Mac OS, Windows NT, and Linux machines) to have their DNS information automatically updated.

Discard A And PTR Records When Lease Is Deleted   This checkbox has a long name but a simple function. When a DHCP lease expires, what should happen to the DNS registration? Obviously, it would be nice if the DNS record associated with a lease vanished when the lease expired; when this checkbox is checked (as it is by default), that's exactly what happens. If you uncheck this box, your DNS will contain entries for expired leases that are no longer valid; when a particular IP address is reissued on a new lease, the DNS will be updated, but in between leases you'll have incorrect data in your DNS—always something to avoid.

Dynamically Update DNS A And PTR Records For DHCP Clients That Do Not Request Updates   This checkbox lets you handle these older clients graciously by making the updates using a separate mechanism.

FIGURE 5.14   The DNS tab of the Scope Properties dialog box

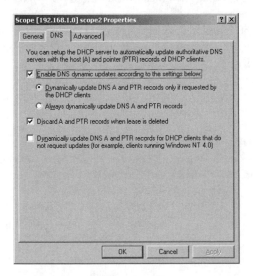

In Exercise 5.6, you will enable a scope to participate in Dynamic DNS updates.

EXERCISE 5.6

Enabling DHCP-DNS Integration

1. Open the DHCP snap-in by selecting Start ➢ Administrative Tools ➢ DHCP.

2. Right-click the DHCP server you configured in Exercise 5.1 and select Properties.

3. The Server Properties dialog box appears. Click the DNS tab.

4. Verify that the Enable DNS Dynamic Updates According To The Settings Below checkbox is checked and verify that the Dynamically Update DNS A And PTR Records Only If Requested By The DHCP Clients radio button is selected. If not, then check it.

5. Verify that the Discard A And PTR Records When Lease Is Deleted checkbox is checked. If not, then check it.

6. Click the OK button to apply your changes and close the Properties dialog box.

 Real World Scenario

Deciding to Implement DHCP in a Static IP Environment

You work for a company that has a static IP environment. Everything about the IP configuration is currently stable, and you have a clearly written procedure for adding new workstations to the network, including the IP configuration. You have read a great deal about DHCP and are interested in it, but you subscribe to the time-tested philosophy that if something isn't broken, don't fix it.

At least, that was your philosophy until you were told yesterday that your company has decided to change its ISP because the CFO cut a deal that will save the company a great deal of money over a two-year period. One thing that she hasn't considered, however, is the time that it will take you to change the DNS entry at every workstation in your network.

A lot has been written about how simple it is to change an IP subnetting design by using DHCP and modifying it by modifying the scope. This is true, but you don't actually change your subnet designs very often. DHCP really pays off, though, when you have to make small changes to the IP configuration. A simple change like a new DNS server can be completed within seconds with DHCP, but alas, with a static network you have to visit and touch every IP stack in your network. As you can imagine, this is going to take at least several minutes for each machine. The more workstations you have, the greater the cost you will pay measured against the savings earned by using DHCP.

Now that you've calculated the cost in your head, here is a tip: The best time to move from static IP to DHCP is when there is no major change in the works. Just create your current environment using scopes in DHCP, test it in a lab, and then touch your workstations for the last time as you move them from static addresses to the automatic addresses available with DHCP.

Monitoring and Troubleshooting DHCP

DHCP doesn't require a lot of ongoing care. However, it's useful to know how to monitor and troubleshoot it for those rare occasions when something does go wrong. In the following sections, you will see how to monitor DHCP leases, log DHCP activity, work with the DHCP server log files and database files, reconcile DHCP scopes, and figure out how to manage multiple DHCP servers and scopes.

Monitoring DHCP Leases

You monitor which DHCP leases have been assigned using the Address Leases view associated with a particular scope. When you open the scope and click the Address Leases item under the scope name, you'll see an easy-to-read list of all the leases currently in force for that scope. This view will show you the client IP address, the client DNS name, the lease's duration, and the client's unique DHCP ID (if there is one).

If you want to remove a client lease, you can do so by right-clicking it in the Address Leases view and selecting Delete. This actually removes the lease, but not before canceling it. Normally, it's better to let leases expire rather than manually canceling them, but sometimes circumstances dictate otherwise.

In Exercise 5.7, you will create a tab-delimited text file containing information about all leases in a scope, the same data that you see in the Address Leases view. You can use this file for analysis or record keeping long after leases have expired or been renewed. In order for this lab to be meaningful, you should have at least one or two leases in use.

EXERCISE 5.7

Inspecting Leases

1. Open the DHCP snap-in by selecting Start ≻ Administrative Tools ≻ DHCP.

2. Expand the target server's node in the MMC until you see the Address Leases node.

3. Right-click the Address Leases node and click Export List on the pop-up menu.

4. When the Save As dialog box appears, select a location for the list file. Type a meaningful name in the Filename field and click the Save button.

5. In WordPad, Word, Excel, or any other tool that honors tab settings, open the file you just created. Notice that the contents of the file mirror exactly what you saw in the DHCP snap-in. If the lease list is empty, you will see only a header row in the text file.

Logging DHCP Activity

In the Windows Server 2003 family, *DHCP server log files* use audit logging so that log files can be used without requiring added monitoring or administering to manage log file growth or to conserve disk resources. By default, the DHCP service automatically logs all DHCP activity to a daily log file in the *systemroot*/System32/DHCP folder. The log file name is DhcpSrvLog-*Day* where *Day* is the three-letter abbreviation for the day of the week.

The following section outlines the format of these log files and how they can be used to gather more information about DHCP Server service operations on the network.

DHCP Server Log File Format

DHCP server logs are comma-delimited text files with each log entry representing a single line of text. Following are the fields (and the order in which they appear) in a log file entry:

`ID, Date, Time, Description, IP Address, Host Name, MAC Address`

Each of these fields is described in detail in Table 5.1.

TABLE 5.1   DHCP Log File Fields

Field	Description
ID	A DHCP server event ID code
Date	The date on which this entry was logged on the DHCP server
Time	The time at which this entry was logged on the DHCP server
Description	A description of this DHCP server event
IP Address	The IP address of the DHCP client
Host Name	The hostname of the DHCP client
MAC Address	The media access control address used by the network adapter hardware of the client

Common DHCP Server Log Event Codes

DHCP server audit log files use reserved event ID codes to provide information about the type of server event or activity logged. Table 5.2 describes these event ID codes in more detail.

TABLE 5.2   Common DHCP Log File Event IDs

Event ID	Description
00	The log was started.
01	The log was stopped.

TABLE 5.2   Common DHCP Log File Event IDs *(continued)*

Event ID	Description
02	The log was temporarily paused due to low disk space.
10	A new IP address was leased to a client.
11	A lease was renewed by a client.
12	A lease was released by a client.
13	An IP address was found in use on the network.
14	A lease request could not be satisfied because the address pool of the scope was exhausted.
15	A lease was denied.
20	A BootP address was leased to a client.

When the DHCP server is configured to perform DNS dynamic updates on behalf of DHCP clients, you can use the DHCP audit logs to monitor update requests by the DHCP server to the DNS server, DNS record update successes, and DNS record update failures. Table 5.3 lists the event IDs that are used for DNS dynamic update events.

TABLE 5.3   DNS Dynamic Update Events

ID number	DHCP Event
30	DNS dynamic update request
31	DNS dynamic update failed
32	DNS dynamic update successful

The IP address of the DHCP client computer is included in the DHCP audit log, providing the ability to track the source in the event of a denial of service attack.

The following shows you a sample output of a DHCP log file:

```
ID,Date,Time,Description,IP Address,Host Name,MAC Address
00,04/10/03,12:36:22,Started,,,,
64,04/10/03,12:36:22,No static IP address bound to DHCP server,,,,
56,04/10/03,12:38:59,Authorization failure, stopped servicing,,sybex.com,,
```

```
24,04/10/03,13:36:25,Database Cleanup Begin,,,,
25,04/10/03,13:36:25,0 leases expired and 0 leases deleted,,,,
25,04/10/03,13:36:25,0 leases expired and 0 leases deleted,,,,
24,04/10/03,14:36:28,Database Cleanup Begin,,,,
25,04/10/03,14:36:28,0 leases expired and 0 leases deleted,,,,
25,04/10/03,14:36:28,0 leases expired and 0 leases deleted,,,,
55,04/10/03,14:44:49,Authorized(servicing),,sybex.com,,
```

As you can see, the DHCP service failed to start at first because the server didn't have a static IP address. Of course, this would also make it impossible to authorize the services, as shown in the next line. After a few database cleanup logs, you can see that DHCP was authorized, probably because an administrator assigned a correct static IP address to the server and manually authorized DHCP.

Examining DHCP Activity in the Event Viewer

DHCP activity is also logged in the system log, which is accessed with the Event Viewer utility, located in the Administrative Tools folder. To quickly look up DHCP events, click the System section and sort the entries by the Source field. Scroll down until you see DHCP entries. The Event Viewer logs most of the same events as the DHCP log.

Working with the DHCP Database Files

DHCP uses a set of database files to maintain its knowledge of scopes, superscopes, and client leases. These files, which live in the *systemroot*\System32\DHCP folder, are always open when the DHCP service is running, and you shouldn't modify or alter them when the service is running. The primary database file is Dhcp.mdb—it has all of the scope data in it. The following files are also part of the DHCP database:

- Dhcp.tmp is a backup copy of the database file created during re-indexing of the database. You normally won't see this file, but if the service fails during re-indexing, it may not remove the file when it should.

- J50.log (plus a number of files named J50*xxxxx*.log) is a log file that stores changes before they're written to the database. The DHCP database engine can recover some changes from these files when it restarts.

- J50.chk is a checkpoint file that tells the DHCP engine which log files it still needs to recover.

In the following sections you will see how to manipulate the DHCP database files.

Removing the Database Files

If you're convinced that your database is corrupt because the lease information you see doesn't match what's on the network, the easiest repair mechanism is to remove the database files and start over with an empty database. (On the other hand, if you're convinced that it's corrupt because the DHCP service fails at startup, you should check the event log.) To start over, stop the DHCP service by typing **net stop dhcpserver** at the command prompt and remove all of the files from the *systemroot*\system32\DHCP folder and then restart the service. Once you've done so, you can reconcile the scope (as described in the section "Reconciling DHCP Scopes" later in this chapter) to rebuild the database contents.

Changing the Database Backup Interval

By default, the DHCP service backs up its databases every 60 minutes. You can adjust this setting by editing the Backup Interval value under HKEY_LOCAL_MACHINE\SYSTEM\Current-ControlSet\Services\DHCPServer\Parameters. This allows you to make backups either more frequently (if your database changes a lot or if you seem to have ongoing corruption problems) or less often (if everything seems to be on an even keel).

Moving the DHCP Database Files

You may find that you need to dismantle or change the role of your DHCP server and offload the DHCP functions to another computer. Rather than spend the time re-creating the DHCP database on the new machine by hand, you can literally copy the database files and use them directly. This is especially helpful if you have a complicated DHCP database with lots of reservations and option assignments.

You also minimize the amount of human error that could be introduced by reentering the information by hand. The steps necessary to move the DHCP database from one Windows 2000 or Server 2003 machine to another are shown in Exercise 5.8.

EXERCISE 5.8

Moving the DHCP Database Between Servers

1. Stop the DHCP service on the source computer by typing **net stop dhcpserver** at the command prompt.

2. Copy the *systemroot*\System32\DHCP folder on the source server to a temporary folder that is accessible from the target server.

3. Run Regedt32.exe and view the HKEY_LOCAL_MACHINE\SOFTWARE\Microsoft\Dhcp-Server\Configuration Registry key. Highlight the Configuration key and select Registry ➢ Save Key. Save the key and note the filename that you used.

4. Install DHCP on the target server and then stop the service by typing **net stop dhcpserver** at the command prompt.

5. Rename the System.mdb file in the temporary folder to System.src.

6. Delete all of the file and subfolders in the *systemroot*\System32\DHCP folder on the target computer. Copy the temporary folder on the source computer to the new *systemroot*\System32\DHCP folder on the target computer.

7. Use REGEDT32 to find the HKEY_LOCAL_MACHINE\SOFTWARE\Microsoft\DhcpServer\Configuration key on the target computer. Highlight the key and select Registry ➢ Restore. Select the file that you saved in step 3 and click Yes to overwrite the current settings.

8. Start the DHCP service on the target computer by typing **net start dhcpserver** at the command prompt and choose Reconcile All Scopes in the DHCP administrative tool (more on this in the next section).

9. If the target computer is part of a Windows 2000 or Server 2003 domain, then it must be authorized.

If you need to transfer the DHCP database from a Windows NT 4 server, you should copy the Edb500.dl_file from the Windows 2000 or Server 2003 CD-ROM and expand it to the System32 folder before proceeding. Also note that you will receive an error message after you start the target DHCP server service. This is normal.

Reconciling DHCP Scopes

As time passes, you may experience what we call DHCP drift, which means the contents of your DHCP database no longer reflect accurately what's on your network. Although Microsoft doesn't make any prominent mention of this fact in the DHCP documentation, the DHCP server actually records lease information in two places: the DHCP database *and* the server's Registry. When you reconcile a scope, the DHCP server will cross-check the database contents with the contents of the Registry, reporting (and fixing) any inconsistencies it finds. You can also reconcile scopes to recover from a corrupt DHCP database. You first remove the database files, then reconcile the server's scopes.

To reconcile a single scope, follow these steps:

1. Open the DHCP snap-in by selecting Start ➢ Administrative Tools ➢ DHCP.

2. Expand the target server's node in the MMC until you see the target scope.

3. Right-click the target scope and choose Reconcile.

4. The Reconcile dialog box appears, but it's empty, as shown in Figure 5.15. To start the reconciliation, click the Verify button.

FIGURE 5.15   The Reconcile dialog box

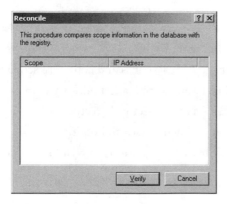

5. If the database is consistent, you'll see a dialog box telling you so. If there are any inconsistencies, the dialog box will list them and allow you to repair them.

You can use a similar procedure to reconcile all scopes on a server. You just right-click the DHCP server and select Reconcile All Scopes instead of just Reconcile (which reconciles an individual scope). To recover a broken DHCP server the preferred way, you first remove the database files and then reconcile all scopes on the server to rebuild the database.

Solving the Problem of Multiple DHCP Servers and Scopes

You would initially think that with multiple DHCP servers and multiple scopes, it makes the most sense to assign each scope to its own DHCP server. However, you will definitely run into a problem if you attempt this solution. If a client computer with an existing lease is rebooted, it will send a DHCP request with its current lease information to any DHCP server that's willing to listen (remember, clients always try to continue using their existing lease). If the first DHCP server to hear the request uses a scope that doesn't include the client's IP address, the DHCP server will send the client a DHCPNACK message. The client then goes into a rebinding state and attempts to obtain a new lease from any DHCP server on the network. If the client happens to receive the new lease from the original DHCP server, then everything is fine. But if the client receives its lease from any other machine, the original DHCP server won't know about the new configuration. It will retain the original lease for the remainder of the lease duration, and the lease will be wasted in the meantime.

Fortunately, there is a solution to this problem. On each DHCP server, simply create a superscope that consists of every other scope on the physical network. On each DHCP server, exclude every address range except the address range the server controls. This prevents the DHCP servers from sending DHCPNACK messages to the client computers.

Summary

The following topics were covered in this chapter:

- How the DHCP lease process issues TCP/IP configuration information to clients in the following stages: IP discovery, IP lease offer, IP lease selection, and IP lease acknowledgment

- How to install and configure the DHCP service on a Windows Server 2003 computer

- How to create and manage DHCP scopes and configure scope options

- How to create and manage superscopes and multicast scopes

- How to authorize DHCP servers in Active Directory

- How to manage and control client leases and options

- How to monitor DHCP lease information, as well as how to interpret the DHCP log files

Exam Essentials

Understand the four stages of the DHCP process. The first phase of the DHCP process is the discovery stage. In the second phase, any DHCP server that received the discover message broadcast and that has valid address information to offer responds with an offer message. Once the client has received at least one offer, the client machine selects an offer from those it received. Once the chosen DHCP server receives the acceptance message from the client, it marks the selected IP address as leased and then sends an acknowledgment message back to the client.

Know how to install and authorize a DHCP server. You install the DHCP service using the Add/Remove Windows Components Wizard. You authorize the DHCP server using the DHCP snap-in. When you authorize a server, you're actually adding its IP address to the Active Directory object that contains a list of the IP addresses of all authorized DHCP servers.

Know how to create a DHCP scope. You use the New Scope Wizard to create a new scope. Before you start, you'll need to know what the IP address range is for the scope you want to create; which IP addresses, if any, you want to exclude from the address pool; which IP addresses, if any, you want to reserve; and the values for the DHCP options you want to set, if any.

Understand the different settings that can be assigned via DHCP. A DHCP server can assign IP addresses, router information, DNS settings, and WINS settings.

Understand the difference between exclusions and reservations. When you want to exclude an entire range of IP addresses, you need to add that range as an exclusion. Any IP addresses within the range for which you want a permanent DHCP lease are known as reservations.

Understand what a superscope is used for. A superscope allows the DHCP server to provide multiple logical subnet addresses to DHCP clients on a single physical network.

Understand how to integrate Dynamic DNS with DHCP. By setting up Dynamic DNS and DHCP integration, you can pass out addresses to DHCP clients and still maintain the integrity (and utility) of your DNS services. You can apply integration at either the scope level or the server level.

Understand how to troubleshoot DHCP problems. If one or more client machines that obtain their address dynamically revert to APIPA, that's usually the first sign that you have a problem. You should make sure the DHCP server is activated and authorized in Active Directory. You can check the DHCP logs files and examine all past DHCP activity. Lease-related problems can be solved by examining lease information in the Address Leases item under the scope name. When lease information on the network doesn't match lease information on the DHCP server, it's a sure sign that the database is corrupt and needs to be reset. When you reconcile a scope, the DHCP server will cross-check the database contents with the contents of the Registry, reporting (and fixing) any inconsistencies it finds. You can also reconcile scopes to recover from a corrupt DHCP database.

Know how to prevent problems with multiple DHCP scopes on multiple DHCP servers You should make sure that you don't place multiple scopes on multiple DHCP servers. Instead, on each DHCP server create a superscope that consists of every other scope on the physical network. On each DHCP server, exclude every address range except the address range the server controls.

Key Terms

Before you take the exam, be certain you are familiar with the following terms:

address pool	discovery
authorization	exclusions
DHCP discover message	lease
DHCP integration	multicast
DHCP relay agent	Multicast Address Dynamic Client Allocation Protocol (MADCAP)
DHCP request message	reservations
DHCP server log files	scope
DHCPACK	superscope
DHCPNACK	unicast

Review Questions

1. You are in the process of upgrading your network to Windows 2000, XP, and Server 2003, and during the process you are including DHCP to help manage the IP addressing. You have created the scope with your 10.0.0.0/16 private address range. You now have 50 Windows Professional workstations completed. You still have 100 Windows 95 workstations to migrate over to Windows 2000 and XP. Everything went smoothly during the migration of the Windows Professional workstations and has worked properly for a month. When you arrived at the office this morning, however, there was havoc everywhere. You were told that the Windows 95 workstations can no longer connect to the Windows Server 2003 computers; the Windows 2000 and XP workstations cannot access the servers, but they can communicate peer to peer. When you look at one of the Windows 2000 workstations, you notice that the address is 169.254.0.27. What is the next step you should take to resolve this problem?

    A. Install the DHCP relay agent on a Windows 2000 Professional workstation.

    B. Attempt to ping the DHCP server from a client with a valid IP address.

    C. Enable the conflict-resolution protocol on the DHCP server.

    D. Enable the APIPA protocol on the Windows 95 clients.

    E. Enable the APIPA protocol on the Windows 2000 and XP clients.

2. You are the administrator of a network in a single location that has grown dramatically. You have a router that you want to use to break the network into three subnets in order to control the overall bandwidth utilization. You also want to avoid the amount of work entailed in changing the static IP configurations if you make changes again in the future. For that reason, you are going to implement DHCP to manage the IP addresses centrally. What should you ensure before you start implementing your plan? (Choose all that apply.)

    A. Make sure that you have identified a Windows 2000 Server computer on each subnet on which to install the DHCP services.

    B. Make sure your router supports BootP.

    C. If your router supports BootP, make sure you install a DHCP server on each subnet.

    D. If your router supports BootP, make sure you install a DHCP relay agent on each subnet.

    E. If your router does not support BootP, make sure you install a DHCP relay agent on each subnet.

3. You administer a network that assigns IP addresses via DHCP. You want to make sure that one of the clients always receives the same IP address from the DHCP server. You create an exclusion for that address, but you find that the computer isn't being properly configured at bootup. What's the problem?

    A. You excluded the wrong IP address.

    B. You need to make a reservation for the client that ties the IP address to the computer's MAC address. Delete the exclusion.

    C. You need to create a superscope for the address.

    D. You must configure the client manually. You cannot assign the address via the DHCP server.

4. Your DHCP server crashed in the middle of the day. You rebooted the server and got it running within 5 minutes and nobody but you seemed to notice that it had gone down at all. What additional steps must you take?

A. None. If there were no lease renewal requests during the 5-minute period in which the DHCP server was down, none of the clients will ever know that it went down.

B. You need to renew all the leases manually.

C. None. The DHCP server automatically assigned new addresses to all the clients on the network transparently.

D. You must reboot all the client machines.

5. Your employer, the Huggy Buggy Bear Company, has used networking for years, starting with LAN Manager in the early 1990s. You migrated to Windows NT as an early adopter, and recently you also migrated to Windows XP and 2003 Server. You are using DHCP on your newly upgraded network, and you still have 100 Windows NT workstations to migrate before you're finished. You have added a new DNS server to the network and modified the scope on the DHCP server to reflect the new addition. You know the command for the Windows NT machines, but what command would you use to verify the IP configuration on the Windows XP Professional machines?

A. w2kipcfg /all

B. ipconfig /all

C. dhcpcfg /all

D. tcpcfg /all

E. winipcfg /all

6. You have just finished migrating all your workstations to Windows 2000 Professional. Along with this migration, you changed all of your static IP addresses over to DHCP. There are four subnets connected by a single router, which supports BootP. The DHCP server has been installed on subnet 1, and it's functioning properly in delivering addresses. When you bring up the clients on subnet 3, the clients boot properly and can communicate with each other, but they cannot communicate with devices on the other subnets. When you run ipconfig /all, you discover that the computers on subnets 2, 3, and 4 are in the 169.254.*x*.*y* address block, which is not the correct network address for any of the subnets. What is the likely cause of this outcome?

A. The DHCP server evaluated the scope for subnet 3, found it invalid, and substituted the default subnet information for the machines in that subnet.

B. The DHCP discover request isn't reaching the DHCP server on subnet 1, and the clients are configuring themselves with APIPA addresses.

C. DHCP servers can support only three subnets, and an additional DHCP server needs to be added to the network.

D. One of the users has brought another DHCP server online, and it's conflicting with the administrator's DHCP server.

7. You are going to modify the IP configuration on your network to take advantage of DHCP. This will be new to your staff, and you need to explain how DHCP works so that they'll be able to troubleshoot problems if they arise. You particularly want your staff to understand how a client obtains an address from the DHCP server. What steps that occur in the initial DHCP lease process do you need to explain to your staff? (Choose all that apply.)

   A. DHCP lease search

   B. DHCP lease offer

   C. DHCP lease acknowledgment

   D. DHCP lease announce

   E. DHCP lease request

   F. DHCP discovery

   G. DHCP lease selection

   H. DHCP selection

8. You assign two DNS server addresses as part of the options for a scope. Later you find a client workstation that isn't using those addresses. What's the most likely cause?

   A. The client didn't get the option information as part of its lease.

   B. The client has been manually configured with a different set of DNS servers.

   C. The client has a reserved IP address in the address pool.

   D. There's a bug in the DHCP server service.

9. Your Spring Flowers Florist Company in Las Vegas has been migrated to Windows XP and Server 2003 using Active Directory to manage the users and desktops with group policies. The company is in one location, and all the machines are on the same subnet. More recently, you decided to use DHCP to manage the address space more efficiently, and so you installed the DHCP server on one of the Windows Server 2003 computers. The scope was created and activated for use. You also configured all the Windows XP Professional workstations to use DHCP. However, when you reboot the Windows XP Professional workstations, they cannot obtain an IP address from the DHCP server. What is the most likely reason for the problem on this network?

   A. The DHCP relay agent has not been enabled for this subnet.

   B. The DHCP server has not been authorized to provide addresses in Active Directory.

   C. The DHCP relay agent needs to be installed on the DHCP server to pass the requests to the DHCP service.

   D. The Windows Server 2003 computer that hosts the DHCP server needs to be rebooted before the DHCP service will start.

10. You are working on a client machine that gets its IP configuration via DHCP. You notice that the client received different configuration information the last few times its lease was renewed. Which of the following would cause this to occur?

A. The DHCP server is not working properly.

B. Another computer on the network has taken over your machine's configuration information since the last renewal.

C. The client is receiving only the information that has changed since the last renewal. An administrator is changing the configuration information between lease renewals.

D. When clients renew their leases, they receive all of their configuration information. An administrator is changing the configuration information between lease renewals.

11. Because of a recent acquisition, your company has two locations, East and West, running Windows NT. The acquired company had been using DHCP on its East network. Soon after the acquisition, you decided to give DHCP a try, and you used BootP through your router to configure your West network to utilize the DHCP server that was running on the East network. Everything worked fine. You then migrated both of your Windows NT networks over to Windows Server 2003, and the DHCP service still works fine. However, all the support staff who ran the East network on the other subnet have left the company, and you now want to have the DHCP East server physically reside on your side of the network so that you can manage the machine more efficiently. What are some of the steps you must take to move the DHCP service on the East server to your subnet on the West server and still use the old DHCP database? (Choose all that apply.)

A. Pause the DHCP service on East.

B. Stop the DHCP service on West.

C. Save the DHCP server Registry subkey of East to a text file.

D. Copy the *systemroot*\System32\DHCP folder from East to West.

E. Scavenge all the scopes in West.

F. Reconcile all the scopes in West.

G. Enter the IP addresses of West and East into the DHCP configuration tools, and select Move Service.

12. You have a Windows Server 2003 network that supports a medium-sized business that refurbishes bowling balls for the Rock & Bowl Lanes in Cleveland, Ohio. You decide to use DHCP to help manage the IP addresses. You configure the DHCP server, two DNS servers, nine file and print servers, and the IIS server with static IP addresses from your private address range of 192.168.1.1 through 192.168.1.254. When you bring up the workstations over the weekend to test your new DHCP network, everything appears to be working fine. But on Monday, you receive calls from some of the users complaining that they cannot access their servers. What is the most likely cause of this sporadic networking problem?

A. You didn't create client reservations for the static IP addresses in the scope.

B. You didn't create a separate scope for the servers that have been configured with the static IP addresses.

C. You didn't exclude the IP addresses of the servers that have been configured with the static IP addresses.

D. You didn't configure the servers that have been configured with static IP addresses for interoperability with a DHCP server.

13. You administer a network that consists of 300 Windows XP and Server 2003 machines, all on a single subnet. You are deploying DHCP using two Windows Server 2003 DHCP servers named Dynamo1 and Dynamo2. Dynamo1 will assign IP addresses in the range 208.45.231.1 through 208.45.231.254. Dynamo2 will assign IP addresses in the range 208.45.232.1 through 208.45.232.254. What should you do to ensure that the DHCP configuration works efficiently?

A. Configure each DHCP server with one superscope and two member scopes. Configure the first member scope on each server with the range 208.45.231.1 through 208.45.231.254 and the second member scope on each server with the range 208.45.232.1 through 208.45.232.254. On Dynamo1, exclude the range 208.45.232.1 through 208.45.232.254. On Dynamo2, exclude the range 208.45.231.1 through 208.45.231.254.

B. Configure a scope on Dynamo1 with the range 208.45.231.1 through 208.45.231.254. Configure a scope on Dynamo2 with the range 208.45.232.1 through 208.45.232.254.

C. Configure a scope on both servers with the range 208.45.231.1 through 208.45.232.254. Exclude the range 208.45.232.1 through 208.45.232.254 on Dynamo1 and exclude the range 208.45.231.1 through 208.45.231.254 on Dynamo2.

D. Configure one superscope and two member scopes on each DHCP server. Configure the first member scope on each server with the range 208.45.231.1 through 208.45.231.254 and the second member scope on each server with the range 208.45.232.1 through 208.45.232.254.

14. Your network consists of three logical subnets named Subnet A, Subnet B, and Subnet C. They are all on the same physical network. Subnet A contains addresses in the range 208.44.0.1–208.44.0.50, Subnet B contains addresses in the range 208.44.0.60–208.44.0.100, and Subnet C contains addresses in the range 208.44.0.110–208.44.0.120. You are setting up a single DHCP server that will provide DHCP services for Subnet A and Subnet B only. The address of the server must be set to 208.44.0.10.

In the following exhibit, each address listed in the Choices column on the left will fit into only one of the empty boxes in the other two columns. Select each address and place it in its appropriate position within the network.

Choices:		Exclusion	Unassigned
208.44.0.32			
208.44.0.113			
208.44.0.78		Scope A	Scope B
208.44.0.10			

15. Your network consists of 100 Windows XP Professional machines, 2 Windows Server 2003 machines, and 3 NetWare clients. All the machines need to access resources on the Windows Server 2003. You want to use the TCP/IP protocol with all the Windows computers and IPX/SPX on all the NetWare computers. You also want to minimize setup time as much as possible.

In the following exhibit, the items in the Choices box represent various configuration options for the three different machine types. Select the configuration options and place them in their appropriate places within the network.

2 Windows Server
2003 machines

Choices:

IP addresses assigned dynamically
DHCP server
Static IP address
Network settings configured manually

100 Windows 2000
Professional machines

3 NetWare clients

Answers to Review Questions

1. **B.** When a DHCP-enabled Windows 2000 or XP workstation cannot locate a DHCP server, it uses APIPA to automatically configure itself with an address in the 169.254.0.0/16 address range. If you cannot ping the DHCP server from a correctly configured machine, it's likely that the DHCP server is down—which is why the Windows 2000 and XP machines have auto-configured themselves. In this particular situation, the Windows Server 2003 computers have configured themselves using APIPA, which is why the other workstations can see the servers. Because the Windows 95 machines didn't participate in the APIPA configuration, they were left without an IP address. Conflict-resolution protocol on a DHCP server is used to determine duplicate addresses, not bad ones. APIPA is already enabled on the Windows 2000 and XP machines, which is why the network is behaving in the manner described. The DHCP relay agent is used to pass requests through routers that don't support the BootP protocol for DHCP broadcasts.

2. **B, E.** DHCP depends on a specific type of broadcast from the client machines in order for them to deliver their IP configuration information. By design, broadcasts are not propagated through routers. However, BootP is a specialized and standard broadcast recognized by many routers and is passed through from one subnet to another, allowing DHCP to function properly. If the routers don't support BootP, you can use a DHCP relay agent, which recognizes the DHCP requests from the clients and passes those requests to DHCP servers through their known IP addresses.

3. **B.** Excluded addresses are just marked as excluded; the DHCP server doesn't maintain any information about them. Reserved addresses are marked as reserved.

4. **A.** When the DHCP server crashed, the scope was effectively deactivated. Deactivating a scope has no effect on the client until it needs to renew the lease.

5. **B.** `Ipconfig /all` is still the command to display the IP configuration on Windows 2000, XP, and Server 2003 machines. The `/all` switch is needed to show the details that include the DNS server address. The `winipcfg` command is used for Windows 9*x* workstations. The other commands are not valid.

6. **B.** TCP/IP is the standard protocol of choice, but it also increases the complexity of configuring both the Windows 2000 and Windows 98 operating systems. Because of this complexity, Microsoft has implemented Automatic Private IP Addressing (APIPA). When an APIPA IP stack is configured for DHCP and a server isn't located, the stack is automatically configured with an address in the 169.254.0.0/16 range, with the intention that an IP network can be set up fairly easily. DHCP servers can support any number of subnets or scopes, within reason. A DHCP server doesn't validate the scope information while clients are communicating with it. Finally, a user cannot bring a DHCP server online because the user needs administrative capability to add the service.

7.   B, C, E, F.   IP lease discovery is used when a DHCP-enabled IP stack is initialized to locate a DHCP server with this specialized broadcast. When a DHCP server receives the discover packet, it sends out an IP lease offer containing an available address. The client responds to the DHCP offer with an IP lease acceptance message, showing that this address is acceptable. Finally, when the DHCP request is received, the server sends out an IP lease acknowledgment, which contains configuration options for the IP stack and adds the information to the DHCP database.

8.   B.   Manual settings override DHCP options.

9.   B.   When you install a DHCP server using Windows Server 2003 and Active Directory, the server won't be permitted to provide DHCP services until it has been authorized. When you authorize a server, you are actually adding its IP address to the Active Directory object that contains a list of DHCP servers. If the address of the server isn't on the list, the DHCP service will fail. DHCP relay agents are used to send DHCP requests across routers that don't support BootP. Windows Server 2003 computers don't need to be rebooted after DHCP has been installed in order to start the service.

10.   D.   During lease renewal, the client gets *all* configuration information offered by the server, not a subset of that information.

11.   B, C, D, F.   Options B, C, D, and F are not *all* the steps necessary to complete this procedure, but all four are necessary. To move the DHCP database from one server to another, you must first stop the DHCP service. Then, copy the *systemroot*\system32\DHCP folder on the East server to a temporary folder that is accessible from the West server. Next, copy the DHCP server Registry key to a text file using REGEDT32. Next, install DHCP on the West server and stop the service and then rename the System.mdb file in the temporary *systemroot*\System32\DHCP folder to System.src. This is followed by copying the temporary *systemroot*\System32\DHCP folder to the new *systemroot*\System32\DHCP folder. Then, use REGEDT32 to restore the DHCP server Registry key to West from the text file saved from the East server. Finally, start the DHCP service on West and choose Reconcile All Scopes.

12.   C.   If you configure static IP addresses and then don't exclude those addresses from the scope in the DHCP server, the same addresses will be available to be delivered to clients and will thus create conflicts. The best practice is to exclude a block of addresses large enough to cover all the devices on your network that should be static. Having just one block also makes it easier for you to recognize the excluded addresses when you're looking at network traffic. Client reservations are used to deliver the same address to the same machine each time and are not used to recognize statically configured clients. A scope identifies a subnet, and the servers and the workstations exist on the same subnet. There is no configuration for a static IP address to interoperate with a DHCP server.

13.   A.   A superscope allows the DHCP server to provide multiple logical subnet addresses to DHCP clients on a single physical network. In each superscope, you should exclude the range of addresses that you want the other server to assign. If you just created a single scope on each DHCP server, you would probably end up with a lot of unused leases.

14.

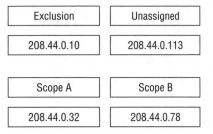

Exclusion	Unassigned
208.44.0.10	208.44.0.113

Scope A	Scope B
208.44.0.32	208.44.0.78

The address 208.44.0.10 needs to be excluded so that the DHCP server can use it. 208.44.0.113 is part of Subnet C and is not assigned by the DHCP server. 208.44.0.32 is part of Scope A, and 208.44.0.78 is part of Scope B.

15.

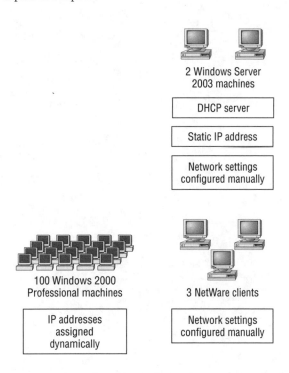

2 Windows Server
2003 machines

DHCP server

Static IP address

Network settings
configured manually

100 Windows 2000
Professional machines

IP addresses
assigned
dynamically

3 NetWare clients

Network settings
configured manually

Because you have a large number of Windows clients that need to use TCP/IP, you should assign IP addresses to them dynamically. To do this, you need to configure the Windows Server 2003 computer as a DHCP server and assign its IP address manually. The NetWare clients will not use TCP/IP, so their network settings cannot be assigned via DHCP.

Chapter

6

Installing and Managing Domain Name Service (DNS)

MICROSOFT EXAM OBJECTIVES COVERED IN THIS CHAPTER:

✓ **Install and configure the DNS Server service.**

- Configure DNS server options.
- Configure DNS zone options.
- Configure DNS forwarding.

✓ **Manage DNS.**

- Manage DNS zone settings.
- Manage DNS record settings.
- Manage DNS server options.

✓ **Monitor DNS. Tools might include System Monitor, Event Viewer, Replication Monitor, and DNS debug logs.**

DNS is one of the most important topics in both Windows Server 2003 network administration and the Windows Server 2003 Network Infrastructure exam. Active Directory depends absolutely on DNS, and many important system functions (including Kerberos authentication and finding domain controllers) are now handled through DNS lookups. Windows 2000 and XP clients use DNS for name resolution, too, but they also use DNS to find Kerberos key distribution centers (KDCs), global catalog servers, and other services that may be registered in DNS.

By the time you finish this chapter, you will have a deeper understanding of how DNS works in general, plus an understanding of how to set up, configure, manage, and troubleshoot DNS in Windows Server 2003.

DNS Fundamentals

The Domain Name Service (DNS) is a hierarchically distributed database. In other words, its layers are arranged in a definite order, and its data is distributed across a wide range of machines. DNS is a standard set of protocols that defines the following:

- A mechanism for querying and updating address information in the database
- A mechanism for replicating the information in the database among servers
- A schema of the database

DNS began in the early days of the Internet when the Internet was a small network created by the Department of Defense for research purposes. Before DNS, computer names, or hostnames, were manually entered into a file located on a centrally administered server. Each site that needed to resolve hostnames had to download this file. As the number of computers on the Internet grew, so did the size of this HOSTS file, and the amount of traffic generated by downloading it. The need for a new system that would offer features such as scalability, decentralized administration, and support for various data types became more and more obvious. The Domain Name Service (DNS), introduced in 1984, became this new system.

With DNS, the hostnames reside in a database that can be distributed among multiple servers, decreasing the load on any one server and providing the ability to administer this naming system on a per-partition basis. DNS supports hierarchical names and allows registration of various data types in addition to the hostname-to-IP-address mapping used in HOSTS files. By virtue of the DNS database being distributed, its size is unlimited and performance does not degrade much when adding more servers.

In the following sections, you will learn more about what DNS is and how it works and see how Windows Server 2003 handles DNS.

What DNS Does

DNS translates between computer hostnames and IP addresses. DNS works at the Application layer of the OSI reference model and uses TCP and UDP at the transport layer. The DNS model is pretty plain: Clients make requests ("what's the IP address for www.chellis.net?") and get back answers ("209.155.222.222"). If a particular server can't answer a query, it can forward it to another, presumably better informed, server.

To really understand how DNS works, it's important to learn about some fundamental parts of the system. We will do that in the following sections.

An Introduction to Domain Naming

The Domain Name System is composed of a distributed database of names that establishes a logical tree structure called the domain name space. Each node, or domain, in that space has a unique name. Therefore, chellis.com and chellis.netchellis.net are two different domains, and they can contain *subdomains*, such as sales.chellis.com and marketing.chellis.netchellis.net.

A domain name identifies the domain's position in the logical DNS hierarchy in relation to its parent domain by separating each branch of the tree with a period. Figure 6.1 shows a few of the top-level domains, where the Microsoft domain fits, and a host called Tigger within the microsoft.com domain. If someone wanted to contact that host, they would use the fully qualified domain name (FQDN) tigger.microsoft.com.

FIGURE 6.1   The DNS hierarchy

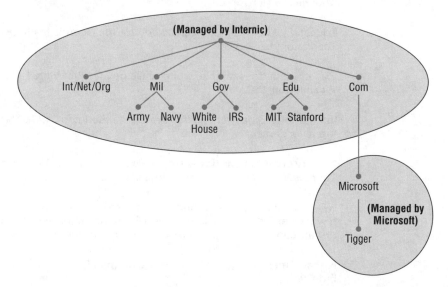

Each domain is associated with a DNS *name server*. In other words, for every domain registered in the DNS, there's some server that can give an authoritative answer to queries about that domain. For example, the chellis.netchellis.net domain is handled by a name server at an Internet provider. This means that any resolver or name server can go straight to the source if it can't resolve a query by looking in its own cache.

Domain names and hostnames must contain only characters *a* to *z*, *A* to *Z*, 0 to 9, and - (hyphen). Other common and useful characters, like the & (ampersand), / (slash), . (period), and _ (underscore), are not allowed. This is in conflict with NetBIOS's naming restrictions. However, you'll find that Windows Server 2003 is smart enough to take a NetBIOS name like Server_1 and turn it into a legal DNS name, like server1.chellis.net.

DNS and the Internet

You're undoubtedly familiar with how DNS works on the Internet; if you've ever sent or received Internet e-mail or browsed web pages on the Net, you've got firsthand experience using DNS. Internet DNS depends on a set of top-level domains that serve as the root of the DNS hierarchy. These top-level domains and their authoritative name servers are managed by the Internet Network Information Center (`www.internic.com`). The top-level domains are organized in two ways: by organization and by country. Table 6.1 shows some of the most common top-level domains.

TABLE 6.1 Common Top-Level DNS Domains

Common Top-Level Domain Names	Type of Organization
Com	Commercial (for example, globalknowledge.com for Global Knowledge Network).
Edu	Educational (for example, gatech.edu for the Georgia Institute of Technology).
Gov	Government (for example, whitehouse.gov for the White House in Washington, D.C.).
Int	International organizations (for example, nato.int for NATO). This top-level domain is fairly rare.
Mil	Military organizations (for example, usmc.mil for the Marine Corps). There is a separate set of root name servers for this domain.
Net	Networking organizations and Internet providers (for example, hiwaay.net for HiWAAY Information Systems). Many commercial organizations have registered names under this domain, too.
Org	Noncommercial organizations (for example, fidonet.org for FidoNet).
AU	Australia.
UK	United Kingdom.

TABLE 6.1   Common Top-Level DNS Domains *(continued)*

Common Top-Level Domain Names	Type of Organization
CA	Canada.
US	United States.
JP	Japan.

Beneath each top-level domain, there can be additional subdomains. For example, commercial organizations in Japan will have .co.jp on the end of their domain names. The local Athens, Alabama, police department has a server in the ci.athens.al.us domain: *ci* for city, *Athens* because the city's name is Athens, *al* for Alabama, and *us* for the top-level domain.

Servers, Clients, and Resolvers

There are a few terms and concepts you will need to know before managing a DNS server. Understanding these terms will make it easier to understand how the Windows Server 2003 DNS server works:

DNS servers   Any computer providing domain name services is a *DNS server*. That being said, not all DNS servers are alike. Earlier implementations of DNS (for example, early versions of the popular Berkeley Internet Name Domain, or BIND) were originally developed for Unix, and they handled a fairly small and simple set of RFC requirements.

There is also the concept of primary and secondary DNS servers to consider. A *primary DNS server* is the "owner" of the zones defined in its database. The primary DNS server has the authority to make changes to the zones it owns. Secondary DNS servers receive a read-only copy of zones through *zone transfers* (discussed later, in the section "Zone Transfers"). The *secondary DNS server* can resolve queries from this read-only copy but cannot make changes or updates. A single DNS server may contain multiple primary and secondary zones (more on zones in a minute).

Any DNS server implementation supporting Service Location Resource Records (see RCF 2052) and Dynamic Updates (RFC 2136) is sufficient to provide the name service for Windows 2000 and newer computers. However, because Windows Server 2003 DNS is designed to fully take advantage of the Windows Active Directory service, it is the recommended DNS server for any networked organization with a significant investment in Windows or extranet partners with Windows-based systems.

Clients   A *DNS client* is any machine issuing queries to a DNS server. The client hostname may or may not be registered in a name server (DNS) database. Clients issue DNS requests through processes called resolvers.

Resolvers   *Resolvers* handle the process of mapping a symbolic name to an actual network address. The resolver (which may reside on another machine) issues queries to name servers. When a resolver receives information from name servers, it caches that information locally in case the same information is requested again.

When a name server is unable to resolve a request, it may reply to the resolver with the name of another name server. The resolver must then address a message to this new name server in the hope that the symbolic name will be resolved.

Queries   There are two types of queries that can be made to a DNS server: recursive and iterative (we'll discuss the difference shortly).

Root servers   When a DNS server processes a recursive query and that query cannot be resolved from local zone files, the query must be escalated to a root DNS server. The *root server* is responsible for returning an authoritative answer for a particular domain *or* a referral to a server that can provide an authoritative answer. Because each DNS server is supposed to have a full set of root hints (which point to root servers for various top-level domains), your DNS server can refer queries recursively to other servers with the assistance of the root servers. You can also configure a DNS server to contain its own root zone; you might want to do so if you don't want your servers to be able to answer queries for names outside your network.

DNS Zones   DNS servers work together to resolve hierarchical names. If they already have information about a name, they simply fulfill the query for the client; otherwise, they query other DNS servers for the appropriate information. The system works well because it distributes the authority of separate parts of the DNS structure to specific servers. A DNS *zone* is a portion of the DNS namespace over which a specific DNS server has authority.

In order to ensure that naming remains accurate in a distributed network environment, one DNS server must be designated as the master database for a specific set of addresses. It is on this server that updates to hostname-to-IP-address mappings can be updated. Whenever a DNS server is unable to resolve a specific DNS name, it simply queries other servers that can provide the information. Zones are necessary because many different DNS servers could otherwise be caching the same information. If changes are made, this information could become outdated. Therefore, one central DNS server must assume the role of the ultimate authority for a specific subset of domain names.

There is an important distinction to make between DNS zones and Active Directory domains. Although both use hierarchical names and require name resolution, DNS zones do not map directly to AD domains.

DNS and Windows Server 2003

Windows Server 2003 relies on TCP/IP, and Active Directory requires DNS—even if you're not connected to the Internet. Naturally, Windows Server 2003 includes a DNS server component and adds some features that are even interoperable with other DNS implementations. In the following sections, you will see how DNS integrates with Windows Server 2003.

Dynamic DNS

In earlier versions of Windows, when you used Dynamic Host Configuration Protocol (DHCP) to assign IP addresses to clients, you had no way to keep the corresponding DNS records up-to-date. For example, if you had a DNS entry for minuteman.chellis.netchellis.net pointing to 192.168.0.202, that's okay until minuteman's DHCP lease is released and it gets a new address. At that point, you'd get the choice of either fixing the DNS record by hand or relying on NetBIOS and WINS for name resolution. You may have a similar problem if you used a dial-up ISP—every time you dial up, you get a different IP address.

The *Dynamic DNS (DDNS) standard*, described in RFC 2136, was designed to solve this very problem. DDNS allows DNS *clients* to update information in the DNS database files. For example, a Windows Server 2003 DHCP server can automatically tell a DDNS server which IP addresses it has assigned and to what machines. Windows 2000 and XP Professional DHCP clients can do this, too, but for security reasons it's better to let the DHCP server do it. The result: IP addresses and DNS records stay in synch so that you can use DNS and DHCP together seamlessly.

Because DDNS is a proposed Internet standard, you can even use Windows Server 2003's DDNS-aware parts with Unix-based DNS servers.

DNS and Active Directory

You can store DNS data in Active Directory (AD) instead of in regular disk files. While it might seem odd to use AD to store information that AD will have to run, it makes sense. Consider a typical DNS zone data file on disk—it's plain text and easily editable. It's not replicated, it's probably not secured, and there's no way to delegate control over it. All of these limitations go away when you build what Microsoft calls an *Active Directory-Integrated (ADI) zone*. In an ADI zone, Active Directory stores all of the DNS zone data in AD, so it gains all of the benefits of AD—especially improved security and seamless replication.

How DNS Works

Knowing how servers and resolvers communicate with each other, and what kind of queries are passed around, is critical to properly configuring your network. That knowledge begins with understanding what's actually in the DNS database itself as well as what's in the zone database file. Once you understand these concepts, you will have a better idea of how DNS resolves names, and you will understand why zone transfers are important. In this section you will also see how to migrate the DNS database files from older systems to Windows Server 2003.

Records in the DNS Database

No matter where your zone information is stored, you can rest assured that it contains a variety of DNS information. Although the DNS snap-in makes it unlikely that you'll ever need to edit these files by hand, it's good to know exactly what data is contained in there.

The first thing to understand is the fact that each zone file consists of a number of *resource records (RRs)*. Each RR contains information about some resource on the network, such as its IP address. There are several types of resource records you need to know about to effectively manage your DNS servers. They are discussed in the sections that follow.

Start of Authority (SOA) Records

The first record in any database file is the start of authority (SOA) record, which looks like this:

```
@ IN SOA source_host contact_e-mail serial_number↵
refresh_time retry_time expiration_time time_to_live
```

The SOA defines the general parameters for the DNS zone, including who the authoritative server is for the zone. Table 6.2 lists the attributes stored in the SOA record.

TABLE 6.2 The SOA Record Structure

Field	Meaning
Source host	The host on which this file is maintained.
Contact e-mail	The Internet e-mail address for the person responsible for this domain's database file.
Serial number	The "version number" of this database file. Increases each time the database file is changed.
Refresh time	The elapsed time (in seconds) that a secondary server will wait between checks to its master server to see if the database file has changed and a zone transfer should be requested.
Retry time	The elapsed time (in seconds) that a secondary server will wait before retrying a failed zone transfer.
Expiration time	The elapsed time (in seconds) that a secondary server will keep trying to download a zone. After this time limit expires, the old zone information will be discarded.
Time to live	The elapsed time (in seconds) that a DNS server is allowed to cache any resource records from this database file. This is the value that is sent out with all query responses from this zone file when the individual resource record doesn't contain an overriding value.

Name Server (NS) Records

Name server (NS) records list the name servers for a domain. This allows other name servers to look up names in your domain. A zone file may contain more than one name server record. The format of these records is simple:

```
domain @ IN NS nameserver_host
```

Domain is the name of your domain, and *nameserver host* is the FQDN of a name server in that domain. There are a couple of interesting shortcuts that can be used in DNS records, such as the following:

▪ In a zone file, the @ symbol represents the root domain of the zone. The *IN* in the records stands for Internet.

- Any domain name in the database file that is *not* terminated with a period will have the root domain appended to the end. For example, an entry that just has the name sales will be expanded by adding the root domain to the end, whereas sales.chellis.net won't be expanded.

What do these records actually look like? Here's a small sample:

```
@ IN NS ns1.chellis.net
@ IN NS ns2.chellis.net
```

NS records play a key role in the referral process that you'll be learning about later in the chapter.

The Host Record

A *host record* (also called an address or an A record) is used to statically associate a host's name to its IP addresses. The format is pretty simple:

```
host_name  IN  A  IP_Address
```

Here's an example from our DNS database:

```
minuteman  IN  A  192.168.0.204
titan      IN  A  192.168.3.144
```

The A record ties a hostname (which is part, you'll recall, of an FQDN) to a specific IP address. This makes them suitable for use when you have devices with statically assigned IP addresses; in that case, you'd create these records manually using the DNS snap-in. As it turns out, if you enable DDNS, your DHCP server can create these for you; that automatic creation is what enables DDNS to work.

The Pointer (PTR) Record

A records are probably the most visible component of the DNS database because Internet users depend on them to turn FQDNs like www.microsoft.com and www.delta-air.com into IP addresses so that browsers and other components can find them. However, the host record has a lesser-known but still important twin: the *pointer (PTR) record*. The format of a pointer record looks like the following:

```
owner ttl class PTR targeted_domain_name
```

The A record maps a hostname to an IP address, and the PTR record does just the opposite. Having both types of records makes it possible to do *reverse lookups*, which occur when a resolver asks a DNS server to cough up the FQDN associated with a particular IP address. This is a useful function for, among other things, preventing people with made-up or illegal domain names from using services like e-mail or FTP servers.

The Alias Record

Almost every company on the Web has a URL of www.*companyname.com*. This is pretty much standard. However, many (if not most) domains don't actually have a machine named www. Instead, they use DNS alias records (more properly known as canonical name, or CNAME, entries, which allow them to use more than one name to point to a single host).

The syntax of an alias record looks like the following:

```
<alias>    IN  CNAME  <hostname>
```

Suppose there was a company with a machine whose real A record name was kingkong.intexas .com. The CNAME records can point the names mail.intexas.com and ftp.intexas.com to that machine. A resolver that queried the company's DNS server for either *mail* or *FTP* would actually get the A record for kingkong back.

Here's how they created the alias:

```
mail       IN  CNAME  kingkong
ftp        IN  CNAME  kingkong
kingkong IN  A      172.30.1.14
```

The Mail Exchange (MX) Record

The mail exchange (MX) record tells you which servers can accept mail bound for this domain. Each MX record contains two parameters—a priority and a mail server—as shown in the following example:

<domain> IN MX <priority> <mailserver host>

Why use MX records? As an example, consider the domain chellis.net. Users in your organization have addresses of `someuser@chellis.net`. To make sure that mail is delivered where you want it to go—to your Exchange server—you'd have two MX records: One points to chellis.net, and one points to your ISP's mail server. When someone on the Internet tries to send SMTP mail to any user whose address ends in chellis.net, their mail server will look to see if that domain contains an MX record. If it does, the sending server will use the host specified in the MX record to deliver the mail.

Attentive readers will notice that we said your domain has *two* MX records. That's because MX records have preferences attached to them. If multiple MX records exist for a domain, the DNS server uses the mail server with the lowest preference and then tries the other mail servers when the most preferred host can't be contacted. For example, the two records you used could look like this:

```
chellis.net. IN MX 100 mail.pair.com
chellis.net. IN MX 10 mail.chellis.net
```

Service Records

Windows Server 2003 depends on some relatively new services, like Lightweight Directory Access Protocol (LDAP) and Kerberos. These protocols postdate the DNS system by quite a while. Normally, clients use DNS to find the IP address of a machine whose name they already know. Microsoft wanted to extend this system by devising a way for a client to locate a particular *service* by making a DNS query.

For example, a Windows 2000 or XP client can query DNS servers for the location of a domain controller. This makes it much easier (for both the client and the administrator) to manage and distribute logon traffic in large-scale networks. For this approach to work, Microsoft had to have some way to register the presence of a service (or, really, a TCP/IP protocol) in DNS, but none of the RR types you've read about so far offer any way to do so. Enter the *service (SRV) record*. SRV records tie together the location of a service (like a domain controller) with information about how to contact the service. Think of a host record: It ties a name to an IP address. The MX record extends the concept by adding another parameter, the preference.

SRV records take it even further by providing seven items of information. Let's look at an example to help clarify this powerful concept:

```
ldap.tcp.chellis.net   SRV   10   100   389   hsv.chellis.net
ldap.tcp.chellis.net   SRV   20   100   389   msy.chellis.net
```

The first field, ldap.tcp.chellis.net, is actually a composite: It contains a service name (*ldap* for LDAP or *kerberos* for Kerberos), a transport protocol (TCP or UDP), and the domain name for which the service is offered. Thus, ldap.tcp.chellis.net indicates that this SRV record is advertising an LDAP server for the chellis.net domain. The next field is just the record type—SRV in this case.

The two numbers following are the priority and the weight. The priority field specifies a preference, just as the preference field in an MX record does. The SRV record with the lowest priority will be used first. The weight is a little different: Service records with equal priority will be chosen according to their weight. Consider the case of three SRV records of priority 0 and weight 100. That tells the DNS server to answer queries by picking one of the three at random because they have equal weight. If one record had a weight of 50 (instead of 100), it would be chosen twice as often as either of the other records.

The next field is the number of the port on which the service is offered: 389 for LDAP or 88 for Kerberos. The final entry in the record defines the DNS name of the server that offers the service (in this case, hsv.chellis.net and msy.chellis.net). You'll read later how these service records are actually used in DNS queries; for now it's enough to understand that they exist.

You can define other types of service records. If your applications support them, they can query DNS to find the services they need.

Zone Database Files

Let's assume that you're not using an ADI zone. The only reason we make that assumption is to illustrate where the zone database files live on a non-ADI server. As it turns out, you can specify names for some, but not all, of these files when you install DNS on your Windows Server 2003 computer. The specific zone database files are discussed in the following sections.

The Domain Name File

Each domain that has a forward lookup zone on your server will have its own database file. For example, when you create a new zone named chellis.net on a Windows Server 2003 DNS server, you'll end up with a new file named chellis.net.dns in the system's DNS directory (*systemroot*\system32\DNS). The file is pretty much empty when you create the zone: It contains only an SOA record for the domain and one NS record listing the name of the server you just created. As you add new A records to the domain, they're stored in this file.

The Reverse Lookup File

This database file holds information on a single reverse lookup zone. These zones are usually named after the IP address range they cover. For example, a reverse lookup zone that can handle queries for the 172.30.1.* block will be named 1.30.172.in-addr.arpa. Notice that the network address is reversed. Remember that the reverse lookup database allows a resolver to provide an IP address and request a matching hostname. It looks like the domain database file (for example, it has SOA and name server records), but instead of A records it has one PTR record for each host designated in the reverse lookup zone.

DNS reverse lookup is frequently used as a sort of backdoor authentication method. For example, most modern mail servers can be configured to refuse incoming mail from servers whose IP address can't be resolved with a reverse lookup. This prevents people with real IP addresses but fake DNS names from using those mail servers (thus, preventing spam). Reverse lookups are also valuable for troubleshooting name resolution problems because you can always find the IP address of a machine even if you're not sure what its domain name is supposed to be.

The Cache File

The cache file contains host information needed to resolve names outside the authoritative domains—in short, it holds a list of the names and addresses of root name servers. If your DNS server will be able to connect to the Internet, you can leave this file alone; if not, you can edit it so that it lists the authoritative roots for your private network.

The Boot File

Consider what a primary DNS server must do when it boots. It has to figure out what zones it's supposed to be serving, decide whether it's authoritative for any of them, and link up with other servers in the zone, if any. You can choose the method by which Windows Server 2003 DNS servers get this information: from AD, from the Registry, or from a BIND-style boot file. The boot file, which must be named *systemroot*\system32\dns\boot, controls the DNS server's startup behavior. Boot files support only four commands:

directory The `directory` command specifies where the other files named in the boot file can be found. This is almost always the *systemroot*\system32\dns directory. You use the command along with a directory path, like this:

```
directory f:\winnt\system32\dns
```

cache The `cache` command specifies the file of root hints used to help your DNS service contact name servers for the root domain. This command, *and* the file it refers to, *must* be present. For example, `cache cache.dns` points the DNS server at the default `cache.dns` file shipped with Windows Server 2003.

primary The `primary` command specifies a domain for which this name server is authoritative, as well as a database file that contains the resource records for that domain. You can use multiple primary commands in a single boot file. Here are a couple of examples:

```
primary chellis.net        chellis.net.dns
primary hsv.chellis.net    hsv.chellis.dns
```

secondary The `secondary` command designates a domain as being one that your server handles as a *secondary domain*. That means your server is authoritative, but it pulls DNS information from one (or more) of the specified master servers. The command also defines the name of the local file for caching this zone. Multiple secondary command records may exist in the boot file. The `secondary` command takes three parameters, as shown by the following syntax:

```
secondary <secondary domain>    <master server>    <local file for caching>
```

Secondary entries would look like this:

```
secondary wuolukka.com    ns.pair.com    wuolukka.dns
secondary chellis.com    ns2.pair.com    chellis.dns
```

How DNS Resolves Names

There are three types of queries that a client can make to a DNS server: recursive, iterative, and inverse. Remember that the client of a DNS server can be a resolver (what you'd normally call a client) or another DNS server.

Iterative queries are the easiest to understand: A client asks the DNS server for an answer, and the server returns the best answer. This type of query is typically sent by one DNS server to another after the original server has received a recursive query from a resolver. The server may not know the answer and may direct you to another server, or it might respond with an actual RR.

Most resolvers, however, use recursive queries. In a recursive query, the client sends a query to one name server, asking it to respond either with the requested answer or with an error. The error states one of two things: that the server can't come up with the right answer or that the domain name doesn't exist. The name server isn't allowed to just refer the client to some other name server. In addition, if your DNS server uses a forwarder, the requests sent by your server to the forwarder will be recursive queries.

Figure 6.2 shows an example of both recursive and iterative queries. In this example, a client within the Microsoft Corporation is querying its DNS server for the IP address for www.whitehouse.gov. Here's what happens to resolve the request:

1. The resolver sends a recursive DNS query to its local DNS server asking for the IP address of www.whitehouse.gov. The local name server is responsible for resolving the name and cannot refer the resolver to another name server.

2. The local name server checks its zones and finds no zones corresponding to the requested domain name.

3. The root name server has authority for the root domain and will reply with the IP address of a name server for the Gov top-level domain.

4. The local name server sends an iterative query for www.whitehouse.gov to the Gov name server.

5. The Gov name server replies with the IP address of the name server servicing the whitehouse .gov domain.

6. The local name server sends an iterative query for www.whitehouse.gov to the whitehouse .gov name server.

7. The whitehouse.gov name server replies with the IP address corresponding to www.whitehouse.gov.

8. The local name server sends the IP address of www.whitehouse.gov back to the original resolver.

FIGURE 6.2 A sample DNS query

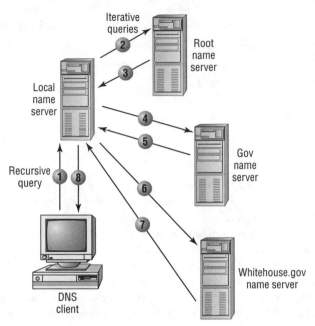

Inverse queries use PTR records. Instead of supplying a name and then asking for an IP address, the client first provides the IP address and then asks for the name. Because there's no direct correlation in the DNS name space between a domain name and its associated IP address, this search would be fruitless without the use of the in-addr.arpa domain. Nodes in the in-addr.arpa domain are named after the numbers in the dotted-octet representation of IP addresses. But because IP addresses get more specific from left to right and domain names get less specific from left to right, the order of IP address octets must be reversed when building the in-addr.arpa tree. With this arrangement, administration of the lower limbs of the DNS in-addr.arpa tree can be given to companies as they are assigned their Class A, B, or C subnet address.

Once the domain tree is built into the DNS database, a special pointer record is added to associate the IP addresses to the corresponding hostnames. In other words, to find a hostname for the IP address 206.131.234.1, the resolver would query the DNS server for a pointer record for 1.234.131.206.in-addr.arpa. If this IP address was outside the local domain, the DNS server would start at the root and sequentially resolve the domain nodes until arriving at 234.131.206 .in-addr.arpa, which would contain the PTR record for the desired host.

You have several specialized options when you configure DNS resolution, as shown in the following sections.

Caching and Time to Live

When a name server is processing a recursive query, it may be required to send out several queries to find the definitive answer. Name servers are allowed to cache all the received information during this process; each record contains something called a time to live (TTL). The TTL specifies how long the record will be valid until it must be resolved again.

The name server owner sets the TTL for each RR on their server. If your data changes a lot, you can use smaller TTL values to help ensure that data about your domain is more consistent across the network on which the name server resides. However, if you make the TTL too small, the load on your name server will go up. That's because once data is cached by a DNS server, the server begins decreasing the TTL from its original value; when it hits zero, the server flushes the RR from its cache. If a query comes in that can be satisfied by this cached data, the TTL that's returned with it equals the current amount of time left before flush time. Client resolvers also have data caches and honor the TTL value so that they too know when to flush.

Load Balancing with Round Robin and Netmask Ordering

The Windows Server 2003 implementation of DNS supports load balancing through the use of round robin and netmask ordering. Load balancing distributes the network load between multiple network cards if they are available. You can create multiple resource records with the same hostname but different IP addresses for multihomed computers. Depending on the options that you select, the DNS server will respond with one of the multihomed computer's addresses.

If round robin is enabled, the first address that was entered in the database is returned to the resolver and then sent to the end of the list. The next time a client attempts to resolve the name, the DNS server will return the second name in the database (which is now the first name) and then send it to the end of the list and so on.

If netmask ordering is enabled, the DNS server will use the first IP address in the database that matches the subnet of the resolver. If none of the IP addresses match the subnet of the resolver, then the DNS server reverts to round robin. If round robin is disabled, the DNS server simply returns the first IP address in the database.

If neither round robin nor netmask ordering is enabled, the DNS server always returns the first IP address in the database. This usually isn't very helpful, so fortunately round robin and netmask ordering are both enabled by default. You will see how to enable and disable round robin and netmask ordering in the section titled "Configuring Advanced Properties."

BIND Options

Earlier we briefly hinted that BIND is a simple DNS implementation primarily used by Unix servers. This is true to an extent, but BIND is really just a set of RFCs that standardize the way DNS operates. Windows Server 2003 is actually compliant with several versions of BIND (specifically, BIND 4.9.7, 8.1.2, 8.2, and 9.1.0), which makes the Server 2003 DNS implementation interoperable with other BIND DNS servers. Windows Server 2003 DNS can also be used on the Internet because BIND is the standard for DNS on almost every computer on the planet.

We don't need to get into the specifics of the different versions of BIND, but you should understand two key points about how BIND can affect your Windows Server 2003 environment:

- When Windows Server 2003 sends a zone transfer to a secondary DNS server, it sends several compressed resource records simultaneously. Unfortunately, BIND versions prior to 4.9.4 don't support compression, and they can only receive one RR at a time. If your secondary servers are running older versions of BIND, you will need to disable these features, as you will see in the section titled "Configuring Advanced Properties."

- Active Directory requires DNS and BIND version 8.1.2. Usually you should use Windows Server 2003 DNS servers with Active Directory–Integrated zones, but some companies have long-established Unix-based DNS servers that they need to continue to use. You may need to upgrade these servers if they don't meet the minimum BIND requirement and you want to use Active Directory.

Queries for Services

Windows Server 2003 uses some special domains (not unlike the in-addr.arpa domain you just read about) to make it possible for domain clients to look up services they need. It turns out that RFC 2052 specifies how this mechanism should work. However, there's a Microsoft twist: The underscore (_) character isn't legal in domain names, so Microsoft uses it to mark its special domains and to keep them from colliding with RFC 2052–compliant domains. There are a total of four of these trick Windows Server 2003 domains:

_msdcs   This domain contains a list of all the Windows Server 2003 domain controllers in a designated normal domain. Each domain controller, global catalog, and PDC emulator is listed here.

_sites   Each site has its own subdomain within the _sites domain. In AD parlance, a site is a group of connected network subnets that have high bandwidth between them.

_tcp   This domain lists service records for services that run on TCP: LDAP, Kerberos, the kpasswd password changer, and the global catalogs.

_udp   This domain lists services that run on UDP: Kerberos and the kpasswd service.

When any network client wants to find a service (for instance, a domain controller), it can query its DNS server for the appropriate SRV record. By making a recursive query, the client can force the local DNS server to poke around in the domain until it finds the desired information.

Zone Transfers

DNS is such an important part of the network that you simply cannot use a single DNS server. If that server fails, the network fails. Adding a secondary server provides DNS redundancy and helps to reduce the load on the primary server because resolvers can distribute their queries across multiple DNS servers.

Secondary DNS servers receive their zone databases through zone transfers. When you configure a secondary server for the first time, you must specify the primary server that is authoritative for the zone and will send the zone transfer. The primary server must also permit the secondary server to request the zone transfer.

Zone transfers occur in one of two ways; full zone transfers (AXFR) and incremental zone transfers (IXFR).

When a new secondary server is configured for the first time, it receives a full zone transfer from the primary DNS server. The full zone transfer contains all of the information in the DNS database. Some DNS implementations always receive full zone transfers.

After the secondary server receives its first full zone transfer, subsequent zone transfers are incremental. The primary name server compares its zone version number with that on the secondary server and sends only the changes that have been made in the interim. This significantly reduces network traffic generated by zone transfers.

  Windows NT 4 does not support incremental zone transfers.

Zone transfers are typically initiated by the secondary server when the refresh interval time for the zone expires or when the secondary server boots. Alternatively, you can configure notify lists on the primary server that notify the secondary servers whenever any changes to the zone database occur. You will see exactly how to accomplish this in the section titled "Setting Zone Properties," later in this chapter.

When you consider your DNS strategy, you must carefully consider the layout of your network. If you have a single domain with offices in separate cities, you want to reduce the number of zone transfers across the potentially slow or expensive WAN links, although this is becoming less of a concern as bandwidth seems to multiply daily.

ADI zones do away with traditional zone transfers altogether. Instead, they replicate across Active Directory with all of the other AD information. This process is seamless, and you can only configure a couple of options, as you will see later in the section "Setting Zone Properties." However, because zone replication is so important, you should monitor replication traffic from time to time, or especially if you encounter DNS zone errors. You will learn how to monitor zone replication later in this chapter in the section "Monitoring DNS in Replication Monitor."

Migrating the DNS Database Files

You can migrate the DNS database files from your older systems to Windows Server 2003 in one of three ways:

Upgrade Windows NT4 or 2000 to Windows Server 2003   When you upgrade to Windows Server 2003 from NT 4 or 2000, all of your zone files remain intact and are stored in the same folder locations.

Manually move the BIND files   Because the Windows Server 2003 DNS service is based on BIND and BIND is based on standardized RFCs, you can literally copy and paste BIND files into the DNS directory on the DNS server. Be aware that some features of Unix BIND files won't be recognized by Windows Server 2003, but that's OK because you never would have been able to implement those features anyway. Be aware that the BIND files you receive from your Unix brethren use a different naming convention, as shown in Table 6.3.

Migrate using zone transfers   You can set up your Windows Server 2003 DNS server with secondary zones for each of your primary zones. Then set up your current primary servers to allow the Server 2003 computer to receive zone transfers and immediately perform a full zone transfer. At this point, the Server 2003 DNS server has everything it needs to be the primary server for the domain. All you need to do is convert the zones on the Server 2003 computer to primary zones. If you want your new primary DNS server to perform zone transfers, you will also need to configure the secondary servers in your network to point to the new server and specify that the secondary servers are valid in the primary server's properties.

TABLE 6.3 BIND Files in Windows and Unix

Windows	Unix
Boot	named.boot
domain_name.dns	db.*domain_name*
IP_network_reverse_notation.dns	db.*IP_network_forward_notation*

 Real World Scenario

What's in a Name?

Your company has a network that contains many different information systems that include platforms from companies such as Sun, Novell, Microsoft, and IBM. Most environments are not as clean as the vendors imply through their marketing efforts. For quite a while, these various systems tended to be isolated, providing services and managed at the departmental level. Over the past few years, these systems have been bumping into each other, and interoperability has been the name of the game for IS departments.

Of course, all the users want is to be able to grab information regardless of the platform that has control over it. They want to share. With the acceptance of standards such as IP and HTTP, connecting these islands has gotten easier these days. But you need more than common protocols and cables to communicate. How do you label these diverse resources on the network so that the nontechnical users can find what they need?

In the real world, this can be more of a political problem than a technical one, although there are surely technical issues. For example, NetBIOS names on Windows 9*x* and Windows NT are limited to 15 characters, whereas Unix machines have a much larger name space.

Before you pull out those disks and install your new OS, take a step back and evaluate how your name space scheme will fit and how it will affect what already exists. What should be your naming standard for a workstation or server? Will that standard help the administrator or the user? Consider that a Windows machine can have more than one name, such as a NetBIOS name and a DNS name. In this situation, it's advisable to keep the host DNS name and the NetBIOS name in harmony so that name resolution will work properly, whether you take the DNS path or the WINS path. Consistency across the network is a good goal, although it's not always attainable.

Installing and Configuring a DNS Server

DNS can be installed before, during, or after installing the Active Directory service. If the Active Directory Installation Wizard cannot locate a DNS server, it will ask you if you would like the Active Directory Installation Wizard to install and configure a DNS server for you. Using this feature is the simplest method of installing a DNS server for the Active Directory service.

The following sections describe the steps to manually prepare a DNS server and how to further configure Windows Server 2003 DNS to fully support your network infrastructure.

Installing a DNS Server

Installing the DNS server is easy because you install it with the same tools you use to add other components. When you install the DNS server, you get the DNS snap-in installed, too. You can open the DNS snap-in by choosing Start ➢ Administrative Tools ➢ DNS. The snap-in is shown in Figure 6.3.

FIGURE 6.3   The DNS snap-in

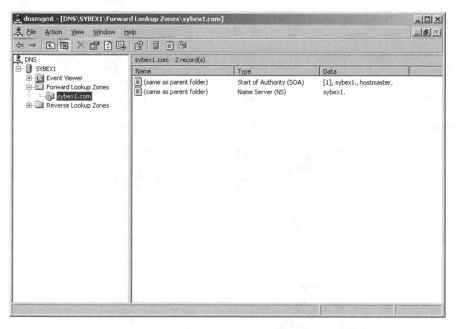

As you can see, it follows the standard Microsoft Management Console (MMC) model. The left-hand pane shows you which servers and zones are available; you can connect to servers in addition to the one you're already talking to. Each server contains subordinate items grouped into folders. Each zone has a folder, which is named after the zone itself. In Figure 6.3, you can see that the server SYBEX1 has a forward lookup zone for sybex1.com.

In Windows Server 2003, DNS is installed and zones are configured at the same time in back-to-back wizards. You will install the DNS service after you have read the following section, "Configuring a DNS Server."

Configuring a DNS Server

Configuring a DNS server ranges from very easy to very difficult, depending on what you're trying to make it do. The simplest configuration is a caching-only server; you don't have to do anything except make sure the server's root hints are set correctly. You can also configure a root name server or set up round robin and netmask ordering, as you will see.

Configuring a Caching-Only Server

Although all DNS name servers cache queries that they have resolved, caching-only servers are DNS name servers that only perform queries, cache the answers, and return the results. They are not authoritative for any domains, and the information that they contain is limited to what has been cached while resolving queries. Accordingly, they don't have any zone files, and they don't participate in zone transfers. When a caching-only server is first started, it has no information in its cache; the cache is gradually built over time.

Caching-only servers are very easy to configure. After installing the DNS service, simply make sure that the root hints are configured properly. Right-click your DNS server and choose the Properties command. When the Properties dialog box appears, switch to the Root Hints tab (Figure 6.4). If your server is connected to the Internet, you should see a list of root hints for the root servers maintained by InterNIC. If not, use the Add button to add root hints as defined in the `cache.dns` file.

FIGURE 6.4   The Root Hints tab of the DNS server Properties dialog box

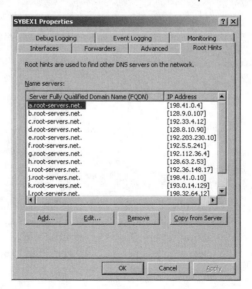

Configuring a Root Name Server

If your Windows Server 2003 computers aren't directly connected to the Internet, or if you want to prevent them from ever referring queries to the Internet, you can configure them to contain their own root zone. Remember that root zones are treated as the authoritative source of information for a top-level domain; by creating your own root zones, you can control exactly which domains your clients can resolve queries for. The process of doing this is pretty simple: the Configure A DNS Server Wizard appears automatically after you install the DNS service (see Exercise 6.1 later in this chapter), or you can do it manually by right-clicking the DNS server and selecting the Configure A DNS Server command.

Configuring Advanced Properties

Earlier in the chapter you saw how round robin and netmask ordering work to load-balance a DNS host. By default, the Windows Server 2003 implementation of DNS enables both round robin and netmask ordering. If you want to disable or enable either of these features, you should select or deselect the appropriate options in the Advanced tab of the server Properties dialog box.

If any of your secondary DNS servers run versions of BIND prior to 4.9.4, they won't be able to process the compressed packets that your Windows Server 2003 computer sends them. You can enable or disable BIND secondaries in the Advanced tab as well.

Creating New Zones

You can use the New Zone Wizard to create a new forward or reverse lookup zone. The process is substantially the same, even though the steps and wizard pages differ somewhat. In either case, you create a new zone first by right-clicking the server you want to host the zone and then selecting New Zone. This starts up the New Zone Wizard. You also create new zones using the Configure A DNS Server Wizard, as you will see in Exercise 6.1, although the steps are slightly different.

Creating a New Forward Lookup Zone

Once you dismiss the Welcome page, the first choice you have to make is on the Zone Type page. Here, you can choose what kind of zone you want this to be. You can choose from primary, secondary, and stub, as well as whether or not the zone will be stored in Active Directory. Which option you'll use depends on what you're doing:

- If you want the DNS server to be authoritative for the zone, select the Primary Zone option.

- If you want to set up your server as a secondary zone server, choose the Secondary radio button. Later in the process, you'll be prompted to specify which primary zone you want to transfer data from.

- Stub zones contain only the information necessary to identify the authoritative DNS servers for a zone. You would typically only select the stub zone option if your DNS server has delegated child zones that it needs to keep track of. You will learn more about zone delegation later in this chapter.

- If you want to store zone data in Active Directory, be sure to check the Store The Zone In Active Directory option. Note that there's no such thing as an ADI secondary zone.

 Real World Scenario

When to Use Stub Zones

Looking at the explanation above of stub zones, you might be wondering to yourself why you would ever use them in the first place. In fact, stub zones become particularly useful in a couple of different scenarios.

Consider what happens when two large companies merge: big.com and bigger.com. In most cases, the DNS zone information from both companies must be available to every employee. You could set up a new zone on each side that acts as a secondary for the other side's primary zone, but administrators tend to be very protective of their DNS databases and they probably wouldn't agree to this plan. Instead, you could add a stub zone to each side that points to the primary server on the other side. When a client in big.com (which you help administer) makes a request for a name in bigger.com, the stub zone on the big.com DNS server would send the client to the primary DNS server for bigger.com without actually resolving the name. At this point it would be up to bigger.com's primary server to resolve the name. An added benefit is that even if the administrators over at bigger.com change their configuration, you won't have to do anything because the changes will automatically replicate to the stub zone just as they would for a secondary server.

Stub zones can also be useful when you administer two domains across a slow connection. Let's change the example above a bit and assume that you have full control over big.com and bigger.com, but they connect through a 56k line. In this case, you wouldn't necessarily mind using secondary zones because you personally administer the entire network, but it could get messy to replicate an entire zone file across that slow line. Instead, use stub zones, which would refer clients to the appropriate primary server at the other site.

No matter which zone type you choose, the next step is to pick whether you want to create a forward or reverse lookup zone. At this point, we'll assume you want to create a forward zone (the steps for creating a reverse zone are covered in the next section).

Forward zones need to have names. You specify the name you want the zone to have using the Zone Name page of the wizard. For an AD-integrated or primary zone, you have to specify the name (including the suffix—microsoft isn't a valid name, but microsoft.com would be). If you're creating a secondary zone, there will be a Browse button you can use to locate the primary zone you want to copy.

If you're building a new AD-integrated zone, you're done once you specify the name. However, if you're setting up a standard primary zone, you must specify where you want the zone data stored on the Zone File page (Figure 6.5). The default filename will be the same as the zone name with .dns on the end, but you can modify it freely. You can also combine more than one zone's data into a single zone file, though that makes it a little harder to sort out what's what.

FIGURE 6.5   The Zone File page of the New Zone Wizard

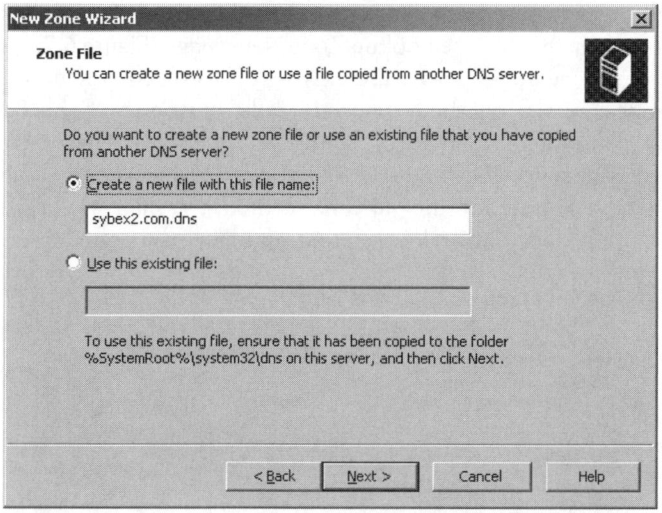

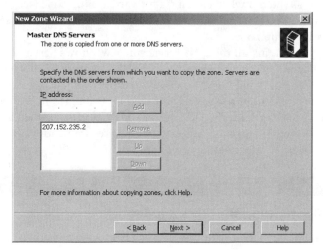

You can also specify how dynamic updates are handled. Specifically, you can choose to allow dynamic updates, allow only secure dynamic updates (on domain controllers only), or not allow dynamic updates.

Because secondary zones have to transfer their zone data from somewhere else, you have to specify where exactly it comes from. Figure 6.6 shows the Master DNS Servers page of the New Zone Wizard. Use the controls here to specify which DNS servers your server will contact to request zone transfers. If you specify more than one server here, your server will try the servers in the order specified.

FIGURE 6.6   The Master DNS Servers page of the New Zone Wizard

Creating a New Reverse Lookup Zone

The process of creating a reverse lookup zone is a little different because reverse lookup zones tie addresses to names. On the Reverse Lookup Zone Name page (Figure 6.7), you can specify the reverse lookup zone's name in two ways. The easy way is to specify the network ID portion of the network the zone covers, using the Network ID radio button and field. The more complex, but equivalent, way is to fill in the name of the reverse zone itself. These two are mostly the same, just inverted: a network ID of 208.15.144 yields a reverse zone name of 144.15.208 .in-addr.arpa. Unless you're used to the old Unix method, use the Network ID radio button— it's less likely that you'll make a mistake with that route.

FIGURE 6.7   The Reverse Lookup Zone Name page of the New Zone Wizard

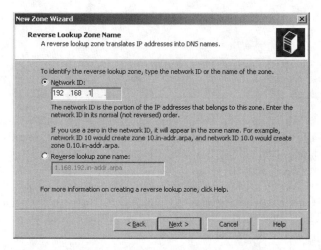

Once you've selected which network you want your reverse zone to point to, you have to select a zone file, just as you did when creating a forward lookup zone (see Figure 6.5 earlier in this chapter). You must also choose how to handle dynamic updates in the same way that you did with the forward lookup zone.

In Exercise 6.1, you will install the DNS service on a Windows Server 2003 and configure your first zone. In Chapter 5, you saw how to install the DHCP server component using the Add Or Remove Programs Control Panel item. You could perform similar steps to install the DNS server component, or you could use the alternate method explained in Exercise 6.1. You'll get the same result with both methods; the DNS server component is installed and appears in the Administrative Tools program group. Microsoft strongly recommends that you configure your DNS servers to use static IP addresses, and we agree.

EXERCISE 6.1

Installing and Configuring the DNS Service

1.   Open the Configure Your Server Wizard by selecting Start ➢ Administrative Tools ➢ Configure Your Server.

EXERCISE 6.1 *(continued)*

2. Click Next to dismiss the Welcome screen and click Next again to dismiss the Preliminary Steps screen.

3. Click the DNS Server item in the Server Role list and click Next to continue.

4. Click Next on the Summary page to complete the DNS installation. You may need to insert the Windows Server 2003 CD into the CD-ROM drive.

5. If your computer is configured with a dynamic IP address, you will be prompted to use a static address. The Local Area Connection Properties dialog box will automatically appear. Once you have made the necessary changes, click the OK button.

6. The Configure A DNS Sever Wizard automatically appears. Click Next to dismiss the Welcome screen.

7. Select the Create Forward And Reverse Lookup Zones radio button and click Next to continue. If you want to create a caching-only server, you can select the Configure Root Hints Only option.

8. Select Yes, Create A Forward Lookup Zone Now and click Next to continue.

9. Select the Primary Zone option. If your DNS server is also a domain controller, you should select the Store The Zone In Active Directory option. Click Next when you are ready.

10. Enter a new zone name in the Zone Name field and click Next to continue.

11. Leave the default zone filename and click Next.

12. Select the Allow Dynamic Updates radio button and click Next.

13. Select No, Don't Create a Reverse Lookup Zone Now and click Next to continue.

14. For now, select the No, It Should Not Forward Queries radio button and click Next to continue.

15. Click Finish to end the wizard. The Configure Your Server wizard reappears and informs you that the DNS service was successfully installed. Click the Finish button.

Setting Zone Properties

There are six tabs on the Properties dialog box you get when you use the Properties command on a forward or reverse lookup zone. You use the Security tab only to control who can change properties and make dynamic updates to records on that zone. The other tabs are discussed in the following sections.

Secondary zones don't have a Security tab, and their SOA tab shows you the contents of the master SOA record, which you can't change.

The General Tab

The General tab (Figure 6.8) includes the following:

- The Status indicator and the associated Pause button lets you see and control whether this zone can be used to answer queries. When the zone is running, the server can use it to answer client queries; when it's paused, the server won't answer any queries it gets for that particular zone.

- The Type indicator and Change button allow you to change the zone type between standard primary, standard secondary, and AD-integrated. As you change the type, the controls you see below the horizontal dividing line will change too. The most interesting controls are the ones you see for AD-integrated zones. For primary zones, you'll see a field that lets you select the zone filename; for secondary zones, you'll get controls that allow you to specify the IP addresses of the primary servers.

- The Replication indicator and Change button allow you to change the replication scope if the zone is stored in Active Directory. You can choose to replicate the zone data to all DNS servers in the Active Directory forest, all DNS servers in a specified domain, all domain controllers in the Active Directory domain (required if you use Windows 2000 domain controllers in your domain), and all domain controllers specified in the replication scope of the application directory partition.

- The Allow Dynamic Updates field gives you a way to specify whether or not you want to support Dynamic DNS updates from compatible DHCP servers. As you learned in Chapter 4, the DHCP server or DHCP client must know about and support Dynamic DNS in order to use it, but the DNS server has to participate, too. You can turn dynamic updates on or off, or you can require that updates must be secured. By default, a standard primary zone won't accept dynamic updates, but an AD-integrated zone will. You can change these settings at will.

FIGURE 6.8 The General tab of the zone Properties dialog box

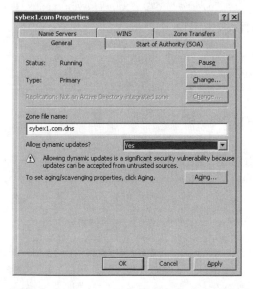

The Start Of Authority (SOA) Tab

The options in the Start Of Authority (SOA) tab (Figure 6.9) control the contents of the SOA record for this zone:

- The Serial Number field indicates which version of the SOA record the server currently holds; every time you change another field, you should increment the serial number so that other servers will notice the change and get a copy of the updated record.

- The Primary Server and Responsible Person fields indicate the location of the primary NS for this zone and the responsible administrator, respectively.

- The Refresh Interval field controls how often any secondary zones of this zone must contact the primary and get any changes that have been posted since the last update.

- The Retry Interval field controls how long secondary servers will wait after a zone transfer fails before they try again. They'll keep trying at the interval you specify (which should be shorter than the refresh interval) until they eventually succeed in transferring zone data.

- The Expires After field tells the secondary servers when to throw away zone data. The default of 24 hours means that a secondary server that hasn't gotten an update in 24 hours will delete its local copy of the zone data.

- The Minimum (Default) TTL field sets the default TTL for all RRs created in the zone; you can still assign different TTLs to individual records if you want.

- The TTL For This Record field controls the TTL for the SOA record itself.

FIGURE 6.9   The Start Of Authority tab of the zone Properties dialog box

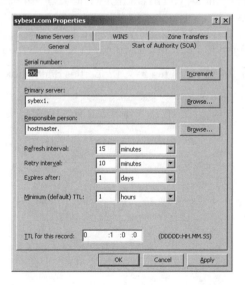

The Name Servers Tab

The name server (NS) record for a zone indicates which name servers are authoritative for the zone. That normally means the zone primary and any secondary servers you've configured for the zone (remember, secondary servers are authoritative read-only copies of the zone). You edit the NS record for a zone with the Name Servers tab (Figure 6.10). To be more specific, the tab shows you which servers are listed, and you use the Add, Edit, and Remove buttons to specify which name servers you want included in the zone's NS record.

FIGURE 6.10   The Name Servers tab of the zone Properties dialog box

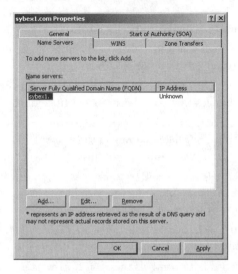

The WINS Tab

The WINS tab (Figure 6.11) allows you to control whether this zone uses WINS forward lookups or not. These lookups pass queries that DNS can't resolve on to WINS for action. This is a useful setup if you're still using WINS on your network. You must explicitly turn this option on with the Use WINS Forward Lookup checkbox in the WINS tab for a particular zone.

FIGURE 6.11   The WINS tab of the zone Properties dialog box

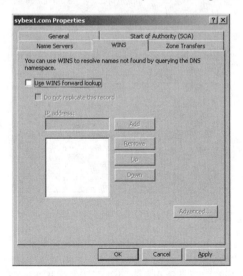

The Zone Transfers Tab

Zone transfers are necessary and useful because they're the mechanism used to propagate zone data between primary and secondary servers. For primary servers (whether AD-integrated or not), you can specify whether or not your servers will allow zone transfers and, if so, to whom. You can use the following controls on the Zone Transfers tab (Figure 6.12) to configure these settings per zone:

- The Allow Zone Transfers checkbox controls whether or not the server will answer zone transfer requests for this zone at all—when it's off, no zone data will be transferred.

- The To Any Server setting allows any server anywhere on the Internet to request a copy of your zone data.

- The Only To Servers Listed On The Name Servers Tab (the default) limits transfers to only those servers listed in the Name Servers tab for this zone. This is a more secure setting than the default because it limits zone transfers to other servers for the same zone.

- The Only To The Following Servers setting, along with its corresponding IP address controls, gives you even more control because you can specify exactly which servers are allowed to request zone transfers—this list can be larger, or smaller, than the list specified on the Name Servers tab.

- The Notify button is for setting up automatic notification triggers that are sent to secondary servers for this zone. Those triggers signal the secondary servers that changes have occurred on the primary; that way, the secondary servers can request updates sooner than they would with their normally scheduled interval. The options in the Notify dialog box are similar to those in the Zone Transfers tab. You can enable automatic notification and then choose either Servers Listed On The Name Servers Tab or The Following Servers.

FIGURE 6.12   The Zone Transfers tab of the Zone Properties dialog box

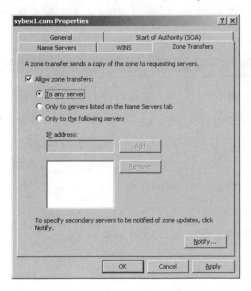

Configuring Zones for Dynamic Updates

Dynamic updates enable DNS client computers to register and dynamically update their resource records with a DNS server whenever changes occur. This reduces the need for manual administration of zone records. The DNS service allows dynamic updates to be enabled or disabled on a per-zone basis at each server. There are some subtleties that you may not have thought of, though.

A Windows 2000 or XP client that has a statically assigned IP address will attempt to register its IP address with a Dynamic DNS server when the IP address changes or when the machine reboots. DHCP clients will update DNS records whenever an IP address assignment changes (for example, when a lease is renewed or issued). In both cases, the DHCP service on the client is responsible for sending the update for all IP addresses assigned to the machine, even those that aren't using DHCP.

What about secure updates? Turning on secure updates has no initial effect on clients because they'll always try unsecured updates first. If an unsecured update fails, the client will try again with a secure update. If that fails, then the update fails. Secure updates will not work on a client unless the client is in the Computers folder in the Active Directory.

What if you're not using Windows 2000 or XP clients? The Windows Server 2003 DHCP server can register DNS data for machines to which it issues leases. In this role, it's called a *DNS proxy* because it's acting on behalf of another set of machines. Although this gives all your computers access to Dynamic DNS registrations, it opens some worrisome security issues because you must add the DHCP servers you want to act as proxies to the DnsProxyUpdate group in Active Directory. This tells the OS that you want those DHCP servers to be able to register clients, but it also means that any DHCP server running on an AD controller has full access to the DNS registration information—meaning that a malicious DHCP client could potentially poison your DNS information.

In Exercise 6.2, you will modify the properties of a forward lookup zone, configuring the zone to use WINS to resolve names not found by querying the DNS name space. In addition, you'll configure the zone to allow dynamic updates.

EXERCISE 6.2

Configuring Zones and Configuring Zones for Dynamic Updates

1. Open the DNS management snap-in by selecting Start ➤ Administrative Tools ➤ DNS.

2. Click the DNS server to expand it and then expand the Forward Lookup Zones folder.

3. Right-click the zone you want to modify (which may be the one you created in the previous exercise) and choose the Properties command.

4. Switch to the WINS tab and click the Use WINS Forward Lookup checkbox.

5. Enter the IP address of a valid WINS server on your network, click Add, and then click OK.

6. Click the General tab.

7. Change the value of the Allow Dynamic Updates control to Yes. Click OK to close the Properties dialog box. Notice that there's now a new WINS Lookup RR in your zone.

Delegating Zones for DNS

DNS provides the ability to divide up the name space into one or more zones, which can then be stored, distributed, and replicated to other DNS servers. When deciding whether to divide your DNS name space to make additional zones, consider the following reasons to use additional zones:

- A need to delegate management of part of your DNS name space to another location or department within your organization.

- A need to divide one large zone into smaller zones for distributing traffic loads among multiple servers, improve DNS name resolution performance, or create a more fault-tolerant DNS environment.

- A need to extend the name space by adding numerous subdomains at once, such as to accommodate the opening of a new branch or site.

Each new delegated zone requires a primary DNS server just like a regular DNS zone. When delegating zones within your name space, be aware that for each new zone you create, you will need to place in other zones delegation records that point to the authoritative DNS servers for the new zone. This is necessary both to transfer authority and to provide correct referral to other DNS servers and clients of the new servers being made authoritative for the new zone.

In Exercise 6.3, you'll create a delegated subdomain of the domain you created back in Exercise 6.1. Note that the name of the server to which you want to delegate the subdomain must be stored in an A or CNAME record in the parent domain.

Creating a Delegated DNS Zone

1. Open the DNS management snap-in by selecting Start ➢ Administrative Tools ➢ DNS.

2. Expand the DNS server and locate the zone you created earlier.

3. Right-click the zone and choose the New Delegation command.

4. The New Delegation Wizard appears. Click Next to dismiss the initial wizard page.

5. Enter **ns1** (or whatever other name you like) in the Delegated Domain field of the Delegated Domain Name page. This is the name of the domain for which you want to delegate authority to another DNS server. It should be a subdomain of the primary domain (for example, to delegate authority for huntsville.chellis.net, you'd enter **huntsville** in the Delegated Domain field). Click Next to complete this step.

EXERCISE 6.3 (continued)

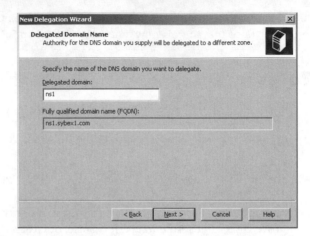

6. When the Name Servers page appears, use the Add button to add the name and IP address(es) of the servers that will be hosting the newly delegated zone. For the purpose of this exercise, enter the zone name you used in Exercise 6.1. Click the Resolve button to automatically resolve this domain name's IP address into the IP address field. Click OK when you are done. Click Next to continue with the wizard.

7. Click the Finish button. The New Delegation wizard disappears and you'll notice the new zone you just created appear beneath the zone you selected in step 4. The newly delegated zone's folder icon is drawn in gray to indicate that control of the zone is delegated.

Manually Creating DNS Records

From time to time you may find it necessary to manually add resource records to your Windows Server 2003 DNS servers. Although Dynamic DNS will free you from the need to fiddle with A and PTR records, other resource types (including MX records, required for the proper flow of SMTP e-mail) still have to be created manually. You can manually create A, PTR, MX, SRV, and 15 other record types.

There are only two important things to remember: You must right-click the zone and use either the New Record command or the Other New Records command, and you must know how to fill in the fields of whatever record type you're using. For example, to create an MX record, you need three pieces of information (the domain, the mail server, and the priority), but to create an SRV record, you need several more.

In Exercise 6.4, you will manually create an MX record for the mailtest server in the domain you created back in Exercise 6.1.

EXERCISE 6.4

Manually Creating DNS RRs

1. Open the DNS management snap-in by selecting Start ➢ Administrative Tools ➢ DNS.

2. Expand your DNS server, right-click its zone, and use the New Mail Exchanger (MX) command.

3. Enter **mailtest** in the Host Or Child Domain field, and enter **mailtest.*yourDomain.com*** (or whatever domain name you used in Exercise 6.1) in the Fully Qualified Domain Name (FQDN) Of Mail Server field and then click OK. Notice that the new record is already visible.

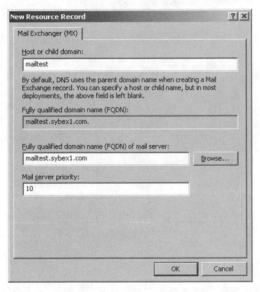

4. Next, create an alias (or CNAME) record to point to the mail server. (It is assumed that you already have an A record for mailtest in your zone.)

5. Right-click the target zone and choose Other New Records. When the Resource Record Type dialog box appears, find Alias in the list and select it.

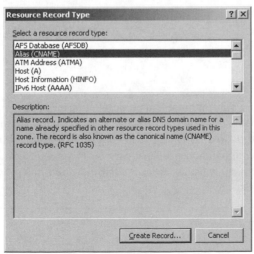

6. Click the Create Record button. The New Resource Record dialog box appears.

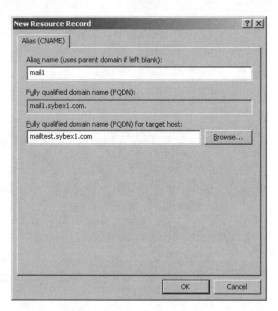

7. Type **mail** into the Alias Name field.

8. Type **mailtest.*yourDomain.com*** into the Fully Qualified Domain Name (FQDN) For Target Host field.

9. Click the OK button and then close the Resource Record Type dialog box.

 Real World Scenario

The Politics of DNS

Your company has made a commitment to a complete migration to Windows Server 2003, mainly to keep up with the next version of NT and to take advantage of the lower cost of administration. You know that the tools to realize this lower cost of administration depend on the global policies, which in turn depend on Active Directory. However, the real issue is that Active Directory depends on DNS, specifically Dynamic DNS, for the registration of Windows 2000, XP, and Server 2003 as resources.

You've spent many hours beefing up your DNS knowledge and are ready to strap DNS into the network. But as soon as you bring it up, you get a nasty message, with incredulous tones, from the Unix guys down the hall, asking, "What in the heck do you think you're doing?" You try to explain how the new version of DNS is dynamic and is used to register services and workstations for the new and improved Windows Server 2003 network. Now that you've wasted your breath, you have to dig in and figure out how to interoperate with your Unix brethren.

Unless your shop is already completely Windows and is already running the company DNS, it's very unlikely that the corporate DNS is going to run on a Microsoft platform. It's also unlikely that the Unix DNS that's running in your shop supports dynamic updates. You are probably going to have an uneasy period in which you'll be given your own zone from the authoritative DNS where you'll create the Windows Server 2003 name space in your own world. This isn't necessarily a bad thing, but you should prepare for it appropriately. One of the ways you can prepare to work with the Unix side is to understand the Unix DNS as well as the Windows version so that you'll know how they will work together and what problems could ensue with issues such as sending updates to their servers.

The Windows Server 2003 DNS is an excellent implementation that follows all the latest RFC standards and will continue to do so. However, as we have all seen, politics plays a growing role in our information systems as they mature and become more and more important in our corporate lives.

Monitoring and Troubleshooting DNS

Now that you have set up and configured your DNS name server and created some resource records, you will want to confirm that it is resolving and replying to client DNS requests. There are tools that allow you to do some basic monitoring and managing. Once you are able to monitor DNS, you'll want to start troubleshooting.

The simplest test is to use the `ping` command to make sure the server is alive. A more exhaustive test would be to use nslookup to verify that you can actually resolve addresses for items on your DNS server.

In the following sections, we'll look at some of these monitoring and management tools, as well as how to troubleshoot DNS.

Monitoring DNS with the DNS Snap-in

You can use the DNS snap-in to do some basic server testing and monitoring. More importantly, you use the snap-in to monitor and set logging options. On the Event Logging tab of the server Properties dialog box (Figure 6.13), you can pick which events you want logged. The more events you select, the more log information you'll get. This is useful when you're trying to track what's happening with your servers, but it can result in a very, very large log file if you're not careful.

FIGURE 6.13 The Event Logging tab of the server Properties dialog box

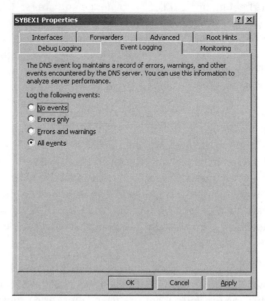

The Monitoring tab (Figure 6.14) gives you some testing tools. The A Simple Query Against This DNS Server test asks for a single record from the local DNS server; it's useful for verifying that the service is running and listening to queries, but not much else. The A Recursive Query To Other DNS Servers test is more sophisticated, using a recursive query to see whether forwarding is working okay. The Test Now button and the Perform Automatic Testing At The Following Interval control allow you to run these tests now or later, as you require.

FIGURE 6.14 The Monitoring tab of the Server Properties dialog box

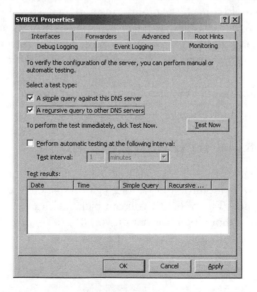

> If the simple query fails, check that the local server contains the zone 1.0.0.127 .in-addr.arpa. If the recursive query fails, check that your root hints are correct and that your root servers are running.

In Exercise 6.5, you will enable logging, use the DNS MMC to test the DNS server, and view the contents of the DNS log.

EXERCISE 6.5

Simple DNS Testing

1. Open the DNS management snap-in by selecting Start ➢ Administrative Tools ➢ DNS.

2. Right-click the DNS server you want to test and select Properties.

3. Switch to the Debug Logging tab, check all the debug logging options except Filter Packets By IP Address, and enter a full path and filename in the File Path And Name field. Click the Apply button.

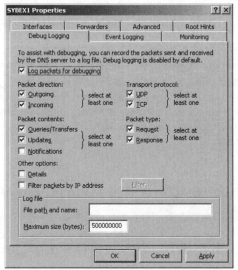

4. Switch to the Monitoring tab, and check both A Simple Query Against This DNS Server and A Recursive Query To Other DNS Servers.

5. Click the Test Now button several times and then click OK.

6. Using Windows Explorer, navigate to the folder that you specified in step 3 and use WordPad to view the contents of the log file.

Monitoring DNS Servers with System Monitor

After you install the DNS service, you will be able to select the DNS object in the Windows Server 2003 System Monitor. This object contains many different counters that are related to monitoring DNS server performance and usage.

Using the System Monitor, you can generate statistics on the following types of information:

- AXFR requests (all-zone transfer requests)
- IXFR requests (incremental zone transfer requests)
- DNS server memory usage
- Dynamic updates
- DNS Notify events
- Recursive queries
- TCP and UDP statistics
- WINS statistics
- Zone transfer issues

All of this information can be analyzed easily using the Chart, Histogram, or Report views of the System Monitor. Additionally, you can use the Alerts function to automatically notify you (or other system administrators) whenever certain performance statistic thresholds are exceeded. For example, if the total number of recursive queries is very high, you might want to be notified so you can examine the situation. Finally, information from Performance Logs And Alerts can be stored to a log data file.

The System Monitor application in Windows Server 2003 is an extremely powerful and useful tool for managing and troubleshooting systems. You should become familiar with its various functions to ensure that system services are operating properly. You should be familiar with working in System Monitor from Chapter 2.

Monitoring DNS Events in the Event Viewer

By default, Windows Server 2003 automatically logs DNS events in the event log under a distinct DNS server heading. Conveniently, the DNS snap-in contains a copy of the DNS event log so that you don't have to switch out of the utility to view the log. Table 6.4 lists some of the more common events.

TABLE 6.4 DNS Event IDs

Event ID	Description
2	The DNS server has started. This message generally appears at startup when either the server computer is started or the DNS Server service is manually started.
3	The DNS server has shut down. This message generally appears when either the server computer is shut down or the DNS Server service is stopped manually.

TABLE 6.4 DNS Event IDs *(continued)*

Event ID	Description
414	The server computer currently has no primary DNS suffix configured. Its DNS name is currently a single label hostname. For example, its currently configured name is host rather than host.example.microsoft.com or another fully qualified name.
708	The DNS server did not detect any zones of either primary or secondary type. It will run as a caching-only server but will not be authoritative for any zones.
3150	The DNS server wrote a new version of zone *zonename* to file *filename*. You can view the new version number by clicking the Record Data tab. This event should appear only if the DNS server is configured to operate as a root server.
6527	Zone *zonename* expired before it could obtain a successful zone transfer or update from a master server acting as its source for the zone. The zone has been shut down.

Monitoring DNS in Replication Monitor

As you saw earlier, ADI zones do not use traditional zone transfers. Instead, they are replicated along with the other Active Directory information. To diagnose ADI zone replication errors, you should look at AD replication itself. Windows Server 2003 does not include support for AD replication monitoring by default. You must install the support tools included on the Windows Server 2003 CD in order to run the *Replication Monitor* utility, as shown in Exercise 6.6.

 The Windows Server 2003 CD must be in the drive or you must have access to the CD via a remote share in order to complete Exercise 6.6. In addition, you should perform the steps of this exercise and the following exercise on a domain controller that is also configured as a DNS server.

EXERCISE 6.6

Installing and Running Replication Monitor

1. In Windows Explorer, navigate to the \SUPPORT\TOOLS\ folder on the Windows Server 2003 CD.

2. Double-click the SUPTOOLS.MSI file that appears in the folder.

3. The Support Tools Installation Wizard guides you through the installation process. To ensure smooth operation of the support tools, be sure to install them to the default directory.

4. After the installation is complete, you can run the Replication Monitor by selecting Start ➢ Run and entering **REPLMON** in the Run dialog box.

The Replication Monitor window is shown in Figure 6.15. When you first start Replication Monitor, the window is empty. You must manually add servers to monitor, as you will see in Exercise 6.7. In the figure, you can see that a server has already been added. The individual components of Active Directory are displayed under the server name.

FIGURE 6.15 The Replication Monitor window

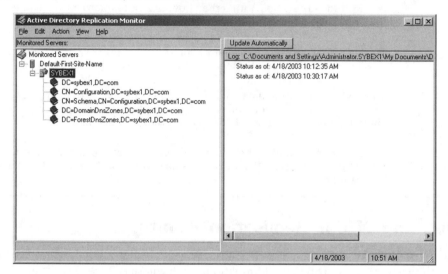

The two most practical uses for Replication Monitor are viewing failed replications and manually initiating replication between domain controllers. If you find that DNS information is not synchronized between servers, you can be sure that replication failed at some point due to any number of reasons (usually a router failure between sites). Replication Monitor will tell you exactly when the replication failed. If you notice a failure and replication isn't scheduled to occur soon, you should manually initiate replication to get those DNS updates immediately.

Exercise 6.7 shows you how to add one or more servers to the Replication Monitor, check for replication failure, and initiate replication manually.

EXERCISE 6.7

Working with Replication Monitor

1. Open Replication Monitor by selecting Start ➢ Run and entering **REPLMON** in the Run dialog box.

2. To add a server to the Replication Monitor window, right-click Monitored Servers and select Add Monitored Server from the pop-up menu.

3. The Add Monitored Server Wizard appears. Select either Add The Server Explicitly By Name or Search The Directory For The Server To Add. If you chose the latter option, you must specify a domain to search in the list of domains. Click Next when you are done.

EXERCISE 6.7 *(continued)*

4. Depending on the option you chose in the previous step, you will be prompted to either enter a server name or choose a server from a list. In either case, enter or choose the server to monitor and click Finish.

5. To search for replication errors, click the Action menu and select Domain ➢ Search Domain Controllers For Replication Errors.

6. The Search Domain Controllers For Replication Failures window appears. Click the Run Search button and enter the name of the domain to search. After a few moments, Replication Monitor should list any failures in the Search Domain Controllers For Replication Failures window. Click Close.

7. You can manually synchronize either the entire Active Directory or just individual pieces. In order to synchronize the domain DNS zones only, right click the DC=DomainDNS-Zones,DC=*domain*,DC=*suffix* item under the monitored server and select Synchronize This Directory Partition With All Servers from the pop-up menu.

8. Depending on how your domain is configured, you can choose the Disable Transitive Replication, Push Mode, or Cross Site Boundaries checkboxes. In this case, leave them blank and click OK.

9. You will be prompted to confirm the replication. Click Yes.

10. Click OK at the success notification.

Troubleshooting DNS

When troubleshooting DNS problems, ask yourself the following basic questions:

- What application is failing? What works? What doesn't work?

- Is the problem basic IP connectivity, or is it name resolution? If the problem is name resolution, does the failing application use NetBIOS names, DNS names, or hostnames?

- How are the things that do and don't work related?

- Have the things that don't work ever worked on this computer or network? If so, what has changed since they last worked?

Windows Server 2003 provides several useful tools that can help you answer these questions. This section discusses the following tools:

- Nslookup, which is used to perform DNS queries and to examine the contents of zone files on local and remote servers

- ipconfig, which is used to view DNS client settings, display and flush the resolver cache, and force a dynamic update client to register its DNS records

- The DNS log file, which monitors certain DNS server events and logs them for your edification

Using Nslookup

Nslookup is a standard command-line tool provided in most DNS server implementations, including Windows Server 2003. It offers the ability to perform query testing of DNS servers and to obtain detailed responses at the command prompt. This information can be useful for diagnosing and solving name resolution problems, for verifying that resource records are added or updated correctly in a zone, and for debugging other server-related problems. You can do a number of useful things with nslookup:

- Use it in noninteractive mode to look up a single piece of data
- Enter interactive mode and use the debug feature
- Perform the following from within interactive mode:
  - Set options for your query
  - Look up a name
  - Look up records in a zone
  - Perform zone transfers
  - Exit nslookup

 When you are entering queries, it is generally a good idea to enter FQDNs so you can control what name is submitted to the server. However, if you want to know which suffixes are added to unqualified names before they are submitted to the server, you can enter nslookup in debug mode and then enter an unqualified name.

Let's start with using nslookup in plain old command-line mode:

`nslookup name server`

This code will look up a DNS name or address named *name* using a server at an IP address specified by *server*. However, nslookup is a lot more useful in interactive mode because you can enter several commands in sequence. Running nslookup by itself (without specifying a query or server) puts it in interactive mode, where it will stay until you type **exit** and press Enter. Before that point, you can look up lots of useful stuff.

While in interactive mode, you can use the `set` command to configure how the resolver will carry out queries. Table 6.5 shows a few of the options available with `set`.

TABLE 6.5 Command-Line Options Available with the set Command

Option	Purpose
set all	Shows all the options available with the set option.
set d2	Puts nslookup in debug mode so you can examine the query and response packets between the resolver and the server.

TABLE 6.5 Command-Line Options Available with the set Command *(continued)*

Option	Purpose
set domain=*domain name*	Tells the resolver what domain name to append for unqualified queries.
set timeout=<timeout>	Tells the resolver which time-out to use. This option is useful for slow links where queries frequently time out and the wait time must be lengthened.
set type=*record type*	Tells the resolver which type of resource records to search for (for example, A, PTR, or SRV). If you want the resolver to query for all types of resource records, type **set type=all**.

While in interactive mode, you can look up a name just by typing it: ***name server***. In this example, *name* is the owner name for the record you are looking for, and *server* is the server that you want to query.

You can use the wildcard character (*) in your query. For example, if you want to look for all resource records that have *K* as the first letter, just type **k*** as your query.

If you want to query for a particular type of record (for instance, an MX record), use the Set Type command:

Set type=mx

This example tells nslookup that you're only interested in seeing MX records that meet your search criteria.

There are a couple of other things you can do with nslookup. You can get a list of the contents of an entire domain with the Ls command. To find all the hosts in the apple.com domain, you'd type **Set type=a** and then type **Ls -t apple.com.**

You can also simulate zone transfers by using the Ls command with the -d switch. This can help you determine whether or not the server you are querying allows zone transfers to your computer. To do this, type the following: **ls -d <*domain name*>.**

A successful nslookup response looks like this:

Server: *Name_of_DNS_server*

Address: *IP_address_of_DNS_server*

Response_data

Nslookup might also return an error. The following message means that the resolver did not locate a PTR resource record (containing the hostname) for the server IP address. Nslookup can still query the DNS server, and the DNS server can still answer queries:

DNS request timed out.

Timeout was *x* seconds.

*** Can't find server name for address <*IP Address*>: Timed out

*** Default servers are not available

Default Server: Unknown

Address: *IP_address_of_DNS_server*

The following message means that a request timed out. This might happen, for example, if the DNS service was not running on the DNS server that is authoritative for the name:

```
*** Request to Server timed-out
```

The following message means that the server is not receiving requests on UDP port 53:

```
*** Server can't find Name_or_IP_address_queried_for: No response from server
```

If the DNS server was unable to find the name of IP address in the authoritative domain, you'd get the following message:

```
*** Server can't find Name_or_IP_address_queried_for: Non-existent domain
```

The authoritative domain might be on the remote DNS server or on another DNS server that this DNS server is able to reach.

The following message generally means that the DNS server is running but is not working properly:

```
*** Server can't find Name_or_IP_address_queried_for: Server failed
```

For example, it might include a corrupted packet, or the zone in which you are querying for a record might be paused. However, this message can also be returned if the client queries for a host in a domain for which the DNS server is not authoritative and the DNS server cannot contact its root servers, or it is not connected to the Internet, or it has no root hints.

In Exercise 6.8, you'll get some hands-on practice with the nslookup tool.

EXERCISE 6.8

Using the nslookup Command

1. Open a Windows Server 2003 command prompt by selecting Start ➤ All Programs ➤ Accessories ➤ Command Prompt.

2. Type **nslookup** and press the Enter key. (For the rest of the exercise, use the Enter key to terminate each command.)

3. Nslookup will start, displaying a message that tells you the name and IP address of the default DNS server. Write these down; you'll need them later.

4. Try looking up a well-known address: type **www.microsoft.com**. Notice that the query returns several IP addresses (Microsoft load-balances Web traffic by using multiple servers in the same DNS record).

5. Try looking up a nonexistent host: type **www.fubijar.com**. Notice that your server complains that it can't find the address. This is normal behavior.

6. Change the server to a nonexistent host (try making up a private IP address that you know isn't a DNS server on your network, like 10.10.10.10). Do this by typing **server ipAddress**. Nslookup will try to turn the IP address into a hostname. Eventually it will display a message telling you that the new default server is using the IP address you specified.

7. Try doing another lookup of a known DNS name. Type **www.microsoft.com**. Notice that nslookup is contacting the server you specified and that the lookup times out after a few seconds.

8. Reset your server to the original address you wrote down in step 3.

9. If doing so won't disrupt your network, unplug your computer from the network and repeat steps 4–8. Notice the difference in behavior.

Using Ipconfig

You can use the command-line tool ipconfig to view your DNS client settings, to view and reset cached information used locally for resolving DNS name queries, and to register the resource records for a dynamic update client. If you use the `ipconfig` command with no parameters, it displays DNS information for each adapter, including the domain name and DNS servers used for that adapter. Table 6.6 shows some command-line options available with `ipconfig`.

TABLE 6.6 Command-Line Options Available for the `ipconfig` Command

Command	What It Does
`ipconfig /all`	Displays additional information about DNS, including the FQDN and the DNS suffix search list.
`ipconfig /flushdns`	Flushes and resets the DNS resolver cache. For more information about this option, see the section "Configuring a DNS Server" earlier in this chapter.
`ipconfig /displaydns`	Displays the contents of the DNS resolver cache. For more information about this option, see "Configuring a DNS Server" earlier in this chapter.
`ipconfig /registerdns`	Refreshes all DHCP leases and registers any related DNS names. This option is available only on Windows 2000 and newer computers that run the DHCP Client service.

Using the DNS Log File

You can configure the DNS server to create a log file that records the following information:

- Queries
- Notification messages from other servers
- Dynamic updates
- Content of the question section for DNS query messages
- Content of the answer section for DNS query messages
- Number of queries this server sends
- Number of queries this server has received
- Number of DNS requests received over a UDP port

- Number of DNS requests received over a TCP port
- Number of full packets sent by the server
- Number of packets written through by the server and back to the zone

The DNS log appears in *systemroot*\System32\dns\Dns.log. Because the log is in RTF format, you must use WordPad or Word to view it.

You can change the directory and filename in which the DNS log appears by adding the following entry to the Registry with the REG_SZ data type:

HKEY_LOCAL_MACHTNE\SYSTEM\CurrentControlSet\Services\DNS\Parameters\LogFilePath

Set the value of LogFilePath equal to the name of the file and path where you want to locate the DNS log.

By default, the maximum file size of Dns.log is 4MB. If you want to change the size, add the following entry to the Registry with the REG_DWORD data type:

HKEY_LOCAL_MACHINE\SYSTEM\CurrentControlSet\Services\DNS↵
\Parameters\LogFileMaxSize

Set the value of *LogFileMaxSize* equal to the desired file size in bytes. The minimum size is 64Kb.

Once the log file reaches the maximum size, Windows Server 2003 writes over the beginning of the file. If you make the value higher, data persists for a longer time but the log file consumes more disk space. If you make the value smaller, the log file uses less disk space but the data persists for a shorter time.

WARNING   Do not leave DNS logging turned on during normal operation because it sucks up both processing and hard disk resources. Enable it only when diagnosing and solving DNS problems.

Summary

DNS was designed to be a robust, scalable, high-performance system for resolving friendly names to TCP/IP host addresses. We started by presenting an overview of the basics of DNS and how DNS names are generated. We then looked at the many features available in Microsoft's version of DNS and focused on how to install, configure, and manage the necessary services.

Important points to remember include the following:

- DNS is based on a widely accepted standard. It is designed to resolve friendly network names to IP addresses.

- DNS names are hierarchical and are read from right (least specific) to left (most specific).

- DNS zones are created to create a database of authoritative information for the hosts in a specific domain.

- Within DNS zones, servers can assume various roles.

- Through the use of replication, multiple DNS servers can remain synchronized.

Exam Essentials

Understand the purpose of DNS.   DNS is a standard set of protocols that defines a mechanism for querying and updating address information in the database, a mechanism for replicating the information in the database among servers, and a schema of the database.

Understand the different parts of the DNS database.   The SOA record defines the general parameters for the DNS zone, including who the authoritative server is for the zone. NS records list the name servers for a domain; they allow other name servers to look up names in your domain. A host record (also called an address or an A record) statically associates a host's name with its IP addresses. Pointer records (PTRs) map an IP address to a hostname, making it possible to do reverse lookups. Alias records allow you to use more than one name to point to a single host. The MX record tells you which servers can accept mail bound for a domain. SRV records tie together the location of a service (like a domain controller) with information about how to contact the service.

Know how DNS resolves names.   With iterative queries, a client asks the DNS server for an answer, and the client, or resolver, returns the best kind of answer it has. In a recursive query, the client sends a query to one name server, asking it to respond either with the requested answer or with an error. The error states either that the server can't come up with the right answer or that the domain name doesn't exist. With inverse queries, instead of supplying a name and then asking for an IP address, the client first provides the IP address and then asks for the name.

Understand the difference between DNS servers, clients, and resolvers.   Any computer providing domain name services is a DNS server. A DNS client is any machine issuing queries to a DNS server. A resolver handles the process of mapping a symbolic name to an actual network address.

Know how to install and configure DNS.   DNS can be installed before, during, or after installing the Active Directory service. When you install the DNS server, the DNS snap-in is installed, too. Configuring a DNS server ranges from very easy to very difficult, depending on what you're trying to make it do. In the simplest configuration, for a caching-only server, you don't have to do anything except make sure the server's root hints are set correctly. You can also configure a root server, a normal forward lookup server, and a reverse lookup server.

Know how to create new forward and reverse lookup zones.   You can use the New Zone Wizard to create a new forward or reverse lookup zone. The process is substantially the same for both types, but the specific steps and wizard pages differ somewhat. The wizard will walk you through the steps, such as specifying a name for the zone (in the case of forward lookup zones) or the network ID portion of the network that the zone covers (in the case of reverse lookup zones).

Know how to configure zones for dynamic updates.   The DNS service allows dynamic updates to be enabled or disabled on a per-zone basis at each server. This is easily done in the DNS snap-in.

Know how to delegate zones for DNS.   DNS provides the ability to divide up the name space into one or more zones, which can then be stored, distributed, and replicated to other DNS servers. When delegating zones within your name space, be aware that for each new zone you create, you'll need delegation records in other zones that point to the authoritative DNS servers for the new zone.

Understand the tools that are available for monitoring and troubleshooting DNS.   You can use the DNS snap-in to do some basic server testing and monitoring. More importantly, you use the snap-in to monitor and set logging options. The DNS object in the Windows Server 2003 System Monitor contains many different counters that are related to monitoring DNS server performance and usage. In addition, Windows Server 2003 automatically logs DNS events in the event log under a distinct DNS server heading. The Replication Monitor can be configured to resolve DNS errors for ADI zones. Nslookup offers the ability to perform query testing of DNS servers and to obtain detailed responses at the command prompt. You can use the command-line tool ipconfig to view your DNS client settings, to view and reset cached information used locally for resolving DNS name queries, and to register the resource records for a dynamic update client. Finally, you can configure the DNS server to create a log file that records queries, notification messages, dynamic updates, and various other DNS information.

Key Terms

Before you take the exam, be certain you are familiar with the following terms:

Active Directory-Integrated (ADI) zone	Replication Monitor
DNS client	resolvers
DNS proxy	resource records (RRs)
DNS server	reverse lookups
Dynamic DNS (DDNS) standard	root server
host record	secondary DNS server
name server	service (SRV) record
name server (NS) records	subdomains
pointer (PTR) record	zone
primary DNS server	zone transfers

Review Questions

1. You are the network administrator for a large sales organization with four distinct regional offices situated in different areas of the United States. Your Windows Server 2003 computers are all in place, and you have almost finished migrating all the workstations to Windows 2000 and XP Professional. Your next step is to implement a single Active Directory tree, but you want to put your DNS infrastructure in place before you start building your tree. Because DNS is a critical component for the proper functioning of Active Directory, you want to make sure that each region will have service for local resources as well as good performance. What should you do to realize these requirements?

   A. Install a single DNS server at your location and create a separate domain name for each region for resolution of local resources.

   B. Install a DNS server at each regional location and create a single domain name for all the regions for resolution of local resources.

   C. Install a single DNS server at your location and create a single domain name for all the regions for resolution of local resources.

   D. Install a DNS server at each regional location and create a separate domain name for each region for resolution of local resources.

2. The following diagram outlines DNS name resolution through recursion. Move each item into the correct position so that the flow of DNS traffic is correct.

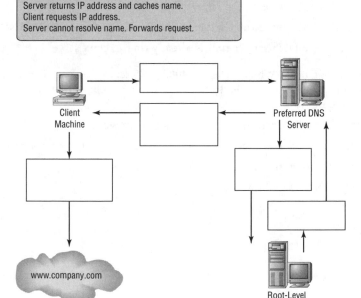

Choices:

Client uses IP address to connect to www.company.com.
Root-level server resolves name.
Server returns IP address and caches name.
Client requests IP address.
Server cannot resolve name. Forwards request.

3. After upgrading your Windows NT network to Windows Server 2003, you decide that you want to implement Active Directory. Your network consists of 3 Windows Server 2003 computers, 65 Windows 2000 and XP Professional workstations, and 3 Unix workstations, one of them running a large laser printer and another a fax server. You've been using a DNS server on one of the Unix boxes for Internet browsing only, but now you'll need DNS for Active Directory. You deploy the Windows Server 2003 DNS service, replacing the DNS on the Unix box and configuring it for dynamic updates. After you deploy Active Directory, everything appears to work fine—the users can connect to resources on the network through hostnames. However, it becomes apparent that the fax server and the laser printer are no longer accessible via their hostnames. What is the most likely cause of this problem?

    A. You need to disable dynamic updates on the DNS server.

    B. You need to install WINS to resolve the hostnames on the Unix machines.

    C. You need to manually add A resource records for the Unix machines.

    D. You need to integrate the primary DNS zone into Active Directory.

4. You have been brought into an organization that has a variety of computer systems. Management is trying to tie these systems together and to at least minimize the administrative efforts required to keep the network-provided services running. The systems consist of 4 Windows NT servers, 7 Windows Server 2003 computers, 300 Windows 2000 and XP Professional workstations, 100 Windows NT workstations, 30 Unix clients, and 3 Unix servers. Management wants to continue the migration toward the new versions of Windows and also to expand the number of Unix servers as the need arises. Presently, they are using WINS running on the Windows NT servers and a DNS service on one of the Unix servers that points to an ISP and provides all hostname resolution. What would be your recommendation for providing name resolution service for this organization?

    A. Install the Windows Server 2003 DNS service on the Windows Server 2003 computer.

    B. Install the WINS service on the Unix server.

    C. Upgrade the DNS on the Unix server to the Windows Server 2003 DNS.

    D. Use the standard DNS service that is already on the Unix server.

5. Jerry wants to configure a Windows Server 2003 DNS server so that it can answer queries for hosts on his intranet but not on the Internet. He can accomplish this by doing which of the following? (Choose two.)

    A. Installing the DNS server inside his company's firewall

    B. Configuring his server as a root server and leaving out root hints for the top-level domains

    C. Leaving forwarding turned off

    D. Disabling recursive lookups

6. Your company has been extraordinarily successful with its e-commerce site. In fact, because your customers have come to expect such a high level of reliability, you want to build several servers that mirror each other; just in case one of them fails, you will still be able to provide excellent service for your customers. The name of the web server is `www.stuffforyou.com`, which you are duplicating on machines on different subnets, and you have made all the necessary host records in the DNS. After a while you notice that only one machine is responding to client requests. You are not the original administrator for the company, so you suspect some of the default settings were changed before you arrived. What must you check so that all the mirrored web servers can be utilized by your customers?

   A. Enable DNS sharing.

   B. Enable IIS sharing.

   C. Enable round robin.

   D. Enable request redirector.

   E. Configure the proper priorities metric for this hostname.

7. Your company has offices in six cities across the country. Each location is relatively autonomous because the locations provide different services under a larger corporate umbrella. As a result, each network has its own support staff. Even though the locations are fairly independent, their standards and deployed technologies are still overseen by the corporate office, to minimize costs. Part of this centralization is supplying primary DNS name resolution services for all the locations. However, the company also uses slow links between the offices, which is causing name resolution performance issues when the requests are for resources across the WAN. You want to resolve this by installing an additional DNS server at each location without increasing zone transfers across the WAN links. Which type of DNS server should you deploy in each location to ensure the results you desire?

   A. Slave server

   B. Caching-only server

   C. Another secondary server

   D. Master server

8. You are almost finished with your migration from Windows NT, NetWare, and Banyan to Windows Server 2003. The various operating systems were a result of several companies coming together during a flurry of mergers. The Banyan portion of the network is gone now, and the NetWare migration is well under way. You also have several Unix servers and workstations that are managed by their own group. You are in the process of building the Windows Server 2003 DNS infrastructure. The Unix group has been running DNS BIND 2.4.1 for the organization because it was primarily used for Internet name resolution. Because DNS is critical to the functioning of Windows Server 2003 Active Directory, there is justification for Windows Server 2003 DNS to have the authority to be the primary zone for the network. However, the Unix group will still maintain the DNS server for the group and use the Windows Server 2003 DNS as the authority. When you finally configure the DNS servers, you cannot get the Unix DNS server to receive zone transfers from the Windows Server 2003 DNS. How must you configure the Windows Server 2003 DNS to send zone transfers to the Unix DNS?

   A. Disable the dynamic updates on the Windows Server 2003 DNS server.

   B. Enable round robin on the Windows Server 2003 DNS server.

   C. Enable dynamic updates on the Unix DNS server.

   D. Configure the BIND secondaries option on the Windows Server 2003 DNS server.

   E. Enable secure updates on the Windows Server 2003 DNS server.

9. The company you work for has six locations around the country. You are part of the administrative team based in the central office, and you have finished upgrading the workstations and servers to Windows XP and Server 2003. Your team is now in the process of deploying DNS in order to support your manager's planned implementation of a single Active Directory tree so you can support the network from your central location. Because you must support name resolution for six offices, you want to provide an efficient and responsive service for the users. Which of the following is the best approach to support your plans for a single Active Directory tree and provide the efficiency and responsiveness for the users in this situation?

   A. Create a single second-level name and maintain all the DNS servers at your central office to ease administration.

   B. Create a single second-level name and deploy a DNS server at each location in the network.

   C. Create a second-level name for each city and maintain all the DNS servers at your central office to ease administration.

   D. Create a second-level name for each city and deploy a DNS server at each location in the network.

10. You want to quickly verify that your DNS service is running and listening to queries. What would you click on or look at in the dialog box shown in the following exhibit in order to do this?

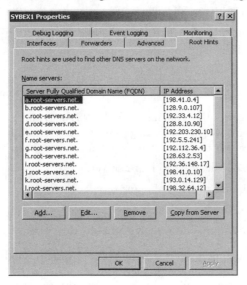

A. The Name Servers area of the Root Hints tab

B. The Add button

C. The Monitoring tab

D. The Interfaces tab

11. Acme Bowling Pin Company, with offices in 4 states, has been acquired by Roadrunner Enterprises, which has offices in 14 states and is a highly diversified organization. Although the various companies are managed independently, the parent company is very interested in minimizing costs by taking advantage of any shared corporate resources; it also wants to have overall central control. This means that you, the network administrator for Acme Bowling Pin Company, will manage your own DNS name space but will still be under the umbrella of the parent organization. Which of the following will best accomplish these goals?

A. Have each location, including yours, register its own name space and manage its DNS system independently.

B. Register a single domain name for Roadrunner Enterprises and use delegated subdomains on a single DNS server at corporate headquarters to provide name resolution across the enterprise.

C. Register a single domain name for Roadrunner Enterprises and use delegated subdomains on DNS servers installed at each location to provide name resolution across the enterprise.

D. Have each location, including yours, register its own name space and add it on a single DNS server at corporate headquarters to provide name resolution across the enterprise.

12. A DNS client sends a recursive query to its local DNS server, asking for the IP address of www.bigbrother.gov. The DNS server finds no local zones corresponding to the requested domain name, so it sends a request to a root name server. What does the root name server reply with?

A. The IP address of the name server for the bigbrother.gov domain

B. The DNS name of the Gov top-level domain

C. The IP address of www.bigbrother.gov

D. The IP address of the name server for the Gov top-level domain

13. You have a private network that contains several DNS zones and servers, including a couple of root name servers. You never need to change any of your DNS data. You find that the load on one of your name servers is inordinately high. What can you do to reduce this load?

A. Increase the TTL on the affected name server.

B. Decrease the TTL on the affected name server.

C. Add a service record to the affected name server.

D. Edit the directory command in the DNS boot file.

14. You are charged with upgrading your Windows NT network to Windows Server 2003. You plan on installing Active Directory and upgrading all your client machines to Windows XP Professional. Your company does not allow Internet access because the company president still views it, as well as e-mail, as a time-wasting toy that distracts the employees. Despite what you feel is a shortsighted view by management, you begin to design the upgrade process. You realize that DNS is an important component of Windows Server 2003, even though you won't be using it to locate resources on the Internet. What DNS records must you include in the configuration of the Windows Server 2003 DNS service in this environment? (Choose all that apply.)

A. Host record

B. Pointer record

C. Alias record

D. Name server records

E. Start of authority record

F. Mail exchange record

G. Service record

15. A spammer is attempting to send junk mail through an unsuspecting mail server. The spammer uses a fake DNS name from which he thinks the mail server will accept mail, but he is rejected anyway. How does the mail server know to reject the spammer's mail?

A. The spammer's DNS name is not in the cache file of the primary DNS server that serves the mail server's domain, so it gets rejected.

B. A fake DNS name is automatically detected if the IP address isn't recognized by the mail server.

C. The mail server employs a reverse lookup zone to verify that DNS names are not fake.

D. The spammer does not have an MX record in the database of the DNS server that serves the mail server's domain.

Answers to Review Questions

1. B.   A DNS server installed at each regional location will provide name and service resolution even if the WAN links go down. The local location will also have better performance because the requests will not have to travel through the WAN links. A single domain name for all the locations is needed because your requirement is to have one Active Directory tree with a contiguous name space.

2.

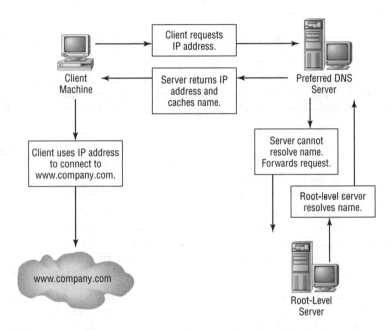

The client machine places its request with its preferred DNS server. If the DNS server doesn't have an entry in its DNS database, it forwards the request to a root-level server. The root-level server resolves the name and sends it back to the preferred DNS server. The DNS server caches the name so that any future requests don't need to be forwarded, and then it sends the IP address to the client. The client then uses the IP address to reach the intended target.

3. C.   Windows 2000 and newer computers will register themselves in the DNS through dynamic updates. However, the Unix machines will not register themselves in the DNS. These machines will have to be added manually into the DNS so that the other clients can locate them. If you disabled the Dynamic DNS updates, you would then have to add all the workstations on the network to the DNS manually. WINS is useful only for NetBIOS name resolution to IP addresses. Integrating the DNS records into Active Directory will have no effect on retrieving the hostnames of machines that don't support Dynamic DNS updates.

4. A. Installing the Windows DNS service on the Windows Server 2003 computer will provide dynamic updates to allow the newer Windows machines to publish themselves and locate the Active Directory services through the SRV records that this version of DNS supports. The Windows Server 2003 DNS will also provide standard DNS services to the Unix and Windows NT machines. In addition, it can point to the DNS server that your ISP is supplying for searches beyond the local network.

No WINS service is available for Unix. It may remain on the Windows NT server until the upgrade is complete and the NetBIOS name resolution is no longer necessary. The DNS service on the Unix server will work, but the manual updates that are necessary make it impractical to use for providing service for a Windows Server 2003 network.

5. B, C. Configuring his server as a root server and leaving forwarding off means that the server will either answer a query (for addresses it knows) or return a failure (for addresses it doesn't know).

6. C. The round robin option allows you to list a hostname with multiple IP addresses and then, as each request comes into the DNS server, to rotate that list, presenting each of the IP addresses in turn. This will balance out the load across all the servers you have mirrored and configured in the DNS.

7. B. Caching-only DNS servers don't perform zone transfers. They build up their information as queries are resolved and thus get smarter over time. If they were deployed in each location, those specific requests would build up in the cache server, thereby reducing the number of requests that would need to be forwarded to the primary DNS server at the corporate office.

A slave server forwards requests it cannot resolve to a DNS server that's specifically used to resolve requests outside your network, so it doesn't apply to this situation. Another secondary server would increase performance for local resolution but wouldn't address other requests. Installing a master server would increase traffic because it's used to perform zone transfers to secondary servers; in this scenario, those servers are already receiving zone transfers from the primary server.

8. D. The BIND secondaries option on the Windows Server 2003 DNS is used for backward compatibility with older versions of DNS. Before BIND version 4.9.5, only one resource record at a time could be transferred. Windows DNS supports fast zone transfers, in which multiple records are transferred simultaneously. Because the Unix DNS in this case is 2.4.1, the old transfer method needs to be used in order to accept the transfers.

Round robin is used to load-balance multiple hosts with the same name using multiple IP addresses. Dynamic updates are not supported in DNS BIND 2.4.1 or even in most current versions of Unix DNS. Secure updates apply only to the DNS zones that are integrated into Active Directory so that access to the records can be controlled by access control lists.

9. B. Installing a DNS server at each city as well as the central office allows the workstations in each city to obtain their name resolution from local servers, thereby providing good response time. If all the DNS servers were in the central office, name resolution would have to cross the routers, introducing latency and the potential for no service if the link ever went down. The namespace in a single Active Directory tree must be contiguous. If you create a second-level domain for each city, you would need to create multiple Active Directory trees.

10. C. From the Monitoring tab, you can perform simple and recursive queries to see if DNS servers are running and listening to queries. You can either run the tests immediately or set a schedule on which the tests will run.

11. C.   DNS has the capability to create subdomains of a central corporate domain, and a subdomain can be delegated to a DNS server in each location for independent management. The entire company could use a single DNS server at corporate headquarters with the multiple domains, but then each name space would not be managed locally at each location.

12. D.   The root name server has authority for the root domain and will reply with the IP address of a name server for the Gov top-level domain.

13. A.   If the TTL is too small, the load on the DNS server will increase.

14. A, D, E, G.   Even though it's best practice to have all the records associated with DNS as a part of each installation, name resolution will still function properly with just the fundamental records. The host record, or A record, is the basic record that contains the mapping between the logical name and the IP address. This is the heart of DNS. The name server records identify the DNS servers that are available for this network. The start of authority record, or SOA record, contains the basic configuration of the DNS service. The service record, while not essential to a traditional DNS, is critical to Active Directory because it's used to identify the domain controllers for login and other query information. The pointer record is used for reverse lookups; although it's very useful, it's not required for standard functionality. The alias record is needed only if you plan to have different names associated with the same physical address. The mail exchange record is necessary only if you are using DNS to locate mail servers.

15. C.   Most mail servers can be configured to reject incoming mail from servers whose IP addresses cannot be resolved with a reverse lookup.

Chapter

7

Managing Remote Access Services

MICROSOFT EXAM OBJECTIVES COVERED IN THIS CHAPTER:

✓ **Configure Routing and Remote Access user authentication.**

- Configure remote access authentication protocols.
- Configure Internet Authentication Service (IAS) to provide authentication for Routing and Remote Access clients.
- Configure Routing and Remote Access policies to permit or deny access.

✓ **Manage DHCP.**

- Manage DHCP Relay Agent.

✓ **Troubleshoot DHCP.**

- Verify that the DHCP Relay Agent is working correctly.

✓ **Manage remote access.**

- Manage devices and ports.
- Manage Routing and Remote Access clients.

Until now, we've focused primarily on communications between computers on the same physical network. This works fine when every machine is located within a single building or campus, but many users need to access the network from remote locations, and standard LAN technology won't provide them with the connections they need. Instead, they must use special dial-up or virtual connections that provide access to the network over telephone lines or through the Internet.

Dial-up networking (on the client side) and remote access services (on the server side) provide another way, in addition to LANs, to carry the network protocols you're already using. In the case of Routing and Remote Access Services (RRAS), some security services necessary to effectively provide remote access are also provided. For example, you'll probably want to have the ability to restrict user dial-up access by group membership, time of day, or other factors, and you'll need a way to specify the various callback, authentication, and encryption options that the protocols support. You'll learn about both dial-up and remote access in this chapter.

You will also learn about virtual private networks (VPNs), which provide remote access to private networks across public connections. Clients can dial in to an ISP and connect to your private network across the Internet. The main benefit of this is reduced cost because long-distance calls are unnecessary. VPNs are becoming more popular due to the increased popularity of high-speed Internet connections such as cable and digital subscriber line (DSL).

Many of the features included in Windows Server 2003 are simply carried over from Windows 2000, with a few minor additions. Thus is the case with the Routing and Remote Access console. RRAS itself actually dates back to the Windows NT 4 Option Pack, and Windows 2000 sported a completely revised version. Windows Server 2003 adds a few new features to RRAS but it remains mostly intact from the previous generation of Windows.

Before you can get into the details of what these features do and how you configure them to provide remote access for your network, you need to understand some of the terms and concepts specific to RRAS remote access. That's where you'll begin in this chapter, and then you'll move on to reviewing the features and configuration settings that you need to understand to meet the exam objectives.

Overview of Dial-Up Networking (DUN)

LANs provide relatively high-speed connectivity to attached machines, but where does that leave those of us who work from home, travel, or need to access data on a remote computer? Until wireless access is available worldwide, we're stuck with the familiar concept of dial-up networking with one computer (the client) dialing a remote server. Once the connection is established, a variety of protocols and services make it possible for us to view Web pages, transfer files and e-mail, and do pretty much anything we could do with a hard-wired LAN connection, albeit at reduced speed.

In the following sections, you will learn more about what dial-up networking does and how it works by examining the specific technologies and protocols associated with remote access.

What DUN Does

From reading Chapter 1, you already understand that Windows Server 2003 network protocols are actually implemented as drivers. These drivers normally work with hardware network interfaces to get data from point A to point B. What about dial-up connections?

Think back to the OSI model. Each layer has a function, and each layer serves as an intermediary between the layer above it and the one below. By substituting one driver for another at some level in the stack, you can dramatically change how things work. That's exactly what Windows Server 2003's DUN subsystem does: It makes the dial-up connection appear to be just another network adapter. The DUN driver takes care of the work of making a slow asynchronous modem appear to work just like a fast LAN interface. Applications and services that use TCP/IP on your DUN connection never know the difference. In fact, you can configure Windows Server 2003 to use your primary connection first and then pass traffic over a secondary connection (like a dial-up link) if the primary connection is down.

On the server side, DUN allows you to host one or more network users who dial into your Windows Server 2003 machine. Windows 2000 Professional and XP Professional allow one dial-up user; Windows Server 2003 allows up to 255, although by the time you allow that many connections, you'll probably be overloading your server. Depending on how you configure the DUN server, users who dial in can either see only resources on the server or see the whole network; you also get to control who can log on, when they can log on, and what they can do once they've logged on. As far as Windows Server 2003 is concerned, a user connected via DUN is no different from one using resources over your LAN, so all the access controls and permissions you apply remain in force for DUN users.

 You will learn more about remote access user authentication in Chapter 8, "Managing User Access to Remote Access Services."

How DUN Works

There are a lot of pieces required to successfully complete a dial-up call from your computer to a server at another physical location. Understanding what these pieces are, how they work, and what they do for you is key. In the following sections, we will look at the DUN infrastructure, how the Point-to-Point Protocol (PPP) helps in this connection, the relationship between PPP and the network protocols, and how multilink can be used to increase the speed and efficiency of your remote connections.

The DUN Infrastructure

Let's start with a look at the physical layer that underlies voice and data calls. Most of the following material will be familiar to anyone who has ever used a modem, but you should still understand the details that you might not have thought of before.

POTS

POTS stands for plain old telephone service. In the early days of dial-up networking, phone lines were used to connect. You were lucky to get 4800bps. At the time, the prevalent modem speed was 300bps. Today, modems offer a theoretical maximum speed of 56Kbps; in practice, many users routinely get connections at 51 or 52Kbps.

The word *modem* is actually an acronym for *modulator-demodulator*. The original Bell System modems took digital data and modulated it into screechy analog audio tones suitable for use on regular phone lines. Because phone lines are purposely designed to pass only the low end of the audible frequency range that most can hear, the amount of data was limited. However, in the early 1990s, some engineers discovered that you could communicate much faster if the path between the sender and receiver was all digital because an all-digital path doesn't have any analog components that induce signal loss, so it preserves the original signal quality faithfully—which in turn makes it possible to put more information into the original signal. As it happens, phone companies nationwide were in the process of making (or had just completed) major upgrades to replace their analog equipment with newer, better, digital equivalents. These upgrades made it possible for people in most areas to get almost-56Kbps speeds without changing any of the wiring in their homes or offices. The connection between the house and the phone office was still analog, but the connections between phone offices were digital, ensuring high-quality connections.

ISDN

In the mid-1970s, Integrated Services Digital Network (ISDN) was designed. At the time, no one had any idea that you'd be able to get 56Kbps speeds out of an ordinary phone line. ISDN's speeds of up to 128Kbps over a single pair of copper wires seemed pretty revolutionary. In addition, ISDN had features like call forwarding, caller ID, and multiple directory numbers (so you could have more than one number, perhaps with different ringing patterns, associated with a single line).

Unfortunately, ISDN requires an all-digital signal path. It also requires special equipment on both ends of the connection. The phone companies were slow to promote ISDN as a faster alternative to regular dial-up service, so customers avoided it.

ISDN still has some advantages, though. Because it's all digital, call setup times are much shorter than they are for analog modems—it only takes about half a second to establish a new ISDN call. Modern ISDN adapters and ISDN-capable routers can seamlessly stitch together multiple ISDN channels to deliver bandwidth in 64Kbps increments. Because you can use ISDN lines for regular analog voice, data, and fax traffic, you can make a single ISDN act like two voice lines, a single 128Kbps data line, or a 64Kbps data line plus a voice line.

ISDN is quickly being replaced by faster broadband services such as DSL and cable modems. In fact, you should only resort to ISDN if these other solutions are not available in your area. Note that DSL and cable modems (a misnomer because they are all digital) do not use PPP—discussed later—so they are technically not considered dial-up connections.

Other Connection Methods

POTS and ISDN aren't available everywhere. For example, suppose your company has a Windows Server 2003 network and has sites on land as well as at sea. The computers at sea must communicate with the land-based offices via a satellite-based connection. In theory, it's a dial-up connection like any other, but in actuality it uses a packet-based protocol called X.25. X.25 can be used to substitute for a regular dial-up connection in Windows Server 2003, assuming you have the right drivers and hardware.

Any other on-demand connection that's established using the *Point-to-Point Protocol (PPP)* can be thought of as a dial-up connection, and Windows Server 2003 doesn't make any distinction between POTS, ISDN, and other dial-ups—they're all treated identically.

Connecting with PPP

The Point-to-Point Protocol enables any two devices to establish a TCP/IP connection over a serial link. That normally means a dial-up modem connection, but it could just as easily be a direct serial cable connection, an infrared connection, or any other type of serial connection. When one machine dials another, the machine that initiates the connection is referred to as a client, and the machine that receives the call is a server—even though the PPP itself makes no such distinction.

PPP negotiation involves three phases that are required to establish a remote access connection. The three phases invoke one or more protocols, as you can see in Figure 7.1.

FIGURE 7.1   The PPP negotiation process

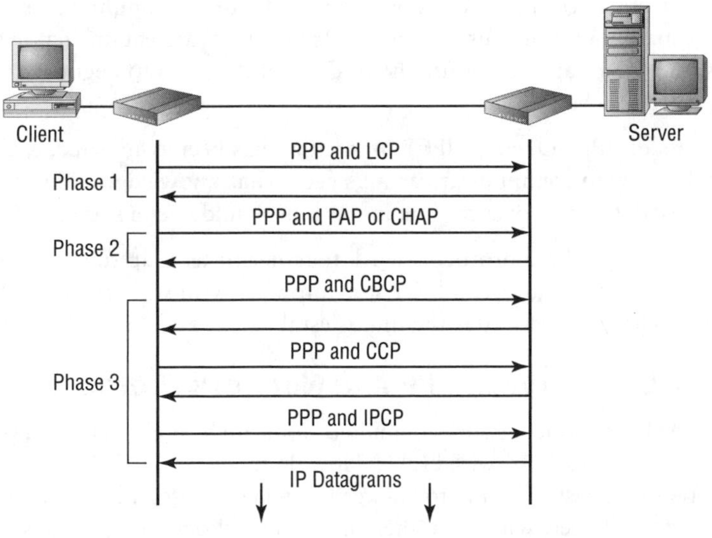

There are actually at least six distinct protocols that run on top of PPP. Understanding what they do helps make the actual PPP negotiation process clearer. These protocols include the following:

The Link Control Protocol (LCP)   The Link Control Protocol (LCP) handles the details of establishing the lowest-level PPP link; in that regard, you can think of it almost as if it were part of the Physical layer. When one PPP device calls another, they use LCP to agree that they want to establish a PPP connection.

The Challenge Handshake Authentication Protocol (CHAP)   *Challenge Handshake Authentication Protocol (CHAP)*—as well as MS-CHAP, PAP, and SPAP, which will be covered in the next chapter—allows the client to authenticate itself to the server. This authentication functions much like a normal network logon; once the client presents its logon credentials, the server can figure out what access to grant.

The Callback Control Protocol (CBCP)   The Callback Control Protocol (CBCP) is used to negotiate whether a callback is required, whether it's permitted, and when it happens. Once the client has authenticated itself, the server can decide whether it should hang up and call the client back. The client can also request a callback at a number it provides; although this isn't as secure as having the server place a call to a predetermined number, it provides some additional flexibility. If a callback occurs, the connection is reestablished and reauthenticated, but the CBCP stage is skipped.

The Compression Control Protocol (CCP)   The Compression Control Protocol (CCP) allows the two sides of the connection to determine what kind of compression, if any, they want to use on the network data. Because PPP traffic actually consists of wrapped-up IP datagrams, and because IP datagram headers tend to be fairly compressible, negotiating effective compression can significantly improve overall PPP throughput.

The IP Control Protocol (IPCP)   At this point in the call, the two sides have agreed to authentication, compression, and a callback. They haven't yet agreed on what IP parameters to use for the connection. These parameters, which include the maximum packet size to be sent over the link (the maximum transmission unit, or MTU), have a great impact on the overall link performance, so the client and server use the IP Control Protocol to negotiate them based on the traffic they expect to be passed.

The Internet Protocol (IP)   Once the IPCP negotiation has been completed, each end has complete knowledge of how to communicate with its peer. That knowledge allows the two sides to begin exchanging IP datagrams over the link just as they would over a standard LAN connection.

Figure 7.1 shows how these protocols work together to lead up to establishing the link. Remember this diagram because you'll see it again when you start reading about PPTP. Now you can see what happens after the link is established and traffic begins flowing.

The Relationship Between PPP and Network Protocols

Normally when you hear about network communication, you hear about using TCP/IP, NetBEUI, AppleTalk, or IPX/SPX on a hard-wired LAN. How do these protocols fit in with PPP? In the case of TCP/IP, that's an easy question to answer: The client routes all (or some) of its outgoing TCP/IP traffic to its PPP peer, which can then inspect the IP datagrams it gets back from the PPP stack to analyze and route them properly.

Windows Server 2003 doesn't just support TCP/IP, so consider what has to happen when a client using NWLink needs to connect over the dial-up Networking. After the LCP negotiation completes, the server will know which protocols the client wishes to use. If the server doesn't want to use one or more of those protocols, it can drop the call or cause the client to warn its user (that's what Windows Server 2003 does). After the other PPP setup steps complete, the client and server can wrap other types of network traffic inside an IP datagram. This process, called *encapsulation*, allows the client to take a packet with some kind of private content, wrap it inside an IP datagram, and send it to the server. The server, in turn, processes the IP datagram, routing real datagrams normally and handling any encapsulated packets with the appropriate protocol. At that point, the client can communicate with the server without knowing that its non-TCP/IP packets are being encapsulated in any way—that detail is hidden deep in the layers of the OSI model.

Understanding the Benefits of Multilink

Many parts of the world don't have high-speed broadband access yet. In fact, many places don't have ISDN or even phone lines that support 56K modems. The multilink extensions to the Point-to-Point Protocol (PPP) provide a way to take several independent PPP connections and make them look like one line so that they act as a single connection.

For example, if you use two phone lines and modems to place a two-line multilink call to your ISP, instead of getting the usual 48Kbps connection, you would end up with an apparent bandwidth of 96Kbps. The multilink PPP software on your Windows Server 2003 machine and on the ISP's router takes care of stringing all of the packets together to make this process seamless. Windows Server 2003's RRAS service supports multilink PPP for inbound and outbound calls. The primary drawback to multilink calls is that they take up more than one phone line apiece.

Overview of Virtual Private Networks

Private networks offer superior security: You own the wires, so you have control over what they're used for, who can use them, and what kind of data passes over them. However, they're not very flexible because you would need to configure and manage costly leased lines between remote locations. To make things worse, most private networks face a dilemma: Implementing enough capacity to handle peak loads almost guarantees that much of that capacity will sit idly much of the time, even though it still has to be paid for.

One way to work around this problem is to maintain private dial-up services so that a field rep in Chicago, for example, can dial the home office in Boston. Dial-ups are expensive, and they have the same excess capacity problem that truly private networks do. As an added detriment, users who need to dial in from long distances have to pay long-distance charges unless they use toll-free numbers (in which case the remote access cost goes up dramatically).

Virtual private networks (VPNs) offer a solution: You get the security of a true private network with the flexibility, ubiquity, and low cost of the Internet. In the following sections, we will look at VPNs: what they are used for, how they work with Windows Server 2003, and how they work in general.

What VPNs Do

At any time, two parties can create a connection over the Internet. The idea behind a VPN is that you can use these connections to let two parties establish an encrypted *tunnel* between them using the Internet as a transportation medium. The VPN software on each end takes care of encrypting the VPN packets as they go; when they leave one end of the tunnel, their payloads are encrypted and encapsulated inside regular IP packets that cause them to be delivered to the remote machine. Figure 7.2 shows one way to conceptualize this process.

FIGURE 7.2 Drilling a tunnel through the Internet

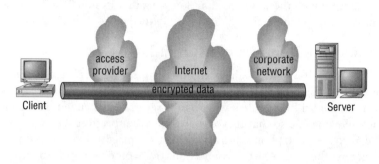

As an example, let's say that you're in the field at a client site. As long as you're somewhere that your ISP serves, you can dial into the client's local point of presence and get connected to the Internet. At that point, you can open a VPN connection back to the servers at your office and do whatever you could do when sitting in front of a normal desktop machine.

VPNs and Windows Server 2003

Windows Server 2003 includes support for the Microsoft proprietary *Point-to-Point Tunneling Protocol (PPTP)* and Cisco's *Layer 2 Tunneling Protocol (L2TP)*. L2TP provides a more generic tunneling mechanism than PPTP; when combined with IPSec, L2TP also allows you to establish VPNs using a wide range of non-Microsoft hardware and software products, including routers and access devices from companies like Cisco, Red Creek, and Nortel.

There are some worthwhile features included in Windows Server 2003's VPN support, including the following:

- You can set up account lockout policies for dial-up and VPN users; this capacity has existed for network and console users for some time.

- The *Extensible Authentication Protocol (EAP)* allows Microsoft or third parties to write modules that implement new authentication methods and retrofit them to fielded servers. One example of EAP is the EAP-TLS module that implements access control based on smart cards and certificates for VPN and dial-up users.

- If you're using Active Directory in native mode, you can use remote access policies to apply and enforce consistent policies to all users in a site, domain, or organizational unit. These policies can include which encryption and authentication protocols users may, or must, use when talking to your servers.

How you enable VPN support on your Windows Server 2003 machine depends on whether you're using a server or a client. Client configuration is easy, as you'll see later in this chapter: Just install the Dial-Up Networking service and then use the Make New Connection Wizard to create a new VPN connection. On the server side, you'll need to install and configure Routing and Remote Access Services and then enable it to accept incoming VPN connections.

How VPNs Work

The VPN client assumes that the VPN server is already connected to the Internet in some way. Here's how the VPN connection process works:

1. The client establishes a connection to the Internet. Dial-Up Networking or any other connection method can be used for this connection. The client must be able to send packets out to the Internet.

2. The client sends a VPN connection request to the server. The exact format of the request varies, depending on whether the VPN is using PPTP or L2TP.

3. The client authenticates itself to the server. Again, the exact process varies according to the VPN protocol in use. If the client can't provide valid credentials, the connection is terminated.

4. The client and server negotiate parameters for the VPN session. This negotiation allows the two ends to agree on an encryption algorithm and strength.

5. The client and server go through the PPP negotiation process described earlier in this chapter because both L2TP and PPTP depend on the lower-level PPP protocols (you will see why later in the section "Configuring a VPN").

Because the contents of data passed around in steps 2 and 3 vary according to the tunneling protocol in use, let's examine the differences. First, though, you should understand encapsulation and how VPNs use it to wrap one kind of data inside another.

An Encapsulation Primer

In the beginning, most networks could carry only one kind of data. Each network vendor had its own protocol, and most of the time there was no way to intermingle data using different protocols on the same line. Over time, vendors began to find ways to allow a single network to carry many different types of traffic, resulting in the current assortment of traffic types found on most large networks. However, the Internet only works with TCP/IP. If you need to send other types of traffic across the Internet, such as IPX or NetBEUI, you can encapsulate it within TCP/IP.

Encapsulation works because software at each level of the OSI model has to see header information to figure out where a packet's coming from and where it's going. But the payload contents aren't important to most of those components. By fabricating the right kind of header and prepending it to whatever you want in the payload, you can route foreign traffic types through IP networks with no trouble.

VPNs depend on encapsulation because their security depends on being able to keep the payload information encrypted. The following steps demonstrate what happens to a typical packet as it goes from being a regular IP datagram to a PPTP packet (see also Figure 7.3):

1. An application creates a block of data bound for a remote host. In this case, it's a web browser.

2. The client-side TCP/IP stack takes the application's data and turns it into a TCP/IP packet, first by adding a TCP header and then by adding an IP header. This can be called the *IP datagram* because it contains all of the necessary addressing information to be delivered by IP.

3. The client is connected via PPP, so it adds a PPP header to the IP datagram. This PPP + IP combination is called a PPP frame.

4. If you were using PPP instead of a VPN protocol, the packet would go across the PPP link without further modification. However, in this example you are using a VPN, so the next step is for the VPN to encrypt the PPP frame, turning it into unreadable information to be transported over the Internet.

5. A Generic Routing Encapsulation (GRE) header is combined with the encrypted payload. GRE really is generic; in this case, the protocol ID fields in the GRE header says that this is an encapsulated PPTP packet.

6. Now that you have a tag to tell you what's in the payload, the PPTP stack can add an IP header (specifying the destination address of the VPN server, not the original host from step 2) and a PPP header.

7. Now the packet can be sent out over your existing PPP connection. The IP header specifies that it should be routed to the VPN server, which can pick it apart and reverse steps 1 through 6 when the packet arrives.

FIGURE 7.3   The encapsulation process

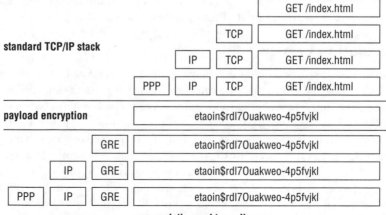

Encapsulation allows the use of VPN data inside ordinary-looking IP datagrams, which is part of what makes VPNs so powerful—you don't have to change any of your applications, routers, or network components (unless they have to be configured to recognize and pass GRE packets).

PPTP Tunneling

PPTP is a pretty straightforward protocol. It works by encapsulating packets using the mechanism described in the previous section. The encryption step (step 4) is performed using the Microsoft Point-to-Point Encryption (MPPE) algorithm. The encryption keys used to encrypt the packets are generated dynamically for each connection; in fact, the keys can be changed periodically during the connection.

When the client and server have successfully established a PPTP tunnel, the authorization process begins. This process is an exchange of credentials that allows the server to decide whether the client is permitted to connect or not. The server sends a challenge message to the client, and the client answers with an encrypted response. When the server gets the response, it can check it to see whether the answer is right. The challenge-response process allows the server to determine which account is trying to make a connection. Once it knows that, it can determine whether the user account is authorized to make a connection. If so, the server accepts the inbound connection; any access controls or remote access restrictions still apply.

L2TP/IPSec Tunneling

L2TP is much more flexible than PPTP, but it's also more complicated. It was designed to be a general-purpose tunneling protocol not limited to VPN use. L2TP itself doesn't offer any kind of security. When you use L2TP, you're setting up an unencrypted, unauthenticated tunnel. Doing so over the Internet would be dangerous because anyone who wanted to could read your traffic. To address this issue, you can use L2TP in conjunction with IPSec, which was discussed in Chapter 4, "Managing IP Security." The overall flow of an L2TP + IPSec tunnel session looks a little different from that of a PPTP session because IPSec security is different. Here's how the L2TP/IPSec combination works:

1. The client and server establish an IPSec security association using the ISAKMP and Oakley protocols discussed in Chapter 4. At this point, the two machines have an encrypted channel between them.

2. The client builds a new L2TP tunnel to the server. Because this happens after the channel has been encrypted, there's no security risk.

3. The server sends an authentication challenge to the client.

4. The client encrypts its answer to the challenge and returns it to the server.

5. The server checks the challenge response to see whether or not it's valid; if so, the server can determine which account is connecting. Subject to whatever access policies you've put in place, at this point the server can accept the inbound connection.

Note that steps 3 through 5 mirror the steps described for PPTP tunneling. This is because the authorization process is a function of the remote access server, not the VPN stack. All the VPN does is provide a secure communications channel, and something else has to decide who gets to use it.

Installing the Routing and Remote Access Services

Now that you understand the principles behind dial-up networking and remote access, you can learn how to actually install and configure remote access services on your server. You can configure a Windows Server 2003 computer as either a remote access client or a remote access server, but usually you install the client component on Windows 2000 Professional and XP Professional computers dialing in to Windows Server 2003 remote access servers. Windows Server 2003 includes RRAS to support remote access services as a server. RRAS is actually installed by default with Windows Server 2003. However, it's not activated until you run the Routing And Remote Access Server Setup Wizard.

Exercise 7.1 will lead you through the process of configuring an RRAS server using the wizard.

EXERCISE 7.1

Installing the Routing and Remote Access Services

1. Open the RRAS MMC console by selecting Start ≻ Administrative Tools ≻ Routing And Remote Access.

2. Select the server you want to configure in the left pane of the MMC. Right-click the server and choose Configure And Enable Routing And Remote Access. The RRAS Setup Wizard appears. Click the Next button.

3. On the Common Configuration page of the wizard, select the Remote Access (Dial-Up Or VPN) radio button and then click the Next button.

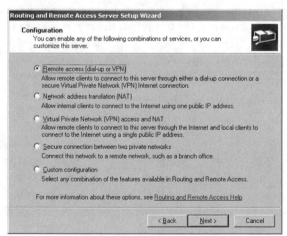

4. The Remote Access page appears, allowing you to select a VPN server and/or a dial-up server. Check both checkboxes because you will configure a VPN server later in this chapter. Note that VPNs require more than one network interface (as you will see later).

If you don't have more than one interface at this time, then just select the Dial-Up option. Click the Next button.

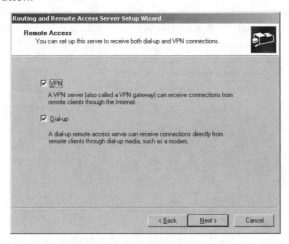

5. The Macintosh Guest Authentication page appears. The Macintosh operating system allows anonymous remote access. If you want your RRAS server to imitate this behavior, click the Allow Unauthenticated Access For All Remote Clients button. Click the Next button. (Note that this page will appear only if Macintosh File and Print services are loaded.)

6. The IP Address Assignment page appears. If you want to use DHCP (either a DHCP server on your network or the built-in address allocator), leave the Automatically radio button selected. If you want to pick out an address range, select the From A Specified Range Of Addresses button. Click the Next button. (If you choose to use static addressing, at this point the wizard will give you the opportunity to define one or more address ranges to be assigned to remote clients.)

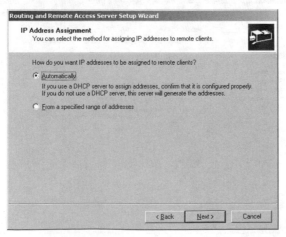

EXERCISE 7.1 *(continued)*

7. The Managing Multiple Remote Access Servers page appears. You use this page to configure your RRAS server to work with other RADIUS-capable servers on your network. In this case, you don't want to use RADIUS, so leave the No, Use Routing And Remote Access To Authenticate Connection Requests button selected and then click the Next button.

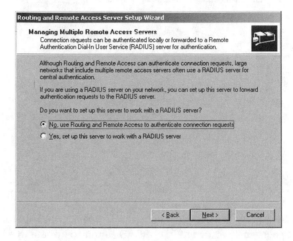

8. The summary page appears. Click the Finish button to start the RRAS service and prepare your server to be configured. You'll see a message indicating that you need to configure the DHCP relay agent (more on that later) if you want to forward DHCP messages to another network.

The RRAS window is shown in Figure 7.4.

FIGURE 7.4 The RRAS window as it appears after completing the RRAS Setup Wizard

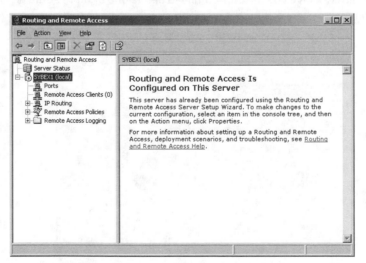

Configuring Your Remote Access Server

Most of the configuration necessary for a remote access server happens at the server level. In particular, you use the server's Properties dialog box to control whether the server allows remote connections at all, what protocols and options it supports, and so forth. You also have to configure settings for your users, which you'll read about in the next section.

To open the RRAS server's Properties dialog box, choose the server you're interested in and select Action ➤ Properties (or right-click the server and select Properties from the context menu). The options in the Properties dialog box are described in the following sections.

Setting General Configuration Options

The General tab of the server Properties dialog box (see Figure 7.5) has only one checkbox of interest for remote access configurations: Remote Access Server. When checked, this option allows the RRAS to act as a remote access server. You need to know this so that you can switch remote access capability on and off without deactivating and reactivating RRAS, which causes the service to erase its settings.

FIGURE 7.5   The General tab of the RRAS server Properties dialog box

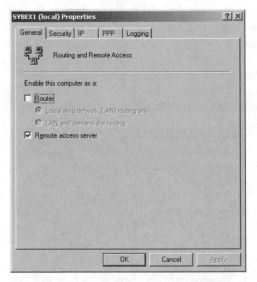

The other tabs in this dialog box control specific settings for different protocols. Note that the tabs you see will depend on which protocols you have installed. For example, on a server that doesn't have IPX installed, you won't have the IPX tab. The other tabs available from this dialog box include the following:

- On the Security tab, you can specify what authentication providers and settings you want the server to use. The controls on this tab are covered in the section "Configuring Security" in Chapter 8.

- The protocol-specific tabs (for example, the IP tab in Figure 7.5) control settings applied to each protocol you have installed. In particular, these tabs govern whether or not the associated protocol can be used for remote access clients as well as whether remote clients can reach the entire network or only the remote access server itself. The next section, "Configuring Inbound Connections," covers each of these tabs independently.

- The PPP tab controls which PPP protocols—including multilink—the clients on this server are allowed to use. The section "Configuring PPP Options" discusses these settings in detail.

- The Logging tab controls what level of log detail is kept for incoming connections. These controls are covered more fully in the section titled "Managing Your Remote Access Server" later in this chapter.

Configuring Inbound Connections

The whole point behind using an RRAS server is to allow remote clients to call it, but it's not an all-or-nothing proposition. You can set separate options for each protocol that the server supports; because all of those protocols are carried via PPP, there are some generic PPP options you can set as well. We will look at these options in the following sections.

Configuring PPP Options

You can use the PPP tab of the RRAS server Properties dialog box (see Figure 7.6) to control the PPP-layer options available to clients that call in. The settings you specify here control whether or not the related PPP options are available to clients; remote access policies can be used to control whether individual connections make use of them or not. There are a total of four checkboxes on this tab.

FIGURE 7.6   The PPP tab of the RRAS server Properties dialog box

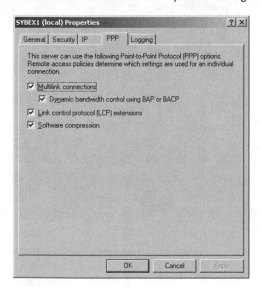

The Multilink Connections checkbox, which is checked by default, controls whether or not the server will allow clients to establish multilink connections when they call in.

The Bandwidth Allocation Protocol (BAP) and Bandwidth Allocation Control Protocol (BACP) allow a client and server to dynamically add or remove links during a multilink session. This is handy because it lets you throttle the amount of available bandwidth up or down on demand—provided you have the Dynamic Bandwidth Control Using BAP Or BACP checkbox checked. It's only available when the Multilink Connections checkbox is checked.

The PPP Link Control Protocol (LCP) is used to establish a PPP link and negotiate its settings. There are a variety of LCP extensions defined in various RFCs; these extensions allow a client and server to dynamically agree on exactly which protocols are being passed back and forth, among other things. The Link Control Protocol (LCP) Extensions checkbox controls whether or not these extensions are available. Windows 9x, NT, 2000, and XP clients depend on the LCP extensions, so you should leave this checkbox marked.

The Software Compression checkbox controls whether RRAS will allow a remote client to use the Compression Control Protocol (CCP) to compress PPP traffic. In some cases, hardware compression at the modem level is more efficient, but not everyone has a compression-capable modem. Leave this checkbox checked as well.

It doesn't make sense to enable multilink connections if you have only one phone line; in addition, you may want to turn them off to keep a small number of users from using all your lines. Exercise 7.2 will take you through the process of controlling multilink for incoming calls.

EXERCISE 7.2

Controlling Multilink for Incoming Calls

1. Open the RRAS MMC console by selecting Start ➢ Administrative Tools ➢ Routing And Remote Access.

2. Right-click the server you want to configure in the left pane of the MMC and choose Properties. The server Properties dialog box appears.

3. Click the PPP tab.

4. To turn multilink capability off, make sure the Multilink Connections checkbox is unchecked. To turn it back on, simply check the checkbox.

5. If you decide to turn multilink capability on, you should also enable the use of BAP/BACP to make it easier for your server to adjust to the load placed on it. To do so, make sure the Dynamic Bandwidth Control Using BAP Or BACP checkbox is marked.

6. Click the OK button.

Configuring IP-Based Connections

TCP/IP is far and away the most commonly used remote access protocol; coincidentally, it's also the most configurable of the protocols that Windows Server 2003 supports. Both of these facts are reflected in the IP tab of the server Properties dialog box (see Figure 7.7).

FIGURE 7.7 The IP tab of the RRAS server Properties dialog box

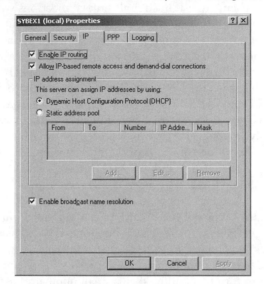

The controls on this tab do the following:

- The Enable IP Routing checkbox controls whether or not RRAS will route IP packets between the remote client and other interfaces on your RRAS server. When this box is checked, as it is by default, remote clients' packets can go to the RRAS server or to any other host to which the RRAS server has a route. To limit clients to only accessing resources on the RRAS server itself, uncheck this box.

- The Allow IP-Based Remote Access And Demand-Dial Connections checkbox controls whether clients may use IP over PPP. It might seem odd to have this choice because the over-whelming majority of PPP connections use IP, but if you want to limit your server to NetBEUI, IPX, or AppleTalk remote clients, you can do so by making sure this box is unchecked.

- The IP Address Assignment control group lets you specify how you want remote clients to get their IP addresses. The default setting here will vary, depending on what you told the RRAS Setup Wizard during setup. If you want to use a DHCP server on your network as the source of IP addresses for remote clients, select the Dynamic Host Configuration Protocol (DHCP) radio button (you need to make that you've got the DHCP relay agent installed and running). If you'd rather use static address allocation, select the Static Address Pool button and then specify which IP address ranges you want issued to clients in the list below.

- The Enable Broadcast Name Resolution option allows remote clients to resolve TCP/IP names without the use of a WINS or DNS server. This feature is enabled by default and is new for Windows Server 2003.

 If you choose to use static addressing, be sure that you don't use any address ranges that are part of a DHCP server's address pool. Better still, you can add the ranges you want reserved for remote access as excluded ranges in the DHCP snap-in.

In Exercise 7.3, you're going to configure your RRAS server so that it only accepts inbound calls that use the IP protocol. You may have to skip some steps (as noted) if you don't have all four network protocols loaded.

EXERCISE 7.3

Configuring Incoming Connections

1. Open the RRAS MMC console by selecting Start ➢ Administrative Tools ➢ Routing And Remote Access.

2. Right-click the server you want to configure in the left pane of the MMC and choose Properties command. The server Properties dialog box appears.

3. Click the IP tab. Verify that both the Enable IP Routing and the Allow IP-Based Remote Access And Demand-Dial Connections checkboxes are marked.

4. Switch to the IPX tab if you have one. Uncheck the Allow IPX-Based Remote Access And Demand-Dial Connections checkbox.

5. If your Properties dialog box has a NetBEUI tab, switch to it and uncheck the Allow NetBEUI-Based Remote Access Clients To Access checkbox.

6. If your Properties dialog box has an AppleTalk tab, switch to it and uncheck the Enable AppleTalk Remote Access checkbox.

7. Click the OK button. After a brief pause, the Properties dialog box disappears and your changes become effective.

Configuring IPX-Based Connections

You may recall that IP and IPX are very similar in many respects. Even though the particulars differ, they both involve addresses that must be assigned to every device on the network. Accordingly, the IP and IPX tabs of the server Properties dialog box aren't that much different. The IPX tab includes two controls that give you power over whether this server speaks IPX or not.

The IPX tabs include the following:

- The Allow IPX-Based Remote Access And Demand-Dial Connections checkbox controls whether this server will accept IPX connections or not.

- The Enable Network Access For Remote Clients And Demand-Dial Connections checkbox controls whether IPX clients can reach only this server or other IPX-capable servers on your network.

Notice that each protocol tab has a checkbox like this but that each one is labeled differently. Make sure you get their names straight for the exam.

In addition, the IPX Network Number Assignment control group gives you a way to have this server automatically assign IPX network numbers to dial-up clients. Your best bet will be to leave the Automatically radio button selected; it tells the server to pass out numbers as it sees fit. If necessary, you can manually assign numbers in a specified range. The two other checkboxes give you some additional control:

- The Use The Same Network Number For All IPX Clients checkbox, which is checked by default, indicates whether you want all IPX clients to get the same network number or not. Normally, you'll want this to be on so that all your IPX resources will be immediately visible to clients.

- The Allow Remote Clients To Request IPX Node Number checkbox is normally unchecked by default because it's a potential security hole. When this checkbox is checked, clients can request a particular IPX node number; in theory, this could allow a malicious remote client to impersonate another IPX device. Leave this box unchecked.

Configuring AppleTalk and NetBEUI Connections

The AppleTalk and NetBEUI tabs control whether or not your server will accept remote connections using those protocols. AppleTalk and NetBEUI are both pretty simple, so there aren't really any configuration options on the tabs—just checkboxes that you use to specify whether your server will allow incoming connections or not. The AppleTalk checkbox is labeled Enable AppleTalk Remote Access, and its NetBEUI counterpart reads Allow NetBEUI-Based Remote Access Clients To Access. The NetBEUI version also has an associated pair of radio buttons that regulate whether NetBEUI clients can see only the RRAS server or the entire network.

Installing a VPN

Conventional dial-up access still works fine, but as you saw earlier, it can be expensive to implement, painful to manage, and vulnerable to attack. VPNs offer a way around these problems by providing low initial and ongoing cost, easy management, and excellent security. Windows Server 2003's Routing and Remote Access Services (RRAS) component includes two complete VPN implementations: one using Microsoft's Point-to-Point Tunneling Protocol (PPTP) and one using a combination of the Internet-standard IPSec protocol and the Layer 2 Tunneling Protocol (L2TP).

The basic process of setting up a VPN is simple, but there are some things to think through before plunging ahead. Getting the VPN installation right may require small hardware or networking changes plus proper configuration of the VPN service itself. We will look at this process in the following sections.

Setting Up Your Server

A VPN it sits between your internal network and the Internet, accepting connections from clients in the outside world. In the Figure 7.8, Clients 1 and 2 are using different ISPs (probably because they're at different physical locations). For example, a packet from Client 1 goes from its computer to its ISP and then through some route, unknown to you, that eventually delivers it to the VPN server, which transforms it into a packet suitable for use on the internal network.

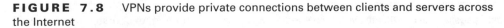

FIGURE 7.8   VPNs provide private connections between clients and servers across the Internet

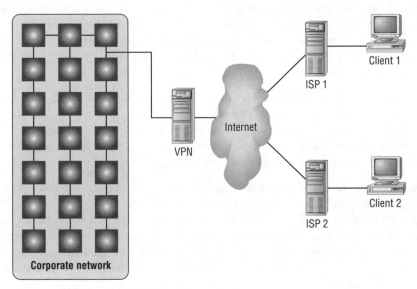

Imagine a line around the internal network and think of it as a security boundary. In general, you'll want your VPN server to be outside any firewalls or network security measures you have in place. The most common configuration is to use two NICs: One connects to the Internet, and the other connects either to the private network or to an intermediate network that itself connects to the private network. Of course, you can use any type of Internet connection you wish for the VPN server: cable modems, DSL, T1, ISDN, or whatever.

The point behind giving the VPN its own network adapter is that your VPN clients need a public IP address to connect to and you probably don't want them calling directly into your internal network. That also means that things will be easiest for your VPN users if the IP address for your VPN server's external interface is statically assigned, so it won't be changing on them when they least expect it.

Avoiding Some Subtle L2TP Pitfalls

As you learned in Chapter 4, IPSec uses a fairly complex process to negotiate security agreements (SAs) between two endpoints of a secure connection. Part of this process involves the use of what Microsoft calls *machine certificates*. These are nothing more than digital certificates issued to machines instead of users. These certificates allow both ends of the connection to authenticate the computers involved, not just the people. In fact, machine-level authentication is a prerequisite step—on an L2TP VPN, the machine endpoints are authenticated before the VPN client ever sends an authentication request.

In most cases, these certificates will be issued automatically, assuming, of course, that you've configured your certificate authority (CA) to issue certificates automatically to machines when they join a Windows Server 2003 domain. If you haven't already made this change, you can manually enroll machines by using the certificate authority tools to request a computer certificate for each machine that needs one; you can also force the CA to issue a certificate to the VPN server by restarting the VPN server or refreshing the local security policy.

In addition, your remote machines must be able to join the domain in the first place. Let's say you want to allow employees to use VPN from home but you don't want those machines joining your domain. In that case, you might be able to issue certificates manually to those users who are running Windows 2000 or newer operating systems, but your best bet will probably be to turn on PPTP instead until the L2TP infrastructure catches up.

With Windows Server 2003, you can also configure a VPN server to use preshared keys instead of certificates. Preshared keys are much easier to configure and manage than certificates because you do not need to set up a certificate server (or use a third-party certificate service), but they are slightly less secure because you need to give the same key to every remote access user. Also, if the preshared key is changed, your users will need to manually change their key configuration, which might not seem like a problem for you, but many users balk at the thought of computer configuration.

Installing RRAS as a VPN Server

To get any use from your VPN, you need two pieces: a VPN client and a VPN server. In Windows Server 2003's case, having a VPN server means that you're very likely to be using RRAS. Because you've already seen how to configure RRAS as a Remote Access Services (RAS) server, this section will give a bare-bones explanation just as a refresher.

Installing A VPN From Scratch

If you don't have RRAS installed at all, you'll need to install it, activate it, and configure it as a VPN server. The easiest way to do this is with the RRAS Setup Wizard. You may remember that the wizard gives you a page with several radio buttons that you use to select the kind of server you want to set up. If you followed the instructions in Exercise 7.1 ("Installing the Routing and Remote Access Services"), you actually already have a VPN server—when you install RRAS as a remote access server, the wizard automatically sets up VPN ports for you.

In Exercise 7.4, you will install an RRAS VPN server from scratch.

EXERCISE 7.4

Installing the Routing and Remote Access Services as a VPN Server

1. Open the RRAS MMC console by selecting Start ⟩ Administrative Tools ⟩ Routing And Remote Access.

2. Select the server you want to configure in the left pane of the MMC. Right-click the server and choose Configure And Enable Routing And Remote Access. The RRAS Setup Wizard appears. Click the Next button.

3. In the Configuration page of the wizard, select the Remote Access (Dial-Up Or VPN) radio button, and then click the Next button.

4. The Remote Access page appears, allowing you to select a VPN server and/or a dial-up server. Check only the VPN checkbox because this exercise focuses on the VPN aspect of RRAS. Click the Next button.

5. The Internet Connections page appears next. This page lists all of the demand-dial and permanent network interfaces known to RRAS; you have to choose an interface to serve as the incoming "phone number" for VPN connections. Pick an interface and click the Next button.

6. The IP Address Assignment page appears. If you want to use DHCP (either a DHCP server on your network or the built-in address allocator), leave the Automatically radio button selected. If you want to pick out an address range, select the From A Specified Range Of Addresses button. Click the Next button.

If you choose to use static addressing, at this point the wizard will give you the opportunity to define one or more address ranges to be assigned to remote clients.

7. The Managing Multiple Remote Access Servers page appears. You use this page to configure your RRAS server to work with other RADIUS-capable servers on your network. In this case, you still don't want to use RADIUS, so leave the No, Use Routing And Remote Access To Authenticate Connection Requests button selected and click the Next button.

8. The summary page appears. Click the Finish button to start the RRAS service and prepare your server to be configured. If the RRAS service is running on the same server as a DHCP server, you'll see a message indicating that you need to configure the DHCP relay agent.

Once you've completed this exercise, you'll have a complete, ready-to-go VPN server that will start accepting connections immediately. However, you may want to configure the available ports to meet your VPN needs; that's covered in the section "Configuring VPN Ports" below.

Enabling RRAS as a VPN

If you're already using RRAS for IP routing or remote access, you can enable it as a VPN server without reinstalling. (Of course, if you want to start from scratch, you can always right-click the server and use the Disable Routing And Remote Access command to wipe out the server's configuration.)

Recall that the General tab of the server Properties dialog box contains controls that you use to specify whether your RRAS server is a router, a remote access server, or both. The first step in converting your existing RRAS server to handle VPN traffic is to make sure the Remote Access Server checkbox is marked on this tab. Making this change requires you to stop and restart the RRAS service, but that's okay because the snap-in will do it for you. Then, you must configure VPN ports, as shown in the following sections.

Configuring a VPN

VPN configuration is extremely simple, at least for PPTP. Either a server can accept VPN calls or it can't. If it can, it will have a certain number of VPN ports, all of which are configured identically. There's very little that you *have* to change or tweak to get a VPN server set up, but there are a few things you can adjust as you like.

Configuring VPN Ports

The biggest opportunity to configure your VPN server is to adjust the number and kind of VPN ports available for clients to use. Windows Server 2003 theoretically supports 16,384 PPTP connections and 30,000 L2TP connections, though this is most likely more than your hardware can handle. In addition, you can enable or disable either PPTP or L2TP, depending on what you want your remote users to have access to. You accomplish this through the Ports Properties dialog box (see Figure 7.9).

FIGURE 7.9 The Ports Properties dialog box

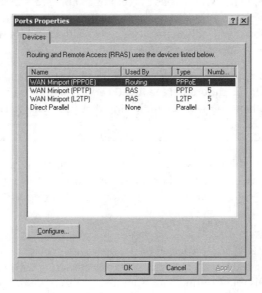

For conventional remote access servers, this dialog box shows you a long list of hardware ports, but for servers that support VPN connections, there are two additional selections: two WAN Miniport devices, one for PPTP and one for L2TP. These aren't really devices; they're actually virtual ports maintained by RRAS for accepting VPN connections. You configure these ports by clicking the Configure button, which displays the Configure Device dialog box (see Figure 7.10).

FIGURE 7.10   The Configure Device dialog box

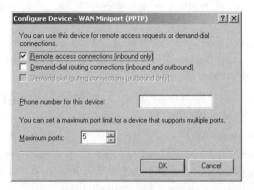

There are three controls pertinent to a VPN configuration:

- The Remote Access Connections (Inbound Only) checkbox must be activated in order to accept VPN connections with this port type. To disable a VPN type (for instance, if you want to turn off L2TP), uncheck this box in the corresponding device's Configure Device dialog box.

- The Demand-Dial Routing Connections (Inbound And Outbound) checkbox controls whether or not this VPN type can be used for demand-dial connections. By default, this box is checked; you'll need to uncheck if you don't want to use VPN connections to link your network with other networks.

- The Maximum Ports control lets you set the number of inbound connections that this port type will support. By default, you get 5 PPTP and 5 L2TP ports when you install RRAS; you can use from 0 to 1000 ports of each type by adjusting the number here.

You can also use the Phone Number For This Device field to enter the IP address of the public interface to which VPN clients connect. You might want to do this if your remote access policies accept or reject connections based on the number called by the client. Because you can assign multiple IP addresses to a single adapter, you can control VPN traffic by throttling which clients can connect to which addresses through a policy.

Remote access policies are discussed in more detail in Chapter 8.

Troubleshooting VPNs

The two primary VPN problems are the inability to establish a connection at all and the inability to reach some needed resource once connected. There's a lot of common ground between the process of troubleshooting a VPN connection and troubleshooting an ordinary remote access connection.

There are some extremely simple—but sometimes overlooked—things to check when your VPN clients can't connect. First, make sure your client can make the underlying connection to its ISP, and then check the following things:

- Is RRAS installed and configured on the server?
  - Is the server configured to allow remote access? Check the General tab of the server Properties dialog box.
  - Is the server configured to allow VPN traffic? Check the Ports Properties dialog box to make sure that the appropriate VPN protocol is enabled and that the number of ports for that protocol is greater than zero.
  - Are there any available VPN ports? If you have only 10 L2TP ports allocated, the 11th caller will be not be able to connect.
- Do the client and server match?
  - Is the VPN protocol used by the client enabled on the server? Windows 2000 and newer clients will try L2TP first and switch to PPTP as a second choice. However, clients on other OSes (including Windows NT) can normally expect either L2TP or PPTP.
  - Are the network protocols for all clients enabled on the server? This is particularly good to check if you have some IPX-using clients.
- Are the client and server authenticated correctly?
  - Are the username and password correct?
  - Does the user account in question have remote access permissions, either directly on the account or through a policy?
  - Do the authentication settings in the server's policies (if any) match the supported set of authentication protocols?

If you check all the simple stuff and find nothing wrong, it's time to move on to some slightly more sophisticated problems. These tend to affect more than one user, as opposed to the simple (and generally user-specific) issues just outlined. The problems include the following:

Policy problems   If you're using a native mode Windows Server 2003 domain and you're using policies, those policies may have some subtle problems that show up under some circumstances:

- Are there any policies whose Allow or Deny settings conflict with each other? Remember that all conditions of all policies must match to gain user access; if any condition of any policy fails, or if there are any policies that deny access, the connection will be denied.
- Does the user match all of the necessary conditions that are in place, such as time and date?

Network problems   If you're using static IP addressing, are there any addresses left in the pool? If the VPN server can't assign an address, it won't accept the connection.

If you're using IPX, be sure that the client and server settings that control whether or not the client can ask for its own node number match; if the server disallows it, the client won't be able to connect unless it already has an assigned number.

Domain problems   Windows Server 2003 RRAS servers can coexist with Windows NT RRAS servers, and both of them can interoperate with RADIUS servers from Microsoft and other vendors. Sometimes, though, this interoperation doesn't work exactly as you'd expect. Some questions to ask include:

- Is the RRAS server's domain membership correct? Your RRAS servers don't have to be domain members unless you want to use native mode features such as remote access policies.

- If you're in a domain, are the server's group memberships correct? The server account must be a member of the RAS group and Internet Authentication Servers security group.

Managing Your Remote Access Server

RRAS server management is generally pretty easy because, in most cases, there's not much to manage. You set up the server and it answers calls. You'll probably find it necessary to monitor the server's ongoing activity, and you may find it necessary to log activity for accounting or security purposes.

You can monitor your server's activity in a number of ways, including having the server keep local copies of its logs or having it send logging data to a remote RADIUS server. In addition, you can always monitor the current status of any of the ports on your system. Microsoft's documentation distinguishes between event logging, which records significant things that happen like startup and shutdown of the RRAS service, and authentication and accounting logging, which tracks things like when a user logged on and logged off. The settings for both types of logging are intermingled in the RRAS snap-in.

In the following sections, you will learn about the various methods at your disposal for monitoring a VPN server.

Monitoring Overall Activity

The Server Status node in the RRAS snap-in shows you a summary of all the RRAS servers known to the system. Depending on whether or not you use the features discussed in Chapter 9, "Managing IP Routing," to manage multiple RRAS servers from one console, you may only see the local server's information here. When you select the Server Status item, the right-hand pane of the MMC will list each known RRAS server. Each entry in the list tells you whether the server is up or not, what kind of server it is, how many ports it has, how many ports are currently in use, and how long the server's been up. You can right-click any Windows Server 2003 RRAS server in this view to start, stop, restart, pause, or resume its RRAS service; disable RRAS on the server; or remove the server's advertisement from Active Directory (provided, of course, that you're using AD).

Controlling Remote Access Logging

A standard RRAS installation will always log some data locally, but that's pretty useless unless you know what gets logged and where it goes. Each RRAS server on your network has its own set of logs, which you manage through the Remote Access Logging folder. Within that folder, you'll normally see a single item labeled Local File, which is the log file stored on that particular server.

If you don't have Windows accounting or Windows authentication turned on, you won't have a local log file. Depending on whether or not you're using RADIUS accounting and logging, you may see additional entries. However, the following sections will stick with local file logging.

Setting Server Logging Properties

The first place from which you can control server logging is at the server level. You use the Logging tab (see Figure 7.11) to control what level of detail you want in the server's event log. It should be noted that these controls regulate *all* logging by RRAS, not just remote access log entries. You have four choices for the level of logged detail:

- The Log Errors Only radio button instructs the server to log errors and nothing else. This gives you adequate indication of problems *after* they happen, but it doesn't point out potential problems noted by warning messages.

- The Log Errors And Warnings radio button is the default choice. This forces the server to log error and warning messages to the event log, giving you a nice balance between information content and log volume.

- The Log All Events radio button causes the RRAS service to log mass quantities of messages, covering literally everything the server does. While this voluminous output is useful for troubleshooting (or even for getting a better understanding of how remote access works), it's overkill for everyday use.

- The Do Not Log Any Events radio button turns off all event logging for RRAS.

 Don't use the Do Not Log Any Events option. It will disallow you from reviewing the service's logs in case of a problem.

FIGURE 7.11   The Logging tab of the server Properties dialog box

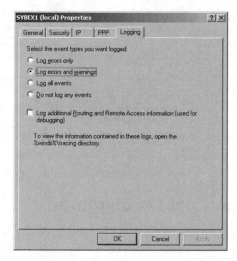

The Log Additional Routing And Remote Access Information checkbox allows you to turn on logging of all PPP negotiations and connections. This can provide valuable information when you're trying to figure out what's wrong, but it adds a lot of unnecessary bulk to your log files. Don't turn it on unless you're trying to pin down a problem.

Setting Log File Properties

You can select an individual log file in the snap-in to control what that log file contains. More precisely, you can control what events should be logged in that file from the time of the change forward. You make these changes by selecting the log file and selecting Action ➤ Properties (or selecting Properties from the pop-up menu) to open the log file Properties dialog box. This dialog box has two tabs: The Settings tab (see Figure 7.12) controls what gets logged in the file, and the Local File tab (see Figure 7.13) controls the format of the file itself.

FIGURE 7.12   The Settings tab of the Local File Properties dialog box

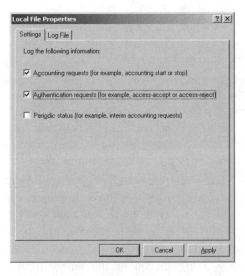

FIGURE 7.13   The Log File tab of the Local File Properties dialog box

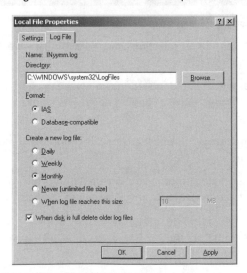

The Settings tab has three checkboxes that control what gets logged:

- Accounting Requests governs whether events related to the accounting service itself will be logged (as well as accounting data). This should always be checked.

- Authentication Requests adjusts whether successful and failed logon requests are logged or not. This too should always be checked.

- Periodic Status controls whether or not interim accounting packets are permanently stored on disk. This should normally be unchecked.

The Log File tab controls how the log file is written to disk. You use this tab to designate three things:

- The Directory field shows where the log file's stored. By default, each server logs its data in *systemroot*\system32\LogFiles\iasLog.log. By using the Log File Directory field, you can change this location to wherever you want.

- The Format controls determine the format of the log file. By default, RRAS will use the older Internet Authentication Service (IAS) format, which was originally used by the IAS component included as part of the Windows NT Option Pack. You can instead choose to use the database-compatible file format, which is available only in Windows 2000 and Server 2003. This format makes it easy for you to take log data and store it in a database, enabling more sophisticated postprocessing for things like billing and chargebacks.

- The Create A New Log File controls determine how often new log files are created. For example, some administrators prefer to get a new log file each week or each month, whereas others are content to let the log file grow without end. You can choose to have RRAS start new log files each day, each week, each month, never, or when the log file reaches a certain size.

Having correct accounting and authorization data is critical to maintaining a good level of security. Exercise 7.5 walks you through configuring remote access logging.

EXERCISE 7.5

Changing Remote Access Logging Settings

1. Open the RRAS MMC snap-in by selecting Start ➤ Administrative Tools ➤ Routing And Remote Access.

2. Navigate to the server whose logging settings you want to change. Expand the target server and select the Remote Access Logging node. The right-hand MMC pane lists the log files on that server.

3. Locate the log file named Local File and then open its Properties dialog box by right-clicking it and choosing Properties.

4. The Local File Properties dialog box appears. On the Settings tab, make sure the Accounting Requests and Authentication Requests checkboxes are marked.

5. Switch to the Log File tab. Select an appropriate time period for log rollover by choosing one of the radio buttons in the Create A New Log File control group.

6. Click the OK button.

Reviewing the Remote Access Event Log

You use the Log File tab to find out exactly where the log file lives, but what do you do with the log information then? Windows Server 2003 online help has an exhaustive list of all the fields logged for each connection attempt and accounting record. You don't need to have all those fields memorized, and you don't have to know how to make sense of the log entries. The Support Tools on the Windows Server 2003 CD includes a handy utility called *iasparse* that will digest an RRAS log in IAS or database format and then produce a readable summary.

Why bother reviewing the logs? One nice feature is that each entry in the authentication log indicates which remote access policy applied (either to accept or reject the connection). This is a good way to identify problems with policies because sometimes multiple policies can combine to have an effect you didn't expect. Furthermore, if it's desirable in your environment, you can use the logged data to generate accounting reports to tell you things like the average utilization of your dial-in ports, the top 10 users of dial-in connect time, or how much online time accounts a certain Windows group used. Unfortunately, though, you're on your own when it comes to building tools to generate reports that will tell you whatever it is you want to know—there aren't any reporting tools included with Windows Server 2003.

Monitoring Ports and Port Activity

You can monitor port status and activity from the RRAS snap-in. The Ports folder under the server contains one entry for each defined port. When you select the Ports folder, you'll see a list of the ports and their current status. The list indicates whether each port is a dial-in or VPN port and whether or not it's active, so you can get a quick summary of your server's workload at any time.

Double-clicking an individual port displays the Port Status dialog box (see Figure 7.14). This dialog box shows things like a port's line speed, the amount of transmitted and received data, and the network addresses for each protocol being carried on the port. This is a useful tool for verifying whether a port is in active use or not, and it gives you a count of the number of transmission and reception errors on the port.

FIGURE 7.14 The Port Status dialog box

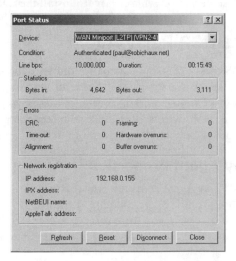

Integrating RRAS with DHCP

As you briefly learned back in Chapter 5, "Managing the Dynamic Host Configuration Protocol," each network that has a DHCP client on it must have either a DHCP server or a DHCP relay agent. Otherwise, the client has no way to reach a DHCP server and get a lease.

What does this mean for your remote access deployment? It depends on your network configuration, as described by the following:

- On a small or simple network, you may choose to use static IP addressing and assign each dial-in client a fixed IP address. In this case, you don't have to fool with DHCP at all.

- If your RRAS server is also a DHCP server, you're OK because dial-in clients will get an IP address from that server's address pool.

- If your RRAS server is on a different IP network from your DHCP servers, or if you want to assign client addresses out of an address range that's not part of any DHCP scope, you need a relay agent.

The RRAS snap-in includes a DHCP relay agent that you install as an additional routing protocol. Once you install and configure it, it can tie your remote access clients to whatever DHCP infrastructure you want to use.

Installing the DHCP Relay Agent

There are a couple of things you should know before installing a DHCP relay agent. First, you can't install the relay agent on a computer that's already acting as a DHCP server. Second, you can't install it on a system running Network Address Translation (NAT) with the addressing component installed.

As long as you meet these requirements, the Server 2003 implementation of RRAS will install the DHCP relay agent automatically when you first enable remote access. You can also install the DHCP relay agent manually if necessary, such as if you recently disabled the DHCP server component on your RRAS server. (You will see how to install the relay agent in Exercise 7.6.)

Configuring the DHCP Relay Agent

As is typical of other RRAS components, you actually configure the DHCP relay agent in two places: from the DHCP Relay Agent Properties dialog box and again on each individual interface. The configuration settings required for each of these two places are different. In the following sections, you will see how to set a DHCP relay agent's properties, how to assign the relay agent to specific interfaces, and how to set an interface's properties.

Setting DHCP Relay Agent Properties

When you select the DHCP Relay Agent item under the IP Routing node in the RRAS snap-in and open its Properties dialog box, you'll see the contents of Figure 7.15. The only thing you can do here is specify to which DHCP servers you want *this particular* DHCP relay agent to forward requests. The only restriction is that the RRAS server that's running the DHCP relay agent must be able to route IP packets to the destination network. The servers you specify here apply to all network interfaces to which you attach the relay agent; there's no way to configure independent forwarding addresses for individual network interfaces.

FIGURE 7.15   The DHCP Relay Agent Properties dialog box

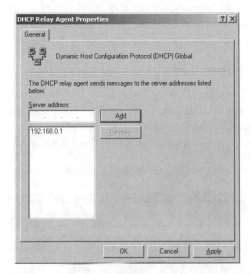

In Exercise 7.6, you will learn how to install the DHCP relay agent on an RRAS server as well as configure it. Note that this will only work if the DHCP relay agent was not previously installed and the local computer isn't running DHCP or NAT.

EXERCISE 7.6

Installing and Configuring the DHCP Relay Agent on an RRAS Server

1.   Open the Routing and Remote Access snap-in by selecting Start ➢ Administrative Tools ➢ Routing And Remote Access.

2.   Locate the server on which you want to install the DHCP relay agent.

3.   Expand the server's configuration until you see the General node. To do this, select the server, then IP Routing, then General.

4.   Right-click the General node and choose the New Routing Protocol command. The New Routing Protocol dialog box appears.

5.   Select DHCP Relay Agent from the list of routing protocols and then click the OK button.

6.   The IP Routing node will now have a child node named DHCP Relay Agent. Select it and choose Properties to open its Properties dialog box.

7.   In the DHCP Relay Agent Properties dialog box, add the IP addresses of the DHCP servers you want DHCP requests forwarded to and then click the OK button.

Assigning the Relay Agent to Specific Interfaces

Once you've configured the list of servers to which you want DHCP requests forwarded, you still have to attach the relay agent to particular network interfaces. To create a relay agent interface, right-click the DHCP Relay Agent item and select New Interface. When the New Interface For DHCP Relay Agent dialog box appears, select the network interface to which you want the relay agent bound. Once you do, the interface-specific properties dialog box (discussed in the following section) appears.

Setting Interface Properties

Each relay-agent-enabled interface has its own set of properties, which are exposed through the interface-specific Properties dialog box (see Figure 7.16). The topmost control, the Relay DHCP Packets checkbox, lets you control whether DHCP relaying is active on this interface or not—you can turn it on or off without restarting the RRAS service.

FIGURE 7.16   The interface-specific Properties dialog box

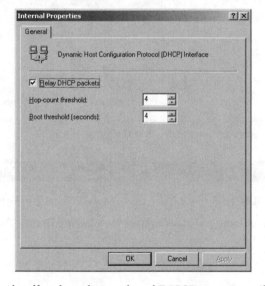

The other two controls affect how long relayed DHCP requests will bounce around your network. The Hop-Count Threshold field sets the number of intervening routers between the client and the DHCP server that the DHCP traffic can traverse, and the Boot Threshold (Seconds) field controls how long the relay agent waits before forwarding any DHCP messages it hears. If you want to give a local DHCP server first crack at incoming requests, adjust the boot threshold up so that the local server has a chance to respond before the message is forwarded.

In Exercise 7.7, you'll add a new DHCP relay agent interface for your LAN connection and then specify configuration parameters for it. In practice, you'd need to add the DHCP relay agent to whichever interface remote clients use, but because we can't assume anything about the configuration of your lab machine, this lab is simplified somewhat.

EXERCISE 7.7

Configuring the DHCP Relay Agent on a Network Interface

1.   Verify that the DHCP relay agent is installed. If not, refer to Exercise 7.6.

2.   Right-click the DHCP Relay Agent item and choose New Interface.

3.   The New Interface For DHCP Relay Agent dialog box appears, listing each of the interfaces to which you could attach the relay agent. Select Local Area Connection and click the OK button.

4.   The interface-specific Properties dialog box appears. If you have a DHCP server on your local network, increase the boot threshold to 5 seconds; if you don't, decrease it to 0.

5.   Click the OK button. Note that the list of DHCP relay agent interfaces has been updated to reflect the new interface.

Configuring a RAS or VPN Client

Dial-up RAS clients and VPN clients are very similar. Almost all of the options that are available when you set up a RAS client are the same as when you set up a VPN client. The main difference is that VPN clients specify the server's IP address, and RAS clients specify the server's phone number. Also, VPN clients require an underlying connection to the Internet. Client configuration is not a focus of the exam, so in this chapter you will only see how to configure a VPN client. Just be sure to remember that the RAS client configuration is extremely similar.

Keep in mind that VPN connections are almost always created on client workstations, so this section describes the settings in Windows XP Professional.

When you establish a virtual private network connection, you're actually building an encrypted tunnel between you and some other machine. The tunneled data is carried over an insecure network, like the Internet. VPN connections are easy to set up and use, as you'll see a little later on in Exercise 7.8.

Once you've created a connection, you can change its properties at any time by opening its Properties dialog box. The Dial-Up Connection Properties dialog box has a total of five tabs you can use to adjust all the pertinent settings for each individual connection.

Don't confuse these settings with the ones present in the Local Area Connection Properties dialog box; they're entirely different.

The General Tab

The General tab of the Dial-Up Connection Properties dialog box is where you specify the IP address of the VPN server or the modem and phone number to use with this particular connection.

In this tab, as with the other tabs in this dialog box, you may recognize the filled-in fields when you use the Network Connection Wizard.

The General tab has a field where you enter the VPN server address or hostname. In addition, the First Connect group lets you specify which dial-up connection, if any, you want brought up before the VPN connection is established.

With the General tab, you can also do the following:

- Change the modem this connection uses, or settings for the modem you already have, with the Configure button. Note that you can also use the Phone And Modem Options control panel to adjust a broader range of modem settings.

- Enter the VPN server address or hostname or enter the phone number to dial.

- For RAS connections, change whether or not dialing rules (for example, "I am now in area code 770") are used when DUN decides how to dial the number for this connection. When the Use Dialing Rules checkbox is checked, the Rules button becomes active, allowing you to define new locations and edit the dialing rules attached to each.

- For VPN connections, specify whether or not to automatically dial another connection first and then specify the connection to dial.

- Change whether or not the connection shows a status/progress icon in the system tray whenever the connection is active. By default, dial-up connections have the Show Icon In Taskbar When Connected checkbox checked.

The Options Tab

The Options tab holds settings that control how DUN dials and redials the connection. The controls in this dialog box are segregated into two groups: The Dialing Options group holds controls that govern DUN's interface behavior while dialing, and the Redialing Options group controls whether or not and how DUN will redial if it doesn't immediately connect.

Dialing Options

There are four separate dialing options available in the Dialing Options group:

- The Display Progress While Connecting checkbox (checked by default) instructs DUN to keep you updated on its progress as it attempts to raise the connection.

- The Prompt For Name And Password, Certificate, Etc. checkbox is also checked by default. When it's on, Windows 2000 will prompt you for any credentials it needs to authenticate your connection to the remote server. This may be a username, a password, a public-key certificate, or some combination of the three, depending on what the remote end requires.

- The Include Windows Logon Domain checkbox is unchecked by default. It forces DUN to include the domain name of the domain you're logged on to as part of the authentication credential. Leave this unchecked unless you're dialing into a Windows NT/2000 network that has a trust relationship with your logon domain.

- For RAS connections, the Prompt For Phone Number checkbox (normally checked) tells DUN to display the phone number in the connection dialog box. This gives you a chance to edit it before dialing; you may want to uncheck it if you (or your users) are prone to making accidental changes.

Redialing Options

The settings in the Redialing Options group control how DUN will attempt to redial the specified number if the remote end is busy or doesn't answer with a recognizable carrier tone. These settings include the following:

- The Redial Attempts field controls how many attempts DUN will make to raise the other end before giving up. The default value is 3, but you can set any value from 0 (meaning that DUN won't attempt to redial) to 999,999,999.

- The Time Between Redial Attempts pull-down menu controls how long DUN will wait after each failed call before it tries again. Values in the pull-down menu range from 1 second all the way to 10 minutes, with various increments in between.

- The Idle Time Before Hanging Up pull-down menu lets you specify an inactivity timer. If your connection is idle for longer than the specified period, your client will terminate the call. Note that the remote end may drop the call sooner than your client, depending on how it's configured. By default, this pull-down menu is set to Never, meaning that your client will never drop a call. If you want an inactivity timer, you can pick values ranging from 1 minute to 24 hours.

- The Redial If Line Is Dropped checkbox automatically redials the number if you are disconnected.

The Security Tab

How useful you find the Security tab will depend on whom you're calling. The default settings it provides will work fine with most Internet Service Providers and corporate dial-up facilities, but Windows XP has a broad range of security settings you can change if you need to. The Security Options group contains controls that directly affect the security of your connection. The Advanced Security Settings tab controls settings such as encryption and authentication protocols.

Security Options

The security options themselves are pretty straightforward. The security settings in effect for this connection are governed by your choice between the Typical (Recommended Settings) and Advanced (Custom Settings) radio buttons. Normally, it's best to stick with the Typical (Recommended Settings) option and use its subordinate controls to pick a canned setting that matches your needs. These subordinate controls include the following:

- The Validate My Identity As Follows pull-down menu lets you choose among unsecured passwords (the default, and the only type of authentication that most networks support), secured passwords, and smart card authentication (useful only when calling another Windows 2000 or Server 2003 network).

- If you choose to require a secured password, the Automatically Use My Windows Logon Name And Password checkbox instructs DUN to offer to the remote end the logon credentials you used to log on to the computer or domain. This is only useful if you're dialing into a network that has access to your domain authentication information.

- If you require a secured password or smart card authentication, the Require Data Encryption checkbox allows you to have either an encrypted connection or none at all. If you check this box, your client and the remote server will attempt to negotiate a common encryption method. If they can't (perhaps because the remote end doesn't offer encryption), your client will hang up.

Advanced Security Settings

If you select the Advanced (Custom Settings) radio button and then click the Settings button, you'll see the Advanced Security Settings dialog box. Its controls are more complex than the ones on the Security tab.

The first field is the Data Encryption pull-down menu. Windows XP offers you the opportunity to encrypt both sides of network connections using IPSec. This capability extends to dial-up connections, too. The pull-down menu gives you the following four choices:

- No Encryption Allowed means that the server will drop your call if it requires encryption because you can't provide it.

- Optional Encryption tells the client to request encryption but to continue the call if it's not available.

- Require Encryption tells the client to request encryption and to refuse to communicate with servers that don't support it.

- Maximum Strength Encryption tells the client to only communicate with servers that offer the same strength encryption it does. For example, with this setting in force, a North American Windows Server 2003 machine running 3DES won't communicate with a French Windows XP machine because the French machine uses the weaker exportable encryption routines.

The Logon Security group controls which authentication protocols this client can use. The default setting, Use Extensible Authentication Protocol (EAP), is what you use if you want to use standard Windows authentication (using the MD5-Challenge method) or certificate-based authentication (using the Smart Card Or Other Certificate choice in the pull-down).

The Allow These Protocols radio button is followed by a long list of authentication protocols. While the specifics of how they work are different, the basic idea behind each of these protocols is the same: Provide a secure way for a client to prove its identity to a server. By selecting the appropriate checkboxes, you can make your client use the same protocols as the remote end. These authentication protocols include the following: PAP, SPAP, CHAP, and MS-CHAP version 1 and version 2.

It is generally recommended that you avoid using PAP and SPAP unless you must talk to some older device that doesn't use CHAP or MS-CHAP. If possible, allow only CHAP and MS-CHAP version 2 on your clients and servers. By default, when you turn on the Allow These Protocols radio button, CHAP, MS-CHAP, and MS-CHAP version 2 will be enabled. This gives you the best mix of flexibility and security.

The Networking Tab

You use the Networking tab to control which protocols your client will attempt to use when communicating with other servers. You have to tell DUN what kind of server it's calling in the first place, using the Type Of Dial-Up Server I Am Calling field. Your choices are PPP or SLIP (the Serial Line Internet Protocol, now relegated to older Unix machines and dial-up hardware). By default, PPP will be selected, and it's unlikely that you'll need to change it. Alternately, the VPN Networking tab uses the top drop-down menu to let you indicate what kind of VPN call you're making. Automatic is the default setting, but you can select a PPTP or L2TP connection if you prefer.

The list box in the middle of the tab shows the network protocols installed on the client. Protocols marked with a check are available for use with this connection. Normally, you'll see TCP/IP and Client For Microsoft Networks marked, which indicates that those two protocols can be used over the connection. The Install, Uninstall, and Properties buttons work just as they do in the Local Area Connection Properties dialog—by using them you can control which protocols are on your machine and what their settings are.

It's worth mentioning that selecting Internet Protocol (TCP/IP) in the protocols list and opening its properties dialog box gives you access to a set of properties that are completely distinct from any TCP/IP settings that may apply to your LAN interfaces. Normally, the dial-up TCP/IP settings are configured to obtain an IP address and DNS information from the remote server, although if you need to you can override these settings.

The Sharing Tab

The Sharing tab contains only two controls: Enable Internet Connection Sharing For This Connection and Enable On-Demand Dialing. This tab is only available with a RAS client. On-Demand Dialing provides a way to automatically dial the connection whenever a computer on the local network attempts to access information on the remote network.

In Exercise 7.8, you will learn how to create a VPN connection on a Windows XP client.

EXERCISE 7.8

Configuring Windows XP Professional as a VPN Client

1. Choose Start, right-click My Network Places, and select Properties.

2. Click the Create A New Connection icon. The New Connection Wizard appears. Click the Next button.

3. Choose the Connect To The Network At My Workplace button and click Next.

4. Choose the VPN Connection radio button and click Next.

5. Enter a descriptive name for the connection and click Next.

6. Choose the Do Not Dial The Initial Connection radio button and click Next.

7. Enter the IP address of the VPN server. Click Next when you're done.

8. The wizard's Summary page appears. Click Finish.

9. The Connect dialog box appears. Make sure that you are connected to the Internet, enter a username and password, and click the Dial button to connect.

Real World Scenario

Servers as Remote Access Clients

We mentioned earlier that remote access clients are usually workstations dialing in to the network from home or on the road. This represents the majority of remote access activity in the world, but you might not realize that servers often communicate with each other across remote access connections as well. Most small businesses (and some medium-sized businesses) with multiple locations cannot afford dedicated leased lines between sites, so they rely on daily, hourly, or even persistent dial-up or VPN connections to replicate their Active Directory databases or to share data between locations. In situations such as this, the server at one location represents the remote access client, and the server at the other end represents the remote access server, even though technically they might be peers in Active Directory.

Server-to-server VPN connections are more and more common as high-speed Internet access becomes ubiquitous. Because most high-speed Internet connections are always on, you don't even need to establish the initial connection to the Internet before "dialing in" to the VPN server. In fact, traditional WAN solutions are rapidly being replaced by persistent VPN connections that are always on and always connected. In this situation, the VPN connection is a two-way initiated connection. The connection is initiated from either one of the servers. Two-way initiated connections require the creation of demand-dial interfaces, remote access policies, IP address pools, and packet filters on the routers on both sides of the connection. In cases such as this, the distinction between the "client" and the "server" is not so clear, so always remember to use those terms with caution.

Summary

In this chapter, you learned about the following topics:

- How to install and configure the Routing and Remote Access Services to handle dial-in connections
- How to configure appropriate encryption and security settings so that communication between the client and server is encrypted and authenticated
- How to install RRAS to provide VPN service using the PPTP and L2TP protocols
- How to configure VPN services on the server and client
- How to troubleshoot common VPN problems

Exam Essentials

Understand how multilink works.   The multilink extensions to the Point-to-Point Protocol (PPP) provide a way to combine several independent PPP connections so that they act as a single connection. Windows Server 2003's RRAS supports multilink PPP for inbound and outbound calls.

Know how to install and configure RAS at the server level.   The RAS installation process is driven by the Routing And Remote Access Server Setup Wizard, which you use to set up a dial-up server. You can specify whether the server acts as a remote access server, specify what authentication providers and settings you want the server to use, control the specific settings applied to each protocol you have installed, specify which PPP protocols (including multilink) the clients on this server are allowed to use, and control what level of log detail is kept for incoming connections.

Know the different components you can use to manage the remote access server.   The Server Status node in the RRAS snap-in shows you a summary of all the RRAS servers known to the system. Each RRAS server on your network has its own set of logs, which you manage through the Remote Access Logging folder. You can monitor port status and activity from the RRAS snap-in, too. The Ports folder under the server contains one entry for each defined port; when you select the Ports folder, you'll see a list of the ports and their current status.

Know how to integrate RRAS with DHCP using the DHCP relay agent.   If there's no DHCP server available on the network where the client is located, you can use a DHCP relay agent to forward DHCP messages from the client to the DHCP server's network. The relay agent acts like a radio repeater, listening for DHCP client requests and retransmitting them on the server's network.

Know how to install and configure a VPN server.   If you don't have RRAS installed, you'll need to install it, activate it, and configure it as a VPN server. If you're already using RRAS for IP routing or remote access, you can enable it as a VPN server without reinstalling. VPN configuration is extremely simple, at least for PPTP. Either a server can accept VPN calls or it can't. If it can, it will have a certain number of VPN ports, all of which are configured identically.

Know how to troubleshoot a VPN.   Verify that the RRAS server is installed and configured on the server, that the client and server protocols match, and that authentication is working properly. Then check for policy problems, network problems, and domain problems.

Know how to configure an RRAS client.   Most client connections are made on Windows 2000 Professional or XP Professional workstations. Dial-in and VPN connections are configured very similarly, but when creating a VPN connection, you must substitute an IP address for a phone number.

Key Terms

Before you take the exam, be certain you are familiar with the following terms:

Challenge Handshake Authentication Protocol (CHAP)

machine certificates

encapsulation

Point-to-Point Protocol (PPP)

Extensible Authentication Protocol (EAP)

Point-to-Point Tunneling Protocol (PPTP)

iasparse

tunnel

IP datagram

virtual private networks (VPNs)

Layer 2 Tunneling Protocol (L2TP)

Review Questions

1. You have a local DHCP server for your dial-in clients, but you also want to use the DHCP relay agent to forward requests to a remote DHCP server if the local server doesn't answer a request. To do this, you must do which of the following?

    A. Add a static route to the remote server.

    B. Adjust the boot threshold on the DHCP relay agent interface for the remote network so that the local server has enough time to respond.

    C. Adjust the DHCP Forwarding Time parameter in the Registry.

    D. Adjust the forwarding time in the DHCP Relay Agent Global Properties dialog box.

2. Your sales force consists of 1000 people who use laptops that are standardized on Windows 98 and Windows NT Workstation. In a migration that's well under way, you have already upgraded all your servers and services to Windows Server 2003 and one-half of your internal Windows NT and Windows 98 machines to Windows 2000 and XP Professional. As soon as you finish the internal migration, you'll begin to bring all the remote users up to Windows 2000 and XP Professional. Recently, you were told that your CEO is concerned with network security, and you were ordered to make sure that all of your external network connections are secure and that any data paths outside your network are encrypted. Which of the following steps can you take to meet these new requirements? (Choose all that apply.)

    A. Configure IPSec for all of your network communications.

    B. Upgrade all of your remote users immediately to Windows 2000 and XP Professional.

    C. Configure your RRAS servers to use MS-CHAP.

    D. Configure your RRAS servers to accept only PPTP and MPPE connections.

    E. Disable remote connections until you complete the Windows Server 2003 migration.

3. Your company has offices in five locations around the country. Most of the users' activity is local to their own network. Occasionally, some of the users in one location need to send confidential information to one of the other four locations or to retrieve information from one of them. The communication between the remote locations is sporadic and relatively infrequent, so you have configured RRAS to use demand-dial lines to set up the connections. Management's only requirement is that any communication between the office locations be appropriately secured. Which of the following steps should you take to ensure compliance with this requirement? (Choose all that apply.)

    A. Configure CHAP on all the RRAS servers.

    B. Configure PAP on all the RRAS servers.

    C. Configure MPPE on all the RRAS servers.

    D. Configure L2TP on all the RRAS servers.

    E. Configure MS-CHAP on all the RRAS servers.

4. Your small financial consulting company has a stand-alone Windows 2000 server that provides a central location for your home-based consultants to upload and download spreadsheet files using Microsoft Windows 98. A few of the consultants use Windows 2000 Professional workstations. You want to set up VPN connections between the consultants and the RRAS server. The RRAS server is connected to a small peer-to-peer network of five Windows 2000 Professional workstations that use the network for storing files, including the files that the consultants are uploading and downloading. What authentication protocol should you use for the VPN?

    A. CHAP

    B. MS-CHAP

    C. EAP-TLS

    D. PAP

5. You recently migrated your company's Windows NT network over to Windows Server 2003. This migration includes 300 Windows XP Professional workstations and 8 Windows Server 2003 servers. Your company has just acquired another company with offices just down the street. They have a Windows NT network that needs to be migrated to Windows Server 2003 as well, and you have already begun to move the servers over to the new operating system and associated services. Because you have a tight cap on expenses for network additions, you presently can't afford leased lines between the buildings. Until you can get support for them, you are going to create a VPN that is both encrypted and authenticated between the two facilities over the Internet connections that already exist. What do you need to implement in order to achieve this goal? (Choose all that apply.)

    A. L2TP

    B. PPTP

    C. IPSec

    D. RADIUS

    E. MS-CHAP

6. You have implemented VPNs to connect the various locations of your organization. These locations include offices in New York, Sacramento, Memphis, and Omaha, with a significant LAN in each one. The RRAS server is set up such that the users aren't aware of the intricacies of the connections. You are beginning to have problems with the connections between the offices, and the resulting support calls are growing dramatically. What configurations could you use to troubleshoot the communication problems?

    A. L2TP using MPPE

    B. L2TP unencrypted

    C. L2TP using IPSec in transport mode

    D. L2TP using IPSec in tunnel mode

7. Your company's 150 sales reps are finally going to receive laptops so that they can communicate with the corporate office whenever they need information stored on the corporate network. The corporate network is fully upgraded to Windows Server 2003, including the default configuration of the RRAS server for the remote connectivity over VPNs. You have installed Windows XP Professional with the default configuration on all the laptops and have added the sales reps to a special group in Active Directory. After testing the laptops, everything appears to work fine. You ship them out, and as they reach the sales reps, you monitor their initial connections. During the next few days, you begin receiving support calls from people complaining that they cannot connect to the network. What is the most likely cause of the problem?

   A. The Windows XP clients are not configured to support a VPN.

   B. The default RRAS configuration does not support VPNs.

   C. The default RRAS configuration does not support enough VPN connections.

   D. The default RRAS configuration does not support L2TP.

   E. The Windows XP client default configuration does not support L2TP.

8. You are the network administrator for a company with two offices: one located on the East Coast, and the other on the West Coast. Sales information needs to be sent from the East Coast office to the West Coast office on the regular basis, and some accounting reports and payroll information needs to be sent back to the East Coast. The owner of your company has been reading stories in the press about security problems on the Internet and refuses to allow any company information to travel through the Internet, regardless of how much you talk about securing those transmissions. The communications between the sites occur approximately once a week. What steps would you take to ensure secure authentication and secure transmission while not spending too much money? (Choose all that apply.)

   A. Configure PAP as the authentication method between the servers.

   B. Install RRAS on a server at each location and keep the line open with an ISDN connection that will always be available for the communication.

   C. Install RRAS on a server at each location and configure dial-on-demand to bring up the connection each time the transmission occurs.

   D. Configure CHAP as the authentication method between the servers.

   E. Configure MS-CHAP as the authentication method between the servers.

   F. Configure IPSec as the encryption method between the servers.

   G. Configure MPPE as the encryption method between the servers.

   H. Configure L2TP as the encryption method between the servers.

9. You are using a RRAS server to manage remote access to your small Windows Server 2003 network that serves a single location. RRAS provides access to several remote users and to the people who have machines on the local network but occasionally want to access the network from home or from hotels when on the road. Regardless of the category of user, everyone is authenticated through Active Directory. You haven't spent much time reviewing the use of this remote connectivity since you configured the system, but now there is a concern about unauthorized users as well as intermittent problems that remote users are experiencing when connecting to the network. You've been asked to prepare a report for management describing the extent of these problems in the company. You recall that when you set up the system, you configured the logging to track all connection attempts using local Windows accounting. Where will you find the logging information that you need for preparing your report?

   A. The Performance Monitor log

   B. Active Directory

   C. The *systemroot*\System32\LogFiles folder

   D. The system event log

   E. The RRAS authentication log

10. Your area of responsibility at the All Terrain Vehicle Rentals Company is to build, deploy, and maintain the remote access system for the Windows Server 2003 network. The system consists of 4 RRAS servers, which serve 200 users across the country. The users often travel from location to location, and they access different servers depending upon where they call in. You put together a management station to monitor all of the RRAS servers so you can keep an eye on this critical aspect of your network. What tool do you use to accomplish this?

   A. The Server Monitor of the RRAS snap-in

   B. The Server Status node of the RRAS snap-in

   C. The System Monitor snap-in

   D. The MMC

11. You have an RRAS server for your dial-in clients, but you want to use the DHCP relay agent to forward requests to a remote DHCP server. You don't want the requests to travel through more than three routers to get to the DHCP server. How can you make this happen?

   A. Add a static route to the DHCP server.

   B. Adjust the boot threshold on the DHCP relay agent interface for the network so that the local server has enough time to respond.

   C. Adjust the hop-count threshold on the DHCP relay agent interface for the network.

   D. Adjust the forwarding time in the DHCP Relay Agent Properties dialog box.

12. After your company acquired another company, you were given the responsibility for connecting the two together. One company is in Los Angeles, and the other is in Sacramento. Both systems ran Windows NT, and you migrated them to Windows 2000, XP, and Server 2003 using Active Directory to manage the users and desktops with group policies. You connected the two locations using one of the Windows Server 2003 computers in Los Angeles. You then decided to use DHCP to mange the address space more efficiently. You installed DHCP service on one of the Windows Server 2003 computers in Los Angeles and installed DHCP relay agent on the multihomed Windows Server 2003 computer that is connecting the two locations. Everything looks great in Los Angeles, but when the clients in Sacramento try to obtain a DHCP lease, there is no reply. What is the most likely problem with this configuration?

A. The DHCP relay agent is configured on the wrong NIC and with the wrong address on the multihomed router.

B. The DHCP relay agent needs to be installed on the DHCP router to forward the requests.

C. None of the addresses have been reserved for the Windows NT machine in Sacramento.

D. The clients in Sacramento need to register with the DHCP server for security purposes.

13. You administer a network consisting of 100 client computers and 2 Windows Server 2003 computers. You must configure a VPN solution for your company using L2TP/IPSec. Unfortunately, you don't have a certificate server in-house, and the management would prefer to not pay for a third-party service. What should you do to ensure that VPN communication is secure? Choose the best answer. (Choose all that apply.)

A. Implement a solution with preshared keys.

B. Use CHAP.

C. Use PPTP.

D. Install a certificate server on the other Windows Server 2003 computer.

14. You recently took over the network administration job at a small company. The network consists of 20 client computers and 2 Windows Server 2003 computers. The network does not contain a DNS or WINS server. Clients on the LAN are able to resolve names to IP addresses without any problem using broadcasts, but you find that remote users cannot do the same. What is the best solution to solve the remote users' problem?

A. Install and enable DNS on one of the Windows Server 2003 computers.

B. Install and enable WINS on one of the Windows Server 2003 computers.

C. Configure the Enable Broadcast Name Resolution option on the RRAS server.

D. Instruct the remote users to access internal computers by IP address.

15. Your RRAS server's NIC is configured with multiple IP addresses. You want to restrict VPN access to only one of the IP addresses. Look at the following graphic to determine the steps you should take to enable this configuration.

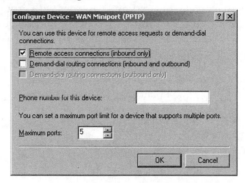

A. Click the Remote Access Connections (Inbound Only) checkbox.

B. Click the Demand-Dial Routing Connections (Inbound And Outbound) checkbox.

C. Enter the appropriate IP address in the Phone Number For This Device field.

D. Increase the number of available ports to match the number of IP addresses assigned to the NIC in the computer.

Answers to Review Questions

1. **B.** The boot threshold for an interface controls how long the relay agent will wait before forwarding DHCP requests it hears on that interface.

2. **C, D.** Because your entire set of client machines are Windows clients, you can use MS-CHAP to provide password encryption when establishing a connection to the network. PPTP and MPPE provide encryption of data between the client machine and the RRAS server. IPSec provides encryption from the client all the way to the resource it's connecting to, which is more than required by the directives. Upgrading the remote clients will not, by itself, provide the encryption required, and the Windows NT clients already support MS-CHAP. Disabling all remote connections until you finish the migration isn't necessary because the pieces are already in place to satisfy the requirements.

3. **C, E.** MS-CHAP provides encrypted and mutual authentication between the respective RRAS locations. MPPE works with MS-CHAP and provides encryption for all the data between the locations. CHAP provides encrypted authentication, but MS-CHAP is needed for MPPE to work. PAP is the lowest level of authentication providing passwords, but in cleartext. L2TP needs to team up with IPSec to provide the data encryption for the secure transfer of information between the locations.

4. **B.** MS-CHAP authentication allows you to create VPN connections with a stand-alone server using PPTP and MPPE. MPPE employs keys that are created via MS-CHAP or EAP-TLS authentication. EAP-TLS is not the correct answer because only domain controllers or member servers support EAP-TLS. Stand-alone servers support only MPPE. Neither PAP nor CHAP is supported with MPPE.

5. **A, C.** L2TP connections can be used to authenticate both sides of the VPN, but PPTP connections only provide encryption. L2TP needs IPSec to provide the encryption for the connection. These two together will provide the secure and authenticated transmission of data across the Internet between the two sites. PPTP can be encrypted using MPPE but doesn't provide authentication between the machines. RADIUS is a service that provides dial-in connectivity. MS-CHAP is an authentication protocol for clients accessing the network.

6. **B.** Both L2TP and IPSec have their own negotiation procedure for making a connection. By removing the IPSec portion of the connection, you can determine whether the problem is resolved. If the problem is alleviated by this action, you can then work on IPSec. If not, you can work on the L2TP portion of the connection. IPSec has two modes: tunnel mode and transport mode. Because L2TP is a tunneling protocol, there is no sense in using IPSec tunneling. IPSec transport mode is used with L2TP and should be set aside as discussed. The L2TP implementation in Windows Server 2003 doesn't support MPPE.

7. **C.** The default configuration for RRAS supports 5 PPTP ports and 5 L2TP ports. There are up to 150 sales reps trying to connect to the server, but only the first 10 will be able to connect. You have to increase the number of ports available, up to 1000, by using the Ports Properties dialog box. The Windows XP Professional clients are by default ready to support VPNs; they will first try L2TP and then switch over to PPTP if ports are unavailable.

8. C, E, G.   RRAS with dial-on-demand will be less expensive than ISDN that is always up. Because the communication is not a continuous or frequent occurrence, it doesn't make sense to have the line always available. MS-CHAP provides encryption and a mutual authentication process. The MPPE provides the encryption of the actual data that travels across the connection. PAP is a cleartext authentication method, and CHAP provides only one-way authentication. L2TP doesn't provide any encryption by itself.

9. C.   When you use Windows accounting, the local Windows account logs are found in the `systemroot\System32\LogFiles` folder. These logs can be stored in either an Open Database Connectivity (ODBC) or in Internet Authentication Service format for later analysis. Performance Monitor Log is the tool that came with Windows NT, and it has been replaced with the system event log. This is used for global service errors such as initialization failures and service starts and stops. There is no RRAS authentication log. You do have RADIUS logging available; when it's used, the log files are stored on the RADIUS servers. This is very useful when you have multiple RRAS servers because you can centralize RRAS authentication requests. Active Directory is not used to log events from the various services in Windows Server 2003.

10. B.   The Server Status node in the RRAS snap-in shows you a summary of all the RRAS servers known to the system. Each server entry displays whether the server is up or not, what kind of server it is, how many ports it has, how many ports are currently in use, and how long the server has been up.

11. C.   The hop count controls the number of intervening routers that the DHCP traffic can traverse between the client and the DHCP server.

12. A.   If the relay agent isn't installed on the subnet that needs the service, the requests cannot be forwarded and the Sacramento subnet won't have DHCP services. You can't install the relay agent on the DHCP server because they share the same UDP ports and will conflict. Client reservations are used to make sure that a machine always receives the same address from the scope; they don't apply in this situation. Clients don't register with DHCP servers for security purposes.

13. A, D.   Windows Server 2003 introduces the ability to use preshared keys with L2TP/IPSec. This can be useful when you don't have access to a certificate server, but you should use certificates if possible because they are more secure.

14. C.   A new feature of Windows Server 2003 allows remote clients to resolve names to IP addresses using broadcasts. Previously, you would have needed a DNS or WINS server in order for remote clients to do this, but this is no longer necessary.

15. C.   Although it may sound strange, you should enter the IP address that you want to apply the VPN to in the Phone Number For This Device field. Then you can configure choice A to accept inbound connections only on the appropriate IP address.

Chapter

8

Managing User Access to Remote Access Services

MICROSOFT EXAM OBJECTIVES COVERED IN THIS CHAPTER:

✓ **Troubleshoot user access to remote access services.**

- Diagnose and resolve issues related to remote access VPNs.
- Diagnose and resolve issues related to establishing a remote access connection.
- Diagnose and resolve user access to resources beyond the remote access server.

Probably the biggest change in remote user access from NT 4 is that Windows 2000 and Server 2003 finally allow you to apply remote access policies. With Windows NT, you could control whether or not individual users could dial in, but there was no way to set that permission for groups of users. The Windows Server 2003 Group Policy Object (GPO) provides a way to apply dial-up permission and capability settings to groups of users.

This chapter explains how remote access policies and profiles are used to grant or deny user access to resources on the network across remote connections. We'll begin by looking at the different authentication protocols included with Windows Server 2003, and you'll see how the operating system handles remote access security. Then we'll dive into the details of configuring user access with profiles and policies. You'll also learn how to configure your server to use Windows Authentication or RADIUS authentication.

Remote Access Security

In the past, remote access was seldom a part of most networks. It was too hard to implement, too hard to manage, and too hard to secure. It's reasonably easy to secure your networks from unauthorized physical access, but doing so for remote access was perceived as being much harder. There are a number of security policies, protocols, and technologies that have been developed to ease this problem. First we'll discuss the user authentication protocols.

User Authentication

One of the first steps in establishing a remote access connection involves allowing the user to present some credentials to the server. You can use any or all of the following five authentication protocols that Windows Server 2003 supports:

Password Authentication Protocol   *Password Authentication Protocol (PAP)* is the simplest—and least secure—authentication protocol. It transmits all authentication information in cleartext with no encryption, which makes it vulnerable to snooping. In addition, it provides no way for a client and server to authenticate each other. Because other protocols offer better security, PAP is falling out of favor, and Microsoft recommends turning it off unless you have clients that cannot use a more secure protocol.

Shiva Password Authentication Protocol   *Shiva Password Authentication Protocol (SPAP)* is a slightly more secure version of PAP that's primarily intended for talking to remote access hardware devices made by the Shiva Corporation. It's included for backward compatibility but isn't widely used.

Challenge Handshake Authentication Protocol *Challenge Handshake Authentication Protocol (CHAP)*—sometimes called MD5-CHAP because it uses the RSA MD5 hash algorithm—has a major security advantage over PAP: It doesn't transmit password information in the clear. Instead, the server sends a challenge encrypted with the DES algorithm to the client, which must decrypt it and return the correct response. This allows the server to verify the user's credentials without sending those credentials across an insecure link.

Although NT's RAS client can use CHAP when dialing into a third-party device, an unmodified NT RAS server will not support CHAP clients. This is because CHAP requires that the server store passwords in cleartext. For security purposes, the Security Account Manager (SAM) database stores NT passwords as a hash, never in cleartext.

Microsoft CHAP *Microsoft CHAP (MS-CHAP)* was created by Microsoft as an extension of the CHAP protocol to allow the use of Windows authentication information. (Among other things, that's what the Log On With Dial-Up Networking checkbox in the Windows Server 2003 Logon dialog box does.) There are actually two separate versions of MS-CHAP. Version 2 is much more secure than version 1, and all Microsoft operating systems upgraded with their respective service packs support version 2. Some other operating systems support MS-CHAP version 1, as well.

Extensible Authentication Protocol *Extensible Authentication Protocol (EAP)* doesn't provide any authentication itself. Instead, it relies on external third-party authentication methods that you can retrofit to your existing servers. Instead of hardwiring any one authentication protocol, a client/server pair that understands EAP can negotiate an authentication method. The computer that asks for authentication is called the authenticator. The authenticator is free to ask for several different pieces of information, making a separate query for each one. This allows the use of almost any authentication method, including secure access tokens like SecurID, one-time password systems like S/Key, or ordinary username/password systems.

Each authentication scheme supported in EAP is called an *EAP type*. Each EAP type, in turn, is implemented as a plug-in module. Windows Server 2003 can support any number of EAP types at once; the Routing and Remote Access Services (RRAS) server can use any EAP type to authenticate if you've allowed that module to be used and the client has the module in question. Windows Server 2003 actually comes with the following two EAP types:

- EAP MD5-CHAP implements the version of CHAP that uses the MD5 hash algorithm. The EAP version of CHAP is identical to the regular version, but the challenges and responses are packaged and sent as EAP messages. This means that if you turn EAP MD5-CHAP on and disable regular CHAP on the server, plain CHAP clients won't be able to authenticate.

- EAP-Transport Level Security (TLS) allows you to use public-key certificates as an authenticator. TLS (which you may recall from Chapter 7, "Managing Remote Access Services") is very similar to the familiar Secure Sockets Layer (SSL) protocol used for web browsers. When EAP-TLS is turned on, the client and server send TLS-encrypted messages back and forth. EAP-TLS is the strongest authentication method you can use; as a bonus, it supports smart cards. However, EAP-TLS requires your RRAS server to be part of a Windows 2000 or Server 2003 domain.

There's a third EAP authentication method included with Windows Server 2003, but it's not really an EAP type. EAP-RADIUS is a fake EAP type that passes any incoming message to a *Remote Authentication for Dial-In User Service (RADIUS)* server for authentication.

Connection Security

There are some additional features you can use to provide connection-level security for your remote access clients. You've already learned about one in Chapter 7: the Callback Control Protocol (CBCP). CBCP allows your RRAS servers or clients to negotiate a callback with the other end. When CBCP is enabled, either the client or the server can ask the server at the other end to call the client back at a number supplied by the client or a prearranged number stored on the server.

Another option is that the RRAS server can be programmed to accept or reject calls based on the caller ID or Automatic Number Identification (ANI) information transmitted by the phone company. For example, you can instruct your primary RRAS server to accept calls from only your home analog line. While this keeps you from calling it when you're on the road, it also keeps the server from talking to strangers.

Finally, you can specify various levels of encryption to protect your connection from interception or tampering. The exact type and kind of encryption used will vary according to the options you specify.

Access Control

Apart from the connection-level measures you can use to prohibit outside callers from talking to your servers, you can restrict which users can make remote connections in a number of ways. First of all, you can allow or disallow remote access from individual user accounts. This is the same limited control you have in Windows NT, but it's just the start for Windows Server 2003.

Besides turning dial-in access on or off for a single user, you can use *remote access policies* to control whether users can get access or not. Like group policies, remote access policies give you an easy way to apply a consistent set of policies to groups of users. However, the policy mechanism is a little different: You create rules that include or exclude the users you want in the policy. Unlike group policies, remote access policies are only available in Windows 2000 native and Server 2003 domain functional level (that is, in domains in which there are no Windows NT domain controllers present). That means that you may not have the option to use remote access policies until your Windows 2000 and Server 2003 deployment is further along.

In the next section, you will learn how to configure user access control.

Configuring User Access

In the previous chapter, you set up the server to accept incoming calls. Now it's time to determine who can actually use the remote access services. You do this in two ways: by setting up *remote access profiles* on individual accounts and by creating and managing remote access policies that apply to groups of users. This distinction is subtle but important because you manage and apply profiles and policies in different places.

Using User Profiles

Windows Server 2003 stores a lot of information for each user account. Collectively, this information is known as the account's profile, and it's normally stored in Active Directory. Some settings in the user's profile are available through one of the two user-management snap-ins: Active Directory Users and Computers if your RRAS server is part of an Active Directory domain or Local Users and Groups if it's not. In either case, the interesting part of the profile is the Dial-In tab of the user's Properties dialog box (see Figure 8.1). This tab has a number of interesting controls that regulate how the user account may be used for dial-in access.

Most aspects of Active Directory are beyond the scope of this book and the related exam. For more information, see the *MCSE: Windows 2003 Active Directory Planning, Implementation, and Maintenance Study Guide* (Sybex, 2003) by Anil Desai with James Chellis.

FIGURE 8.1   The Dial-In tab of the user's Properties dialog box

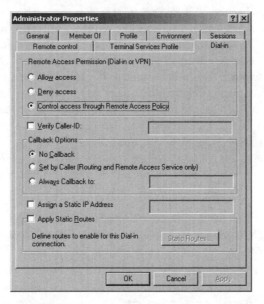

These controls include the following:

The Remote Access Permission (Dial-in Or VPN) control group   The first, and probably most familiar, controls on this tab are in the Remote Access Permission control group. They control whether the user has dial-in permission or not. They're similar to the controls you may remember from the Windows NT User Manager; however, Windows Server 2003 has a new feature. In addition to explicitly allowing or denying access, you can leave the access decision up to a remote access policy provided you're using Windows Server 2003 in native mode.

The Verify Caller-ID checkbox   RRAS can verify a user's caller ID information and use the results to allow or deny access. When you check the Verify Caller-ID checkbox and enter a phone number in the field, you're telling RRAS to reject a call from anyone who provides that username and password but whose caller ID information doesn't match what you enter.

The Callback Options control group   The Callback Options control group gives you three choices for regulating callback. The first (and default setting), No Callback, means the server will never honor callback requests from this account. If you choose the Set By Caller radio button instead, the calling system can specify a number at which it wants to be called and the RRAS server will call the client back at that number. The final choice, Always Callback To, allows you to enter a number that the server will call back no matter where the client's actually calling from. This is less flexible, but more secure, than the second option.

The Assign A Static IP Address checkbox   If you want one particular user to always get the same static IP address, you can arrange it by checking the Assign A Static IP Address checkbox and then entering the desired IP address. This allows you to set up nondynamic DNS records for individual users, guaranteeing that their machines will always have a usable DNS entry. On the other hand, this is much more error prone than the dynamic DNS-DHCP combination you could be using instead.

The Apply Static Routes checkbox   In an ordinary LAN, you don't have to do anything special to clients to enable them to route packets—just configure them with a default gateway and the gateway handles the rest. For dial-up connections, though, you may want to define a list of static routes that will enable the remote client to reach hosts on your network, or elsewhere, without requiring that packets be sent to a gateway in between. If you want to define a set of static routes on the client, you'll have to do it manually. If you want to assign static routes on the server, check the Apply Static Routes checkbox and then use the Static Routes button to add and remove routes as necessary.

Remember that these settings apply to individual users, so you can assign different routes, caller ID, or callback settings to each user.

You might not want to apply static routes on your production systems because it may reduce your ability to dial in and fix problems.

Using Remote Access Policies

Windows Server 2003 includes support for two additional configuration systems: remote access policies and remote access profiles (we will look at remote access profiles in the section "Using Remote Access Profiles" later in this chapter). Policies determine who may and may not connect; you define rules with conditions that the system evaluates to see whether a particular user can connect or not.

You can have any number of policies in a native Windows Server 2003 domain; each policy may have exactly one profile associated with it.

> Settings in an individual user's profile override settings in a remote access policy.

You manage remote access policies through the Remote Access Policies folder in the RRAS snap-in. Policies contain conditions that you pick from a list. When a caller connects, the policy's conditions are evaluated, one by one, to see whether the caller gets in or not. All of the conditions in the policy must match for the user to gain access. If there are multiple policies, they're evaluated according to an order you specify.

In the following sections, you will see how to create and configure remote access policies.

Creating a New Policy

To create a policy, right-click the Remote Access Policies folder and select New Remote Access Policy. This command starts the New Remote Access Policy Wizard, which uses a series of steps to help you define the policy. You use the Policy Configuration Method page (see Figure 8.2) to tell the wizard if you want to configure a custom or a built-in policy and define a friendly name for the policy. This is the name that appears in the snap-in's policy list.

FIGURE 8.2   The Policy Configuration Method page of the New Remote Access Policy Wizard

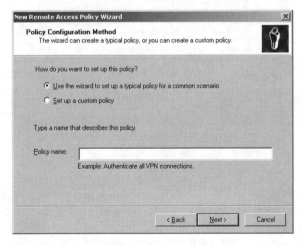

If you chose to configure a custom policy, the Policy Conditions page (see Figure 8.3) will be next. This page will initially be blank. To create a condition for the policy, click the Add button, which will bring up the Select Attribute dialog box (see Figure 8.4).

> If you want to restrict dial-in access based on an account's group membership, check out the Windows Groups attribute.

FIGURE 8.3   The Policy Conditions page of the New Remote Access Policy Wizard

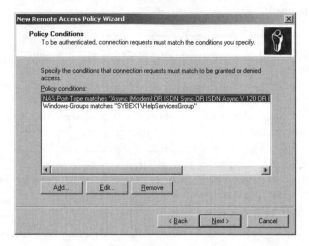

FIGURE 8.4   The Select Attribute dialog box

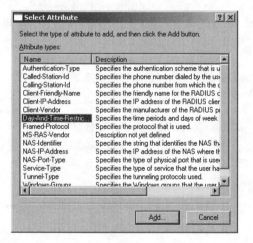

The Select Attribute dialog box lists all of the attributes that you can evaluate in a policy (see Table 8.1; attributes marked as "IAS only" work only with the Internet Authentication Service). These attributes are drawn from the RADIUS standards, so you can (and in some cases, should) intermix your Windows Server 2003 RRAS servers with RADIUS servers.

TABLE 8.1   Remote Access Policy Attributes

Attribute Name	What It Specifies
Called-Station-Id	Phone number of remote access port called by the caller
Calling-Station-Id	Caller's phone number

TABLE 8.1 Remote Access Policy Attributes *(continued)*

Attribute Name	What It Specifies
Client-Friendly-Name	(IAS only) Name of the RADIUS server that's attempting to validate the connection
Client-IP-Address	(IAS only) IP address of the RADIUS server that's attempting to validate the connection
Client-Vendor	(IAS only) Vendor of remote access server that originally accepted the connection; used to set different policies for different hardware
Day-And-Time-Restrictions	Weekdays and times when connection attempts are accepted or rejected
Framed-Protocol	Protocol to be used for framing incoming packets (e.g., PPP, SLIP, etc.)
NAS-Identifier	(IAS only) Friendly name of the remote access server that originally accepted the connection
NAS-IP-Address	(IAS only) IP address of the remote access server that originally accepted the connection
NAS-Port-Type	Physical connection (e.g., ISDN, POTS) used by the caller
Service-Type	Framed (for PPP) or login (Telnet)
Tunnel-Type	Which tunneling protocol should be used (L2TP or PPTP)
Windows-Groups	Which Windows groups are allowed access

Once you choose an attribute and click the Add button, its corresponding editor appears. With this editor, you can edit the value of the attribute. For example, if you select the Day-And-Time-Restrictions attribute, you'll see the Time Of Day Constraints dialog box, which is a calendar grid that lets you select which days and times are available for logging on. Each attribute has its own unique editor. After you select an attribute and give it a value, you can add more attributes or move to the next page by clicking the Next button on the Policy Conditions page.

The Permissions page of the wizard has only two radio buttons, which specify whether the policy you create allows or prevents users from connecting: Grant Remote Access Permissions and Deny Remote Access Permissions. Once you choose a permission and click the Next button, the Profile page appears. The Edit Profile button allows you to edit the user profile attached to the policy. You don't have to edit the profile when you create the policy; you can always come back to it later. Once you create the policy, it will appear in the snap-in and you can manage it independently of the other policies.

In Exercise 8.1, you'll create an adjunct policy that adds time and day restrictions to the default policy. This exercise requires you to be in Windows 2000 native or Server 2003 domain functional level, and you must have completed the exercises in Chapter 7.

EXERCISE 8.1

Creating a Remote Access Policy

1. Open the RRAS MMC snap-in by selecting Start ➢ Administrative Tools ➢ Routing And Remote Access.

2. Expand the server you want to configure in the left pane of the MMC.

3. Select the Remote Access Policies folder.

4. Select Action ➢ New Remote Access Policy. The New Remote Access Policy Wizard starts. Click Next to dismiss the Welcome page and continue with the wizard.

5. On the Policy Configuration Method page, select the Set Up A Custom Policy radio button, type **Working Hours Restrictions** in the Policy Name field, and then click the Next button.

6. On the Policy Conditions page, click the Add button. The Select Attributes dialog box appears.

7. Select the Day-and-Time-Restrictions attribute and then click the Add button.

8. The Time Of Day Constraints dialog box appears. Use the calendar controls to allow remote access Monday through Saturday from 7 A.M. to 7 P.M. and then click the OK button.

9. The Conditions page reappears, this time with the new condition listed. Click the Next button.

10. The Permissions page appears. Select the Grant Remote Access Permission radio button and click Next to continue.

11. The User Profile page appears. Click the Next button (you'll edit the profile in the next exercise).

12. Click the Finish button on the confirmation screen to close the wizard and save your changes.

Working with Existing Policies

After you complete Exercise 8.1, you'll be better equipped to see a couple of additional policy-management features. To begin, you can reorder policies by right-clicking a policy in the MMC window and selecting Move Up and Move Down. Because policies are evaluated in the order of their appearance in the snap-in, and because all conditions of all policies must match for a user to get access, this is a good way to establish a set of policies that filter out some users. For example, you could create one policy that only allows members of the marketing department to dial in between 8 A.M. and 5 P.M. and then add another that allows engineers free rein to dial in anytime.

In addition, when you open the policy's Properties dialog box (see Figure 8.5), you can add to and remove them from the policy, change the policy's name, and control whether a user whose connection matches the policy's conditions will be granted or denied access.

In addition, you can delete a policy you no longer need by right-clicking it and using the Delete command; the snap-in will prompt you for confirmation before it removes the policy.

FIGURE 8.5   The policy's Properties dialog box

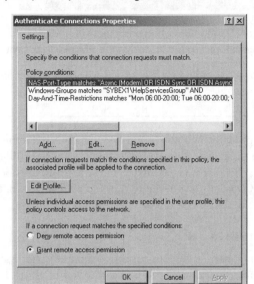

Using Remote Access Profiles

Remote access profiles are an integral part of remote access policies. Profiles contain settings that determine what happens during call setup and completion. (Don't confuse remote access profiles with the dial-in settings associated with a user profile.) Each policy has a profile associated with it; the profile determines what settings will be applied to connections that meet the conditions stated in the policy.

For security reasons, it's usually a good idea to limit access to the administrative accounts on your network. In particular, we usually tell clients to restrict remote access for the Administrator account; that way, the potential exposure from a dial-up compromise is somewhat reduced. In Exercise 8.2, you will learn how to configure the Administrator account's user profile to restrict dial-up access.

EXERCISE 8.2

Configuring a User Profile for Dial-In Access

1. Log on to your computer using an account that has administrative privileges.

2. If you're using an RRAS server that's part of an AD domain, open the Active Directory Users and Computers snap-in by selecting Start ➢ Administrative Tools ➢ Active Directory Users And Computers. If not, open the Local Users and Groups snap-in by selecting Start ➢ Administrative Tools ➢ Local Users And Groups.

3. Expand the tree to the Users folder. Right-click the Administrator account in the right-hand pane and choose Properties. The Administrator Properties dialog box appears.

4. Switch to the Dial-In tab. On machines that participate in Active Directory, the Control Access Through Remote Access Policy radio button in the Permissions group should be set.

5. Click the Deny Access radio button to prevent the use of this account over a dial-in connection.

6. Click the OK button.

You can create one profile for each policy, either when you create the policy or later (by using the Edit Profile button in the policy's Properties dialog box). The profile contains settings that fit into six distinct areas; each area has its own tab in the profile Properties dialog box. These tabs include the Dial-In Constraints tab, the IP tab, the Multilink tab, the Authentication tab, the Encryption tab, and the Advanced tab.

The Dial-In Constraints Tab

The Dial-In Constraints tab (see Figure 8.6) has most of the settings that you think of when you consider dial-in access controls. The controls here allow you to adjust how long the connection may be idle before it gets dropped, how long it can be up, the dates and times for establishing the connection, and what dial-in port and medium can be used to connect.

FIGURE 8.6   The Dial-In Constraints tab of the Edit Dial-In Profile Properties dialog box

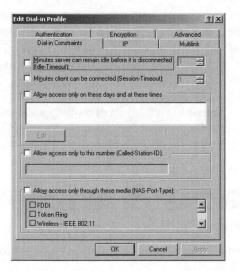

The IP Tab

The IP tab (see Figure 8.7) gives you control over the IP-related settings associated with an incoming call. If you think back to the server-specific settings covered in the previous chapter, you'll remember that the server preferences include settings for other protocols besides IP; this is not so in the remote access profile. In the remote access profile, you can specify where the client gets its IP address. As a bonus, you can define IP packet filters that screen out particular types of traffic to and from the client.

FIGURE 8.7   The IP tab of the Edit Dial-In Profile Properties dialog box

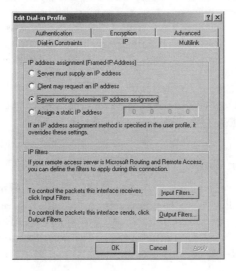

The Multilink Tab

The profile mechanism also gives you a degree of control over how the server handles multilink calls; you exert this control through the Multilink tab (see Figure 8.8) of the profile Properties dialog box. Your first choice is to decide whether to allow them at all and, if so, how many ports you want to allow a single client to use at once. Normally, this setting is configured so that the server-specific settings take precedence, but you can override them.

FIGURE 8.8   The Multilink tab of the Edit Dial-In Profile Properties dialog box

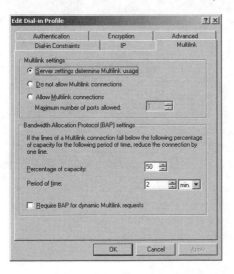

The Bandwidth Allocation Protocol (BAP) Settings control group gives you a way to control what happens during a multilink call when the bandwidth usage drops below a certain threshold. For example, why tie up three analog lines to provide 168Kbps of bandwidth when the connection is only using 56Kbps? You can tweak the capacity and time thresholds; by default, a multilink call will drop one line every time the bandwidth usage falls below 50 percent of the available bandwidth and stays there for two minutes. The Require BAP For Dynamic Multilink Requests checkbox allows you to refuse calls from clients that don't support BAP; this is an easy way to make sure that no client can hog your multilink bandwidth.

The settings you specify on the Multilink tab will be ignored unless you have multilink and BAP/BACP enabled on the server.

The Authentication Tab

On the Authentication tab (see Figure 8.9), you can specify which authentication methods are allowed on this specific policy. Note that these settings, like the other policy settings, will be useful only if the server's settings match. For example, if you turn EAP authentication off in the server Properties dialog box, turning it on in the Authentication tab of the profile Properties dialog box will have no effect.

FIGURE 8.9   The Authentication tab of the Edit Dial-In Profile Properties dialog box

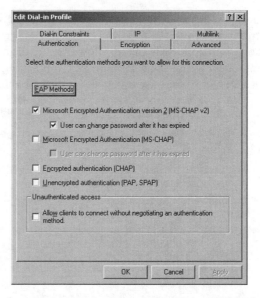

You'll notice each authentication method has a checkbox. Check the appropriate boxes to control the protocols that you want this profile to use. If you enable EAP, you can also choose which specific EAP type you want the profile to support. You can also choose to allow totally unauthenticated access (which is unchecked by default).

The Encryption Tab

The Encryption tab (see Figure 8.10) controls which type of encryption you want your remote users to have access to. The following radio buttons are listed on the Encryption tab:

- Basic Encryption (MPPE 40-Bit) means single DES (Data Encryption Standard) for IPSec or 40-bit Microsoft Point-to-Point Encryption (MPPE) for Point-to-Point Tunneling Protocol (PPTP).

- Strong Encryption (MPPE 56 Bit) means 56-bit encryption (single DES for IPSec; 56-bit MPPE for PPTP).

- Strongest Encryption (MPPE 128 Bit) means triple DES for IPSec or 128-bit MPPE for PPTP connections.

- No Encryption allows users to connect using no encryption at all. When unchecked, a remote connection must be encrypted or it'll be rejected.

FIGURE 8.10   The Encryption tab of the Edit Dial-In Profile Properties dialog box

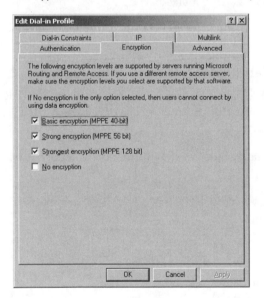

In Exercise 8.3, you'll force all connections to your server to use encryption. Any client that can't use encryption will be dropped. You must complete Exercise 8.1 before you do this exercise.

WARNING   Don't do this exercise on your production RRAS server unless you're sure that all of your clients are encryption capable.

EXERCISE 8.3

Configuring Encryption

1. Open the RRAS snap-in by selecting Start ➢ Administrative Tools ➢ Routing And Remote Access.

2. Expand the server you want to configure in the left pane of the MMC.

3. Select the Remote Access Policies folder. The right pane of the MMC displays the policies defined for this server. Select the Working Hours Restrictions policy that you created in Exercise 8.1.

4. Select Action ➢ Properties. The policy Properties dialog box appears.

5. Click the Edit Profile button. The Edit Dial-In Profile dialog box appears. Select the Encryption tab.

6. Uncheck the No Encryption checkbox. Make sure that the Basic, Strong, and Strongest (if present) checkboxes are all marked.

7. Click the OK button. When the policy Properties dialog box reappears, click the OK button.

The Advanced Tab

The Advanced tab (see Figure 8.11) is primarily used if you want your RRAS server to interoperate with RADIUS equipment from other vendors. The tab allows you to specify additional attributes you want incorporated into the profile.

FIGURE 8.11 The Advanced tab of the Edit Dial-In Profile Properties dialog box

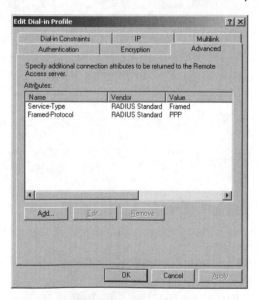

When you first open the tab, you'll see only two attributes specified: Service-Type (with a value of Framed) and Framed-Protocol (with a value of PPP). That combination allows the RRAS server to tell its peers that it's handling a framed PPP connection. There are several dozen additional attributes available, and each can be added with the Add button. Some are defined in the RADIUS standard, while others are specific to particular vendors. It's not necessary to know what attributes are on this list, only that you use the Advanced tab to add additional attributes when combining RRAS with third-party RADIUS-based solutions.

 Real World Scenario

Remote Access Is More than Technology

You are the network administrator of a Windows Server 2003 network that supports the sales organization of a national training company. In an effort to cut costs, your management wants the sales representatives to work out of their homes and on the road. You jump to the task with the immediate intention of implementing RRAS, which you know has the necessary components to provide secure remote access.

However, one thing you want to keep in mind is that the simplicity of RRAS creates a tendency for administrators to rely too much on the technology and to take their eyes off the ball of proper processes and procedures. If your users can get into your network, then unauthorized intruders will surely try. The first step in dealing with the losers and maladjusted purveyors of mischief is to prepare a properly detailed written remote access policy. This should include a description of how you want to enable remote access, what resources should be available, and what consistent type of technical mechanism you will deploy to facilitate remote access. There is no one right or wrong answer for every organization, but there needs to be a well thought-out rationale for how you deploy remote services. As you can see, this is not simply a technical problem to solve.

The approach to this remote access policy should be based on an analysis of risk and liability. The analysis should cover what the implications would be if various levels of information were breached. Then the cost necessary to protect the resource could be objectively determined. This determination will affect all decisions regarding the variety of technologies that are included with RRAS, such as types of authentication, control of who can access the network remotely, encryption levels, and callback. A failure to complete a process of this nature will most likely result in a situation in which unauthorized access results in damage to your network—and by extension, damage to your career.

Setting Up a VPN Remote Access Policy

Earlier in this chapter, you learned how to use the remote access policy mechanism on a Windows Server 2003 native-mode domain. Now it's time to apply what you've learned to a virtual private network (VPN). Recall that there are two ways to control which specific users can access a remote access server: You can grant and deny dial-up permission to individual users in each user's Properties dialog box, or you can create a remote access policy that embodies whatever restrictions you want to impose. It turns out that you can do the same thing for VPN connections, but there are a few additional things to consider.

Granting and Denying Per-User Access

To grant or deny VPN access to individual users, all you have to do is make the appropriate change on the Dial-In tab of each user's Properties dialog box. Although this is the easiest method to understand, it gets tedious quickly if you need to change VPN permissions for more than a few users. Furthermore, there's no way to distinguish between dial-in and VPN permission.

Creating a Remote Access Policy for VPNs

You may find it helpful to create remote access policies that enforce the permissions you want end users to have. There are a number of ways to accomplish this result; which one you use will depend on your overall use of remote access policies.

The simplest way is to create a policy that allows all of your users to use a VPN. Earlier in this chapter, you learned how to create remote access policies and specify settings for them; one thing you may have noticed was that there's a NAS-Port-Type attribute that you can use in the policy's conditions. That attribute is the cornerstone of building a policy that allows or denies remote access via VPN because you use it to accept or reject connections arriving over a particular type of VPN connection. For best results, you'll use Tunnel-Type in conjunction with the NAS-Port-Type attribute, as described in Exercise 8.4.

 Remember that you can use remote access policies only if you're in a native mode Windows 2000 or Server 2003 domain functional level.

EXERCISE 8.4

Creating a VPN Remote Access Policy

1. Open the RRAS MMC console by selecting Start ➢ Administrative Tools ➢ Routing And Remote Access.

2. Navigate to the server on which you want to create the policy and expand the server node until you see the Remote Access Policies node.

3. Right-click the Remote Access Policies folder and choose the New Remote Access Policy command. This starts the New Remote Access Policy Wizard.

4. Name the policy VPN Access or something else that clearly indicates what it's for and then click the Next button.

5. When the Policy Conditions page of the wizard appears, click the Add button to add this condition: NAS-Port-Type Attribute Set To "Virtual (VPN)." If you want to restrict VPN users to either PPTP or L2TP, add this other condition: Tunnel-Type Attribute Set To The Appropriate Protocol. Click the next button.

6. In the Permissions page of the wizard, make sure the Grant Remote Access Permission radio button is selected (unless you're trying to *prevent* VPN users from connecting). Click the Next button.

7. The Profile page appears next. If you want to create a specific profile (perhaps to restrict which authentication types VPN clients may use), use the Edit Profile button to specify the new profile. At a minimum, you should clear the No Encryption option on the Encryption tab of the remote access profile. When you're done editing the profile, click the Next button, then click the Finish button to create and activate the policy.

If you don't want to grant VPN access to everyone, there are some changes you can make to the process in Exercise 8.4 to fine-tune it. When you add the policy described in the exercise, it will end up at the end of the policy list. This means that the default policies will take effect before the VPN-specific policy does, so you'll probably want to move the VPN policy to the top of the list.

For example, if you want to allow everyone dial-up access but you also want VPN capability to be reserved for a smaller group, create an Active Directory group and put your VPN users in it. You can then create a policy using the two conditions outlined in the exercise *plus* a condition that uses the Windows-Groups attribute to specify the new group. As with the ordinary VPN policy in Exercise 8.4.

 Real World Scenario

Planning VPN Security

The CEO of your company has just returned from a seminar that promised lower communication costs through the use of VPNs tunneled through the Internet. She can't wait to start ripping out the fixed leased lines so that she can see the saved dollars move down to the bottom line. As the network administrator, you are now charged with implementing VPNs to provide secure communications across the network.

You know that along with the increase of mobile computing there has been a correlating increase in the use of VPNs. This trend has been, and will continue to be, a boon to productivity. This growth is akin to the benefit that the public highway system has provided to private organizations for their economic activities. For this reason, VPNs will continue to grow in importance in the explosion of remote communication that's taking place today.

However, you know that a VPN is only a part of an overall security implementation for a network; you can't assume that a company's communications are secure simply because it's using a VPN. As mentioned previously, a written remote access policy needs to include a written security policy that is based on an analysis of risk and liability. You can make the effort to create a VPN solution for the users on your network, but they may have NetBIOS enabled on their network connection, with file- and printer-sharing enabled. With this type of configuration, you may have secure communications with your network, but any confidential company information that the users have downloaded to their computers is now exposed to the Internet.

Other things to consider are that clients may download Java applets and ActiveX controls that have the capability to run their own remote control activities, hidden from view, or that hackers may use your system to gain access to your network so that they can use it as a platform for a future denial of service (DoS) attack on another network.

Ensure that you have considered as many aspects as possible when you are planning your remote systems. As you deploy VPNs to secure your company's communications, make sure that you aren't plugging one narrow crack in your system while leaving another gaping hole that's too big to see.

Configuring Security

There are several aspects involved with remote access security configuration, the most fundamental of which involves configuring the types of authentication and encryption the server will use when accepting client requests. We will look at each of these in the following sections.

Controlling Server Security

The Security tab of the server's Properties dialog box (see Figure 8.12) allows you to specify which authentication and accounting methods RRAS uses. You can choose one of two authentication providers by using the Authentication Provider drop-down list. Your choices include the following:

Windows Authentication   This is a built-in authentication suite included with Windows Server 2003.

RADIUS Authentication   This allows you to send all authentication requests heard by your server on to a RADIUS server for approval or denial.

You can also use the Accounting Provider drop-down list on the Security tab to choose between Microsoft-developed accounting, in which connection requests are maintained in the event log, and RADIUS accounting, in which all accounting events are sent to a RADIUS server for action.

When you select the RADIUS Authentication option from the Authentication Provider drop-down menu, you are enabling a RADIUS client that passes authentication duties to a RADIUS server. Click the Configure button to open the RADIUS Authentication dialog box. From here, you can click the Add button to add the name or address of a RADIUS server that the RAS server will pass authentication duties to. You must also enter the correct secret, which is initially set by the RADIUS server. The secret is similar to a password but adds a layer of security to the connection between the RAS server and the RADIUS server. The Time-Out option determines how long the RAS server will attempt to authenticate the remote user before giving up. The Initial Score option is similar to the cost value used by routers. The RAS server will attempt to authenticate users on the RADIUS server with the highest score first. If that attempt fails, the RAS server will use the RADIUS server with the next highest score and so on. Finally, the Port option can be changed, but the default setting is part of RFC 2866, "RADIUS Accounting," and should not be altered unless extraordinary circumstances dictate such.

FIGURE 8.12   The Security tab of the RRAS server Properties dialog box

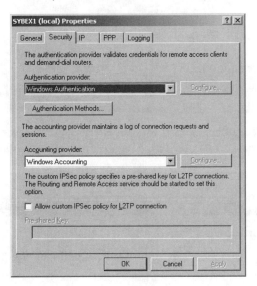

Select the Windows Authentication option from the Authentication Provider drop-down menu if you want the local machine to authenticate your remote access users. To configure the server by telling it which authentication methods you want it to use, click the Authentication Methods button, which displays the Authentication Methods dialog box (see Figure 8.13). If you look back over the list of authentication protocols earlier in the chapter, you'll find that each one has a corresponding checkbox here: EAP, MS-CHAP v2, MS-CHAP, CHAP, SPAP, and PAP. You can turn on totally unauthenticated access by checking the Allow Remote Systems To Connect Without Authentication checkbox, but that is not recommended because it allows anyone to connect to, and use, your server (and thus by extension your network).

There's actually a special set of requirements for using CHAP because it requires access to each user's encrypted password. Windows Server 2003 normally doesn't store user passwords in a format that CHAP can use, so you have to take some additional steps if you want to use CHAP. First, enable CHAP at the server and policy levels. Next, you need to edit the default domain GPO's Password Policy object to turn on the Store Password Using Reversible Encryption For All Users policy setting. After you've done that, each user's password must be either reset or changed, which forces Windows Server 2003 to store the password in reversibly encrypted form. After these steps are completed for an account, that account can be used with CHAP. These steps aren't required for MS-CHAP or MS-CHAP v2; for those protocols, you just enable the desired version of MS-CHAP at the server and policy levels.

FIGURE 8.13 The Authentication Methods dialog box

In Exercise 8.5, you're going to configure your RRAS server so that it accepts only inbound calls that use the IP protocol. You may have to skip some steps (as noted) if you don't have all of the four network protocols loaded.

EXERCISE 8.5

Configuring Authentication Protocols

1. Open the RRAS MMC snap-in by selecting Start ➢ Administrative Tools ➢ Routing And Remote Access.

2. Navigate to the server whose authentication support you want to change. Select the server and then select Action ➢ Properties to open the server Properties dialog box.

3. Switch to the Security tab. Make sure that Windows Authentication is selected in the Authentication Provider drop-down.

4. Click the Authentication Methods button. The Authentication Methods dialog box appears.

5. Select the Extensible Authentication Protocol (EAP) checkbox.

6. Select the two MS-CHAP checkboxes.

7. Select the CHAP checkbox.

8. Verify that the SPAP and PAP checkboxes are cleared.

9. Verify that the Allow Remote Systems To Connect Without Authentication checkbox is cleared.

10. Click the OK button; when the server Properties dialog box reappears, click its OK button.

11. You will be asked if you want to view the help files associated with configuring authentication protocols. Click No to finish the exercise.

Controlling Security at the Policy Level

You can apply authentication restrictions at the policy level, too. As you saw in the preceding sections, policy-level settings don't exactly override the server settings. For example, you could configure your server to allow CHAP, MS-CHAP, and MS-CHAP v2 and then set up a policy that would prevent some users from using CHAP. On the other hand, if you disable CHAP at the server level, you can't build a policy that will magically allow it.

Having said that, one key point to remember is to configure your server with the sum of the authentication methods you want to be able to use and then create specific policies that limit which authentication methods (and other settings, particularly dial-in constraints) individuals or groups can use on that server.

Configuring a RADIUS (IAS) Server

Microsoft's implementation of RADIUS is called *Internet Authentication Service (IAS)*. IAS provides RADIUS clients (described earlier) and proxy servers with authentication services. It is particularly useful when you have several remote access servers because it centralizes the authentication, authorization, and accounting for all of your remote access users. When an IAS server is part of an Active Directory domain, it uses Active Directory to authenticate users. The IAS console includes a Remote Access Policies node that is used in exactly the same way you use the Remote Access Policies node on a RAS server, which you saw earlier in this chapter.

You install IAS using the Add/Remove Windows Components Wizard. Select the Networking Components option, click the Details button, and select Internet Authentication Service. After IAS is installed, you can access it through the Internet Authentication Service MMC in the Administrative Tools program group.

Perform the following steps to add a list of RADIUS clients to the IAS server:

1. From within the IAS snap-in, right-click the RADIUS Clients folder and select the New RADIUS Client command.

2. Enter a friendly name and the name or IP address of your RADIUS client and click Next.

3. Select the client-vendor type (the default of RADIUS Standard typically works fine) and enter and confirm the shared secret. Remember that the RADIUS client must enter the shared secret as well in order to use the IAS server.

4. Click the Finish button and you will see the RADIUS client listed in the right pane.

To delete a client from the list, right-click the client name and select the Delete command. To change the attributes of the client, such as the IP address or shared secret, double-click the client name to open the Client Properties dialog box.

Summary

In this chapter you learned about the following topics:

-   That the user authentication protocols included with Windows Server 2003 are PAP, SPAP, CHAP, MS-CHAP, and EAP

- That the Dial-In tab of a user's Properties dialog box has a number of interesting controls that regulate how the user account may be used for dial-in access

- How remote access policies determine who may and may not connect and how you define rules with conditions that the system evaluates to see whether a particular user can connect or not

- How to use remote access profiles, which contain settings that determine what happens during call setup and completion

- How to configure which accounting and authentication methods RRAS uses

Exam Essentials

Know how to use remote access policies. Policies determine who may and may not connect; you define rules with conditions that the system evaluates to see whether a particular user can connect or not. You manage remote access policies through the Remote Access Policies folder in the RRAS snap-in. Policies contain conditions that you pick from a list. When a caller connects, the policy's conditions are evaluated, one by one, to see whether the caller gets in or not.

Know how to use remote access profiles. Each remote access policy has a profile associated with it; the profile determines what settings will be applied to connections that meet the conditions stated in the policy. The settings fit into six distinct areas, and each area has its own tab in the profile Properties dialog box. These tabs are named Dial-In Constraints, IP, Multilink, Authentication, Encryption, and Advanced.

Know how to configure remote access security. There are several different aspects involved with remote access security configuration, the most fundamental of which involves configuring the types of authentication and encryption the server will use when accepting client requests. You can choose one of two authentication providers by using the Authentication Provider drop-down list; they are Windows Authentication and RADIUS. You can apply authentication restrictions at the policy level, too.

Know how to create a remote access policy for VPNs. The simplest way is to create a policy that allows all your users to use a VPN. To allow VPN access to a smaller group, create an Active Directory group and put your VPN users in it. You can then create a policy using the following conditions: NAS-Port-Type Attribute Set To "Virtual (VPN)" and Tunnel-Type Attribute Set To The Appropriate Protocol. Use the Windows-Groups attribute to specify the new group.

Know how to troubleshoot user access. The main things to look for are missing or misconfigured policies. Without a default remote access policy, no user will be allowed access through the RRAS server. All connection requests are evaluated against the criteria contained in the remote access policy. If there is no remote access policy, there are no conditions to compare and any request is thereby denied.

Know how to configure a RADIUS (IAS) server. You install IAS using the Add/Remove Windows Components Wizard. To add a list of RADIUS clients to the IAS server, right-click the RADIUS Clients folder and select the New RADIUS Client command. You will be prompted to enter information about the clients, such as their IP address and client-vendor type.

Key Terms

Before you take the exam, be certain you are familiar with the following terms:

Challenge Handshake Authentication Protocol (CHAP)

Password Authentication Protocol (PAP)

EAP type

remote access policies

Extensible Authentication Protocol (EAP)

remote access profiles

Internet Authentication Service (IAS)

Remote Authentication for Dial-In User Service (RADIUS)

Microsoft CHAP (MS-CHAP)

Shiva Password Authentication Protocol (SPAP)

Review Questions

1. You are the network administrator for Worldwide Sales Organization, Inc., and you have hundreds of salespeople who need to connect to the network from all over the world. The sales representatives' computers all have smart cards that they use with a Cisco RADIUS server for authentication into the network. The network consists of a Windows NT LAN as well as several Unix servers and a mainframe. You are in the process of migrating the Windows NT portion of the network to Windows Server 2003. You have included Windows Server 2003 RRAS, and you want to incorporate the RADIUS authentication for use with the RRAS server. Which authentication protocol should you select for the RRAS server to use the RADIUS server?

   A. MS-CHAP

   B. Kerberos

   C. EAP

   D. PAP

2. You receive a phone call from Carlos, the new network administrator for the Enterprise Shoe Sales To Your Door Company. The majority of the users are the hundreds of remote salespeople who connect throughout the day to the network to update and track sales orders. For quite a while, they have been experiencing intermittent problems, which have actually grown since the last administrator left the company. Carlos attempted to modify the default remote access policy with little success, so he decided to begin from scratch. In order to make sure that no one is negatively affected by the modifications, he deleted the now-confusing default remote access policy that he was trying to modify. During his telephone call, Carlos asks for your help in building the new remote access policy. What will happen to the remote users until the new remote policy is created?

   A. Only users who have standard remote access permission set to Allow Access will connect to the server.

   B. All connection attempts will be rejected.

   C. Anyone who dials the server will be connected.

   D. Only users in Active Directory will be connected.

   E. All users will be connected except those who are configured to be allowed access through the remote access policy.

3. You are building an ISP around the technology available with Windows Server 2003. You are marketing personalized services that will ultimately allow you to provide voice, data, and video services to your customers by integrating Active Directory with the infrastructure of the network. For example, you plan to sell bandwidth on demand based on the customer's account in Active Directory. Your long-range plans notwithstanding, you start providing basic services to your customers by offering both dynamic and static IP addressing. Most ISPs offer static IP addresses based on a particular machine, but you want to provide a particular address based on the individual user. How can you provide this level of service for the users?

   A. Create an IP address reservation for the user in the Windows Server 2003 DHCP server.

   B. Assign a unique IP address to the user account in Active Directory.

   C. Create a remote access policy that provides an assigned static IP address to the appropriate users.

   D. You can't provide a static IP address per user using Windows Server 2003 services.

4. You are the network administrator for the Beach Party Bingo Apparel Company. You serve offices in three cities, with support people for the network in each location. The support people need to access the network from home occasionally when they get paged for network problems during weekends and evenings. You also have more than 100 salespeople who travel incessantly as they try to get your company's product in boutiques across the country. They need to access the network on a regular basis. You want all remote communication to be logged so that for security purposes you can track the locations where connections originate. How can you configure the RRAS server to accommodate these requirements?

   A. Configure Set By Caller for the sales staff and No Callback for the support staff.

   B. Configure Set By Caller for the sales staff and for the support staff.

   C. Configure Set By Caller for the sales staff and Always Callback for the support staff.

   D. Configure No Callback for the sales staff and Set By Caller for the support staff.

   E. Configure Set By Caller for the sales staff.

5. You are configuring RAS on your network, and you have installed RRAS on a Windows Server 2003 server. Users can dial in to one of two phone numbers, 420-4200 and 420-4201, in order to establish RAS connectivity. The Remote Access Permission for each user is set to Control Access Through Remote Access Policy.

You are required to apply the following rules. Administrators and power users can connect at any time, but power users must dial in to 420-4200. If a user is a member of both the Administrators group and the Power Users group, that user must be treated as an administrator. Members of the Domain Users group can connect only between the hours of 5 P.M. and 11 P.M. but may connect to either phone number.

Using the following exhibit, design the simplest remote access policies possible by selecting the items in the Choices column and placing them in the appropriate empty boxes. Policy A is always processed first, and Policy C is always processed last. The default remote access policy has been deleted. Use the Default item if the default setting is required for an element. If no setting is required, then leave its box blank. Note that some items might be used more than once, and some items might not be used at all.

Choices:

- 420-4200
- 420-4201
- 5 P.M.–11 P.M.
- 11 P.M.–5 P.M.
- Administrators
- Allow
- Default
- Deny
- Domain Users
- Power Users

	Conditions	Permission	Profile
Policy A			
Policy B			
Policy C			

6. The AVO import/export company has offices in Canada and throughout South America. The buyers for the company have laptop computers that dial into the network, usually from hotels and from company facilities of AVO's clients. Because financial and proprietary client information will be included in these communications, you want to make sure that they are secure. You plan to encrypt the authentication and data transfers during the VPN communication sessions. Many of the remote sites don't support 128-bit encryption, but you do want to make sure that all sessions are using 56-bit keys. How do you configure the remote access policy for the RRAS server to support these requirements?

A. Basic Encryption

B. Enhanced Encryption

C. Strong Encryption

D. Strongest Encryption

7. Mildred's Natural Pharmaceuticals is in the process of gobbling up other health food and homeopathic companies and integrating them into a national organization. Because the acquisition process for many of the companies that are coming on board hasn't been completed, you don't want them to have complete access to your network. Your company is halfway through a migration from Windows NT and 2000 to Windows Server 2003 at the corporate level. You are still running the Windows 2000 network using Active Directory running in mixed mode. Most of the new locations are small, mom-and-pop health food stores, and many of them aren't computerized at all. You are in the process of sending out stand-alone Windows Server 2003 servers so that each of those locations can connect to the corporate RRAS server. The other locations represent a mix of Windows 95, Windows 98, and Windows NT workstations. You want to use VPNs to enable each location to connect to the corporate network through the location's local Internet connection. What is the best way for you to grant and control VPN access to the RRAS server for all the locations for which the acquisition process has been completed?

    A. Use the default remote access policy for VPN.

    B. Grant access per user.

    C. Create a remote access policy with a NAS port type that uses tunnel type.

    D. Create an Active Directory group containing your VPN users, add a condition that uses the Windows-Groups attribute, and put this policy ahead of the default remote access policy in order to ensure execution.

8. You are the network administrator of the New Products Development Company, which has offices in Southern California. The employees at the corporate office are a combination of administrative support staff and technical engineers in the lab. The engineers also frequently work from home at all hours of the night, and they are supported via RRAS. You were involved with the migration of the network from a hodgepodge of different network operating systems, but predominately Windows clients and a smattering of Macintosh client computers. The CIO decided that the network operating system would be based upon Windows Server 2003 and that the Novell and Banyan hardware would be removed. This was completed last year and everything appears to be fine. Recently, and increasingly, you have been getting calls from development engineers who are working with the Linux operating system complaining that they cannot connect to the RAS server. You are now told that even though the fundamental network for the company will remain Windows Server 2003 based, it is still important to support the work of the development engineers. What steps do you need to take in order for the Linux clients to be able to connect to the RRAS servers so that they can securely access resources at the office from home? (Choose all that apply.)

    A. Select Store Password Using Reversible Encryption For All Users in the GPO for the engineers.

    B. Select The User Must Change Password At Next Logon for the engineers.

    C. Reset the passwords for the engineers.

    D. Enable PAP on RRAS and in the engineers' remote access policy.

    E. Enable MS-CHAP v2 on RRAS and in the engineers' remote access policy.

    F. Enable CHAP on RRAS and in the engineers' remote access policy.

9. The Risk Assessment Insurance Company has five main offices across the United States. The cities are Los Angeles, Dallas, Atlanta, Chicago, and New York. Each city acts as the hub for the many individual sales offices each agent represents in their respective region. You have been involved in the migration from Windows NT to Windows Server 2003 over the last year. The main reason for the migration as directed by the CIO was to reduce administrative costs, a benefit promised by the new operating system platform. The migration has been completed, and the domain has finally been switched over from mixed mode to native mode. Although the software has been upgraded across all the workstations and servers, you still have not taken full advantage of the administrative opportunities available with the system. You still spend a great deal of time managing all of the remote connections used by the agents from their home offices. You are instructed to reduce the amount of time you spend supporting these tasks. What should you do to accomplish this?

   A. Create and implement consistent remote access rules for the agents in a Group Policy object and place it in the root domain of the forest with the No Override option set.

   B. Create and implement consistent remote access rules for the agents in a Group Policy object and place it in each domain of the forest with the No Override option set.

   C. Create a master remote access policy and implement it systematically on each RRAS server.

   D. Implement Internet Authentication Service and configure all of the RRAS servers to participate.

10. Rick needs to set up RRAS callbacks for a single group of users who work from home. He could accomplish this by enabling callbacks for each individual user in each user's Properties dialog box or by doing which of the following?

   A. Creating a Windows Server 2003 security group and then configuring a remote access policy for the group

   B. Creating a remote access profile for the group

   C. Moving the users to a server that has callbacks enabled

   D. Enabling callbacks on the server

11. Hannah's manager has asked her to configure a remote access server so that it restricts what times of day users can dial in. She creates a remote access policy that contains time-of-day restrictions, but it doesn't work. What is the most likely cause?

   A. The Day-And-Time-Restrictions policy hasn't been replicated throughout the domain.

   B. The Day-And-Time-Restrictions policy doesn't have a high enough priority.

   C. The Day-And-Time-Restrictions policy has a priority that's too high.

   D. The Day-And-Time-Restrictions policy is not linked to an active remote access profile.

12. You have already upgraded all your network servers and the services that run on them, including RRAS, to Windows Server 2003. You are responsible for building the remote access system for all your remote users. The requirements are that you must support Windows 98, Windows NT, Windows 2000/XP Professional, and also the growing number of Linux machines that the users are authorized to use from home or on the road. Because most of the users have machines on the local network as well as the need to connect from home, another requirement is that all forms of authentication use encrypted passwords to protect the passwords across the Internet and the ISP networks through which users connect to the RRAS servers. What authentication protocol should you use to satisfy these requirements?

A. MS-CHAP v1

B. MS-CHAP v2

C. CHAP

D. PAP

E. EAP

13. The Windows Server 2003 network that you administer has about 250 people with accounts that give them access to resources. Of these 250 people, only 35 are supposed to have remote access while they are on the road. Another 10 managers are allowed access at certain specified times. In addition, five administrators are authorized to have remote access from home so they can support the network. You have implemented remote access polices to make sure that only the people you have approved have access to the Windows Server 2003 network. Some of the people are in more than one group. These people are having problems accessing the network remotely, and so you take a look at the various policies to find the cause. How are remote access policies evaluated?

A. The most restrictive policy first

B. By name

C. By date of creation

D. By priority

14. William's Sailing Company provides weeklong trips up and down the Atlantic and Pacific coasts of the United States. The company's administrative offices are in North Carolina, providing support to the crews on the six ships in the fleet. You have built a policy-based remote access system that includes several conditions. When a crewmember under the policy tries to access the network to download the guest lists and their meal requests, he is denied access. As the network administrator, you are trying to troubleshoot the problem. Which of the following is true regarding remote access policies?

A. The crewmember does not need to meet any of the policy conditions as long as he has dial-in permission.

B. The crewmember must meet at least one condition in order to be granted access.

C. The crewmember must meet all conditions in order to be granted access.

D. The crewmember does not need to meet any of the conditions as long as the correct credentials are supplied.

15. The Happy Trails Riding Club has a small network of about 25 Windows XP Professional work-stations and one Windows Server 2003 computer. The company provides its clients with weeklong vacations in the mountains featuring a rugged outdoor experience. The owner of the company and two sales representatives need remote access to the network. As the network administrator, you must make sure that the remote access network is always available to these three users but that it is restricted to normal business hours for all other users. What steps should you take to accomplish this task? (Choose all that apply.)

A. Create a new group and add only the three users.

B. Create a policy that includes the Day-And-Time Restrictions and the Windows-Groups policies for the three-user group.

C. Create a new group and add every employee except for the three users.

D. Create a policy that includes the Windows-Groups policy for the three-user group.

E. Create a policy that includes the Day-And-Time Restrictions and the Windows-Groups policies for the larger group.

Answers to Review Questions

1. **C.** RRAS supports multiple authentication methods that can be used for different purposes. The Extensible Authentication Protocol (EAP) allows requests to the RRAS server to be properly formatted and forwarded to the RADIUS server. MS-CHAP is the Microsoft Challenge Handshake Authentication Protocol, which is used in a pure Microsoft environment. Kerberos is a standard that's used to authenticate a user to Active Directory. PAP stands for Password Authentication Protocol, a simple protocol that provides little security and does not forward requests to third-party authentication authorities.

2. **B.** Without a default remote access policy, no user will be allowed access through the RRAS server. All connection requests are evaluated against the criteria contained in the remote access policy. If there is no remote access policy, there are no conditions to compare and any request is thereby denied. Removing the remote access policy does not leave the remote connection to your network open. Therefore, partial connectivity to your network is not possible if there is no remote access policy. The options are either granularity of access through policy or no access at all with no policy.

3. **B.** In Active Directory, dial-in users can be assigned a static IP address associated with their user account. You need to make sure that you have removed these IP addresses from any scope that is being delivered through DHCP so that you won't create conflicts. DHCP delivers addresses based on the machine, and reservations are assigned based on a particular MAC address. Remote policies don't allow you to deliver a unique IP address.

4. **C.** The Always Callback option for the support staff will ensure that their remote connections are always made from their homes. The Set By Caller option for the sales staff will allow them to travel around the country and enter the number where they are at any given time for the callback, thereby allowing you to keep records of all connections. Using No Callback would allow anyone configured with this option to call from anywhere and connect to the system without any callback requirements.

5.

	Conditions		Permission	Profile
Policy A	Administrators		Allow	Default
Policy B	Power Users		Allow	420-4200
Policy C	Domain Users		Allow	Default
	5 P.M.–11 P.M.			

Administrators need to be able to connect to either line at any time of the day, so this policy should be listed first. The policy allowing members of the Power Users group to connect should come second; this will make it possible for members of both the Administrators and the Power Users groups to take advantage of the unlimited access enjoyed by administrators. The policy that applies to Domain Users needs to come last; otherwise, users who are members of both Power Users and Domain Users would be allowed to dial in to 420-4201.

6. C.   Strong Encryption in the remote access policy will configure the RRAS server to use 56-bit DES encryption for L2TP/IPSec VPN connections as well as 56-bit MPPE dial-up connections. Basic Encryption will support L2TP/IPSec 56-bit encryption but only 40-bit encryption for MPPE dial-up connections. Strongest Encryption uses 128-bit encryption for MPPE dial-up connections and supports triple DES encryption for L2TP/IPSec connections. Enhanced Encryption is not a valid option in RRAS.

7. B.   In this situation, you are forced to grant access per user because you can implement remote access policies only if you are running your Windows Server 2003 Active Directory network in Windows 2000 native mode or Windows Server 2003 domain functional level. Ideally, you would use Active Directory and create groups so that you could manage access to the network via remote access policies, but this solution doesn't apply in this situation.

8. A, C, F.   PAP uses cleartext passwords and MS-CHAP supports only Microsoft clients, so they are not options for the Linux clients. CHAP supports encryption across the wire but not in storage, so the encryption must be reversible. Selecting this option does not affect existing passwords, so after you select this option, you need to reset the engineers' passwords. However, if you select the option that forces a password change at the next login, then the engineers will be unable to access the system in the first place from their Linux machines because CHAP does not support this feature.

9. D.   The Windows Server 2003 RRAS server can be configured to behave as a RADIUS server. This allows configuration information to be shared by multiple machines through Internet Authentication Service. In this configuration, when the RRAS server receives a request, it forwards that request to the IAS server for processing and authorizes or denies access based upon a centralized policy. Remote access polices cannot be set in GPOs. The problem of creating a master policy and trying to keep all of the RRAS servers in sync will expand geometrically as the number of servers you are trying to manage increases.

10. A.   Remote access policies allow you to create policies that target specific groups (provided you're in Windows 2000 native or 2003 domain functional level).

11. B.   Policies are evaluated in order, so if the time-of-day restrictions have too low a priority, another policy may allow the connection to proceed instead of stopping it.

12. C.   The Challenge Handshake Authentication Protocol (CHAP) is a standard remote access authentication that is available on Microsoft and non-Microsoft clients. It provides the use of encrypted passwords. The MS-CHAP protocol is based on CHAP but is not available for non-Microsoft clients. If MS-CHAP is the only authentication protocol available on the RRAS server, the Linux clients won't be able to connect to the server. PAP is available on Linux clients, but it doesn't provide the encryption that you need. EAP is an authentication protocol that allows RRAS to interact with other authentication enforcement entities such as RADIUS servers.

13. D.   Policies are evaluated in the order of their priority. If a policy set to restrict remote access has a lower priority and another policy set to allow the connection to proceed has a higher priority, the latter will prevail.

14. C.   In order to gain access to the system, users must meet all of the conditions in at least one remote policy as well as have dial-in permission and supply the correct credentials.

15. A, C, D, E.   In this case, you should create two groups, one for the three unique users and one for the other users in the company. Then apply a policy that allows access unconditionally to the smaller group and a policy that includes Day-And-Time Restrictions and Windows-Groups policies for the larger group.

Chapter

9

Managing IP Routing

MICROSOFT EXAM OBJECTIVES COVERED IN THIS CHAPTER:

✓ **Manage Remote Access.**

 ▪ Manage packet filters.

 ▪ Manage Routing and Remote Access routing interfaces.

 ▪ Manage routing protocols.

✓ **Manage TCP/IP routing.**

 ▪ Manage routing protocols.

 ▪ Manage routing tables.

 ▪ Manage routing ports.

✓ **Implement secure access between private networks.**

✓ **Troubleshoot Routing and Remote Access routing.**

 ▪ Troubleshoot demand-dial routing.

 ▪ Troubleshoot router-to-router VPNs.

As the use of IP internetworking has grown, so has the demand for easy-to-install and easy-to-configure routers. Not every small business that wants to connect to the Internet or connect two remote offices can afford an expensive router and a certified professional to administer it. Microsoft's first attempt to solve this problem was the version of the Routing and Remote Access Services (RRAS) included in the Windows NT 4.0 Option Pack, which is the direct ancestor of the RRAS components included in Windows Server 2003.

The Windows Server 2003 version of RRAS is a fully functional multiprotocol router. It can handle routing Internet Protocol (IP), Internetwork Packet Exchange (IPX), and AppleTalk traffic, and it can be extended by third parties to add additional network protocols or routing methods. The idea behind using RRAS for routing is that you can just enable RRAS on a Windows Server 2003 machine and use it as a router in addition to whatever else you have it doing. For example, you could use a Windows Server 2003 computer with RRAS for routing, IIS for Simple Mail Transfer Protocol (SMTP) mail and web service, and two network interface cards (NICs) to serve as a combination firewall, router, and Internet server.

 Although RRAS supports routing for IPX and AppleTalk networks, in this chapter we'll discuss IP routing because that's what Microsoft emphasizes on the exam.

We will begin the chapter by discussing how IP routing works and looking at the ways that routing is integrated into Windows Server 2003. Next we'll show you how to install and configure RRAS for routing, and we'll take a look at TCP/IP and VPN packet filters. We'll end the chapter with a discussion on managing and troubleshooting IP routing.

Understanding IP Routing

Routing is the process of delivering traffic to the correct destination. IP routing is simple to understand at the most basic level: Packets have addresses, and the process of routing involves getting a packet from its source to its destination. The mechanics of how that happens are a little more complicated, though. In the following sections, we will see exactly what routing does, how routing works, and how Windows Server 2003 handles routing.

What Routing Does

An internetwork is just a network of networks. A sample internetwork might contain five distinct networks: Atlanta, Boston, Orlando, Portland, and San Diego. The internetwork is the collection of all of these networks, any of which could ordinarily stand alone. (Don't confuse an internetwork with the Internet; the Internet we all use is actually just a really large, really complex internetwork.)

Complex internetworks like the Internet support, and even require, routing. Consider what happens when you try to send a file over the Internet. Suppose you're on the East Coast, and the destination is in California. If you look at a map of the physical topology of the Internet, you'll see that there are a large number of potential routes to get from here to there. Some may be better than others; for instance, one route would carry packets east, across the Atlantic, through Europe, and across Russia and the Pacific Ocean to the West Coast of the U.S. That's a legal route, but it would be inefficient.

Routing combines the idea that each packet on a network has a source and destination with the idea of associating routes with costs. Routing systems allow administrators to attach a *metric*, or cost, to each leg of a route. In a bit, you'll see how routing systems use this metric information to calculate the most efficient route for packets to take.

> The actual way in which the metric information is used in calculations varies between Routing Information Protocol (RIP) version 1, RIP version 2, and Open Shortest Path First (OSPF); the important point to remember is that all three routing protocols (discussed in more detail throughout this chapter) use metrics to figure out the "best" route in any situation.

How Routing Works

The basic underlying idea in the routing process is that each packet on a network has a source address and a destination address, which means that any device that receives the packet can inspect its headers to determine where it came from and where it's going. If such a device also has some information about the network's design and implementation—like how long it takes packets to travel over a particular link—it can intelligently change the routing to minimize the total cost.

> In this section, the discussion of routing theory and practice will be confined to IP routing, even though the same concepts apply to IPX/SPX and AppleTalk routing.

> According to the Open Systems Interconnection (OSI) model, a gateway and a router are two different things. However, Microsoft uses the terms interchangeably, and so will we.

Figure 9.1 shows an imaginary network made up of six interconnected local networks. These networks, named A through F, are connected by links of varying speeds and costs. This accurately mirrors what happens in the real world, where it's common for internal networks (or Internet providers) to have multiple ways to establish a link between two points.

FIGURE 9.1 An example network

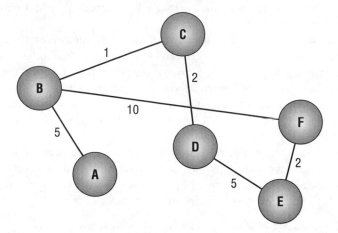

Imagine that a client machine on network B wants to send traffic to a machine on network E. The most obvious route would probably be B to F to E, but you could also use B to C to D to E. Notice the costs: B-F-E has a total cost of 12, while the seemingly longer B-C-D-E actually has a lower cost of 8. That doesn't appear to make sense because the latter route has a longer path. When you consider what cost really means, though, you'll understand why it makes sense.

Assigning link costs is entirely up to you. Normally, you assign costs that reflect your preference for how you want traffic to flow. An expensive or slow link would probably deserve a higher cost than a cheaper or faster link; if you assign a high cost to your most financially expensive links (for example, metered ISDN connections), they would not be used if there were more cost-efficient links available.

Now, revisit Figure 9.1 with the assumption that each circle is really a router. After all, you can hide all the complexity of the network behind a router because only the router is in charge of moving packets. Call your client machine X and your server Y. When X wants to send traffic to Y, it already knows the destination IP address of its target. X will build a packet, including its IP address as the source and Y's address as the destination. X will then use its default gateway setting to send that packet to router B.

Router B receives the packet and has both source and destination address information. By examining the IP addresses, it can determine that it doesn't "know" a direct route to the network where Y is located. However, there are two intermediate nodes that claim to know how to reach Y: C and F. Because C has the lowest link cost, the router at B will send the packet to C in a simple routing algorithm. When C receives it, it will go through the same process, forwarding the packet on to D, and so on. Eventually the packet arrives at its destination.

Let's take a look at some of the specific ways in which RRAS actually performs the steps in the preceding example.

Routing Tables

A routing table is a database that stores route information. Think of it as like a road map for the internetwork—the routing table lists which routes exist between networks, so the router or host can look up the necessary information when it encounters a packet bound for a foreign network. Each entry in the routing table contains the following four pieces of information:

- The network address of the remote host or network
- The forwarding address to which traffic for the remote network should be sent
- The network interface that should be used to send the packet to the forwarding address
- A cost, or metric, that indicates what relative priority should be assigned to this route

For example, you could write the San Diego—Atlanta route as 10.1.1.0:10.10.1.254:ATL:1, assuming that the interface name is ATL and you want to use a metric of 1. The actual format of how these entries are stored isn't important (in fact, it's not visible in RRAS); what's important for you to know is that every routing table entry contains that information.

Routing tables actually can contain these three different kinds of routes:

- *Network routes* provide a route to an entire network. For example, the San Diego-to-Atlanta route is a network route because it can be used to route traffic from any host in San Diego to any host in Atlanta.
- *Host routes* provide a route to a single system. Think of them as shortcuts—they provide a slightly more efficient way for a router to "know" how to get traffic to a remote machine, so they're normally used when you want to direct traffic to remote networks through a particular machine.
- *Default routes* are where packets go when there's no explicit route for them. This is similar to the default gateway you're used to configuring for TCP/IP clients. Any time a router encounters a packet bound for some remote network, it will first search the routing table; if it can't find a network or host route, it will use the default route instead. This saves you from having to configure a network or host route for every network you might ever want to talk to.

Static Routing

Static routing provides predefined routes in a static routing table. Static routing systems don't make any attempt to discover other routers or systems on their networks. Instead, you manually tell the routing engine how to get data to other networks; specifically, you tell it what other networks are reachable from your network by specifying the network addresses, subnet masks, and a metric for each network. This information goes into the system's routing table. When an outgoing packet arrives at the routing engine, the engine can examine the routing table to select the lowest-cost route to the destination. If there's no explicit entry in the routing table for that network, the packet goes to the default gateway, which is then entrusted with getting the packet to where it needs to go.

Static routing is faster and more efficient than dynamic routing. Static routing works well when your network doesn't change much. You can identify the remote networks to which you want to route and then add static routes to them to reflect the costs and topology of your network. In Windows Server 2003, you maintain static routes with the route command, which allows you to either see the contents of the routing table or modify it by adding and removing static routes to individual networks.

Dynamic Routing

Unlike static routing, *dynamic routing* doesn't depend on your adding fixed, unchangeable routes to remote networks. Instead, a dynamic routing engine can discover its surroundings by finding and communicating with other nearby routers in an internetwork.

This process, usually called *router discovery*, enables a newly added (or rebooted) router to configure itself. This is roughly equivalent to the process that happens when you move into a new neighborhood. Within a short time of your arrival, you'll probably meet most of the people who live nearby, either because they come to you or because you go to them. At that point, you have useful information about the surrounding environment that could only come from people who were already there.

The two dynamic routing protocols in Windows Server 2003 are the Routing Information Protocol (RIP) and the Open Shortest Path First (OSPF) protocol. Each has its advantages and disadvantages, but they share some common features and functionality. Each router (whether a hardware device, a Windows Server 2003 machine, or whatever) is connected to at least two separate physical networks. When the router starts, the only information it has is drawn from its internal routing table. Normally, that means it knows about all the attached networks plus whatever static routes have been previously defined. The router then receives configuration information that tells it about the state and topology of the network.

As time goes on, the network's physical topology can change. For example, take a look at the network in Figure 9.2. If network G suddenly lost its connection, the routers in sites A, D, and E would need to readjust their routing tables because they could no longer route traffic directly to G. The process by which this adjustment happens is what makes routing dynamic, and it's also the largest area of difference between the two dynamic routing protocols for IP.

FIGURE 9.2   A more complex, dynamically routed network

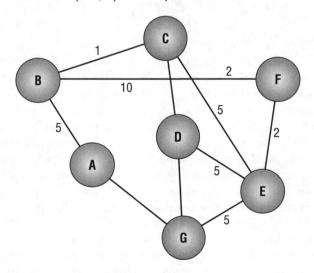

In the following sections, we will look at both RIP and OSPF more closely.

The Routing Information Protocol (RIP)

The *Routing Information Protocol (RIP)* is simple and easy to configure, but it has performance limitations that restrict its usefulness on medium-to-large networks. RIP routers begin with a basically empty routing table, but they immediately begin sending out announcements that they know will reach the networks to which they're connected. These announcements may be broadcast or multicast. Routers on other networks that hear these announcements can add those routes to their own routing tables. The process works both ways, of course; your router will hear announcements from other routers and add those routes to its list of places it knows how to reach. Unfortunately, RIP only supports a maximum of 15 hop counts (the number of routers that a packet can pass through).

Microsoft's RIP implementation in Server 2003 supports RIPv1 and RIPv2. The primary difference between the two versions is the manner in which updates are sent; RIPv1 uses broadcasts every 30 seconds, and RIPv2 uses multicasts only when routes change. RIPv2 also supports simple (e.g., plain text) username/password authentication, which is handy to prevent unwanted changes from cluttering your routing tables. RIPv2 routers also add the ability to receive triggered updates. When you know that your network topology is changing (perhaps because you've added connectivity to another network), you can send out a trigger that contains information about the changes. This trigger forces all the RIP routers you own to assimilate the changes immediately. Triggered updates are also useful because routers that detect a link or router failure can update their routing tables and announce the change, making their neighbors aware of it sooner rather than later.

You can use the RRAS snap-in to set up two kinds of filters that screen out some types of RIP updates. *Route filters* allow you to pick and choose the networks that you want to admit knowing about and for which you want to accept announcements. *Peer filters* give you control over which neighboring routers your router will listen to.

RIP also incorporates features that attempt to prevent route loops. In Figure 9.2, the network topology has the potential to cause a route loop. For instance, say that someone in E wants to send a packet to a machine in A, but the G-to-A and D-to-C links are down. E sends the packet to G, which recognizes that it can't reach A. G also knows that the route D-C-B-A will work, so it sends the packet to D. When the packet reaches D, D knows it can't talk to C, so it sends the packet to E because E-G-A is normally a valid route. Thus you can see that the packet will never reach its destination and will loop continually. This might seem like a contrived example, but in real life, where internetwork links are often concentrated among a small number of physical links, it's a real problem. RIP offers several methods for resolving and preventing loops, including the split-horizon and poison reverse algorithms. Despite their cool names, it's not important to understand how they work to pass the exam—it's enough to know what they're for and that RIP implements them to protect against routing loops.

RIP has two operation modes. In *periodic update mode*, a RIP router sends out its list of known routes at periodic intervals (which you define). The router marks any routes it learns from other routers as RIP routes, which means they remain active only while the router is running. If the router is stopped, the routes vanish. This mode is the default for RIP on LAN interfaces, but it's not suitable for demand-dial connections because you don't want your router bringing up a connection just to announce its presence.

In *auto-static update mode*, the RRAS router broadcasts the contents of its routing table only when a remote router asks for it. Better still, the routes that the RRAS router learns from its RIP neighbors are marked as static routes in the routing table, and they persist until you manually delete them—even if the router is stopped and restarted or if RIP is disabled for that interface. Auto-static mode is the default for demand-dial interfaces.

The Open Shortest Path First (OSPF) Protocol

RIP is designed for fairly small networks; as it turns out, it can handle only 15 router-to-router hops. If you have a network that spans more than 16 routers at any point, RIP won't be able to cache routes for it; some parts of the network will appear to be (or in fact will be) unreachable. The *Open Shortest Path First (OSPF)* protocol is designed for use on large or very large networks. It's much more efficient than RIP, but it also requires more knowledge and experience to set up and administer.

RIP routers continually exchange routing data with one another, which allows incorrect route entries to propagate. Instead of exchanging routing data, each OSPF router maintains a map of the state of the internetwork. This map, called a *link-state map*, provides a continually updated reference to the state of each internetwork link. Neighboring routers group into an *adjacency* (think neighborhood); within an adjacency, routers synchronize any changes to the link-state map. When the network topology changes, whichever router notices it first floods the internetwork with change notifications. Each router that receives the notification updates its copy of the link map and then recalculates its internal routing table.

The "shortest path first" in OSPF refers to the algorithm that OSPF systems use to calculate routes: Routes are calculated so that the shortest path (the one with the lowest cost) is used first. SPF-calculated routes are always free of loops, which is another nice advantage over RIP.

OSPF networks are broken down into areas; an area is a collection of interconnected networks. Think of an area as a subsection of an internetwork. Areas are interconnected by backbones. Each OSPF router keeps a link-state database only for the areas it's connected to. Special OSPF routers called *area border routers* interlink areas. Figure 9.3 shows how this looks.

FIGURE 9.3   A simple OSPF network

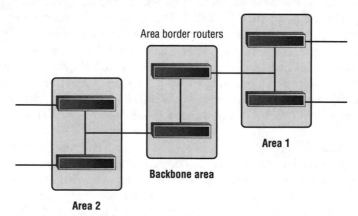

Microsoft's OSPF implementation supports (but doesn't require) the use of *route filters*, so any Windows Server 2003 OSPF router can choose to accept routing information either from other OSPF routers or from other types of routers (e.g., those using RIP). In addition, a desirable feature not always found in OSPF routers is that you can change any of the OSPF settings discussed later in this chapter and have them take effect immediately without having to stop and restart the router.

Border Routing

Internal routing refers to routing that occurs within your internetwork. By contrast, *border routing* is what happens when packets leave your internetwork and go to another one someplace else. Consider what happens when you use your home computer to browse a website. TCP/IP packets from your machine go to your ISP (probably via PPP, over an analog, cable, DSL, or ISDN connection). The ISP examines the destination address of the packets and determines that they should go to some other network that it doesn't have a direct connection to.

For example, when you want to fetch a web page from Microsoft's website, you're dialed into a local ISP (such as `hiwaay.net`), which is connected to several upper-tier providers, including Sprint and Cable & Wireless. Microsoft uses so much bandwidth that it acts as its own ISP, but its web server farm is located on yet another network.

Figure 9.4 shows this internetwork with a border area around each piece of the internetwork: one for HiWAAY, one for Cable & Wireless, one for `msft.net`, and one for Microsoft proper. The thick black lines between borders indicate *backbone* links that join border areas together.

FIGURE 9.4   Networks are divided into border areas linked by backbones.

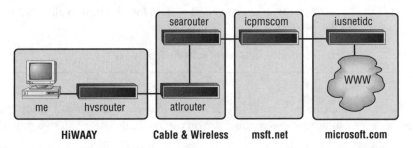

In a border routing network, some routers are responsible for handling packets inside the area, while others manage network communication with other areas. These border routers are responsible for storing routes to other borders that they can reach over the backbone. Because this represents a huge number of potential routes, border routing normally uses dynamic routing protocols like OSPF and RIPv2 to allow, for example, a border router at HiWAAY to discover routes in the adjacent Cable & Wireless border area.

Multicast Routing

IP multicasting works by sending to a single IP address a packet that is read by many hosts. The hosts all have individual IP addresses, but they belong to a multicast group that shares a single, separate IP address. As you saw in Chapter 5, "Managing the Dynamic Host Configuration Protocol," multicast group membership is dynamic, and groups can contain unlimited hosts on separate IP networks provided that routers between the networks support multicast traffic. In fact, computers that aren't part of a multicast group can send multicast packets.

Multicasting uses a special range of IP addresses, called the Class D address space, reserved exclusively for multicasting. The multicast address range contains the IP addresses 224.0.0.0 through 239.255.255.255. Each multicast group uses a single address in the Class D address space. In addition, just as with regular IP addresses, the multicast address range reserves a few special addresses used for specific purposes. Table 9.1 details a partial list these special multicast addresses.

TABLE 9.1   Special Multicast Addresses

Address	Description
224.0.0.0	Base address (reserved)
224.0.0.1	All Hosts, all systems on the same network segment
224.0.0.2	All Routers, all routers on the same network segment
224.0.0.5	All OSPF Routers, used to send routing information to all OSPF routers on the network
224.0.0.6	All Designated OSPF Routers, used to send routing information to all designated OSPF routers
224.0.0.9	All RIP 2 Routers, used to send routing information to all RIPv2 routers on the network
224.0.1.24	Used to support replication for WINS servers

Internet Group Management Protocol (IGMP) is used to exchange multicast group membership information between multicast-capable routers. You can configure RRAS in two modes:

IGMP router mode   IGMP router mode listens for IGMP membership report packets and tracks group membership. IGMP router mode must be attached to any interfaces that connect to multicast-configured hosts.

IGMP proxy mode   IGMP proxy mode essentially acts like a multicast host, except that it forwards IGMP membership report packets to an IGMP router. This provides a list of multicast-enabled hosts to an upstream router that normally wouldn't be aware of the hosts. Typically, IGMP proxy is used on single-router networks connected to the Internet. The IGMP proxy sends the list of multicast hosts to the multicast-capable portion of the Internet known as the Internet multicast backbone, or MBone, so that the hosts can receive multicast packets.

You may find the need to send multicast traffic across non-multicast-compatible routers. This is made possible through the use of IP-in-IP interfaces (or IP-in-IP tunnel). An IP-in-IP interface actually encapsulates packets with an additional IP header. The encapsulated packets can be sent across any router because they appear to be ordinary IP packets. The way you create and manage IP-in-IP interfaces in RRAS is similar to the way you configure other interfaces.

🌐 Real World Scenario

Is a Multihomed Computer a Router?

For several years, your company has been growing steadily, from a small network of 50 Windows NT workstations and 5 Windows NT servers to a medium-sized network of more than 200 Windows 2000 and XP Professional workstations and more than 10 Windows Server 2003 servers. Everything functions properly, but performance is beginning to suffer. After analyzing the network traffic, you realize that you need to segment the network into subnets to control the traffic and improve the performance. You are considering using multihomed computers to save money on the purchase price of dedicated routers.

There is a great deal to be said about the level of sophistication in Windows Server 2003, such as the expanded support with routing protocols. For years, RIP has been used to build fairly large networks, while OSPF has been used for huge, complex networks. However, to get that functionality, one has to fork over pretty big bucks for those specialized machines. But before you leap at the cost savings of using a multihomed Windows Server 2003, you want to take a closer look.

Despite the cost, there is a lot to be said for using specialized routing computers for the connection points in networks. When there is a significant utilization of bandwidth across your network, it's questionable whether the multihomed host will be able to provide the level of service that you need. General-purpose operating systems such as Windows Server 2003 will always pale in comparison to a computer that's designed to perform singular tasks. In addition, with the basic routing protocol, there are many tools and services that are used to guarantee levels of service and to set up filters and access control lists.

Windows Server 2003 really makes sense as a router, though, if you want to connect a small satellite office to a larger network. This will provide the basic routing functionality to make the connection; the more refined services are not necessary. But you can be sure that Sprint and AT&T won't be replacing their Cisco and Nortel routers with Windows Server 2003. Make sure you are applying these Windows Server 2003 routing services in the areas that are appropriate for the particular load and scale of your situation.

Routing and Windows Server 2003

RRAS provides a multiprotocol router—in other words, the RRAS routing engine can handle multiple network protocols and multiple routing methods on multiple NICs. RRAS provides some specific features that are of interest when the conversation turns to network routing. These features include the following:

- It can bring up connections to specific networks when the router receives packets addressed to those networks. This is *demand-dial routing*, and it allows you to use on-demand links instead of permanent connections. This is especially nice for Integrated Services Digital Network (ISDN), which combines per-minute fees in most places with really fast call setup times. Point-to-Point Tunneling Protocol (PPTP) connections can be demand-dialed, too, or you can use demand-dial interfaces to make long-distance connections only when they're needed.

- You can establish static routes that specify where packets bound for certain networks should go. The most common use of this feature is to link a remote network with your LAN; the remote network gets one static route that basically says, "Any traffic leaving my subnet should be sent to the router." RRAS handles it from there.

- It provides dynamic routing using RIPv1 and RIPv2 and the OSPF protocol. These protocols provide two different ways for your router to share routing information with other routers "near" it in network space.

- It provides *packet filtering* to screen out undesirable packcts in both directions. For example, you can create a packet filter to keep out FTP traffic, or you can add a filter to a demand-dial interface so that it will be brought up only for Web or mail traffic. Other traffic types will pass if the link is up, but they won't cause RRAS to open the link if it's not already open. (See the section "Configuring TCP/IP Packet Filters" later in the chapter for more details.)

- It supports *unicast routing*, in which one machine sends directly to one destination address. It also supports *multicast routing*, where one machine sends to an entire network.

- It supports *Network Address Translation (NAT)*, a service that allows multiple LAN clients to share a single public IP address and Internet connection.

Installing RRAS

The RRAS components are installed on computers running Windows Server 2003 whether or not you choose to activate them. Before your server will be able to route IP packets, you have to activate and configure RRAS. This process is normally handled through the RRAS Setup Wizard. Exercise 9.1 leads you through the process of installing Routing and Remote Access Services as a router.

EXERCISE 9.1

Installing the Routing and Remote Access Services for IP Routing

1. Open the RRAS MMC console by selecting Start ➢ Administrative Tools ➢ Routing And Remote Access.

2. Select the server you want to configure in the left pane of the MMC. Right-click the server and choose Configure And Enable Routing And Remote Access. The Routing And Remote Access Server Setup Wizard appears. Click the Next button.

3. In the Configuration dialog box, ensure that the Secure Connection Between Two Private Networks radio button is selected and then click the Next button.

4. The Demand-Dial Connections page appears. It's only there to ask if you want to use demand-dialed connections or not; you still have to set the connections up (either manually or using the Demand-Dial Wizard) after you complete the RRAS Setup Wizard. Select Yes to use demand-dial connections. Click Next to continue.

5. On the IP Address Assignment page, you can choose how RRAS assigns IP addresses to incoming demand-dial calls. If you want to use DHCP (either a DHCP server on your network or the built-in address allocator), leave the Automatically radio button selected. If you want to pick out an address range, select the From A Specified Range Of Addresses button. Click the Next button.

6. If you chose to manually pass out IP addresses, the next page that appears is the Address Range Assignment page. You use this page to specify which IP address ranges you want handed out to incoming calls (whether demand-dial or from remote access users). Use the New, Edit, and Delete buttons to specify the address ranges you want to use and then click the Next button.

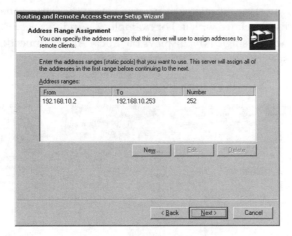

7. Click the Finish button on the Summary page to close the wizard. If you chose to create a demand-dial interface, the Demand-Dial Interface Wizard appears automatically. Leave the computer in its current state because the next exercise in this chapter will walk you through the Demand-Dial Interface Wizard.

Configuring IP Routing

When the summary page of the RRAS Setup Wizard appears, it's going to remind you to do either two or three of the following things, depending on whether or not you chose to use demand-dial connections:

- Add demand-dial interfaces if you want to support demand dialing.

- Give each routable interface a network address for each protocol it carries. For example, if you're using TCP/IP and IPX on a computer with three NICs, each NIC that participates in routing needs to have distinct TCP/IP and IPX addresses.

- Install and configure the routing protocols (e.g., OSPF or RIP for IP in this case) on the interfaces that should support them.

These three steps form the core of what you must do to make your RRAS server into an IP router. You begin by examining how RRAS treats LAN, demand-dial, RIP, and OSPF interfaces. Next, we'll look at how to configure properties that affect RRAS in general, such as error logging and route preferences. You'll also learn how to install and configure the RIP and OSPF protocols. Finally, you'll see how to manage static routes with the route command.

Creating and Managing Interfaces

The Network Interfaces node in the RRAS snap-in (shown in Figure 9.5) shows you a summary of the routable interfaces available on your machine for *all* protocols. It lists all of the LAN and demand-dial interfaces, plus two special interfaces maintained by RRAS: loopback and internal. Each of the interfaces displayed has a type, a status (either enabled or disabled), and a connection status associated with it. For example, a Windows Server 2003 machine in the default configuration with a single NIC displays the Local Area Connection interface. Each of those interfaces represents a potential destination for routed packets.

FIGURE 9.5   The Network Interfaces node

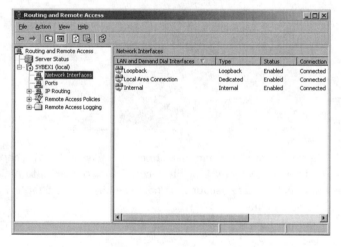

You can right-click each interface to get a pop-up menu with some useful commands, including Disable, Enable, and Unreachability Reason (which tells you why an interface is marked as "unreachable"). There are some commands specific to demand-dial interfaces, which will be covered in the following sections.

What "Unreachable" Really Means

A demand-dial interface can have several different states. First, the enabled and disabled states that appear in the Status column indicate whether the link is administratively available—that is, whether you're allowing people to use it or not. The Connection State column shows you whether the connection is *working* or not, which makes it more useful. The default state for a demand-dial connection is disconnected, which is perfectly reasonable. When RRAS tries to establish a connection, the state changes to connected—also eminently logical. In both the connected and disconnected states, any static routes tied to the demand-dial interface are available.

When RRAS tries to dial a number and fails to connect, it will continue to try until it reaches the redial limit set in the Dialing tab of the interface's Properties dialog box. If the redial limit is reached, the interface will be marked as Unreachable for a time-out period. As long as the interface is unreachable, any static routes pointing to it will be unavailable—they'll actually disappear from the routing table. After the time-out period, RRAS will try again to dial; if it fails this time, it tacks another 10 minutes onto the time-out and tries again. The time-out starts at 10 minutes and works up from there; if it reaches 6 hours, the counter will stop incrementing so the time-out will stay there until a successful connection is made or until you restart the RRAS service.

Fortunately, you can adjust both the minimum and maximum values for this time-out from their defaults (10 minutes and 6 hours, respectively). You make this change by adding two REG_DWORD values to HKLM\System\CurrentControlSet\Services\Router\Interfaces*Interface-Name* (where *InterfaceName* matches the name of the interface for which you want to change the time). The MinUnreachabilityInterval value controls both the minimum retry interval *and* how much the retry interval is incremented after each failure; the MaxUnreachabilityInterval sets the upper limit. Both of these values must be expressed in seconds.

Managing LAN Interfaces

Each LAN interface has properties of its own. These interfaces, which appear when you select the General node under the IP Routing node in RRAS, correspond to the LAN interfaces you've defined in RRAS. You can set general properties for the interfaces; once you add specific routing protocols to the interfaces, you can configure those protocols individually (as you'll see in a short while). To see the properties for an interface, just select the General node in the console, click the interface of interest in the right-hand pane, and select Action ➤ Properties, which brings up the Local Area Connection Properties dialog box.

In the following sections, we'll look at the various configuration options that are available for LAN interfaces.

The General Tab

The General tab (Figure 9.6) allows you to set some useful parameters for the entire interface, including whether or not this interface will send out router discovery advertisements so that other routers on your network can find it.

The controls on the General tab do the following:

- The Enable IP Router Manager checkbox controls whether this interface allows IP routing at all. When it's checked, the administrative status of this interface will appear as "Up," indicating that it's available for routing traffic. When it's unchecked, the interface will be marked as "Down," and it won't route any packets, nor will other routers be able to communicate with it.

FIGURE 9.6 The General tab of the Local Area Connection Properties dialog box

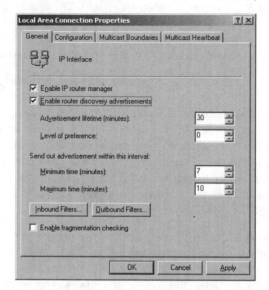

- The Enable Router Discovery Advertisements checkbox controls whether or not this router will broadcast *router discovery messages*. These messages allow clients to find a "nearby" (in network terms) router without any manual configuration on your part. When this checkbox is enabled, the controls below it become active so you can set the following properties:
  - How long advertisements are valid, in the Advertisement Lifetime (Minutes) field. Clients will ignore any advertisement they receive after its lifetime has expired.
  - What preference level is assigned to this particular router, in the Level Of Preference field. Clients use routers with higher preferences first; if there's more than one router with equal preference levels, the client can randomly select one.
  - The minimum and maximum time intervals for sending advertisements. RRAS will send out advertisements at a randomly chosen interval that falls between the minimum and maximum; with the default settings, that means RRAS will send an advertisement every 7 to 10 minutes.
- The Inbound Filters and Outbound Filters buttons allow you to selectively accept or reject packets on the specified interface. You can accept all packets that don't trigger a filter or accept only those packets that match filter criteria. Each type of filter can use the source or destination IP address and net mask as filter criteria. For example, you can construct a filter that rejects all packets from 206.151.234.0 with a net mask of 255.255.255.0; that effectively screens out any traffic from that subnet.
- The Enable Fragmentation Checking checkbox tells your router to reject any fragmented IP packets instead of accepting them for processing. Because flooding a router with fragmented IP packets is a popular denial of service attack, you may want to check this box.

The Configuration Tab

The Configuration tab (Figure 9.7) may seem out of place in the Local Area Connection Properties dialog box because it essentially duplicates what you see when you edit the properties of a LAN interface from the Network and Dial-Up Connections folder. You use this tab to set the IP address, subnet mask, and default gateway for an interface if you want it to use a different set of parameters than the ones defined for the interface. The Advanced button allows you to specify multiple IP addresses and default gateways, just as the TCP/IP Properties dialog box does.

FIGURE 9.7   The Configuration tab of the Local Area Connection Properties dialog box

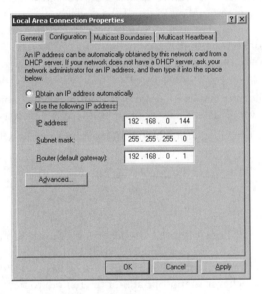

Setting Up Demand-Dial Interfaces

When you install RRAS, it will automatically create an interface for each LAN connection it can find. If you want to create new demand-dial interfaces, you'll have to do it yourself. Fortunately, there's an easy way to do this with the Demand-Dial Interface Wizard, which you activate with the New Demand-Dial Interface command (available when you right-click the Network Interfaces node in the RRAS console).

In the following sections, we will look at the separate steps involved in setting up demand-dial interfaces.

Naming the Interface

The first page in the wizard is the Interface Name page, where you specify the name you want the new interface to have. This is the name you'll see in the RRAS console, so you should choose some name that identifies the source and destination of the connection (for example, HSV-ATL for a connection between Huntsville and Atlanta). This is particularly useful when you want to use one RRAS console somewhere on a network to manage many RRAS servers—having an easy way to see which link you're working with can be very valuable.

Choosing a Connection Type

The Connection Type page of the wizard allows you to specify which type of demand-dial interface you will create. Demand-dial interfaces can use a physical device (like a modem or an ISDN adapter) or a virtual private network (VPN) connection. For example, you can have a demand-dial connection that opens a VPN tunnel to a remote network when it sees traffic destined for that network. Depending on which option you choose here, the remaining wizard pages will differ.

Assuming you choose to use a physical device as the basis for your network, the Select A Device page of the wizard prompts you to choose a device (like a modem or ISDN terminal adapter) to use for this demand-dial interface. If the device you want to use doesn't already exist, you'll need to add it; for that reason, you're probably better off adding and configuring modems and so on before setting up RRAS.

If you specify that you want to use a VPN connection, you'll see the VPN Type page, where you can specify what type of VPN connection to use. You have the following three choices:

- The Automatic radio button tells RRAS to figure out the connection type when negotiating with the remote server. This is the most flexible choice, so it's selected by default.

- The Point-To-Point Tunneling Protocol (PPTP) radio button tells RRAS that this connection will always use PPTP.

- Likewise, the Layer 2 Tunneling Protocol (L2TP) radio button indicates that you want this connection to always use L2TP.

Determining Who to Call

The next step is the same for both VPN and physical connections, even though the wizard page is labeled differently. For VPNs, you'll see the Network Address page, and for ordinary dial-up connections, the page is labeled Phone Number. In either case, you should enter the phone number or IP address (whichever is appropriate) of the remote router.

Setting Routing and Security Options

The next page is the Protocols And Security page (Figure 9.8), which contains four configuration checkboxes:

- The Route IP Packets On This Interface and Route IPX Packets On This Interface checkboxes control whether this interface will handle the specified packet types or not. By default, IP routing is enabled but IPX routing isn't.

- If you want to add a user account so that a remote router (running RRAS or not) can dial in, check the Add A User Account So A Remote Router Can Dial In checkbox.

- Some routers can handle Password Authentication Protocol (PAP), Challenge Handshake Authentication Protocol (CHAP), or Microsoft Challenge Handshake Authentication Protocol (MS-CHAP) authentication, but others can only handle PAP. If your remote partner falls into this latter group, make sure that Send A Plain-Text Password If That Is The Only Way To Connect is checked.

- If the system that your RRAS server is calling isn't running RRAS, it may expect you to manually interact with it, perhaps through a terminal window. This is what the last checkbox, Use Scripting To Complete The Connection With The Remote Router, is for—check it and you'll get a terminal window after the modem connects so you can provide whatever commands or authenticators you need.

FIGURE 9.8   The Protocols and Security page

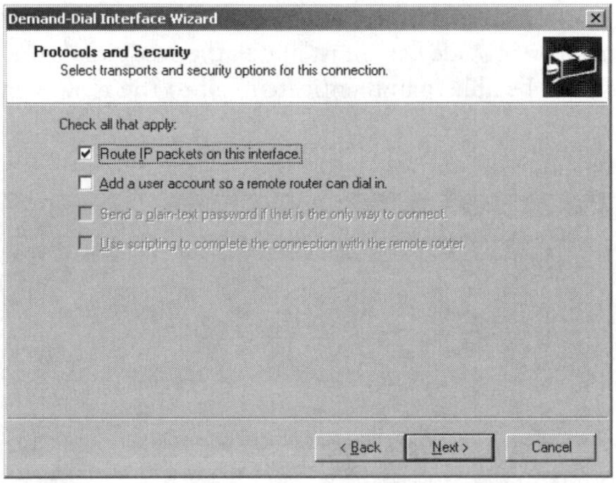

Setting Dial-In Credentials

If you choose to allow remote routers to dial in to the RRAS machine you're setting up, you'll have to create a user account with appropriate permissions. The Demand-Dial Interface Wizard handles the account creation process for you, assuming you fill out the Dial In Credentials page (Figure 9.9).

FIGURE 9.9   The Dial In Credentials page

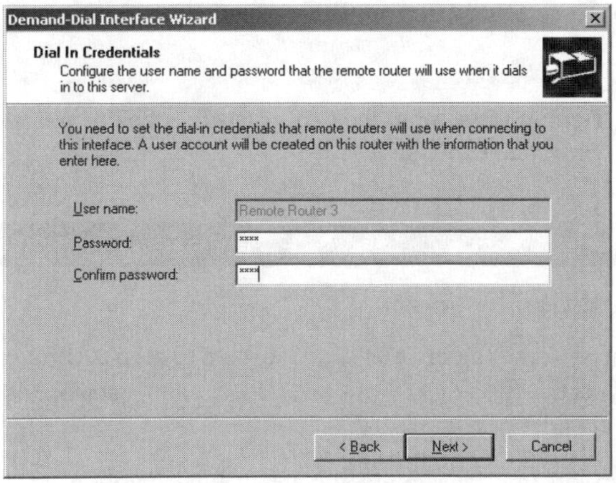

Microsoft recommends that you pick a username that makes it evident which routers use the link; in this case, HSV-MCO tells you right away that this account is used for the Huntsville-Orlando link. You can use ICAO airport identifiers, city names, or whatever else you like.

Setting Dial-Out Credentials

If you want your router to initiate calls to another router, you'll need to tell your local RRAS installation what credentials to use when it makes an outgoing call. Although RRAS uses the information you enter in the Dial In Credentials page, it makes no attempt to do anything with the credentials you provide on the Dial Out Credentials page (Figure 9.10). (Actually, it does check the two password fields to make sure you've typed the same password into each one, but that's it.) The credentials you provide here must match the credentials the remote router expects to see or your router won't be able to authenticate itself to the remote end.

FIGURE 9.10 The Dial Out Credentials page

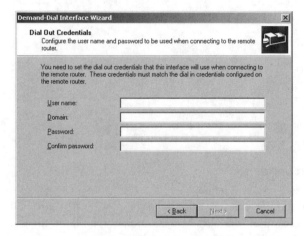

In Exercise 9.2 you will continue from the previous exercise with the Demand-Dial Interface Wizard. In this exercise, you'll create a simple demand-dial interface. This requires you to have the phone number, username, and password for the remote end as well as demand-dial capable device installed in the machine.

 The Demand-Dial Interface Wizard automatically appears immediately after you complete Exercise 9.1.

EXERCISE 9.2

Creating a Demand-Dial Interface

1. If you are continuing from the previous exercise, skip to step 3. Otherwise, open the RRAS MMC console, select the server you want to create the interface on, and select its Network Interfaces node.

2. Right-click the Network Interfaces node and select New Demand Dial Interface. This starts the Demand-Dial Interface Wizard.

3. Click the Next button on the Welcome page (and after each of the subsequent steps). Specify a name for the interface on the Interface Name page.

4. The Connection Type dialog page will appear. Select the Connect Using A Modem, ISDN Adapter, Or Other Physical Device radio button on the Connection Type page if you have one of these devices installed. Select the Connect Using Virtual Private Networking (VPN) radio button if you want to connect to the remote router via a VPN interface. Alternately, you can choose to connect through a Point to Point over Ethernet (PPPoE) connection. For the rest of this exercise we will assume that you chose the first option.

5. Select your device from the list of devices that appears on the Select A Device page.

6. On the Protocols And Security page, make sure the Route IP Packets On This Interface checkbox is the only one selected.

7. If you have not defined any static routes yet, you will be asked to do so before you can activate the demand-dial connection. On the Static Routes For Remote Networks page, click the Add button and enter the IP address, subnet mask, and metric of the remote router. Click OK when you're done. You will notice the new static route in the list.

8. In the Dial Out Credentials page, fill in the username, domain (if any), and password needed to connect to the remote network.

9. When the wizard summary page appears, click the Finish button to create the interface.

Creating and Removing RIP or OSPF Interfaces

After you create the physical interfaces (using either demand-dial or LAN interfaces), the next thing you have to do is create an interface for the routing protocol you want to use. You do this by right-clicking either the RIP or OSPF nodes in the RRAS console (which appear after you install the routing protocols, as shown a little later in the section "Managing Routing Protocols") and choosing New Interface. That displays the New Interface dialog box, which lists all the physical interfaces that are available for the selected protocol. For example, if you have two NICs in a computer and have already bound RIP to both of them, you can add OSPF to either or both, but when you try to add another RIP interface, you'll get an error message.

Once you select the interface you want to use and if RRAS can create the interface, it adds the interface to the appropriate item in the console and opens the corresponding Properties dialog box.

You can remove a RIP or OSPF interface by selecting it in the appropriate folder and pressing the Delete key, by selecting Action ➤ Delete, or by choosing Delete from the pop-up menu.

Setting RIP Interface Properties

RIP interfaces have their own properties, all of which are specific to the RIP. You adjust these settings by selecting the RIP node, clicking the appropriate RIP interface in the right window pane, and selecting Properties from the pop-up or Action menus.

Now let's take a look at the various options available in a RIP interface's Properties dialog box.

The General Tab

The General tab of the RIP interface Properties dialog box (Figure 9.11) lets you control the router's operational mode, which protocols it uses to send and accept packets, and a couple of other useful things.

FIGURE 9.11 The General tab of the RIP interface Properties dialog box

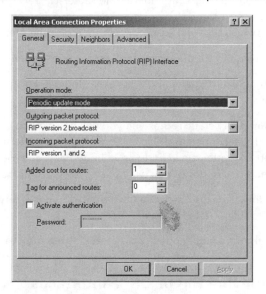

Here's what you can do with the General tab:

- The Operation Mode drop-down list controls the router's mode. By default, demand-dial interfaces will be set to Auto-Static Update Mode, while LAN interfaces will be set to Periodic Update Mode.

- The Outgoing Packet Protocol drop-down list controls what kind of RIP packets this router sends out. If your network has all RIPv2 routers, choose RIP Version 2 Multicast to make RRAS send out efficient RIP multicasts; if you have a version 1 or a mix of version 1 and version 2, there are selections for those, too. The fourth choice, Silent RIP, is useful when you want your RRAS router to listen to other routers' routes but not advertise any of its own. Typically, you'll use Silent RIP when you're using RRAS to connect a small network (like a branch office) that doesn't have any other routers to a larger network—the small network doesn't have any routes to advertise because it's connected to only one remote network.

- Use the Incoming Packet Protocol drop-down list to specify what kinds of RIP packets this interface will accept. You can choose to accept only RIP version 1 packets, only RIP version 2 packets, both version 1 and version 2 packets, or none at all. The default setting is to accept both version 1 and version 2 packets.

- The Added Cost For Routes field lets you control how much this router will increase the route cost. Normally, it's best to leave this as 1 because setting it too high may increase the interface's cost so much that no one uses it.

- The Tag For Announced Routes field gives you a way to supply a tag included in all RIP packets sent by this router. RRAS doesn't use RIP tags, but other routers can use them.

- The Activate Authentication checkbox and Password field give you an identification tool for use with your routers. If you turn on authentication, all incoming and outgoing RIP packets must contain the specified password. Therefore, all of this router's neighbors need to use the same password. The password is transmitted as cleartext, so this option doesn't provide you with any security.

The Security Tab

The Security tab (see Figure 9.12) helps you regulate which routes your RIP interface will accept from and broadcast to its peers. There are good reasons to be careful about which routes you accept into your routing table because a malicious attacker can simply flood your router with bogus routes and watch, laughing, as your routers send traffic off on a wild goose chase. Likewise, you may not want to advertise every route in your routing table, particularly if the same routers handle both Internet and intranet traffic. You can use the controls on this tab to discard routes that fall within a particular range of addresses, or you can accept only those routes that fall within a particular range.

FIGURE 9.12   The Security tab of the RIP interface Properties dialog box

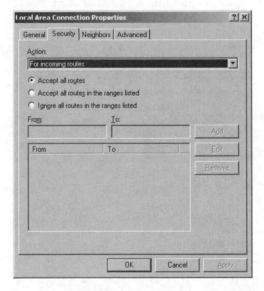

The default setting is to accept all routes, but you can change it using these controls:

- The Action drop-down list lets you choose whether you want to impose settings on incoming routes that your router hears from its peers or on outgoing routes that it announces. Depending on which of these options you choose, the wording of the three radio buttons below the drop-down will change.

- The From and To fields, the Add, Edit, and Remove buttons, and the address range list are all used to specify which set of addresses you want to use with the restriction radio buttons.

- The restriction radio buttons in the center of the dialog box control the action applied to incoming or outgoing routes:

    - The default setting, Announce All Routes (for outgoing routes) or Process All Routes (for incoming routes) does just that—all routes are accepted or announced, no matter the source.

    - Selecting Announce All Routes In The Ranges Listed (outgoing) or Accept All Routes In The Range Listed (incoming) causes RRAS to silently ignore any routes that fall outside of the specified ranges. You normally use this option when you want to limit the scope of routes over which your router can exchange traffic.

    - The Do Not Announce All Routes In The Range Listed (outgoing) and Ignore All Routes In The Ranges Listed (incoming) settings tells RRAS to silently ignore any routes that fall within the specified ranges. This is useful for filtering out routes that you don't want to make available or those you don't want to use to reach remote systems.

The Neighbors Tab

The Neighbors tab (Figure 9.13) gives you a finer degree of control over how this particular interface interacts with its peer RIP routers. By specifying a list of trusted neighbor routers (an OSPF concept that Microsoft's mixed in to its RIP implementation), you can choose to use neighboring routers' routes in addition to, or instead of, broadcast and multicast RIP announcements.

FIGURE 9.13   The Neighbors tab of the RIP interface Properties dialog box

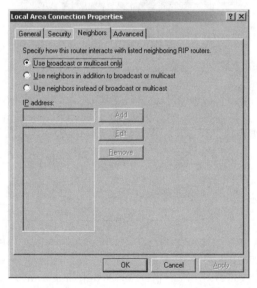

You will see the following radio buttons on the Neighbors tab:

- The Use Broadcast Or Multicast Only radio button tells RRAS to ignore any RIP neighbors. This is the default setting. It means that any router that can successfully broadcast or multicast routes to you can load its routes into your routing table.

- The Use Neighbors In Addition To Broadcast Or Multicast radio button tells RRAS to accept routes from RIP peers as well as from the neighbors you've specified.

- The Use Neighbors Instead Of Broadcast Or Multicast radio button indicates that you don't trust RIP announcements that your router picks up from the network; instead, you're telling RRAS to trust only those neighbors that are defined in the neighbor list.

You manage the list of trusted neighbor routers using the IP Address field, the Add, Edit, and Remove buttons, and the list itself. These controls are enabled when you specify that you want to use neighbor-supplied routing information; once the controls are activated, you can add router IP addresses to the neighbor list.

The Advanced Tab

The Advanced tab (Figure 9.14) contains 12 controls that govern some fairly esoteric RIP behavior.

FIGURE 9.14   The Advanced tab of the RIP interface Properties dialog box

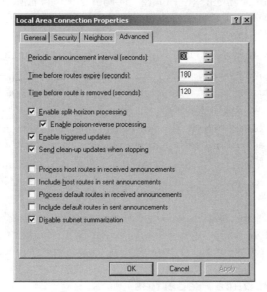

The first three controls are only active when you turn on Periodic Update Mode on the General tab:

- The Periodic Announcement Interval (Seconds) field controls the interval at which periodic router announcements are made.

- The Time Before Routes Expire (Seconds) field controls how long the route may stay in the routing table before it's considered to be expired. The arrival of a new RIP announcement for the route resets the timer—it will be marked as invalid only if it reaches the expiration timer without being renewed through a new announcement.

- The Time Before Route Is Removed (Seconds) field controls the interval that may pass between the time a route expires and the time it's removed.

The next group of checkboxes controls update processing and loop detection:

- The Enable Split-Horizon Processing checkbox turns on split-horizon processing, in which a route learned by a RIP router on a network is not rebroadcast to that network. Split-horizon processing helps prevent routing loops, so it's on by default.

  - The Enable Poison-Reverse Processing checkbox (which is active only when the Enable Split-Horizon Processing checkbox is on) modifies the way split-horizon processing works. When poison-reverse is turned on, routes learned from a network are rebroadcast to the network with a metric of 16, a special value that tells other routers that the route is unreachable. It also prevents routing loops while still keeping the routing tables up-to-date.

- The Enable Triggered Updates checkbox indicates whether you want routing table changes to be immediately sent out when they're noticed (the default) or not. Triggered updates help keep the routing table up-to-date with minimum latency.

- The Send Clean-Up Updates When Stopping checkbox controls whether or not RRAS will send out announcements that mark the routes it was handling as unavailable. This immediately lets its RIP peers know that the routes it was servicing are no longer usable.

The last set of controls governs what happens with host and default routes:

- By default, RRAS ignores any host routes it sees in RIP announcements. Turn on the Process Host Routes In Received Announcements checkbox if you want it to honor those routes instead of ignoring them.

- The Include Host Routes In Sent Announcements checkbox directs RRAS to send host route information as part of its RIP announcements; normally it won't do this.

- The Process Default Routes In Received Announcements and Include Default Routes In Sent Announcements checkboxes have the same function as their host route checkboxes described earlier.

- The Disable Subnet Summarization checkbox is active only if you have RIP version 2 specified as the outbound packet type for the router. When subnet summarization is turned off, RIP won't advertise subnets to routers that are on other subnets.

Setting OSPF Interface Properties

OSPF has its own set of properties that you can set on OSPF-enabled interfaces. Setting these properties is both simpler and more complex than RIP—simpler because there aren't as many of them because OSPF is largely self-tuning, but the properties you *can* set tend to be somewhat more abstruse. You open an OSPF interface's Properties dialog box by selecting the OSPF node, clicking the interface in the right window pane, and selecting Properties from the Action menu.

Let's take a look at the options available in an OSPF interface's Properties dialog box.

The General Tab

The General tab (Figure 9.15) of the OSPF Properties dialog box controls, among other things, whether or not OSPF is enabled on a particular interface address.

FIGURE 9.15 The General tab of the OSPF Properties dialog box

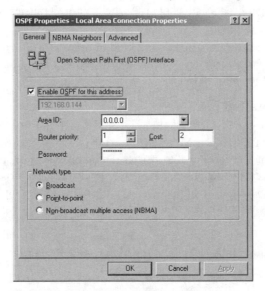

Here's what you can do with the controls on the General tab:

- The Enable OSPF For This Address checkbox, combined with the address drop-down menu, specify whether OSPF is active or not on the *selected* address. Because a single interface can have multiple IP addresses, you use this checkbox and drop-down to specify which IP addresses are OSPF capable. The settings you make in the OSPF Properties dialog box apply to the IP address you select here.

- The Area ID drop-down allows you to select which OSPF area this interface is a part of. There's a simple rule: One IP address can be in one area. If you have multiple IP addresses defined, each one must be in a separate area.

- The Router Priority field controls the priority of this interface relative to other OSPF routers in the same area. OSPF supports the concept of a designated router in an area; that router serves as the default router for the area it's in. The router with the highest priority will become the designated router unless there's already an existing designated router.

- The Cost field controls the metric attached to this router's routes in the link-state database.

- The Password field works just like it does for RIP—all routers within an area can share a common plaintext password for identification. This does nothing for access control (especially since the default password is an easy-to-guess 12345678).

The Network Type controls influence how this router interacts with its peers, but to understand what its controls do you have to know the following:

- A *broadcast router* is one that can talk to any number of other routers—like a typical LAN router, which can see any number of other routers on the LAN.

- A *point-to-point router* is one that has only one peer. For example, a typical Digital Subscriber Line (DSL) installation will have one router on your end and one on the ISP end—that's a point-to-point configuration.

- A *non-broadcast multiple access (NBMA) router* is a single router that can talk to multiple peers without using a broadcast, as in an Asynchronous Transfer Mode (ATM) or X.25 network.

You use these radio buttons to specify what kind of network your router is participating in. If you set the router to NBMA mode, you can use the NBMA Neighbors tab to specify which routers your NBMA router should talk to.

The NBMA Neighbors Tab

Think back to the description of RIP neighbors; you learned that Microsoft had recycled an OSPF concept for use in RIP. The NBMA Neighbors tab (see Figure 9.16), then, should look like the Neighbors tab of the RIP interface Properties dialog box; as it happens, the two are very similar. The IP Address drop-down list lets you pick the IP address whose neighbors you're configuring. Once you've picked an IP address, you can use the remaining controls in the tab to specify the IP addresses and priorities of the NBMA neighbors you want this router interface to talk to.

FIGURE 9.16 The NBMA Neighbors tab of the OSPF Properties dialog box

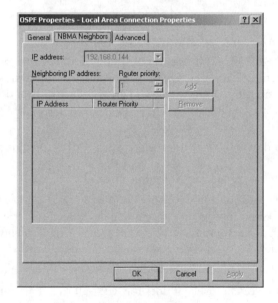

The Advanced Tab

The Advanced tab (shown in Figure 9.17) contains the advanced features of the OSPF Properties dialog box. First, you can choose which IP address you're configuring. Next, you'll need to use the six fields that give you access to some inner OSPF workings.

The six fields of the Advanced tab include the following:

- The Transit Delay (Seconds) field specifies how long you think it will take for a link-state update to propagate outward from this router; this value is used by the OSPF engine to decide how stale route information is when it arrives.

FIGURE 9.17   The Advanced tab of the OSPF Properties dialog box

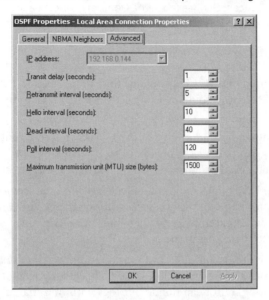

- The Retransmit Interval (Seconds) field is for your best estimate of the round-trip delay required for two routers to communicate—if it takes longer than this interval for a packet to arrive, it will be retransmitted.

- The Hello Interval (Seconds) field controls how often OSPF routers send out "here I am" packets to discover other routers. This value must be the same for all routers on the same network; lowering the interval will speed up the discovery of topology changes at the expense of generating more OSPF traffic.

- The Dead Interval (Seconds) field controls the interval after which a router is marked as "dead" by its peers. Microsoft recommends using an integral multiple of the hello interval for the dead interval; for example, if your hello interval is set to the default of 10 seconds, the default dead interval of 40 seconds will work fine.

- The Poll Interval (Seconds) field controls how long an NBMA router will wait before attempting to contact an apparently dead router to see whether it's really dead or not. This interval should be set to at least twice the dead interval.

- The Maximum Transmission Unit (MTU) Size (Bytes) field regulates how big an OSPF IP packet can be. Your best bet is to leave this value alone.

Setting IP Routing Properties

The IP Routing node in the RRAS console has several subnodes, including the General node. When you click the General node and select Properties from the Action menu, you'll find that there are settings you can change that apply to all installed IP routing protocols on the server. These settings give you some additional control over how routing works.

In the following sections, we'll look at the options in the General Properties dialog box. These options are available for configuring settings that apply to IP routing in general.

The Multicast Scopes tab of the General Properties dialog box is for setting and managing multicast scopes.

The Logging Tab

The Logging tab (shown in Figure 9.18) contains four radio buttons that you use to control what information the IP routing components of RRAS log. These radio buttons include the following:

- The Log Errors Only radio button instructs the server to log IP routing–related errors and nothing else. This gives you adequate indication of problems *after* they happen, but it doesn't point out potential problems noted by warning messages.

- The Log Errors And Warnings radio button is the default choice; it instructs RRAS to log error and warning messages to the event log without adding any informational messages. If you get in the habit of carefully reviewing your event logs, these warning messages may give you welcome forewarning of incipient problems.

- The Log The Maximum Amount Of Information radio button causes the IP routing stack to log messages about almost everything it does. This gives you a lot of useful fodder when you're troubleshooting, but it can flood your logs with minutiae if you're not careful— don't turn it on unless you're trying to isolate and fix a problem.

- The Disable Event Logging radio button turns off all IP routing event logging.

Don't use the Disable Event Logging option because it will keep you from being able to review the service's logs in case of a problem.

FIGURE 9.18 The Logging tab of the General Properties dialog box

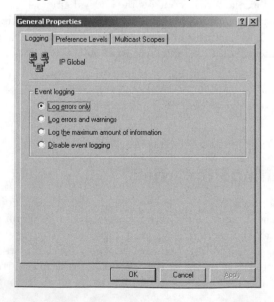

The Preference Levels Tab

The Preference Levels tab (Figure 9.19) gives you a way to change the router's behavior by telling it what class of routes to prefer. In the earlier discussion of routing, you read that the router selects routes based on cost metric information. There's another factor that comes into play: the preference level of the routing source. The default configuration for RRAS causes it to prefer local and static routes over dynamically discovered routes.

FIGURE 9.19   The Preference Levels tab

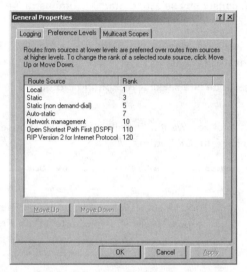

For example, say there are two routing table entries indicating routes to 216.80.*—one that you've entered as a static route and one that your router has discovered via a RIP peer. In this example, the router will always try to use the static route first; if it can't, it will try to use the RIP-generated route. You can change the router's class preference by selecting the class you want to change and using the Move Up and Move Down buttons.

Managing Routing Protocols

Routing protocols typically don't take a lot of management; once you install RIP or OSPF, the protocol engine takes care of exchanging routes with remote routers. Unlike what you may be accustomed to with dedicated routers using a router OS like Cisco's IOS, there's no way to directly edit the contents of the routing table generated by dynamic routing protocols. That means your management of these protocols is pretty much limited to installing them, configuring them to meet your needs, and watching them as they run.

In the following sections, you will examine the details of installing routing protocols and setting routing protocol properties.

Installing RIP and OSPF

You add routing protocols from the General subnode beneath the IP Routing node in RRAS. This is quite different from the way you manage network protocols in Windows NT, but it makes sense—there's no reason to install RIP or OSPF unless you're using RRAS, so it's logical that you would install it from there.

Exercise 9.3 explains how to install the RIP and OSPF protocols; you'll need them installed for the later exercises in the chapter.

EXERCISE 9.3

Installing the RIP and OSPF Protocols

1. Open the RRAS MMC console by selecting Start ➢ Administrative Tools ➢ Routing And Remote Access.

2. Select the server you want to configure in the left pane of the MMC. Expand it until you see the General node beneath IP Routing.

3. Right-click the General node and select New Routing Protocol. The New Routing Protocol dialog box appears.

4. Select the routing protocol you want to install. In this case, choose RIP Version 2 For Internet Protocol and click the OK button.

5. The RRAS console refreshes its display, revealing a new node labeled RIP under the IP Routing node.

6. Right-click the General node and select New Routing Protocol. This time when the New Routing Protocol dialog box appears, select Open Shortest Path First (OSPF) and click the OK button.

Setting RIP Properties

The RIP protocol is pretty much self-tuning. Once you configure a RRAS router to use the RIP protocol, it will look for peer routers, and exchange routing information without a whole lot of effort on your part. There is a small group of settings you can change through the RIP Properties dialog box (which you open by selecting the RIP node under IP Routing in the RRAS console and then choosing Action ➢ Properties).

We will look at the various tabs of the RIP Properties dialog box in the following sections.

The General Tab

The General tab (Figure 9.20) has the same logging controls you saw on the General tab of the IP Routing Properties dialog box. The Maximum Delay (Seconds) control governs how long the router will wait to send an update notification to its peers.

The Security Tab

The Security tab (Figure 9.21) lets you control what router announcements your router will accept. By default, the RRAS RIP implementation will ingest routes supplied by any other router; you can restrict this behavior by supplying either a list of routers to trust or a list of routers whose routes you want to reject.

FIGURE 9.20   The General tab of the RIP Properties dialog box

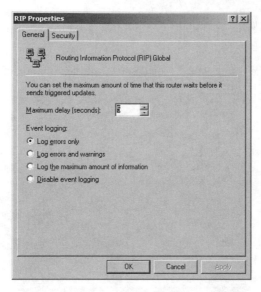

FIGURE 9.21   The Security tab of the RIP Properties dialog box

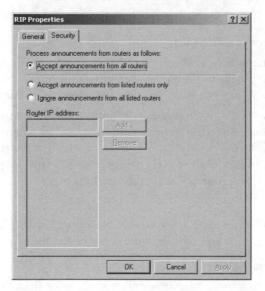

Setting OSPF Properties

You can also set some OSPF-specific properties by selecting the OSPF node under the IP Routing item in the RRAS console and opening the OSPF Properties dialog box.

The General Tab

The General tab of the OSPF Properties dialog box (Figure 9.22) contains the logging controls that you've already seen twice in this chapter, plus two additional controls that you'll probably have occasion to use.

FIGURE 9.22 The General tab of the OSPF Properties dialog box

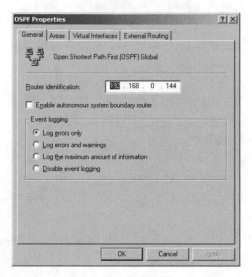

These controls include the following:

- The Router Identification field allows you to enter an IP address that your router uses to identify itself. Although it's not a good idea to assign a bogus IP address as your router's identifier, you may want to choose the public IP address, even for internal interfaces.

- The Enable Autonomous System Boundary Router checkbox controls whether or not your OSPF router will advertise routes it finds from other sources (including its static routes and routes it learns via RIP) to the outside world. The External Routing tab won't be enabled unless you check this box; check it only if you want this particular RRAS router to try to exchange OSPF routing information with its peers.

The Areas Tab

The Areas tab lists the OSPF areas that your router knows about. You can add, edit, or remove areas from the list using the corresponding buttons below the list box.

The Virtual Interfaces Tab

The Virtual Interfaces tab is used to create and edit virtual links. Recall that OSPF conceptually divides networks into areas, some of which may be part of the backbone and some of which aren't. Because a non-backbone router won't be connected to the backbone, there has to be some other way to allow backbone and non-backbone routers to share routing information. A virtual link connects a backbone area border router and a non-backbone area border router. Once the link is created, the two routers can share routing information just as though they were connected to the same physical network.

The External Routing Tab

The External Routing tab (Figure 9.23) allows you to control which additional routing sources the OSPF components will use. OSPF isn't the only potential source for routing information—your router can acquire routes from a number of other sources. You might not want all of those routes to be accepted and used, though.

FIGURE 9.23   The External Routing tab of the OSPF Properties dialog box

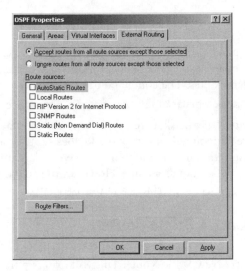

You can use the two radio buttons at the top, Accept Routes From All Route Sources Except Those Selected and Ignore Routes From All Route Sources Except Those Selected, to control the meaning of the checkboxes in the Route Sources list. By default, OSPF will accept all routes from all sources. To turn off individual route sources (for instance, static routes), check the appropriate box. If you want to reject all route sources *except* for a particular group, use the Ignore Routes From All Route Sources Except Those Selected radio button and then check the route sources you do want to use.

The External Routing tab will be active only if you check the Enable Autonomous System Boundary Router checkbox on the General tab.

The Route Filters button allows you to either ignore or accept individual routes. This is a handy way to screen out particular routes that you don't want without disallowing entire classes of route source information.

Managing Static Routes

Static routes are simple to manage and configure because they don't participate in any kind of automatic discovery process. Static routes are conceptually very simple—they combine a destination network address with a subnet mask to provide a list of potential destinations.

The destination addresses are reached through a particular interface on your router, and they're sent to a specified gateway (normally another router, either on your end or on some remote network). Finally, there's a metric associated with the static route.

You create new static routes in two ways: by using the `route add` command from the command line or by right-clicking the Static Routes node in the RRAS console and selecting New Static Route.

In the following sections, we'll take a look at how those methods work.

Using *route add* to Create a Static Route

With the `route add` command, you can add new static routes; you can choose whether these routes remain in the routing table after the system reboots. Routes that stick around in this manner are called persistent routes. The command itself is simple:

```
route add destination mask netMask gateWay metric interface
```

You specify the destination, net mask, gateway, metric, and interface name on the command line. These parameters are all required, and `route add` does some basic checking to make sure that the net mask and destination match and that you haven't left anything out. You have to specify the interface as a number, not as a name. However, the `route print` command (which will be covered a little later) lists its interfaces and the associated numbers.

Using RRAS to Create a Static Route

To create a new static route using the RRAS console, right-click the Static Routes node in the RRAS console and select New Static Route. This will bring up the Static Route dialog box (Figure 9.24).

FIGURE 9.24   Use the Static Route dialog box to create new static routes.

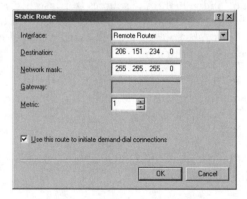

You have to provide the same parameters as with the `route add` command—the interface you want to use to connect, the destination and network mask, the gateway for the outbound packets, and a metric. If you're creating a route that's not bound to a LAN interface, you can also use the Use This Route To Initiate Demand-Dial Connections checkbox to specify that the route should bring up a new demand-dial connection on the specified interface.

Exercise 9.4 shows you how to add and remove static routes.

Adding and Removing Static Routes

1. Open the RRAS MMC console by selecting Start ➢ Administrative Tools ➢ Routing And Remote Access.

2. Select the server you want to configure in the left pane of the MMC. Expand it until you see the Static Routes node beneath IP Routing.

3. Right-click the Static Routes node and select New Static Route. The Static Route dialog box appears.

4. Select the interface you want to use from the Interface drop-down list; you can use the internal interface or any other interface you've already defined.

5. Enter the destination address (try 216.92.80.0) and a net mask of 255.255.255.0.

6. For the gateway address, enter the IP address of your RRAS server.

7. Click the OK button. The RRAS console reappears.

8. Right-click the Static Routes item and choose Show IP Routing Table. The IP Routing Table window appears. Verify that your newly added static route is present in the table.

9. Select the Static Routes item. Note that the right pane of the MMC changes to list all static routes that you've defined. Compare the list with the contents of the IP Routing Table window.

10. Right-click the static route you added and use the Delete command to remove it.

Configuring TCP/IP Packet Filters

One of the most useful features in RRAS is its ability to selectively filter TCP/IP packets in both directions. You can construct filters that allow or deny traffic into or out of your network based on rules that specify source and destination addresses and ports. The basic idea behind packet filtering is simple: You specify filter rules and incoming packets are measured against those rules. You have two choices: Accept all packets except those prohibited by a rule or drop all packets except those permitted by a rule.

Filters are normally used to block out undesirable traffic. In general, the idea is to keep out packets that your machines shouldn't see. For example, you could configure a packet filter that would block all packets to a web server except those on TCP ports 80 and 443.

On the other hand, you could just as easily create a filter that blocks all outgoing packets on the ports used by the MSN and AOL instant messaging tools. Another example (and one that might be more helpful) is the use of filters for a PPTP or L2TP server; these filters screen out everything except VPN traffic so that you can expose a Windows Server 2003 VPN server without fear of compromise.

Filters are associated with a particular interface; the filters assigned to one interface are totally independent of those on all other interfaces, and inbound and outbound filters are likewise separate. You create and remove filters by using the Input Packet Filters and Output Packet Filters buttons on the General tab of the Local Area Network Properties dialog box (refer back to Figure 9.6). The mechanics of working with the filters are identical; just remember that you create inbound filters to screen traffic coming to the interface and outbound filters to screen traffic going back out through that interface.

To create a filter, find the interface on which you want the filter and then open its Properties dialog box. Click the appropriate packet filter button and you'll see the Inbound Filter dialog box (Figure 9.25).

FIGURE 9.25 The Inbound Filters dialog box

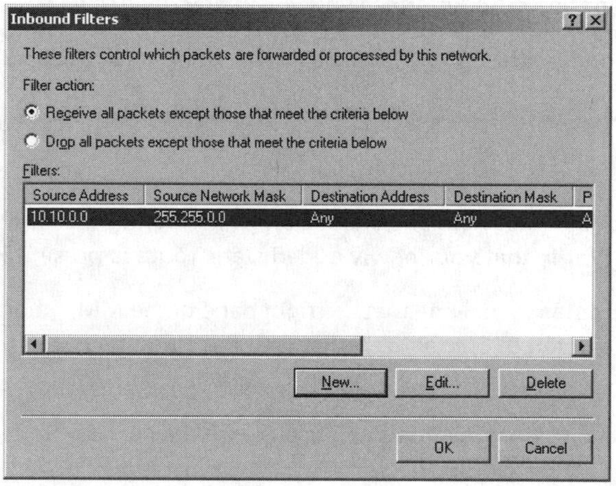

This dialog box has the following six salient parts:

- The Receive All Packets Except Those That Meet The Criteria Below and the Drop All Packets Except Those That Meet The Criteria Below radio buttons control what this filter does. To make a filter that excludes only those packets you specify, select the Receive All Packets Except Those That Meet The Criteria Below radio button. To do the opposite, and accept only those packets that meet your rule, select the Drop All Packets Except Those That Meet The Criteria Below radio button. Note that these buttons will be inactive until you create a filter rule.

- The Filters list, which is initially empty, shows you which filters are defined on this interface. Each filter's entry in the list shows you the source address and mask, the destination address and mask, and the protocol, port, and traffic type specified in the rule.

- You can add, edit, and remove filters using the New, Edit, and Delete buttons.

To create a filter, click the New button and you'll see the Add IP Filter dialog box (Figure 9.26). The conditions you specify here must *all* be true to trigger the rule. For example, if you specify both the source and destination addresses, only traffic from the defined source to the defined destination will be filtered.

FIGURE 9.26   The Add IP Filter dialog box

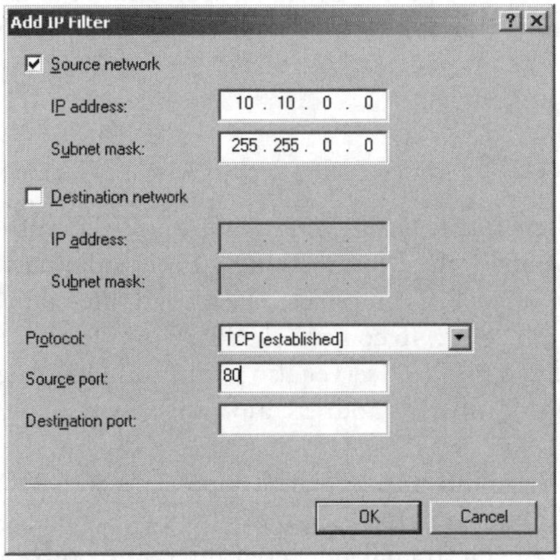

Follow these steps to fill out the Add IP Filter dialog box:

- To create a filter that blocks packets by their origin or source address, check the Source Network checkbox and supply the IP address and subnet mask for the source you want to block.

- To create a filter that blocks according to destination, check the Destination Network checkbox and fill in the appropriate address and subnet mask.

- To filter by protocol, choose the protocol you want to block:

  - Any, which blocks everything

  - TCP

  - TCP (established)

  - IP

  - UDP

  - ICMP

  - Other, with a fill-in field for the protocol

For each of these protocols, you'll have to enter some additional information; for example, if you select TCP, you have to specify the source or destination port numbers (or both), whereas for Other, you'll have to enter a protocol number (more on that in Exercise 9.5).

Once you've specified the filter you want, click the OK button and you'll see it in the filter list. Filters go into effect as soon as you close the interface's Properties dialog box; you can always go back and add, edit, or remove filters at any time.

Configuring VPN Packet Filters

Packet filters provide a useful security mechanism for blocking unwanted traffic on particular machines. It's a good idea to use packet filters to keep non-VPN traffic out of your VPN servers. The rules for doing this are fairly straightforward, as you will see in the following sections.

PPTP Packet Filters

You need at least two filters to adequately screen out non-PPTP traffic. The first filter allows traffic with a protocol ID of 47, the Generic Routing Encapsulation (GRE) protocol, to pass to the destination address of the PPTP interface. The second filter allows inbound traffic bound for TCP port 1723 (the PPTP port) to come to the PPTP interface.

You can add a third filter if the PPTP server also works as a PPTP client; in that case, the third filter needs the interface's destination address, a protocol type of TCP (established), and a source port of 1723.

Once you've created these filters, select the Drop All Packets Except Those That Meet The Criteria Below radio button in the Inbound Filters dialog box and close it. You have to repeat the process on the Outbound side, creating two or three corresponding output filters that screen out any traffic not originating from the VPN interface and using the correct protocols.

In Exercise 9.5, you'll set up RRAS IP packet filters that block everything except PPTP traffic on the specified interface.

WARNING   Don't attempt this on your production VPN server until you've been successful in trying it on another, less-critical machine.

EXERCISE 9.5

Configure PPTP Packet Filters

1.   Open the RRAS console by selecting Start ➢ Administrative Tools ➢ Routing And Remote Access and expand the server and IP Routing nodes to expose the General node of the server you're working on. Select the General node.

2.   Right-click the appropriate interface and choose Properties.

3.   In the General tab of the interface Properties dialog box, click the Inbound Filters button. The Inbound Filters dialog box appears.

4.   Click the New button and the Add IP Filter dialog box appears.

5. Fill out the Add IP Filter dialog box as follows:

    ▪   Check the Destination Network checkbox.

    ▪   Fill in the destination IP address field with the IP address of the remote VPN interface.

    ▪   Supply a destination subnet mask of 255.255.255.255.

    ▪   Select a protocol type of TCP and then specify a source port of 0 and a destination port of 1723.

    Click the OK button.

6. The Inbound Filters dialog box reappears, listing the new filter you created in step 5. Repeat step 5, but this time specify Other in the Protocol field and fill in a protocol ID of 47. When you're done, click the OK button and you'll go back to the Inbound Filters dialog box.

7. In the Inbound Filters dialog box, click the Drop All Packets Except Those That Meet The Criteria Below radio button and click the OK button.

8. Repeat steps 3–7, but this time create output filters. Make sure to specify the IP address of the VPN adapter as the source, not the destination!

9. Close the interface Properties dialog box.

L2TP Packet Filters

To use L2TP packet filters, you have to go through the same basic process, but the filters you need are slightly different. There are a total of four filters required—two input filters and two output filters:

▪   An input filter with a destination of the VPN interface address and a net mask of 255.255.255.255, filtering UDP with a source and destination port of 500

▪   An input filter with a destination of the VPN interface address and a net mask of 255.255.255.255, filtering UDP with a source and destination port of 1701

▪   An output filter with a source of the VPN interface address and a net mask of 255.255.255.255, filtering UDP with a source and destination port of 500

▪   An output filter with a source of the VPN interface address and a net mask of 255.255.255.255, filtering UDP with a source and destination port of 1701

Managing IP Routing

Managing IP routing is fairly simple: if you understand how the options described earlier in this chapter work, you know most of what you need to know to keep IP routing working smoothly.

All of the remaining skills you need center around monitoring your routers to make sure traffic is flowing smoothly and troubleshooting the occasional problem.

There are a number of status displays built into the RRAS console. Knowing that they exist, and what they display, makes it much easier to see all of the various health and status data that RRAS maintains. Each of these commands shows you something different:

The General ➢ Show TCP/IP Information command   As you would expect, this display shows a broad general selection of IP routing data, including the number of routes in the route table, the number of IP and UDP datagrams received and forwarded, and the number of connection attempts. You can use the Select Columns command (right-click in the TCP/IP Information window) to customize what you see in this view.

The Static Routes ➢ Show IP Routing Table command   This command shows you the entire contents of the routing table, including the destination, net mask, and gateway for each route. This version of the routing table doesn't show you where the route came from (e.g., whether it was learned by RIP or OSPF).

The RIP ➢ Show Neighbors command   This command shows you which RIP neighbors exist; for each router, you can see how many bad packets and bad routes that neighbor has tried to foist off on your router.

The OSPF ➢ Show Areas command   This command shows you a list of all the defined areas (keep in mind there will only be one area per interface). For each area, you can see whether that area is up or not, as well as the number of shortest-path computations performed on the link.

The OSPF ➢ Show Link-State Database command   This command presents a view of the entire contents of the link-state database, which is far outside the scope of this book.

The OSPF ➢ Show Neighbors command   This command shows you everything RRAS knows about the OSPF neighbors of this router, including the type of neighbor (point-to-point, broadcast, or NBMA), the neighbor's state, and its router ID.

The OSPF ➢ Show Virtual Interfaces command   This command shows you a list of virtual interfaces for this OSPF router. Unless you have a fairly complicated OSPF network, this is likely to be blank.

Exercise 9.6 shows you how to monitor IP routing.

EXERCISE 9.6

Monitoring Routing Status

1. Open the RRAS MMC console by selecting Start ➢ Administrative Tools ➢ Routing And Remote Access.

2. Select the server whose status you want to monitor in the left pane of the MMC. Expand it until you see the IP Routing node.

3. Select the Network Interfaces node. Note that the right pane of the MMC now lists all known interfaces along with their status and connection state.

4. Select the General node beneath IP Routing. Note that the right pane of the MMC updates to show the IP routing interfaces, their IP addresses, their administrative and operational states, and whether or not IP filtering is enabled on each interface.

5. Right-click the General node and choose the Show TCP/IP Information command. Check the number of IP routes shown.

6. Right-click the Static Routes node and choose the Show IP Routing Table command. Note that the number of routes listed corresponds to the route count in the TCP/IP Information window and that some of the routes listed are automatically generated.

Now let's revisit the route command that you saw earlier, but in the context of route monitoring.

Using the *route print* Command

You already learned how to use the `route add` command to add a new static route from the command line. However, the `route print` command can show you all or part of the routing table from the command line. Just typing **route print** into a command window will give you a complete dump of the entire routing table; adding a wildcard IP address (for example: **route print 206.151.***) will display only routes that match 206.151.

Troubleshooting IP Routing

A comprehensive overview of IP routing troubleshooting is beyond the scope of this book. Microsoft's online help is pretty good at suggesting probable causes and solutions for most routing problems. If you understand the topics presented in this chapter, then you shouldn't have many troubleshooting problems in RRAS as long as you verify the following points:

- The RRAS service is running and configured to act as an IP router.
- The router's TCP/IP configuration is correct (including a static IP address).
- You have IP routing protocols attached to each interface on which you need them.

   Next, you need to verify the following routing-specific settings and behaviors:

- If you're using OSPF, make sure that the Enable OSPF For This Interface checkbox is turned on in the interface's OSPF Properties dialog box.
- Check to be sure that your router is receiving routes from its peers. Do this by opening the routing table and looking at the Protocol column. Seeing entries marked as OSPF or RIP tells you that at least some peers are getting routing information through. If you don't see any RIP or OSPF routes, that's a bad sign.

- You need to have a static default route enabled if your router hasn't received any default routes. To do this, add a new static route with a destination of 0.0.0.0, a net mask of 0.0.0.0, and either a demand-dial or LAN interface appropriate for your network setup.

 Real World Scenario

Bringing In Experts to Help the Experts

Your company has finally realized that using its multihomed computers as routers isn't the most effective means for supporting your network. You decide to explore using dedicated routers and switches to segment and control network traffic. You also want to make sure that you have evaluated the differences between the two approaches thoroughly and professionally. How exactly should you proceed?

Part of the MCSE certification covered in this chapter is TCP/IP routing and the RIP and OSPF routing protocols. Those concepts are important because you are most likely placing the Windows Server 2003 information system in a routed environment. Just as it is important to understand that expertise regarding Windows Server 2003 is essential, it's also important to understand the need for experts in the world of OSPF and other routing protocols.

Although the concepts are covered in this book, and although the certification exam tests your understanding of the concepts, the book and certification don't fully prepare you to design an OSPF network with all the nuances that the operating systems from vendors such as Cisco, Nortel, and Lucent provide. This is a deep field, just as Windows Server 2003 is a deep field. Both a vascular surgeon and an orthopedic surgeon are technically proficient, and there is a great deal of crossover knowledge between the two. However, when your bones are sticking out and the blood is flowing, you want the two doctors to cover their own fields. The same is true in networking. If you are not as experienced and knowledgeable in internetworking as you are in networking, you would be well served to run your routing or IP designs by an internetworking specialist. The specialist may have some insight that has been honed over time, which will reap benefits to your information system. No single person knows everything, and one of the hallmarks of a professional is to know when to call in another professional. Both professionals need to work together to build an infrastructure that will support the requirements of the new services available in Windows Server 2003.

Summary

In this chapter, you learned about the following topics:

- How IP routing connects networks by intelligently delivering network traffic to the correct destination in the internetwork

- How to create and manage demand-dial, RIP, and OSPF interfaces for IP routing
- How to install OSPF and RIP and set routing parameters
- How to manage static routes with the `route add` command and the RRAS console
- How to configure TCP/IP packet filters for blocking undesirable traffic
- How to manage demand-dial routing

Exam Essentials

Know the difference between static routing and dynamic routing. *Static routing* systems don't make any attempt to discover other routers or systems on their networks. Instead, you tell the routing engine how to get data to other networks. Dynamic routing doesn't depend on your adding fixed, unchangeable routes to remote networks. Instead, a *dynamic routing* engine can discover its surroundings by finding and communicating with other nearby routers in an internetwork.

Understand RRAS. RRAS provides Windows Server 2003 computers with routing capabilities. You can establish static routes that specify where packets bound for certain networks should go. RRAS provides dynamic routing using the Open Shortest Path First (OSPF) protocol and versions 1 and 2 of the Routing Information Protocol (RIP). It also provides packet filtering to screen out undesirable packets in both directions.

Understand the difference between RIP and OSPF. A RIP-capable router periodically sends out announcements while simultaneously receiving announcements from its peers. This exchange of routing information enables each router to learn what routers exist on the network and which destination networks each router knows how to reach. OSPF networks are broken down into areas; an area is a collection of interconnected networks. Think of an area as a subsection of an internetwork. Areas are interconnected by backbones. Each OSPF router keeps a link-state database only for the areas to which it's connected.

Know how to install RRAS and configure IP routing. The RRAS components are installed on computers running Windows Server 2003 and Enterprise Server whether or not you choose to activate them. To enable your server to route IP packets, you have to activate and configure RRAS using the Routing And Remote Access Server Setup Wizard in the RRAS MMC console. You then need to add demand-dial interfaces if you want to support demand-dialing, give each routable interface a network address for each protocol it carries, and install and configure the routing protocols on the interfaces that should support them.

Know how to configure TCP/IP packet filters. You can construct filters that allow or deny traffic into or out of your network based on rules that specify source and destination addresses and ports. To create a filter, find the interface on which you want the filter, open its Properties dialog box, and click the appropriate packet filter button.

Key Terms

Before you take the exam, be certain you are familiar with the following terms:

adjacency	Network Address Translation (NAT)
area border routers	network routes
auto-static update mode	non-broadcast multiple access (NBMA) router
backbone	Open Shortest Path First (OSPF)
border routing	packet filtering
broadcast router	peer filters
default routes	periodic update mode
demand-dial routing	point-to-point router
dynamic routing	route filters
host routes	router discovery messages
internal routing	Routing Information Protocol (RIP)
link-state map	static routing
metric	unicast routing
multicast routing	

Review Questions

1. You work on a network with four subnets whose addresses are 208.45.231.0, 208.45.232.0, 208.45.233.0, and 208.45.234.0. Your routers are configured with these IP addresses:

   Router 1: 208.45.231.1 and 208.45.232.1

   Router 2: 208.45.231.2 and 208.45.233.1

   Router 3: 208.45.232.2 and 208.45.234.1

   Router 4: 208.45.233.2 and 208.45.234.2

   Router 2 is connected to the Internet. The connection between Router 2 and Router 4 is a very slow 56K dial-up line. Your computer's IP address is 208.45.231.25. Your default gateway is 208.45.231.2 because that's the address of the router that's connected to the Internet. You want to make sure that your computer always routes information to 208.45.234.0 through Router 1 unless Router 1 becomes unavailable because the 56K line is so slow. Which command should you use to accomplish this?

   A. route add 208.45.231.1 mask 255.255.255.0 208.45.234.0 metric 1
      route add 208.45.231.2 mask 255.255.255.0 208.45.234.0 metric 2

   B. route add 208.45.234.0 mask 255.255.255.0 208.45.231.1 metric 2
      route add 208.45.234.0 mask 255.255.255.0 208.45.231.2 metric 1

   C. route add 208.45.234.0 mask 255.255.255.0 208.45.231.1 metric 1
      route add 208.45.234.0 mask 255.255.255.0 208.45.231.2 metric 2

   D. route add 208.45.234.0 mask 255.255.255.0 208.45.232.1 metric 1
      route add 208.45.234.0 mask 255.255.255.0 208.45.233.1 metric 2

2. You administer a network that consists of four subnets. Your manager wants to reduce costs as much as possible. You decide to configure at least one Windows Server 2003 computer on each subnet with RRAS and a nonpersistent demand-dial connection. You would prefer that routing updates not be broadcast to the network, but any changes should be propagated to the other RRAS computers. Which of the following should you use to accomplish these goals?

   A. RIP version 2

   B. OSPF

   C. RIP version 1

   D. Area border routers

3. Leigh is setting up an RRAS router at a remote site so that it can connect back to the corporate LAN. Which of the following interfaces will Leigh need?

   A. A demand-dial interface for connecting the remote and LAN routers

   B. RIP or OSPF for routing discovery

   C. A demand-dial interface as well as RIP or OSPF

   D. None of the above

4. You upgraded all your locations to Windows Server 2003 and implemented the routing capability built into the servers. Because you didn't want to deal with the complexity of the OSPF routing protocol, you chose to implement RIP. After implementing the routers, you discover that routes that you don't want your network to consider are updating your RIP routing tables. What can you do to control which networks the RIP routing protocol will communicate with on your network?

   A. Configure TCP/IP filtering.

   B. Configure RIP route filtering.

   C. Configure IP packet filtering.

   D. Configure RIP peer filtering.

   E. There is no way to control this behavior.

5. You can configure a single LAN interface with multiple IP addresses. If you do, which of the following statements is *not* true?

   A. You can configure OSPF independently on each of the IP addresses.

   B. Each IP address can participate in the same OSPF area.

   C. One IP address may not be another IP address's RIP or OSPF neighbor.

   D. You may not have only one of the IP addresses participating in RIP.

6. Joe set up a new RRAS router that seems to be functioning properly, but it isn't routing traffic. He has already verified that RRAS is running and properly configured. Which of the following are possible causes of the problem? (Choose all that apply.)

   A. No routes are being learned from peer routers.

   B. There is no static default route.

   C. No RIP neighbors are defined.

   D. The router's authentication credentials are wrong.

7. Your company has six locations that have been connected together in a hub and spoke design with your location as the center. The network is designed that way because it grew over time and you simply added another connection to your Windows NT RAS server each time one was needed. You are concerned that if your connection goes down, the entire network will go down and all your users across the country will lose connectivity. You have now migrated all your servers to Windows Server 2003, and you are well on your way in migrating the Windows NT workstations to Windows 2000 and XP Professional. You decide that each RRAS server will have at least three separate connections to other RRAS servers in the network so that you will always have a way to find a path through the network. You want to accomplish this with the least amount of administrative effort, router update traffic, and convergence time for changes in the connections. How should you configure the RRAS computers to ensure these objectives?

   A. Configure RIP version 2 on all routing interfaces.

   B. Configure OSPF on all routing interfaces.

   C. Configure RIP version 1 on all routing interfaces.

   D. Configure static routes.

   E. Configure RIP version 2 and OSPF on all routing interfaces.

8. You work for a very large accounting company that has more than 1000 workstations in three locations over a routed network. You have upgraded all the servers to Windows Server 2003 and are well under way in bringing all the workstations to Windows 2000 and XP Professional. Two of the locations are connected to the central office, which has a T1 connection to the Internet. All the users on all three networks are funneled through this RRAS server for Internet access. Your company has a policy that personal Internet browsing from company equipment is not acceptable. The main purposes of Internet access within the company are e-mail connectivity and VPN traffic to your business partners. Also, some staff members occasionally download new regulations and forms from a few government websites. How can you implement this policy using the tools and services on your Windows Server 2003 network?

   A. Configure TCP/IP filters to control access to the Internet.

   B. Configure IP packet filters to control access to the Internet.

   C. Configure the Internet browsers through global policies to control which websites users can and cannot visit.

   D. Create static routing tables to control which websites, based on address, the users can reach.

9. You notice that packets sent to your RRAS router aren't being routed. You determine that the packets are indeed reaching the router. What should you check in order to troubleshoot the problem?

   A. The RRAS service status

   B. The RRAS routing configuration

   C. The RRAS server's TCP/IP configuration

   D. All of the above

10. You are the administrator of a network consisting of six subnets that are routed together through an ISP that doesn't support multicasting. You are connected to the ISP at all locations with Windows Server 2003 RRAS servers. The marketing department is interested in providing audio and video presentations between the corporate office and one of the other locations; these presentations will be a test of how audio and video presentations could be used throughout the entire company. Your company is growing rapidly, and you plan to build a private network to support more flexibility in your routing capability—but that isn't going to happen in time for the test. What can you do on your side of the network to allow the multicasting traffic to reach the intended destinations?

   A. Configure multicast boundaries on each of the appropriate RRAS routers.

   B. Install RIP version 2 and OSPF to carry the multicast traffic.

   C. Configure an IP-in-IP tunnel interface on the appropriate RRAS routers.

   D. Configure the multicast heartbeat on the appropriate RRAS routers.

11. You are the network administrator for your company. You're planning to upgrade the network to Windows 2003 to take advantage of the various new services available and the general overall stability that it promises to provide. Your network is located in one large building and is not connected to remote locations; the entire network is on one subnet, and has poor performance due to the amount of network traffic it is supporting. You want to break the network into smaller pieces, but your company doesn't want to spend money on a third party dedicated router. After you get your servers up and running Windows 2003, you plan to build one Windows 2003 server with multiple NICs so that you can break the network into four subnets. When you're ready to set up this solution for this network, what would be the best way to configure the multihomed Windows 2003 router?

    A. Install and configure the OSPF routing protocol and let it figure out the routing tables automatically.

    B. Install and configure RIPv1 so that the broadcasts will fill in the tables and keep them up-to-date automatically.

    C. Install and configure RIPv2 so that the broadcasts will fill in the tables and keep them up-to-date automatically.

    D. Configure the multihomed host with a static routing table.

    E. Install and configure RIPv1 and RIPv2 so that the broadcasts will fill in the tables and keep them up-to-date automatically.

12. You are part of a small support staff of a medium-sized company that is growing. No one on your staff is experienced with routers, and because your company has a hiring freeze that extends to your support staff, you cannot bring routing expertise on board in the foreseeable future. However, you are charged with connecting eight offices together. You are almost finished upgrading your servers to Windows 2003 Server, and you've read that you can use them as routers. When it comes time to connect the servers between the various offices using the routing functionality offered in Windows 2003, what routing protocol would make the most sense for your particular situation?

    A. OSPF

    B. RIP

    C. BGP

    D. Dynamic routing file

    E. Static routing tables

13. Your network has eight subnets; each subnet has at least two connections to the other subnets, and some have three or four connections to the other subnets. This design was created because you wanted to make sure that every subnet was accessible from every other network if any connection went down. You want to implement this design as effectively as possible, and you want the network to recover as quickly as possible if a link should go down. You are going to implement this design in the near future and use Windows 2003 Server servers as the routers as you bring each subnet online. Which routing protocol supported by Windows 2003 Server would be most appropriate for this design?

A. RIPv1

B. RIPv2

C. OSPF

D. Static routing tables as a backup to RIP

E. Static routing tables as a backup to OSPF

14. You are building four networks—each in a different city—to support the regional activities of the Sunrise Flower Shop. Each region needs to communicate with each of the others so that it can take orders for the other regions and then transmit the delivery instructions, including JPEG images, to the appropriate location. To save costs, you decide to set up demand-dial connections with a bandwidth that's sufficient to support the images. However, you don't want routing updates to be broadcast throughout the network—although you do want any changes to the network to be sent to the other routers so that communications can be reliable. Which routing protocol should you use when you configure the Windows 2003 Server servers that you are using for the connection points?

A. OSPF

B. RIPv2

C. Static routing tables

D. RIPv1

E. CHAP

15. You need to create a new demand-dial interface. What would you do in the following exhibit in order to begin the Demand-Dial Interface Wizard?

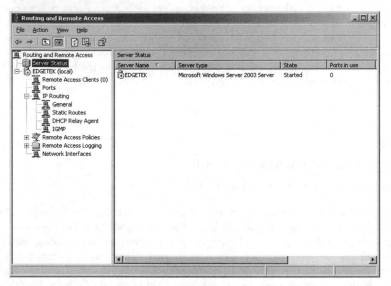

A. Right-click EDGETEK, select New, and select Interface.

B. Right-click Routing Interfaces and select New Demand-Dial Interface.

C. Right-click EDGETEK and select Properties.

D. Right-click Routing Interfaces and select Properties.

Answers to Review Questions

1. C. The correct syntax for the `route add` command is as follows: `route add` *destination mask subnet mask gateway metric cost metric*. In option A, the destination and gateway addresses are reversed. Option B uses incorrect metrics. Option D uses gateways that are not on the host's subnet.

2. A. The only way to accomplish all the goals is to use RIP version 2. RIP version 1 broadcasts changes to the entire network, so that choice wouldn't work. OSPF cannot be used because the connection is a nonpersistent demand-dial interface. Area border routers are simply special versions of OSPF routers.

3. A. RIP and OSPF are optional; you can use static routes on a remote dial-up router to avoid dealing with dynamic routing protocols.

4. B. RIP route filters allow you to configure your routers to either ignore or accept updates from specific network addresses or a range of addresses. TCP/IP filtering is configured at each individual host to control the traffic at a granular level, such as specific address, UDP port, or TCP port. IP packet filtering is used on the router interface to control IP traffic based on subnet masks, IP address, or port. RIP peer filtering is used to control communication between individual routers rather than control the entire network address.

5. B. A single interface can take part in only one OSPF area.

6. A, B, D. RIP neighbors are optional. If no routes are arriving or if there is no static default route, the router may not be able to route traffic.

7. B. The OSPF protocol has less overhead on the network than either version of RIP. If the network changes, the information will be propagated to the other routers immediately instead of at a set broadcast time. Although there is more up-front administrative overhead for configuring OSPF than for configuring RIP, once everything is set up, less effort will be required for subsequent administrative duties.

    RIP is a distance-vector protocol that periodically broadcasts routes to the other servers. It's useful for a very simple routed network, but when you want to set up many multiple and complex routes, it creates a great deal of traffic. Your environment is much too complex to configure static routes. Every time something changed, you would have to modify all the routing tables manually.

8. B. IP packet filters are applied at the RRAS server and can control access based on rules that act on source and destination addresses and ports. For example, you could build a rule that specifies the IP address of all acceptable Web destinations while dropping all other requests, or you could create a rule that would use IP addresses to prevent requests from reaching specific sites. You could also build a rule that would not allow services such as CHAT to work through your RRAS server. By applying this governor at the RRAS server, you wouldn't have to keep track of each individual workstation.

    TCP/IP filters are configured at each workstation; although they can control specific communication, the administrative overhead is unacceptable for a broad-based policy. Configuring each browser through global policies is not a valid option. Using static routing tables applies only to communication between routers, not concerned as to the ultimate destinations of the packets.

9. D. Any of these factors could prevent traffic from flowing and therefore should be checked.

10. C. An IP-in-IP tunnel encapsulates IP datagrams inside other IP headers. This allows you to send packets that are not supported, such as multicasts in this situation, to other locations that *are* supported. Multicast boundaries use the multicast scope, rate of traffic, or IP header to control the forwarding of the traffic, but this does not allow that traffic to flow across a section of the network that does not support it. This is also the case for multicast heartbeat, which is used to look for multicast support connectivity on the network. RIP and OSPF are routing protocols that manage the tables that locate routes through the network. They are not involved in the support or lack of support of multicast traffic.

11. D. Configuring the multihomed router with a static routing table is the simplest approach for this environment. Although you could spend the time configuring the server with the more sophisticated routing protocols, there is no compelling advantage in this situation because every subnet will always be one hop away from the others. The more sophisticated protocols become useful when there are multiple routes available or when there are subnets that are across multiple routers. Also remember that OSPF doesn't figure out routes automatically until you have configured OSPF properly. There is nothing automatic about it.

12. B. RIP is the easiest dynamic routing protocol among the choices you have with Windows 2003. RIP will automatically discover the other RIP routers and build the tables necessary for the routing to take place. Although there is broadcast traffic associated with RIP on a small network, it won't have an impact. OSPF demands up-front planning and the understanding of how it functions. It also isn't particularly useful in a small network that's not going to change very often. Even as you add new paths to this network, RIP will update its tables appropriately. Static routing tables are a bit too cumbersome and error prone for a network with multiple routes. There is no such thing as a dynamic routing file. BGP (Border Gateway Protocol) is used to connect large, independently managed networks and isn't an option with the Windows 2003 product.

13. C. OSPF is best suited for routed networks that have multiple connections and that can change abruptly without severely impacting the availability of the other networks. Both versions of RIP are better suited for simple networks with straightforward routes. Building static routes to back up dynamic routing protocols is self-defeating.

14. B. RIP version 2 uses a multicast method for communicating changes to the other routers when routing changes are detected on the network. This minimizes any traffic on the network, but this protocol is still easy to configure and is reliable. RIPv1 broadcasts every 30 seconds to communicate with the other routers. OSPF has a great deal of overhead and is designed to manage the convergence of large networks when links go down. Static routing tables must be edited manually and won't update other routers. CHAP is an authentication protocol, not a routing protocol.

15. B. To create a new demand-dial interface, you need to right-click the Routing Interfaces node that is under the server on which you want to create the interface. Then select New Demand-Dial Interface from the pop-up menu.

Glossary

A

account lockout policy   A Windows 2003 policy used to specify how many invalid logon attempts should be tolerated before a user account is locked out. Account lockout policies are set through account policies.

account policies   Windows 2003 policies used to determine password and logon requirements. Account policies are set through the Microsoft Management Console (MMC) Local Computer Policy or Domain Controllers Policy snap-in.

Active Directory (AD)   A directory service available with the Windows Server 2003 platform. The Active Directory stores information in a central database and allows users to have a single user account (called a *domain user account* or Active Directory user account) for the network.

Active Directory user account   A user account that is stored in the Windows Server 2003 Active Directory's central database. An Active Directory user account can provide a user with a single user account for a network. Also called a *domain user account*.

Active Directory Users and Computers   On Windows Server 2003 domain controllers, the main tool used for managing the Active Directory users, groups, and computers.

Active Directory-Integrated (ADI) zone   Zone data is stored in the Active Directory and is available across the entire domain.

address pool   The range of IP addresses that the DHCP server can actually assign.

adjacency   A term used to describe neighboring routers which are grouped into an *adjacency* (think neighborhood). Within an adjacency, routers synchronize any changes to the link-state map. When the network topology changes, whichever router notices it first floods the internetwork with change notifications.

Administrator account   A Windows 2003 special account that has the ultimate set of security permissions and can assign any permission to any user or group.

area border router   A special OSPF router that connects adjacent areas.

audit policy   A Windows 2003 policy that tracks the success or failure of specified security events. Audit policies are set through Local Computer Policy or Domain Controllers Policy.

authentication   The process required to log on to a computer locally. Authentication requires a valid username and a password that exists in the local accounts database. An access token will be created if the information presented matches the account in the database.

authentication header (AH)   Header used to digitally sign the entire contents of each packet.

Authorization   In the context of DHCP, a process used with Active Directory to ensure that only DHCP servers that have been approved or authorized are allowed to allocate DHCP addresses.

Automatic Update Extends the functionality of Windows Update by automating the update process.

auto-static update mode RIP update mode in which the RIP router only broadcasts the contents of its routing table when a peer router asks for it. See also *periodic update mode*.

B

backbone A technology associated with interconnecting networks through a central backbone network. With the OSPF protocol, connects all OSPF areas, allowing any router in the AS (area) to connect to any other AS via tunnels.

binding The process of linking together software components, such as network protocols and network adapters.

border routing The passing of packets from one internetwork to another.

broadcast router A type of router that can talk to any number of other routers—like a typical LAN router, which can see any number of other routers on the LAN.

C

capture buffer A resizable storage area in memory to copy frames that are captured by Network Monitor. The default size is 1MB; you can adjust the size manually as needed. The buffer is a memory-mapped file and occupies disk space.

capture filter This configuration of Network Monitor is used to either collect or reject frames based upon specific criteria.

certificate The codes exchanged to allow for encrypted information interchange. Each party has its own certificate identifying (uniquely) the party sending or receiving information.

Challenge Handshake Authentication Protocol (CHAP) Remote access authentication protocol that uses encrypted challenge and response messages instead of sending passwords and usernames in plain text.

cyclic redundancy check (CRC) A mathmatical calculation that is computed on a packet at the source and destination that is used to determine whether or not a packet has been damaged in transmission.

D

default gateway A TCP/IP configuration option that specifies the gateway (router's address) that will be used if the destination address is outside of the local network.

default response rule   IP filtering rule that governs what the IP filtering stack does when no other more explicit filter rule applies.

default route   The route packets take when there is no explicit route; if a router encounters a packet bound for some remote network whose route cannot be resolved in the routing table, the packet takes the default route.

default subnet mask   Network IDs and host IDs within an IP address are distinguished by using a subnet mask. The default subnet mask is assigned to a Class A, B, or C address. These addresses are characterized by 8, 16, or 24 bits to specify the network number in the address.

delegation   When a higher security authority assigns administrative permissions to a lesser authority.

demand-dial routing   Type of routing that allows the use of an impermanent connection, like an analog modem or ISDN, to imitate a dedicated Internet connection.

DHCP authorization   The process of enabling a DHCP server to lease addresses by registering the server in Active Directory.

DHCP discover message   Message broadcast by a DHCP client that's looking for a nearby DHCP server; the discover message contains the hardware MAC address and NetBIOS name of the client, which the server can use to direct the response.

DHCP integration   Feature that allows you to pass out addresses to DHCP clients while still maintaining the integrity of your DNS services. When a client receives an address from the DHCP that information is registered in DNS automatically.

DHCP relay agent   A service used with DHCP that allows DHCP requests to be processed on a multisegment network. The DHCP relay agent or proxy is used to forward requests through a router to a DHCP server.

DHCP request message   A message a client sends to the DHCP server to request or renew lease of its IP address.

DHCP server log files   Files that contain logs of all DHCP activity. Log files can be used without requiring added monitoring or administration to manage log file growth or to conserve disk resources. By default, the DHCP service automatically logs all DHCP activity to a daily log file in the *systemroot*/System32/DHCP folder.

DHCPACK   An acknowledgment message sent by the DHCP server to the client after the server marks the selected IP address as leased.

DHCPNACK   A negative acknowledgment sent by the DHCP server to the client. This generally occurs when the client is attempting to renew a lease for its old IP address after it has been reassigned.

discovery   Used within the DHCP process to locate a DHCP server and determine what IP addresses are available.

disk quota policies   Policies used to specify how much disk space can be allocated by users.

distribution group   A type of group that can be created on a Windows 2003 domain controller in the Active Directory. A distribution group is a logical group of users who have common characteristics. Distribution groups can be used by applications and e-mail programs.

DNS client   The network node that needs to resolve a hostname to an IP address. This is also commonly referred to as the resolver.

DNS proxy   A technology used with DHCP servers that allows them to register DNS data for the computers that they issue leases to. The DHCP server acts as a proxy for the DNS server. The DHCP server must be registered with Active Directory through the DnsProxyUpdate group.

DNS server   A server that uses DNS to resolve domain or hostnames to IP addresses.

domain   In Microsoft networks, an arrangement of client and server computers referenced by a specific name that shares a single security permissions database. On the Internet, a domain is a named collection of hosts and subdomains registered with a unique name by the InterNIC.

domain controller   A Windows Server 2003 computer that is configured to store the domain database, commonly referred to as *Active Directory*.

domain local group   A scope for a group on a Windows 2003 domain controller. A domain local group is used to assign permissions to resources. Local groups can contain user accounts, universal groups, and global groups from any domain in the domain tree or domain forest. A domain local group can also contain other domain local groups from its own local domain.

domain policies   Policies applied at the domain level that allow administrators to control what a user can do after logging on. Domain policies include audit policies, security option policies, and user rights policies. These policies are set through Domain Controllers Policy.

domain user account   A user account that is stored in the Windows Server 2003 Active Directory's central database. A domain user account can provide a user with a single user account for a network. Also called an Active Directory user account.

Dynamic DNS (DDNS) standard   The RFC that specifies how Dynamic DNS needs to be implemented to ensure interoperability between the various vendors' DDNS products.

dynamic routing   Type of routing in which a router can discover its surroundings by finding and communicating with other nearby routers.

E

EAP type   Authentication scheme supported in Extensible Authentication Protocol (EAP).

Encapsulating Security Payload (ESP)   Protocol used to encrypt the entire payload of an IPSec packet, rendering it undecipherable by anyone other than the intended recipient. It provides confidentiality only.

encapsulation   A process where a client sending data wraps the data or encapsulates it within an IP datagram before it is sent through the network.

encryption   The process of translating data into code that is not easily accessible to increase security. Once data has been encrypted, a user must have a password or key to decrypt it.

end-to-end mode   Mode in which network traffic is protected before it leaves the originating machine and remains secured until the receiving machine gets it and decrypts it when you use IPSec to encrypt or authenticate connections between two machines. Also called *transport mode*.

exclusion   Any IP addresses, within the scope range, that you never want the DHCP server to automatically assign.

Extensible Authentication Protocol (EAP)   A protocol that allows third parties to write modules that implement new authentication methods and retrofit them to fielded servers.

F

filter action   Associated with the use of filters. When you specify a filter action within a filter it dictates which action should be taken when a security filter match occurs.

filter list   Groups of individual filters that allow you to easily build rules that enforce complicated behavior and then distribute those rules throughout your network as necessary.

forward lookup zone   A name-to-address database that helps computers translate DNS names into IP addresses and provides information about available resources.

G

global group   A scope for a group on a Windows 2003 domain controller. A global group is used to organize users who have similar network access requirements. Global groups can contain users and global groups from the local domain.

Group Policy policies   These policies specify how group policies are applied to a computer.

Guest account   A Windows 2003 user account created to provide a mechanism to allow users to access the computer even if they do not have a unique username and password. This account normally has very limited privileges on the computer. It is disabled by default.

Guests group   A Windows 2003 built-in group that has limited access to the computer. This group can access only specific areas. Most administrators do not allow Guests group access because it poses a potential security risk.

H

hierarchical address   In a hierarchical address, instead of treating an IP address's entire 32 bits as a unique identifier, one part of the IP address is designated as the network address, and the other part as a node address, giving the address a layered, hierarchical structure.

host record   Associates a host's name to its IP addresses.

host route   A route to a single system; normally used when you want to direct traffic to remote networks through a particular machine.

I

iasparse   A utility (included in the Windows 2003 Resource Kit) that digests an RRAS log, in IAS or database formats, and then produces a readable summary.

information hiding   Process by which routers on the Internet see only one external address for the network, hiding the complexity of a network from the rest of the Internet.

inheritance   Parent folder permissions that are applied to (or inherited by) files and subfolders of the parent folder. In Windows 2003, the default is for parent folder permissions to be applied to any files or subfolders in that folder.

internal routing   Term that refers to the process of moving packets around on your own internetwork.

Internet Authentication Service (IAS)   The Microsoft implementation of a RADIUS server that is used to provide RADIUS clients and proxy servers with authentication services.

Internet Control Message Protocol (ICMP)   Protocol designed to pass control and status information between TCP/IP devices.

Internet Protocol (IP)   The Network layer protocol upon which the Internet is based. IP provides a simple connectionless packet exchange. Other protocols such as TCP use IP to perform their connection-oriented (or guaranteed delivery) services.

Internet Protocol Security Extensions (IPSec)   A process that makes it possible to transfer sensitive information to other hosts across the Internet without fear of compromise. IPSec provides authentication and encryption for transmitted data.

IP address   Logical IP address by which each TCP/IP host is identified. This address is unique for each host that communicates by using TCP/IP. Each 32-bit IP address identifies a location of a host system on the network in the same way that a street address identifies a house on a city street. Also called node address.

IP datagram   The structure that enables a client and server to transfer other types of data by wrapping the data within an IP packet.

ipconfig   A command used to display the computer's IP configuration.

ipconfig tool   Command-line tool provided by Windows 2003 used to configure, and to see the configuration of, TCP/IP interfaces on your local machine.

IPSec client   The computer that attempts to establish a connection to another machine. See also *IPSec server*.

IPSec Policy Agent   A service running on a Windows 2003 machine that connects to an Active Directory server and fetches the IPSec policy and then passes it to the IPSec code.

IPSec SA   A security association (SA) is a set of parameters that defines the services and mechanisms necessary for IPSec to properly secure IP communications.

IPSec server   The server that services security requests (for a security key and to initiate a secure communications channel) from IPSec clients.

K

Kerberos   A security protocol that is used in Windows Server 2003 to authenticate users and network services. This is called dual verification, or *mutual authentication.*

Kerberos policies   Policies that are used to configure computer security settings for Kerberos authentication. Kerberos policies are set through account policies.

key distribution center (KDC)   A domain controller that is responsible for holding all of the client passwords and account information. When a Windows Server 2003 computer is installed as a domain controller, it automatically becomes a KDC.

L

Layer 2 Tunneling Protocol (L2TP)   A generic tunneling protocol that allows encapsulation of one network protocol's data within another protocol. Used in conjunction with IPSec to enable virtual private network (VPN) access to Windows 2003 networks.

lease   The offer of service provided by a DHCP server to a client upon successful negotiation.

link-state map   A routing table that contains the current links or paths that are available for routers to use and determines what router should service a route request.

LMHOSTS file   A file that consists of NetBIOS computer name–to–IP address mappings. Used in name resolution if the broadcast doesn't generate a useful answer.

local group   A group that is stored on the local computer's accounts database. Administrators can add users to local groups and manage them directly on a Windows 2003 computer, but Microsoft recommends adding a global to a local group and not adding users directly to local groups.

local policies   Policies that allow administrators to control what a user can do after logging on. Local policies include audit policies, security option policies, and user rights policies. These policies are set through Local Computer Policy.

local user account   A user account stored locally in the user accounts database of a computer that is running Windows 2003.

Local Users and Groups   A utility that is used to create and manage local user and group accounts on Windows 2000 Professional, Windows XP Professional computers and Windows 2000 and Windows 2003 member servers.

Logical Link Control (LLC) sublayer   A sublayer in the Data-Link layer of the Open Systems Interconnection (OSI) model. The LLC sublayer defines flow control.

logon   The process of opening a session with a Windows Server 2003 computer or a network by providing a valid authentication consisting of a user account name and a password. After logon, network resources are available to the user according to the user's assigned permissions.

logon policies   These policies specify the restrictions that are associated with a user logging onto a Windows 2003 computer or domain.

M

machine certificates   Digital certificates issued to machines instead of to people.

Media Access Control (MAC) sublayer   A sublayer in the Data-Link layer of the Open Systems Interconnection (OSI) model. The MAC sublayer is used for physical addressing.

metric   Cost information used to calculate the most efficient route for packets to take.

Microsoft Baseline Security Analyzer (MBSA)   A utility you can download from the Microsoft website to ensure that you have the most current security updates.

Microsoft CHAP (MS-CHAP)   A remote access authentication protocol and is Microsoft's extension to CHAP. It is designed to work with computers and networks that are using Windows 98, Windows Me, Windows NT 4 (all versions), Windows 2000 (all versions), Windows XP (all versions), and Windows Server 2003.

Microsoft Management Console (MMC)   A console framework for management applications. The MMC provides a common environment for *snap-ins*.

Microsoft Software Update Services (SUS)   Services used to deploy a limited version of Windows Update to a corporate server, which in turn provides the Windows updates to client computers within the corporate network.

mirrored filter   A mirrored filter creates two separate rules with opposite effects. For example, an inbound filter rule allowing traffic from any address to TCP port 80 will, when mirrored, create a rule allowing traffic to any address on TCP port 80.

multicast   The process of sending IP packets to selected IP addresses.

Multicast Address Dynamic Client Allocation Protocol (MADCAP)   A protocol that issues leases for multicast addresses only.

multicast routing   A special type of routing where a packet is sent to multiple host computers based on a special Class D IP address.

multicast scope   Range in which multicast addresses may be assigned.

multihoming   The process of adding multiple IP addresses on a single physical network connection.

mutual authentication   The type of authentication used with Kerberos version 5. With mutual authentication, the user is authenticated to the service and the service is authenticated to the user.

N

name server   A DNS server that can give an authoritative answer to queries about its domain.

name server (NS) records   A file that contains all of the name servers within the domain and is used by other name servers to look up names within the domain.

NetBIOS Extended User Interface (NetBEUI)   A simple Network layer transport protocol developed to support NetBIOS installations. NetBEUI is not routable, and so it is not appropriate for larger networks. NetBEUI is no longer supported in Windows 2003.

network address   The network address uniquely identifies each network. Every machine on the same network shares that network address as part of its IP address. In the IP address 130.57.30.56, for example, 130.57 is the network address.

Network Address Translation (NAT)   A service that allows multiple LAN clients to share a single public IP address and Internet connection by translating and modifying packets to reflect the correct addressing information.

network binding   Binding that links a protocol to an adapter so that the adapter can carry traffic using that protocol.

Network Driver Interface Specification (NDIS)   A driver interface developed by Microsoft to bind multiple protocols to one card or the same protocol to multiple cards.

network route   TCP/IP network segments are interconnected by IP routers, which pass IP datagrams from one network segment to another. Network routes are the paths that are in the configurations of the routers.

node address   Assigned to and uniquely identifies each machine in a network.

non-broadcast multiple access (NBMA)   A single router that can talk to multiple peers without using a broadcast.

nslookup   A tool that allows a resolver or server to query a DNS server to see what information it holds for a host record.

NWLink IPX/SPX/NetBIOS Compatible Transport   Microsoft's implementation of the Novell IPX/SPX protocol stack.

O

Open Datalink Interface (ODI)   Driver interfaces that allow multiple cards to be bound to multiple protocols; developed by Apple and Novell.

Open Shortest Path First (OSPF)   A routing protocol that is designed for use on large or very large networks. It's much more efficient than RIP, but it also requires more knowledge and experience to set up and administer.

Open Systems Interconnection (OSI)   The organization responsible for maintaining the information and requirements in the OSI model. Also called International Standards Organization.

Open Systems Interconnection (OSI) model   A reference model for network component interoperability developed by the International Standards Organization (ISO) to promote cross-vendor compatibility of hardware and software network systems. The OSI model splits the process of networking into seven distinct services, or layers. Each layer uses the services of the layer below it to provide its service to the layer above.

organizational unit (OU)   An Active Directory object that contains other objects. Each domain can consist of multiple OUs, logically organized in a hierarchical structure. OUs may contain users, groups, security policies, computers, printers, file shares, and other Active Directory objects.

P

packet   Small chunks of data that are constructed, modified, and disassembled by network protocols at various levels of the OSI model. Each packet consists of three parts: a header, data, and a trailer.

packet filtering   A technology that filters what type of traffic is allowed into and out of the router.

packet payload   The data within a network packet that is being transmitted to a remote computer.

passthrough action   A security filter action, this "Permit" action tells the IPSec filter to take no action. It neither accepts nor rejects the connection based on security rules, meaning that it adds zero security. It allows traffic to pass without modification.

Password Authentication Protocol (PAP)   The simplest and least secure authentication protocol; it transmits all authentication information in cleartext, which makes it vulnerable to snooping.

password policies   Windows 2003 policies used to enforce security requirements on the computer. Password policies are set on a per-computer or domain basis, and they cannot be configured for specific users. Password policies are set through account policies.

payload   The data to be transmitted to the remote computer.

peer filters   A technology used by routers that specifies which neighboring routers a local router will listen to.

periodic update mode   RIP update mode in which routing table updates are automatically sent to all other RIP routers on the internetwork. See also *auto-static update mode*.

ping   Command used to send an Internet Control Message Protocol (ICMP) echo request and echo reply to verify that a remote computer is available.

Point-to-Point Protocol (PPP)   A set of remote authentication protocols used by Windows during remote access for interoperability with third-party remote access software.

point-to-point router   Router with only one peer. For example, a typical DSL installation will have one router on your end and one on the ISP end—that's a point-to-point configuration.

Point-to-Point Tunneling Protocol (PPTP)   A Microsoft-specific VPN protocol that encapsulates IP, IPX, or NetBEUI information inside IP packets, hiding data from onlookers.

pointer (PTR) record   Record that associates an IP address to a hostname.

preshared key   A shared, secret key that is previously agreed upon by two users. It is quick to use and does not require the client to run the Kerberos protocol or to have a public-key certificate.

primary DNS server   The "owner" of the zone files defined in the DNS database. The primary DNS server has authority to make changes to the zone files it owns.

promiscuous mode   Mode in which a node on a network accepts all packets regardless of their destination addresses.

protocol stack   A group of protocols that implements an entire communication process. TCP/IP is an example of a protocol stack.

R

remote access policies   Like group policies, remote access policies allow the administrator to control whether users can get access or not. Unlike group policies, remote access policies are available only in native Windows 2003 domains.

remote access profiles   A profile associated with a user that allows an administrator to determine who can actually use dial-up capabilities. Remote access profiles work on individual accounts, whereas remote access policies work on groups of users.

Remote Access Service (RAS)   A service that allows network connections to be established over a modem connection, an Integrated Services Digital Network (ISDN) connection, or a null-modem cable. The computer initiating the connection is called the RAS client; the answering computer is called the RAS server.

Remote Authentication Dial-In User Service (RADIUS)   A common authentication scheme, used by (for example) ISPs using non-Microsoft systems.

Replication Monitor   A utility included with Windows 2003 server that is used to monitor Active Directory replication.

reservation   An IP-to-MAC mapping that allows a DHCP server to always give the same IP address to a DHCP client.

resolver   DNS client computer that makes requests to a DNS server; these requests ask the server to resolve a client DNS name into the corresponding IP address or vice versa.

resource record (RR)   Record that contains information about some resource on the network. There are several types of resource records.

reverse lookup   In DNS, a query process by which the IP address of a host computer is searched to find its friendly DNS domain name.

reverse lookup zone   A database which stores a mapping of IP address to friendly DNS domain names. In DNS Manager, reverse lookup zones are based on the in-addr.arpa domain name and typically hold pointer (PTR) resource records.

root server   The root is the highest or uppermost level in a hierarchically organized set of information. A root server is the DNS server that is authoritative for the root of the namespace.

route filters   Filters that are used by routers that allow you to configure what networks you want to accept network traffic from.

router discovery messages   These messages allow clients to find a "nearby" (in network terms) router without any manual configuration on your part.

Routing Information Protocol (RIP)   An IP routing protocol that allows routers to exchange information about the presence and routes of other routers on the network.

S

scope   Contiguous range of addresses.

secondary DNS server   Server that pulls DNS information from the specified master server. Secondary DNS servers receive a read-only copy of zone files. The secondary DNS server can resolve queries from this read-only copy but cannot make changes or updates.

security association (SA)   An association that provides all the information needed for two computers to communicate securely. It contains a policy agreement that controls which algorithms and key lengths the two machines will use plus the actual security database used to securely exchange information.

Security Configuration and Analysis tool   A Windows 2003 utility that is used to analyze and to help configure a computer's local security settings. Security Configuration and Analysis works by comparing the computer's actual security configuration to a security database configured with the desired settings.

security group   A type of group that can be created on a Windows 2003 domain controller in the Active Directory. A security group is a logical group of users who need to access specific resources. Security groups are used to assign permissions to resources.

security method   A pre-specified encryption algorithm with a negotiated key length and key lifetime.

security options   Policies used to configure security for the computer. Security option policies apply to computers rather than to users or groups. These policies are set through Local Computer Policy or Domain Controllers Policy.

Service Access Point (SAP)   A technology provided by the LLC sublayer so that other computers can transfer information through this sublayer to the upper OSI layers.

Service (SRV) record   Record that links the location of a service such as a domain controller with information about how to contact the service. It provides seven items of information: service name, a transport protocol, the domain name for which the service is offered, the priority, the weight, the port number on which the service is offered, and the DNS name of the server that offers the service.

Shiva Password Authentication Protocol (SPAP)   A remote access authentication method that encrypts passwords with a two-way encryption scheme. With this option, Windows XP Professional, Windows 2000 Server, and Windows Server 2003 are able to dial into Shiva network access servers. Conversely, Shiva clients can remotely access Windows XP Professional, Windows 2000 Servers, and Windows Server 2003 computers using SPAP.

site   A term used within the Active Directory to represent different geographical locations.

Start of Authority (SOA) record   Record that defines the general parameters for the DNS zone, including who the authoritative server is for the zone.

static routing   A specification of where packets bound for certain networks should go based on static route tables.

subdomain   Branches of a network.

subnet   If an organization is large and has a lot of computers, or if its computers are geographically dispersed, it makes good sense to divide its colossal network into smaller ones connected together by routers. These smaller nets are called *subnets*.

subnet address   An address associated with subnetting in TCP/IP. Subnetting is the process of carving a single IP network into smaller logical subnetworks. This trick is achieved by dividing the host portion of an IP address to create something called a subnet address.

subnet mask   A number mathematically applied to an IP addresses to differentiate the network address from the node address.

superscope   Allows you to group two or more scopes (IP network addresses) together into a single logical network.

System Monitor   A Windows 2003 utility used to monitor real-time system activity or view data from a log file.

T

tracert   A tool used to map out the path that the packets are taking as they flow to a remote system.

Transmission Control Protocol (TCP)   A Transport layer protocol that implements guaranteed packet delivery using the IP protocol.

Transmission Control Protocol/Internet Protocol (TCP/IP)   A suite of Internet protocols upon which the global Internet is based. TCP/IP is a general term that can refer either to the TCP and IP protocols used together or to the complete set of Internet protocols. TCP/IP is the default protocol for Windows 2003.

transport mode   Another name for the end-to-end mode, in which IPSec is used to encrypt before data is sent and decrypted at the other end; the data is protected during transport (obviously).

tunnel   A technology associated with VPNs that establishes a secure channel of communications over the Internet.

tunnel endpoint   The systems at the end of a two-way IPSec tunnel.

tunnel mode   The use of IPSec to secure traffic that's being passed over someone else's wire.

U

unicast   A type of network communication where a packet is sent from a source host to a single destination host.

unicast routing   Routing in which one machine sends data directly to one destination address.

Unicast scope   DHCP scope used to assign unicast (point-to-point) addresses. Compare with *Multicast Address Dynamic Client Allocation Protocol (MADCAP)*.

universal group   A scope for a group on a Windows 2003 domain controller. A universal group is used to logically organize users and appears in the global catalog (a special listing that contains limited information about every object in the Active Directory). Universal groups can contain users from anywhere in the domain tree or domain forest, other universal groups, and global groups.

User Datagram Protocol (UDP)   A connectionless Internet transport protocol included in the TCP/IP protocol standard.

user profile   A profile that stores a user's *Desktop* configuration and other preferences. A user profile can contain a user's Desktop arrangement, program items, personal program groups, network and printer connections, screen colors, mouse settings, and other personal preferences.

user rights policies   Policies that control the rights that users and groups have to accomplish network tasks. User rights policies are set through Local Computer Policy or Domain Controllers Policy.

V

virtual private network (VPN)   A private network that uses links across private or public networks (such as the Internet). When data is sent over the remote link, it is encapsulated, encrypted, and requires authentication services.

W

Windows file protection policies   These policies are used to specify how Windows file protection will be configured.

Windows Update   A utility that connects the computer to Microsoft's website and checks the files to make sure that they are the most up-to-date versions.

Z

zone   Subtree of the DNS database that is considered a single unit.

zone transfer   Action in which information is copied from a primary DNS server to a secondary DNS server.

Index

Note to the Reader: Throughout this index **boldfaced** page numbers indicate primary discussions of a topic. *Italicized* page numbers indicate illustrations.

M

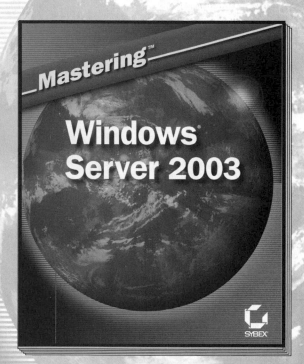

The Official
Juniper™ Networks Certification Study Guides
From Sybex

The Juniper Networks Technical Certification Program offers a four-tiered certification program that validates knowledge and skills related to Juniper Networks technologies:

- JNCIA (Juniper Networks Certified Internet Associate)
- JNCIS (Juniper Networks Certified Internet Specialist)
- JNCIP (Juniper Networks Certified Internet Professional)
- JNCIE (Juniper Networks Certified Internet Expert)

The JNCIA and JNCIS certifications require candidates to pass written exams, while the JNCIP and JNCIE certifications require candidates to pass one-day hands-on laboratory exams.

The Only OFFICIAL Juniper Networks Study Guides Are From Sybex

Written and reviewed by Juniper employees, the Juniper Networks Study Guides are the only official Study Guides for the Juniper Networks Technical Certification Program. Each book provides in-depth coverage of all exam objectives and detailed perspectives and insights into working with Juniper Networks technologies in the real world.

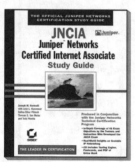

JNCIA: Juniper Networks Certified Internet Associate Study Guide
ISBN: 0-7821-4071-8

JNCIS: Juniper Networks Certified Internet Specialist Study Guide
ISBN: 0-7821-4072-6

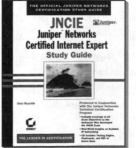

JNCIP: Juniper Networks Certified Internet Professional Study Guide
ISBN: 0-7821-4073-4

JNCIE: Juniper Networks Certified Internet Expert Study Guide
ISBN: 0-7821-4069-6

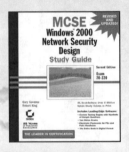

TELL US WHAT YOU THINK!

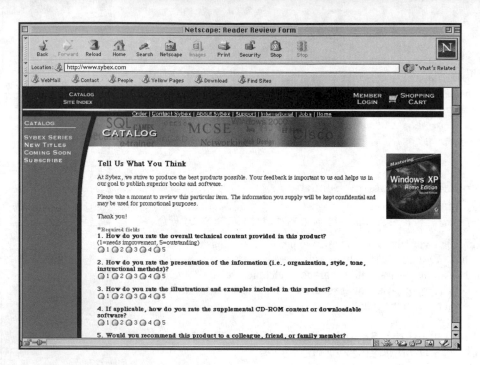

Your feedback is critical to our efforts to provide you with the best books and software on the market. Tell us what you think about the products you've purchased. It's simple:

1. Go to the Sybex website.
2. Find your book by typing the ISBN or title into the Search field.
3. Click on the book title when it appears.
4. Click **Submit a Review.**
5. Fill out the questionnaire and comments.
6. Click **Submit.**

With your feedback, we can continue to publish the highest quality computer books and software products that today's busy IT professionals deserve.

www.sybex.com

SYBEX Inc. • 1151 Marina Village Parkway, Alameda, CA 94501 • 510-523-8233

Sybex Offers the Complete Solution

SYBEX®

MCSA/MCSE: Windows Server 2003 Environment Management and Maintenance Study Guide
ISBN 0-7821-4260-5 • $49.99

MCSA/MCSE: Windows XP Professional Study Guide, Second Edition
ISBN 0-7821-4241-9 • $49.99

MCSA: Windows 2003 Core Requirements
ISBN 0-7821-4264-8 • $119.99

The Microsoft Certified Systems Administrator (MCSA) will put you on the path to manage and maintain the computing environment of medium- to large-sized companies.

MCSA 2003 Track

Choose ONE Client OS Requirement

Exam #	Exam
70-210	Installing, Configuring and Administering Microsoft Windows 2000 Professional
70-270	Installing, Configuring and Administering Windows XP Professional

2 Network Operating System Requirements

Exam #	Exam
70-290	Managing and Maintaining a Microsoft Windows Server 2003 Environment
70-291	Implementing, Managing, and Maintaining a Microsoft Windows Server 2003 Network Infrastructure

Choose ONE Elective

Exam #	Exam
70-086	Implementing and Supporting Microsoft Systems Management Server 2.0
70-227	Installing, Configuring, and Administering Microsoft Internet Security and Acceleration (ISA) 2000
70-228	Installing, Configuring and Administering SQL Server 2000
	CompTIA A+ and Network+ combo
	CompTIA A+ and Server+ combo

For a list of all Sybex products that will help prepare you for any of the MCSA exams, visit **www.sybex.com**.